Bruce Eckel

C++ Inside & Out

Osborne **McGraw-Hill**
Berkeley New York St. Louis San Francisco
Auckland Bogotá Hamburg London Madrid
Mexico City Milan Montreal New Delhi Panama City
Paris São Paulo Singapore Sydney
Tokyo Toronto

This book is printed on acid-free paper.

Osborne **McGraw-Hill**
2600 Tenth Street
Berkeley, California 94710 U.S.A.

For information on translations and book distributors outside of the U.S.A., please write to Osborne **McGraw-Hill** at the above address.

C++ Inside & Out

890 DOC 998765

ISBN 0-07-881809-5

Publisher
Kenna S. Wood

Acquisitions Editor
Jeffrey M. Pepper

Associate Editor
Emily Rader

Project Editor
Erica Spaberg

Copy Editor
Paul Medoff

Technical Editor
Jeffrey Hsu

Proofreaders
Audrey Johnson
K. D. Sullivan
Mick Arellano

Indexers
Matthew Spence
Bruce Eckel

Computer Designer
Stefany Otis

Illustrator
Marla Shelasky

Cover Designer
Bay Graphics Design, Inc.
Mason Fong

*Dedicated to my family and friends, who nurture me,
and to my Idea Fairy, who inspires me*

About the Author...

Bruce Eckel, a member of the ANSI C++ Committee, is a veteran C++ programmer and seasoned author on object-oriented programming who has written the Osborne top-seller **Using C++**. Eckel is also the author of Borland's *World of C++* video training course. He was a columnist for *Micro Cornucopia* for four years, the C++ editor for the *C Gazette*, and the features editor of *The C++ Report*. He is a contributor to various publications including *Computer Language* and *Dr. Dobb's Journal* and speaks regularly on C++ for Borland's OOP world tours and various other conferences. He owns Revolution2, a firm specializing in C++ consulting.

Contents

2 *Using Predefined Classes* 27

11 Complete Examples 597

Acknowledgments

Two technical readers donated their time to this book and were very helpful. Leigh Sneddon helped make Chapters 1 through 6 easier to understand, and Eric Nagler reviewed Chapter 10. On the first edition, Ron Burk was greatly responsible for making the book accurate; I also received feedback from John Carolan (Glockenspiel), Walter Bright (Zortech), and Brian McElhinney (who taught me much of what I learned about C while working at Fluke in Seattle).

Thanks to Gene Wang, David Intersimone, and Borland for making consulting more than I ever hoped: a stimulating, challenging adventure. Thanks to Koann and the folks at Software Development for including me in such an exciting event.

Thanks especially to Bjarne Stroustrup for his tireless efforts in creating and developing his brainchild, and for never getting sloppy (also, for answering my questions without making me feel stupid). The ANSI C++ Committee has been a great experience, despite what everyone warned me about committees. Maybe we're special, somehow. Thanks to everyone on the committee for working so hard, and to Dan Saks (the secretary of the committee) for clarifying obscure corners of the language for me.

I've met people in the computer field who have been more than computer experts; they've also had insights and interests and a sense of humor in other areas, and we've become good friends: Larry Fogg, who disavows interest in computers since Micro Cornucopia died (but who still loves technology in his heart), founder of Fogg's Vacation Training Institute ("We unBend Your Mind"). Andrew Binstock, whom I came to know over the phone as the editor of *The C Gazette*, but who turned out to be a French Lit major who told me about Napoleon while we walked the streets of Paris. Zack Urlocker, fellow speaker and co-explorer on two world tours, including that great trip to the Zen monastery in Japan (equal only to the Adventures in Eating there). Richard Hale Shaw, erstwhile guitarist, philosopher, and rebel, who taught me pragmatism in this field as well as being clear on what you want, and remembering what you're fighting for. Carl Haflinger (yes, I don't call but I *think* about it ...).

Personal: My brother Todd, sister Lynn, and their families. Chris and Laura Strand, Joe Lordi, Robert Herald, Dave and Brenda Bartlett, Rich Lyons and Pam Allenstien, Rick and Susan Maney-O'Leary, Jeff and Bridget Lynch, the Longwood Gradual Students. Mike Sequeira and Karen Theodore. Sonia Lee, a computer artist. Peter and Marty Almquist. Brad Jerbic and his accidental magic. My great friend Mark Bennett Western who continues to open horizons for me—I can only hope that my life will have more friends like you. Dave Rentschler, who taught me how to ask questions and be aggressive about learning. The Moelter families, who know how to enjoy life. The Robbins families for their endurance. The Zoehrers. The COMA group: Marilyn the Ph.D. who will be an artist; John Pollock, Mark Mabry, Richard Sudek, and Michael Wilk—may you all find the happiness you deserve. And to all my friends who have been misplaced over the years, I still think of you sometimes.

My friend Daniel Will-Harris has been a creative influence on my life since the day I met him, the first day of junior high school in boy's choir. He continues to lead me in directions I haven't thought of before, and to be a sounding board for new ideas and ventures.

Finally, to Melinda, who has changed my life beyond what I ever thought it could be, who has challenged me beyond my limits, and has given me what we all fear most but hope for passionately in the deepest places in our heart: an adventure, which has made me grow beyond my boundaries and become something new.

Preface

Although C++ is easily taught to C programmers, the audience of this
book is intended to be those who have programmed in another
language. The closer your language is to C, the easier time you'll have;
for example, a Pascal programmer will have an easy transition. However,
it should also be possible for a FORTRAN (or even BASIC, my own first
language) programmer to learn C++ from this book. The ANSI C language
(supported by virtually all commercial compilers) is taught along with
C++ in the early parts of the book and as the book progresses. Elements
which are part of ANSI C are clearly specified, and any incompatibilities
are shown.

From the success of the first edition of this book (*Using C++*, 1989)
and the comments I've gotten from readers, I think I took the right path.
That is, C++ cannot effectively be treated as just an extension to C. You
cannot take a C book and add a couple of chapters on classes and
inheritance and have a C++ book. C++ is a different language.

This may seem confusing at first, because C++ is indeed a superset of
C, and a C programmer can begin using a C++ compiler with virtually no
effort. Much of the value of C++ to C programmers, at least initially, is
that C++ is pickier and will find numerous errors that a C compiler allows.
(For this reason, a C++ compiler is an even better way to learn C!)
However, C++ is an entirely different approach to programming. The
beauty of it is that, as a procedural programmer, you'll have a much

easier time adapting to the new features since the old features are familiar.

Creativity Versus Complexity

It seems that the most creative and innovative software is developed by small teams. As software projects have become larger and more sophisticated, development teams have grown larger in an attempt to cope with complexity and deadlines. We have seen these teams, and the companies that manage them, lose the clarity of their vision about a project, or simply lose the ability to implement it in a timely manner. The project either fails to materialize, or the delivery date slips and slips and slips.

C++ is an object-oriented extension to the C programming language. An object-oriented language allows, among other things, the complexity of a program to be hidden. Most languages come with built-in data types and ways for you to use those data types (add them, pass them around, print them, and so on). C++ and other object-oriented programming (OOP) languages allow you to *define your own data types* and the ways to use those types. This is a powerful ability, but it also opens up many new questions: How will you pass objects around? Will you add them? If so, how? How will an object handle errors? Most users of a language don't need to think about these details (neither do C++ programmers who use someone else's libraries of data types), but when you begin defining your own types, each of these questions must be answered. This book serves as a guide to answering the many new types of programming questions you will have when you begin using C++.

Why C++

C++ improves productivity. It does this not by imposing a structure that you must follow if you want the program to come out "right," but by creating a framework in which building an easy-to-read, robust, maintainable, extensible program is the most natural path. It just *feels* right to do it that way. This is true whether you are experimenting or creating production code—in fact, you will find that much of the code you create while experimenting survives into production.

The size of the problem a team can manage depends on their abilities and the sophistication of their tools. One of the great benefits I see in C++ is that it puts the power needed to build large, complex projects back in the hands of the small team. This means we may start seeing the kind of wild innovation that was so refreshing in the early days of the computer revolution (which I start counting from the time computers got cheap enough that you weren't forced to do "serious" work on them all the time—people aren't creative when they have to be serious). C++ certainly isn't limited to small projects—a main goal was to support large programming projects. The language provides a way to communicate interface specifications between members of a large programming team and to enforce the correctness of those interfaces at compile time. In addition, the ability to easily create and maintain large libraries of useful tools will be a benefit to one-person projects as well as very large teams.

There are numerous advantages to using C++. Some of the design goals of the language are

☐ To simplify the building and use of libraries

☐ To allow code reuse. If a library function doesn't suit your needs, you can easily modify a portion of it without understanding the whole thing—whether or not you have access to the source code.

☐ To improve "maintainability" of code. Since the language supports object-oriented design, code is generally much easier to understand, fix, and modify.

☐ To allow you to create "extensible" programs to which you can easily add functionality.

Many people who learn the language discover a more mysterious benefit. Once a program compiles, it often seems to "just work right the first time." I doubt there's a way to measure or verify this benefit, but it is probably due to the stronger type checking C++ has over C, and the structure even the most avid hackers are seduced into using when creating new data types.

C++ is the first object-oriented language with efficiency as one of its primary goals. Inefficiency and lack of compile-time error checking has held object-oriented languages back from being practical in many production programming situations.

I see the language from an individual viewpoint. One of my favorite things about C++ is that it makes me think about programming in ways I've never considered before. Most commonly used procedural languages make you think about programming; C++ helps you think about problem solving.

I've had the same experience with C++ as I had when I learned calculus. Before I learned calculus, algebra and trigonometry were interesting but only marginally useful. I didn't connect with or remember them very well. When I learned calculus, a lot of things about algebra and trigonometry became very clear, and I quickly learned their intricacies because I had to use them, without thinking about it, on a daily basis. C++, like calculus, added a new dimension to my thinking. From this new perspective, I could easily see the reasoning behind most of the features in my previous framework of thinking (which was C and Pascal). My knowledge of C has improved greatly since I started programming in C++ — except for operator precedence. I've never found a way to make that stick.

Book Organization

The first four chapters of the book present the syntax of ANSI C and draft-ANSI C++. (We must say "draft" until the specification is approved, a process that will no doubt result in another edition of this book.) These chapters cover the features that are common between the two languages, describing the extensions that C++ adds to ANSI C and especially flagging the places where they are different. These chapters focus on more than just the syntax of the language, however. When you begin writing larger programs in C++, you inevitably create many files that must be managed and compiled properly. In the first chapters you will learn the proper construction of multifile projects, emphasizing header files and the **make** utility. (Virtually all C and C++ compilers come with a **make**.) All the programs in each chapter are compiled with the **makefile**, which describes the relationships in the projects. The **makefile** is placed at the end of each chapter.

The remaining chapters in the book cover object-oriented programming in C++. Here, you learn how to use the features presented in the first four chapters, and other new features in C++. Chapter 5 shows you how to overload operators and functions. Operator overloading means you can give an operator like **+** or **–** a special meaning when used with a new data type you create. Function overloading means you can create several meanings for the same function identifier, depending on the argument list.

Chapter 6 shows how to create objects at run time, for situations when you don't know at compile time how many objects you will need or what their lifetimes will be. Creating objects at run time is an extremely powerful feature of C++.

Chapter 7 demonstrates how code can be reused in C++, both by using objects inside of other objects (*composition*), and through the mechanism of *inheritance*.

Chapter 8 shows how to use inheritance to build extensible programs. Once you've built an extensible program, you or someone else can easily add features without ripping apart the existing code. The creation of extensible programs and the reuse of libraries are the two features of C++ that will save the most money in development projects.

Chapters 9 through 11 cover more advanced topics. Chapter 9 considers the thorny problems of passing and returning objects by value into and out of functions. Much emphasis is placed on the copy constructor **X(X&)**, which often causes new C++ programmers a lot of grief.

Chapter 10 covers the very important OOP concept of container classes and their associated iterators. These always make me think of Winnie-the-Pooh arriving at Eeyore's birthday party and explaining his gift: "A pot...to *put* things in." (On the way, he ate the honey inside.) Containers are objects that hold other objects, and iterators are objects which point inside containers, move around, and fetch objects back out. These are classes you write or get from someone and are not built into the core language, but you use them almost as often as you use the other OOP language features. If they're so important, why isn't there direct language support? The **template** keyword is essentially language support for container classes, and Chapter 10 has extensive coverage of templates.

Throughout the book, I've tried to use interesting examples. I've tried to avoid repeating the typical textbook examples in favor of programs that have been useful, fascinating, or both. One of the more difficult problems in teaching this language seems to be the order in which concepts are introduced. Great efforts have been made to ensure a concept is introduced before it is used in an example, or at least to tell you where a concept is explained more fully, in the few cases where they are used prematurely. But for someone who loves the language like I do, it's very difficult to hold back from using a great feature because it hasn't been introduced yet. Therefore Chapter 11 is a relief, because I've introduced everything and can pull out the stops. (In my *next* book, the equivalent of Chapter 11 will come sooner, because if you don't know some of the basics I'll refer you back to *this* book.) This chapter has several complete examples, which provide you with some projects to sink your teeth into.

Changes From the First Edition

The original intent of this second edition was to update the book to match the new version of the language that is being supported by most compilers, to take out or update anachronistic material (for example, the common file extension custom used to be .HXX and .CXX or .HPP and .CPP, and now it has become the more sensible .H and .CPP), to support iostreams throughout the book rather than the less-powerful **printf()** family of functions, and also to include a chapter on templates and an appendix on exception handling.

However, as I reviewed more of the material and studied the code, I discovered places where I could greatly improve the explanations, and that some of the code designs were embarrassingly flawed. I am somewhat comforted by reminding myself that with pragmatic object-oriented design, you'll get it working the first time but you may not always get it *right*, and that at least the code can be improved easily. This turned out to be true—the fixes weren't as painful as they would be in another language.

Also, I began to realize that a lot of people who bought *Using C++* were going to buy the new one, and I wanted to give them something that would make them feel it was worth it. In many places I got some inspirations, which I hope will justify the cost of buying another book (see the last examples in Chapter 9 and the new examples in Chapter 11).

Code Organization

The code is an essential part of this book, and its accuracy is imperative. To make understanding and using the code as easy as possible, I invented a style of program creation that allowed the code to be included automatically into the book, with no changes. As a result, the chances of error are vastly reduced. But the biggest advantage of this is that the code you see in the book actually compiled. Each file begins with a special comment that looks like this:

```
//: FILENAME.CPP—A brief description of the file,
//. with continuing description lines.
```

The // begins a C++ comment, which continues to the end of the line. The //: is my own notation indicating that this is a file description line. The filename follows, then two dashes, and a one-line description of the first line of the description, which may continue onto following lines using the //. comment form.

Although the filename is always available to anyone actually editing the file, as soon as the file is printed that information is lost. Thus, it's important to repeat it in the file, especially for this book. This way the file can be referred to and you'll know where it is.

The : and the . comment form serve two purposes. First, as a visual cue to the reader that this information is about the file and is relatively important. Second, this form allows search programs to find the information. For example, you can print all the comment lines in a directory with the following command, using the commonly available program called GREP:

```
grep //: *.h *.cpp
```

We will look at a more powerful program called AWK, which performs elaborate searching and substitution, later in the book. Text-manipulation programs like this can be very useful when dealing with large numbers of files; they can even allow you to automatically build documentation if you use the above form in your source-code files.

I also use a particular coding style, which seasoned C programmers may find peculiar, but which I maintain is easier to understand (of course, every programmer maintains that *their* style is better). It is also more compact, which is important not only in books, but especially in the presentations I give. These run much more smoothly if I can minimize slide movement when the audience is looking at a particular piece of code. You can find the description and reasoning behind the style in the early chapters.

28 Up

There's a classic British documentary called *28 Up*, which chronicles the lives of a group of people starting at age 7, at 7-year intervals. It turned out that they seemed to know themselves best, at least in terms of what they wanted to be, at age 7. When I was that age, the closest thing I could come up with was "inventor." I did in fact invent things—I bought myself a file cabinet and filled it with drawings of things that I thought would be neat to have. Then I would go pester my father, a builder and master carpenter, to try to get him to make the things I had invented. Dad is nothing if not a practical man, and he would explain to me how difficult it would be to build the car or catapult or whatever had seized my fancy at the moment. Fortunately for Dad, 7-year-olds are easily distracted, so he didn't have to build too many of my ideas. Mom, for her part, provided some of this distraction by trying to teach me to be organized. She tried, she really tried. It probably shows up more in my programming than in the organization of my office.

I actually consider myself an inventor now—I've fulfilled the dream of my 7-year-old self. However, my filing cabinet is now a disk drive, and the inventions are my thoughts. Dad doesn't have to talk me out of trying something too complicated. (Is that maturity—when you can see something is too hard without your dad pointing it out to you?) When I create something I think is particularly clever, or that I've been trying to figure out for years, the euphoria can last for days. I hope some of the projects I've created will give you the same feeling.

Source-Code Disk and Video

As mentioned earlier, all the source-code files are compiled exactly as you see them in the text. Part of the motivation behind the organization of the code is to be able to offer it on disk, which saves you the trouble of typing it in. In addition, other tools and projects have been added to the disk, including code from the first edition of the book which for various reasons didn't go into the second, along with a free version of AWK. The code can be purchased by mail using the order form at the end of the preface.

Because of the success of *The World of C++* video training tape, which I wrote for Borland, I've seen the value of video as an aid to learning. To help you assimilate this book, I've created a video (available April, 1993) of approximately four hours, comprised of a lesson for each chapter of the book. It's not quite as good as having me there in person, but it can help. The video can be purchased by mail using the order form at the end of the preface.

Feedback

I have endeavored to ensure the correctness of the code and the information in this book, but errors occasionally slip through. If you find a problem, please send the correction to me so I can make the change in a subsequent printing. Also, if you have comments on the book I would like to hear them.

The best way to communicate (especially with code) is via electronic mail. On Compuserve, I am 72070,3256. I can be reached from internet via the Compuserve bridge at 72070.3256@compuserve.com. On MCI Mail, I am 456-6744. If you don't have access to any of those, my distribution company, EckelBits, will forward mail to me. Their address is EckelBits, 5343 Valle Vista, La Mesa, CA 91941-4259.

Consulting

I began working with C++ in 1987, on a research project with Dr. Tom Keffer at the University of Washington School of Oceanography where he was a physical oceanographer (that is, a physicist who specializes in the ocean). He and his colleagues (and the Navy, who funded us) had noticed that, although all the mathematical routines written in FORTRAN were quite reliable, there seemed to be a distinct productivity disadvantage to using that language. Our goal was to make a suite of tools in a more productive language. (The project was called DAIMS: Data Analysis and Interactive Modeling System.) We chose C++ despite the claim that most scientists and engineers will give up FORTRAN only when their cold, dead fingers are pried from the manuals.

On a small scale, the project was a success—we got a matrix class working, as well as an interpreter which created and manipulated matrices, and we showed how much simpler it was to model equations using the C++ tools than FORTRAN. However, because of the state of the language at the time, the compiler (which was buggy), and the lack of tutorial information in the C++ community, the project was a bit too ambitious. The tax dollars still appear to have been well-spent, as we both ended up serving the C++ community. Tom went on to create Rogue Wave (an oceanographic reference that may suggest a certain maverick nature in that academic community), a company that provides some of the best C++ tools around. One of their packages, Math++, looks strikingly similar to the goals of the original DAIMS project and includes a much more sophisticated set of matrices. They've also converted the famous Linpack FORTRAN math libraries into C++ classes. He's still trying to lure those scientists away.

I went on to write this book, and my magazine articles (formerly about building hardware projects and controlling them with C, the subject of my first, self-published book, *Computer Interfacing with Pascal & C*) have since become exclusively about C++. I began speaking at conferences and had the good fortune to be Borland's C++ speaker for their OOP World Tours 1-3, so I've literally traveled the world speaking about C++.

But my first love is still inventing, and I get great enjoyment from helping companies build their projects. I certainly enjoy creating and solving my own problems, but there's nothing quite as satisfying as solving someone else's problem. If you're working on a project, and think I might be able to help, I can be reached (at my consulting company, Revolution2) via the same channels listed above under "Feedback."

Code Disk & Video Order Form

Quantity	Item	price
	C++ Inside & Out Source-Code Disk, 3.5" High-Density. Includes all source code from book plus additional code from first edition, tools and free version of **awk**.	$25 ea postpaid
	If you live in CA: 7.75% Sales Tax for above	$1.94
	Above with Overseas shipping/handling	$32 ea postpaid
	C++ Inside & Out video training tapes. Approx 4 hours on 2 tapes, with a lesson for each chapter in the book. VHS/NTSC version for U.S. (Available April 1993)	$99 ea postpaid
	If you live in CA: 7.75% Sales Tax for above	$7.67
	C++ Inside & Out video training tapes for overseas (PAL version). (Available April 1993)	$119 ea postpaid
	Total Amount Enclosed:	

Name: _____

Company: _____

2nd Address Line: _____

Street: _____

City: _____

State: _____

Country if not US: _____

Zip:_____

Please send check with order. Foreign orders, please use a check in US funds drawn on a US bank. There is a $5 handling charge for invoicing or special requests. Send to:

**EckelBits
5343 Valle Vista
La Mesa, CA   91941- 4259**

Osborne/McGraw-Hill assumes NO responsibility for this offer. This is solely an offer of the distribution company EckelBits, and not of Osborne/McGraw-Hill.

Comments & corrections are appreciated.

CHAPTER

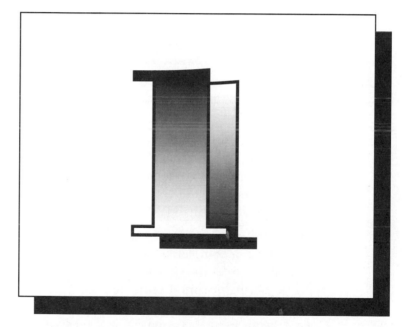

Introduction to Object-Oriented Languages

*T*his chapter lays the groundwork for the book. To learn C++, you need some programming experience (described here). The rest of the chapter discusses ideas behind object-oriented programming, especially as they apply to C++.

If all the ideas don't make sense to you as you read them, *don't panic.* The object-oriented approach is a new way to think about programming. You may need to "unlearn" some old ideas before the object-oriented ideas drop into place (many teachers find that nonprogrammers pick up object-oriented programming more quickly than programmers). However, one of the primary goals of C++ is to add the power of object-oriented programming on top of what you already know about procedural programming.

Prerequisites

Although it is not absolutely necessary, you will have the easiest time with this book if you are proficient in a procedural programming language such as Pascal or C and have experience creating and using data structures (for example, **record** in Pascal and **struct** in C). C++ and other object-oriented languages combine data structures and functions (which will be reviewed in the book).

This book covers many of the fundamentals of the C language. It is not, however, a complete reference. Many fine books on C are available. The definitive reference is *The C Programming Language*, Second Edition, by Brian Kernighan and Dennis Ritchie (Prentice-Hall 1988). The second edition follows the ANSI C standard. Since many of the new features of ANSI C were taken from C++, non-ANSI C books will be more confusing than helpful. (ANSI, the American National Standards Institute, is a standard-setting group). The C language described in this book is ANSI C.

Occasionally, references will be made to the "ARM." *The Annotated C++ Reference Manual* (Bjarne Stroustrup and Margaret Ellis, Addison-Wesley 1990) is the base document for ANSI C++ (as specified by the ANSI Committee X3J16, which was still in progress at this writing). It isn't an introductory text but it resolves language issues and is used, with the ANSI C++ draft, as the authority on C++. The C++ language described in this book conforms to the ANSI C++ draft that was available at the time the book was written.

Terminology

Italics will be used in this book to introduce a new word or concept and emphasize a word or phrase. Keywords, variable names, and function names are in **boldface**.

In this book, the *programmer* is someone who creates a collection of related functions that are made available to the *user*, who writes programs using these functions. The related functions are generally delivered as a *library*. The source code for the library may or may not be available. The programmer must understand the internals of the library, while the user generally has no desire to. Thus, unlike books that describe *end-user* (the people who use the programs) applications, the word "user" (also known as an *application developer*) in this book refers to someone who writes programs, but is a user of a library.

A *procedural language* emphasizes functions over data. Functions are treated as black boxes. Pieces of data move into a function, other pieces of data move out of the function. Procedural languages are often modeled with *data-flow diagrams*, which show data flowing through a system, into and out of functions. The most widely-known procedural languages are Pascal and C.

Why Use an Object-Oriented Language?

Object-oriented programming (often abbreviated as OOP) is a new way of thinking about problem solving with computers. Instead of trying to mold the problem into something familiar to the computer, the object-oriented approach adapts the computer to the problem. The problem is examined for independent entities that relate to other parts of the problem—these entities are not chosen based on their "computerizability," but because they actually exist and have some physical or conceptual boundary that divides them from the rest of the problem. These entities are represented as *objects* in the computer program. The goal is to have a one-to-one correspondence between entities in the physical problem and objects in the program.

You may have trouble choosing objects because the process is too obvious—you get used to the mental transformation required to force a problem into the arbitrary solution space of conventional computer programming. It can be a hard habit to break, but try to look at a problem in simple terms. For example, if you're creating a simulation of a parking lot, your objects will be cars, parking spaces, and toll booths. Objects for an oil field might be wells or blasts (for geological mapping). Shape objects can be used in a drawing program. A statistical analysis program might need matrix objects. The more simple and obvious your objects are, the easier it will be to create and maintain your program.

Object-Oriented Terminology

Programming in an object-oriented language means creating new types of data (called *classes*) and "teaching" those data types how to handle *messages*. You "teach" a class what to do with a message by creating a *method*, which is simply a function associated with the class. The user creates variables of a data type (objects or *instances*) and sends messages to those objects. Objects can even seem to take on life: "send a message to an object, and let the object figure out what to do with it."

History

It is suggested that object-oriented programming is a direct result of the chaos that occurs when conventional languages are applied to very large problems. As languages develop, so does their ability to handle complexity. In the evolution of each language, there comes a point when programmers begin to have difficulty managing programs of a certain size and sophistication.

The pioneers developed the first programming languages to trim mistakes on the part of the human reader, by translating from programming concepts (albeit very basic ones, like moving data in and out of machine registers) to machine representation. These languages used English-like words, and allowed the replacement of memory locations with names chosen by the programmer. This support for *mnemonic devices* to trigger mental association meant that the human spent more time on *semantics* (what the code means) and less time on *syntax* (how the words and phrases are assembled).

Procedural Languages

Complexity expands to fill available resources. Early programmers soon discovered difficulties in creating large, elaborate programs that worked correctly. Procedural languages were the next step in language evolution.

The model used in procedural languages is the *black box.* Every piece of a program is boxed off so the complexity of that piece is hidden. These "boxes" are *functions* in C, *procedures* in Pascal. The finished program is, at the top level, a collection of function calls.

The ideal black box doesn't make changes to data outside its boundaries (that is, it doesn't introduce *side effects*). In practice this is too severe a constraint, and black boxes modify data outside their boundaries. This introduces a weakness (often referred to as *coupling*) to the box, since the data isn't completely under its control.

Programs written in early, nonprocedural languages tended to be small, partly because programming itself was still young, but more often because the limits to complexity are reached early with these languages. When the move was made to procedural languages, the code was not difficult to rewrite. Procedural languages, however, are powerful enough to write large and complicated programs that cannot be cheaply abandoned.

The designers of procedural languages made an unconscious assumption when using the model of the black box that goes something like this: *Maintenance shouldn't happen. Needs don't change. Once the code is working, debugged, and correct, it should be epoxied into its black box.* This assumption works fine as long as project size is limited, but it can cause surprising disasters as complexity creeps into the "large" category.

The Software Crisis

Programming languages manage complexity. In the late '60s and early '70s, practitioners saw the limits of procedural languages in managing complexity and began the long, drawn-out complaint called "the software crisis."

The crisis sneaks up on people. There is no abrupt, chaotic edge when software suddenly becomes unmanageable. It slowly becomes harder to change the software, harder to get the bugs out, and harder to find programmers who want to do maintenance work. Managers are frustrated and bewildered, because they know it is *possible* to fix the program if only they can get someone to stick with it long enough. It is also expensive to abandon old code, so people keep trying to save it, rather than looking for a new way to program.

Structured Development

Procedural languages do not provide enough support to structure large programs for ease of modification and maintenance. The reaction to this problem was to force structure into the programs from outside through a methodology called *structured development*.

Structured development techniques salvage procedural languages for use in large projects. These techniques require a great deal of forethought and planning so the project assembles quickly, correctly, and is bug free and easy to maintain. Because it is an attempt to salvage a particular group of languages and not an insight into the needs of programmers, structured development tends to sound better than it works.

The selection of the problem to solve may have been skewed by perspective. Because the original programmers often didn't document their code, and because programmers who were brought into an existing project to maintain it often couldn't figure out what was going on by reading the code, it appeared that the solution to the software crisis was a methodology that guaranteed the production of good documentation to accompany the code. If you study the structured techniques, you'll find that this is where their focus is: a series of documents representing the system you wish to create. While the techniques may lead to a good design, they were driven by the need to create documentation.

Documentation is certainly an important aspect of a system, but the emphasis should *first* be on a good design. In addition, the concept of documentation should be replaced by the drive to make the program clear in whatever way is best—this can sometimes be accomplished simply by thoughtful naming of identifiers. A system that demands, for example, that each function have a manual page will not only create much unnecessary, tedious work (and the associated loss of enthusiasm that is so hard to quantify, yet so critical to success), but you'll also end up with a system that won't get maintained ("I'm still thinking about the problem; I'll fix the documentation later").

The important thing is to be able to extract *accurate* information somehow. Ideally, this will be from a wonderfully written book that describes the program in exquisite detail. Such things may exist. They may even have been accurate at one point in time. But without vigilance and money (which companies often don't wish to spend, preferring instead to fix it quickly) documentation inevitably gets out of sync with programs. A practical system will not only rely on a good design, but on brief, easy-to-maintain documentation that is tightly bound with the code, possibly in the form of special comments.

The final criticism of the structured techniques is that people learn and create through experimentation, not planning. Programmers are no different, and they often have shorter attention spans than most during management planning meetings. Programmers need a system that supports experimentation and salvages as many experiments as possible, not one that requires an entire project to be planned out before any code can be written.

An Evolution in Programming

Many useful techniques came from structured development, but it was not a "magic band-aid," merely a logical progression in programming. Whenever the traditional system is found to be flawed, an attempt is made to salvage it. The next step is the creation of a new system that accepts the limitations the old system attempted to deny (this is called a "paradigm shift"). Object-oriented programming is one such system. It probably isn't the last one we'll see.

Object-oriented techniques tend to emphasize (and support) design even more than structured techniques. You might even think of object-oriented programming as "better structured development."

Be aware, however, that creating and proselytizing design methodologies is a very lucrative business. Many folks may have gone into it not because they have experience in object-oriented programming that has provided insights into design, but instead because there is a big demand for OOP design methodologies. While a good OOP design methodology is certainly desirable, you should be suspicious of any that are presented to you as the best and correct way, especially if they look like a rehash of the structured methodologies. Some design pointers will be presented in this book, but no methodologies.

Supporting Experiments and Structure

Using assembly language, the programmer could stop decoding numbers and instead think about words. Procedural languages hid the complexity of the operations upon data. Object-oriented languages hide the data and the complexity of the program.

An object-oriented language emphasizes data types and the intrinsic operations that may be performed on those data types. Data are seen as inseparable from how they are used. Data do not flow openly around a system (as portrayed in data-flow diagrams used in the structured techniques), but are protected from accidental modification. In object-oriented programming, *messages* (rather than data) move around the system. Instead of the functional approach ("invoke a function on a piece of data"), in an object-oriented language you "send a message to an object."

An object-oriented language supports experimentation in two ways:

☐   Objects are neat, robust packages that don't break simply because other objects are around. A programmer may introduce new objects and code, knowing that bugs in the new code will be isolated from the rest of the system.

☐   New object types may be derived from old ones. This saves programmer time and supports quick explorations. It also localizes bugs to
the code for the derived object type, since the original type is
assumed to be working correctly.

The support for natural "packaging" of objects has another important
effect. Programmers choose to structure a program in an object-oriented
language *because it helps them code,* not because it has some unseen future
benefit. Good style becomes the path of least resistance rather than a
"cultural revolution." Planning is minimized and action is maximized.

The Process of Language Translation

To further describe object-oriented programming, some background
in language translation is necessary.

All computer languages are *translated* from something that tends to
be (relatively) easy for a human to understand into something that is
executed on a computer (*machine instructions*), but is very difficult (if not
impossible) for a human to understand. Traditionally, translators fall into
two classes: *interpreters* and *compilers.*

Interpreters

An *interpreter* translates *source code* (written in the programming
language) into activities (which may comprise groups of machine instructions) and immediately executes those activities. BASIC is the most
popular interpreted language. BASIC interpreters translate and execute
one line at a time and then forget the line has been translated. This makes
them slow, since they must retranslate any repeated code. More modern
interpreters translate the entire program into an intermediate language
that is executed by a much faster interpreter.

Interpreters have many advantages. The transition from writing code
to executing code is almost immediate, and the source code is always
available so the interpreter can be much more specific when an error

occurs. The benefits often cited for interpreters are ease of interaction and rapid development (but not execution) of programs.

Interpreters usually have severe limitations when building large projects. The interpreter (or a reduced version) must always be in memory to execute the code, and even the fastest interpreter may introduce unacceptable speed restrictions. Most interpreters require that the complete source code be brought into the interpreter all at once. Not only does this introduce a space limitation, it can also cause more difficult bugs if the language doesn't provide facilities to localize the effect of different pieces of code.

Compilers

A *compiler* translates source code directly into assembly language or machine instructions (often called *object code*). This is an involved process, and usually takes several steps. The transition from writing code to executing code is significantly longer with a compiler.

Depending on the acumen of the compiler writer, programs generated by a compiler tend to require much less space to run, and run much more quickly. Although size and speed are probably the most often cited reasons for using a compiler, in many situations they aren't the most important reasons. Some languages (such as C) are designed to allow pieces of a program to be compiled independently. These pieces are eventually combined into a final *executable program* by a program called the *linker.* This is called *separate compilation.*

Separate compilation has many benefits. A program that, taken all at once, would exceed the limits of the compiler or the compiling environment can be compiled in pieces. Programs can be built and tested a piece at a time. Once a piece is working, it can be saved and forgotten. Collections of tested and working pieces can be combined into libraries for use by other programmers. As each piece is created, the complexity of the other pieces is hidden. All these features support the creation of large programs.

Compiler debugging features have improved significantly. Early compilers only generated machine code, and the programmer inserted print statements to see what was going on. This was not always effective.

Recent compilers can insert information about the source code into the executable program. This information is used by powerful *source-level debuggers* to show exactly what is happening in a program by tracing its progress through the source code.

Some compilers tackle the compilation-speed problem by performing *in-memory compilation*. Most compilers work with files, reading and writing them in each step of the compilation process. In-memory compilers keep the program in RAM. For small programs, this can seem as responsive as an interpreter.

The Compilation Process

If you are going to create large programs, you need to understand the steps and tools in the compilation process. Some languages (C and C++, in particular) start compilation by running a *preprocessor* on the source code. The preprocessor is a simple program that replaces patterns in the source code with other patterns the programmer has defined (using *preprocessor directives*). Preprocessor directives are used to save typing and to increase the readability of the code (later in the book, you'll learn how the design of C++ is meant to discourage much of the use of the preprocessor, since it can cause subtle bugs). The preprocessed code is written to an intermediate file.

Compilers often do their work in two passes. The first pass *parses* the preprocessed code. The compiler breaks the source code into small units and organizes it into a structure called a *tree*. In the expression **A + B**, the elements **A**, **+**, and **B** are leaves on the parse tree. The parser generates a second intermediate file containing the parse tree.

A *global optimizer* is sometimes used between the first and second passes to produce smaller, faster code.

In the second pass, the *code generator* walks through the parse tree and generates either assembly language code or machine code for the nodes of the tree. If the code generator creates assembly code, the assembler is run. The end result in both cases is an *object module* (a file with an extension of **.o** or **.obj**). A *peephole optimizer* is sometimes used in the second pass to look for pieces of code containing redundant assembly language statements.

The use of the word "object" to describe chunks of machine code is an unfortunate artifact. The word came into use before anyone thought of object-oriented programming. "Object" is used in the same sense as "goal" when discussing compilation, while in object-oriented programming it means "a thing with boundaries."

The *linker* combines a list of object modules into an executable program that can be loaded and run by the operating system. When a function in one object module makes a reference to a function or variable in another object module, the linker resolves these references. The linker brings in a special object module to perform startup activities.

The linker can also search through special files called libraries. A library contains a collection of object modules in a single file. A library is created and maintained by a program called a *librarian*.

Static Type Checking

The compiler performs *type checking* during the first pass. Type checking tests for the proper use of arguments in functions (ensuring that a function receives the proper *data type*, for example, an integer or a text string that it expects) and prevents many kinds of programming errors. Since type checking occurs during compilation rather than when the program is running, it is called *static type checking.*

Some object-oriented languages (notably Smalltalk) perform all type checking at run time (*dynamic type checking*). Dynamic type checking is less restrictive during development, since you can send *any* message to *any* object (the object figures out whether the message is an error at run time). It also adds overhead to program execution and leaves the program open for run-time errors that can only be detected through exhaustive testing.

C++ uses static type checking because the language cannot assume any particular run-time support for bad messages. Static type checking notifies the programmer about misuse of types right away and maximizes execution speed. As you learn C++, you will see that most of the language design decisions favor the same kind of high-speed, robust, production-oriented programming the C language is famous for.

You can disable static type checking. You can also do your own dynamic type checking—you just need to write the code.

Why You Need Objects

Now that some of the framework is in place, the specific problems with traditional programming languages and the solutions offered by C++ will be examined.

Creating Multiple Entities

When using a procedural language, the programmer often creates functions that cannot easily be adapted to new situations. A common pitfall is the "one-function solution." Here, it is assumed that there is only one of something, and that fact is wired into the system. When a new situation with more than one arises, the program must be redesigned.

As an example, when displaying information, you can fall into the habit of programming as if the (one) screen were the only way to talk to the end user. If a window system is used, however, your whole way of thinking must change—now there are many screens, each of which must be treated as a separate entity.

To manage multiple entities in a procedural language, a data structure must be declared to hold all the information necessary for each entity. For example, a window structure has an X,Y location, a size, foreground and background colors, a place to store data, etc. Functions are defined to initialize, clean up, and manipulate the entities.

It takes effort to think of the display as a single screen and then switch to thinking of multiple windows. After the code is written, creating multiple entities is fairly simple; a data structure is declared for each entity, and functions are called with the address of a structure as a parameter. It is as easy to create one entity as to create many.

This system works fine, but there is a lot of room for bookkeeping errors. The user of the library must remember to initialize and clean up the structures. Sometimes the programmer forces the user to do this via direct manipulation of the structure, rather than through functions. This can be confusing, since there are usually structure elements that are used internally by the system, but are visible to the user.

The visibility of structure elements presents another problem: the user's functions may also manipulate structure elements, sometimes intentionally, sometimes accidentally. The user can inadvertently change structure elements, causing bizarre and untraceable results.

Data Abstraction

C++ supports multiple entities and libraries using *data abstraction.* Data abstraction means you can combine the data structure and the operations on that data structure together into a new *abstract data type.* An abstract data type behaves just like data types that are built into the language, except they aren't part of the language definition; they are something the programmer has created.

When you create a data structure in a procedural language, you usually create separate functions to manipulate the structure. Those functions can only be used on that structure. Other functions don't know how to manipulate the structure, since the structure isn't a built-in type. It makes sense, then, to bind into one unit the data structure and the functions that will manipulate the data structure. In C++, this unit is called a *class* (also called a *user-defined type*). Variables, or *instances* of that class, are called *objects.*

As a user of a procedural language, you don't think about what goes on when you declare and use a built-in data type or what the variable looks like inside. The functionality of a data type is built into the compiler, and it's complicated.

An IEEE (Institute of Electrical and Electronic Engineers) floating-point number, for example, contains an exponent, a mantissa, and a sign bit, all of which must be initialized properly. When you use floating-point numbers, the compiler calls special floating-point functions. To prevent accidental errors, you don't have explicit control over the exponent, mantissa, or sign data—these are only manipulated by the special functions called by the compiler.

Abstract data typing works the same way. The data elements of a structure may be *private,* so the user cannot directly manipulate them. Private data elements may only be manipulated by special functions that are part of the class (*member functions*) or nonmember functions that have been given special permission (*friend functions*). This prevents accidental modification of the data and makes it much easier to track down bugs.

Each class has two types of member functions that are special. One, called the *constructor*, takes care of initialization when a new object is created. The other, the *destructor*, automatically cleans up an object when it is no longer needed. In the case of a window object, a constructor might create space in memory and paint the window on the screen. The destructor removes the window from the screen and frees the memory. Constructors and destructors prevent the existence of objects that haven't been initialized properly, and thus remove a significant source of bugs.

Some languages, such as C, can define an *alias* for a structure or built-in type and use the alias as if it were a new type. In C, the keyword for this is **typedef**, which suggests abstract data typing, but true abstract data typing differs from aliasing with **typedef**. In abstract data typing, the programmer defines a data structure, the private elements and functions that are used only with that structure, and the initialization and cleanup functions. The resulting abstract data type is treated by the compiler almost as if it were a built-in data type. The compiler ensures that the type is used properly and that only specific functions modify the data in the object.

Organizing Code

In C++, the *interface* description and the *implementation* of a class are separate. The interface describes *what* the class does, and the implementation defines *how* the class works. Compilation (but not final linking) can occur with only the interface description. A different implementation can be created at a later date and linked in, without recompiling the rest of the project.

This feature has a number of benefits. Bugs (and bug fixes) tend to be isolated; they don't ripple through the rest of the code. Improvements and modifications can be made without concern for destroying the correct behavior of some other part of the system.

Software engineers think the separation of interface and implementation is very helpful. You can describe and compile a system to ensure that it all fits together without writing an implementation. The compiler is, in effect, a "design checker." Once the interfaces are specified, the implementation proceeds with the knowledge that system integration has already occurred.

Finding the Objects in Your System

Classes also support a logical breakdown of code components. The best way to define classes is to look for distinct elements in the problem description. An object in the computer program (the solution domain) should correspond as closely as possible to an object in the problem domain. One approach to this is to write down the description of the project in words and then look for the nouns to find the objects and the verbs to find the messages/functions. A well-designed object-oriented program is much simpler to describe to nonprogrammers, and it prevents the phenomenon often seen in programming where every solution "looks like a computer" rather than like a weather system, a controller, a multimeter, and so on. A solution that is a reflection of the problem domain is much easier to understand, repair, and modify (and thus cheaper to maintain).

C++ is intended to support library use. It guides the programmer toward a particular style of program organization. In addition, a particular interface is not just a suggestion to be used or discarded by the user. While the structured approach relies upon human organizations to make sure the implementation doesn't stray from the specification, the C++ translator *enforces* the proper use of data types (classes). This feature supports the construction of very large projects; the specification language is the **class** declaration, and the compiler checks for accurate implementation and use.

Inheritance

In an object-oriented language, one user-defined type (**class**) can *inherit* the characteristics of another. When you inherit, you say: "this new class is an old one, plus a few additions and modifications" (or "with a few restrictions"). The compiler effectively makes a copy of the original class into the new one and allows you to add or modify members without corrupting the original class code.

Conserving Effort

Inheritance is useful in two ways. It conserves coding effort. If you have a debugged, operational class that you or someone else has written, inheritance helps you reuse the code in the class. You don't need to fight through the source code and understand the implementation. You also don't have to make a copy of the original code for your new project (a typical practice in C that requires the maintenance of multiple different versions of the code). You make changes where you need them and reuse old code. You might otherwise start from scratch rather than struggle to figure out how the code works.

Creating Extensible Programs

The second use for inheritance is more subtle and powerful. The object-oriented concept of *subclassing* helps the programmer organize a solution to make it easy to maintain and extend.

When a *derived class* inherits from a *base class*, the objects of the derived class still retain membership in the base class. By deriving many classes from the same base class, you can create a group of classes that have the same interface but different implementations. The main program manages a group of these objects. It can send any message to any object, but the effect will be different, depending on the specific subclass.

For example, suppose you are designing an air-traffic control system. All objects on the display will be of the class **plane**, but they will each have their own pattern on the screen. The base class in this system is **plane**, and the interface to **plane** says that "a **plane** object knows how to draw itself and move itself," even though a **plane** can't know how to perform these operations until it knows whether it's an **airliner** or a small private **aircraft**. The different types of **plane**s are derived from **plane**, and each is given methods to draw and move themselves. The air-traffic control system handles **plane** objects, it sends messages to the objects telling them to draw and move themselves and the objects figure out what to do with the messages.

Using identical interfaces with different implementations is called *polymorphism.* Like many C++ features, polymorphism improves program clarity. A program designed around polymorphism is easy to maintain and extend.

Since the program is only a manager for a set of generic objects, bugs are automatically isolated in the objects themselves. Once a base class is debugged, any errors in a derived class must be due to the new code in the derived class.

To extend a polymorphic program, simply derive a new subclass from the same base class the other generic objects inherited. The new subclass can be managed by the same program without modification.

A classic example of polymorphism is the "shape" program (shown later in the book), that manages generic **shape** objects. **shape** has an interface that includes methods to **draw()** and **erase()**. If you derive **circle**, **square**, and **line** subclasses from **shape**, they can have specific implementations of **draw()** and **erase()**. Then the program sends, for example, the **draw()** message to a **shape** object, ignorant of whether it is a **circle**, **square**, or **line**. The object figures out how to draw itself. The program never needs to know the specific type of the object, only that it is a **shape**.

To extend this program, derive a new subclass (for example, a **triangle**) from **shape** and implement the methods to **draw()** and **erase()** a **triangle**. That's all there is to it—the program already knows how to send all possible messages to objects of type **triangle**, since **triangle** is just another **shape**.

Late Binding

Resolving a function call is the process of inserting the address (or some other reference) of the function definition at the point where the function is called. When the program executes, the function is executed by performing an assembly language call to that address.

A typical procedural language resolves function calls at compile time.

A program designed around polymorphism manages a collection of base-class objects. The precise result of a message sent to one of these objects cannot be determined at compile time, since only the base class of the object is known, not the subclass. The specific function that is called must thus be determined at run time, rather than compile time. The ability to delay function resolution until run time is called *late binding*. Late binding is an essential feature of an object-oriented language because it is the mechanism that implements polymorphism.

Overloading

The idea of an "intelligent object" deciding what to do with a message has one more aspect in C++.

Overloading means that one function name can be used in many different ways. As an example, suppose a class has a method called **print()**. You can overload **print()** so it will display the contents of an object when called without arguments, or display the object and some text when called with a string argument, or display some other kind of information when called with other arguments. Therefore you can call **print()** with a variety of different arguments, and (in effect) the object "figures out what to do with the message."

Ordinary functions (not class methods) may be overloaded in C++, providing a single function name and many argument lists. C++ also allows operators (**+**, **−**, **=**, etc.) to be overloaded so that mathematically oriented objects may be used with a familiar syntax. For example, you will find a **matrix** class in the appendices. Matrices may be added, subtracted, multiplied, etc. The code looks just like the mathematical equations, so it's a better match to the problem being solved.

Your Transformation to OOP

As you learn object-oriented programming in C++, you'll probably have the same experience as most other people who have made the transformation from a procedural language. This transformation seems to consist of a series of steps coupled with two phases of understanding for each step. These phases correspond to two different ways of viewing the benefits of programming in C++.

The first benefit may be thought of as simply a "mechanical advantage": programming is easier because the compiler performs better error checking than C and because C++ allows you to organize your code in a better fashion and reuse that code more expediently. For example, tying code together with data promotes ease and safety in using libraries (which may be the most common use for the bulk of programmers). A second powerful example is the use of inheritance to customize an application framework for your particular program. The "mechanical advantage" view of C++ is very important for saving money: reusing code easily and quickly, without introducing bugs into existing code.

The second benefit, and the second "phase" of your understanding of each "step," is object-oriented programming. While the mechanical advantage can be thought of as an extension to procedural programming, OOP is a different way of thinking about programming altogether. To understand OOP, you'll have to look at some aspects of programming with "new eyes," and this might take some time. The benefits are dramatic and well worth the effort. Because you think of the problem in its own terms rather than the terms of the computer, OOP makes it easier for you to conceptualize the problem and keep the complexity of the solution under control. The class mechanism creates a "firewall" between pieces of code, which makes it much easier to assemble the system and to change the design during assembly as your insights grow. Also, and possibly most important, OOP makes it easy to extend the system, so it reduces the cost of maintenance.

"Aha!" Experiences with C++

People commonly have a series of experiences with C++ that seem to be an insight into what the language is all about. Later, they discover that such an experience doesn't represent the entirety of understanding, but simply a portion of it, and they move on to the next step. Each step is valid; you will be seeing genuine improvements, but try to keep your mind open to further benefits so you can smoothly move your understanding into full object-oriented programming.

First you understand the concept of simple data abstraction: now you can add functions to structures, so the functions are intimately associated with the structures they modify. This is what you've probably (consciously or unconsciously) been wanting to do in your procedural language when creating structures and the functions that operate on them, so it seems to clarify things a lot and make your code neater. Additional features like better type checking, constructors, and destructors to reduce errors by guaranteeing initialization and cleanup, dynamic object creation for easy and safe creation of variables at run-time, and operator overloading all add up to a stepwise improvement in the language. You can see how this makes library use easier and your code more robust (and indeed, just by using these features you'll see a significant improvement in your programming). So you say, "Now I know what C++ is all about."

Then you discover the basics of inheritance. This makes a lot of sense because it means you can stop breaking existing code every time you want to extend its functionality; in particular, if you have a library that doesn't quite do what you want, you don't need to delve into the source code for all the functions to adapt its behavior to your needs. You simply inherit, and the compiler copies the class data structure and functionality into your new class. Then you can add or change what you want without touching the original code. In addition, all the member functions in the base class are used directly, without duplicating them, which provides a potential for reduced code space. All this is even more impressive than wrapping functions and data together inside a class, and it has much greater potential. So you say "I didn't understand C++ before, but now I *really* do."

Finally you stop ignoring the **virtual** keyword, and start wondering what it's actually for. This step has been said to take the new programmer as long as nine months, but perhaps other stimulation can shorten the C++ learning curve (see, for example, *The World of C++* video course from Borland, written by the author, or the video tape created for this book). With the understanding of why the **virtual** keyword exists in C++ and what it means, comes a whole new way of looking at the language, the reasons behind abstraction and inheritance, and the motivations for design of object-oriented programming. When you understand **virtual**, you understand the core of C++.

What's OOP Really All About?

An object-oriented language supports three key features:

☐ **Abstract data typing** The programmer can create new data types to adapt the programming environment to the need at hand (or use someone else's types). This generally takes the form of tying the data structure together with its operations (functions). Put another way, you can provide both characteristics and behaviors for the new data type. Various OOP languages provide other features to make the abstract data type more robust; C++ provides *access control* to data with the keywords **public**, **private**, and **protected**, as well as guaranteed initialization and cleanup with constructors and destructors. (Note that "abstract" is sometimes considered an unfortunate designation, since the new data type seems as "real" as an **int** or **float**. No doubt the term was intended to describe the process of abstraction from the entity in the real-world problem into the representation in the computer).

☐ **Inheritance** Once you have a type defined, you can specify other types based on that type. For example, dogs, cats, birds, and hamsters can all be described as types of pets, with certain common characteristics (they all have an age) and behaviors (you must clean up after them). Inheritance defines the relationship between the base type and the derived types. In C++, the compiler physically implements inheritance by making a copy of the data structure and providing access to the member functions in the base class. However, inheritance is much more than this—it's a conceptual relationship between the two types, which should reflect the same relationship in the problem space. If a base class can receive a message, any message you send to an object derived from that base should generate an appropriate response.

☐ **Polymorphism** "Generating an appropriate response" as described in the previous paragraph has some subtle implications. Deriving a class from an existing class means you're making a new type of the existing class. You can send any message to a derived type that you can send to the base type. For example, a **shape** can accept the messages **draw()** and **erase()**. Anything derived from a **shape** is a type of **shape**, and can receive the same messages. Now what happens when you send a message (**draw()**, for example) to something you and the compiler perceive as the base type, **shape**, but is actually a more specific derived type like a **circle** or **triangle**? You want the appropriate drawing activities to be performed, without knowing exactly what type of object you're dealing with. The proper behavior of a derived-class object when treated as a base-class object is referred to as *polymorphism*. Polymorphism is the third pivotal feature of an object-oriented programming language.

This magical behavior is not an anomaly, but instead a design objective when you're writing OOP programs—the code manipulating objects should use the generic interface and know nothing about the specifics of the objects. This way, that code doesn't have to be changed when new types of objects are added to the system through inheritance—the new types take the same messages; they just perform different actions. This is the concept of an *extensible program.*

Once you have the necessary classes, solving the problem only entails making some objects and sending messages to them. As long as the objects respond to the messages in the desired fashion, the relationship between classes or how the classes are created isn't that important. Thus, object-oriented programming is often summed up as "sending messages to objects."

☐ **Other features** The definition of OOP does not generally include features other than the key three (although this can be the subject of hot debate). However, many OOP languages either directly support or don't stand in the way of things like concurrency (multitasking), persistence (variables that exist between the invocations of a program), and exception handling.

Summary: The Activities of Object-Oriented Programming

The primary activity in object-oriented programming is the creation of new abstract data types (classes); these data types may be created through inheritance, and they may have polymorphic behaviors.

The user of a class creates objects and sends messages to the objects. An object "figures out" what to do with a message.

Data abstraction and hiding reduces intermodule dependence. This means that modifying code in one section won't affect code in another section—changes are isolated and don't propagate through the system.

Inheritance helps you reuse code. When used with polymorphism, inheritance helps you reuse program designs and create extensible programs. This isn't automatic; you must build it into the system.

How C++ Supports Object-Oriented Programming

C++ supports abstract data typing with the **class** construct. Elements of the **class** (*members*) can be built-in data types, objects, or functions. Members can be **public** (available to everyone), **private** (only available to other members), or **protected** (available to **class** members and members of inherited classes). Combining like functions and data is called *encapsulation*. Removing data from public view is called *data hiding*.

C++ supports inheritance. You can derive a new user-defined type from an old one and make changes only where you need them. Inheritance promotes easy code reuse, and it is essential to implement polymorphism.

C++ supports polymorphism with the **virtual** keyword. A **virtual** function created in a base class and redefined in a derived class may act polymorphically. When the function is called as a member of the base class, the proper code is called via late binding.

Function overloading provides support for the general idea of "send a message to an object, and let the object figure out what to do with it."

C++ supports object-oriented programming without losing the efficiency of C.

A Note About Smalltalk

Smalltalk and similar object-oriented languages are different from C++. They generally provide much more of an "environment" for programming. Many implementations of Smalltalk go so far as to replace the operating system. Often, all the function binding occurs at run time, and there is no static type checking. Debugging is built into every object. Every object is derived from the same base class and the *activation record* (containing the primary information about each object) is the same size, so all objects can be manipulated by the debugger.

For these reasons, Smalltalk and similar languages have a much different feel than C++, and a common claim from Smalltalk programmers is that C++ is not truly object oriented.

C++ was designed to provide support for object-oriented programming and bring the benefits of that system into the mainstream development world. On the way, some compromises were made. In particular, Stroustrup was unwilling to give up the run-time efficiency of C. In addition, robust programs require static type checking. Demanding that all objects be derived from the same base class is an impractical constraint upon the programmer. Debugging in the manner of Smalltalk isn't possible, so conventional compiled-language debuggers are used instead.

C++ combines the benefits of object-oriented programming with the practical speed of C. It was designed for and is used in real programming projects in all situations: switching systems, operating systems, desktop publishing systems, computer-aided design programs, embedded software, mathematical analysis—virtually any programming project can benefit from C++. What's important to you is that it increases your programming power.

A Better C

If, after this brief and somewhat philosophical introduction to object-oriented programming, you don't feel that you can dive in and instantly use all the features, fear not. You can still write working programs. One of the objectives of C++ is to retain the experience of the enormous number of C programmers (since Pascal is a cousin to C—at least in spirit—this extends to Pascal programmers). You can start using C++ by programming in your usual procedural style and add features as you learn them. Don't worry, though. The features are enticing. Once you get an appetite for new ones, you will want to try others.

CHAPTER

Using Predefined Classes

*T*he user-defined data type, or class, is what distinguishes C++ from traditional procedural languages. A class is a new data type that you or someone else creates to solve a particular type of problem. Once a class is created, anyone can use it without knowing the specifics of how it works, or even how classes are built. This chapter will teach you enough of the basics of C and C++ so you can utilize a class that someone else has written. The quick coverage of C++ features that are similar to C features will continue in Chapters 3 and 4.

This chapter treats classes as if they are just another built-in data type available for use in programs. So you don't see any undefined concepts, the process of writing your own classes must be delayed until the last part of Chapter 3. This may cause a tedious delay for experienced C programmers. However, to leap past the necessary basics would hopelessly confuse programmers attempting to move to C++ from other languages.

Unless otherwise noted, all descriptions in this book refer to C++ that conforms to AT&T release 3.0. All references to C, unless otherwise noted, mean ANSI C.

If you program with Pascal or some other procedural language, this chapter gives you a decent background in the style of C used in C++. If you are familiar with the style of C described in the first edition of Kernighan & Ritchie (often called K&R C) you will find some new and different features in C++, as well as ANSI C. If you are familiar with ANSI C, and in particular with function prototypes, you should skim through this chapter looking for features that are particular to C++.

Classes that someone else has created are often packaged into a library. This chapter uses the iostream library of classes, which comes with all C++ implementations. Iostreams are a very useful way to read from files and the keyboard, and to write to files and the display. After covering the basics of building a program in C and C++, iostreams will be used to show how easy it is to utilize a predefined library of classes.

To create your first program you must understand the tools used to build applications.

Tools for Separate Compilation

Chapter 1 discussed the importance of separate compilation when building large projects. In C and C++, a program can be created in small, manageable, independently tested pieces. Programs created with separate compilation can be much larger than programs created by languages that require the entire program to be contained in a single file, such as BASIC and early versions of Turbo Pascal.

Programming in a language that supports separate compilation is different from putting the program in a single file. To create a program with multiple files, functions in one file must access functions and data in other files. When compiling a file, the C or C++ compiler must know about the functions and data in the other files: their names and proper usage. The compiler ensures the functions and data are used correctly. This process of "telling the compiler" the names of external functions and data and what they should look like is called *declaration*. Once you declare a function or variable, the compiler knows how to check to make sure it is used properly.

At the end of the compilation process, the executable program is constructed from the object modules and libraries. The compiler produces object modules from the source code. These are files with extensions of .o or .obj, and should not be confused with object-oriented programming "objects."

The linker must go through all the object modules and *resolve* all the external references—that is, make sure that all the external functions and data you claimed existed in declarations during compilation actually exist.

Declarations vs. Definitions

A *declaration* tells the compiler, "This function or this piece of data exists somewhere else, and here is what it should look like." A *definition* tells the compiler, "Make this piece of data here" or "make this function here." You can declare a piece of data or a function in many different places, but there must only be one definition in C and C++. When the linker is uniting all the object modules, it will complain if it finds more than one definition for the same function or piece of data.

Declarations normally go in header files with an extension of .h. Definitions normally go in implementation files with extensions of .cpp.

Almost all C/C++ programs require declarations. Before you can write your first program, you need to understand the proper way to write a declaration.

Function Declaration Syntax

A function declaration in ANSI C and C++ gives the function name, the argument types passed to the function, and the return value of the function. For example, here is a declaration for a function called **func1()** that takes two integer arguments (integers are denoted in C/C++ with the keyword **int**) and returns an integer:

```
int func1(int,int);
```

C programmers should note that this is different from function declarations in K&R C. The first keyword you see is the return value, all by itself: **int**. The arguments are enclosed in parentheses after the function name in the order they are used. The semicolon indicates the end of a statement; in this case, it tells the compiler "that's all—there is no function definition here!"

C/C++ declarations attempt to mimic the form of the item's use. For example, if A is another integer, the above function might be used this way:

```
A = func1(2,3);
```

Since **func1()** returns an integer, the C or C++ compiler will check the use of **func1()** to make sure that **A** is an integer and both arguments are integers.

In C and C++, arguments in function declarations may have names. The compiler ignores the names, but they can be helpful as mnemonic devices for the user. For example, we can declare **func1()** in a different fashion that has the same meaning:

```
int func1(int length, int width);
```

A Gotcha

There is a significant difference between C (both ANSI and K&R) and C++ for functions with empty argument lists. In C, the declaration

```
int func2();
```

means "a function with any number and type of argument." This prevents type-checking, so in C++ it means "a function with *no* arguments."

 Remember   If you declare a function with an empty argument list in C++, it's different from what you might be used to in C.

Function Definitions

Function definitions look like function declarations except they have bodies. A *body* is a collection of statements enclosed in curly braces. Braces denote the beginning and ending of a block of code; they have the same purpose as the **begin** and **end** keywords in Pascal. To give **func1()** a definition that is an empty body (a body containing no code), write this:

```
int func1(int length, int width) { }
```

Notice that in the function definition, the braces replace the semicolon. Since braces surround a statement or group of statements, you don't need a semicolon. Notice also that the arguments in the function definition must have names if you want to use the arguments in the function body (since they are never used here, they are optional).

Function definitions are explored in Chapter 3.

Variable Declaration Syntax

The meaning attributed to the phrase "variable declaration" has historically been confusing and contradictory, and it's important that you understand the correct definition so you can read code properly. A variable declaration tells the compiler what a variable looks like. It says "I know you haven't seen this name before, but I promise it exists someplace, and it's a variable of *X* type."

In a function declaration, you give a type (the return value), the function name, the argument list, and a semicolon. That's enough for the compiler to figure out that it's a declaration, and what the function should look like. By inference, a variable declaration might be a type followed by a name. For example,

```
int A;
```

could declare the variable **A** as an integer, using the above logic.

Here's the conflict: there is enough information in the above code for the compiler to create space for an integer called **A**, and that's what happens. To resolve this dilemma, a keyword is necessary for C and C++ to say "this is only a declaration; it's defined elsewhere." The keyword is **extern**. It can mean the definition is external to the file, or later in the file.

Declaring a variable without defining it means using the **extern** keyword before a description of the variable, like this:

```
extern int A;
```

The **extern** keyword can also apply to function declarations. For **func1()**, it looks like this:

```
extern int func1(int length, int width);
```

This statement is equivalent to the previous **func1()** declarations. Since there is no function body, the compiler must treat it as a function declaration rather than a function definition.

The **extern** keyword is superfluous and optional for function declarations. It is probably unfortunate that the designers of C did not require the use of **extern** for function declarations; it would have been more consistent and less confusing (but would have required more typing, which certainly explains what they did).

Including Headers

Most libraries contain significant numbers of functions and variables. To save work and ensure consistency when making the external declarations for these items, C/C++ uses a device called the *header file*. A header file is a file containing the external declarations for a library; it conventionally has a filename extension of .h, like this:

headerfile.h

You may also see some older code using different extensions like .hxx or .hpp.

The programmer who creates the library provides the header file. To declare the functions and external variables in the library, the user simply includes the header file. To include a header file, use the **#include** preprocessor directive. This tells the preprocessor to open the named header file and insert its contents where the **#include** statement appears. Files may be named in a **#include** statement in two ways: in double quotes, or in angle brackets (**<>**). Filenames in double quotes, such as:

```
#include "local.h"
```

tell the preprocessor to search the current directory for the file and report an error if the file does not exist. Filenames in angle brackets tell the preprocessor to look through a search path specified in the environment. Setting the search path varies between machines, operating systems and C++ implementations. To include the iostream header file, you say:

```
#include <iostream.h>
```

The preprocessor will find the iostream header file (often in a subdirectory called INCLUDE) and insert it.

In C, a header file should not contain any function or data definitions because the header can be included in more than one file. At link time, the linker would then find multiple definitions and complain. In C++, there are two exceptions: **inline** functions and **const** constants (described in Chapter 3) can both be safely placed in header files.

Linking

The linker collects object modules (with filename extensions of .o or .obj) generated by the compiler into an executable program the operating system can load and run. It is the last phase of the compilation process.

Linker characteristics vary from system to system. Generally, you just tell the linker the names of the object modules and libraries you want linked together and the name of the executable, and it goes to work. Some systems require you to invoke the linker yourself. With most C++ packages, you invoke the linker through C++. In many situations, the linker is invoked for you invisibly.

Some linkers won't search object files and libraries more than once, and they search through the list you give them from left to right. This means that the order of object files and libraries can be important. If you have a mysterious problem that doesn't show up until link time, one possibility is the order in which the files are given to the linker.

Using Libraries

Now that you know the basic terminology, you can understand how to use a library. To use a library:

1. Include the library's header file.

2. Use the functions and variables in the library.

3. Link the library into the executable program.

These steps also apply when the object modules aren't combined into a library. Including a header file and linking the object modules are the basic steps for separate compilation in both C and C++.

How the Linker Searches a Library

When you make an external reference to a function or variable in C or C++, the linker, upon encountering this reference, can do one of two things. If it has not already encountered the definition for the function or variable, it adds it to its list of "unresolved references." If the linker has already encountered the definition, the reference is resolved.

If the linker cannot find the definition in the list of object modules, it searches the libraries. Libraries have some sort of indexing, so the linker doesn't need to look through all the object modules in the library—it just looks in the index. When the linker finds a definition in a library, the entire object module, not just the function definition, is linked into the executable program. Note that the whole library isn't linked, just the object module in the library that contains the definition you want (otherwise programs would be unnecessarily large). If you want to minimize executable program size, you might consider putting a single function in each source code file when you build your own libraries. This requires more editing, but it can be helpful to the user.

 Note Because the linker searches files in the order you give them, you can preempt the use of a library function by inserting a file with your own function, using the same function name, into the list before the library name appears. Since the linker will resolve any references to this function by using your function before it searches the library, your function is used instead of the library function.

Secret Additions

When a C or C++ executable program is created, certain items are secretly linked in. One of these is the startup module, which contains initialization routines that must be run any time a C or C++ program executes. These routines set up the stack and initialize certain variables in the program.

The linker always searches the standard library for the compiled versions of any "standard" functions called in the program. The iostream functions, for example, are in the standard C++ library.

Because the standard library is always searched, you can use any function (or class, in C++) in the library by including the appropriate header file in your program. To use the iostream functions, you just include the **iostream.h** header file.

In non-ANSI implementations of C (and C++ C-code generators that use non-ANSI implementations of C), commonly used functions are not always contained in the library that is searched by default. Math functions, in particular, are often kept in a separate library. You must explicitly add the library name to the list of files handed to the linker.

Using Plain C Libraries

Just because you are writing code in C++, you are not prevented from using C library functions. There has been a tremendous amount of work done for you in these functions, so they can save you a lot of time. You should hunt through the manuals for your C and/or C++ compiler before writing new functions.

This book will use C library functions when convenient (ANSI C library functions will be used to increase the portability of the programs).

Using predefined C library functions is very strightforward—just include the appropriate header file and use the function.

 Note Since ANSI C header files use function prototyping, their function declarations agree with C++. If, however, your C header files use the older K&R C "empty-argument-list" style for function declarations, you will have trouble because the C++ compiler takes these to mean "functions with no arguments." To fix the problem, you must create new header files and either put the proper argument lists in the declarations or simply put ellipses (...) in the argument list, which mean "any number and type of arguments."

If your C functions have been compiled with a compatible C compiler, and the header files have not been explicitly prepared for C++, you'll have to do one other thing. C++ uses different names inside the compiler for its identifiers than C does (you'll understand why as you learn the language). To tell the compiler you're using a C library, with C names, you use an *alternate-linkage specification*. Here's what it looks like, for a file called **myheader.h**:

```
extern "C" { #include <myheader.h> }
```

The "C" tells the compiler how to generate names when it sees the declarations in the header file. This way, the linker will see the proper names for function calls when it searches the C library. Header files for C libraries that have been prepared for C++ already contain alternate-linkage specifications.

Your First C++ Program

You now know enough of the basics to create and compile a program. The program will use the predefined C++ **iostream** class that comes with all C++ packages. The **iostream** class handles input and output for files, with the console, and with "standard" input and output (which may be redirected to files or devices). In this very simple program, a stream object will be used to print a message on the screen.

Using the iostream Classes

To declare the functions and external data in the **iostream** class, include the header file with the statement

```
#include <iostream.h>
```

The first program uses the concept of standard output, which means "a general-purpose place to send output." You will see other examples using standard output in different ways, but here it will just go to the screen. The iostream package automatically defines a variable (an object) called **cout** that accepts all data bound for standard output.

To send data to standard output, use the operator **<<**. C programmers know this operator as the bitwise left shift. C++ allows operators to be overloaded. When you overload an operator, you give it a new meaning when that operator is used with an object of a particular type. With iostream objects, the operator **<<** means "send to." For example:

```
cout << "howdy!";
```

sends the string "howdy!" to the object called **cout**.

Chapter 5 covers operator overloading in detail.

Fundamentals of Program Structure

A C/C++ program is a collection of variables, function definitions, and function calls. When the program starts, it executes initialization code and calls a special function, **main()**. You put the primary code for the program here. (All functions in this book use parentheses after the function name.)

A function definition consists of a return value type (which defaults to integer if none is specified), a function name, an argument list in parentheses, and the function code contained in braces. Here is a sample function definition for a function named **function()**:

```
void function() {
  // function code here (this is a comment)
}
```

The above function has an empty argument list and a body that only contains a comment.

There can be many sets of braces within a function definition, but there must always be at least one set surrounding the function body. Since **main()** is a function, it must follow these rules. Unless you intend to return a value from your program (some operating systems can utilize a return value from a program), **main()** should have a return type of **void**, so the compiler won't issue a warning message.

C and C++ are free-form languages. With few exceptions, the compiler ignores carriage returns and white space, so it must have some way to determine the end of a statement. In C/C++, statements are delimited by semicolons.

C comments start with **/*** and end with ***/**. They can include carriage returns. C++ uses C-style comments and adds a new type of comment: **//**. The **//** starts a comment that terminates with a carriage return. It is more convenient than **/* */** for one-line comments, and is used extensively in this book.

Hello, World!

And now, finally, the first program:

```
//: HELLO.CPP — Saying Hello with C++
#include <iostream.h> // stream declarations

void main() {
  cout << "Hello, World! I am " << 8 << " Today!" << endl;
}
```

The **cout** object is handed a series of arguments, which it prints out in left-to-right order. With iostreams, you can string together a series of arguments like this, which makes the class easy to use.

Text inside double quotes is called a *string*. The compiler creates space for strings and stores the ASCII equivalent for each character in this space. The string is terminated with a value of 0 to indicate the end of the string. The special iostream manipulator **endl** outputs the line and a newline.

Inside a character string, you can insert special characters that do not print using escape sequences. These consist of a backslash (\) followed by a special code. For example **\n** means new line. Your compiler manual or local ANSI C guide gives a complete set of escape sequences; others include **\t** (tab), **** (backslash), and **\b** (backspace).

Notice that the entire phrase terminates with a semicolon.

String arguments and constant numbers are mixed in the **cout** statement. Because the operator **<<** is overloaded with a variety of meanings when used with **cout**, you can send **cout** a variety of different arguments, and it will "figure out what to do with the message."

Note the **:** in the first (in this case the only) comment (**//**) line (and a period in the second comment line, when there is one). The purpose of these is explained in "Comment Notation," near the end of the chapter.

Running the Compiler

To compile the program, edit it into a plain text file called HELLO.CPP and invoke the compiler with HELLO.CPP as the argument. For simple, one-file programs like this one, most compilers will take you all the way through the process. To run Borland C++, the command line is:

bcc hello.cpp

or simply

bcc hello

Microsoft C++ compiles only with:

cl hello.cpp

The UNIX C++ packages vary. Plain vanilla **cfront** from AT&T uses a capital CC to run C++, but you should check your particular installation.

C++ *Translation Strategies*

Chapter 1 stated that all languages are implemented with translators. There are two types of translators for C++: C-code generators and native-code compilers. The activities you see when you invoke C++ depend upon the approach used in your translator.

C-Code Generation

When Bjarne Stroustrup created C++, he realized that a large hurdle in its acceptance is availability. To hasten availability, he created a C-code generator that quickly ports to any platform with a C compiler. The C-code generator translates C++ into C and feeds it to the local C compiler. Most packages for UNIX are derived from AT&T **cfront**, and are thus C-code generators. Some packages for other platforms including PCs are also C-code generators derived from **cfront**.

C-code generators have several advantages. Because they are derived from the original AT&T sources, C++ programs tend to be transportable between different platforms running C-code generators (this used to be more of a problem than it is now, since compilers tend to conform much more). The debugged C-code generator can be quickly moved to another environment. When attempting to decipher the meaning of a C++ statement, it is possible (though often painful) to discern meaning from the generated C code. C-code generators benefit from the libraries and tools developed for their companion C compiler.

C-code generators tend to be slower than native-code compilers because once the C-code generator finishes, the C compiler must run. The maximum size and complexity of the source code file they can compile is usually less than for native-code compilers (you can sometimes fix this by breaking the program into smaller files). C-code generators are dependent upon the vagaries of their companion C compiler. For example, some C compilers truncate function and variable names after 32 characters. Since C++ tends to generate long variable names, this can cause problems.

C-code generators also tend to be more expensive than native-code compilers, since the companies marketing them must pay royalties to AT&T.

Native-Code C++ Compilers

Native-code C++ compilers perform all the activities of the C-code generator and the C compiler combined. They tend to run much faster and compile larger source code files than C-code generators.

Native-code compilers are built from scratch. This means the compiler-writer has control over the entire compilation process, and the system can be optimized for C++. It also means a much bigger job, and more opportunities for errors.

Native-code compilers do not use AT&T sources, so they can be cheaper (no royalties to AT&T), and they don't inherit the bugs and limitations of the C-code generator. It is generally agreed that the native-code compiler is the most desirable implementation and that C-code generators are a temporary phase to aid acceptance.

Although a number of native code compilers are available for many platforms, this book was developed on a PC, and the code was tested using Borland C++ and Microsoft C++. The code was written with portability in mind, so most compilers should handle the examples unchanged.

Terminology

Both C-code generators and native-code compilers are a type of compiler: they take code in one form and produce code in another form.

This book will use the more comfortable term "compiler" when discussing both C-code generators and native-code compilers. When a distinction is necessary, the more specific "C-code generator" or "native-code compiler" will be used.

Make: An Essential Tool for Separate Compilation

There is one more tool you should understand before creating programs in C++. The **make** utility manages all the individual files in a project. When you edit the files in a project, **make** ensures that only the source files that were changed, and other files that are affected by the modified files, are recompiled. By using **make**, you don't have to recompile all the files in your project every time you make a change. Also, **make** remembers all the commands to put your project together. Learning to use **make** will save you a lot of time and frustration.

The **make** utility was developed on UNIX. The C language was developed to write the UNIX operating system. As programs encompassed more and more files, the job of deciding which files should be recompiled because of changes became tedious and error-prone, so **make** was invented. Most C compilers come with a **make** program. All C++ packages either come with a **make**, or are used with a C compiler that has a **make**.

Make Activities

When you type **make**, the **make** program looks in the current directory for a file called a *makefile*, which you've created if it's your project. This file lists dependencies between source code files. **make** looks at the dates on files. If a dependent file has an older date than a file it depends on, **make** executes the rule given after the dependency.

All comments in makefiles start with a # and continue to the end of the line.

As a simple example, the makefile for the "hello" program might contain:

```
# a comment
hello.exe: hello.cpp
        bcc hello.cpp
```

This says that HELLO.EXE (the target) depends on HELLO.CPP. When HELLO.CPP has a newer date than HELLO.EXE, **make** executes the rule **bcc hello.cpp**. There may be multiple dependencies and multiple rules. All the rules must begin with a tab (in many versions of **make**).

By creating groups of interdependent dependency-rule sets, you can modify source code files, type **make**, and be certain that all the affected files will be recompiled correctly.

Macros

A makefile may contain *macros*, small programs called with a single word. Macros allow convenient string replacement. The makefiles in this book use a macro to invoke the C++ compiler. For example,

```
#Macro to invoke Borland C++
CPP = bcc
hello.exe: hello.cpp
        $(CPP) hello.cpp
```

The **$** and parentheses expand the macro. To expand means to replace the macro call **$(CPP)** with the string **bcc**. With the above macro, if you want to change to a different compiler (Microsoft, for example), you just change the macro to

```
CPP = cl
```

You can also add compiler flags, etc., to the macro.

Makefiles in This Book

Throughout this book, makefiles are used at the end of chapters to compile all the programs in the chapter. Because implementations of **make** vary from system to system, only the common features are used. You should be aware that there are many advanced shortcuts that can save a lot of time when using **make**. Your documentation will describe the further features of **make**.

More About iostreams

So far you have seen only the most rudimentary aspect of the **iostream** class. The output formatting available with iostreams includes number formatting in decimal, octal, and hex. Here's another example of the use of iostreams:

```
//: STREAM2.CPP -- more streams features
#include <iostream.h>

void main() {
  // specifying formats with manipulators:
  cout << "a number in decimal: " << dec << 15 << endl;
  cout << "in octal: " << oct << 15 << endl;
  cout << "in hex: " << hex << 15 << endl;
  cout << "a floating-point number: " << 3.14159 << endl;
  cout << "nonprinting char (escape): " << char(27) << endl;
}
```

This example shows the **iostream** class printing numbers in decimal, octal, and hexadecimal using iostream *manipulators* (which don't print anything, but change the state of the output stream). Floating-point numbers are determined automatically by the compiler. In addition, any character can be sent to a stream object using a *cast* to a character (a **char** is a data type designed to hold characters), which looks like a function call: **char()**, along with the character's ASCII value. In the above program, an escape is sent to **cout**.

String Concatenation

An important feature of the ANSI C preprocessor is *string concatenation*. This feature is used in some of the C++ examples in this book. If two quoted strings are adjacent, and no punctuation is between them, the compiler will paste the strings together as a single string. This is particularly useful when printing code listings in books and magazines that have width restrictions:

```
//: CONCAT.CPP -- String Concatenation
#include <iostream.h>

void main() {
  cout << "This string is far too long to put on a single "
    "line but it can be broken up with no ill effects\n"
    "as long as there is no punctuation separating "
    "adjacent strings.\n";
}
```

Reading Input

The **iostream** class provides the ability to read input. The object used for standard input, **cin**, normally expects input from the console, but input can be redirected from other sources. An example of redirection is shown later in this chapter.

The iostreams operator used with **cin** is **>>**. This operator waits for the same kind of input as its argument. For example, if you give it an integer argument, it waits for an integer from the console. Here's an example program that converts number bases:

```
//: NUMCONV.CPP -- Converts decimal to octal and hex
#include <iostream.h>

void main() {
  int number;
  cout << "Enter a decimal number: ";
  cin >> number;
  // Using format manipulators:
  cout << "value in octal = 0" << oct << number << endl;
  cout << "value in hex = 0x" << hex << number << endl;
}
```

Notice the definition of the integer **number** at the beginning of **main()**. Since the **extern** keyword isn't used, the compiler creates space for **number** at that point.

Simple File Manipulation

Standard I/O provides a very simple way to read and write files, called I/O redirection. If a program takes input from standard input (**cin** for iostreams) and sends its output to standard output (**cout** for iostreams), that input and output can be redirected—input can be taken from a file, and output can be sent to a file. To redirect I/O on the command line, use the **<** sign to redirect input and the **>** sign to redirect output. For example, if we have a fictitious program FICTION.EXE (or simply FICTION in UNIX), which reads from standard input and writes to standard output, you can redirect standard input from the file STUFF and redirect the output to the file SUCH with the command

fiction < stuff > such

Since the files are opened for you, the job is much easier (although you'll see later that iostream has a very simple mechanism for opening files).

As a useful example, suppose you want to record the number of times you perform an activity, but the program that records the incidents must be loaded and run many times, and the machine might be turned off. To keep a permanent record of the incidents, you must store the data in a file. This file will be called INCIDENT.DAT and will initially contain the character 0. For easy reading, it will always contain ASCII digits representing the number of incidents.

The program to increment the number is very simple:

```
//: INCR.CPP — Read a number, add one and write it
#include <iostream.h>

void main() {
  int num;
  cin >> num;
  cout << num + 1;
}
```

To test the program, run it and type a number followed by a carriage return (press RETURN). The program should print a number one larger than the one you typed.

The program can be called from inside another program using the ANSI C **system()** function, which is declared in the header file **stdlib.h**:

```
//: INCIDENT.CPP — Records an incident using INCR
#include <stdlib.h> // declare the system() function

void main() {
  // other code here...
  system("incr < incident.dat > incident.dat");
}
```

To use the **system()** function, you give it a string that you would normally type at the operating system command prompt. The command executes, and control returns to the program.

Notice that the file INCIDENT.DAT is read and written using I/O redirection. Since the single > is used, the file is overwritten. Although it works fine here, reading and writing the same file isn't always a safe thing to do—if you aren't careful you can end up with garbage in the file.

If a double **>>** is used instead of a single **>**, the output is appended to the file (and this program wouldn't work correctly).

This program shows you how easy it is to use plain C library functions in C++: just include the header file and call the function. The upward compatibility from C to C++ is a big advantage if you are learning the language starting from a background in C.

Controlling Execution in C/C++

This section covers the execution control statements in C++. You must be familiar with these statements before you can read C or C++ code.

C++ uses all C's execution control statements. These include **if-else**, **while**, **do-while**, **for**, and a selection statement called **switch**. C++ also allows the infamous **goto**, which will be avoided in this book.

True and False in C

An expression is true if it produces a nonzero integral value. An expression is false if it produces an integral zero.

All conditional statements use the truth or falsehood of a conditional expression to determine the execution path. An example of a conditional expression is **A == B**. This uses the conditional operator **==** to see if the variable **A** is equivalent to the variable **B**. The expression returns 1 if the statement is true and 0 if it is false. Other conditional operators are **>**, **<**, **>=**, **<=**, and **!=**. The next chapter covers conditional statements.

if-else

The **if-else** statement can exist in two forms: with or without the else. The two forms are:

```
if(expression)
  statement
```

or

```
if(expression)
  statement
else
  statement
```

The *expression* evaluates to true or false. The *statement* means either a simple statement terminated by a semicolon or compound statement, which is a group of simple statements enclosed in braces. Any time the word "statement" is used, it is always implied that the statement can be simple or compound. Note this *statement* can also be another **if**, so they can be strung together.

Pascal programmers should notice that the "then" is implied in C and C++, which are terse languages. "Then" isn't essential, so it was left out.

```cpp
//: IFTHEN.CPP -- Demonstration of if and
//. if-else conditionals
#include <iostream.h>

void main() {
  int i;
  cout << "type a number and a carriage return" << endl;
  cin >> i;
  if ( i > 5 )
    cout << "the number was greater than 5 " << endl;
  else
    if ( i < 5 )
      cout << "the number was less than 5 " << endl;
    else
      cout << "the number must be equal to 5 " << endl;

  cout << "type a number and a carriage return" << endl;
  cin >> i;
  if ( i < 10 )
    if ( i > 5 )  // "if" is just another type of statement
      cout << "5 < i < 10 " << endl;
    else
      cout << "i <= 5 " << endl;
  else // matches "if ( i < 10 ) "
    cout << "i >= 10 " << endl;
}
```

Indentation makes C/C++ code easier to read. Since C and C++ are free-form languages, the extra spaces, tabs, and carriage returns do not affect the resulting program. It is conventional to indent the body of a control-flow statement so the reader may easily determine where it begins and ends. (Note that all conventions seem to end after the agreement that some sort of indentation take place. The feud between styles of code formatting is unending.)

while

The **while**, **do-while**, and **for** commands control looping. A statement repeats until the controlling expression evaluates to false.

The form for a **while** loop is

```
while(expression)
  statement
```

The *expression* is evaluated once at the beginning of the loop, and again before each further iteration of the *statement*.

This example stays in the body of the **while** loop until you type the secret number or press CTRL-C.

```
//: GUESS.CPP -- Guess a number (demonstrates "while")
#include <iostream.h>

void main() {
  int secret = 15;
  int guess = 0;
  // "!=" is the "not-equal" conditional:
  while ( guess != secret ) { // compound statement
    cout << "guess the number: ";
    cin >> guess;
  }
  cout << "You got it!" << endl;
}
```

do-while

The form for **do-while** is

```
do
  statement
while(expression);
```

The **do-while** is different from the while because the statement always executes at least once, even if the *expression* evaluates to false the first time. In a simple **while**, if the conditional is false the first time the *statement* never executes.

If a **do-while** is used in the GUESS program, the variable **guess** does not need an initial dummy value, since it is initialized by the **cin** statement before it is tested:

```
//: GUESS2.CPP -- The guess program using do-while
#include <iostream.h>

void main() {
  int secret = 15;
  int guess; // no initialization needed this time
  do {
    cout << "guess the number: ";
    cin >> guess;
  }  while ( guess != secret );
  cout << "You got it!" << endl;
}
```

for

A **for** loop performs initialization before the first iteration. Then it performs conditional testing and, at the end of each iteration, some form of "stepping." The form of the **for** loop is

```
for(initialization; expression; step)
 statement
```

Any of *initialization*, *expression*, or *step* may be empty. The initialization code executes once at the very beginning. The *expression* is tested before each iteration (if it evaluates to false at the beginning, the *statement* never executes). At the end of each loop, the step executes.

Usually, **for** loops are used for "counting" tasks, for example:

```
//: CHARLIST.CPP -- Display all the ASCII characters.
//. Demonstrates "for."
#include <iostream.h>

void main() {
  for( int i = 0; i < 128; i = i + 1 )
    if (i != 26 )  // ANSI Terminal/ANSI.SYS Clear screen
      cout << " value: " << i <<
        " character: " << char(i) << endl; // type conversion
}
```

You might notice that the variable **i** is defined at the point where it is used, instead of at the beginning of the block denoted by the open curly brace {. Traditional procedural languages require that all variables be defined at the beginning of the block so when the compiler creates a block it can allocate space for those variables.

Defining all variables at the beginning of the block requires the programmer to write in a particular way because of the implementation details of the language. Most people don't know all the variables they are going to use before they write the code, so they must keep jumping back to the beginning of the block to insert new variables, which is awkward and causes errors. It is confusing to read the code because each block starts with a clump of variable declarations, and the variables might not be used until much later in the block.

In C++ (not in C), you can spread your variable definitions throughout the block. Whenever you need a new variable, you can define it right where you use it. In addition, you can initialize the variable at the point you declare it, which prevents an important class of errors. Defining variables at any point in a scope allows a more natural coding style and makes code easier to understand. C++ compilers search for all the variable definitions in the block and allocate storage for them at the beginning of the block.

The break *and* continue *Keywords*

Inside the body of any of the looping constructs you can control the flow of the loop using **break** and **continue**. The **break** keyword quits the loop without executing the rest of the statements in the loop. The **continue** keyword stops the execution of the current iteration and goes back to the beginning of the loop to begin a new iteration.

As an example of the use of **break** and **continue**, this program is a very simple menu system:

```
//: MENU.CPP -- simple menu program demonstrating
//. the use of "break" and "continue"
#include <iostream.h>

void main() {
  char c; // to hold response
  while(1) {
    cout << "MAIN MENU:" << endl;
    cout << "l for left, r for right, q to quit: ";
```

```cpp
    cin >> c;
    if ( c == 'q')
      break; // out of "while(1)"
    if ( c == 'l') {
      cout << "LEFT MENU:" << endl;
      cout << "select a or b: ";
      cin >> c;
      if ( c == 'a' ) {
        cout << "you chose 'a'" << endl;
        continue; // back to main menu
      }
      if ( c == 'b' ) {
        cout << "you chose 'b'" << endl;
        continue; // back to main menu
      }
      else {
        cout << "you didn't choose a or b!" << endl;
        continue; // back to main menu
      }
    }
    if ( c == 'r' ) {
      cout << "RIGHT MENU:" << endl;
      cout << "select c or d: ";
      cin >> c;
      if ( c == 'c' ) {
        cout << "you chose 'c'" << endl;
        continue; // back to main menu
      }
      if ( c == 'd' ) {
        cout << "you chose 'd'" << endl;
        continue; // back to main menu
      }
      else {
        cout << "you didn't choose c or d!" << endl;
        continue; // back to main menu
      }
    }
    cout << "you must type l or r or q!" << endl;
  }
  cout << "quitting menu..." << endl;
}
```

If the user selects q in the main menu, the **break** keyword is used to quit; otherwise the program just continues to execute indefinitely. After each of the submenu selections, the **continue** keyword is used to pop back up to the beginning of the while loop.

The **while(1)** statement is the equivalent of saying "do this loop forever." The **break** statement allows you to break out of this infinite while loop when the user types **q**.

switch

A **switch** statement selects from among pieces of code based on the value of an integral expression. Its form is:

```
switch(selector) {
  case integral-value1 : statement; break;
  case integral-value2 : statement; break;
  case integral-value3 : statement; break;
  case integral-value4 : statement; break;
  case integral-value5 : statement; break;
          (...)
  default: statement;
}
```

Selector is an expression that produces an integral value. The **switch** compares the result of *selector* to each *integral-value*. If it finds a match, the corresponding *statement* (simple or compound) executes. If no match occurs, the default *statement* executes.

You will notice in the above definition that each **case** ends with a **break**, which causes execution to jump to the end of the **switch** body. This is the conventional way to build a **switch** statement, but the **break** is optional. If it is missing, the code for the following **case** statements execute until a **break** is encountered. Although you don't usually want this kind of behavior, it can be useful to an experienced C programmer.

The **switch** statement is a very clean way to implement multipath selection (selecting from among a number of different execution paths), but it requires a selector that evaluates to an integral value. If you want to use, for example, a string as a selector, it won't work in a **switch** statement. For a string selector, you must use instead a series of **if** statements and compare the string inside the conditional.

Menus often lend themselves neatly to a **switch**, as in the following:

```
//: MENU2.CPP -- a menu using a switch statement
#include <iostream.h>

void main() {
  char response; // the user's response
  int quit = 0;  // flag for quitting
  while ( quit == 0 ) {
    cout << "Select a, b, c or q to quit: ";
    cin >> response;
    switch(response) {
      case 'a' : cout << "you chose 'a'" << endl;
                 break;
      case 'b' : cout << "you chose 'b'" << endl;
                 break;
      case 'c' : cout << "you chose 'c'" << endl;
                 break;
      case 'q' : cout << "quitting menu..." << endl;
                 quit = 1;
                 break;
      default  : cout << "you must use a,b,c, or q!" << endl;
    }
  }
}
```

Notice that selecting q sets the **quit** flag to 1. The next time the selector is evaluated, **quit == 0** returns false so the body of the **while** does not execute.

Introduction to C and C++ Operators

You can think of *operators* as a special type of function (C++ operator overloading treats operators precisely that way). An operator takes one or more arguments and produces a new value. The arguments are in a different form than ordinary function calls, but the effect is the same.

You should be reasonably comfortable with the operators used so far from your previous programming experience. The concepts of addition (**+**), subtraction and unary minus (**–**), multiplication (*****), division (**/**), and assignment(**=**) all work much the same in any programming language. The full set of operators is enumerated in the next chapter.

Precedence

Operator precedence defines the order in which an expression evaluates when several different operators are present. C and C++ have specific rules to determine the order of evaluation. The easiest to remember is that multiplication and division happen before addition and subtraction. After that, if an expression isn't transparent to you, it probably won't be for anyone reading the code, so you should use parentheses to make the order of evaluation explicit. For example:

```
A = X + Y - 2 / 2 + Z;
```

has a very different meaning from the same statement with a particular grouping of parentheses:

```
A = X + (Y - 2) / (2 + Z);
```

Autoincrement and Autodecrement

C and C++ are full of shortcuts. Shortcuts can make code much easier to type, and sometimes much harder to read. Perhaps the designers thought it would be easier to understand a tricky piece of code if your eyes didn't have to scan as large an area of print.

One of the nicer shortcuts is the autoincrement and autodecrement operators. You often use these to change loop variables, which control the number of times a loop executes.

The autodecrement operator is **--** and means "decrease by one unit." The autoincrement operator is **++** and means "increase by one unit." If **A** is an **int**, for example, the expression **++A** is equivalent to (**A = A + 1**). Autoincrement and autodecrement operators produce the value of the variable as a result. If the operator appears before the variable (for example, **++A**), the operation is performed and the value is produced. If the operator appears after the variable (for example, **A++**), the value is produced and then the operation is performed. As an example:

```
//: AUTOINC.CPP -- Shows use of autoincrement
//. and autodecrement operators.
#include <iostream.h>

void main() {
  int i = 0;
  int j - 0;
  cout << ++i << endl; // pre-increment
  cout << j++ << endl; // post-increment
  cout << --i << endl; // pre decrement
  cout << j-- << endl; // post decrement
}
```

If you've been wondering about the name "C++," now you understand—
it implies "one step beyond C."

Using Standard I/O for Easy File Handling

The **iostream** class contains functions to read and write files. Often,
however, it is easiest to read from **cin** and write to **cout**. The program
can be tested by typing at the console, and when it is working, files can
be manipulated via redirection on the command line (in UNIX and
MS-DOS).

Simple "cat" Program

So far, all the messages you've seen are sent via operator overloading
to stream objects. In C++, a message is usually sent to an object by calling
a *member function* for that object. A member function looks like a regular
function—it has a name, argument list, and return value. However, it
must always be connected to an object. It can never be called by itself. A
member function is always selected for a particular object via the dot (**.**)
member-selection operator.

The **iostream** class has several nonoperator member functions. One of these is **get()**, which can be used to fetch a single character (or a string, if it is called differently). The following program uses **get()** to read characters from the **cin** object. The program uses the complementary member function **put()** to send characters the **cout** object. Characters are read from standard input and written to standard output.

```
//: CAT.CPP -- Demonstrates member function calls
//. and simple file i/o.
#include <iostream.h>

void main() {
  char c;
  while ( cin.get(c) )
    cout.put(c);
}
```

Above, **get()** returns a value that is tested to determine when the end of the input is reached. As long as the return value is nonzero (true), there is more input available and the body of the **while** loop is executed, but when the expression **cin.get(c)** produces a result of **0**, there is no more input, so it stops looping.

To use CAT, simply redirect a file into it, as follows; the results will appear on the screen:

```
cat < infile
```

If you redirect the output file you've created a simple "copy" program:

```
cat < infile > outfile
```

Pass By Reference

C programmers may find the above program puzzling. According to plain C syntax, the character variable **c** looks like it is passed by value to the member function **get()**. Yet **c** is used in the **put()** member function as if **get()** had modified the value of **c**, which is impossible if it was passed by value! What goes on here?

C++ has added another kind of argument passing: *pass by reference*. If a function argument is defined as pass by reference, the *compiler* takes the address of the variable when the function is called. The argument of the stream function **get()** is defined as pass by reference, so the above program works correctly.

Chapter 4 describes passing by reference in more detail. The first part of that chapter describes addresses, which you must understand before references make any sense.

Handling Spaces in Input

To read and use more than a character at a time from standard input, you will need to use a *buffer*. A buffer is a data-storage area used to hold and manipulate a group of data items with identical types.

In C and C++, you can create a buffer to hold text with an array of characters. Arrays in C and C++ are denoted with the bracket operator (**[]**). To define an array, give the data type, a name for the array, and the size in brackets. For an array of characters (a character buffer) called **buf** the definition could be

```
char buf[100];  // space for 100 contiguous characters
```

To read an entire word instead of a character, use **cin** and the **>>** operator, but send the input to a character buffer instead of just a single character. The operator **>>** is overloaded so you can use it with a number of different types of arguments. The idea is the same in each case: you want to get some input. You need different kinds of input, but you don't have to worry about it because the language takes care of the differentiation for you.

Here's a program to read and echo a word:

```
//: READWORD.CPP -- Read and echo a word from standard input
#include <iostream.h>

void main() {
  char buf[100];
  cout << "type a word: ";
  cin >> buf;
  cout << "the word you typed is: " << buf << endl;
}
```

You will notice the program works fine if you type a word, but if you type more than one word, it only takes the first one. The **>>** operator is word-oriented; it looks for white space, which it doesn't copy into the buffer, to break up the input. You must type a carriage return (press RETURN) before any of the input is read.

To read and manipulate anything more than a simple character or word using iostreams, it is best to use the **get()** function. **get()** doesn't discard white space, and it can be used with a single character, as shown in the CAT.CPP program, or a character buffer (**get()** is an overloaded function). When used with a character buffer, **get()** needs to know the maximum number of characters it should read (usually the size of the buffer) and optionally the terminating character it should look for before it stops reading input.

This terminating character that **get()** looks for (the delimiter) defaults to a newline (**\n**). You don't need to change the delimiter if you just want to read the input a line at a time. To change the delimiter, add the character you wish to be the delimiter in single quotes as the third argument in the list. When **get()** matches the delimiter with the terminating character, the terminating character isn't copied into the character buffer; it stays on the input stream. This means you must read the terminating character and throw it away; otherwise the next time you try to fill your character buffer using **get()**, the function will immediately read the terminating character and stop.

Here's a program that reads input a line at a time using **get()**:

```
//: GETLINE.CPP -- Stream input by lines
#include <iostream.h>

void main() {
  char buf[100];
  char trash;
  while( cin.get(buf,100) ) { // get chars until '\n'
    cin.get(trash); // throw away the terminator
    cout << buf << "\n";  // add the '\n' at the end
  }
}
```

The **get()** function reads input and places it into buf until either 100 characters are read, or a **\n** is found. The **get()** function puts the zero byte, required for all strings, at the end of the string in **buf**. The character

trash is only used for throwing away the line terminator (a more convenient iostream function to use is **getline()**). Because the newline character was never put in **buf**, you must send one out when you print the line.

The return value of **cin.get()** for lines is the same as the overloaded version of the same function for single characters. It is true as long as it reads some input (so the body of the loop is executed) and false when the end of the input is reached.

Try redirecting the contents of a text file into GETLINE.

Aside: Examining Header Files

As your knowledge of C++ increases, you will find that the best way to discover the capabilities of the **iostream** class, or any class, is to look at the header file where the class is declared. The header file will contain the class declaration. You won't completely understand the class declaration until you've read the next chapter. The class declaration contains some **private** and **protected** elements, which you don't have access to, and a list of **public** elements, usually functions, that you as the user of the class may utilize. Although there isn't necessarily a description of the functions in the class declaration, the function names are often helpful and the class declaration acts as a sort of "table of contents."

Header files for predefined classes like **iostream**s are usually located in a subdirectory, often called INCLUDE, under the installation directory for your C++ package or the associated C package, if you use a C-code generator. On UNIX, you must ask your system administrator where the C++ INCLUDE files are located.

Utility Programs Using iostreams and Standard I/O

Now that you've had an introduction to iostreams and you know how to manipulate files with I/O redirection, you can write some simple programs. This section contains examples of useful utilities.

Pipes

Notice that in UNIX and MS-DOS, you can also use *pipes* on the command line for I/O redirection. Pipes feed the output of one program into the input of another program if both programs use standard I/O. If **prog1** writes to standard I/O and **prog2** reads from standard I/O, you can pipe the output of **prog1** into the input of **prog2** with the following command

```
prog1 | prog2
```

where I is the pipe symbol. If all the following programs use standard I/O, you can chain them together like this:

```
prog1 | prog2 | prog3 | prog4
```

Text-Analysis Program

The following program counts the number of words and lines in a file and checks to make sure no line is greater than **maxwidth**. It uses two functions from the ANSI C library, both of which are declared in the header file **string.h**. The **strlen()** function finds the length of a string, not including the zero byte that terminates all strings. The **strtok()** function is used to count the number of words in a line; it breaks the line up into chunks that are separated by any of the characters in the second argument. For this program, a word is separated by white space, which is a space or a tab. The first time you call **strtok()**, you hand it the character buffer, and all the subsequent times you hand it a zero, which tells it to use the same buffer it used for the last call (moving ahead each time **strtok()** is called). When it can't find any more words in the line, **strtok()** returns zero.

```cpp
//: TEXTCHEK.CPP — Counts words and lines in a text file.
//. Checks to see that no line is wider than maxwidth
#include <iostream.h>
#include <string.h> // ANSI C strlen() & strtok() declarations

void main() {
  const int maxwidth = 64;  // const means "you can't change it"
  int linecount = 0;
```

```
int wordcount = 0;
char buf[100], c, trash;
while ( cin.getline(buf,100) ) {
  linecount++; // we just read a whole line
  if ( strtok(buf," \t") ) {
    wordcount++;  // count the first word
    while ( strtok(0," \t") )
      wordcount++; // count the rest of the words
  }
  if ( strlen(buf) > maxwidth )
    cout << "line " << linecount << "is too long." << endl;
}
cout << "number of lines: " << linecount << endl;
cout << "number of words: " << wordcount << endl;
}
```

In this program, the more convenient **getline()** is used instead of **get()**. Notice the use of the autoincrement to count lines and words. Since the value produced by autoincrementing the variable is ignored, it doesn't matter whether you put the increment first or last.

To count words, **strtok()** is set up for the first call by handing it the text buffer **buf**. If it finds a word, the word is counted. If there are more words, they are counted.

The keyword **const** is used to prevent **maxwidth** from being changed. The keyword **const** was invented for C++ and later added to ANSI C. The compiler will generate an error message if you ever try to change the value, and an optimizer can use the fact that a variable is **const** to create better code. It is always a good idea to make a variable **const** if you know it should never change.

Notice the way **buf**, **c**, and **trash** are all declared with a single **char** statement. You can declare all types of data this way, just by separating the variable names with commas.

Expanding Tabs

Some text-processing systems cannot handle tabs in files, but word processing programs often insert them. Here's a program that replaces tabs with spaces:

```
//: DETAB.CPP -- Replace tabs with spaces
#include <iostream.h>

void main() {
  const int tabsize = 8;
  char c;
  while( cin.get(c) ) {
    if ( c == '\t') {
      for(int i = 0; i < tabsize; i++)
        cout << " ";
    }
    else
      cout.put(c);
  }
}
```

When a tab is found, the spaces are counted out using a **for** loop. The **for** loop allows you to easily change the number of spaces per tab. Notice that the space is output with a double-quoted space—this could also have been a single-quoted space character. Also, **put()** is used to output **c**, but you could also have said **cout << c**.

iostream Support for File Manipulation

All the examples in this chapter have used I/O redirection to handle input and output. Although this approach works fine, iostreams have a much faster and safer way to read and write files. This is accomplished by including **fstream.h** instead of (or in addition to) **iostream.h** and then creating and using **fstream** objects in almost the identical fashion you use ordinary **iostream** objects. Here's a program that copies one file onto another (you'll learn later how to use command-line arguments so the filenames aren't fixed):

```
//: IOCOPY.CPP -- fstreams for opening files
//. Copies itself to TMP.TXT
#include <fstream.h>

void main() {
  ifstream infile("iocopy.cpp");
  if(!infile) cerr << "couldn't open iocopy.cpp" << endl;
  ofstream outfile("tmp.txt");
  if(!outfile) cerr << "couldn't open tmp.txt" << endl;
```

```
char ch;
while(infile.get(ch))
  outfile.put(ch);
}
```

The first line creates an **ifstream** object called **infile** and hands it the name of the file (which happens to be the same name as the source-code file). An **ifstream** object is a special type of **iostream** object declared in **fstream.h** that opens and reads from a file. The second line checks to see if the file was successfully opened, using an **if** conditional that simply checks to see if the object is nonzero (using the "logical NOT" operator **!**, which you'll learn about in the next chapter). The third line creates an **ofstream** operator that is just like an **ifstream**, except it writes to a file. This is also checked for successful opening.

The **while** loop simply gets characters from **infile** with the member function **get()**, and puts them into **outfile** with **put()**, until the **get()** returns false (that is, zero). The files are automatically closed when the objects are destroyed, which is another benefit of using fstreams for manipulating files—you don't have to remember to close the files.

There's also a set of iostream classes for doing in-memory formatting, in the header file **strstream.h**.

Comment Notation

You may be wondering about the comment notation used in this book. Each file has a "headline" at the top, indicated by the **//:** comment. The filename appears first, because even though your editing program may know the name of the file, when you print it on paper you don't have that information. Following the double dash is a very brief description of the file. Lines in the file that start with **//.** are supplementary comments, intended to give additional information about the file.

Other documentation methods either require the use of a special preprocessor (Knuth's "WEB" language, for example) or are too complex (a problem with my earlier attempts). This technique is for those people who need to easily extract documentation comments from source-code, but want an easy-to-remember syntax.

One of the best things about this documentation comment syntax is that it can be used immediately. There are many different versions of the GREP program floating around (some are shareware or public domain); an excellent one comes with Borland C++. To use GREP for file header block information, the command is:

```
grep //[:\.] *.h *.cpp
```

The square brackets contain a set of characters, any one of which will match (note that the **.** is a special character, and must be escaped with a backslash). This will look for **//** followed by either the **:** or **.** character.

You can get better results if you have any implementation of AWK, a text-processing interpreter with a C-like syntax (a public-domain version is included with this book's source-code disk). You can extract comment headers from all the files in a directory with the following command:

```
awk "/\/\/:|\/\/\./ { print substr($0, 5) }" *.h *.cpp
```

In AWK-speak, this means: "for each input line that contains **//:** or **//**" (notice the use of **|** to indicate "or," and that **/** and **.** must be escaped using ****), "print the line" (**$0** means the whole line) "starting from character 5." The AWK **substr()** function eliminates the comment characters, so you just get text. Similarly, if you just want the headlines you say

```
awk "/\/\/:/ { print substr($0, 5) }" *.h *.cpp
```

AWK is a tremendous tool for programmers. The best reference is the book by the original authors of the program (Aho, Kernighan & Weinberger, *The AWK Programming Language*, Addison-Wesley 1988).

Makefile for Chapter Examples

Here is the makefile for all the examples shown in this chapter:

```
# MAKEFILE for the examples in Chapter 2
# set CPP to your particular compiler's command-line name:
CPP = BCC
```

```
.cpp.exe:
    $(CPP) $<

all: hello.exe stream2.exe concat.exe numconv.exe \
    incr.exe incident.exe ifthen.exe guess.exe \
    guess2.exe guess3.exe charlist.exe menu.exe menu2.exe \
    autoinc.exe cat.exe readword.exe getline.exe \
    textchek.exe detab.exe iocopy.cpp
```

The macro CPP is set to the name of the compiler. To use a different compiler, you can either edit the **makefile** or change the value of the macro on the command line, like this:

```
make CPP=CL
```

This makefile uses a feature of **make**, called *rules* (or *implicit rules* or *inference rules*). A rule is the way to teach **make** how to convert a file with one type of extension (.cpp) into a file with another type of extension (.obj or .cxc). This eliminates a lot of redundancy in a **makefile**. Once you teach **make** the rules for producing one kind of file from another, all you have to do is tell **make** which files depend on which other files. When **make** finds a file with a date earlier than the file it depends on (which means the source file has been changed and not yet recompiled), it uses the rule to create a new file.

The implicit rule tells **make** that it doesn't need explicit rules to build everything, but instead it can figure out how to build things based on their file extension. In this case it says: "to build a file that ends in .exe from one which ends in .cpp, invoke the following command." The command is the compiler name, followed by a special built-in macro. This macro, **$<**, will produce the name of the source file (sometimes called the dependent). Although the makefile contains no explicit dependencies, the implicit conversion implies the proper dependencies.

The **make** program looks at the first target (item to be made) in the makefile unless you specify one on the command line, such as:

```
make textchek.exe
```

Thus, if you want to make all the files in a subdirectory by typing **make**, the first target should be a dummy name that depends on all the other targets in the file. In the above makefile, the dummy target is called **all**.

When a line is too long in a makefile, you can continue it on the next line by using a backslash (\). White space is ignored here, so you can format for readability.

Summary

This chapter has covered the basic tools you need to create programs and the general form of C and C++ programs. It has also demonstrated how to use predefined classes by including the header file to define the class and sending messages to objects.

The next chapter will show you how to write your own classes in C++. First, built-in data types, operators, and functions for C and C++ are introduced, followed by classes and other class-like items (structures, enumerated data types, and unions). Finally, some debugging hints are presented.

Chapter 4 is the last of the chapters covering issues common to C and C++. It explains the concept of addresses, which are manipulated with pointers in C and C++, and references in C++.

The remainder of the book covers subjects that are unique to C++ and object-oriented programming.

CHAPTER

Creating Classes in C++

Chapter 2 introduced enough of the C and C++ languages so you can use predefined classes. This chapter teaches you to define your own classes in C++. Chapter 4 discusses the very important subject of addresses in C and C++.

This chapter begins by discussing the different types of data built into C and C++. Before you can define your own data types, you must understand how to create methods for those data types. Methods take the form of functions in C++. This chapter shows you how to create functions and demonstrates the extensions C++ has added for functions. Finally, you will see how to package data and functions together into an abstract data type: the class.

Keep in mind this is an introduction and guide, not a reference manual. The final word for C is the ANSI C specification (which is tedious to read and not recommended unless you are inclined to those kinds of things) and the second edition of Kernighan and Ritchie (K&R). Unless otherwise specified, all the descriptions here are based on ANSI C. The final word on C++ is the ANSI C++ specification, when it is finished. At this writing, the X3J16 document is in draft form, so you are forced to use the ARM, but the ARM will suffice for most issues.

Introduction to C++ Data

Data types can be *built-in* or *abstract*. A *built-in data type* is one that the compiler intrinsically understands, one that "comes with the compiler." The types of built-in data are identical in C and C++. A *user-defined data type* is one you or another programmer create as a class. These are commonly referred to as *abstract data types*. The compiler knows how to handle built-in types when it starts up; it "learns" how to handle abstract data types by reading header files containing class declarations.

Basic Built-in Types

The ANSI C specification doesn't say how many bits each of the built-in types must contain. Instead, it stipulates the minimum and maximum values the built-in type must be able to hold. When a machine is based on binary, this maximum value is directly translated into bits. For example, if a machine uses binary-coded decimal (BCD) to represent numbers, the amount of space in the machine required to hold the maximum numbers for each data type will change. The minimum and maximum values that can be stored in the various data types are defined in the system header files **limits.h** and **float.h**.

C and C++ have four basic built-in data types, described here for binary-based machines. A **char** is for character storage and uses a minimum of one byte of storage. An **int** stores an integral number and uses a minimum of two bytes of storage. The **float** and **double** types store floating-point numbers, often in IEEE floating-point format. The **float** is for single-precision floating point and **double** is for double-precision floating point.

You can define and initialize variables at the same time. Here's how to define variables using the four basic data types:

```
//: BASIC.CPP—Defining the four basic data
//. types in C & C++

void main() {
  // Definition without initialization:
  char protein;
  int carbohydrates;
  float fiber;
  double fat;
  // Definition & initialization at the same time:
  char pizza = 'A', pop = 'Z';
  int DongDings = 100, Twinkles = 150, HeeHos = 200;
  float chocolate = 3.14159;
  double fudge_ripple = 6e-4; // exponential notation
}
```

The first part of the program defines variables of the four basic data types without initializing them. If you don't initialize a variable, its contents are undefined (although some compilers will initialize to 0). The second part of the program defines and initializes variables at the same time. Notice the use of exponential notation in the constant **6e–4**, meaning: "6 times 10 to the minus fourth power."

Specifiers

Specifiers modify the meanings of the basic built-in types, and expand the built-in types to a much larger set. There are four specifiers: **long**, **short**, **signed**, and **unsigned**.

The **long** and **short** specifiers modify the maximum and minimum values a data type will hold. A plain **int** must be at least the size of a **short**. The size hierarchy for integral types is: **short int**, **int**, **long int**. All the sizes could conceivably be the same, as long as they satisfy the minimum/maximum value requirements. On a machine with a 64-bit word, for example, all the data types might be 64 bits.

The size hierarchy for floating-point numbers is: **float**, **double**, and **long double**. The **long float** is not allowed in ANSI C. There are no **short** floating-point numbers.

The **signed** and **unsigned** specifiers tell the compiler how to use the sign bit with integral types and characters (floating-point numbers always contain a sign). The maximum **unsigned** number can be twice as large as the maximum **signed** number; **char** may or may not default to **signed**. By specifying **signed char**, you force the sign bit to be used. The default, **signed**, is only necessary with **char**; **char** may or may not default to **signed**. By specifying **signed char**, you force the sign bit to be used.

The following example shows the size of the data in bytes using the **sizeof()** operator, introduced later in this chapter:

```
//: SPECIFY.CPP—Demonstrates the use of specifiers
#include <iostream.h>

void main() {
  char c;
  unsigned char cu;
  int i;
  unsigned int iu;
  short int is;
  short iis; // same as short int
  unsigned short int isu;
  unsigned short iisu;
  long int il;
  long iil;  // same as long int
  unsigned long int ilu;
```

```
    unsigned long iilu;
    float f;
    double d;
    long double ld;
    cout << "sizeof(char) = " << sizeof(c) << endl;
    cout << "sizeof(unsigned char) = " << sizeof(cu) << endl;
    cout << "sizeof(int) = " << sizeof(i) << endl;
    cout << "sizeof(unsigned int) = " << sizeof(iu) << endl;
    cout << "sizeof(short) = " << sizeof(is) << endl;
    cout << "sizeof(unsigned short) = " << sizeof(isu) << endl;
    cout << "sizeof(long) = " << sizeof(il) << endl;
    cout << "sizeof(unsigned long) = " << sizeof(ilu) << endl;
    cout << "sizeof(float) = " << sizeof(f) << endl;
    cout << "sizeof(double) = " << sizeof(d) << endl;
    cout << "sizeof(long double) = " << sizeof(ld) << endl;
}
```

When you are modifying an **int** with **short** or **long**, the keyword **int** is optional, as shown above.

Scoping

Scoping rules tell you where a variable is valid, where it is created and where it gets destroyed (*goes out of scope*). The *scope* of a variable extends from the point where it is defined to the first closing brace matching the closest opening brace before the variable is declared. To illustrate:

```
//: SCOPE.CPP—How variables are scoped

void main() {
  int scp1;
  // scp1 visible here
  {
    // scp1 still visible here
    //......
    int scp2;
    // scp2 visible here
    //......
    {
      // scp1 & scp2 still visible here
      //...
      int scp3;
```

```
    // scp1, scp2 & scp3 visible here
    // ...
  } // <—scp3 destroyed here
  // scp3 not available here
  // scp1 & scp2 still visible here
  // ...
} // <—scp2 destroyed here
// scp3 & scp2 not available here
// scp1 still visible here
//...
} // <—scp1 destroyed here
```

The above example shows when variables are visible and when they are unavailable (*go out of scope*). A variable can only be used when inside its scope. Scopes can be *nested*, indicated by matched pairs of braces inside other matched pairs of braces. Nesting means you can access a variable in a scope that encloses the scope you are in. In the above example, the variable **scp1** is available inside all of the other scopes, while **scp3** is only available in the innermost scope.

Defining Variables on the Fly

There is a significant difference between C and C++ when defining variables. Both languages require that variables be defined before they are used, but C requires all the variable definitions at the beginning of a scope. While reading C code, a block of variable definitions is often the first thing you see when entering a scope. These variable definitions don't usually mean much to the reader because they appear apart from the context in which they are used.

C++ allows you to define variables anywhere in the scope, so you can define a variable right before you use it. This makes the code much easier to write and reduces the errors you get from being forced to jump back and forth within a scope. It makes the code easier to understand because you see the variable definition in the context of its use. This is especially important when you are defining and initializing a variable at the same time—you can see the meaning of the initialization value by the way the variable is used.

Here's an example showing on-the-fly variable definitions:

```
//: ONTHEFLY.CPP—On-the-fly data definitions

void main() {
  //...
  { // begin a new scope
    int q = 0; // plain C requires definitions here
    //...
    for(int i = 0; i < 100; i++) { // define at point of use
      q++;
      // notice q comes from a larger scope
      int p = 12; // definition at the end of the scope
    }
    int p = 1;  // A different p
  } // end scope containing q & outer p
}
```

In the innermost scope, **p** is defined right before the scope ends, so it is really a useless gesture (but it shows you can define a variable *anywhere*). The **p** in the outer scope is in the same situation.

The definition of **i** in the **for** loop is rather tricky. You might think that **i** is only valid within the scope bounded by the opening brace that appears after the **for**. The variable **i** is actually valid from the point where it is defined to the end of the scope that *encloses* the **for** loop. This is consistent with C, where the variable **i** must be defined at the beginning of the scope enclosing the **for** if it is to be used by the **for**.

Specifying Storage Allocation

When creating a variable, you have a number of options to specify the lifetime of the variable, where the storage is allocated, and how the variable is treated by the compiler.

Global Variables

Global variables are defined outside all function bodies and are available to all parts of the program (even code in other files). Global variables are unaffected by scopes and are always available (the *lifetime* of a global variable lasts until the program ends). If the existence of a global variable in one file is declared using the **extern** keyword in another file, the variable is available for use by the second file. Here's an example of the use of global variables:

```
//: GLOBAL.CPP—Demonstration of global variables

int global;

void main() {
  global = 12;
}
```

Here's a file that accesses **global** as an **extern**:

```
//: GLOBAL2.CPP—accessing external global variables

extern int global;  // the linker resolves the reference

void foo() {
  global = 47;
}
```

Storage for the variable **global** is created by the definition in GLOBAL.CPP, and that same variable is accessed by the code in GLOBAL2.CPP. Since the code in GLOBAL2.CPP is compiled separately from the code in GLOBAL.CPP, the compiler must be informed that the variable exists elsewhere by the declaration

```
extern int global;
```

Local Variables

Local variables occur within a scope; they are "local" to a function. They are often called "automatic" variables because they automatically come into being when the scope is entered, and go away when the scope closes. The keyword **auto** makes this explicit, but local variables default to **auto**, so it is never necessary to declare something as an **auto**.

Register *Variables*

A *register variable* is a type of local variable. The **register** keyword tells the compiler "make accesses to this variable as fast as possible." Increasing the access speed is implementation dependent but, as the name suggests, it is often done by placing the variable in a register. There is no guarantee that the variable will be placed in a register or even that the access speed will increase—it is a hint to the compiler.

There are restrictions to the use of register variables. You cannot take or compute the address of a register variable. A register variable can only be declared within a block (you cannot have global or **static register** variables). You can, however, use a **register** variable as a formal argument in a function (in the argument list).

static

The **static** keyword has several distinct meanings. Normally, variables defined local to a function disappear at the end of the function scope. When you call the function again, storage for the variables is created anew and the data is reinitialized. If you want the data to be extant throughout the life of the program, you can define that variable to be **static** and give it an initial value. The initialization is only performed when the program begins to execute, and the data retains its value between function calls. This way, a function can "remember" a piece of information between function calls.

You might wonder why global data isn't used instead. The beauty of **static** data is that it is unavailable outside the scope of the function, so it can't be inadvertently changed. This localizes errors.

An example of the use of static data is:

```
//: STATIC.CPP—Using static data in a function
#include <iostream.h>

void func() {
  static int i = 0;
  cout << "i = " << ++i << endl;
}
```

```
void main() {
  for(int x = 0; x < 10; x++)
    func();
}
```

Each time **func()** is called in the **for** loop, it prints a different value. If the keyword **static** is not used, the value printed will always be 1.

The second meaning of **static** is related to the first in the "unavailable outside a certain scope" sense. When **static** is applied to a function name or to a variable that is outside of all functions, it means "this name is unavailable outside of this file." The function name or variable is *local to the file* or has *file scope*. As a demonstration, compiling and linking the following two files will cause a linker error:

```
//: FILESTAT.CPP—file scope demonstration
// compiling and linking this file with FSTAT2.CPP
// will cause a linker error

static int fs; // file scope: only available in this file

void main() {
  fs = 1;
}
```

Even though the variable **fs** is claimed to exist as an **extern** in the following file, the linker won't find it because it has been declared **static** in FILESTAT.CPP, shown here:

```
//: FSTAT2.CPP—Trying to reference fs
extern int fs;

void func() {
  fs = 100;
}
```

The **static** specifier may also be used inside a class. This definition will be delayed until after classes have been described later in the chapter.

extern

The **extern** keyword was briefly described in Chapter 2. It tells the compiler that a piece of data or a function exists, even if the compiler hasn't yet seen it in the file currently being compiled. This piece of data or function may exist in another file (as was described in Chapter 2) or further on in the current file. As an example of the latter:

```
//: FORWARD.CPP—Forward function & data declarations
#include <iostream.h>

extern int i; // not actually external, but the compiler
              // must be told it exists somewhere
extern void foo();

void main() {
  i = 0;
  foo();
}

int i; // the data definition

void foo() {
  i++;
  cout << i;
}
```

When the compiler encounters the declaration **extern int i;**, it knows that the definition for **i** must exist somewhere as a global variable. This definition can be in the current file, later on, or in a separate file. When the compiler reaches the definition of **i**, no other declaration is visible, so it knows it has found the same **i** declared earlier in the file. If you were to define **i** as **static**, you would be telling the compiler that **i** is defined globally (via the **extern**), but it also has file scope (via the **static**), so the compiler will generate an error.

Linkage

To understand the behavior of C & C++ programs, you need to know about *linkage*. Linkage describes the storage created in memory to represent an identifier *as it is seen by the linker*. An identifier is represented by storage in memory that holds a variable or a compiled function body. There are two types of linkage: *internal linkage* and *external linkage*.

Internal linkage means that storage is created to represent the identifier for the file being compiled *only*. Other files may use the same identifier with internal linkage or for a global variable, and no conflicts will be found by the linker—separate storage is created for each identifier. Internal linkage is specified by the keyword **static** in C and C++.

External linkage means that a single piece of storage is created to represent the identifier *for all files being compiled*. The storage is created *once*, and the linker must resolve all other references to that storage. Global variables and function names have external linkage. These are accessed from other files by declaring them with the keyword **extern**. Variables defined outside all functions (with the exception of **const** in C++) and function definitions default to external linkage. You can specifically force them to have internal linkage using the **static** keyword. You can explicitly state that an identifier has external linkage by defining it with the **extern** keyword. Defining a variable or function with **extern** is not necessary in C, but it is sometimes necessary for **const** in C++.

Automatic (local) variables exist only temporarily, on the stack, while a function is being called. The linker doesn't know about automatic variables, and they have *no linkage*.

Constants

In old (pre-ANSI) C, if you want to make a constant, you have to use the preprocessor. For example:

```
#define PI 3.14159
```

Everywhere you use **PI**, the value is substituted by the preprocessor (you can still use this method in C and C++).

When you use the preprocessor to create constants, you place control of those constants outside the scope of the compiler. No type checking is performed on the name **PI**, and you can't take the address of **PI** (so you can't pass a pointer or a reference to **PI**). **PI** cannot be a variable of a user-defined type. The meaning of **PI** lasts from the point it is defined to the end of the file; the preprocessor doesn't recognize scoping.

C++ introduces the concept of a *named constant* that is just like a variable, except its value cannot be changed. The modifier **const** tells the compiler that a name represents a constant. Any data type, built-in or user-defined, may be defined as **const**. If you define something as **const** and then attempt to modify it, the compiler will generate an error.

As with **short** and **long**, if you use the **const** modifier alone, it defaults to **int**:

```
const x = 10; // means: const int x = 10;
```

In ANSI C and C++, you can use a named constant in an argument list, even if the argument it fills is a pointer or a reference (that is, you can take the address of a **const**). A **const** has a scope, just like a regular variable, so you can "hide" a **const** inside a function and be sure that the name will not affect the rest of the program.

The **const** was taken from C++ and incorporated into ANSI C, albeit quite differently. In ANSI C, the compiler treats a **const** just like a variable that has a special tag attached that says "don't change me." When you define a **const** in ANSI C, the compiler creates storage for it, so if you define more than one **const** with the same name in two different files (or put the definition in a header file), the linker will generate error messages about conflicts. The intended use of **const** in ANSI C is quite different from its intended use in C++.

Differences in const *Between C++ and ANSI C*

In C++, **const** replaces the use of **#define** in most situations requiring a constant value with an associated name. In C++, **const** is *meant* to go into header files, and to be used in places where you would normally use a **#define** name. For example, C++ lets you use a **const** in declarations such as arrays:

```
const sz = 100;
int buf[sz]; // not allowed in ANSI C !
```

In ANSI C, a **const** cannot be used where the compiler is expecting a constant expression.

A **const** must have an initializer in C++. ANSI C doesn't require an initializer; if none is given, it initializes the **const** to 0.

In C++, a **const** doesn't necessarily create storage—in ANSI C a **const** *always* creates storage. Whether or not storage is reserved for a **const** in C++ depends on how it is used. In general, if a **const** is used simply to replace a name with a value (just as you would use a **#define**), storage doesn't have to be created for the **const**. If no storage is created (this depends on the complexity of the data type and the sophistication of the compiler), the values may be folded into the code for greater efficiency— *after* type checking, not before, as with **#define**. If, however, you take an address of a **const** (even unknowingly, by passing it to a function that takes a reference argument) *or* you define it as **extern**, storage is created for the **const**.

In C++, a **const** that is outside all functions has file scope (it is invisible outside the file). That is, it defaults to internal linkage. This is very different from all other identifiers in C++ (and from **const** in ANSI C!) that default to *external* linkage. Thus, if you declare a **const** of the same name in two different files and you don't take the address or define that name as **extern**, the ideal compiler won't allocate storage for the **const**, but simply fold it into the code (admittedly very difficult for complicated types). Because **const** has implied file scope, you can put it in header files (in C++ only) with no conflicts at link time.

Since a **const** in C++ defaults to internal linkage, you can't just define a **const** in one file and reference it as an **extern** in another file. To give a **const** external linkage so it can be referenced from another file, you must explicitly define it as **extern**, like this:

```
extern const x = 1;
```

Notice that by giving it an initializer *and* saying it is **extern**, you force storage to be created for the **const** (although the compiler still has the option of doing constant folding here). The initialization establishes this as a definition, not a declaration. The declaration

```
extern const x;
```

in C++ means that the definition exists elsewhere (again, this is *not* necessarily true in ANSI C). You can see now why C++ requires a **const** definition to have an initializer: The initializer distinguishes a declaration from a definition (in ANSI C it's *always* a definition, so no initializer is necessary). With an external **const** declaration, the compiler cannot do constant folding because it doesn't know the value.

Constant Values

In C++, a **const** must always have an initialization value (in ANSI C, this is not true). Constant values for built-in types are expressed as decimal, octal, hexadecimal, or floating-point numbers (sadly, binary numbers were not considered important), or as characters.

In the absence of any other clues, the compiler assumes a constant value is a decimal number. The numbers 47, 0, and 1101 are all treated as decimal numbers.

A constant value with a leading 0 is treated as an octal number (base 8). Base 8 numbers can only contain digits 0-7; the compiler flags other digits as an error. A legitimate octal number is 017 (15 in base 10).

A constant value with a leading 0x is treated as a hexadecimal number (base 16). Base 16 numbers contain the digits 0-9 and a-f or A-F. A legitimate hexadecimal number is 0x1fe (510 in base 10).

Floating point numbers can contain decimal points and exponential powers (represented by e, which means "10 to the power"). Both the decimal point and the e are optional. If you assign a constant to a floating-point variable, the compiler will take the constant value and convert it to a floating-point number (this process is called *implicit type conversion*). However, it is a good idea to use either a decimal point or an **e** to remind the reader you are using a floating-point number; some older compilers also need the hint.

Legitimate floating-point constant values are: 1e4, 1.0001, 47.0, 0.0 and –1.159e–77. You can add *suffixes* to force the type of floating-point number: f or F forces a **float**, L or l forces a **long double**; otherwise the number will be a **double**.

Character constants are characters surrounded by single quotes, as: 'A', '0', ' '. Notice there is a big difference between the character '0' (ASCII 96) and the value 0. Special characters are represented with the "backslash escape": '\n' (new-line), '\t' (tab), '\\' (backslash), '\r' (carriage return), '\"' (double quote), '\'' (single quotes), and so on. You can also express char constants in octal: '\17' or hexadecimal: '\xff'.

volatile

Whereas the qualifier **const** tells the compiler "this never changes" (which allows the compiler to perform extra optimizations) the qualifier **volatile** tells the compiler "you never know when this will change," and *prevents* the compiler from performing any optimizations. Use this keyword when you read some value outside the control of the system, such as a register in a piece of communication hardware. A **volatile** variable is always read whenever its value is required, even if it was just read the line before.

C/C++ *Operators and Their Use*

Operators were briefly introduced in Chapter 2. This section covers all the operators in C and C++.

All operators produce a value from their operands. This value is produced without modifying the operands, except with assignment, increment, and decrement operators. Modifying an operand is called a *side effect*. The most common use for operators that modify their operands is to generate the side effect, but you should keep in mind that the value produced is available for your use just as in operators without side effects.

Assignment

Assignment is performed with the operator **=**. It means "take the right-hand side (often called the *rvalue*) and copy it into the left-hand side (often called the *lvalue*)". An rvalue is any constant, variable, or expression that can produce a value, but an lvalue must be a distinct, named variable (that is, there must be a physical space to store a value). For example, you can assign a constant value to a variable (**A = 4;**), but you cannot assign anything to constant value—it cannot be an lvalue (you can't say **4 = A;**).

Mathematical Operators

The basic mathematical operators are the same as the ones available in most programming languages: addition (**+**), subtraction (**–**), division (**/**), multiplication (*****) and modulus (**%**, this produces the remainder from integer division). Integer division truncates the result (it doesn't round). The modulus operator cannot be used with floating-point numbers.

C/C++ also introduces a shorthand notation to perform an operation and an assignment at the same time. This is denoted by an operator followed by an equal sign and is consistent with all the operators in the language (whenever it makes sense). For example, to add 4 to the variable **x** and assign **x** to the result, you say: **x += 4;**.

This example shows the use of the mathematical operators:

```
//: MATHOPS.CPP—mathematical operators
#include <iostream.h>

// A macro to display a string and a value.
#define print(str, var) cout << str " = " << var << endl

void main() {
  int i, j, k;
  float u,v,w;  // applies to doubles, too

  cout << "enter an integer: ";
  cin >> j;
  cout << "enter another integer: ";
  cin >> k;
  print("j",j);  print("k",k);
  i = j + k; print("j + k",i);
  i = j - k; print("j - k",i);
  i = k / j; print("k / j",i);
  i = k * j; print("k * j",i);
  i = k % j; print("k % j",i);
  // the following only works with integers:
  j %= k; print("j %= k", j);

  cout << "enter a floating-point number: ";
  cin >> v;
  cout << "enter another floating-point number: ";
  cin >> w;
  print("v",v); print("w",w);
  u = v + w; print("v + w", u);
```

```
u = v - w; print("v - w", u);
u = v * w; print("v * w", u);
u = v / w; print("v / w", u);

// the following works for ints, chars, and doubles too:
u += v; print("u += v", u);
u -= v; print("u -= v", u);
u *= v; print("u *= v", u);
u /= v; print("u /= v", u);
}
```

The rvalues of all the assignments can, of course, be much more complex.

Introduction to Preprocessor Macros

Notice the use of the macro **print()** in the previous example to save typing (and typing errors!). The arguments in the parenthesized list following the macro name are substituted in all the code following the closing parenthesis. The preprocessor removes the name **print** and substitutes the code wherever the macro is called, so the compiler cannot generate any error messages using the macro name, and it doesn't do any type checking on the arguments (the latter can be beneficial, as shown in the debugging macros at the end of the chapter).

Operators are Just a Different Kind of Function Call

There are two differences between the use of an operator and an ordinary function call. The syntax is different; an operator is often "called" by placing it *between* or sometimes *after* the arguments. The second difference is that the compiler determines what function to call. For example, if you are using the operator **+** with floating-point arguments, the compiler "calls" the function to perform floating-point addition (this "call" is sometimes the action of inserting inline code or a floating-point coprocessor instruction). If you use operator **+** with a floating-point number and an integer, the compiler "calls" a special function to turn the **int** into a **float**, and then "calls" the floating-point addition code.

It is important to be aware that operators are simply a different kind of function call. In C++ you can define your own functions for the compiler to call when it encounters operators used with your abstract data types. This feature is called *operator overloading* and is described in Chapter 5.

Relational Operators

Relational operators establish a relationship between the values of the operands. They produce a value of 1 if the relationship is true, and a value of 0 if the relationship is false. The relational operators are less than (**<**), greater than (**>**), less than or equal to (**<=**), greater than or equal to (**>=**), equivalent (**==**) and not equivalent (**!=**). They may be used with all built-in data types in C and C++. They may be given special definitions for user-defined data types in C++.

Logical Operators

The *logical operators* AND (**&&**) and OR (**| |**) produce a true (1) or false (0) based on the logical relationship of its arguments. Remember that in C and C++, a statement is true if it has a nonzero value and false if it has a zero value.

The following example uses the relational and logical operators:

```
//: BOOLEAN.CPP—Relational and logical operators.
#include <iostream.h>

void main() {
  int i,j;
  cout << "enter an integer: ";
  cin >> i;
  cout << "enter another integer: ";
  cin >> j;
  cout << "i > j is " << (i > j) << endl;
  cout << "i < j is " << (i < j) << endl;
  cout << "i >= j is " << (i >= j) << endl;
  cout << "i <= j is " << (i <= j) << endl;
```

```
cout << "i == j is " << (i == j) << endl;
cout << "i != j is " << (i != j) << endl;
cout << "i && j is " << (i && j) << endl;
cout << "i || j is " << (i || j) << endl;
cout << " (i < 10) && (j < 10) is "
     << ((i < 10) && (j < 10)) << endl;
}
```

You can replace the definition for **int** with **float** or **double** in this program. Be aware, however, that the comparison of a floating-point number with the value of zero is very strict: A number that is the tiniest fraction different from another number is still "not equal." A number that is the tiniest bit above zero is still true.

Bitwise Operators

The *bitwise operators* allow you to manipulate individual bits in a number (thus they only work with integral numbers). Bitwise operators perform boolean algebra on the corresponding bits in the two arguments to produce the result.

The bitwise AND operator (**&**) produces a 1 in the output bit if both input bits are 1; otherwise it produces a 0. The bitwise OR operator (**|**) produces a 1 in the output bit if either input bit is a 1 and only produces a 0 if both input bits are 0. The bitwise, eXclusive OR, or XOR (**^**) produces a 1 in the output bit if one or the other input bit is a 1, but not both. The bitwise NOT (**~**, also called the *one's complement operator*) is a *unary operator*—it only takes one argument (all other bitwise operators are *binary operators*). Bitwise NOT produces the opposite of the input bit—a 1 if the input bit is 0, a 0 if the input bit is 1. The operator performs the inversion on all bits in the data.

Bitwise operators can be combined with the **=** sign to unite the operation and assignment: **&=**, **|=** and **^=** are all legitimate (since **~** is a unary operator, it cannot be combined with the **=** sign).

Shift Operators

The *shift operators* also manipulate bits. The left-shift operator (**<<**) produces the operand to the left of the operator shifted to the left by the number of bits specified after the operator. The right-shift operator (**>>**)

produces the operand to the left of the operator shifted to the right by the number of bits specified after the operator. These are shifts, and not rotates—even though a rotate command is usually available in assembly language, you can build your own rotate command, so presumably, the designers of C felt justified in leaving "rotate" off (aiming, as they said, for a minimal language).

If the value after the shift operator is greater than the number of bits in the left-hand operand, the result is undefined. If the left-hand operand is unsigned, the right shift is a *logical shift* so the upper bits will be filled with zeros. If the left-hand operand is signed, the right shift may or may not be a logical shift.

Shifts can be combined with the equal sign (**<<=** and **>>=**). The lvalue is replaced by the lvalue shifted by the rvalue.

Here's an example that demonstrates the use of all the operators involving bits:

```
//: BITWISE.CPP—demonstration of bit manipulation
#include <iostream.h>

// A macro to print a newline (saves typing):
#define NL cout << endl
// Notice the trailing ';' is omitted—this forces the
// programmer to use it and maintain consistent syntax

// This function takes a single byte and displays it
// bit-by-bit. The (1 << i) produces a one in each
// successive bit position; in binary: 00000001, 00000010, etc.
// If this bit bitwise ANDed with val is nonzero, it means
// there was a one in that position in val.
void print_binary(const unsigned char val) {
  for(int i = 7; i >= 0; i--)
    if( val & (1 << i) )
      cout << "1";
    else
      cout << "0";
}
// Generally, you don't want signs when you are working with
// bytes, so you use an unsigned char.

void main() {
  // an int must be used instead of a char here because the
  // "cin >>" statement will otherwise treat the first digit
  // as a character. By assigning getval to a and b, the value
```

```
    // is converted to a single byte (by truncating it)
    unsigned int getval;
    unsigned char a,b;
    cout << "enter a number between 0 and 255: ";
    cin >> getval; a = getval;
    cout << "a in binary: "; print_binary(a); cout << endl;
    cout << "enter another number between 0 and 255: ";
    cin >> getval; b = getval;
    cout << "b in binary: "; print_binary(b); NL;
    cout << "a | b = "; print_binary(a | b); NL;
    cout << "a & b = "; print_binary(a & b); NL;
    cout << "a ^ b = "; print_binary(a ^ b); NL;
    cout << "~a = "; print_binary(~a); NL;
    cout << "~b = "; print_binary(~b); NL;
    unsigned char c = 0x5A; // interesting bit pattern
    cout << "c in binary: "; print_binary(c); NL;
    a |= c;
    cout << "a |= c; a = "; print_binary(a); NL;
    b &= c;
    cout << "b &= c; b = "; print_binary(b); NL;
    b ^= a;
    cout << "b ^= a; b = "; print_binary(b); NL;
}
```

Here are functions to perform left and right rotations:

```
//: ROLROR.CPP—Perform left and right rotations

unsigned char ROL(unsigned char val) {
  int highbit;
  if ( val & 0x80 ) // 0x80 is the high bit only
    highbit = 1;
  else
    highbit = 0;
  val <<= 1;  // left shift (bottom bit becomes 0)
  val |= highbit;  // rotate the high bit onto the bottom
  return val;  // this becomes the function value
}

unsigned char ROR(unsigned char val) {
  int lowbit;
  if ( val & 1 ) // check the low bit
    lowbit = 1;
  else
    lowbit = 0;
  val >>= 1; // right shift by one position
  val |= (lowbit << 7); // rotate the low bit onto the top
```

```
    return val;
}
```

Try using these functions in the BITWISE program. Notice the definitions (or at least declarations) of **ROL()** and **ROR()** must be seen by the compiler in BITWISE.CPP before the functions are used.

The bitwise functions are generally extremely efficient to use because they translate directly into assembly language statements. Sometimes a single C or C++ statement will generate a single line of assembly code.

Unary Operators

Bitwise NOT isn't the only operator that takes a single argument. Its companion, the logical NOT (**!**), will take a true value (nonzero) and produce a false value (zero). The unary minus (**–**) and unary plus (**+**) are the same operators as binary minus and plus—the compiler figures out which usage is intended by the way you write the expression. For example, the statement

```
x = -a;
```

has an obvious meaning.

The compiler can figure out:

```
x = a * -b;
```

but the reader might get confused, so it is safer to say

```
x = a * (-b);
```

The unary minus produces the negative of the value. Unary plus provides symmetry with unary minus, although it doesn't do much.

The increment and decrement operators (**++** and **--**) were introduced in Chapter 2. These are the only operators other than those involving assignment that have side effects. The increment operator increases the variable by one unit ("unit" can have different meanings according to the data type—see Chapter 4) and the decrement operator decreases the variable by one unit. The value produced depends on whether the operator is used as a *prefix operator* or a *postfix operator* (before or after the variable). Used as a prefix, the operator changes the variable and produces the changed value. As a postfix, the operator produces the unchanged value and *then* the variable is modified.

The last unary operators are the address-of (**&**), dereference (*), and cast operators in C and C++ and **new** and **delete** in C++. Address-of and dereference are used with pointers, which will be described in Chapter 4. Casting is described later in this chapter, and **new** and **delete** are described in Chapter 6.

Conditional Operator or Ternary Operator (? :)

The *conditional operator* or *ternary operator* (**?** :) is unusual because it has three operands. It is truly an operator because it produces a value, unlike the ordinary **if-else** statement. It consists of three expressions: if the first expression (followed by a **?**) evaluates to true, the expression following the **?** is evaluated, and its result becomes the value produced by the operator. If the first expression is false, the third expression (following a :) is executed and its result becomes the value produced by the operator.

The conditional operator can be used for its side effects or for the value it produces. Here's a code fragment that demonstrates both:

```
A = --B ? B : (B = -99);
```

Here, the conditional produces the rvalue. **A** is assigned to the value of **B** if the result of decrementing **B** is nonzero. If **B** became 0, **A** and **B** are both assigned to –99. **B** is always decremented, but it is only assigned to –99 if the decrement causes **B** to become 0. A similar statement can be used without the "**A =**" just for its side effects:

```
--B ? B : (B = -99);
```

Here the second **B** is superfluous, since the value produced by the operator is unused. An expression is required between the **?** and :. In this case, the expression could simply be a constant that might make the code run a bit faster.

The Comma Operator

The comma is not restricted to separating variable names in multiple definitions (such as **int i, j, k;**). When used as an operator to separate expressions, it produces only the value of the last expression. All the rest of the expressions in the comma-separated list are only evaluated for their side effects. The following code fragment increments a list of variables and uses the last one as the rvalue:

```
A = (B++,C++,D++,E++);
```

The parentheses are critical here. Without them, the statement will evaluate to

```
(A = B++), C++, D++, E++;
```

Common Pitfalls When Using Operators

As you have just read, one of the pitfalls when using operators is trying to get away without parentheses when you are even the least bit uncertain about how an expression will evaluate (consult your local C manual for the order of expression evaluation).

Another extremely common error looks like this:

```
//: PITFALL.CPP—operator mistakes

void main() {
  int a = 1, b = 1;
  while( a = b ) {
    // ....
  }
}
```

The statement **a = b** will always evaluate to true when **b** is not 0. The variable **a** is assigned to the value of **b**, and the value of **b** is also produced by the operator **=**. Usually you want to use the equivalence operator **==**, not assignment, inside a conditional statement. This one bites a lot of programmers.

A similar problem is using bitwise AND and OR instead of logical. Bitwise AND and OR use one of the characters (**&** or **|**) while logical AND and OR use two (**&&** and **||**). Just as with **=** and **==**, it's easy to just type one character instead of two. A mnemonic may help: bits are smaller, bitwise AND and OR operators are smaller than logical AND and OR operators.

Casting Operators

Cast in C is used in the sense of "casting into a mold." C will automatically change one type of data into another if it makes sense to the compiler. For example, if you assign an integral value to a floating-point variable, the compiler will secretly call a function (or, more probably, insert code) to convert the **int** to a **float**. Casting allows you to make this type conversion explicit—to force it when it wouldn't normally happen.

To perform a cast, put the desired data type (including all modifiers) inside parentheses to the left of the value. This value can be a variable, constant, the value produced by an expression, or the return value of a function. Here's an example:

```
int B = 200;
A = (unsigned long int)B;
```

You can even define casting operators for user-defined data types. Casting is very powerful, but it can cause headaches because in some situations it forces the compiler to treat data as if it were, for example, larger than it really is, so it will occupy more space in memory. This can trample over other data. This usually occurs when casting pointers, not when making simple casts like the one shown above.

C++ has an additional kind of casting syntax that follows the "function-call" syntax used with constructors (defined later in this chapter). This syntax puts the parentheses around the argument, like a function call, rather than around the data type, for example:

```
float A = float(200);
```

This is equivalent to:

```
float A = (float)200;
```

sizeof()—*An Operator by Itself*

The **sizeof()** operator stands alone because it satisfies an unusual need—it gives you information about the amount of memory allocated for data items. As described earlier in this chapter, **sizeof()** tells you the number of bytes used by any particular variable. It can also give the size of a data type (with no variable name):

```
printf("sizeof(double) = %d\n", sizeof(double));
```

The **sizeof()** operator can also give you the sizes of user-defined data types. This is used later in the book.

Creating Functions in C and C++

Most modern languages have an ability to create named subroutines or subprograms, and C and C++ are not exceptions. In C/C++, a subprogram is called a *function*. All functions have return values (although that value can be "nothing"), so functions in C are very similar to functions in Pascal. (The Pascal *procedure* is the specialized case of a function with no return value. From that perspective, it hardly seems worth the brouhaha to give it a separate name....)

Function Prototyping

Function prototyping is another improvement invented in C++ that propagated back into ANSI C. You have been seeing function prototyping in this book described as "telling the compiler that a function exists and how it is called." Now it's time for more details.

In old (pre-ANSI) C, you could call a function with any number or type of arguments, and the compiler wouldn't complain. Everything seemed fine until you ran the program. You got mysterious results (or worse, the program crashed) with no hints as to why. The lack of help with argument passing and the enigmatic bugs that resulted are probably prime reasons why C has been dubbed a "high-level assembly language."

C programmers just adapted to it. When Stroustrup designed C++, he decided that something must be done about the problem, so he added *function prototyping*. With function prototyping, you always use a *prototype*, an example, when declaring and defining a function. When the function is called, the compiler uses the prototype to ensure that the proper arguments are passed in and that the return value is treated correctly. If the programmer makes a mistake when calling the function, the compiler catches the mistake.

Telling the Compiler How Arguments Are Passed

In a function prototype, the *argument list* (which follows the name and is surrounded by parentheses) contains the types of arguments that must be passed to the function and (optionally for the declaration) the names of the arguments. The order and type (but not the names) of the arguments must match in the declaration, definition, and function call. Here's an example of a function prototype in a declaration:

```
int translate(float x, float y, float z);
```

You cannot use the same form when defining variables in function argument lists as you do in ordinary variable definitions, for example, **float x, y, z**. You must indicate the type of each argument. In a function declaration, the following form is also acceptable,

```
int translate(float, float, float);
```

since the compiler doesn't do anything but check for types when the function is called.

In the function definition, names are required because the arguments are referenced inside the function:

```
int translate(float x, float y, float z) {
  x = y = z;
```

```
// ...
}
```

The only exception to this rule occurs in C++ as follows: an argument may be unnamed in the argument list of the function definition. Since it is unnamed, you cannot use it in the function body, however. The reason unnamed arguments are allowed is to give the programmer a way to "reserve space in the argument list." You must still call the function with the proper arguments, but you can *use* the argument in the future without modifying any of the other code. This option of ignoring an argument in the list is possible if you leave the name in, but you will get an obnoxious warning message about the value being unused every time you compile the function. The warning is eliminated if you remove the name.

ANSI C and C++ have two other ways to declare an argument list. If you have an empty argument list, you can declare it as **foo()** in C++. Remember this only means an empty argument list in C++. In ANSI C it means "an indeterminate number of arguments." In both ANSI C and C++, the declaration **foo(void);** means an empty argument list. The **void** keyword means "nothing" in this case (it can also mean "no type" when applied to certain variables).

The other option for argument lists occurs when you don't know how many arguments or what type of arguments you will have; this is called a *variadic function.* This "uncertain argument list" is represented by ellipses (**...**). Defining a variadic function is significantly more complicated than a plain function. You can use a variadic function declaration for a function that has a fixed set of arguments if (for some reason) you want to disable the error checks of function prototyping. Handling variadic argument lists is described in the library section of your local ANSI C guide.

Function Return Values

A function prototype may also specify the return value of a function. The type of this value precedes the function name. If no type is given, the return value type defaults to **int** (most things in C default to **int**). If you want to specify that no value is returned, as in a Pascal procedure, the **void** keyword is used. This will generate an error if you try to return a value from the function. Here are some complete function prototypes:

```
foo1(void); // returns an int, takes no arguments
foo2(); // like foo2() in C++ but not in ANSI C!
float foo3(float, int, char, double); // returns a float
void foo4(void); // takes no arguments, returns nothing
```

At this point, you may wonder how to specify a return value in the function definition. This is done with the **return** statement. The **return** keyword exits the function back to the point right after the function call. If **return** has an argument, that becomes the return value of the function. You can have more than one **return** statement in a function definition, as in this example:

```
//: RETURN.CPP—Use of "return"
#include <iostream.h>

char cfunc(const int i) {
  if(i == 0)
    return 'a';
  if(i == 1)
    return 'g';
  if(i == 5)
    return 'z';
  return 'c';
}

void main() {
  cout << "type an integer: ";
  int val;
  cin >> val;
  cout << cfunc(val) << endl;
}
```

The code in **cfunc()** acts like an **if-else** statement. The **else** is unnecessary because the first **if** that evaluates true causes an exit of the function via the **return** statement. Notice that a function declaration is not necessary because the function definition appears before it is used in **main()**, so the compiler knows about it. Arguments and return values are covered in detail in Chapter 9.

Using the C Function Library

All the functions in your local C function library are available while you are programming in C++. You should look hard at the function library before defining your own function—chances are, someone has solved the problem for you and probably given it a lot more thought (as well as debugging!).

A word of caution, though: many compilers include a lot of extra functions that make life even easier and are very tempting to use, but are not part of the ANSI C library. If you are certain you will never want to move the application to another platform (and who is certain of that?), go ahead—use those functions and make your life easier. If you want your application to be portable, you should restrict yourself to ANSI C functions (this is safe because the ANSI C library is part of C++). Keep a guide to ANSI C handy and refer to that when looking for a function rather than your local C or C++ guide. If you must perform platform-specific activities, try to isolate that code in one spot so it can easily be changed when porting to another platform. Platform-specific activities are often encapsulated in a class—this is the ideal solution.

The formula for using a library function is as follows: first, find the function in your guidebook (many guidebooks will index the function by category as well as alphabetically). The description of the function should include a section that demonstrates the syntax of the code. The top of this section usually has at least one **#include** line, showing you the header file containing the function prototype. Duplicate this **#include** line in your file, so the function is properly declared. Now you can call the function in the same way it appears in the syntax section. If you make a mistake, the compiler will discover it by comparing your function call to the function prototype in the header, and will tell you about your error. The linker searches the standard library by default, so that's all you need to do—include the header file and call the function.

Creating Your Own Libraries with the Librarian

You can collect your own functions together into a library, or add new functions to the library the linker secretly searches (you should back up the old one before doing this). Most packages come with a *librarian*, which manages groups of object modules. Each librarian has its own commands, but the general idea is this: If you want to create a library, make a header file containing the function prototypes for all the functions in your library. Put this header file somewhere in the preprocessor's search path, either in the local directory (so it can be found by **#include** "*header*") or in the INCLUDE directory (so it can be found by **#include** <*header*>). Now take all the object modules and hand them to the librarian along with a name for the finished library (most librarians require a common extension, such as .lib). Place the finished library in the same spot the other libraries reside, so the linker can find it. When you use your library, you will have to add something to the command line so the linker knows to search the library for the functions you call. You must find all the details in your local manual, since they vary from system to system.

Unique Features of C++ Functions

C++ functions have a number of improvements over C functions, designed to make them easier to program and use.

Inline *Functions*

The preprocessor macro function introduced earlier in this chapter for the MATHOPS program saves typing, improves readability, reduces errors and eliminates the overhead of a function call. Preprocessor macro functions are popular in C, but they have the drawback that they are not "real" functions, so the usual error checking doesn't occur during compilation.

C++ encourages (sometimes even requires) the use of small functions. The programmer concerned with speed, however, might opt to use preprocessor macros rather than functions to avoid the overhead of a function call. To eliminate the cost of calls to small functions, C++ has *inline functions*. These functions are specified with the **inline** keyword:

```
inline int one() { return 1; }
```

Notice the definition accompanies the **inline** keyword. When the compiler encounters an **inline** definition, it doesn't generate code as it does with an ordinary function definition. Instead, it remembers the code for the function. In an **inline** function call, (which looks like a call to any other function), the compiler checks for proper usage as it does with any function call and then substitutes the code for the function call. Thus, the efficiency of preprocessor macros is combined with the error checking of ordinary functions.

The inline function is another tough nut when it comes to terminology. Because the body of the function doesn't actually reserve any storage for the function code, it is tempting to call it a declaration rather than a definition. Indeed, you cannot "declare" an inline function in the usual sense. In the "declaration"

```
inline int one();
```

the **inline** keyword has no effect—it does the compiler no good to know that a function is an **inline** if it doesn't have the code to substitute when it encounters a function call. The **inline** function definitions must occur before they are used, just like ordinary function declarations. Generally, this is accomplished by putting the **inline** function definition in a header file. There is nothing else that could be called a definition other than the place where the function body is, so it is called a definition.

Saving Space

Because an inline function duplicates the code for every function call, you might think it automatically increases code space. For small functions (which inlines were designed for) this isn't necessarily true. Keep in mind that a function call requires code to pass arguments, make the call, and handle the return value; this code isn't present for an inline function. If your inline function turns out to be smaller than the amount of code necessary for the ordinary call, you are actually *saving* space. In addition, if the **inline** function is never called, no code is ever generated. With an ordinary function, code for that function is there (only once) whether you call it or not.

The **inline** keyword is actually just a hint to the compiler. The compiler may ignore the **inline** and simply generate code for the function someplace.

inline *Abuse*

A big advantage to inline functions is that they save a lot of typing—your function is declared and defined in one place. The code is often clearer to the reader, as well. The result is often an abuse of inline functions; they are used because they are easier and clearer rather than because they are faster. This abuse is most rampant in (of all places) articles and books on programming in C++. As you will see, some projects in this book push the boundaries of good sense when using **inline**.

The problem is this: the C++ compiler must remember the definition for the inline function, rather than simply compiling it and moving on as with an ordinary function. Inline functions can take up a lot more space than the other items a compiler must remember—enough space, in fact, to crash some implementations of C++. (This rarely happens anymore because of the use of better memory-management techniques in compilers and the low cost of RAM.)

The speed benefits of inline functions tend to diminish as the function grows in size. At some point, the overhead of the function call becomes small compared to the execution of the function body, and the benefit is lost.

C++ *Function Overloading*

C++ introduces the concept of *function overloading*. This means you can call the same function name in a variety of ways, depending on your needs. An overloaded **print()** function might be able to handle **float**s, **int**s, and strings, for example,

```
print(3.14);
print(47);
print("this is a string");
```

where the function **print()** is overloaded with several different meanings.

The most useful place to overload functions is in classes, as we shall see later. You can also overload ordinary functions by using the **overload** keyword in earlier releases of the language. The keyword is still available, but obsolete, in modern releases of C++. You may still see it in old code, but you should never use it.

The **overload** keyword is placed before any of the function declarations:

```
overload print; // warn C++ we are overloading this name
void print(float);
void print(int);
void print(char *); // for strings; see Chapter 4
```

In the last declaration, you see a new type of argument: **char ***. The "*" indicates that this argument isn't an actual argument, but instead a *pointer* to the argument. Pointers are discussed in detail in Chapter 4, but they are such an integral part of C and C++ that a brief introduction is necessary here. A pointer is a variable that holds the *address* of another variable. Because you don't know how long a string is at compile time, the compiler can't know how to pass the string to the **print()** function. If we tell **print()** "where the string lives" by passing the address, the function can figure out for itself where to get the characters in the string and how long the string is (at run time instead of compile time).

Distinguishing Overloaded Functions

For the compiler to tell the difference between one use of the function and another, it must have a unique set of arguments each time the function is overloaded. These can even be the same arguments, as long as the order is different, for example:

```
//: OVERLOAD.CPP—same parameters, different order
#include <iostream.h>

void print(int x, char c) {
  cout << "first function : int, char" << endl;
}

void print(char c, int x) {
  cout << "second function : char, int" << endl;
}

void main() {
  int i = 0;
  char c = 'x';
  print(i,c);
  print(c,i);
}
```

Overloading functions and operators is covered in detail in Chapter 5. Improvements to overloading are described in Chapter 11.

Is Overloading Object Oriented?

Object-oriented programming can be perceived as one more step in the long process of shifting the petty details of managing a program from the programmer onto the computer. The motto might be: "let the programmer think more about the design, and let the computer handle more of the implementation." If you use this rather generous interpretation, then any construct that allows the programmer to fire off a message and let the system figure out what to do with the message is an object-oriented feature. Function overloading allows you to use the same message name with different arguments and the compiler figures out how to handle it. You don't have to remember as many message names—you do less work, the computer does more work, so it's object oriented, right?

It depends. Much of the history of object-oriented programming happened in an interpreted environment, where all messages are resolved during program execution. Resolving messages at compile time rather than run time is not considered an object-oriented feature if you come from this background.

Resolving all messages at run time introduces a lot of overhead to the system. In addition, the compiler can't do static type checking (and error detection). Both these drawbacks are counter to C++'s design philosophy.

Whether function overloading is object oriented really depends upon where you draw the boundary. If you are willing to be casual and say "I write the code and the computer takes care of it. I don't care how," then function overloading can be thought of as object oriented. If you insist that all messages must be resolved at run time, then function overloading (as well as many other implementation details of C++) isn't object oriented.

Default Arguments

C++ functions may have *default arguments* that are substituted by the compiler if you don't supply your own. Default arguments are specified in the function declaration, for example:

```
void foo(int i = 0);
```

You can now call the function as **foo()** (which is the same as **foo(0)**) or **foo(47)**. Default arguments seem like function overloading to the client programmer. Note that the variable name **i** is optional in the declaration, even with default arguments.

You can have more than one default argument in a list, but all the default arguments must be at the end of the list, and once you start using defaults, all the arguments in the rest of the list must be defaulted, as shown here:

```
void foo2(int q, int r, int u = 4, int v = 5, int w = 6);
```

The class: Defining Boundaries

Now you know enough about data types, operators, and functions to understand the creation of the central construct for object-oriented programming in C++: the class. Predefined classes were used in the last chapter, and now you can start defining your own classes.

A class is a way to package associated pieces of data together with functions that operate on that data. It allows you to hide data and functions, if desired, from the general purview. When you create a class, you are creating a new type of data (an abstract data type) and the operations for that type. It is a data type like a **float** is a data type. When you add two **float**s, the compiler knows what to do. A class definition "teaches" the compiler what to do with your new data type.

A class definition consists of the name of the class followed by a body, enclosed in braces, followed by a semicolon (remember the semicolon—leaving it off causes strange errors). The class body contains variable definitions and function declarations. These variables and functions are an intimate part of the class, only used in association with an object belonging to that class. Although the variable definitions look like the ordinary definitions of local variables inside a function, no storage is allocated for them until a variable (object) of the class type is created. When this happens, all the storage for the variables is allocated at once, in a clump.

The variables and functions (collectively called *members*) of a class are normally hidden from the outside world—the user cannot access them. These variables and functions are called *private*. You make the privacy explicit with the **private** keyword; members in a class default to **private**. To allow the client programmer access to members, use the **public** keyword.

Here's a simple class definition:

```
class nurtz {
 int i; // default to private
public: // everything past here is public
 void set(int v) { i = v; } // inline function
 int read() { return i; } // inline function
};
```

Class **nurtz** has three members: the data item **i** and two functions. You can only change the value of **i** by calling the member function **set()**; you can only read it by calling the member function **read()**. The **set()** and **read()** functions are sometimes called *access functions*, since their sole purpose is to provide access to the **private** data. It is important to remember that only member functions (and friend functions, described later) may read or change the values of **private** variables.

As you can see, **set()** and **read()** are inline functions, but the **inline** keyword isn't used! Because a class is so unique, the compiler doesn't need any hints to know that a function is **inline**.

To create and use some variables (objects) of class **nurtz**, you define them just like you define any other variables:

```
nurtz A, B, C;
```

To use the objects, you call member functions using a dot, like this:

```
A.set(2);
int q = A.read();
```

Member functions are not like ordinary functions—you can only call them in association with an object.

Thinking About Objects

You can think of an object as an entity with an *internal state* and *external operations*. The "external operations" in C++ are member functions. The functions that execute the messages in an object-oriented language are called *methods*. *Messages* are the actual function calls. The concept of *state* means an object remembers things about itself when you are not using it. An ordinary C function (one without any **static** variables) is *stateless* because it always starts at the same point whenever you use it. Since an object has a state, however, you can have a function that does something different each time you call it. For example:

```
//: STATE.CPP—a state-transition class
#include <iostream.h>

// See "enum" defined later in this chapter for a better
// way to do this:
const idle = 0;
const pre_wash = 1;
const spin1 = 2;
const wash = 3;
const spin2 = 4;
const rinse = 5;
const spin3 = 6;

class washing_machine {
  int current_cycle;
 public:
  void start() { current_cycle = idle; }
  void next();
};

void washing_machine::next() {
  switch(current_cycle) {
    case idle : current_cycle = pre_wash; break;
    case pre_wash  : current_cycle = spin1; break;
    case spin1 : current_cycle = wash; break;
    case wash: current_cycle = spin2; break;
    case spin2 : current_cycle = rinse; break;
    case rinse: current_cycle = spin3; break;
```

```
    case spin3 : current_cycle = idle; break;
    default : current_cycle = idle;
  }
  cout << "current_cycle = " << current_cycle << endl;
}

void main() {
  washing_machine WM;
  WM.start();
  for (int i = 0; i < 7; i++)
    WM.next();
}
```

The **state** variable **WM** shows a washing machine going through all its cycles, one for each time you call **next()**.

Design Benefits

One of the design benefits of C++ is that it separates the interface from the *implementation*. The interface in C++ is the class definition. The interface says: "here's what an object looks like, and here are the methods for the object." It doesn't specify (except in the case of inline functions) *how* the methods work. The implementation shows *how* the methods work, and consists of all the member function definitions. While the interface must have been seen by the compiler anyplace you use the class, the implementation can only exist in one spot. If, at some point in the future, the programmer wishes to improve the implementation, it doesn't disturb the interface or all the code compiled using the interface. The implementation can be changed, and the whole system relinked (only the implementation code must be recompiled). Assuming the interface is well planned, code changes are very isolated, which prevents the propagation of bugs.

In a similar vein, you can design and code the interface and delay writing the implementation code. The interface is used as if the implementation code exists ("only the linker knows for sure"). This means you can make the equivalent of a "rough sketch" of your system and check to see that everything fits together properly by compiling all the modules that use the interface.

Declaration Versus Definition (Again)

Although ANSI has established a clear picture of "declaration" and "definition" for C, with the C++ class it again grows fuzzy. It can be argued that a class description reserves no storage (except in the case of static members), and it is really just a model of a new data type and not an actual variable, so it should be called a declaration.

The common terminology is as follows. A class name without a description of the class, such as

```
class foobar;
```

will be called a *class name declaration.*

A name declaration followed by a body, such as:

```
class foobar {
 int i;
 //...
};
```

is a *class declaration.*

Constructors and Destructors (Initialization and Cleanup)

When you define an instance of a built-in type (such as an **int**), the compiler creates storage for that variable. If you choose to assign a value when reserving storage for the variable, the compiler does that too. In effect, the compiler *constructs* the variable for you.

When a variable of a built-in type goes out of scope, the compiler cleans up the storage for that variable by freeing it; in effect, it *destroys* the variable.

C++ allows you to ensure that user-defined types (classes) are always properly initialized and cleaned up. This means the compiler needs a function to call when the variable is created (a *constructor*) and a function to call when the variable goes out of scope (a *destructor*). If the programmer doesn't supply constructors (there can be more than one overloaded constructor) and a destructor (there can only be one) for a class, the compiler assumes the simplest actions.

The constructor is a member function with the same name as the class. The constructor assumes that the storage has been allocated for all the variables in the object's structure when it is called. Here's an example of a constructor:

```
//: CONSTRUC.CPP—a class with constructors
#include <iostream.h>

class thizbin {
  int i, j, k;
public:
  thizbin() { i = j = k = 0; }  // constructor
  thizbin(int q) { i = j = k = q; } // overloaded constructor
  thizbin(int u, int v, int w) {
    i = u;
    j = v;
    k = w;
  }  // more overloading
  void print(char * msg) {
    cout << msg << ": " << endl;
    cout << "i = " << i << endl;
    cout << "j = " << j << endl;
    cout << "k = " << k << endl;
  }
};

void main() {
  thizbin A;  // calls constructor with no arguments
  thizbin B(47); // calls constructor with 1 argument
  thizbin C(9,11,47); // calls constructor with 3 arguments
  A.print("A--no argument constructor");
  B.print("B--1 argument constructor");
  C.print("C--3 argument constructor");
}
```

Class **thizbin** has three overloaded constructors, one that takes no arguments (used in the definition of **A**), one that takes one **int** (used for **B**), and one that takes three **int**s (used for **C**). The **print()** method displays the private values of the objects after they are initialized.

The name of the destructor is the class name with a tilde attached at the beginning. For the above example, the destructor name would be **~thizbin()**. The destructor never takes any arguments; it is only called by the compiler and cannot be called explicitly by the programmer (except for one unusual situation, when it is used to place an object at a specific location in memory). See Chapter 6 for more information.

While you will almost always want to perform various types of initialization on an object, the "default destructor" (doing nothing) is often sufficient, and you may not need to define a destructor. However, if your object initializes some hardware (for example, puts a window up on the screen) or changes a global value, you may need to undo the effect of the object (close the window) when the object is destroyed. For this, you need a destructor.

As an example, the following program keeps track of the number of objects in existence by modifying a global variable:

```cpp
//: OBJCOUNT.CPP—Counts objects in existence
#include <iostream.h>

int count = 0;

class obj {
 public:
  obj() {
    count++;
    cout << "number of objects: " << count << endl;
  }
  ~obj() {
    count--;
    cout << "number of objects: " << count << endl;
  }
};

void main() {
  obj A, B, C, D, E;
  {
    obj F;
  }
  {
    obj G;
  }
}
```

As the objects are created, they increase the count, and as they go out of scope, they decrease the count. Notice that after the first group of variables is created, **F** is created and then destroyed, and **G** is created and then destroyed; then the rest of the variables are destroyed. When the closing brace of a scope is encountered, destructors are called for each variable in the scope.

static *Class Members*

Every time you define an object that belongs to a particular class, all the data elements in that class are duplicated for the variable. It is possible, however, to define a variable in a class such that only one instance of the variable is created for all the objects ever defined for that class. Each object has access to this one piece of data, but the data is shared among all the objects instead of being duplicated for each object. To achieve this effect, declare the variable **static** (a third meaning of the keyword **static**).

You often use **static** member variables to communicate between objects, for example:

```
//: STATVAR.CPP—Static member variable in a class
#include <iostream.h>

class common {
  static i;  // declaration, NOT definition!
 public:
  common() { i++; }
  ~common() { i--; }
  void look_around() {
    if( i > 1 )
      cout << "there are other objects of this class" << "endl";
    else
      cout << "no other objects of this class" << endl;
  }
};

// you must provide a definition for a static member:
int common::i = 0;

void main() {
  common A;
  A.look_around();
```

```
  {
    common B;
    B.look_around();
  }  // B destroyed here
  A.look_around();
}  // A destroyed here
```

This example also shows another need for the destructor: to keep track of information about objects. For a more sophisticated example of this, see Chapter 9.

You must explicitly reserve storage for, and initialize, all static objects. Storage isn't created for you, since only one piece of storage is needed for the whole program. You can't initialize a class **static** variable as you do a function **static** variable:

```
class bad {
  static int i = 33; // won't compile
};
```

Instead, you must use the explicit syntax for static members. This repeats the type of the object but uses the class name and the scope resolution operator with the identifier. Other than that, it's the same as an ordinary global object definition, as shown here:

```
int bad::i = 33;
```

The definition and initialization occur outside of all class and function bodies. There can only be one such definition, so even though it looks like privacy is compromised, no one else can access the variable in the same manner.

const *Class Members*

You can make a member of a class **const**, but the meaning reverts to that of C. That is, storage is always allocated for a **const** data member, so a **const** occupies space inside a class. The other rules of C++ still apply—in particular, a **const** must be initialized at the point it is defined. What does this mean, in the case of a class? Storage isn't allocated for a variable until an object is created, and that is the point where the **const** must be initialized. Therefore, the meaning of **const** for class members is "constant for that object for its lifetime."

The initialization of a **const** must occur in the constructor. It is a special action, and must happen in a special way, so that its value is guaranteed to be set at all times. This is performed in the *constructor initializer list*, which occurs after the constructor's argument list but before its body, to indicate that the code is executed before the constructor body is entered. The constructor initializer list has a number of purposes, but one is to initialize **const** members, like this:

```
//: CONSTMEM.CPP—Constant data members of a class

class counter {
  int count;
  const int max;  // 'int' is optional
public:
  counter(int Max = 10, int init = 0) : max(Max) {
    count = init;
  }
  int incr() {
    if(++count == max) return 1;
    return 0;
  }
};

void main() {
  counter A, B(14), C(5,4);
  while(!B.incr())
    if(A.incr())
      C.incr();
}
```

The statement **max(Max)** performs the initialization. Notice that it looks like a constructor call. It is indeed intended to mimic a constructor call, but the meaning of this syntax for built-in types in the constructor initializer list is simply assignment. The assignment of **count** could also have been moved to the constructor initializer list, like this:

```
counter(int Max = 10, int init = 0) : max(Max), count(init) {}
```

True Constants Inside Classes

The treatment of **const** inside classes creates an inconvenient situation when you're creating an array inside a class. (The array was briefly introduced in Chapter 2.) When dealing with ordinary arrays (not inside classes) the best programming practice is to use a named constant to define the size of the array, like this:

```
const sz = 10;
char array[sz];
```

This way, any code that refers to the size of the array uses **sz**, and if you need to change the size, you only change it in one place, at the **const** definition.

You cannot use a **const** data inside an array definition in a class, because the compiler must know the size of the array when it is defined and because a **const** inside a class always allocates storage (the compiler cannot know the contents of a storage location).

Fortunately, there is a convenient way to work around this problem. The enumerated data type **enum** (described later in this chapter) is designed to associate names with integral numbers. Normally **enum** is used to distinguish a set of names by letting the compiler automatically assign numbers to them. However, you can force a name to be associated with a particular number, as follows:

```
enum { sz = 100 };
```

This introduces a name called **sz** that has the integral value **100**.

Storage is never allocated for enumeration names, so the compiler always has the values available. This provides a technique (sometimes disparagingly referred to as the "enum hack") to solve the problem of using names for array sizes (without reverting back to the barbarity of the preprocessor):

```
class array {
  enum { size = 10 };
  int A[size];
};
```

Since enumerations can only be integral types, this technique is primarily useful for creating arrays.

The Header File

When you create a class, you are creating a new data type. Generally, you want this type to be easily accessible to yourself and others. In addition, you want to separate the interface (the class declaration) from the implementation (the definition of the class member functions) so the implementation can be changed without forcing a recompile of the entire system. You achieve this end by putting the class declaration in a header file.

Function Libraries and Separate Compilation

Instead of putting the class declaration, the definition of the member functions and the **main()** function in the same file, it is best to isolate the class declaration in a header file that is included in every file where the class is used. The definitions of the class member functions are also separated into their own file. The member functions are debugged and compiled once and are then available as an object module (or in a library, if the librarian is used) for anyone who wants to use the class. The user of the class simply includes the header file, creates objects (instances) of that class, and links in the object module or library (the compiled code).

The concept of a library of associated functions combined into the same object module or library and a header file containing all the declarations for the functions is very standard when building large projects in C. It is a must in C++: you could throw any function into a library in C, but the class in C++ determines which functions are associated by dint of their common access to the private data. Any member function for a class *must* be declared in the class declaration; you cannot put it in some separate file. The use of function libraries was encouraged in C and institutionalized in C++.

Importance of Using a Common Header File

When using a function from a library, C allows you the option of ignoring the header file and simply declaring the function by hand. You may want the compiler to speed up just a bit by avoiding the task of opening and including the file. For example, here's an extremely lazy declaration of the C function **printf()**:

```
printf(...);
```

It says, "**printf()** has some number of arguments, and they all have some type, but just take whatever arguments you see and accept them." By using this kind of declaration, you suspend all error checking on the arguments.

This practice can cause subtle problems. If you declare functions by hand in each different file, you may make a mistake the compiler accepts in a particular file. The program will link correctly, but the use of the function in that one file will be faulty. This is a tough error to find and is easily avoided.

If you place all your function declarations in a header file and include that file everywhere you use the function (and especially where you define the function), you ensure a consistent declaration across the whole system. You also ensure that the declaration and the definition match by including the header in the definition file.

C does not enforce this practice. It is very easy, for example, to leave the header file out of the function definition file. Header files often confuse the novice programmer (who may ignore them or use them improperly).

If a class is declared in a header file in C++, you *must* include the header file everywhere a class is used and where class member functions are defined. The compiler will give an error message if you try to call a function without declaring it first. By enforcing the proper use of header files, the language ensures consistency in libraries and reduces bugs by forcing the same interface to be used everywhere.

There was an additional problem in earlier releases of the language. When you overloaded ordinary (nonmember) functions, the *order* of overloading was important. If you used the same function names in separate header files, you could change the order of overloading without knowing it, simply by including the files in a different order. The compiler didn't complain, but the linker did—it was mystifying. This problem existed in C++ compilers following AT&T releases up through 1.2. It was solved by a change in the language called *type-safe linkage* (described later in the book).

Preventing Redeclaration of Classes

When you put a class declaration in a header file, it is possible for the file to be included more than once in a complicated program. The iostream classes are a good example. Any time a class does I/O (especially in inline functions), it may include the iostream header. If the file you are working on uses more than one kind of class, you run the risk of including the iostream header more than once and redeclaring classes.

The compiler considers the redeclaration of a class to be an error, since it would otherwise allow you to use the same name for different classes. To prevent this error when multiple header files are included, you need to build some intelligence into your header files using the preprocessor (the **stream** class already has this "intelligence").

The Preprocessor Directives #define, #ifdef, and #endif

As shown earlier in this chapter, **#define** will create *preprocessor macros*, which look similar to function definitions. The **#define** statement can also create flags. You have two choices: you can simply tell the preprocessor that the flag is defined, without specifying a value

```
#define FLAG
```

or you can give it a value (which is the pre-ANSI C way to define a constant)

```
#define PI 3.14159
```

In either case, the label can now be tested by the preprocessor to see if it has been defined. For example,

```
#ifdef FLAG
```

will yield a true result, and the code following the **#ifdef** will be included in the package sent to the compiler. This inclusion stops when the preprocessor encounters the statement

```
#endif
```

or

```
#endif FLAG
```

Any text after the **#endif** on the same line is ignored in C++ (although it isn't legal ANSI C) and may be used as comments. The **#ifdef/#endif** pairs may be nested within each other.

The complement of **#define** is **#undef** (short for "UNDEFine"), which will make an **#ifdef** statement using the same variable yield a false result. An **#undef** statement will also cause the preprocessor to stop using a macro. The complement of **#ifdef** is **#ifndef**, which yields true if the label has *not* been defined (this is the one we use in header files).

There are other useful features in the preprocessor (especially the ANSI preprocessor). You should check your local guide for the full set.

A Standard for Each Class Header File

In each header file that contains a class, you should first check to see if the file has already been included in this particular code file. You do this by checking a preprocessor flag. If the flag isn't set, the file wasn't included, and you should set the flag (so the class can't get redeclared) and declare the class. If the flag was set, the class has already been declared, so you should just ignore the code declaring the class. Here's how the header file should look:

```
#ifndef CLASS_FLAG_
#define CLASS_FLAG_
// Class declaration here...
#endif CLASS_FLAG_
```

As you can see, the first time the header file is included, the class declaration will be included by the preprocessor, but the class declaration will be ignored all the subsequent times.

The name **CLASS_FLAG_** can be any unique name, but a reliable standard to follow is to take the name of the header file and replace periods with underscores and follow it with a trailing underscore (leading underscores are reserved by ANSI C for system names). Here's an example:

```
//: SIMPLE.H—Simple class which prevents redefinition

#ifndef SIMPLE_H_
#define SIMPLE_H_

class simple {
  int i,j,k;
public:
  simple() { i = j = k = 0; }
};

#endif // SIMPLE_H_
```

Although the **SIMPLE_H_** after the **#endif** is ignored by the preprocessor, it is useful for documentation.

Portable Inclusion of Header Files

C++ was created in a UNIX environment, where the filenames have case sensitivity. Thus, UNIX programmers could name C header files as **header.h** and C++ header files with a capital H, as **header.H**. This didn't translate to some other systems such as MS-DOS, so programmers there distinguished C++ header files with **.hxx** or **.hpp**. Thus you will sometimes see old header files with these extensions. However, the common practice now is to name C++ header files the same as C header files: **header.h**. It turns out that using the same naming convention as C is not a problem, since programmers must know what they are doing when including a header file, and the compiler will catch the error if you try to include a C++ header in a C compilation. All header files in this book use the **.h** convention.

Defining Class Member Functions

All the member function definitions so far have been **inline**. In the general case, functions will be defined in a separate code file. This section shows the specifics of defining member functions.

The Scope Resolution Operator (::)

To define a member function, you must first tell the compiler that the function you are defining is associated with a particular class. This is accomplished using the *scope resolution operator* (::). For example:

```
//: SCOPERES.CPP—Defining a non-inline member function
#include <iostream.h>

class example {
  int i, j, k;
 public:
  example(); // declare the function
  void print(); // ditto
};

example::example() { // the constructor
  i = 12;
  j = 100;
  k = 47;
}

void example::print() {
  cout << "i = " << i;
  cout << ", j = " << j;
  cout << ", k = " << k << endl;
}

void main() {
  example test;
  test.print();
}
```

As you can see, the member function is associated with the class name by attaching the class name followed by the scope resolution operator. The functions will now be compiled as normal functions instead of inline functions.

Use the scope resolution operator any time you are not sure which definition the compiler will use. You can also use scope resolution to select a definition other than the normal default. For example, if you create a class in which you define your own **puts()** function (**puts()** is an ANSI C library function that puts a string to standard output), you can select the global **puts()** as follows:

```
//: DISPLAY.CPP—A class with it's own puts() function
#include <stdio.h>  // contains the puts() declaration

class display {
 public:
  void puts(char *); // declare the function
};

void display::puts(char * msg) {
  ::puts("inside my puts function");
  ::puts(msg);
}

void main() {
  display A;
  A.puts("calling A.puts()");
}
```

If, inside **display::puts()**, the **puts()** function was called without the scope resolution operator, the compiler would call **display::puts()** instead of the library function **puts()**. If the scope resolution operator is used with no name preceding it, it means "use the global name."

Calling Other Member Functions

As the previous example implies, you can call member functions from inside other member functions. It was stated earlier that a member function can never be called unless it is associated with an object, so this might look a bit confusing at first. If you are defining a member function, that function is already associated with an object (the *current object*, also referred to with the keyword **this**). A member function can be called by just using its name inside another member function (no object name and dot is necessary inside a member function). To illustrate, here's an example that creates a "smart array" (one that checks boundaries):

```
//: SMART.CPP—An array that checks boundaries
#include <iostream.h>
#include <stdlib.h> // for exit() declaration

class array {
  enum { size = 10 };
  int a[size];
  void check_index(const int index); // private function
public:
  array(const int initval = 0); // default argument value
  void setval(const int index, const int value);
  int readval(const int index);
};

// constructor (don't duplicate the default value!):
array::array(const int intval) {
  for (int i = 0; i < size; i++ )
    setval(i, intval);  // call another member function
}

void array::check_index(const int index) {
  if ( index < 0 || index >= size ) { // logical OR
    cerr << "array error: setval index out of bounds" << endl;
    exit(1);  // ANSI C library function; quits program
  }
}

void array::setval(const int index, const int value) {
  check_index(index);
  a[index] = value;
}

int array::readval(const int index) {
  check_index(index);
  return a[index];
}

void main() {
  array A, B(47);
  int x = B.readval(10); // out of bounds—see what happens
}
```

Check_index() is a **private** member function that can only be called by other member functions. Whenever the user wants to set or read a value,

check_index() is called first to make sure the array boundaries are not exceeded.

You can see that C and C++ try to make the definition of a variable mimic its use (this doesn't always succeed). For an array, the definition might be

```
int values[100];
```

To use the array, you write

```
int y = values[4];
```

to read element 4 or write

```
values[99] = 128;
```

to assign to element 99. Remember that elements are counted from 0, so if you define an array with 100 elements, you must start at element 0 and stop at element 99.

friend: *Access to Private Elements of Another Class*

There are times when the program design just won't work out right. You can't always make everything fit neatly into one class; sometimes other functions must have access to private elements of your class for everything to work together harmoniously. You could make some elements **public**, but this is a bad idea unless you really want the client programmer to change the data.

The solution in C++ is to create **friend** functions. These are functions that are not class members (although they can be members of some other class; in fact, an entire class can be declared a **friend**). A **friend** has the same access privileges as a member function, but it isn't associated with an object of the host class (so you can't call member functions of the host class without associating the functions with objects). The host class has control over granting **friend** privileges to other functions, so you always know who has the ability to change your private data (it's much easier to trace bugs that way).

As an example, suppose you have two different classes, both of which keep some kind of internal time: a **watch** and a **microwave_oven**, and you want to be able to synchronize the clocks in the two separate classes. Your program might look like this:

```
//: FRIENDLY.CPP—Demonstration of friend functions.
// The synchronize() function has arguments from both watch
// and microwave_oven. The first time synchronize() is declared
// as a friend in watch, the compiler won't know that
// microwave_oven exists unless we declare its name first:
class microwave_oven;

class watch {
  int time;   // a measure of time
  int alarm;  // when the alarm goes off
  int date;   // other things a watch should know
public:
  // constructor sets starting state:
  watch() { time = alarm = date = 0; }
  void tick() { time++; } // very simple transition
  // declare a friend function.
  // (see text for meaning of '&')
  friend void synchronize(watch&, microwave_oven &);
};

class microwave_oven {
  int time;
  int start_time;
  int stop_time;
  int intensity;
public:
  microwave_oven() {
    time = 0;
    start_time = stop_time = 0;
    intensity = 0;
  }
  void tick() { time++; }
  friend void synchronize(watch&, microwave_oven &);
};

void synchronize(watch& objA, microwave_oven & objB) {
  objA.time = objB.time = 15;  // set both to a common state
}

void main() {
  watch que_hora;
```

```
microwave_oven nuke;
que_hora.tick();
que_hora.tick();
nuke.tick();
synchronize(que_hora,nuke);
}
```

Since **synchronize()** is a **friend** function to both **watch** and **micro-wave_oven**, it has access to the private elements of both. In a non-**friend** function, the references to **objA.time** and **objB.time** would be illegal.

References

Something new is introduced in this example: the **&** in the argument list for **synchronize()**. Normally, when you pass an argument to a function, the variable you specify in the argument list is *copied* and handed to the function. If you change something in the copy, it has no effect on the original. When the function ends, the copy goes out of scope and the original is untouched. If you want to change the original variable, you must tell the function *where the original variable lives* instead of making a copy of the original variable. As described earlier in this chapter, a *pointer* is one way of telling a function where the original variable lives. In that example, the address of a string was passed to a function called **print(char *)**. It was necessary to use the address because the compiler couldn't know how long the string was. A *reference*, specified by the operator **&**, is the second way to pass an address. It is often a much nicer way to pass an address to a function, and it is only available in C++.

A reference quietly takes the address of an object. Inside the function, the reference lets you treat the name as if it were a real variable, and not just the address of a variable.

As you can see in the definition for **synchronize()**, the elements of **objA** and **objB** are selected using the dot, just as if **objA** and **objB** were objects, and not addresses of objects. The compiler takes care of every-thing else. References are described in detail in Chapter 4.

Notice that **synchronize()** can reach right in and modify the **private** elements of both **objA** and **objB**. This is only true because **synchronize()** was declared a **friend** of both classes. An alternative solution is to declare an entire class a friend and make **synchronize()** one of the member functions, as in this example:

```
//: FRIEND2.CPP—Making an entire class a friend

class watch {
  int time;   // a measure of time
  int alarm;  // when the alarm goes off
  int date;    // other things a watch should know
public:
  // constructor sets starting state:
  watch() { time = alarm = date = 0; }
  void tick() { time++; } // very simple transition
  // Allow all members of microwave_oven access to private
  // elements of watch:
  friend class microwave_oven;
};

class microwave_oven {
  int time;
  int start_time;
  int stop_time;
  int intensity;
public:
  microwave_oven() {
    time = 0;
    start_time = stop_time = 0;
    intensity = 0;
  }
  void tick() { time++; }
  void synchronize(watch& WA) {
    time = WA.time - 15;  // set both to a common state
  }
};

void main() {
  watch que_hora;
  microwave_oven nuker;
  que_hora.tick();
  que_hora.tick();
  nuker.tick();
  nuker.synchronize(que_hora);
}
```

This program is identical to FRIENDLY.CPP, except **synchronize()** is a member function of **microwave_oven**. Notice that **synchronize()** only takes one argument here, since a member function already knows about the object it is called for. Also notice that the name declaration for

microwave_oven is unnecessary before class **watch**, since it is included in the **friend** declaration.

Often, the choice of whether to use member functions or nonmember functions comes down to your preference for the way the syntax should look.

Declaring a friend Member Function

It is also possible to select a single member function from another class to be a **friend**. Here, however, the compiler must see everything in the right order. Here's the same example as before with just the function **synchronize()** as a **friend**:

```
//: FRIEND3.CPP—A friend member function

class watch;  // class name declaration

class microwave_oven {
  int time;
  int start_time;
  int stop_time;
  int intensity;
public:
  microwave_oven() {
    time = 0;
    start_time = stop_time = 0;
    intensity = 0;
  }
  void tick() { time++; }
  void synchronize(watch& WA);
};

class watch {
  int time;  // a measure of time
  int alarm;  // when the alarm goes off
  int date;   // other things a watch should know
public:
  // constructor sets starting state:
  watch() { time = alarm = date = 0; }
  void tick() { time++; } // very simple transition
  // Allow all members of microwave_oven access to private
  // elements of watch:
  friend void microwave_oven::synchronize(watch& WA);
};
```

```
void microwave_oven::synchronize(watch& WA) {
    time = WA.time = 15;  // set both to a common state
}

void main() {
  watch que_hora;
  microwave_oven nuke;
  que_hora.tick();
  que_hora.tick();
  nuke.tick();
  nuke.synchronize(que_hora);
}
```

In class **watch**, **microwave_oven::synchronize()** is declared a **friend**, so the compiler must see the declaration for class **microwave_oven** before class **watch** to verify that member function exists. Since **synchronize(watch&)** has an argument that is a reference to **class watch**, the class name declaration for **watch** must appear before the declaration for **microwave_oven**, so the compiler knows **watch** is a legitimate name.

The **synchronize()** member function can no longer be inline, because the definition refers to inner details of **watch**, which haven't been declared yet. The definition must appear after the declaration of class **watch**.

There is no problem in class **microwave_oven** when **synchronize(watch&)** is declared, because a reference has a fixed size and the compiler knows how to pass it (the same is true for a pointer). However, if you were passing by value, this example would not compile because you must be able to use a function immediately after it is declared, and if the declaration were **synchronize(watch)** (pass by value), the compiler wouldn't know at that point how big a **watch** object is, so it wouldn't know how to pass it. This generates a compiler error and points out that it is possible to get into a loop in trying to do forward declarations when you are passing by value. The only solution is to pass a pointer or reference.

Other Class–like Items

There are several other constructs in C++ that have declarations similar to the class. Each of these constructs has a different purpose.

They include the "plain" structure **struct**, the enumerated data type **enum**, and the space-saving **union**.

struct: *A Class with All Elements Public*

The data structure keyword **struct** was developed for C so a programmer could group together several pieces of data and treat them as a single data item. As you can imagine, the **struct** is an early attempt at abstract data typing (without the associated member functions). In C, you must create nonmember functions that take your **struct** as an argument. There is no concept of private data, so anyone (not just the functions you define) can change the elements of a **struct**.

C++ will accept any **struct** you can declare in C (so it's upward compatible). However, C++ expands the definition of a **struct** so it is just like a class, except a class defaults to **private**, while a **struct** defaults to **public**. Any **struct** you define in C++ can have member functions, constructors and a destructor, and so on. Although the **struct** is an artifact from C, it emphasizes that all elements are public. You can make a class in C++ work just like a **struct** in C++ by putting **public:** at the beginning of your class. Notice that a **struct** in ANSI C doesn't have constructors, destructors, or member functions.

As you can see from the following example, all the elements in a **struct** are **public**:

```
//: STRUCT.CPP—demonstration of structures vs. classes

class CL {
  int i, j, k;
public:
  CL(int init = 0 ) { i = j = k = init; }
};

struct ST {
  int i, j, k;
  // don't need to say "public."  Everything is public!
  ST (int init = 0 ) { i = j = k = init; }
};

void main() {
  CL A(10);
```

```
  ST B(11);
  B.i = 44; // this is OK
// A.i = 44; // this will cause an error!
}
```

Clarifying Programs with enum

Enumerations are a way of attaching names to numbers, thereby giving more meaning to anyone reading the code. The **enum** keyword (from C) automatically enumerates any list of words you give it by assigning them values of 0, 1, 2, and so on. You can declare **enum** variables (which are always **int**s). The declaration of an **enum** looks similar to a class declaration, but an **enum** cannot have any member functions.

Enumerations are very useful when you want to keep track of some sort of feature, for example:

```
//: ENUM.CPP—Keeping track of shapes.

enum shape_type {
  circle,
  square,
  rectangle
};  // must end with a semicolon like a class

void main() {
  shape_type shape = circle;
  // activities here....
  // now do something based on what the shape is:
  switch(shape) {
    case circle:  /* circle stuff */ break;
    case square:  /* square stuff */ break;
    case rectangle:  /* rectangle stuff */ break;
  }
}
```

Shape is a variable of the **shape_type** enumeration, and its value is compared with the value in the enumeration. Since **shape** is really just an **int**, however, it can be any value an **int** can hold (including a negative number). You can also compare an **int** variable with a value in the enumeration.

If you don't like the way the compiler assigns values, you can do it yourself, like this:

```
enum shape_type { circle = 10, square = 20, rectangle = 50 };
```

If you give values to some names and not to others, the compiler will use the next integral value. For example,

```
enum snap { crackle = 25, pop };
```

The compiler gives **pop** the value 26.

You can see how much more readable the code is when you use enumerations.

Saving Memory with **union**

Sometimes a program will handle different types of data using the same variable. In this situation, you have two choices: you can create a **class** or **struct** containing all the possible different types you might need to store, or you can use a **union**. A **union** piles all the data into a single space; it figures out the amount of space necessary for the largest item you've put in the **union**, and makes that the size of the **union**. Use a union to save memory.

Anytime you place a value in a union, the value always starts in the same place at the beginning of the union, but only uses as much space as is necessary inside the union. Thus, you create a "supervariable," capable of holding any of the union variables. All the addresses of the **union** variables are the same (in a class or **struct**, the addresses are different).

Here's a simple use of **union**. Try removing various elements and see what effect it has on the size of the union. Notice that it makes no sense to declare more than one instance of a single data type in a union (unless you're just doing it to use a different name).

```
//: UNION.CPP—The size and simple use of a union
#include <iostream.h>

union packed { // declaration similar to a class
```

```
    char i;
    short j;
    int k;
    long l;
    float f;
    double d;   // the union will be the size of a double,
                // since it's the largest element
};   // semicolon ends a union, like a class


void main() {
  cout << "sizeof(packed) = " << sizeof(packed) << endl;
  packed X;
  X.i = 'c';
  X.d = 3.14159;
}
```

The compiler performs the proper assignment according to the **union** member you select.

Once you perform an assignment, the compiler doesn't care what you do with the **union**. In this example, you could assign a floating-point value to **X** as follows:

```
X.f = 2.222;
```

and then send it to the output as if it were an **int**:

```
cout << X.i;
```

This produces garbage.

C++ allows a union to have a constructor, destructor, and member functions just like a class:

```
//: UNION2.CPP—Unions with constructors and member functions

union U {
  int i;
  float f;
  U(int a) { i = a; }
  U(float b) { f = b;}
  ~U() { f = 0; }
  int read_int() { return i; }
  float read_float() { return f; }
};
```

```
void main() {
  U X(12), Y(1.9F);
  X.i = 44;
  X.read_int();
  Y.read_float();
}
```

Although the member functions civilize access to the union somewhat, there is still no way to prevent the user from selecting the wrong element once the union is initialized. A "safe" union can be encapsulated in a class (notice how the **enum** clarifies the code) like this:

```
//: SUPERVAR.CPP—A supervariable
#include <iostream.h>

class super_var {
  enum {
    character,
    integer,
    floating_point
  } vartype;  // define one
  union {  // anonymous union
    char c;
    int i;
    float f;
  };
public:
  super_var(char ch) {
    vartype = character;
    c = ch;
  }
  super_var(int ii) {
    vartype = integer;
    i = ii;
  }
  super_var(float ff) {
    vartype = floating_point;
    f = ff;
  }
  void print();
};
```

```
void super_var::print() {
  switch (vartype) {
    case character:
      cout << "character: " << c << endl;
      break;
    case integer:
      cout << "integer: " << i << endl;
      break;
    case floating_point:
      cout << "float: " << f << endl;
      break;
  }
}

void main() {
  super_var A('c'), B(12), C(1.44F);
  A.print();
  B.print();
  C.print();
}
```

In this code, the **enum** has no type name (it is an *untagged enumeration*). This is acceptable if you are going to define instances of the **enum** immediately, as is done here. There is no need to refer to the **enum**'s type in the future, so the type is optional.

The **union** has no type name and no variable name. This is called an *anonymous union*. It creates space for the **union** but doesn't require accessing the **union** elements with a variable name and the dot operator. For example, if your anonymous **union** is

```
union { int i, float f };
```

you access members by saying

```
i = 12;
f = 1.22;
```

just like other variables. The only difference is that both variables occupy the same space.

If the anonymous union is at file scope (outside all functions and classes), it must be declared **static** so it has internal linkage.

static *Member Functions*

Static data members are useful because they work for the class *as a whole*, not for a particular instance/object of a class. One effect of a static data member is that it doesn't occupy space in each object, so the size of each object is reduced.

Although a member function doesn't occupy space in an object, that function must somehow know which object data it is accessing when a function is called. This is done by the compiler, secretly, by passing the starting address of the object into the member function. You can access the starting address while inside the member function using the keyword **this**. The extra overhead of the member function call when passing **this** is analogous to the extra size in an object when adding data members. In line with this analogy, you can remove the extra time involved in a member function call by making the member function **static**.

Like a static data member, a static member function acts for the class as a whole, not for a particular object of the class. The starting address of the object (**this**) is *not* passed to a static member function, so it cannot access non-**static** data members (the compiler will give you an error if you try). The only data members that can be accessed by a static member function are static data members.

You can call a static member function in the ordinary way, with the dot or the arrow, in association with an object. However, you can also call a static member function by itself, without any specific object, using the scope-resolution operator, like this:

```
class X {
public:
  static void f();
};
X::f();
```

When you see a static member function in a class, remember that the designer intended that function to be conceptually associated with the class as a whole. That function will have the faster calling time of an ordinary, global function, but its name will be visible only within the class, so it won't clash with global function names.

const *and* volatile *Member Functions*

C++ allows you to restrict the use of a particular member function so that, as the programmer, you can ensure that the user can only use it in the appropriate context. This is accomplished with the keywords **const** and **volatile**. You will see **const** member functions used far more often than **volatile** member functions, but the syntax works the same way for both.

const *Objects*

The keyword **const** tells the compiler that a variable will not change throughout its lifetime. This applies to variables of built-in types, as you've seen. When the compiler sees a **const** like this, it stores the value in its symbol table and inserts it directly, after performing type-checking (remember that this is an improvement in C++, which acts differently than C). In addition, it prevents you from changing the value of a **const**. The reason to declare an object of a built-in type as **const** is so the compiler will ensure that it isn't changed.

You can also tell the compiler that an object of a user-defined type is a **const**. Although it is conceptually possible that the compiler could store such an object in its symbol table and generate compile-time calls to member functions (so all the values associated with a **const** object would be available at compile time), in practice it isn't feasible. However, the other aspect of a **const**—that it cannot be changed during its lifetime—is still valid and can be enforced.

const *Member Functions*

The compiler can tell when you're trying to change a simple variable and can generate an error. The concept of **const**ness can also be applied to an object of a user-defined type, and it means the same thing: the internal state of a **const** object cannot be changed. This can only be enforced if there is some way to ensure that all operations performed on a **const** object won't change it. C++ provides a special syntax to tell the compiler that a member function doesn't change an object.

The keyword **const** placed after the argument list of a member function tells the compiler that this member function can only read data members, but it cannot write them. Creating a **const** member function is actually a contract that the compiler enforces. If you declare a member function like this,

```
class X {
  int i;
public:
  int f() const;
};
```

then **f()** can be called for any **const** object, and the compiler knows that it's a safe thing to do because you've said the function is **const**. However, the compiler also ensures that the function definition conforms to the **const** specifier. Not only are you forced to use the **const** specifier when you define the function (otherwise the compiler won't recognize that the function is a member), but you cannot change any data members inside the function or the compiler will generate an error, for example:

```
int X::f() const { return i++; }   // compiler reports an error
```

The **const** function can be used on a **const** object because the declaration *claims* it is safe, and the compiler *ensures* that the definition conforms to this claim. Notice that the **const** keyword must be used in both the declaration *and* the definition. This is illustrated in the following program:

```
//: CONSTF.CPP—const member functions
//. Compiler checks for proper use of const

class cmembers {
  int x;
public:
  cmembers(int X) { x = X; }
  int X() const { return x; }
  int XX() { return x; }  // non-const, doesn't modify
  int incr() const { return ++x; } // error
  void g() const; // non-inline
};
```

```
void cmembers::g() const {
  x++;  // error
}

void main() {
  cmembers A(1);
  const cmembers B(2);
  A.X();  // Can call any member function for non-const objects
  A.XX();
  A.incr();
  A.g();
  B.X(); // Can only call const members for const objects
  B.incr();
  B.g();
  B.XX();    // error
}
```

Notice that even though **XX()** doesn't actually modify any data members, it hasn't been defined as a **const** member function so it can't be used with **B**. Also, the compiler will verify that a function doesn't modify any data members if you say it's a **const**, whether or not that function is defined inline.

Member functions that are **const** can be called for non-**const** objects, but non-**const** functions cannot be called for **const** objects. Therefore, for the greatest flexibility of your classes, you should declare functions as **const** when possible, since you never know when the user might want to call such a function for a **const** object.

Casting Away const Status

In some rare cases you may wish to modify certain members of an object, even if the object is a **const**. That is, you may want to leave the **const** on all the members except a select few. You can do this with a rather odd-looking cast. Remember that a cast tells the compiler to suspend its normal assumptions and to let you take over the type checking. Thus it is inherently dangerous and not something you want to do casually. However, the need sometimes occurs.

To cast away the **const**ness of an object, you select a member with the **this** pointer. Since **this** is just the address of the current object, it seems redundant. However, by preceeding **this** with a cast to itself, you implicitly remove the **const** (because **const** isn't part of the cast). Here's an example:

```
//: CASTAWAY.CPP—casting away the const-ness of an object

class fishing_pole {
  int rod, reel;
public:
  fishing_pole() { rod = reel = 0; }
  void cast_away() const {
    (((fishing_pole*)this)->reel)++;
  }
};

void main() {
  const fishing_pole fp;
  fp.cast_away();
}
```

Inside **cast_away()**, the cast of **this** to type **fishing_pole** (*without* the **const**) removes the **const**ness of **reel**, while leaving **rod** as a **const**. Of course, this isn't the most straightforward code in the world—when you do this kind of thing, you're intentionally breaking the type-safety mechanism, and that is usually an ugly process. You should know what it looks like, but you should try not to do it.

volatile *Objects and Member Functions*

A *volatile object* is one that might be changed by forces outside the program's control. For example, in a data communication program or alarm system, some piece of hardware might cause a change to a variable, while the program itself might never change the variable. The reason it's important to be able to declare a variable **volatile** is to prevent the compiler from making assumptions about code associated with that variable. The primary concern here is optimizations. If you read a variable, and (without changing it) read it again sometime later, the optimizer might assume that the variable hasn't changed and delete the second read. If the variable was declared **volatile**, however, the optimizer won't touch any code associated with the variable.

The syntax for **const** and **volatile** member functions is identical. Only **volatile** member functions may be called for **volatile** objects. In addition, objects and member functions can be both **const** and **volatile**, as shown here:

```
//: CONSTVOL.CPP—const AND volatile together

class comm {
  unsigned char databyte;
public:
  comm() { databyte = 0; }
  unsigned char read() const volatile {
    return databyte;
  }
};

void main() {
  const volatile comm port;
  port.read();
}
```

Ostensibly, **databyte** is where the data is placed (by hardware, or perhaps an interrupt control routine). Since **port** is both **const** and **volatile**, it can only be read, and the compiler won't optimize away any reads of that location.

By the previous logic, you should declare as many functions as possible both **const** *and* **volatile** so they would always be usable with objects that are **const** and/or **volatile**. In practice, however, **volatile** is used far less frequently than **const**.

Debugging Hints

When you're writing your own classes, you can use the features of C++ to your advantage and build in debugging tools. In particular, each class should have a function called **dump()** (or some similar name) that will display the contents of an object. This way you can use **dump()** to dump a display of your objects at various points in your program to trace their progress. If you build the **dump()** function in from the start, you won't have as much mental resistance to running a trace as you might otherwise.

The following class has a built-in **dump()** function:

```
//: DEBUG1.CPP—A class with a dump() function
#include <iostream.h>

class debuggable {
  int counter; // some sort of internal counter
  float a, b;  // data the user is aware of
public:
  debuggable(float x = 0.0, float y = 0.0) {
    a = x; b = y; counter = 2;
  }
  void set_a(float x) { a = x; counter++; }
  float read_a() { return a; counter++; }
  void set_b(float y) { b = y; counter++; }
  float read_b() { counter++; return b; }
  void dump(char * msg = "") {
    cout << msg << ":" << endl;
    cout << "a = " << a << endl;
    cout << "b = " << b << endl;
    cout << "counter = " << counter << endl;
  }
};

void main() {
  debuggable U, V(3.14), W(1.1,2.2);
  U.set_a(99);
  U.dump("After 1 set_a");
  U.read_b();
  U.dump("After 1 read_b");
  // other operations ...
  V.dump("V");
  W.dump();  // string argument is optional
}
```

Because the argument **msg** is given a default value of an empty string, providing a message when you call **dump()** is optional. In this program, the variable **counter** is normally completely hidden from the user's view, and no functions are provided to access it. The variable **counter** keeps track of internal information. When debugging, this information might be essential. It is best to provide as much information as possible, as well as optional messages, in the **dump()** function.

Debugging Flags

If you hard-wire your debugging code into a program, you can run into problems. You start to get too much information, which makes the bugs difficult to isolate. When you think you've found the bug you start tearing out debugging code, only to find you need to put it back in again. You can solve these problems with two types of *debugging flags*: preprocessor debugging flags and run-time debugging flags.

Preprocessor Debugging Flags

By using the preprocessor **#define** to insert one or more debugging flags (preferably in a header file), you can test a flag using a **#ifdef** statement to conditionally include debugging code. When you think your debugging is finished, you can simply use **#undef** to remove the flag(s), and the code will automatically be removed (you'll also reduce the size of your executable file).

It is best to decide on names for debugging flags before you begin building your project so the names will be consistent. Preprocessor flags are often distinguished from variables by writing them in all uppercase letters. A common flag name is DEBUG (but be careful you don't use NDEBUG, which is reserved in ANSI C). The sequence of statements might be

```
#define DEBUG // probably in a header file
//....
#ifdef DEBUG // check to see if flag is defined
/* debugging code here */
#endif DEBUG
```

Many C and C++ implementations will even let you **#define** and **#undef** flags from the compiler command line, so you can recompile code and insert debugging information with a single command (preferably via the makefile). Check your local guide for details.

Run-Time Debugging Flags

In some situations it is more convenient to turn debugging flags on and off during program execution (it is much more elegant to turn flags on and off when the program starts up using the command line. See Chapter 4 for details of using the command line). Large programs are tedious to recompile just to insert debugging code.

You can create integer flags and use the fact that nonzero values are true to increase the readability of your code. For example:

```
int debug = 0; // default off
//...
cout << "turn debugger on? (y/n): ";
cin >> reply;
if ( reply == 'y') debug++; // turn flag on
//...
if(debug) {
 // debugging code here
}
```

Notice that the variable is in lowercase letters to remind the reader it isn't a preprocessor flag.

Turning a Variable Name into a String

When writing debugging code, it is tedious to write print expressions consisting of a string containing the variable name followed by the variable. Fortunately, ANSI C has introduced the "string-ize" operator **#**. When you put a **#** before an argument in a preprocessor macro, that argument is turned into a string by putting quotes around it. This, combined with the fact that strings with no intervening punctuation are concatenated into a single string, allows us to make a very convenient macro for printing the values of variables during debugging like this:

```
#define PR(x) cout << #x " = " << x << endl;
```

If you print the variable **A** by calling the macro **PR(A)**, it will have the same effect as the following code:

```
cout << "A = " << A << endl;
```

The ANSI C assert() Macro

The **assert()** macro is a very convenient debugging macro. When you use **assert()**, you give it an argument that is an expression you are "asserting to be true." The preprocessor generates code that will test the assertion. If the assertion isn't true, the program will stop after it issues an error message telling you what the assertion was and that it failed. Here's a trivial example:

```
//: ASSERT.CPP—Use of the assert() debugging macro
#include <assert.h>  // contains the macro

void main() {
  int i = 100;
  assert(i != 100);
}
```

The ANSI C library header file **assert.h** contains the macro for assertion. When you are finished debugging, you can remove the code generated by the macro simply by placing the line

```
#define NDEBUG
```

in the program before the inclusion of **assert.h** or by defining **NDEBUG** on the compiler command line. **NDEBUG** is a flag used in **assert.h** to change the way code is generated by the macros.

Debugging Techniques Combined

By combining the techniques discussed in this section, a framework arises that you can follow when writing your own debugging code. Keep in mind that if you want to isolate certain types of debugging code, you can create variables **debug1**, **debug2**, and so on, and preprocessor flags **DEBUG1**, **DEBUG2**, and so on.

The following example shows the use of command-line flags, formally introduced in the next chapter. It is better to show you the right way to do something and risk confusing you for a bit rather than to teach you a method that will later need to be unlearned.

The flags on the command line are accessed through the arguments **argc** and **argv** to **main()** as follows

```cpp
//: DEBUG2.CPP—Framework for writing debug code
#include <iostream.h>
#include <fstream.h>
#include <stdlib.h>
#define DEBUG

void main( int argc, char * argv[]) {
  int debug = 0;
  if ( argc > 1 ) { // if more than one argument
    if (*argv[1] == 'd')
      debug++; // set the debug flag
    else {
      cout << "usage: debug2   OR   debug2 d" << endl;
        "optional flag turns debugger on.";
      exit(1);  // quit program
    }
  }
  // ....
#ifdef DEBUG
  if(debug)
    cout << "debugger on" << endl;
#endif // DEBUG
  // ...
}
```

All the debugging code occurs between the **#ifdef DEBUG** and **#endif //DEBUG** lines.

If you type

```
debug2
```

on the command line, nothing will happen, but if you type

```
debug2 d
```

the "debugger" will be turned on. When you want to remove the debugging code at some later date to reduce the size of the executable program, you need only change the **#define DEBUG** to **#undef DEBUG** (or better yet, do it from the compiler command line).

Formatting Style

You might notice that the formatting style in this book is different from many traditional C styles. Of course, everyone feels their own style is the most rational. However, the style used here has a simple logic behind it, which will be presented here mixed in with ideas on why some of the other styles developed.

The formatting style is motivated by one thing: presentation, both in print and in live seminars. You might feel your needs are different because you don't make a lot of presentations, but working code is read much more than it is written, so it should be easy for the reader to perceive. My two most important criteria are "scannability" (how easy it is for the reader to grasp the meaning of a single line) and the number of lines that can fit on a page. The latter may sound funny, but when you are giving a live presentation, it's very distracting to shuffle back and forth between slides, and a few wasted lines can cause this.

Everyone seems to agree that code inside braces should be indented. What people don't agree on, and the place where there's the most inconsistency within formatting styles, is this: where does the opening brace go? This one question, I feel, is what causes such inconsistencies among coding styles. (For an enumeration of coding styles, see *C++ Programming Guidelines,* by Tom Plum and Dan Saks, Plum Hall 1991.) I'll try to convince you that many of today's coding styles come from pre-ANSI C constraints (before function prototypes) and are thus inappropriate now.

First, my answer to the question: the opening brace should always go on the same line as the "precursor" (by which I mean "whatever the body is about: a class, function, object definition, **if** statement, and so on"). This is a single, consistent rule I apply to all the code I write, and it makes formatting much simpler. It makes the "scannability" easier.

When you look at this line:

```
void foo(int a);
```

you know, by the semicolon at the end of the line, that this is a declaration and it goes no further, but when you see the following line:

```
void foo(int a) {
```

you immediately know it's a definition because the line finishes with an opening brace, and not a semicolon.

Similarly, for a class,

```
class string;
```

is a class name declaration, and

```
class string {
```

is a class declaration. You can tell by looking at the single line in all cases whether it's a declaration or definition. Also, putting the opening brace on the same line instead of a line by itself allows you to fit more lines on a page.

So why do we have so many other styles? In particular, you'll notice that most people create classes following the above style (which Stroustrup uses in *The C++ Programming Language*, 2nd ed., Addison-Wesley, 1991) but create function definitions by putting the opening brace on a single line by itself (which also engenders many different indentation styles). Stroustrup does this *except* for short inline functions. The style I advocate doesn't cause an exception here—the opening brace is the same for short inlines and ordinary function definitions.

The style of function definition used by many folks might come from pre-function-prototyping C, where you had to say

```
void bar()
 int x,
 float y
{
 /* body here */
}
```

Here, it would be quite ungainly to put the opening brace on the same line, so no one did it. However, they did make various decisions about whether the braces should be indented with the body of the code, or whether they should be at the level of the "precursor." Thus we got many different formatting styles.

The approach I use removes all the exceptions and special cases, and logically produces a single style of indentation, as well. Even within a function body, the consistency holds, as in the following:

```
for(int i = 0; i < 100; i++) {
  cout << i << endl;
  cout << x * i << endl;
}
```

The style is very easy to teach and remember—you use a single, consistent rule for all your formatting, not one for classes, one for functions, and possibly others for **for** loops, **if** statements, and so on. The consistency alone, I feel, makes it worthy of consideration.

Above all, C++ is a new language, and (although we must make many concessions to C) we shouldn't be carrying too many artifacts with us that cause problems in the future. Small problems multiplied by many lines of code become big problems.

In the end, everyone will format code in the style they find comfortable—after all, it *is* a free-form language. If you get code in one style which you find unreadable, there are code formatting tools that reformat the code into other styles.

Makefile for Chapter 3 Examples

Here is the makefile for the chapter examples.

This makefile also uses a *built-in macro*, of which there are several in **make**. Calling a built-in macro is just like calling a regular macro except you leave out the parentheses. One built-in macro used here is **$***, which means "the file to produce" (also called the *target file*) *without* the file extension. The target without the extension is called the *base name*.

Here's the first rule used in the **makefile**:

```
.cpp.exe :
    $(CPP) $*.cpp
```

It says "to take a file with an extension of .cpp and create a file with an extension of .exe, run C++ on the base name with an extension of .cpp." Notice that there is no space between .cpp and .exe, and that the command must be preceded with a tab.

The second rule is similar, and creates a .obj file from a .cpp file.

You will notice in the "master dependency list" **all**, that most of the dependencies are on .exe files, so the first rule will be used. One dependency, ROLROR.OBJ, will use the second rule. In all cases, if **make** cannot find the appropriate .cpp file in the current directory, it will complain that it "cannot create" that .cpp file.

There are two programs that depend on more than one file. These programs are GLOBAL.EXE and FILESTAT.EXE. When **make** encounters these names in the **all** list, it checks for other dependencies before executing the rules. The dependencies exist, so **make** uses those *instead* of the rules. The commands use another built-in macro: **$**** that means "the full list of out-of-date dependencies" (in this case, all the .obj files that are out of date). This macro is available on most versions of **make** on the PC, but isn't part of many UNIX **make**s. If you are using UNIX, replace the **$**** with the list of dependencies. When **make** goes to create GLOBAL.EXE or FILESTAT.EXE, it first uses the default rule to create the .obj files from the .cpp files and then runs the linker on all the .obj files in the dependency list.

By learning to use rules and built-in macros, you will create smaller, more error-free makefiles.

Here is the makefile for this chapter:

```
# MAKEFILE for examples in Chapter 3
# Borland BC++, with the following
# warnings turned off:
# aus: identifier assigned a value which is never used
# eff: code has no effect
# par: parameter "parameter" is never used
CPP = bcc -w-aus -w-eff -w-par
# nmake CPP=cl     # Microsoft C++ command line

.cpp.exe:
    $(CPP) $*.cpp

.cpp.obj:
    $(CPP) -c $*.cpp
```

```
all: basic.exe specify.exe scope.exe onthefly.exe \
     static.exe global.exe \
     forward.exe mathops.exe boolean.exe bitwise.exe \
     rolror.obj pitfall.exe return.exe overload.exe state.exe \
     construc.exe objcount.exe statvar.exe \
     scoperes.exe display.exe smart.exe friendly.exe \
     friend2.exe friend3.exe struct.exe enum.exe union.exe \
     union2.exe supervar.exe debug1.exe assert.exe \
     dcbug2.exe constmem.exe constvol.exe castaway.exe

errors: constf.exe

global.exe : global.obj global2.obj
     $(CPP) $**

# This should generate warnings/errors:
reminder.exe : reminder.cpp

# running "make filestat.exe" should cause a linker error:
filestat.exe : filestat.obj fstat2.obj
     $(CPP) $**
```

CHAPTER

Pointers and References

Many high-level languages (even BASIC) have the ability to take the address of a variable and manipulate addresses at run time. In perhaps no other languages is it so essential to understand how this works than in C and C++. This chapter covers the ins and outs of manipulating addresses in C and C++.

Addresses Are Just Like Mailboxes

All data and code in a program are stored in memory while a program is running. Each memory cell can be individually selected by using its address, like the address on your mailbox. The fact that variables and code live in memory opens up a new way to refer to them: by their *starting address*, the address of the first byte of the variable or piece of code.

While writing code, you refer to starting addresses with *symbolic names* (the identifiers you give your variables or functions). The compiler uses symbolic names for functions, global variables, and static variables. The names are often modified during translation, but some form of the name exists all the way through into the object modules. Only at link time (or sometimes during loading) are symbolic names resolved into addresses; at this time, all information about the names is removed and doesn't exist in the executable file. It's usually possible to tell the compiler and linker to leave special information for use by a symbolic debugger, but this is unavailable to the executing program. This means that if you want to perform an operation on a variable or function without knowing all the details about that variable or function at compile time, you must use its address.

Local (also called *automatic*) variables are created on the stack and are referred to via their starting address on the stack. Global variables may also be used via their addresses.

Pointers

There exists a special type of variable that is designed to manipulate addresses. It's called a *pointer*, and is denoted by the unary operator *.

This is different from the binary multiplication operator *. Operators, like overloaded functions, are called according to the context in which they are used. A pointer is really an additional data type—it has its own rules and can be manipulated with all the operators available for the "ordinary" data types **char**, **int**, **float**, and **double**.

Pointers allow you to select and manipulate the addresses of variables and functions at run time. Some programs aren't possible without this flexibility. Pointers have four primary uses: in arrays, as function arguments, for direct memory access, and in dynamic memory allocation.

Use of Pointers in Arrays

An *array* has a single name but refers to a block of variables (all of the same type). To select any of the variables in the block, you can index into the array using the bracket operator **[]**, or you can use pointer arithmetic. The name of the array by itself (without the brackets) actually *is* the starting address of the block of variables.

Arrays were previously introduced when creating character buffers. You define an array of ten characters like this:

```
char array[10];
```

Notice the use of the bracket operator in the definition. Remember that in C and C++, the definition of a variable attempts to mimic the use of the variable. So to produce an element in the array, use the bracket operator in the same way:

```
char c = array[9];
```

This produces the value of the tenth element in the array (since you start counting at zero, this is the last element). Array indexing can also be used as an lvalue. The statement:

```
array[0] = 'A';
```

sets the first element of the array to the character value 'A' (ASCII 65). The starting address is produced by simply saying **array**. You are not restricted to constants inside the brackets. Generally, arrays are used to choose elements at run time, so expressions are valid within arrays:

```
c = array[2*i];
```

There is no bounds checking for arrays in C or C++. The compiler may perform compile-time checking and/or add code to impose run-time range constraints, but most do not. This means that just because you declare an array to be ten elements, there's nothing to stop you from selecting the 100th element of the array:

```
c = array[99];   // who knows what this will be?
```

You may also create multidimensional arrays, for example:

```
float TWO_D[10][5];   // a two-dimensional array
float THREE_D[10][15][12];   // a three-dimensional array
  // etc...
```

Strings: A Special Type of Array

Quoted text strings are treated specially by the compiler. When you use a string, as when sending a string to the console with **cout**,

```
cout << "This is a string";
```

the compiler takes the characters inside the double quotes, turns them into their equivalent ASCII numbers, adds a zero byte (to indicate the end of the string), and stashes the whole thing away in memory somewhere. Then it places the starting address of that memory in the argument list. This means that whenever you create or use a string like "A String," what you are really talking about is the starting address of that string.

You can treat a string as an array like this:

```
char * ca = "A String Is Really An Array";
```

You can select elements of the array by using brackets: **ca[0]** produces A, **ca[2]** produces S, and so on. Examples of the use of string pointers will be seen through the rest of this book.

Functions That Modify Their Arguments

An important use for pointers is as function arguments, when you want to affect the function argument rather than simply copy the contents of the argument into a local variable inside the function. In this discussion, the variable that is outside the scope of the function, and originates the function argument either by being copied into the function or by having its address taken, will be called the *outside variable*.

In a function with ordinary arguments, like

```
int ordinary_args(int j) {
  //...
  j = 10;
}
```

the variable **j** is a local variable. When you call it by saying **ordinary_args(x)**, a local variable **j** is created, and the contents of **x**, the outside variable, are copied into **j**. When **j** is assigned the value 10, as shown, only the local variable is affected. When the function ends, the local variable goes out of scope. The value of the outside variable **x** is unchanged through all this.

Often, you want to change the value of the outside variable. You can pass the value back as the return value of the function and assign the outside variable to the new value. This is the preferred method, since it clarifies what is going on, but it only works for one variable. What if you want a function to change more than one outside variable, or you're already using the return value of the function for something (like an error code)?

The answer is to pass the address of the outside variable. Since the function now knows where the outside variable lives (rather than simply getting a copy of its contents), it can go out and manipulate the outside variable directly. In the previous example, the function definition becomes:

```
int pointer_args(int * j) {
  // ...
  *j = 10;
}
```

The * in the argument list says "this argument is a pointer to an integer, rather than an integer." The ***j** says "what the pointer points to." Using the * here is called *dereferencing* the pointer.

If you use **j** by itself, as in

```
//: COUTPTR.CPP—printing pointers
#include <iostream.h>
#include <stdio.h>

void main() {
  int i;
  int* ip = &i;        // printing pointer contents:
  cout << ip << endl; // with iostreams
  printf("%p\n", ip); // with printf
}
```

you get the contents of the pointer, which is an address in memory. To get at what the pointer points to, you must dereference the pointer with a *. So ***j = 10;** says "set the value (not the pointer) to 10."

Memory Access

There are numerous reasons why you may want to access memory directly. For example, video memory in a PC can be changed more quickly via direct access than by calling operating system functions. Some computers are designed with memory-mapped I/O, in which hardware devices are located in the memory space—pointers allow you to access these devices. Sometimes a pointer is simply the most expedient way to access portions of memory.

Dynamic Memory Allocation

There are situations when you don't know the quantity or type of object until run time, or you don't want the objects to be subject to normal scoping rules. Normally, you define and use all your objects at compile time, but the concept of dynamic memory allocation (covered in Chapter 6) allows you to create and destroy objects at run time. Dynamic memory allocation is an important part of programming in C and C++, since it frees you from the normal limitations of being forced to know everything at compile time.

When you create an object dynamically (using the **new** keyword), you get an address back (that you assign to a pointer), and you must access the object through the pointer. When you destroy a dynamic object (using the **delete** keyword), you must give the address of the object to **delete**.

Using Pointers and Addresses

A pointer is just like any other variable—it contains a value that can be manipulated by operators, passed as a function argument, used as an index in a **for** loop, and so on. The only difference is that the value is treated as an address, and so the pointer always points somewhere (even if that somewhere is nonsense). Because the pointer contains an address, its contents are always treated as a positive integral value (so you can't assign a pointer to a floating-point value).

The distinction between the definition of an ordinary variable and the definition of a pointer is the *****. The ***** means "what's in the box at this address." Thus, when you define a pointer, such as

```
int * ip;
```

the definition says "an **int** is in the box at the address contained in **ip**." Remember that C and C++ variable definitions attempt to mimic their use. When you use a pointer by dereferencing it, like this,

```
*ip = 2;
```

it says, "change the contents of the box at the address contained in **ip** to 2."

When you create a pointer, it doesn't point to anything intelligent unless you first *initialize* it. To initialize a pointer, you must set it to an address. You have several choices when doing this:

❑   If you know what the address is, (for example, if you want to point to some piece of hardware, or video memory) assign the pointer to a specific number.

☐   If you are working with a string or inside a function dealing with a pointer argument, the address is handed to you.

☐   The address of a function or array is simply the name of the function without the argument list or the name of the array without the brackets.

☐   If you are using dynamic memory allocation, the keyword **new** returns the starting address of the object you create.

☐   If you want to use the address of an existing variable, you must use the address-of operator, **&**. This is a unary operator that produces the address of whatever variable it precedes. If you want to create a pointer and initialize it to the address of another variable, you say:

```
int A = 47;   // define an ordinary int
int * ap;     // define an int pointer
ap = &A;      // set the int pointer to the address of the int
int * aap = &A;  // create and initialize simultaneously
```

☐   If you want to pass an address to be used as a pointer argument for the function **pointer_args()**, you say **pointer_args(&A);**. Note that since a pointer name without the * also produces the address, you can say **pointer_args(ap);** as well.

Pointer Arithmetic

When you use operators on pointers, the arithmetic comes out a bit differently. In fact, the way pointer arithmetic is performed depends on the type of pointer involved. To see why this is necessary, imagine you have an array of **char** and a pointer to the start of that array (element 0). If you want to look at element 1, you need the address of the next **char** in the array. Since a **char** is one byte long, element 1 lives at the starting address plus 1.

Now imagine you have an array of **double** and a pointer to element 0. An IEEE **double** (IEEE is the International Association of Electrical and Electronic Engineers, whose format for floating-point number representation in computers is the most common standard used) is eight bytes long, so element 1 lives at the starting address plus eight bytes.

Fortunately, you don't have to figure this out every time you calculate an address. Pointer arithmetic is automatic, as this example shows:

```
//: PTRARITH.CPP—Demonstration of pointer arithmetic
#include <iostream.h>

void main() {
  char A = 'a';
  char * cp = &A;  // create and initialize a char pointer
  double d = 1.119;
  double * dp = &d; // create and initialize a double pointer

  cout << "Addition & Subtraction: " << endl;
  char * cp2 = cp + 1;
  double * dp2 = dp + 1;
  cout << "cp2 = cp +1; dp2 = dp + 1;" << endl;
  cout << "cp2 - cp = " << cp2 - cp << endl;
  cout << "dp2 - dp = " << dp2 - dp << endl;
  cout << "(int)cp2 - (int)cp = " << (int)cp2 - (int)cp << endl;
  cout << "(int)dp2 - (int)dp = " << (int)dp2 - (int)dp << endl;
  cout << "increment & decrement:" << endl;
  cout << "cp2 = cp; dp2 = dp; cp2--;cp2--;  dp2++; dp2++;"
       << endl;
  cp2 = cp; dp2 = dp;
  cp2--;cp2--;
  dp2++; dp2++;
  cout << "cp - cp2 = " << cp - cp2 << endl;
  cout << "dp2 - dp - " << dp2 - dp << endl;
  cout << "(int)cp - (int)cp2 = " << (int)cp - (int)cp2 << endl;
  cout << "(int)dp2 - (int)dp = " << (int)dp2 - (int)dp << endl;
}
```

This example demonstrates pointer arithmetic by showing you the result of pointer calculations. For comparison, calculations are made with both **char** pointers and **double** pointers. The results are printed both in terms of pointers and in terms of bytes. The result of the pointer calculation can be printed directly, but to see the result in bytes you must first cast the pointers to integer values.

The use of casting is very important here. The **(int)** cast tells the compiler, "I know this is actually some other type, but treat it like an **int** for this operation." When you run the program, you will see that pointer arithmetic always takes the size of the pointer into account. If you add 1 to a **double** pointer, for example, the pointer is incremented by 8 bytes, which is the size of a **double**. However, if you subtract 2 pointers that point to adjacent **double** locations (as shown in the program), you don't get 8, the size of the **double**, you get 1, the number of **double** variables between two adjacent **double** pointers. A pointer is really another kind of built-in data type that has its own kind of arithmetic.

To see the actual integer values of the pointers, you must cast the pointer to an **int** so that integer operations, not pointer operations, are performed on the pointer.

The program also demonstrates that the increment and decrement operators use pointer arithmetic. Modify the program and try other operators and other types of pointers.

Variable Pointers

Any data type (built-in or user-defined) can have a pointer, and the way you define a pointer is always the same: the name of the data type, a star, and the variable name. Here's a program with many kinds of pointers to variables, including an object pointer:

```
//: VARPTRS.CPP—Different kinds of pointers to variables

class CLS {};  // an empty class definition

void main() {
  int A;
  int * ap = &A;
  unsigned char B;
  unsigned char * bp = &B;  // pointer must be same type
  long double C;
  long double * cp = &C;
  CLS D;
  CLS * dp = &D;
  // Note pointers don't have to be initialized when
  // you create them:
  CLS * ep;  // this points somewhere random...
}
```

You can even take the address of a constant, as follows:

```
//: CONSTPTR.CPP—Taking the address of a constant

void main() {
  const int X = 100;
  const int * XP = &X;
}
```

Notice that you can't assign a nonconstant pointer to the address of a constant. The language won't allow this because you could then change the contents of the **const** variable. The variable that is constant depends on where the modifier **const** is placed in the definition. For example,

```
const int * XP;
```

means that **XP** points to a constant integer, so **XP** can be changed but ***XP** cannot. In contrast,

```
int * const XPC;
```

means **XPC** is a constant that points to an integer value, which can be changed, so ***XPC** can be modified, while **XPC** cannot.

It is often helpful to use constant pointers to ensure that a variable cannot be changed. This is especially true when passing pointers to functions; you might want to pass a pointer, but you might not want the outside variable to be changed:

```
//: CONSTARG.CPP—Passing a pointer to a constant argument

struct sam {
  int i;
  float j;
  double k;
};

void func(const sam * arg) {
  if(arg->i == 0 ) { // reading values is OK
    // ...
  }
  // arg->k = 1.23;  // writing values is an error
}

void main() {
```

```
sam A;
A.i = 1;
A.j = 1.1;
A.k = 2.2;
func(&A);
}
```

Since **sam** is a struct, all its members are **public**, so anyone can change them. In **main()**, elements of the variable **sam A** are changed with no error message from the compiler. However, in the definition of **func()**, the argument is **const**, so the compiler will generate an error if you try to do anything but read the argument (or call member functions). If you uncomment the line that changes private data,

```
// arg->k = 1.23;
```

you will get an error message from the compiler.

Void Pointers

A variable can reside in any part of data memory (not necessarily program memory—processors that use a Harvard architecture separate program and data memory). Because a **char** can have the same address as a **long**, you might come to the conclusion that a pointer to a **char** is the same size as a pointer to a **long**. While this is indeed true in many architectures, it is not always the case. If you assume it is true, you will not write portable code.

For example, consider a machine that uses a 32-bit word. Its addressing may be designed to use 32-bit boundaries, so a **long** fits nicely inside a single word, and the ordinary address works nicely as a pointer. However, a **char** might be implemented in 8 bits on such a machine, which means that 4 **char**s would fit inside a word. This means a **char** pointer might require some extra information to locate a particular byte inside a word. Thus, the **char** pointer might be a different size than a **long** pointer.

The concept of a pointer as "a variable containing the address of another variable" has intriguing possibilities. If you always know how big a pointer is, you can pass an address of any type to a function. The function can then cast that address to a pointer of the proper type (based on some other piece of information) and perform operations on the result. This way, you can create functions that operate on a number of different data types.

C++ invented the **void** pointer for this purpose. The use of the keyword **void** to describe a pointer is different from its use to describe function argument lists and return values (which mean "nothing"). A **void** pointer means a pointer to any type of data. Thus, a function like

```
funcv(void * vp) {
  //...
}
```

can take a pointer to any piece of data. If you have **int i** and **float f**, the function calls **funcv(&i)** and **funcv(&f)** are both valid. The definition of a **void *** guarantees that it is at least as large as the largest typed pointer implemented, so it can contain a pointer of any type.

Of course, inside the function call you will need to know exactly what kind of data type was passed (you could pass a flag, or check an outside variable).

Once you know what data type the **void** pointer references, you must cast it to a pointer of that type so it's treated properly. For example, here's a function called **print()** that takes a character, an integer, or a floating-point number:

```
//: PRINTV.CPP—A Print Function Using Void Pointers
#include <iostream.h>

enum numtype { floating, character, integer };

void print( void * number, numtype type ) {
  switch(type) {
    case floating:
      cout << "float : " << *( (float *)number ) << endl;
      break;
    case character:
      cout << "character : " << char(*((char *)number)) << endl;
      break;
    case integer:
      cout << "integer : " << *( (int *)number ) << endl;
      break;
  }
}
```

```
void main() {
  int i = 47;
  float f = 6.28;
  char c = 'Z';
  print( &i, integer);
  print( &f, floating);
  print( &c, character);
}
```

Notice that after the **void** pointer is cast to the correct type of pointer (**(float *)**, **(int *)** or **(char *)**), it must be dereferenced with the ***** operator so the value at the address is produced. If it weren't dereferenced, the address in the pointer would be produced instead.

If you recall the section on function overloading in the last chapter, you might think it makes more sense to simply overload the function and let the compiler figure out which one you are calling. This, however, means you must know the data type at compile time. The previous **print()** function lets you delay the specific knowledge of the data type until run time.

Chapters 7 and 8 contain much better solutions to this type of problem (using simple inheritance in Chapter 7 and virtual functions in Chapter 8).

Array Pointers

Any time you need to manipulate a group of identical variables, especially when you need to calculate which variable to select from the block at run time, you can use an array. You can create an array of multiple dimensions for any type of variable (even a user-defined type).

In C and C++, whenever you calculate the address of a variable at run time, you are using a pointer. It turns out that an array is really another type of pointer. In fact, arrays and pointers are almost interchangeable, as shown here:

```
//: ARRAYPTR.CPP—A pointer to the starting address of
//. an array can be treated like the array itself.
#include <iostream.h>

// The compiler initializes global arrays for you:
```

```
int c[] = { 1,2,3,4,5,6,7,8,9,10 };

void main() {
  // int * c is the same as int c[], if c isn't external:
  for(int i = 0; i < 10; i++)
    cout << "c[" << i << "] = " << c[i] << endl;
  int * cp = c;
  for(i = 0; i < 10; i++, cp++)
    cout << "i = " << i << ", *cp = " << *cp << endl;
  int a[10];   // allocates space for 10 integers
  int *b = a;  // b & a are now equivalent
  for(i = 0; i < 10; i++)
    b[i] = i * 10;  // put some values in
  for(i = 0; i < 10; i++)
    cout << "a[" << i << "] = " << a[i] << endl;
    // the same value comes out of a[i] as was
    // installed with b[i] !
}
```

Once the pointer **cp** is assigned to the starting address of **c**, you can index into the array with **cp**, just as you can with **c**. The same is shown for the pointer **b** and the starting address of **a**.

Notice that array names and pointers are not identical. A pointer is a variable that holds a value, while an array name is an identifier that is used with brackets to manipulate an array element, and by itself to produce the starting address of an array. You cannot modify an array name. For the previous code example, the expressions

```
a++;
```

and

```
c = cp;
```

are illegal.

How to Count When Using Arrays

A common pitfall when using arrays is the so-called "off-by-one" error. Since you define an array of, for example, ten elements as **array[10]**, it is easy to think that you index the array all the way up to and including

10. However, the first element of the array is right at the starting address: the name of the array plus zero offset (**array[0]**). Thus you must count a ten-element array from 0-9.

Arrays are actually indexed at run time by taking the starting address and adding the number of bytes necessary to produce the address of the desired element. (If you index an array using a constant expression such as **A[4]**, many compilers will fold this calculation so the indexing actually happens at compile time.) Since pointer arithmetic is used in C and C++, you don't have to worry about counting the bytes in the data type; it's taken care of for you. For example, **array[0]** is equivalent to ***(array + 0)**, **array[1]** is the same as ***(array + 1)**, and so on. Here's an example that emphasizes how arrays are indexed:

```
//: INDEX.CPP—Demonstration of array indexing
#include <iostream.h>

void main() {
  int x[10];
  for(int i = 0; i < 10; i++)
    x[i] = 100 - i * i; // for interesting numbers
  // Three different ways of selecting the zeroth element:
  cout << "x[0] = " << x[0] << endl;
  cout << "*(x + 0) = " << *(x+0) << endl;
  cout << "*x = " << *x << endl;

  // print the array using pointer addition:
  for(i = 0; i < 10; i++)
    cout << "*(x + " << i << ") = " << *(x + i) << endl;
}
```

If you study this code, you'll be convinced that indexes must start at 0.

Initialization of Aggregates

In ARRAYPTR.CPP you see an interesting definition:

```
int c[] = { 1,2,3,4,5,6,7,8,9,10 };
```

This creates a global array and initializes all the array elements to the values inside the braces. This is called *aggregate initialization*, and it's a very convenient feature, since the compiler saves you a lot of typing and potential errors. With a global variable, the compiler causes the initialization to occur once when the code is loaded. If an automatic aggregate is initialized, it means that every time the scope is entered (in a function, every time the function was called) some special code must initialize the variables.

You can use aggregate initialization for more than just arrays. Here are some other alternatives:

```cpp
//: AGREGATE.CPP—Aggregate initialization
#include <iostream.h>

struct simple {
  int i, j, k;
};

simple A = { 100, 200, 300 };

struct {  // no type name needed on the structure ...
  int i;
  char * name;
  float f;
} array_of_struct[] = { // ... since an instance is defined
  1, "first", 1.1,
  2, "second", 2.2,
  3, "third", 3.3,
  4, "fourth", 4.4
};

void function() {
  simple A[] = { 1,2,3, 4,5,6, 7,8,9 };
  // statics work too:
  static simple B[] = { 1,2,3, 4,5,6, 7,8,9 };
}

class X {
  int i;
  char * name;
  float f;
public:
  X(int ii = 0, char * nm = "", float ff = 0.0) {
    i = ii; name = nm; f = ff;
  }
  void print(char* id = "") {
    if(*id) cout << id << " ";
    cout << "i = " << i << " name = " << name
```

```
              << " f = " << f << endl;
  }
};

void main() {
  X z[] = { X(1, "1", 1.1), X(2, "2", 2.2), X(3, "3", 3.3) };
  const zsize = sizeof(z)/sizeof(z[0]);
  for(int i = 0; i < zsize; i++)
    z[i].print();

  // notice you can declare an array of objects without an
  // aggregate initialization list ONLY if
  // the class has a constructor with no arguments:
  X arr[10];

  for(int p = 0; p < 4; p++) {
    cout << "array_of_struct[" << p << "].i = "
         << array_of_struct[p].i << endl;
    cout << "array_of_struct[" << p << "].name = "
         << array_of_struct[p].name << endl;
    cout << "array_of_struct[" << p << "].f = "
         << array_of_struct[p].f << endl;
  }
}
```

The first example shows the aggregate initialization of an instance of **struct simple**. The initialization values are copied into the array elements in the order in which they appear (**i** gets 100, **j** gets 200, **k** gets 300). The second example shows a **struct** with no type name. The type name is unnecessary here because the name is never used; an instance of the **struct** is immediately created. The instance in this case is an array. Each set of three items in the initialization list is used as an element of the array. The third example shows how both ordinary and **static** variables within a function can use aggregate initialization.

The first line inside **main()** shows aggregate initialization for an array of objects with **private** members. Notice that each array element is initialized with a constructor call—this is the proper form when the class has a constructor. Notice also that the array definition doesn't have a size. The compiler performs *automatic counting* to determine the size of the array. On the next line, a **const** is created containing the calculated size of the array:

```
const zsize = sizeof(z)/sizeof(z[0]);
```

This may seem strange at first—on one line let the compiler determine the size of the array, and on the next line calculate it yourself. It turns out that this is a very robust and desirable programming practice because the size of the array is determined in only one place. From then on, you use **zsize** to refer to the array size (for example, as an index boundary). If you want to change the number of elements in the array, you only need to add or subtract initializers in the aggregate initialization list. Because you make only one change in one place, bugs are greatly reduced.

The last example shows how you can define an array of objects without an aggregate initialization list. You can do this only if the class either has no **private** member data or functions (in which case it looks like a **struct**), or if it has a *default constructor*, a constructor with no arguments or with all default arguments. Class **X** has a default constructor.

Strings

Strings are another form of aggregate initialization. A *string literal* is really just an array of characters initialized to the ASCII values of the letters inside the quotes. However, a string literal is significantly different from normal arrays—there is no analog in other data types to the way quoted strings are handled by the compiler. For one thing, a quoted string is not always a constant; you may be able to modify the characters in a quoted string at run time (ANSI C doesn't allow this). Also, you can perform what looks like aggregate initialization of an automatic string array. You can do the following:

```
void localstring() {
  char * hello = "hello, world!\n";
  cout << hello[4];  // you can treat it like an array!
  //...
}
```

Although you are using pointer notation to define the array, the end result acts like an array. The difference is the string is actually **static**, so if you modify the string (not a portable activity) it will hold your changes between function calls. The following example illustrates this and tests to see if your compiler allows modification of string literals:

```
//: STATCSTR.CPP—Strings are actually static arrays.
#include <string.h>  // prototype for strlen()
```

```
#include <iostream.h>

int StringHolder() {
  static int i = 0; // to count through the string
  char * st = "This is a static string\n";
  if (i < strlen(st)) { // counts chars in the string
    st[i] = 'X';
    i++;  // point to next character
    cout << st;  // print the string
    return 1;  // indicate there's still some string left
  } else
    return 0; // indicate there's no string left
}

void main() {
  while( StringHolder() )
    ; // do it until there's none left
}
```

Each function call in this example will write over another character in the string.

Similarities Between Arrays and Pointers

With strings, the global definitions **char cha[] = "string";** and **char * chp = "string";** have the same effect. A string is created and its starting address is used for **cha** or **chp**. An **int** pointer (or any other data type except string) cannot be initialized to an array of **int** values like this.

There is a significant difference between **char cha[]** and **char * chp**. The latter is a pointer variable, so you can modify it; **chp = cha** and **chp++** are both legal. However, **cha[]** is an array and not a pointer. When you say **cha**, you produce the starting address of the array, but **cha** is not a variable, so you cannot say **cha = chp** or **cha++**. If you create an array in one file and declare the array as an **extern** pointer in another file, you will have problems because there is no external pointer variable.

String literals are only initialized once, when the program starts up. In contrast, single constant variables may be initialized, but sometimes the compiler builds their values right into the code—this is called *constant folding.* After startup, the act of "initializing" a local string pointer means copying its starting address to the pointer.

An example may clarify this. Suppose you create a character array inside a function body like this:

```
void function() {
  char * A - "This is a string";
  cout << A[6];
}
```

Notice pointer notation is used to define **A**. If you were to say **char A[17]**, the compiler would make local space for an array of 17 characters and then initialize that local array by copying from the character string every time the function is called.

When you use this type of pointer notation, here's what happens. When the program starts up, space is created in a special area for constants, and the ASCII characters for "This is a string" are copied into that space, followed by a 0 byte to indicate the end of the string. Then, every time **function()** is called, local space is allocated for **char * A** and the starting address of the string is copied into the pointer **A**.

Similarly, if you make a call to a function that takes a string argument, such as the ANSI C library function **puts()**,

```
puts("hello");
```

it is equivalent to making a global pointer or array

```
char * cp = "hello";
char cp2[] = "hello";
```

and passing the starting address (via the pointer) as the argument of **puts()**, like this:

```
puts(cp);
puts(cp2);
```

It is often useful to imagine these activities when you are trying to figure out how the compiler is translating your code.

String Examples

Because strings are so important, it is helpful to see a few working examples. The first example centers some lines of text on the screen (assuming an 80-column display). To do this, the number of characters are counted by looking for the 0 byte that terminates every string (this is just a demonstration—if you want to count the characters in a string you should use the library function **strlen()**). The text-centering example looks like this:

```
//: CENTER.CPP—centers text on display.
#include <iostream.h>

const width = 80; // width of screen
char str1[] = "This is the first line of text";
char *str2 = "second line";
char str3[] = "This is the third and last line of text";

void center(char * string) {
  char * cp = string;
  for(int len = 0; *cp != 0; cp++, len++)
    ; // empty statement—all the work is done in the "if"
  // at this point, len contains the number of chars in
  // the string
  for(int col = 0; col < (width - len)/2; col++)
    cout << " ";
  cout << string << endl;
}

void main() {
  center(str1);
  center(str2);
  center(str3);
  center("that's all, folks!");
}
```

In the function **center()**, the first **for** loop does all the work with the initialization and stepping, so the body of the loop is empty. Notice that the comma operator is used in the stepping section, so two operations are performed instead of just one. Before the initialization clause, the character pointer **cp** is created and initialized to the pointer argument. Then **cp** and the integer **i** are incremented until the variable **cp** points to is 0 (which means the end of the string). At this point, the count in **i** is the number of characters in the string.

Code like this (combining two operations into a clause with the comma operator) is sometimes considered to be "too clever," but you will encounter it.

Here's a program that is more fun. It consists of two functions, **encrypt()** and **decrypt()**. The **encrypt()** function takes a string to be coded and an encryption key (a second string), and replaces the string with an encrypted value. The **decrypt()** function reverses the process.

```
//: ENCRYPT.CPP—Captain Midnight Secret Decoder Ring
#include <iostream.h>

void encrypt(char * msg, char * key) {
  unsigned char ckey = 0;
  for(char * cp = key; *cp != 0; cp++)
    ckey += *cp;  // generate a number from the key
  for(cp = msg; *cp != 0; cp++)
    *cp += ckey;  // use the number to encrypt the msg
}

void decrypt(char * msg, char * key) {
  unsigned char ckey = 0;
  for(char * cp = key; *cp != 0; cp++)
    ckey += *cp;  // generate a number from the key
  for(cp = msg; *cp != 0; cp++)
    *cp -= ckey;  // use the number to decrypt the msg
}

char * msg = "this is the message";
void main() {
  cout << msg << endl;
  encrypt(msg, "mom");
  cout << msg << endl;
  decrypt(msg, "mom");
  cout << msg << endl;
}
```

The encryption process is trivial; an encryption key is generated by summing up all the numerical values of the characters in the key string. The encryption key is added to each character in the **msg** string to generate an encrypted message. The process is reversed for decryption.

You can also stash the text in an object and create methods to encrypt and decrypt the information. Here is a program using classes that has the same effect:

```
//: ENCODE.H—A Class to hold a text string,
//. encrypt and decrypt it.
#ifndef ENCODE_H_
#define ENCODE_H_
class encode {
  char * encrypted_string;
  unsigned char make_key(char *);
public:
  encode(char * msg, char * key);  // install a message
  char * decode(char * key);  // decode it and read it back
};
#endif // ENCODE_H_
```

The following file contains the methods for **encode** and a program to test the class. You should remove the **#define TEST** for normal use, for example, when you're linking with a file that contains a **main()**.

```
//: ENCODE.CPP—Methods for the encryption/decryption class
#define TEST
#include <iostream.h>
#include "encode.h"

// private function to create a key from a string:
unsigned char encode::make_key(char * keystring) {
  unsigned char ckey = 0;
  for(char * cp = keystring; *cp != 0; cp++)
    ckey += *cp;  // generate a number from the key
  return ckey;
}

encode::encode(char * msg, char * key) {
  unsigned char ckey = make_key(key);
  encrypted_string = msg;  // save the pointer to the message
  for(char * cp = encrypted_string; *cp != 0; cp++)
    *cp += ckey;  // use the key to encrypt the msg
}

char * encode::decode(char * key) {
 unsigned char ckey = make_key(key);
 for(char * cp = encrypted_string; *cp != 0; cp++)
   *cp -= ckey;  // use the key to decrypt the string
 return encrypted_string;
}

#ifdef TEST
```

```
void main() {
  encode hidden_message("This is a test string", "key string");
  cout << hidden_message.decode("key string") << endl;
}

#endif // TEST
```

The process of creating a key now has its own **private** function. Encrypting a message is built into the constructor. Because the encryption and decryption schemes are hidden inside the methods, you can modify them without changing the interface.

To construct the object, **class encode** stashes the address of the string argument in its private pointer. This means that it is using the space of the global string to hold its data. You might not want to rely on the creation of global text strings to hold your data. For example, if you are working with a string, you might want to stash an encrypted copy away in the object and then go on working with your string. To do this, you must use the **new** operator to create space for the string and then copy the string. Chapter 6 contains examples of this.

Arrays of Pointers

In C and C++ you are not restricted to making simple arrays and simple pointers. You can combine the two into a very useful construct: an *array of pointers*.

An array of pointers is exactly what it sounds like. You have an array, and the elements in that array contain the addresses of other data objects (which can be pointers themselves. Yes, you can have an array of pointers to pointers to pointers to...). The most common place you will see an array of pointers is in the command-line arguments for **main()**:

```
void main(int argc, char * argv[]) {
  //...
}
```

The use of the empty brackets in an argument declaration is different from a global or static definition. In a global or static definition, the empty brackets in **int A[] = { 1, 2, 3 };** mean "create enough space for this array," but in an argument list (or **extern** declaration), the empty brackets cause a pointer to be created. Since pointers can always be dereferenced using the bracket operator instead of the star, you can also say (and this is quite common) the following:

```
void main(int argc, char ** argv) {
  // ...
}
```

When a C or C++ program starts up, **argc** and **argv** are initialized by the startup code. The **argc** is the number of arguments, and **argv** is an array of pointers to the argument strings. The startup code counts the arguments and places the count in **argc** (including the command itself, so a command line with no arguments has an **argc** of 1). Then it takes each space-delimited argument, builds a string from it, and places the pointers to the strings in the array **argv[]**. Since you never know how big this array is until the program starts up, you can use the count in **argc** to know when to stop pulling string pointers out of **argv**. The ANSI C standard requires that the last **argv** be NULL, so you can also check the value of **argv** to find the end of the list.

You index into the array of pointers just like an ordinary array. However, the result is a pointer, not a character, so you must treat it appropriately.

The following example takes command-line arguments and concatenates them (you might use this in a shell script in UNIX or batch file on a PC to generate potential names for your company from pieces of names):

```
//: NAMECAT.CPP—Concatenates the command line together
#include <iostream.h>

void main(int argc, char * argv[]) {
  char namebuf[200];  // to hold the concatenated string
  char * np = namebuf; // to put characters in namebuf
  for(int i = 1; i < argc; i++) {
    for(char * cp = argv[i]; *cp !=0; cp++)
      *np++ = *cp;
  }
  *np = 0;  // zero byte terminates a string
  cout << namebuf << endl;
}
```

This program first creates a local character buffer **namebuf** to hold the finished string. Then the program defines a pointer and assigns it to the starting address of the buffer. The pointer is used to stuff characters into the buffer.

The outer **for** loop simply steps through the command-line arguments until there are no more left (that is, until **i** is not less than **argc**). For each of these arguments, the inner **for** loop is executed; the character pointer **cp** is assigned to the starting address of the command-line argument, and the pointer is stepped through all the characters in the argument. For each step, the character in the argument is stuffed into the output buffer **namebuf**. The command-line argument ends (as all strings do) with a zero byte. This is tested with the expression in the **for**: ***cp != 0**.

In the statement that performs the actual stuffing of the character into the output buffer, ***np++ = *cp;**, the increment applies to the pointer, not to the variable pointed to. This statement says, "put the value **cp** points to into the slot **np** points to and then move **np** to the next slot." If you say **(*np)++;**, it means "add 1 to the character **np** points to."

If you don't put the statement ***np = 0;** after all the strings have been copied, your command-line arguments will print followed by unpredictable garbage—**cout** will just keep printing until it finds a zero byte.

Although this example helps you understand how pointers work, there is a function in the ANSI C library called **strcat()** that has the same effect—you should always use that rather than trying to write and debug your own version.

The Size of a Pointer (Memory Models)

While the size of a built-in data type depends on the variable to be stored, the size of a pointer only depends on one thing: the size of the address (since that's all you store in the pointer). On many computers, the size of a pointer only depends on the type of data. These are called linear address space machines.

The Intel 80*x*86 microprocessors (including the 8088, 8086, 80286, 80386, 80486, and so on.) upon which PCs are based use a segmented addressing scheme, which breaks the address into two pieces, a segment and an offset. The segment can be thought of as selecting the city where the address is located, and the offset chooses the specific apartment within the city. While a linear addressing scheme generates unique addresses for an apartment in Vienna and one in Denver, a segmented scheme might have the same offset for both apartments.

The size of a pointer in a 80x86 processor varies depending on the memory model selected during compilation. The memory model tells the compiler how large your code and data will be. Some programs are very small and don't need very much data space. For these, the segment for the program counter (a "hardware pointer" built into the processor; it points to the next instruction to be executed), and the segments for all the data pointers in the program never change. This program spends its whole life in the same small town, so the pointers can be the size of the offsets (that's the only part that changes).

Some programs, however, contain a large amount of code (more than fits in one segment), and their data pointers must range all over the map, just like a program on a linear-address-space machine. These programs must calculate segment addresses as well as offset addresses for both the program counter and all the data pointers, so pointers are larger. On the PC, the memory model selected is based on a combination of the size the program and the size of the data.

Novice programmers and programmers familiar with linear-address processors find the 80x86 frustrating (it is unquestionably a nemesis to programmers). Their solutions range from ignoring the problem to always using the largest memory model and pretending they are on a linear-address-space machine (indeed, 80386 processors and on support both segmented and linear addressing).

Ignoring the problem is a good way to start, and compilers support this by choosing a default memory model. You will run into problems, however, when you try to address an absolute location outside your program's segment area. Also, if you want to manage a large amount of data (larger than 64K bytes on the PC), you will need a different memory model.

You might wonder why you can't just use the largest memory model. You can, but there's a price. If all your data is in one segment, the pointer is the size of the offset, and the calculations are straightforward when you change a pointer (increment it, for example). However, if your data ranges all over the map, your pointer is the size of the segment and the offset, and both must be calculated every time you change the pointer. This can slow your program significantly.

Far Pointers

One of the problems with using various memory models is that you don't always know the exact model you will be using when you are writing code. A program designed, for example, for a small data space might someday need to access a large data space. You might also encounter situations when you want to keep all your pointers small and fast, but you must access some absolute location in memory (video memory on the PC, for example).

Many C and C++ implementations on 80x86 allow you to override the default pointer size for specific variables by using the nonportable, implementation-specific **near** and **far** keywords. The **near** keyword forces an offset-only pointer when the pointers would normally default to segment + offset. The **near** keyword is generally used to increase speed. The **far** keyword forces a segment + offset pointer when the pointers would normally default to offset-only. If you know you are addressing a specific location or you will always be pointing to a chunk of data larger than 64K, you should declare your pointer **far**. A **far** pointer always does the right thing, regardless of the memory model used.

Example Showing Pointer Sizes

If you are on a 80x86 machine, you should try compiling and running the following program with the various memory models available with your compiler. For each different memory model, it will show you the size of various different pointers—the "default" pointer (which is affected by the memory model) and the **near** and **far** pointers (which are not affected by the memory model). The program uses the "stringize" preprocessor directive # in the **SIZE()** macro so the name of the pointer can automatically be printed, as well as its size. The program looks like this:

```
//: PTRSIZE.CPP—The sizes of pointers with various memory
//. models on a segmented-addressing processor (won't compile
//. with linear-addressing processors).
```

```
#include <iostream.h>

// A macro to display the name and size of a pointer:
#define SIZE(PP) cout << "sizeof(" #PP ")= " << \
        sizeof(PP) << endl;

void main() {
  char * byte_ptr;   // points to the smallest kind of data
  long double * longd_ptr; // the biggest kind of data

  char far * far_byte_ptr;
  long double far * far_longd_ptr;

  char near * near_byte_ptr;
  long double near * near_longd_ptr;

  SIZE(byte_ptr);
  SIZE(longd_ptr);
  SIZE(far_byte_ptr);
  SIZE(far_longd_ptr);
  SIZE(near_byte_ptr);
  SIZE(near_longd_ptr);
}
```

Consult your local guide for the specifics of compiling with various memory models and building **near** and **far** pointers to absolute locations. This is not a straightforward topic.

Function Addresses

Once a function is compiled and loaded into the computer to be executed, it occupies a chunk of memory. That memory, and thus the function itself, has an address.

C has never been a language to bar entry where others fear to tread. You can use function addresses just as you can use variable addresses—with pointers. The declaration and use of function pointers looks a bit opaque at first, but it follows the format of the rest of the language.

Defining a Function Pointer

To define a pointer to a function, you say

```
void (*func_ptr)();
```

When you are looking at a complex definition like this, the best way to attack it is to start in the middle and work your way out. "Starting in the middle" means starting at the variable name, which is **func_ptr**. "Working your way out" means looking to the right for the nearest item (nothing in this case; the right parenthesis stops you short), looking to the left (a pointer, denoted by the star), looking to the right again (an empty argument list indicating a function), and then looking to the left (**void**, which indicates the function has no return value). This right-left-right motion works with most declarations.

To review, "start in the middle" ("**func_ptr** is a ..."), go to the right (nothing there—you're stopped by the right parenthesis), go to the left and find the * ("... pointer to a ..."), go to the right and find the empty argument list ("... function ... "), and go to the left and find the **void** ("**func_ptr** is a pointer to a function returning **void**").

You might wonder why ***func_ptr** requires parentheses. If you didn't use them, the compiler would see

```
void *func_ptr();
```

You would be declaring a function rather than defining a variable. You can think of the compiler as going through the same process you do when it figures out what a declaration or definition is supposed to be. It needs those parentheses to "bump up against" so it goes back to the left and finds the *, instead of continuing to the right and finding the empty argument list.

Aside: Complicated Declarations and Definitions

Once you figure out how the C and C++ declaration syntax works you can create much more complicated items. For example:

```
//: DECL.CPP—Some complicated definitions

/* 1. */      void * (*(*fp1)(int))[10];

/* 2. */      float (*(*fp2)(int,int,float))(int);

/* 3. */      typedef double (*(*(*fp3)())[10])();
              fp3 A;

/* 4. */      (*(*f4())[10])();
```

Walk through each one and figure it out. Number 1 says "**fp1** is a pointer to a function taking an integer argument and returning a pointer to an array of ten **void** pointers (pointers with unspecified type)."

Number 2 says "**fp2** is a pointer to a function taking three arguments (**int**, **int**, and **float**) and returning a pointer to a function taking an integer argument and returning a **float**."

If you are creating a lot of complicated definitions, you might want to use a **typedef**. Number 3 shows how a **typedef** saves typing the complicated description every time. It says, "An **fp3** is a pointer to a function returning a pointer to an array of ten pointers to functions taking no arguments and returning doubles." Then it says "**A** is one of these **fp3** types." You can also use **typedef** to build complicated descriptions from simple ones.

Number 4 is a function declaration instead of a variable definition. It says "**f4** is a function returning a pointer to an array of 10 pointers to functions returning integers." The outer functions each return an **int** by implication, since C and C++ default to **int** if a data type isn't specified.

You will rarely if ever need such complicated declarations and definitions as these; however if you go through the exercise of figuring them out, you will not even be mildly disturbed with the slightly complicated ones you may encounter in real life.

Using a Function Pointer

Once you define a pointer to a function, you must assign it to a function address before you can use it. Just as the address of an array **arr[10]** is produced by the array name without the brackets (**arr**) the address of a function **func()** is produced by the function name without the argument list (**func**). You can also use the more explicit syntax **&func**. To call the function, you dereference the pointer in the same way that you declared it (remember that C and C++ always try to make definitions look the same as the way they are used). The following example shows how a pointer to a function is defined and used:

```
//: PTRFUNC.CPP—Defining and using a pointer to a function
#include <iostream.h>

void func() {
  cout << "func() called..." << endl;
}

void main() {
  void (*fp)();  // define a function pointer
  fp = func;  // initialize it
  (*fp)();     // dereference it to call the function

  void (*fp2)() = &func;  // define and init at the same time
  (*fp2)();
}
```

After the pointer to function **fp** is defined, it is assigned to the address of a function **func()** using **fp = func;**. Notice the argument list is missing on the function name. The second case shows simultaneous definition and initialization and the use of the alternate form to produce the function address.

Array of Pointers to Functions

One of the more interesting constructs you can create is an array of pointers to functions. To select a function, you just index into the array and dereference the pointer. This supports the concept of table-driven code—instead of using conditionals or **case** statements, you select functions to execute based on a state variable (or combination of state variables). This kind of design can be very useful if you often add or delete functions from the table (or if you want to create or change such a table dynamically).

The following example creates some dummy functions using a preprocessor macro and then creates an array of pointers to those functions using automatic aggregate initialization. As you can see, it is very easy to add or remove functions from the table (and thus, functionality from the program).

```
//: FUNCTABL.CPP—Using an array of pointers to functions
#include <iostream.h>

// A macro to define dummy functions:
#define DF(N) void N() { \
  cout << "function " #N " called..." << endl; \
}

DF(A); DF(B); DF(C); DF(D); DF(E); DF(F); DF(G);

void (*func_table[])()  = { A, B, C, D, E, F, G };

void main() {
  while(1) {
    cout << "press a key from 'a' to 'g' or q to quit" << endl;
    char c;
    cin.get(c); cin.get(c); // second one for CR
    if ( c == 'q' ) break; // ... out of while(1)
    if ( c < 'a' || c > 'g' ) continue;
    (*func_table[c - 'a'])();
  }
}
```

A problem occurs when you add or remove functions from the list in the above program. To keep from running off the end of the function table, you must change the bounds checking. A neater solution is to encapsulate the array inside a class. The following program adds the functions to the list at run time rather than at compile time. You can imagine how this class could be useful when creating some sort of interpreter or list processing program.

```
//: DYNAFUNC.H—Class that holds an array of pointers
//. to functions. The functions are inserted into
//. the array at run time.
#ifndef DYNAFUNC_H_
#define DYNAFUNC_H_

class function_holder {
  int func_count; // number of functions in array
  enum { size = 100 }; // max size of array
  void (*function_ptr[size])(); // array
```

```
    void error(char * msg1, char * msg2 = "");
public:
  function_holder();
  void add_function( void (*fp)() );
  void remove_function( int fnum );
  int last_function() { return func_count; }
  void run(int fnum);
  void run_all();
};
#endif // DYNAFUNC_H_
```

Here are the methods for **function_holder**, and a built-in test program that is removed by deleting the **#define TEST**:

```
//: DYNAFUNC.CPP—function_holder methods
// remove the following line when you've finished testing
#define TEST
#include "dynafunc.h"
#include <iostream.h>
#include <stdlib.h>

void function_holder::error(char * msg1, char * msg2) {
  cerr << "function_holder error: " << msg1 << msg2 << endl;
  exit(1);
}

function_holder::function_holder() {
  func_count = 0;
  for(int i = 0; i < size; i++)
    function_ptr[i] = 0;
}

// The argument is a pointer to a function returning nothing
void function_holder::add_function( void (*fp)() ) {
  if ( func_count >= size )
    error("add_function: no more space in array");
  function_ptr[func_count++] = fp;
}

void function_holder::remove_function( int fnum ) {
  if ( fnum < 0 || fnum >= size )
    error("remove_function: index out of bounds");
  // move up all the function definitions by one:
  for(int i = fnum; i < func_count; i++)
    function_ptr[i] = function_ptr[i + 1];
  function_ptr[func_count] = 0;
```

```
    func_count--; // we just removed a function from the list
}

void function_holder::run(int fnum) {
  if ( fnum < 0 || fnum >= size )
    error("run: index out of bounds");
  (*function_ptr[fnum])();  // call the function
}

void function_holder::run_all() {
  for (int i = 0; i < func_count; i++)
    (*function_ptr[i])();
}

#ifdef TEST

#define FDEF(NM) void NM() { \
  cout << "this is function " #NM << endl; \
}

FDEF(f1); FDEF(f2); FDEF(f3); FDEF(foo); FDEF(bar); FDEF(fred);

void main() {
  function_holder machine;
  machine.add_function(f1);
  machine.add_function(f2);
  machine.add_function(f3);
  machine.add_function(foo);
  machine.add_function(bar);
  machine.add_function(fred);
  machine.run_all();
  machine.remove_function(3);
  machine.run_all();
}
#endif // TEST
```

The method **add_function()** assumes that **func_count** indexes the first empty element in the array. All functions are added to the end. The method **remove_function()** moves up all the functions after the one to be removed. This deletes the function from the list and automatically reclaims the space previously used by that function. The methods **run()** and **run_all()** call functions in the list. The preprocessor macro **FDEF()** allows quick creation of dummy functions for testing.

Ideas for Improvements to **function_holder**

There are a number of improvements you can make to the class. The functions don't take arguments or return values—you can easily modify the array definition to accept arguments, but the argument list is always fixed. What if you use a variadic argument list, which allows you to pass any number or kind of arguments? You would then have to write code to ensure that the proper arguments are passed before the function is called or use the macros for handling variable argument lists (in **stdarg.h**) to manage the arguments inside the function.

You might want to add a method to change the sequence of the functions or insert a new function in the middle of the list, so you can dynamically alter the order in which the functions are called.

Finally, you might not want to be limited by the **enum size**, which establishes the maximum size of the array at compile time. What if you don't know how big the array will be? You can create a dynamically sized array by using the **new** keyword in the constructor (see Chapter 6).

You can also create new **function_holder** objects at run time using **new**.

Examples of Pointer Use

To give you a better feeling for the use of pointers, this section presents several examples of pointer use.

Character Statistics in a File

The first program takes standard input (which you can redirect from a file) and counts all the various kinds of characters, including tabs and spaces. After the file ends, it displays the statistics showing the number of occurrences of each kind of character.

```
//: STATS.CPP—Statistics on a character file
#include <fstream.h>
```

```
// limits.h contains the definition of CHAR_MAX, which
// is the maximum value a char can hold:
#include <limits.h>
#include <assert.h>

void main(int argc, char *argv[]) {
  assert(argc > 1);
  ifstream in(argv[1]);
  assert(in); // ensure it's opened OK
  // one place for each character:
  int stat_array[CHAR_MAX + 1];
  char c;
  for(int i = 0; i <= CHAR_MAX; i++)
    stat_array[i] = 0;  // initialize array
  while(in.get(c))  // do for all chars in input
    stat_array[c]++;  // use char as index; increment count
  for(i = 0; i <= CHAR_MAX; i++)
    if(stat_array[i] != 0)
      cout << "number of char #" << i <<", '" <<
          char(i) << "' : " << stat_array[i] << endl;
}
```

This program uses command-line arguments. First, it ensures that there is at least one command-line argument by testing **argc** with the **assert()** macro. Then it creates an **ifstream** object called **in** using the first argument on the command line as the filename. All the input for the program is taken from this file. Notice that the **ifstream** destructor automatically closes the file.

Each time a character is read, it is used as an array index into **stat_array[]**. The array variable corresponding to the character count is selected and incremented in a single statement:

```
stat_array[c]++;
```

Passing Arguments of Unknown Size

There are many situations in C and C++ when you want to pass a piece of data to a function, but there is no way to know at compile time how big the piece of data is. The most common example of this is a string, which is really an array of characters.

In this situation, you have no choice but to pass a pointer. Since a pointer is a fixed size depending only on the pointer type, it is not affected by the size of the data it points to. Thus, there is no ambiguity at compile time. Of course, when the program is running and the function is called, you must somehow divine how big the piece of data really is. With strings, this is done by looking for the 0 byte at the end of the string. If you are passing an array of another type, you can either place some sort of terminator flag at the end of the array or you can pass an extra argument to indicate how long the array is (this is one of the approaches taken with the command line).

Here are two functions that each show one of these approaches:

```
//: PASSARRY.CPP—How to pass arrays
#include <iostream.h>

void printa(const int x[], int size) {  //2nd arg = array size
  for(int i = 0; i < size; i++)
    cout << "x[" << i << "] = " << x[i] << endl;
}

void printb(const int y[]) { // array has terminator flag
  int i = 0;
  while(y[i] != -1)  // you have to use some sort of end flag
                     // that puts a restriction on your data
    cout << "y[" << i << "] = " << y[i++] << endl;
}

int z[] = { 1, 3, 47, 74, 99, 212, 77, 11, 9, -1 };

void main() {
  printa(z, sizeof(z)/sizeof(z[0]));
  printb(z);
}
```

The number of elements in the array is calculated with a useful trick. The expression **sizeof(z)/sizeof(z[0])** yields the size of the entire array in bytes divided by the size of an individual element. On the PC, the size of the array is 20, since there are 10 elements and each int element is 2 bytes, so you get 10 (you get 10 on any machine). By performing this calculation, you can change the size of the array without modifying the rest of the program. This trick can be used for arrays of any data type. Alternately, you can say **sizeof(z)/sizeof(*z)**.

Notice that the arrays are passed as pointers, which means the functions **printa()** and **printb()** could change them. To prevent this, and to show anyone reading the code that it won't happen, the arguments are declared as **const**.

Functions That Modify Outside Variables

If you can manage it, the "cleanest" way for a function to affect its environment is by a return value. There are times, however, when this approach is unsatisfactory and you must modify outside variables. (Another alternative is for the function to modify a global variable. This is generally considered to be hostile toward efforts to create maintainable code). The only way to modify an outside variable is to pass its address to the function.

There are a number of instances where this approach was taken with the ANSI C library. One of these is the math function **frexp()**, which takes a floating-point number and breaks it into an integer exponent (to be used as a power of 2) and a mantissa with an absolute value between 0.5 and 1.0. Since there are two values to return, the designers chose to return the mantissa through the normal return mechanism. The exponent is returned through an integer pointer argument. The prototype for the library function is

```
double frexp(double val, int  * exponent);
```

where **exponent** is the address where you want the integer exponent delivered. This function will be used shortly.

To write a function that modifies an outside variable, you must dereference the argument pointer inside the function body. For example:

```
//: MODIFY.CPP—A function that modifies an outside variable

void addten(int * val){
  *val += 10;
}

void main() {
  int X = 37;
  addten(&X);  // you must explicitly take the address of
```

```
                        // a variable for a pointer argument
}
```

When you create a function that modifies an outside variable and install that function in a library with a header file, you must ensure that the user knows it requires a pointer argument, so the user will take the address of an argument instead of just blindly handing the variable to the function. With old C, this error would pass through with no complaint, causing endless headaches. Function prototyping causes error messages if the user gets it wrong.

Forcing the user to be concerned about how function parameters are passed ("let the user beware") is not in the spirit of C++, which might be thought of as "don't bother the user with details the compiler can handle." C++ has a construct called a *reference* to solve this problem (described later in this chapter).

You should be aware that you aren't limited to returning only one variable. If you want to affect more than one variable and you don't want to modify the function arguments, you can package all your variables together into a **struct** and return that, as shown here:

```cpp
//: RETSTRUC.CPP—Returning a structure to modify more than
//. one variable in the environment.
#include <iostream.h>

struct X {
  int i;
  float j;
  long k;
};

X fred(int ii, float jj, long kk) {
  X local;
  local.i = ii;
  local.j = jj;
  local.k = kk;
  return local;  // return all values packaged in a struct
}

void main() {
  X a;
  a = fred(99, 2.15, 3000);
  cout << "a.i = " << a.i << ", a.j = " << a.j
```

```
        << ", a.k = " << a.k << endl;
}
```

Returning a **struct** has its own limitations, which are outlined in Chapter 9.

Passing struct and Object Pointers

You often need to write functions that take structures (in C and C++) or objects (in C++) as arguments. You can do this two ways: by value, in which a local copy of the structure or object is made inside the function, or by passing an address (via either a pointer or a reference). It is generally more efficient to pass an address than to pass a value, especially because structures and objects tend to be larger than built-in types.

When you pass a pointer to a structure or object, you must dereference that pointer in a special way, using the structure pointer operator (**->**). You may wonder why different dereferencing operators are necessary for structures and objects. The ***** operator refers to the entire structure, so you can't select individual members using *****. The following example demonstrates what happens when ***** is applied to a structure:

```
//: DEREFSTR.CPP—What happens when you dereference an
//. entire structure using the *, instead of individual
//. elements using ->
#include <iostream.h>

struct x {
  int i, j, k;
  float f;
};

#define PR(z) cout << #z " = " << z << endl

void main() {
  x A, B;
  x *xpa = &A, *xpb = &B;
  A.i = A.j = A.k = 0; A.f = 0.0;
  B.i = B.j = B.k = 91; B.f = 1.99;
  *xpa = *xpb;  // dereferencing the whole structure
  PR(A.i);
  PR(A.j);
```

```
    PR(A.k);
    cout << "A.f = " << A.f << endl;
}
```

You will see that the entire structure is copied from **B** to **A**.

The next example shows how to select individual members of a structure or a class using the structure pointer operator (**->**):

```
//: PTRSTRUC.CPP—Selecting members when you have a pointer
//. to a structure or object.
#include <iostream.h>

struct A {
  char c;
  int i;
  float f;
};

class B {
  char c;
  int i;
  float f;
public:
  B(char cc = 0, int ii = 0, float ff = 0.0) {
    c = cc; i = ii; f = ff;
  }
  void print(char * msg = "") {
    cout << msg << ": c = " << c << ", i = " << i
         << ", f = " << f << endl;
  }
};

void main() {
  A u;    // make a structure
  A * up = &u;  // make a pointer to the structure
  B v((char)'c',88);    // make an object
  B * vp = &v;  // make a pointer to the object
  up->i = 100;  // select a member of the structure
  vp->print("vp"); // call a member function of the object
  // notice that B->i = 100; is illegal since i is private
}
```

The expression **up->i = 100;** selects the member **i** of the structure variable **u** that **up** points to. The expression

```
vp->print("vp");
```

calls the member function **print()** of the object **v** that **vp** points to.

Notice that selecting a function is the same as selecting a variable; you need only add the argument list to call the function. If you didn't include the argument list, you would produce the starting address of the function.

Examining the Contents of a **float**

This example demonstrates a more sophisticated use of pointers. An IEEE floating-point number consists of an exponent, a mantissa, and a sign bit, all packed together into 4 bytes for a **float** and 8 bytes for a double. A **float** uses 1 bit for the sign, 7 bits for the exponent, and 24 bits for the mantissa. The high bit of the mantissa is not actually stored in the **float**—there will always be a 1 in the high bit, so it doesn't need to be stored.

If your system uses IEEE floating point, it is very educational to look at the contents of these bytes to see how a number is constructed. The following program will print the exponent and mantissa of a **float** and the bit pattern of the internal floating-point representation, broken up into its individual parts. The program works on a PC or a machine with similar byte ordering; you might have to modify the byte ordering to make it work on your particular machine.

```
//: SEEFLOAT.CPP—Examine the bit pattern of a float
#include <math.h>
#include <iostream.h>
#include <stdlib.h>

// this function displays the bit number bitnum in byte
// as a 1 or a 0.
void display_bit(const unsigned char * byte, int bitnum) {
  cout << (*byte & (1 << bitnum) ? '1' : '0');
}

void main(int argc, char * argv[]) {
  if ( argc < 2 ) {
    cerr << "usage: seefloat number" << endl;
    exit(1);
```

```
}
float f = atof(argv[1]); // 1st arg is float value
int exponent;
// display the exponent and mantissa:
double mantissa = frexp(f, &exponent);
cout << "exponent in base 2 = " <<  exponent << endl;
cout << "mantissa = " << mantissa << endl;
// Now display the binary representation:
cout << "Binary representation: " << endl;
// cast the starting address of the floating point number
// into a byte pointer:
unsigned char * bytewise = (unsigned char *)&f;
// Now use the byte pointer as an array, and pick out the
// bytes one by one. Notice the byte ordering in a
// floating-point number is very machine dependent; yours
// may work differently. On the PC, the starting address + 3
// is the high byte and they count down from there.
cout << "sign: ";
// The address of the third element is given to display_bit():
display_bit(&(bytewise[3]), 7);
cout << endl << "exponent: ";
for(int i = 6; i >= 0; i--)
  display_bit(&(bytewise[3]), i);
// the last bit of the exponent is in the next byte:
display_bit(&(bytewise[2]), 7);
cout << endl << "mantissa: 1";  // high bit is always 1
// display the rest of the byte:
for(i = 6; i >= 0; i  )
  display_bit(&(bytewise[2]), i);
// display the other 2 bytes in their entirety:
for(int j = 1; j >= 0; j--)
  for(i = 7; i >= 0; i--)
    display_bit(&(bytewise[j]), i);
cout << endl << "all: ";
for(j = 3; j >= 0; j--) {
  for(i = 7; i >= 0; i--)
    display_bit(&(bytewise[j]), i);
  cout << " ";
}
}
```

A number of new features have been introduced here. First, the floating-point number is plucked off the command line. If the command-line argument isn't there, the program sends an error message to standard error using **cerr**, which sends output to *standard error*, and then exits. The **exit()** function sets the error value for the program.

The floating-point number is converted from the command-line argument (a string) with the ANSI C library function **atof()**, which means "ASCII to **float**." It takes an ASCII string and returns a floating-point **double**. Since the result of the function is going to a **float**, the compiler performs an automatic type conversion from **double** to **float**.

The ANSI C library function **frexp()** (mentioned earlier) is used to print one version of the exponent and mantissa, and the function **display_bit()** is used to display the individual bits of the floating-point number. You hand **display_bit()** a pointer to a byte and the number of the bit you wish to display.

A pointer called **bytewise** is created to point to individual bytes. The **bytewise** pointer is assigned to the starting address of the floating-point number. Since **bytewise** is a character pointer, you can select each of the bytes in the floating-point number by treating **bytewise** as an array. Since **display_bit()** must be given an address and not a value, the address of the array element must be taken, which produces expressions like **&(bytewise[3])**.

When you are experimenting with this program, try numbers whose patterns you recognize in base 2, such as 1, 2, 8, 15, 31, 255. Notice that the exponent is in an "offset binary format"—an exponent of 0 is represented with 01111111, an exponent of 1 is 10000000, and so on. This allows the representation of negative exponents. If you want to know more about floating-point numbers, a good reference is *Numerical Recipes in C*, by William Press and Brian Flannery, Cambridge University Press, 1987.

References

When building function libraries, a good design philosophy is to make the use of a function as transparent as possible for the user. Generally, a user will want to hunt through a function library (or class library, in C++), grab a function, and use it without spending a lot of time figuring out how it works.

Functions in C and C++ that take addresses as arguments or return addresses force the user to be concerned with the implementation mechanics of a solution. The evolution of programming languages has been away from forcing the user to cope with details and towards allowing the user to spend more time thinking about "the big picture." In this spirit, C++ contains a feature called the *reference*, which allows the programmer to take responsibility for the way arguments are passed to functions. References were not added to ANSI C or any other version of C.

An example will illustrate. If a function in C or C++ takes a pointer argument

```
void func(const datatype * x);
```

and you want to call it for a variable **A**, you are responsible for passing the address of **A** to **func()**. You must explicitly take the address using the "address-of" operator (**&**):

```
func(&A);
```

Forcing the user to take the address of a variable doesn't add much to the semantics of the program. Because of this, it's easy to forget.

If a function returns an address, you can write code that makes the function call part of an lvalue. For example, if you have a class called **matrix** and a member function **float * val(int,int)** that returns a pointer to a floating-point element of the matrix, you can assign

```
matrix m;
//...
*(m.val(3,5)) = 1.19;
```

to that element.

You can also use **matrix** elements in expressions, for example:

```
float f = *(m.val(1,1)) - *(m.val(3,4));
```

Again, the use of pointers doesn't add to the meaning of the expressions. The pointers talk about how a value is produced or a variable is changed, not what the program does. If anything, dereferencing the pointers makes the code harder to read.

Using References in C++

Since references are solely a feature of C++, the rest of this chapter refers only to C++.

A reference in C++ is like a pointer because it contains an address and like an ordinary variable because you don't have to dereference it. If a function takes a reference argument

```
void funcr(int & x);
```

you simply call the function the same way you call it if you are passing by value—**funcr(A);**. The fact that you are taking an address is invisible (this isn't a panacea; see the comments later in this chapter).

In the **matrix** example, if the member function is redefined to return a reference to a floating-point number instead of a pointer, its prototype will be **float & valr(int, int);**. Now, to use it, you say

```
m.valr(2,3) = 2.159;
float ff = m.valr(1,1) + m.valr(4,7);
```

Since the notation is cleaner, the user can focus on what the program does rather than how it is accomplished.

Void references (**void&**) are not allowed.

Reference Syntax

The only place you will notice references is in the function argument list. You can pass an argument by reference and return a reference to a variable. Everywhere else in a function body, the argument looks like an ordinary variable—that is, as if you had passed it by value. In fact, one of the bonuses of using references is that you can switch back and forth between pass-by-value and pass-by-reference styles by simply changing the argument list. Here's an example showing passing and returning by value, by pointer, and by reference:

```cpp
//: PASSING.CPP—Demonstration of passing arguments and
//. returning values by value, by pointer, and by reference
#include <iostream.h>

class demo {
  int i, j, k;
public:
  demo(int u = 0, int v = 0, int w = 0 ) {
    i = u; j = v; k = w;
  }
  demo byvalue(demo X);   // pass in and out by value
  demo * bypointer(demo * X); // pass in and out by pointer
  demo & byreference(demo & X);  // pass in and out by reference
  void print(char * msg = "") {
    cout << msg << ": i = " << i << " j = " << j
         << " k = " <<  k << endl;
  }
};

// Notice the private data in X can be changed because this is
// a member function. A copy of X is created local to the
// function, and the return value is copied out.
demo demo::byvalue(demo X) {
  X.i = X.j = X.k = 999;
  return X;   // return an object
}

// In both the bypointer() and byreference() functions, the
// address of the modified argument is returned because, here,
// it is the only "safe" object (because it's an outside
// variable. You shouldn't return the address of a local
// variable.
demo * demo::bypointer(demo * X) {
  X->i = X->j = X->k = 888;
  return X;   // X is actually a pointer in this function
}

// Now notice that using X when it is passed by reference is
// exactly the same as when it is passed by value:
demo & demo::byreference(demo & X) {
  X.i = X.j = X.k = 777;
  return X;   // return a reference
}
```

```
void main() {
  demo A, B;
  A.byvalue(B).print("result of byvalue()");
  A.bypointer(&B)->print("result of bypointer()");
  A.byreference(B).print("result of byreference()");
}
```

In each case, the member function **print()** is being called for the return value of the function, which is either an object or the address of an object. Notice the calling syntax is identical when values are used and when references are used.

Although passing and returning objects by value happens automatically here, it is not a trivial subject (Chapter 9 is devoted to this topic).

Why References Are Essential

References often cause a lot of confusion, and people approach them differently. Someone without a strong background in C will often begin using references everywhere except where pointers are essential. C programmers who learn C++ will often avoid references, thinking of them as just another way to pass an address. Since pointers can do the job, they use pointers.

There is a situation where references are essential, and for which they were introduced to C++ (in general, features have not been capriciously added to the language—each one is carefully considered). To understand the necessity, a sneak preview of *operator overloading* is necessary (operator overloading is covered in Chapter 5).

When you overload an operator, you create a function that is exactly the same as any other function except for its name. The name of the function always consists of the keyword **operator** followed by the character(s) used for the operator. For example, addition for a **class foo** might look like **foo foo::operator+(foo)**. The rest of the function is the same (although there are limitations on the number of arguments—you don't add to more than one thing at a time). The compiler quietly calls the overloaded function when it sees the appropriate data types being used with that operator.

Here's a simple example of a class with an overloaded addition operator:

```
//: OPERPLUS.CPP—Class with an overloaded + operator
#include <iostream.h>

class plus {
  int i;
public:
  plus(int x = 0) { i = x; }
  plus operator+(plus arg) { return plus(i + arg.i); }
  void print(char * msg = "") {
    cout << msg << ": i = " <<  i << endl;
  }
};

void main() {
  plus A(13), B(34);
  plus C = A + B;
  C.print("C = A + B");
}
```

The **operator+()** takes a single argument, which is the value to the right of the **+** sign. Remember, this function is invoked for the object on the left of the **+** sign. The **operator+()** function creates a new plus object by calling the **plus** constructor. The argument to the **plus** constructor is the sum of the private data parts of the two objects. The **plus** constructor creates a new (temporary) **plus** object, which is copied out of the function as the return value of the operator.

Everything works fine in the above example; all the objects are passed and returned by value. However, there are many occasions when you need to pass the address of an object. For example, objects may be too large to pass by value without destroying the efficiency of the program. Suppose you take the above program and modify it to use pointers:

```
//: OPERPL2.CPP—Trying pointers in operator overloading
#include <iostream.h>

class plus {
  int i;
public:
  plus(int x = 0) { i = x; }
```

```
   plus operator+(plus * arg) { return plus(i + arg->i); }
   void print(char * msg = "") {
     cout << msg << ": i = " <<  i << endl;
   }
};

void main() {
   plus A(13), B(34);
   plus C = A + &B;
   C.print("C = A + B");
}
```

This program works, but the syntax **A + &B** lands somewhere between confusing and horrendous. As a last ditch, you could attempt to make the syntax homogeneous: **&A + &B**. This might work with a **friend operator+()** function instead of a member. It might, but it doesn't. The C++ compiler must have some way of determining that you want to call the **operator+()** for a particular class. If you say **&A + &B**, the compiler's best guess is that you are adding two pointers.

References allow you to pass addresses to overloaded operator functions and still retain the clean notation of **A + B**. Here's how **class plus** works using references:

```
//: OPERPL3.CPP—Using references for operator overloading
//. when you need to pass an address instead of a value.
#include <iostream.h>

class plus {
   int i;
public:
   plus(int x = 0) { i = x; }
   plus operator+(plus & arg) { return plus(i + arg.i); }
   void print(char * msg = "") {
     cout << msg << ": i = " << i << endl;
   }
};

void main() {
   plus A(13), B(34);
   plus C = A + B;    // The syntax is as clean as pass-by-value
   C.print("C = A + B");
}
```

With references, you can use operator overloading and still pass addresses when using large objects.

Independent References

References are designed for argument passing and return values, but the language strives to be consistent in all its aspects. Even though it is not a good practice, you can create independent references that are not associated with function arguments. While a pointer doesn't have to point to anything in particular when it is created, a reference must always be initialized.

An independent reference can only be initialized to an existing variable of the correct type, or to a constant. The syntax for creating an independent reference is

```
int A;
int & ar = A;
```

As is always the case with references, the address of **A** is automatically taken.

At this point, you have two ways to refer to the same variable, both of which look and act exactly the same. You might think this sounds messy. It is, and you should think very hard before you decide you must use an independent reference. Remember they were included for syntactic completeness, not necessarily because they are a good idea.

You can even do equally questionable things like casting a variable of one data type into a reference of another data type. For example:

```
float f;
int & x = (int &)f;
```

You cannot create arrays of references. Object-oriented programming often deals with collections of objects, so the array is a useful tool; the fact that you can't use it with references is one more reason to avoid independent reference variables and use pointers instead.

Notice that the subject here is "independent references" and not "independent reference variables." A reference is quite different from a pointer. A pointer is a variable—it can be reassigned to other addresses. A reference, however, must be initialized when it is created, and it can never refer to a different variable. When you say

```
int X = 10, Y = 100;
int & xr = X;
xr = Y;
```

you don't cause **xr** to refer to **Y**. Since the compiler always dereferences the address for you, the above code will copy the value in **Y** into **X**.

You can also create references to constant values like this:

```
int & aa = 47;
```

The compiler creates a temporary variable, copies the constant value into it, and uses the address of the temporary variable in the reference. This means that any function that takes a reference argument can also take a constant argument.

What It Means to Return an Address

If you return an address from a function by either a reference or a pointer, you are giving the user a memory address. The user can read the value at the address, and if you haven't declared the pointer type to be **const**, the user can also write the value.

By returning an address, you are giving the user permission to read and (for non-**const** pointer types) write to **private** data. This is a significant design decision.

Don't Do This

You must be certain that you *never* return the address of a local variable. Syntactically, this is a completely acceptable thing to do, as shown here:

```
//: RETLOCAL.CPP—Returning the address of a local variable
#include <iostream.h>

int * fred() {
  int A = 100;
  return &A;
}

int * bob() {
  int B = 200;
  return &B;
}

void main() {
  int * x = fred();
  bob();
  cout << "fred() = " << *x << endl;
}
```

Not only does the compiler accept the function **fred()**, but it actually does what you want some of the time! For example, in this test (which only works on a particular version of a particular compiler, and may not be the same for you), if the call to **bob()** is not made, the value of ***x** is 100. However, if **bob()** is called, the value of ***x** becomes 200.

Here's what happens. When **fred()** is called, local space is created on the stack for the variable **A**, and the value 100 is stored there; **fred()** returns the address of this local variable. If another function with local variables is called, those local variables will write over the space where **A** used to be, so the value at the old address of **A** gets changed. Since **x** still points to that variable, the value at ***x** gets changed. Since **bob()** is a function that is identical to **fred()** and its local variable **B** sits right in the space where **A** was, assigning **B** to 200 will also change ***x** to 200. This, of course, is very dependent on the order the functions are called and the machine architecture, so you should never plan on it acting in any particular fashion.

You may see code where, at first glance, it might appear that addresses of local variables are being returned. For example:

```
//: RETSTAT.CPP—Functions which appear to be returning
//. addresses to local variables.

char * LooksLocal() {
  char * ts = "This looks like a local variable";
```

```
    return ts;
}

int & ReturnStatic() {
  static int X = 200;  // this has local visibility
  return X;
}
```

In both cases the variables are actually **static**, so while they have local visibility, they have global lifetime. Thus it is generally safe and acceptable to return their addresses. The only trick here is remembering that a quoted string constant creates a **static** variable even though it isn't explicitly declared **static**, so although it might look wrong, it is OK.

Dangers of Returning References and Pointers

When you return a pointer from a function, the user can assign it to a pointer variable and instantly have unchecked access to the private data elements in your class. This includes the ability to index off the end of arrays, as shown here:

```
//: RETPTR.CPP—Problems returning pointers from functions
#include <iostream.h>
#include <stdlib.h>
const size = 100;

class vec {
  int v[size];
  void error(char * msg = "") {
    cerr << "vec error: " << msg << endl;
    exit(1);
  }
public:
  int * operator[](int index) {
    if(index < 0 || index >= size)
      error("index out of range");
    return &(v[index]);
  }
};

void main() {
  vec vector;
  *vector[5] = 88;  // the way it's supposed to be used, ugly
                    // syntax and all.
```

```
int * x = vector[0];
x++;  // now we can point to the next element
*x = 47;  // and change that.
x[1000] - 4;  // Bad news—the user has control over
              // private elements of the class, and can index
              // off the end of the vector.
}
```

In class **vec**, the overloaded **operator[]()** function allows you to index into the **vec** array. Since it returns a pointer, you must dereference the pointer to access the array element; this obfuscates the code. You can also easily take the pointer returned by **operator[]()** and use it to index off the end of the array, as shown in the last statement.

Since a reference is bound to one address when it is created, and the address can't be changed, it is more difficult to gain control of private data. Returning a reference is thus the preferred method when you must return an address from a function.

It isn't impossible to muck around in the private data when you return a reference, as shown here:

```
//: RETREF.CPP—Returning a reference from a function
#include <iostream.h>
#include <stdlib.h>
const size = 15;

class vec2 {
  int v[size];
  void error(char * msg = "") {
    cerr << "vec2 error: " <<  msg << endl;
    exit(1);
  }
public:
  vec2(int ival = 0);
  int & operator[](int index) {
    if(index < 0 || index >= size)
      error("index out of range");
    return v[index];
  }
  void print(char * msg = "");
};

vec2::vec2(int ival) {
  for (int i = 0; i < size; i++)
```

```
      v[i] = ival;
}

void vec2::print(char * msg) {
  if (*msg) // "" contains only the zero-byte terminator
    cout << msg << endl;
  for (int i = 0; i < size; i++)
    cout << v[i] << "  ";
  cout << endl;
}

void main() {
  vec2 vector(7);
  vector[7] = 88;  // Much more readable syntax

  int & x = vector[0];
  // You can't index using x, and there's no pointer to
  // increment. In fact, x is glued to vector[0].
  // The user can change the value at vector[0], but you've
  // explicitly given permission to do that:
  x = 100;
  vector.print("vector after vector[0] = 100");
  // Of course, there always seems to be a way around these
  // things. However, it's much more obscure and harder to
  // use than x[1] is in RETPTR.CPP.
  *(&x + 1) = 99;  // changing vector[1]
  vector.print("vector after *(&x + 1) = 99");
}
```

This example is very similar to the previous example, but **operator[]()** returns a reference instead of a pointer. The reference means you get the much more readable syntax, like this:

```
vector[7] = 88;  // no dereferencing necessary!
```

Finally, the example shows that it's still possible to abuse references, but it is much harder. You can explicitly prevent the user from modifying the contents of the reference by returning a reference to a **const**.

Pointers and References to Objects

When you pass a pointer or reference to an object as a function argument, you select members (either data or functions) using the structure pointer operator for pointers and the structure member operator for references, as in this example:

```
//: SELECT.CPP—Selecting members for address arguments
#include <iostream.h>

class PrintMe {
  char * phrase;
public:
  PrintMe(char * msg = "") {
    phrase = msg;
  }
  void print(char * msg2 = "") {
    cout << msg2 <<": " <<  phrase << endl;
  }
};

void ByPointer(PrintMe * P) {
  // arrow selects function from pointer:
  P->print("inside ByPointer");
}

void ByReference(PrintMe & P) {
  // dot selects function from reference:
  P.print("inside ByReference");
}

void main() {
  PrintMe One("This is phrase 1"),
          Two("This is phrase 2");
  ByPointer(&One);
  ByReference(Two);
}
```

Both **ByPointer()** and **ByReference()** can only select **public** data or function elements. To select **private** elements, the functions must be declared as **friend** functions inside the class definition.

Reference Members of a class

There are only two situations where you can mention a reference without giving an initializer. One case, as you might guess, is if you are declaring an external variable. For example:

```
extern int & X;
```

It is also possible to use references (instead of pointers) as class members. When you use reference members, they must be initialized in the constructor initializer list:

```
//: REFMEMBR.CPP—References as class members
#include <iostream.h>

class michael {
  int & refmem;  // no initializer in class definition
public:
  michael(int * j) : refmem(*j) {} // special construction
  michael(int & j) : refmem(j) {}
  void set(int newval) { refmem = newval; }
};

void main() {
  int A = 100, B = 200;
  cout << "A = " << A << " B = " <<  B << endl;
  michael W(&A);
  michael W2(B); // constructor michael(int&) called
  cout << "A = " << A << " B = " <<  B << endl;
  W.set(44); // value of A gets changed.
  W2.set(88); // value of B gets changed.
  cout << "A = " << A << " B = " <<  B << endl;
}
```

When to Use References

When it was necessary or beneficial to pass an address to a function or return an address from a function in C, there was no choice: you used a pointer. In C++, you often have a choice about how to pass and return addresses. This section examines some of the tradeoffs.

Although it is syntactically possible to use independent references (just as it is possible to return addresses of local variables) it is rarely a good idea, and will not be considered further in this book.

Advantages of References

Here are some of the advantages of using references in C++:

☐   References have the advantage of notational cleanliness. When you are trying to understand the meaning of a piece of code, you don't have to fight through the details of how parameters are passed. A good example is the **matrix** class in the appendices; it is possible to write equations using **matrix** objects that look and act very similar to the mathematical equations describing the desired matrix manipulation. This means the user can concentrate on the meaning of the equations rather than their implementation.

☐   References put the responsibility for argument passing on the programmer who writes the functions, not on the individual who uses them. This makes the language do more of the bookkeeping work and the user less (and so reduces errors). References are a necessary complement to operator overloading, as shown earlier.

☐   The efficiency of passing an address varies depending on machine (some machines have special instructions that make passing by value more efficient). You can easily compare passing by value to passing by reference, since the only part you need to change is the argument list.

Problems with References

Although references are notationally cleaner and they put the responsibility of knowing how parameters are passed on the programmer, there are some situations in which they can hide bugs. For example, the iostream function **get()** can be called with a character argument: **cin.get(c);**. Because a reference hides the type of argument passing that the function uses, you can't tell from looking at the function call whether **c** is passed by value or passed by reference. If you are trying to track down a problem associated with the variable **c**, you will probably read right past **cin.get(c)**, thinking that **c** is passed by value, so it wasn't modified by the function call (when, in fact, it was).

This is a valid complaint: a function may have side effects that aren't apparent from its calling syntax. There are a number of reasons you shouldn't abandon references, however.

☐ The problem exists primarily with built-in data types, in which all the "data elements" are public. That is, anyone can change an **int**. To make the method of argument passing explicit so the user knows a variable may be changed, you can use a pointer instead of a reference when passing built-in data types. Actually, passing an argument by value is usually very efficient for built-in types, so the only reason you would pass an address instead of a value for a built-in type is if the function modifies the argument. Therefore, while you shouldn't abandon references completely, you probably shouldn't use them for built-in types.

☐ User-defined types have data-hiding mechanisms to protect their data from being unknowingly modified. Since you can force all modifications of internal data to be performed through member functions or friend functions, "unseen side effects" are much easier to monitor. You can even put statements in member functions to notify you if private data is changed.

☐ User-defined types are often large enough that it is more efficient to pass an address than to pass by value (passing by value copies the entire object, and not just an address). However, the efficiency depends on the particular system you are using. Some computers are optimized to manipulate large chunks of data—with a machine like this, it might be more efficient to pass by value than to pass an address and dereference the address every time an element is used.

Guidelines for Passing Arguments

"So," you may ask, "How should I pass arguments?" The answer, in the spirit of C, is: "any way you want to." However, here are a few guidelines that can help you make the decision:

❑ If a function does not modify an argument that is a built-in data type or a "small" user-defined type, pass arguments by value, as **const**. The meaning of "small" depends on your system.

❑ If a function modifies an argument that is a built-in type, pass a pointer. This makes it explicit to anyone reading the code that the built-in type is being modified.

❑ If a function modifies an argument that is a user-defined type, pass a reference. Any function that modifies private data in an object must either be a member function or a friend function. This means the class has control over the functions that can modify its private data. Just because you hand the address of an object to a function doesn't mean the function can secretly change the private data in the object. Thus, the clue that a C pointer gives ("this function modifies an outside variable") is not as useful with user-defined types in C++, since the modifications can be traced directly through functions that have permission to change private data.

When debugging, you should instead ask "who has permission to modify this object?" The answer is conveniently located in the class itself, instead of being scattered about in random functions. Since references reduce effort and confusion on the part of the user, they should be used for objects.

❑ To pass "non-small" objects that are not modified, pass references to constants, on the premise that it is more efficient. The meaning of "non-small" is often obvious for a particular class, but it must be tested for your particular implementation. Testing is easy, since it only involves adding/removing the **&** in the argument list. Since the argument is never modified, it is again clearer to the user if a reference is passed.

Here's an example that shows the various types of parameter passing just suggested in this list:

```
//: PASSARGS.CPP—Demonstration of argument passing guidelines

// Built in types:
```

```
int F1(int x);  // function doesn't modify outside variable
int F2(int * x);  // function modifies outside variable

// Small User-defined Types:

class XX {
  int i;
public:
  //...
  friend int F4(XX &); // explicit permission to change
    // private data
};

int F3(XX arg); // function doesn't modify outside variable
int F4(XX & arg); // function modifies outside variable by
                  // directly manipulating its private data
int F5(XX & arg); // function modifies outside variable by
                  // calling a member function, since this
                  // was not declared "friend"

// Large User-defined Types:

class big {
  enum { size = 50 };
  int * data[size][size];  // 50 x 50 matrix
public:
  // ....
  friend int F7(big &); // explicit permission to change
      // private data
};

int F6(const big & arg); // function doesn't modify outside var
int F7(big & arg);  // function modifies outside var by
                    // directly manipulating its private data
int F8(big & arg);  // function modifies outside var by calling
                    // member functions
```

Makefile for Chapter 4 Examples

Here is the makefile for all the examples in this chapter:

```
# makefile for examples in Chapter 4
# Borland C++ compiler, with the following
```

```
# warnings turned off:
# aus: identifier assigned a value which is never used
# nmake CPP=cl  # Microsoft C++ command line
CPP = bcc -w-aus

.cpp.exe:
    $(CPP) $<

.cpp.obj:
    $(CPP) -c $*.cpp

all:  ptrarith.exe varptrs.exe constptr.exe constarg.exe \
    printv.exe arrayptr.exe index.exe agregate.exe \
    statcstr.exe center.exe encrypt.exe encode.exe \
    namecat.exe ptrsize.exe decl.obj ptrfunc.exe \
    functabl.exe dynafunc.exe stats.exe passarry.exe \
    modify.exe retstruc.exe derefstr.exe ptrstruc.exe \
    seefloat.exe passing.exe operplus.exe operpl2.exe \
    operpl3.exe retlocal.exe retstat.obj retptr.exe \
    retref.exe select.exe passargs.obj refmembr.exe \
    contptr.exe

encode.exe : encode.cpp encode.h
dynafunc.exe : dynafunc.cpp dynafunc.h
```

CHAPTER

Overloading Functions and Operators

Computer language development seems to be a history of "necessary conveniences." Perhaps some of the first programmers, working in machine code, thought of assembly language as an overblown solution to the programming problem (though it's hard to imagine how). Perhaps assembly language programmers thought of the first interpreters and compilers as slow, filled with arbitrary features, and not worth the effort (it certainly seems worthwhile now). Some programmers of early languages probably found concepts like data structures, functions, and separate compilation unnecessary and confusing. However, once you get used to any of these features, they go from curious inventions of the ivory-tower computer scientists to absolutely necessary features of any civilized computer language.

There is a faction in the C++ community that believes that the language should follow C's "minimalist" philosophy. (There is the complementary faction that feels there aren't enough features to do proper object-oriented programming. The two factions, and those in the middle, make up the synthesis of conflicting impulses that seem to characterize "life" in a project.) Many of these people feel that the ability to change the meaning of an operator is both confusing and superfluous. As discussed in Chapter 4, operator overloading was also the feature that "forced" the addition of references to C++; without operator overloading, references are a convenient feature but not an essential one. By getting rid of operator overloading, you get rid of references too, and remove a lot of complexity and confusion. Wouldn't this be better?

From the standpoint of a traditional procedural language, it probably would be better. However, C++ is striking out in a new direction. Although it is possible to create and maintain large projects and libraries with languages like C, they don't really have the features to support this kind of activity. These languages were really designed to solve one computer problem at a time. When the problem was solved, a few changes might be made, but long term maintenance and significant program modifications are not supported.

Instead of asking, "How do we solve the problem of writing this computer program?" C++ asks, "How do we solve the problem of programming and of thinking about programming? How do we support the creation of programs which are cheap to maintain and easy to modify? How do we avoid throwing away old code?" These questions go in a new direction and require a new approach.

The approach taken by C++ and other object-oriented languages is *extensibility.* Instead of making a program more complex as the problems get more complex (and further away from a model that is easily represented by the computer language), extensibility allows you to change the model of the computer language to fit your problem. Once you adapt the language to your problem, the solution can be expressed in a clean and concise manner. This means your program will be easy to understand and easy to change.

Extensibility has received some bad press due to languages like FORTH, which is completely extensible, without bounds or restrictions. While FORTH is a brilliant language and a fascinating experiment, its lack of boundaries often produces programs that can only be understood by their authors.

Like FORTH, C++ allows you to essentially create a new language by extending the old one. The difference is that the new language elements (classes) you create in C++ must conform to a strict set of rules that are enforced by the C++ compiler. Your classes must, syntactically, fit seamlessly into the old language.

All data types have certain operations that may be performed upon them. The operations allowed for a user-defined type may be ordinary member functions; most of the examples up to this point have taken this approach. An operator, however, is another way of expressing functionality, and for some data types it is more natural to use an operator than a member function. To completely integrate a new user-defined data type into the language, you must have the ability to give operators a special meaning for that data type.

The Syntax of Operator Overloading

To overload an operator (as with function overloading, overload means "give it an additional meaning"), you define a function for the compiler to call when that operator is used with the appropriate data types. Whenever the compiler sees those data types used with the operator, it calls the function. You can have multiple functions to overload a single operator, but they must all take different arguments (so the compiler can differentiate them).

The function definition syntax for operator overloading is different than for normal functions. The function name is the keyword **operator**, followed by the operator itself, followed by the argument list and the function body. Thus, using the nonoperator @ to represent the selected operator, the syntax is:

```
returntype operator@(argumentlist) { functionbody }
```

for a friend function, and:

```
returntype classname::operator@(argument) { functionbody }
```

for a class member.

A friend function has one argument for a unary operator and two arguments for a binary operator, while a member function has zero arguments for a unary operator and one argument for a binary operator. This is true because a member function is automatically dealing with one variable already: the object it was called for. The reasons for choosing member functions vs. friend functions will be discussed later in the chapter.

Examples of Operator Overloading

This section contains two examples of operator overloading. The most common situation in which operator overloading is useful is when you are dealing with a mathematically oriented object, as shown in the first example. Often, however, a particular operator may lend itself well to nonmathematical functionality; this is demonstrated in the second example.

A Mathematical Class

This class shows an exhaustive example of all the operators. A simple class called **point** is created to hold coordinates of a point in space, and all the operators are defined for **point** so you can see how to create each type of operator.

```
//: POINT.H—Declaration of a class to represent a point in
// space. Demonstrates operator overloading.
#ifndef POINT_H_
#define POINT_H_

class point {
protected:
  float x, y;
public:
  point(float xx = 0, float yy = 0) {
    x = xx; y = yy;
  }
  point operator=(point); // assignment
  float magnitude();  // vector equivalents
  float angle();
  point operator+(point); // add two points
  point operator+(); // unary plus
  point operator-(point); // subtract two points
  point operator-(); // unary minus
  point operator*(float); // multiply a point by a scalar
  point operator/(float); // divide a point by a scalar
  point operator%(point); // nontraditional modulus
  point operator+=(point); // same operators with '='
  point operator-=(point);
  point operator*=(float);
  point operator/=(float);
  point operator%=(point);
  point operator++(); // increment (prefix)
  point operator++(int); // increment (postfix)
  point operator--(); // decrement (prefix)
  point operator--(int); // decrement (postfix)
  point operator[](float); // rotate the vector
  point operator<<(float); // shift the vector along the x-coord
  point operator>>(float); // shift the vector along the y-coord
  point operator<<=(float); // shift and assign
  point operator>>=(float);
  int operator<(point);  // relational comparison of points
  int operator>(point);  // returns 1 if true, 0 if false
  int operator<=(point);
  int operator>=(point);
  int operator==(point);
  int operator!=(point);
  int operator!();        // 1 if a point is zero
  int operator&&(point); // 0 if either is zero
  int operator||(point); // 0 only if both are zero
  float operator&(point); // cross-product (magnitude only)
  float operator|(point); // dot-product
```

```
  float operator^(point); // angle between two vectors
  point operator&=(point); // multiply point by cp magnitude
  point operator|=(point); // multiply point by dp magnitude
  point operator^=(point); // multiply point by angle
  void print(char * msg = "");
};
#endif // POINT_H_
```

Each operator that takes a **point** as an argument or returns a **point** passes or returns the object by value.

Using **this**

Many of the methods for **point** have rather strange-looking **return** statements, such as:

```
return *this;
```

The keyword **this** is unique to C++. It means "the starting address of the object for which this function was called." The starting address is the same as the address of the first variable in the **class** structure. Before looking at the methods for **point**, here is a small program that illustrates the meaning of **this**:

```
//: THIS.CPP—Illustration of the "this" keyword
#include <iostream.h>

class charles {
  int i;
  float f;
public:
  long L;  // public data
  char C;
  charles(int ii = 0, float ff = 0.0,
          long ll = 0, char cc = 0 ) {
    i = ii;
    f = ff;
    L = ll;
    C = cc;
  }
  void test_this() {
    void * vp = this;
    cout << "i = " << *( (int*)vp ) << endl;
    ( (int *&)vp )++; // move past the int
```

```
      cout << "f = " << *( (float*)vp ) << endl;
      ( (float *&)vp )++; // move past the float
      cout << "L = " << *( (long*)vp ) << endl;
      ( (long *&)vp )++; // move past the long
      cout << "C = " << *( (char*)vp ) << endl;
  }
};

void main() {
  charles X(1957, 7.865, 100000, 'X');
  X.test_this();
}
```

The member function **test_this()** creates a **void** pointer **vp** and gives it the value of **this**, the address of the current object. This is often the address of the first element in the structure, which is **i**. To test this premise, **vp** is cast to an **int** pointer and dereferenced with the expression *((int *)vp)**. The result is sent to **cout**. To point **vp** to the next element in the structure, it is cast to a reference to an **int** pointer and then incremented, in the statement **((int *&)vp)++;**. The pointer is now, presumably, pointing to the element **f**. This premise is tested by casting it to a **float** *, dereferencing it, and printing the result. The same type of actions are performed for **L** and **C**. This isn't terribly useful information, since it's much easier to access the elements by name. However, it is interesting.

Although you can produce a value by casting **vp** (a **void***) to a pointer to a specific type, you cannot modify **vp** using the same notation. That is, you cannot say **((int *)vp)++**, even though it looks like it might make sense (and is, in fact, supported by some C++ compilers for backward compatibility with C code). The problem is that while the cast can produce a pointer with the right value and the right type, it isn't a modifiable **lvalue**—it can be a copy of the original pointer, and incrementing a copy will not affect the original pointer. To increment the pointer itself as if it were a different type, the pointer must be cast not only to a pointer of the desired type, but to a *reference* to a pointer of that type, like this: **((int *&)vp)++**. The value produced by this cast is a reference, which *can* be used as an lvalue. This ensures that **vp** is incremented, and not a copy. If you try to increment **((int *)vp)++**, a compiler that is performing strict checking will issue an error.

The order of elements within a section with the same access (**public**, **private**, **protected**) is the same order that you define them. However, there is no guarantee that the sections will appear in the order you defined them. The **private** section may appear after the **public** section, even if you defined it first. Thus, the program above might not work as expected. The element **L** will appear before **C**, and **i** will appear before **f**, but **L** and **C** might appear before **i** and **f**. It is generally not a good idea to plan on the elements being ordered in any particular fashion.

Since **this** is a pointer to the beginning of the **class** structure, you can select structure elements using the arrow operator **->**. Of course, you don't have to do this inside a member function (which is the only place you have access to **this**)—you just refer to the elements by name.

If you want to refer to the entire structure of the object you are in, you say: ***this**. Remember the dereference operator ***** produces the contents at the address contained in the pointer. Since **this** points to an entire structure, ***this** is the structure (and **return *this** produces a copy of the structure as the return value).

It is important to return the resulting value of an operation when you overload an operator, because operators can generally be used in complicated expressions and are not necessarily used alone like ordinary function calls. Thus the expression **A + B + C** relies on the result of the operation **A + B** being passed to the second operation and added to **C**. In the case of **operator+()**, you don't usually modify the operands when you are adding two values together (although you can do anything you want when you overload an operator). If you look at the code for **operator+()**, you see a brand new **point** is created and returned. In the case of **operator+=()**, however, the lvalue is modified and becomes the result.

You should return a copy of the result when you do any kind of assignment. Assignment, too, can be used in a complex statement like the other operators:

```
X = A + (Y = 1);
```

Here are the methods for **point**:

```
//: POINT.CPP—Methods for class to represent point in space.
// Notice that not all these definitions make sense; they just
// show you how to overload operators.
#include "point.h"
#include <math.h>
#include <iostream.h>
// Used to determine zero:
```

```
const float tiny = 0.0001;

point point::operator=(point rv) {
  x = rv.x; // copy the rvalue
  y = rv.y;
  return *this;  // return a copy of this object
}

float point::magnitude() {
  return sqrt(x*x + y*y);
}

float point::angle() {
  return atan2(y,x);
}

point point::operator+(point p) {
  return point(x + p.x, y + p.y);
}

point point::operator+() {
  return *this;  // unary + normally doesn't do anything.
}

point point::operator-(point p) {
  return point(x - p.x, y - p.y);
}

point point::operator-() {
  return point(-x, -y);
}

point point::operator*(float f) {
  return point(x * f, y * f);
}

point point::operator/(float f) {
  return point(x / f, y / f);
}

point point::operator%(point p) {
  // fmod() is the "floating point remainder" function
  return point(fmod(x, p.x), fmod(y, p.y));
}

point point::operator+=(point p) {
  x += p.x;
```

```cpp
  y += p.y;
  return *this;
}

point point::operator-=(point p) {
  x -= p.x;
  y -= p.y;
  return *this;
}

point point::operator*=(float f) {
  x *= f;
  y *= f;
  return *this;
}

point point::operator/=(float f) {
  x /= f;
  y /= f;
  return *this;
}

point point::operator%=(point p) {
  x = floor(x / p.x);
  y = floor(y / p.y);
  return *this;
}

// Prefix form:
point point::operator++() {
  x += 1.0;
  y += 1.0;
  return *this;
}

// Postfix form:
point point::operator++(int) {
  return operator++();
}

// Prefix form:
point point::operator--() {
  x -= 1.0;
  y -= 1.0;
  return *this;
}
```

```
// Postfix form:
point point::operator--(int) {
  return operator--();
}

point point::operator[](float f) {
  float new_x - magnitude() * cos(angle() * f);
  float new_y = magnitude() * sin(angle() * f);
  return point(new_x, new_y);
}

point point::operator<<(float f) {
  return point(x + f, y);
}

point point::operator>>(float f) {
  return point(x, y + f);
}

point point::operator<<-(float f) {
  x += f;
  return *this;
}

point point::operator>>=(float f) {
  y += f;
  return *this;
}

int point::operator<(point p) {
  if ( x < p.x && y < p.y )
    return 1;
  return 0;
}

int point::operator>(point p) {
  if ( x > p.x && y > p.y )
    return 1;
  return 0;
}

int point::operator<=(point p) {
  if ( x <= p.x && y <= p.y )
    return 1;
  return 0;
}
```

```
int point::operator>=(point p) {
  if ( x >= p.x && y >= p.y )
    return 1;
  return 0;
}

int point::operator==(point p) {
  if ( x == p.x && y == p.y )
    return 1;
  return 0;
}

int point::operator!=(point p) {
  if ( x != p.x && y != p.y )
    return 1;
  return 0;
}

int point::operator!() {
  if ( fabs(x) < tiny && fabs(y) < tiny )
    return 1;
  return 0;
}

int point::operator&&(point p) {
  if ( fabs(x) < tiny && fabs(y) < tiny )
    return 0;
  if ( fabs(p.x) < tiny && fabs(p.y) < tiny )
    return 0;
  return 1;
}

int point::operator||(point p) {
  if ( fabs(x) < tiny && fabs(y) < tiny &&
       fabs(p.x) < tiny && fabs(p.y) < tiny )
    return 0;
  return 1;
}

float point::operator&(point p) {
  return magnitude() * p.magnitude() *
         sin(point::operator^(p));
}

float point::operator|(point p) {
  return magnitude() * p.magnitude() *
         cos(point::operator^(p));
```

```
}

float point::operator^(point p) {
  return fabs(angle() - p.angle());
}

point point::operator&=(point p) {
  float cross = operator&(p);
  x *= cross;
  y *= cross;
  return *this;
}

point point::operator|=(point p) {
  float dot = operator|(p);
  x *= dot;
  y *= dot;
  return *this;
}

point point::operator^=(point p) {
  float arc =  operator^(p);
  x *= arc;
  y *= arc;
  return *this;
}

void point::print(char * msg) {
  if (*msg) cout << msg << " : ";
  cout << "x = " << x << " << y = " << y << endl;
}
```

Many of the methods use ANSI C math library functions, contained in **math.h**.

Each operator shown here is overloaded only once, but you can overload any operator multiple times, as long as the argument is different for each overload.

All the methods in this **class** pass and return by value, which is generally efficient for a **class** this size. This becomes a problem with complicated classes (ones that contain pointers) as shown in Chapter 9. Note that in the postfix form of **operator++**, the return value is the result of the function call to the prefix value of **operator++**, which is also a **point**.

Remember that you are making important design decisions when you overload an operator. You should ask yourself whether you are making life easier or harder for the user. For example, in the preceding code the operator **&** was overloaded to mean "cross product." Will this be meaningful to someone using the class, or to someone reading the code in which the class is used?

Creating Temporary Objects

A number of the methods in class **point** use an unfamiliar form in their **return** statements. For example, in **operator[]**, the **return** statement is

```
return point(new_x, new_y);
```

What does it mean when you use a class name with an argument list like this? When the compiler sees a construct like this it treats it as a constructor call for a *temporary object*, which is an object with no name and usually a very brief lifetime. In the above example, space is created inside the function **operator[]** to hold a **point** object, and the constructor **point::point(float,float)** is called to initialize that object. Finally, the temporary **point** object is copied to the outside of the function via the **return** mechanism, and the temporary **point** object goes out of scope.

You can create your own temporary objects any place where a non-temporary object can be used. For example, if there is a function **fp(point)** which takes a **point** object as an argument, you would normally hand it an initialized point, like this:

```
point A(1.1,2.2);
fp(A);
```

but you can also create a temporary object for the express purpose of handing it to the function as an argument, like this:

```
fp(point(1.1,2.2));
```

Using temporary objects can make your code briefer, more efficient and easier to read.

Distinguishing Prefix and Postfix for Operators ++ and - -

In the declarations and definitions for **operator++()** and **operator- -()**, the compiler distinguishes between the prefix and postfix versions of those operators by calling the operator functions with no argument or one **int** argument, respectively. If for a point **p** you say **++p**, the compiler will call **point::operator++()**, but if you say **p++**, the compiler calls **point::operator++(int)**. This way, you can generate two different functions with two different signatures, and produce a different effect for the pre- and postfix operators. Because older versions of C++ did not make the distinction between prefix and postfix, some newer compilers might allow both calls to be made with only the prefix definition of **operator++ ()** or **operator- -()** (although they will usually issue a warning).

Notice that the argument **int** has no identifier, so it is not used in the function—it is only there to generate a different function signature. Because there is no identifier, the compiler will not complain that a variable has been "created but not used." You can also use this technique as a placeholder in your functions if you think you will need a variable later on, but you don't want to generate compiler warnings.

Short-Circuiting

In C and C++, the nonoverloaded operators **&&** (logical AND) and **||** (logical OR) have the "short-circuit" feature: if the truth or falsehood of the expression containing **&&** or **||** can be determined at some point early in the expression, the entire expression isn't evaluated. For example:

```
int cond1(), cond2();
if( cond1() && cond2() )
  // ...
if( cond2() || cond1() )
  // ...
```

In the first **if** statement, if **cond1()** evaluates to 0 (false), then there is no point in evaluating **cond2()**, because you already know the expression will be false. If the second **if** statement, if **cond2()** is true, you know the whole expression will be true, so **cond1()** is not evaluated.

C and C++ "short-circuit" the expression when its truth or falsehood can be determined. However, if you overload **operator&&()** or **operator||()**, short-circuiting is not performed in expressions using those overloaded operators—the entire expression is always evaluated.

Here are a few exercises for **class point**:

```
//: POINTTST.CPP—A few tests for the point class
#include "point.h"
#include <iostream.h>

void main() {
  point A, B(1.1, 2.2), C(3.3, 4.4), D(5.5, 6.6);
  B.print("B");
  C.print("C");
  D.print("D");
  A = B + C - D;
  A.print("A = B + C - D");
  A += (B << 8.2) + (D >> 4.1);
  A.print("A += (B << 8.2) + (D >> 4.1)");
  cout << "magnitude of A = " << A.magnitude()
       << ", angle of A = " << A.angle() << endl;
  cout << "Angle C ^ D = " <<  (C ^ D) << endl;
}
```

When designing the external operations for a class, remember that all the user usually sees is those operations. If the operations don't contribute to readable code, you should think hard before you do it that way. This is especially true for operator overloading.

Esoteric Operator Overloading

The **point** class shows the overloading of the more common operators. C++ doesn't stop there, however—you can overload operators you wouldn't normally think of redefining, like the "address-of" operator **&**, the pointer dereference operator *, and even the function-call parentheses! The **class** shown in the following example has an element **index** before the array **vv[]**, so if you try to access the array directly using **this**, you will get **index** instead (as mentioned before, it is a bad idea to rely on the implementation-dependent ordering of the elements in a **class** structure). Both the **&** and the * select the starting address of **vv[]** instead of **index**, though you can return anything you want.

One reason overloading the function call is valuable is that it allows you to use an operator syntax with multiple arguments. This also allows many different kinds of overloading. The example shown here simply sets an array element to a value.

```
//: VECTOR.H—Esoteric operator overloading
#ifndef VECTOR_H_
#define VECTOR_H_

static const size = 20;

class vector {
  int index;
  float vv[size];
  void error(char * msg);
public:
  vector(float initval = 0.0);
  float & operator[](int index);
  // use the "address-of" operator to return the start
  // of the floating-point array:
  const float * operator&() { return vv; }
  float operator*() { return vv[0]; }
  // Here's a strange one. You can overload the "function call"
  // operator. The function shown here sets element el to the
  // value f, and returns the new value. Notice it is the only
  // overloaded operator that allows an argument list of more
  // than one for a member function (more than two for a
  // friend):
  float operator()(int el, float f);
  void print(char * msg = "");
};
#endif // VECTOR_H_
```

Here are the methods for **class vector**:

```
//: VECTOR.CPP—Methods for class vector
#include <iostream.h>
#include "vector.h"
#include <stdlib.h>

void vector::error(char * msg) {
  cout << "vector error: " << msg << endl;
  exit(1);
```

```
}

vector::vector(float initval) {
  for(int i = 0; i < size; i++)
    vv[i] = initval;
}

float & vector::operator[](int index) {
  if(index < 0 || index >= size)
    error("operator out of range");
  return vv[index];
}

float vector::operator()(int el, float f) {
  if(el < 0 || el >= size)
    error("operator out of range");
  vv[el] = f;
  return f;
}

void vector::print(char * msg) {
  if (*msg) cout << msg << ":" << endl;
  for(int i = 0; i < size; i++) {
    cout.precision(6);
    cout << vv[i] << " ";
    if ( i % 5 == 4) // linefeed every 5
      cout << endl;
  }
  cout << endl << endl;
}
```

The following program exercises the overloaded operators in **vector**:

```
//: VECTEST.CPP—Test for class vector.
#include "vector.h"
#include <iostream.h>

void main() {
  vector V(1.1);
  V.print("V");
  for(int i = 0; i < size; i++)
    V[i] = (float)(i * 1.5);
  V[0] = 33.119;
  V.print("V after V[i] = (float)(i * 1.5); V[0] = 33.119;");
  const float * startval = &V;
  cout << "*startval = " << *startval << endl;
  V(4, 999.99);
```

```
    V.print("V after V(4, 999.99)");
    cout << "*V = " << *V << endl;
}
```

You will notice in **class vector** that the overloaded indexing brackets **operator[]()** specifically allow the result to be used as an lvalue (that is, you can change the selected value in the **vector**). As noted in Chapter 4, this is an important design decision—if you don't want to allow the user to change the value, you should explicitly say so by declaring the return value **const**.

Multiple Dimensions with operator[]

One of the most frequently asked questions about operator overloading is, "Can I make **operator[]** work with multiple dimensions?" There are a number of situations where this is a helpful model for the user; one is the **matrix** class, which you can find in Appendix B.

To understand how it works, consider the way the compiler evaluates an expression with **[][]**. For example:

```
A[i][j] = 1;
```

The compiler finds the object **A** and sees the set of brackets associated with that object, so it calls **A.operator[](i)** (assuming the overloaded operator has been defined; otherwise an error is produced). Now here's the trick: the result of the inner **operator[]** must produce an object or a reference to an object. That object's class must also have an **operator[]**! The expression thus evaluates to **A.operator[](i).operator[](j)**.

Notice how important references are in this situation. To achieve the familiar array-indexing syntax, you *must* have references in the language, otherwise you would be forced to return objects by value. If you didn't have references and you were dealing with objects that had to be returned by address, you would end up with a choice between these two unpleasant alternatives:

```
*A[1]->operator[](2) = 20;
```

or

```
*(*A[1])[2] = 20;
```

Without references, operator overloading would be seriously impaired.

To see how to overload two levels of brackets, here's a simple example:

```
//: BSIMPLE.CPP—Simple test of double bracket operator
#include <iostream.h>

class inner {
  int x;
public:
  inner(int X = 0) : x(X) {}
  int& operator[](int) { return x; }
};

class outer {
  inner i;
public:
  outer(int I = 0) : i(I) {}
  inner& operator[](int) { return i; }
};

void main() {
  outer o(21);
  for(int i = 0; i < 5; i++)
    for(int j = 0; j < 3; j++)
      cout << "o[" << i << "][" << j
           << "] = " << o[i][j] << endl;
  o[1][2] = 19;
  cout << o[3][4] << endl;
}
```

In **main()**, the object **o** only refers to a single storage location, even though you can choose any index. That's because the index is ignored in both the **inner** and **outer** definitions of **operator[]**. Notice how the syntax works out and how the references allow you to use the result as both an lvalue and an rvalue.

A more interesting example is a container, and one that is particularly appropriate for two levels of indexing is an interface to a database table. Consider the abstraction (which isn't very far from the truth): a table is an array of records, and a record is an array of fields. Here's how you might do it by double-indexing **operator[]**:

```
//: BRACKETS.CPP—Overloading multilevels of square brackets
#include <string.h>
#include <stdlib.h>
#include <iostream.h>
#include <fstream.h>

class field {
  char * data;
public:
  field(char * d = "") : data(strdup(d)) {}
  ~field() { free(data); }
  void operator=(char * d) {
    free(data);
    data = strdup(d);
  }
  operator int() { return strlen(data); }
  friend ostream& operator<<(ostream& os, field& f) {
    return os << f.data;
  }
};

class record {
  field ** Field;
  int size;
  void copygrow(int newsize) {
    field** temp = new field*[newsize];
    for(int i = 0; i < size; i++)
      temp[i] = Field[i];
    while(i < newsize)
      temp[i++] = new field;
    size = newsize;
    delete Field;
    Field = temp;
  }
  enum { bumpsize = 10 }; // amount to increase
public:
  record() : size(0), Field(0) {}
  ~record() {
    for(int i = 0; i < size; i++)
      delete Field[i];
    delete Field;
  }
  field& operator[](int i) {
    if(i < 0) { cerr << "record: negative index"; exit(0); }
    if(i >= size) copygrow(i + bumpsize);
    return *Field[i];
  }
```

```cpp
};

class table {
  record ** Record;
  int size;
  void copygrow(int newsize) {
    record** temp = new record*[newsize];
    for(int i = 0; i < size; i++)
      temp[i] = Record[i];
    while(i < newsize)
      temp[i++] = new record;
    size = newsize;
    delete Record;
    Record = temp;
  }
  enum { bumpsize = 10 }; // amount to increase
public:
  table() : size(0), Record(0) {}
  ~table() {
    for(int i = 0; i < size; i++)
      delete Record[i];
    delete Record;
  }
  record& operator[](int i) {
    if(i < 0) { cerr << "table: negative index"; exit(0); }
    if(i >= size) copygrow(i + bumpsize);
    return *Record[i];
  }
};

void main(int argc, char* argv[]) {
  if(argc < 3) { cerr << "usage: brackets file index"; exit(0);}
  ifstream in(argv[1]);
  if(!in) { cerr << "can't open " << argv[1]; exit(0); }
  const index = atoi(argv[2]);
  const bsz = 120; char buf[bsz];
  table Tbl;
  int lines = 0;
  while(in.getline(buf, bsz)) {
    int j = 0;
    char * p = strtok(buf, " \t\n");
    while(p) {
      Tbl[lines][j++] = p;
      p = strtok(0, " \t\n");
    }
    lines++;
  }
```

```
  // Print entire table:
  for(int k = 0; k < lines; k++) {
    for(int i = 0; Tbl[k][i]; i++)
      cout << Tbl[k][i] << " ";
    cout << endl;
  }
  // print index element:
  for(k = 0; k < lines; k++)
    cout << Tbl[k][index] << endl;
}
```

The string class, **class field**, is the most rudimentary form of a string class. The **strdup()** function (from the ANSI C library) is used because it creates storage *and* copies in one step. However, because **strdup()** uses **malloc()**, **free()** must be called in the destructor. Then **operator=()** is overloaded so you can perform assignment to character strings, and an automatic type conversion operator is created for the cast to **(int)**, primarily so the field can be checked to see if it has a nonzero length.

The overloaded **operator<<()** is actually a nonmember function because it is preceeded by **friend**. This is the basic form you need to use when creating an overloaded iostream operator for a specific class. The arguments indicate that an **ostream** object is on the left of the **<<** and a **field** object is on the right. Inside the function, you need only send the desired parts of the **field** object to the output stream and then return that output stream so it may be used in the rest of the user's expression.

The classes **record** and **table** are designed almost identically (in Chapter 10 they're turned into a single template!). The key feature of both is that they will expand themselves to fit any index you choose via the **operator[]**. This is a particularly elegant solution because there's usually a problem when dealing with **operator[]** and references—you must always return an object of some type, even when the user goes out of bounds (unless you want to simply abort the program, as is done in the preceding example with negative values, or you have an exception-handling compiler). With this technique, there's never a question about what to return if the bounds are exceeded, because the boundaries are expanded to whatever you ask for! The function **copygrow()** expands the array in each class. The array is started from zero and expanded every time you choose an index greater than the current **size**.

The only **public** member function (other than the constructor) is the **operator[]** for both classes. That's because you can use it to both put things in and get things out. Notice that even if you choose an element that you didn't initialize and is way out in the array, you'll get a usable value back—in this case, an empty character string. This is because **operator[]** calls the **private** member function **copygrow()** if you try to index out of its bounds. Notice that the objects grow by amounts of **bumpsize**, which can be modified to increase run-time efficiency.

The function **copygrow()** has the same form for both **record** and **table**. Looking at **record**'s **copygrow()**, it creates a new **field*** array that has the new, larger size (this returns a pointer to an array of pointers); then it goes through and copies the old pointers from **Field** into the new array (notice that the size of a **record** always *increases*, so this can never go off the end). Next, it initializes the rest of the array pointers to new **field** objects, so they all point to something valid (the default **field** constructor is called here, which produces an empty string). Then **copygrow()** changes the size of the **record** and calls **delete** for the old **Field** pointer, which deletes the storage previously allocated. Note that the storage is an array of **field** *pointers*, so there are no destructor calls (which we wouldn't want anyway, since those **field** pointers are being used in the expanded array). Finally, **Field** is assigned to **temp**, so it points to the larger array of pointers.

In **main()**, the command-line argument is checked, and the first argument is used to open a file by creating an **ifstream** object, which automatically closes the file when it goes out of scope (notice how much nicer it is to use the **iostream** file functions than the ANSI C functions). To ensure the file was successfully opened, the overloaded **iostream operator!** is used—it returns true or false to indicate the validity of the file. Each line is of the file is read with the iostream function **getline()**, which takes as its first argument the destination buffer, and as the second argument the maximum size of the buffer. The line is then parsed into a **table** object called **Tbl** using the ANSI C library function **strtok()**, which *tokenizes* a character buffer (breaks it up into discrete pieces).

You tell **strtok()** how to break it up by the characters in the second argument. It creates a token until it sees any of the characters in the delimiter string, then it returns a pointer to that token. The first time you call **strtok()** for a buffer, you give it the name of the buffer as the first argument. After that, you hand it 0 as the first argument to continue working on the rest of the same buffer.

To insert something into a table, assignment is used with the bracket operators, so that **field**'s **operator=** is called.

Printing is perfomed by looping through the table. Each line is printed until **Tbl[k][i]** produces 0 (via its **operator int** automatic type conversion). In the last part, only the selected word is printed.

You can try this on any text file. It will first print the contents of the file (with only one space between any of the words and with no indentation, but with the line breaks intact) and then print the chosen index. Try it on the source code to the program.

Zero vs. NULL

In the successive calls to **strtok()**, you can see that zero is used instead of NULL. C programmers are familiar with the use of NULL everywhere you want a zero value, and that's the proper form in C. In C++, however, you should always use numerical 0 instead. Although this may initially sound surprising, here's the explanation, from *C++ Programming Guidelines* (Plum & Saks, Plum-Hall Publishing, 1991):

"A constant expression that evaluates to 0 is converted to a pointer, commonly called the null pointer, whenever it is assigned, compared or uscd to initialize a pointer. ... The *Annotated C++ Reference Manual*, by Ellis and Stroustrup (Addison-Wesley, 1990) does not guarantee that the defined constant NULL is compatible with all pointer types. Some implementations define NULL as **(void*)0**, which cannot be assigned to another pointer type without a cast. The symbol NULL is actually an artifact of old C. Before C had prototypes, NULL was needed to assure that null pointer arguments had the correct size."

Thus, you should always use 0, never NULL, in C++.

Overloading the Comma Operator

In a sequence of expressions separated by commas, the expressions are evaluated (including the side effects) from left to right. All the values resulting from the evaluation of the expressions are discarded except for the final value, which is the result of the entire comma-separated sequence. Thus, all the expressions except for the last one are only used for their side effects.

When the expression to the left of the comma is an object or produces an object, the comma operator can be overloaded to generate a user-defined side-effect appropriate for that object. Here is an example:

```
// CRISPY.CPP—Overloading the comma operator
#include <stdio.h>

class crispy {
  static int i;
public:
  crispy operator,(crispy &);
};

int crispy::i = 0; // static member definition

crispy crispy::operator,(crispy & c) {
  switch(c.i) {
    case 0 : i++; puts("snap!"); break;
    case 1 : i++; puts("crackle!"); break;
    case 2 : puts("pop!"); break;
    default : i = 2; break;
  }
  return c;
}

void main() {
  crispy rice1, rice2, rice3, rice4;
  // rice4 gets the value of rice3 (with i = 2):
  rice4 = (rice1, rice2, rice3, rice3);
}
```

The parentheses are necessary because the = operator has higher precedence than the comma operator.

Smart Pointers

You can only define the unary **operator->()** as a member function for a class, and it cannot be a static member. The use of a smart pointer is a little counterintuitive, because the pointer is used on an *object* of the class, and not a *pointer to an object*, which is what you normally use the

-> operator for. This means that the object is meant to *represent* a pointer, but one that does something different than an ordinary pointer; perhaps some error checking (that's the "smart" part of the pointer).

If **C** is a class with an **operator->()** member function, and **el** is a member of that class or some other **class**, **struct**, or **union**, then

```
C cobj;
cobj->el;
```

is evaluated as

```
(cobj.operator->())->el;
```

This means that **operator->()** must return either:

☐ A pointer to a class object containing the element **el**. The "normal" dereferencing using the -> operator is performed to select **el**.

☐ An object of another class. This other class must contain a definition for **operator->()**. In this case, the **operator->()** is called again for the new object. This process is repeated recursively until the result is a pointer to a class object containing the element **el**.

Here's an example that uses the recursive-dereferencing property of the smart pointer:

```
// SMART.CPP—"Smart pointer" example
#include <iostream.h>
#include <string.h>
#include <stdlib.h>

struct String {
  char * s;
  String(char * S) : s(strdup(S)) {}
  ~String() { free(s); }
};

class String_pointer {
  String * m;
public:
  String_pointer(String & S) : m(&S) {}
  String* operator->() {
    // (perform a test)
    return m;
```

```
  }
};

void main() {
  String_pointer X(String("hello, world!\n"));
  cout << X->s;
}
```

String_pointer holds the pointer to a **String** and returns it, assuming the test is passed safely. In the expression **X->s**, **String_pointer::operator->()** is called, which returns **m** (not **s**); but the compiler knows it can go further, so it continues and fetches **s** from **m**, which is a **String** pointer. Note that this recursive activity can continue for multiple levels.

The Copy Constructor and Operator=() Can Be Created by the Compiler

New C++ programmers often have difficulty dealing with the *copy constructor* and **operator=()**. The copy constructor, also referred to as **X(X&)**, is a constructor that takes as its argument a reference to an object of the same class. It is a function that is used quietly by the compiler to copy objects by value *into* a function when the objects are used as arguments, and *out of* a function when an object is returned by value. For example:

```
X thizbin(X c) {  // c is passed by value; X(X&) called
  return c;  // c is returned by value; X(X&) called
}
```

The copy constructor is also used to initialize a new object from an old one in the following expression:

```
X a;
X b = a;  // X(X&) called here
```

Prior to AT&T cfront 2.0 (and compilers conforming to that release), if the programmer did not define a copy constructor (which often happened because new programmers don't see the need for it, since it is never called explicitly) the compiler resorted to a *bitwise copy*, which means that the structure of one object is directly copied into the structure of another copy. This works fine for very simple objects (for example, ones that don't contain pointers or instances of other classes) but is definitely not the desired effect when the object contains pointers or members which are other objects. Prior to 2.0, the programmer was forced to write the copy constructor to handle these cases.

Similarly, **operator=()** is called when one already initialized object is assigned to another already initialized object. For example:

```
X d;
X e = d;   // X(X&) called
X f;
f = d;     // X::operator=(X&) called
```

If **f** contains pointers or member objects, **operator=()** is responsible for cleaning those up.

As with the copy constructor, if **operator=()** was not defined by the programmer in C++ implementations prior to release 2.0, the compiler resorted to a bitwise copy of the right side onto the left side, ignoring the need to clean up the left side first. This resulted in real problems because if the left-side object contains pointers to free store, the old pointers are copied over, and the address of the block of free store is lost, which may eventually cause the program to run out of memory. The programmer who writes the **operator=()** must be sure to properly clean up the left side before performing the assignment activities.

In draft-ANSI C++, the programmer may still take over the duties of copy initialization and assignment by writing **X(X&)** and **operator=()**. As before, those who do so are completely responsible for the activities during copy initialization and assignment, since the default activity (bitwise copy before 2.0) is disabled when these functions are defined. Draft-ANSI C++ has an improvement when the programmer doesn't define either **X(X&)** or **operator=()**. Instead of the previous bitwise copy, C++ automatically generates a copy initializer (if you didn't define one) and an **operator=()** (if you didn't define one) that use *memberwise initialization* and *memberwise assignment*, respectively. Memberwise initialization calls the copy constructors for each member object in a class. If a member object contains member objects, the copy constructors for those objects are called, and so on. Memberwise assignment calls the **operator=()** functions for each member object in a class. If a member object contains member objects, their **operator=()** functions are called, and so on. These activities more closely match "the right thing to do" when the programmer doesn't define a copy constructor or **operator=()**, and removes a lot of confusion from new C++ programmers.

Note that if any version of the copy constructor has been defined, the compiler will not generate a default copy constructor. If any version of the **operator=()** has been defined, the compiler will not generate a default assignment operator. This is true even if the version doesn't solve your particular problem.

Creating Your Own Type-Conversion Operators

C++ gives you the ability to make a user-defined type look and act almost exactly like a built-in type. This extends to casting—you can define a casting operator so your new type can be converted to some other type, either built-in or user-defined. When the compiler sees your type being used where the other type is required (and it has no way to use your type directly), it quietly calls your casting operator. Here's an example:

```
//: CASTING.CPP—Type conversion for user-defined types

class number {
  float f;
public:
  number(float x = 0.0) { f = x; }
  operator int() {  // return value established by function name
    return (int)f;
  }
};

class number2 {
  int i;
public:
  number2(int x = 0) { i = x; }
  operator number() {  // cast to another user-defined type
    return number((float)i);
  }
};
```

```
void brian(number X) {}

void main() {
  number n(9.7);
  number2 n2(25);
  int x = n;  // implicit call to number::operator int()
  n = n2; // implicit call to number2::operator number()
  brian(n2); // implicit call to number2::operator number()
}
```

Here, two possible implicit type conversions are specified. In **class number**, **operator int()** is a way to make an **int** from a **number**. Note that you don't need to designate the return value on a type-conversion operator—the name of the operator is the same as the return value. In **class number2**, **operator number()** is a way to make a **number** from a **number2**. The statement

```
int x = n;
```

causes the compiler to call the first type-conversion operator, and the statement

```
n = n2;
```

causes the compiler to call the second type-conversion operator.

In the preceding listing, the conversion is performed by calling a function in the argument's class. You can also make the destination class perform the type conversion by creating constructors that take a single argument which is the other user-defined type. The source class must either give explicit access privileges to the destination class (by declaring the destination class constructor to be a friend) or provide adequate access functions so the destination object's constructor can read the necessary data. Both of these alternatives are shown in the following example:

```
//: CONSTCNV.CPP—Single-argument constructors to perform
//. type conversion. Two different alternatives are shown
//. to allow the destination object access to the source
//. object's private data.
class micah;  // declare the class

class shani {
  float f1, f2;
```

```
public:
  shani(float x1 = 0.0, float x2 = 0.0) {
    f1 = x1;   f2 = x2;
  }
  shani(micah &);   // type-conversion constructor
  float f_one() { return f1; }  // access functions
  float f_two() { return f2; }
};

class micah {   // define the class
  int i1, i2;
public:
  micah(int y1 = 0, int y2 = 0) {
    i1 = y1;   i2 = y2;
  }
  micah(shani &);   // type-conversion constructor
  friend shani::shani(micah &);   // allow access to private data
};

// This constructor has permission to read the private data in
// micah, since it's a friend function:
shani::shani(micah & m) {
  f1 = m.i1;  // implicit (float) cast
  f2 = m.i2;
}


// This constructor uses the access functions in shani to read
// the private data. It isn't a friend, so it must get the data
// some other way than by directly reading the elements:
micah::micah(shani & s) {
  i1 = (int)s.f_one();
  i2 = (int)s.f_two();
}

void function1(shani s) {}
void function2(micah m) {}

void main() {
  shani S;
  micah M;
  M = S;  // micah::micah(shani &) called
  S = M;  // shani::shani(micah &) called
  function1(M);   // shani::shani(micah &) called
  function2(S);   // micah::micah(shani &) called
}
```

Here you see a class name declaration at the beginning of the file. Since **shani** uses **micah** in the argument list for the type-conversion constructor, the compiler must know that **micah** is a legal class name. The **class shani** has the access functions **f_one()** and **f_two()** that provide the constructor **micah::micah(shani &)** with enough information to make a **micah** from a **shani**. However, **class micah** does not contain these access functions. For the constructor **shani::shani(micah &)** to have enough information to make a **shani** from a **micah**, it must be given **friend** status in **micah** so it can access **private** data in **micah**.

Choosing Between Casting Operators and Constructor Conversion

As you can see from the two examples, the compiler doesn't seem to care whether you've defined a casting operator or a constructor to perform the type conversion—if a conversion path exists, it will perform the implicit type conversion whenever it can. So, how do you decide which form of type conversion to use?

The compiler sees them both the same way—as a function to call implicitly to perform the type conversion when the need arises. The decision about which one to use is often made for you—if you own the class that needs to be converted, you can write a casting operator for it. If you don't own it and you can extract enough information, you can write a type-conversion constructor for the destination class. Also, you must use the casting operator when converting a user-defined type to a built-in type, since you can't define a constructor for a built-in type.

It is important that you don't use both a constructor and a casting operator for the same type conversion, since this introduces an ambiguity as to how the conversion should be performed. The compiler generates an error message if you try to do both.

Dangers of Too Much Type Conversion

Automatic type conversion is very convenient and can greatly reduce the number of function definitions you need to write. For example, with no automatic type conversions you must have two overloaded versions of **Daniel()** here:

```
void Daniel(book);
void Daniel(play);
```

However, if there is a type conversion function **book::operator play()** or **play::play(book)**, you only need the single version of **Daniel()**:

```
void Daniel(play);
```

Now if you call **Daniel()** with a **play**, the function matches exactly, and if you use a **book** as an argument, the compiler automatically converts it to a **play**.

Because it saves work and makes life more convenient, you might be tempted to go a bit wild with automatic type conversion operators. This can get you in trouble in two ways:

First, if you have two ways to perform the same type conversion, the compiler cannot resolve the ambiguity. The following program uses two ways to get from **lucy** to **ricky**.

```
//: DUALCONV.CPP—Two ways to perform the same type conversion
//. The translator should generate an error message.

// declare the class so ricky can use the name:
class lucy;

class ricky {
  double straight;
public:
  ricky(double f = 0.0) { straight = f; }
  ricky(lucy);  // type conversion from lucy to ricky
};

class lucy {
  double whacky;
public:
  lucy(double f = 0.0) { whacky = f; }
  // a second way to convert lucy to ricky:
  operator ricky() { return ricky(whacky); }
};

void ethel(ricky) {}

void main() {
  lucy L;
```

```
  ethel(L);  // which implicit type conversion is used?
}
```

The compiler should generate an error message. This type of problem is straightforward, since you get an error message the instant you try to create the second form of type conversion in the new **class**.

Second, a more insidious problem occurs when you can convert to more than one type from a single class. If an overloaded function can take more than one argument that has an automatic type conversion, you'll have trouble. Here's an example:

```
//: AMBIG.CPP—Too much automatic type conversion
//. causes ambiguity

class ricky;
class lucy;

class fred {
  short bald;
public:
  fred(int i = 0) { bald = i; }
  operator ricky();
  operator lucy();
};

void ethel(ricky);
void ethel(lucy);

void main() {
  fred F;
  ethel(F);  // should we make a ricky or a lucy from a fred?
}
```

The design problem here is that you don't see the difficulty right away. The class works fine until some poor unfortunate overloads a function to take arguments of both **ricky** and **lucy**. The problem is compounded because the user might not own the original code and thus might have no control over the situation.

If the designer of the class doesn't exercise restraint when creating implicit type conversions, the user can get stuck with the results. The only way to repair the problem is for the user to modify the header file—by commenting out the undesirable automatic type conversion, the remaining conversion becomes unambiguous. Modifying the header file when you don't own the source code is risky, and should only be undertaken after you know it won't damage the rest of the system.

Design Guidelines for Type Conversion

R.B. Murray has suggested guidelines for type conversion.

First, don't create more than one implicit type conversion from each user-defined type unless you absolutely must. This will eliminate the problem shown in the preceding listing (AMBIG.CPP).

This doesn't mean you are limited to the number of types you can convert to. It just means that only one conversion should be allowed implicitly. Here's an example that shows multiple conversions with only a single implicit conversion:

```
//: MULTCONV.CPP—Multiple type conversions, but only a single
//. implicit conversion. This design of this class will prevent
//. future problems.

class craig;
class charles;
class john;

class todd {
  long i;
public:
  todd(int x = 0) { i = x; }
  operator craig();  // single implicit type conversion.
  // The rest of the conversion functions cannot be called
  // secretly by the compiler; they must be called explicitly
  // by the user:
  charles To_charles();  // make a charles from a todd
  john To_john();        // make a john from a todd
};
```

Second, a conversion operator should always take a more complex type and generate a simpler type. If a type is a logical extension of another type, the conversion operator should take the extension and create the simpler type from it. Since extensions usually proliferate from simpler types, choosing to go from the simpler type to one particular extension may cause trouble if you want to treat all the extensions in a similar fashion in a later application. The following example shows the proper "direction" for conversion operators:

```
//: SIMPLIFY.CPP—Conversion operators should always simplify
//. more complex types.
#include <iostream.h>

class price {
  unsigned long base;      // in pennies
  unsigned long sales_tax;
public:
  void set_base(unsigned long b) { base = b;}
  void set_tax(unsigned long st) { sales_tax = st; }
  void print(char * msg = "") {
    if(*msg) cout << msg << ": " << endl;
    cout << "price = $ " << base/100 << "." << base%100 << endl;
    cout << "tax = $ " << sales_tax/100 << "."
         <<   sales_tax % 100 << endl;
    cout << "total = $ " << (base + sales_tax)/100
         << "." <<   (base + sales_tax)%100 << endl;
  }
  unsigned long base_price() {return base;} // access functions
  unsigned long tax() {return sales_tax;}
};

class non_deductible {
  char * name;
  price cost;
public:
  non_deductible(char * nm, unsigned long p, unsigned long st) {
    name = nm;  // OK if using a constant character string
    cost.set_base(p);  // there's an easier design for this type
    cost.set_tax(st);  // of programming. See Chapter 7.
  }
  void print() {
    cout << "non_deductible, ";
    cost.print(name);
  }
  // Automatic type conversion from more complicated type to
  // simpler type:
  operator price() { return cost; }
};

class deductible {
  char * name;
  char * category;
```

```cpp
    int percent_deductible;
    price cost;
public:
  deductible(char * nm, char * ct, unsigned long p,
      unsigned long st, int percent) {
    name = nm;
    category = ct;
    cost.set_base(p);
    cost.set_tax(st);
    percent_deductible = percent;
  }
  void print() {
    cout << "deductible category " << category << ", ";
    cost.print(name);
    cout << "percent deductible: "
        << percent_deductible << endl;
  }
  // Automatic type conversion from more complicated type to
  // simpler type:
  operator price() { return cost; }
};

// and finally, a class to add up all the prices:
class price_total {
  unsigned long sum;
public:
  price_total() { sum = 0; }
  void print() {
    cout << "total is: $ " << sum/100 << "." << sum%100 << endl;
  }
  void add(price p) {
    sum += p.base_price();
    sum += p.tax();
  }
};

void main() {
  non_deductible Refrigerator("Refrigerator", 74595, 5623);
  deductible stamps("Stamps", "postage", 24000, 0, 100);
  deductible mag1("DDJ", "publications", 2000, 0, 100);
  deductible mag2("C Gazette", "publications", 1800, 0, 100);
  non_deductible Dinner("Food", 2253, 180);
  price_total total;
  total.print();
  Refrigerator.print();
  total.add(Refrigerator);
  total.print();
```

```
    stamps.print();
    total.add(stamps);
    total.print();
    mag1.print();
    total.add(mag1);
    total.print();
    mag2.print();
    total.add(mag2);
    total.print();
    Dinner.print();
    total.add(Dinner);
    total.print();
}
```

Here both the **non_deductible** and **deductible** classes have implicit type-conversion operators to produce the simpler type **price**. **Class price_total** has a method called **add()**, which takes as an argument a **price**. Because of the implicit type-conversion operators, you can **add()** both **deductible** and **non_deductible** objects without the necessity of overloading **add()**.

Third, it is acceptable to provide mutual conversions between two classes. Not all classes are logical extensions. Murray gives the example that the numbers represented by **double** includes all numbers in a class called **rational**, so mutual conversion between **double** and **rational** makes sense. A function overloaded to take either a **double** or a **rational** will match either argument exactly; if the function only takes one type of argument, the type conversion will be called automatically for the other type of argument. Thus there is no ambiguity with mutual conversions.

Finally, don't use implicit type conversion unless it's necessary. If implicit type conversion is used arbitrarily, it can cause problems for future users of your class.

Example: Creating Your Own iostream Functions

One of the most immediately useful applications for overloading is the creation of iostream output functions for your user-defined type. Then you can say the following,

```
MyType X;
cout << X;
```

which works very nicely, especially when you are debugging.

The **operator<<()** has already been overloaded for the **iostream** class, but you can easily overload it for your new class. The following example is a vector of X-Y pairs with both a stream input function and a stream output function:

```
//: XYVEC.H—Vector of X-Y pairs with stream output function
#ifndef XYVEC_H_
#define XYVEC_H_
#include <iostream.h>

const size = 20;

class XYvec {
  float X[size];
  float Y[size];
  void error(char * msg);
public:
  XYvec(float xinit = 0, float xstep = 0,
        float yinit = 0, float ystep = 0);
  // modify values by overloading the function call operator:
  void operator()(int index, float xval, float yval);
  // Stream input and output:
  friend ostream& operator<<(ostream& s, XYvec& v);
  friend istream& operator>>(istream& s, XYvec& v);
};
#endif // XYVEC_H_
```

You'll notice that the header file **xyvec.h** must include the **iostream.h** header file because of the declarations for **operator<<()** and **operator>>()**. The **xinit** and **xstep** in the constructor are initialization and step values. The first element in the X vector is set to the initialization value, the second is set to the first value plus the step value, etc. The same is true for **yinit** and **ystep** for the Y vector.

Here are the methods for **XYvec**:

```
//: XYVEC.CPP—Methods for X-Y pair vector
#include "xyvec.h"
#include <stdlib.h>

void XYvec::error(char * msg) {
```

```
  cerr << "XYvec error: " << msg << endl;
  exit(1);
}

XYvec::XYvec(float xinit, float xstep,
             float yinit,float ystep) {
  for(int i = 0; i < size; i++) {
    X[i] = xinit + i * xstep;
    Y[i] = yinit + i * ystep;
  }
}

void XYvec::operator()(int index, float xval, float yval) {
  if(index < 0 || index >= size)
    error("index out of range");
  X[index] = xval;
  Y[index] = yval;
}

ostream& operator<<(ostream& s, XYvec& v) {
  s << "\t   X\t\t   Y" << endl;
  s.precision(6);
  for(int i = 0; i < size; i++)
    s << "\t" << v.X[i] << "\t" <<  v.Y[i] << endl;
  return s;
}

istream& operator>>(istream& s, XYvec& v) {
  float val;
  int index = 0;
  while(!s.bad() && !s.eof()) {
    s >> val;
    v.X[index] = val;
    if(s.bad() || s.eof()) break;
    s >> val;
    v.Y[index++] = val;
    if(index == size) break;
  }
  return s;
}
```

The function-call **operator()** is useful as the only operator that can take an arbitrary number of arguments. In this case it is overloaded to allow you to set the X-Y values of a particular pair.

Because of the design of iostreams, an overloaded **operator<<()** or **operator>>()** must be a global **friend** function, and it must take arguments of an iostream object (either **istream** or **ostream**, depending on the operator) followed by an object of your user-defined type. The function must return the same stream object it takes as an argument. It is important that the stream object be passed into and out of the function, so you can have expressions of the form:

```
cout << "arg1: " << arg1 << "arg2" << arg2; // etc...
```

In effect, each argument is added to the stream, and then the stream is passed down the line.

Here is a small program to test **class XYvec**:

```
//: XYTEST.CPP—Test program for class XYvec
#include "xyvec.h"

void main() {
  XYvec A(3.14, 0.47, 2.59, .939);
  A(4, 77.77, 111.9);  // change pair #4
  cout << "A =" << A << endl;  // print it
  XYvec B;
  cin >> B;
  cout << "B =" << B << endl;
}
```

To test the input function, redirect the output to a file, edit the first two lines out of the file, run the program, and redirect the file as input.

Selecting Friend or Member Functions for Operator Overloading

In many situations you get equivalent results by using either a friend function or a member function when you overload an operator. A friend function simply contains an extra argument (the friend function must have both objects passed to it, while the member function only needs a single argument). Why are both alternatives available? If you use a member function and an argument of a different type, the member function only allows the new type to be on the right side of the operator.

That is, **A + 2** may be legal, but **2 + A** is not. A friend function allows both combinations. These variations are shown in the following example:

```
//: FRIEND.CPP—Why everybody need friends

class integer {
  int i;
public:
  // notice there's no constructor with a single int
  // argument, so no implicit type conversion can
  // happen from int to integer.
  void set(int ii = 0) { i = ii; }
  // operator overloading with a member functions:
  integer operator+(int);
  integer operator+(integer);
};

integer integer::operator+(int x) {
  // tedious without a constructor:
  integer result;
  result.set(i + x);
  return result;
}

integer integer::operator+(integer x) {
  integer result;
  result.set(i + x.i);
  return result;
}

class integer2 {
  int i;
public:
  void set(int ii = 0) { i = ii; }
  // operator overloading with a friend functions. Note
  // you need a function for each possible combination:
  friend integer2 operator+(integer2, integer2);
  friend integer2 operator+(integer2, int);
  friend integer2 operator+(int, integer2);
};

integer2 operator+(integer2 x, integer2 y) {
  integer2 result;
  result.set(x.i + y.i);
  return result;
}
```

```
integer2 operator+(integer2 x, int a) {
  integer2 result;
  result.set(x.i + a);
  return result;
}

integer2 operator+(int a, integer2 x) {
  integer2 result;
  result.set(x.i + a);
  return result;
}

void main() {
  integer A; A.set(10);
  integer B;
  integer C; C.set(20);
  B = A + 4;  // This is legal for class integer
  B = A + C;  // This is legal for class integer
// B = 4 + A;  // This isn't legal for class integer
  integer2 D; D.set(100);
  integer2 E;
  integer2 F; F.set(200);
  E = D + 40;  // This is legal for class integer2
  E = D + F;  // This is legal for class integer2
  E = 40 + D;  // This is also legal for integer2
}
```

In **class integer**, there are two overloaded versions of **operator+()**: one that takes an **int** argument and one that takes an **integer** argument. This, as demonstrated in **main()**, means that you can add an **integer** to an **int**, and an **integer** to an **integer**, but you can't add an **int** to an **integer**.

In **class integer2**, the **operator+()** is defined as **friend**. This means that **integer2** allows the combination that **integer** wouldn't: an **int** plus an **integer2**. Thus, a **friend** function allows a more natural syntax.

In the prededing example, you can see how tedious it gets when you have to redefine the same function **operator+(integer2, int)** and **operator+(int, integer2)**. Implicit type conversion can eliminate both definitions, as shown in this example:

```
//: SUCCINCT.CPP—Implicit type conversion can eliminate
//. repetitive coding.
```

```
class integer3 {
  int i;
public:
  // by creating a constructor that takes an int, the
  // translator can perform implicit type conversion...
  integer3(int ii = 0) { i = ii; }
  // ...so only one operator+() definition is required:
  friend integer3 operator+(integer3, integer3);
};

integer3 operator+(integer3 x, integer3 y) {
  return integer3(x.i + y.i);
}

void main() {
  integer3 A(10), B(20), C;
  C = A + B;  // legal
  C = A + 4;  // also legal
  C = 4 + A;  // also legal
}
```

To summarize: use a member function for notational convenience if you have no other compelling needs. Also use a member function if you want to force a particular syntax (using a member function **operator=(int)** prevents the user from saying **1 = A**). If your syntax requires that the arguments be order independent, use a **friend** (and, possibly, an implicit type conversion operator to reduce coding).

Function Overloading

Operator overloading is only one example of the general idea of function overloading. Function overloading means you can create many different functions, all with the same name but with different argument lists.

The most common type of function overloading is seen in class constructors: more than one constructor is usually required for a class to handle different types of initialization. Inside a class, function overloading happens automatically; the programmer doesn't need to do anything except define more than one function with the same name. For example:

```
//: WIDGET.CPP—Member functions are automatically, safely
//. overloaded.

class widget {
  int i;
public:
  widget() { i = 0; }
  widget(int j) { i = j; }
  widget(double d) { i = (int)d; }
};
```

Here we see the constructor for **widget** has been automatically overloaded.

Functions that aren't associated with a class (nonmember functions) may also be overloaded. The compiler automatically "mangles" the names so there is no conflict. Here's an example:

```
//: FROB.CPP—Nonmember function overloading
int frob(int);  // overload declarations
double frob(int, int);
void frob();

void main () {
  frob(1);
  frob(1,2);
  frob();
}
```

In an early version of the language, you had to tell the compiler that a function was about to be overloaded by using the **overload** keyword. Although you may see this keyword used in old code, it is obsolete, and you should never use it.

A compiler can differentiate one overloaded function call from another by the function arguments. However, the linker just sees a name, not an accompanying argument list, so the name of an overloaded function with one argument list must be different than the function with a different argument list. So the linker can differentiate between one type of overloaded function and another, the compiler "mangles" the names: it adds characters to the names. These additional characters contain information about the argument types of the functions, so the internal representations of two functions with the same name are different if they have different argument lists. In addition, class member functions have the name of the class mangled in (which effects class member scoping). If you want to see how this works for your particular compiler (there is no standard for name mangling), you can compile the file with a flag set to generate assembly code, and then look at the names used for the assembler.

Taking the Address of an Overloaded Function

Attempting to take the address of an overloaded function introduces an ambiguity, because there is more than one function for the compiler to choose from. This ambiguity must be resolved by specifying the argument types of the function pointer that will receive the address of the overloaded function. For example:

```
void foo(int);
void foo(float);
void (*foo_ptr_int)(int) = foo;
void (*foo_ptr_float)(float) = foo;
```

Type-Safe Linkage

In AT&T C++ releases 1.2 and earlier, the scheme for function mangling was different. So the C++ code could call plain C functions without any problems, nonoverloaded functions were just turned into plain C names. When a function was overloaded, the first name was turned into a plain C name, and only the subsequent names were mangled.

This design caused trouble when declarations were mixed around. If you have a plain C **frob** (in a separate C file) and two C++ **frob**s, it is very important which **frob** was declared first, since it was the one turned into the plain C name. For example, if **int frob(int)** was the plain C name and you had some other file and declared **void frob()** first, the linker would quietly cause the plain C **frob** to be called for **int frob(int)** calls in the first file, while calling it for **void frob()** in the second file. As you can imagine, this caused some pretty subtle bugs.

The real trouble occurred with header files. If you overloaded a function name declared in two separate header files and you switched the order of inclusion of the header files in various definition files, the name mangling happened differently. This was a particular problem when overloading a library function like **sin()** for a user-defined type. If the header containing your declaration came first, the C library **sin()** function was mangled, which wasn't what you wanted at all.

All current C++ compilers solve the problem using an approach called *type-safe linkage*. Type-safe linkage mangles all names. It uses a consistent algorithm depending only on the arguments, so it won't matter what order the functions are declared. To allow plain C naming (so you can call external C functions) C++ contains an escape mechanism based upon an extension of the meaning of the **extern** keyword. If you follow the keyword by a character string describing the type of linkage you desire, the compile will alter the way it creates names. The two types of linkage that must be supported by a C++ compiler are "C" and "C++" (although the latter is not often used). If you want to declare a single function using C linkage, you say:

```
extern "C" void foo(int);
```

If you want to include an entire header file using C linkage, you put it in braces, like this:

```
extern "C" {
#include "myfile.h"
#include <sysfile.h>
}
```

The alternate linkage specification applies to everything within the braces.

Generally, header files that are intended to be included in both C and C++ files are already modified to provide C linkage, but in many cases you will have to do it yourself.
The declaration of objects in other files can also be modified, but the effect is implementation and language dependent. For example,

```
extern "C" {
  special_buf foo[10];
}
```

gives **foo** C linkage.

Makefile for Chapter 5 Examples

Here is the **makefile** for all the examples in this chapter:

```
# maketile for examples in Chapter 5
# Borland C++ compiler, with the following
# warnings turned off:
# aus: identifier assigned a value which is never used
# par: parameter "parameter" is never used
# inl: function not expanded inline
CPP = bcc -w-aus -w-par -w-inl
# nmake CPP=cl    # Microsoft C++ command line

.cpp.exe:
        $(CPP) $<

.cpp.obj:
        $(CPP) -c $*.cpp

all:    this.exe vectest.exe casting.exe \
        constcnv.exe multconv.obj simplify.exe \
        xytest.exe friend.exe succinct.exe widget.obj frob.obj \
        dualconv.exe pointtst.exe bsimple.exe brackets.exe \
        crispy.exe smart.exe

errors: ambig.exe

vectest.exe : vectest.obj vector.obj
        $(CPP) $**

pointtst.exe : pointtst.obj point.obj
        $(CPP) $**

xytest.exe : xytest.obj xyvec.obj
        $(CPP) $**

vectest.obj : vector.h vectest.cpp
vector.obj : vector.h vector.cpp
point.obj : point.cpp point.h
pointtst.obj : pointtst.cpp point.h
xyvec.obj : xyvec.cpp xyvec.h
xytest.obj : xytest.cpp xyvec.h
```

CHAPTER

Creating Objects at Run Time

*O*ne of the most important ways modern humans interact with their environment is through language. Not only does language give people tools to interact, it shapes those interactions and even the thoughts behind the interactions. If you understand the limitations of your language, you can understand some of the limitations in your thinking and creativity.

Many popular computer languages have built-in biases toward particular ways of thinking, design, and programming. Since these languages are often learned first, new programmers close down the scope of their creativity and think in terms of "the correct way." As a result, there are entire classes of problems they are unable to solve.

The bias that will be examined here can be broadly cast as the idea that *you always know all the facts when you write the program.* As you will see in later chapters, this bias actually extends to program design *(you always know all the problems the program must solve when you design it),* but this chapter will focus on the way variables are treated in other languages, how that affects your programming, and the improvements in C++ that free the way you think about certain types of problems.

The Bias of Some Popular Languages

Many popular languages, such as FORTRAN, Pascal, and C, lean toward the idea that you always know how many variables you will need when the program is running, and when they will be created and destroyed (their scope). When you encounter a problem that relies on some other constraint to determine how many variables you need and when they will be created and destroyed, you either can't solve the problem or you solve it the hard way and end up with an inflexible design.

For example, consider the game of *Life*. Life is a computer simulation that models the population patterns of a simple creature that lives on a two-dimensional grid. The rules for the creature's existence are very simple. If there are a certain number of adjacent creatures to an empty spot on the grid, a new creature is born. If a creature has too many neighbors, or too few neighbors, it dies. By changing the initial conditions and the rules, you can generate all sorts of fascinating patterns.

In the Life simulation, objects are constantly appearing and disappearing. The quantity and lifetime of the objects are not dictated by some fixed design inside the computer program. Instead, they depend on the number of other objects around the object. This is an example of a simulation problem. Most simulation problems are much more complicated than Life. While Life has been programmed in many languages, a "real" simulation problem is much more manageable when written in an object-oriented language. In fact, the first OOP language (Simula, developed in 1967) was created to ease the task of building simulations.

As another example of a situation when you don't know the number or lifetime of variables, consider a computer-aided design system. Here, the number of shapes and how long the shapes remain on the screen is up to the user.

You can see that the arbitrary restriction of knowing the quantity, point of creation, and lifetime of an object excludes a lot of interesting problems. The fact that you might have learned to think in a particular way because of your programming language prevents you from even conceiving of some very interesting solutions.

To be fair, C and Pascal *do* have a method to create space for variables at run time (FORTRAN, however, has none). This feature is called *dynamic memory allocation*, and it allows the programmer to grab chunks of memory to be used as variables. As you will see, the support for creating variables at run time in C++ is much more complete; creating an object at run time is as easy as creating one at compile time.

Languages like LISP and Smalltalk take the opposite approach. In these languages, *all* variables are created dynamically—when you need a variable, you just create it; when you're done with it you just "let it go." The lifetimes of these variables are not determined by normal scoping rules. Since variables are not destroyed based on their scope, they can proliferate to the point of filling up memory. When the memory is full, these languages run a *garbage-collection routine* to free the space occupied by unused variables. Languages with garbage collectors free the programmer from concerns about the lifetime of a variable, which is good. They are limited, however, in the kinds of problems they can solve—you wouldn't want a critical real-time process interrupted because the system just happened to run out of memory at that point.

Dynamic Object Creation

C++ takes the middle ground between languages that support dynamic memory allocation and languages in which all variables are dynamically allocated. In this book, the C++ approach will be called *dynamic object creation*. While C++ supports objects with scoped lifetimes (*stack-based objects*), it also supports objects with arbitrary lifetimes (*heap-based objects*). C++ is different than Pascal or C because it doesn't just allocate memory for an object, it *initializes* the object. Thus, when you use dynamic object creation in C++, you get back a live, initialized object, not just a chunk of memory big enough to hold an object. (When you dynamically allocate a built-in type, however, no initialization is performed, so the traditional term "dynamic memory allocation" will still be used when built-in types are involved.)

Because C++ supports both objects with scoped lifetimes and objects with arbitrary lifetimes, you are forced to know more about what is going on in a program and to choose between stack-based and heap-based objects. This language design decision is often considered repugnant to users of more "pure" object-oriented languages (ones that contain garbage collectors). As you will see, however, it gives you the choice of optimizing your program for speed and real-time applications if you want. If you don't need a garbage collector or if it would make your application unusable, you aren't automatically saddled with a garbage collector. If you want to create an application that works best with garbage collection, you can build a garbage collector for objects of specific types (thus retaining efficiency everywhere else).

To understand dynamic object creation, you need some background.

The Stack

When you define an object at compile time by saying,

```
void Fogg() {
  int obj = 100;
  // ...
}
```

the compiler generates code that moves the stack pointer down to create enough space on the stack for an **int** and to put the integer value 100 in that space. Whenever the variable **obj** is used, code is generated to find that slot on the stack. Note that all storage for a particular scope is allocated at the opening brace of that scope, even if the variables are not defined until much later.

This activity takes place any time **Fogg()** is called. Thus, the memory is always created when the function is called, regardless of where the stack pointer is at the time. Functions in C and C++ that only use local variables do not depend on the state of the program when the function is called, so they may be called at any time. Because of this, functions in C and C++ that only use local variables are said to be *reentrant*—you can call them any time, even in the middle of a call to the same function.

C and C++ also support *recursive* functions. You can design a function that calls itself. For example:

```
//: DAVE.CPP—A recursive function
#include <iostream.h>

const stupid = 100;

void Dave(int pun) {
  if (pun != stupid)
    Dave(++pun);
  else
    cout << "stop! " << pun << " puns is enough!" << endl;
}

void main() {
  Dave(0);
}
```

A more useful example is the recursive scanner shown in the TAWK example in Chapter 11.

When a scope closes (with a)), the compiler generates code to move the stack pointer up past all the local variables that have been created. Thus, when a local variable goes out of scope, the memory for it is automatically freed. In C++, the destructor is called (if one exists) before the stack pointer is moved. C++ does more than just free the space occupied by the variable, it cleans up the variable.

The Free Store

You can think of the stack pointer as moving down from the top of the memory available for use by the program (although the actual direction depends on your implementation, and whether you are standing on your head). When a function is called that has local variables, the stack pointer moves down (actually, the return address is also stored on the stack when a call is executed, so the pointer always moves down for a function call).

At the "other end" of the memory set aside for your program is the *free store*, also called the *heap*. When you request a chunk of memory, it comes from the free store, and when you release a chunk of memory it returns to the free store.

In ANSI C, library functions **malloc()**, **calloc()**, and **realloc()** are used to allocate free store, and **free()** is used to release the allocated memory back to the free store. In Pascal, the predefined subprograms **new()** and **dispose()** manage the free store.

In C++ the concept of dynamic memory allocation has been extended and built into the core of the language. Not only do the C++ keywords **new** and **delete** allocate and deallocate free store, but creating an object with **new** also calls the constructor, and destroying an object with **delete** also calls the destructor. Thus, calling **new** is almost exactly like creating a local variable, and calling **delete** is almost exactly the same as when the local variable goes out of scope. This is the reason the term "dynamic object creation" was chosen rather than "dynamic memory allocation." A lot more is going on than just memory allocation.

You might have noticed the phrase "almost exactly" in the last paragraph. Where is the difference? The **new** and **delete** keywords handle pointers, rather than the objects themselves—**new** returns a pointer to the initialized object, and **delete** takes a pointer to an object that was previously created on the free store using **new**. Other than the fact that you are manipulating an address instead of an entire object, you can treat objects created on the free store just like they were local variables. Here's an example comparing a local object to one created on the free store. The example uses a class called **tracker** that shows you when constructors and destructors are called:

```
//: TRACKER.H—A Class to track construction & destruction
#ifndef TRACKER_H_
```

```
#define TRACKER_H_
#include <iostream.h>

class tracker {
  int i;
public:
  tracker(int x = 0) {
    cout << "constructor called with argument " << x << endl;
    i = x;
  }
  ~tracker() {
    cout << "destructor called for object w/ i = " << i << endl;
  }
  void print() {
    cout << "tracker::print(); i = " << i << endl;
  }
};
#endif // TRACKER_H_
```

Now you can create objects either on the stack (as local variables) or on the free store, for example:

```
//: FREESTOR.CPP—Local objects vs. Dynamic Object Creation
#include "tracker.h"

void Toni() {
  tracker local(10);  // create a local object
  tracker * free = new tracker(20); // free store object
  local.print(); // calling a member function for a variable
  free->print(); // calling a member function for a pointer
}

void main() {
  Toni();
}

// Notice the destructor is called only once, for the local
// object!  The pointer "free" goes out of scope, but the
// object it points to is still valid!
```

When you create an object using **new**, you give the class name followed by an argument list containing the constructor arguments (if there are no arguments, you can leave off the list). Storage is allocated on the heap and then the constructor is called for that storage using the arguments in the list. It's very straightforward.

It is very important to notice that the destructor is only called automatically for the stack-based object as it goes out of scope. Remember that *you* are responsible for destroying any objects you create on the free store. If you don't destroy them, the pointer may go out of scope (as it does above, when **Toni()** ends), but the object hangs around on the free store. This is the worst situation—the object is there, but you can't get to it since the pointer has gone out of scope, so you can't destroy it. It's important that you destroy an object before you lose track of it, as in this example:

```
//: DELETE.CPP—How to destroy an object on the free store
#include "tracker.h"

void f() {
  tracker * free = new tracker(20);
  free->print(); // calling a member function for a pointer
  delete free; // delete must be handed the starting address
            // of the object created by "new."
}

void main() {
  f();
}
```

Life: A Framework for Simulation and Modeling

Many systems that simulate or model real-world processes require that information units representing elements of the process be created and destroyed at run time. The creation and destruction of these units is governed by a criterion that relates directly to the process, rather than scopes in the source code. Dynamic object creation in C++ is ideal for solving these kinds of problems.

This section presents a version of the famous Life program, but with a new twist. Because it is designed and implemented in an object-oriented manner, it is very easy for you to change the rules for the simulation. For example, you might want to endow each element (called a **LifeUnit** in the program) with a life span, so a **LifeUnit** that is too young or too old cannot bear children. You could allow a **LifeUnit** to be mobile, or groups of

LifeUnits to band together into tribes. Because the main system simply asks a **LifeUnit** if it will live to the next generation, the "rule" for Life is focused in one place and can easily be changed. You can also add new kinds of rules: whether a **LifeUnit** will move, catch the bubonic plague, win a million dollars, get married, buy a dog, and so on. The rules can be tested at various times in the life span ("**LifeUnit** fails driver's license test"), or for various other reasons ("**LifeUnit** overfeeds goldfish. **LifeUnit** flushes goldfish and buys hamster."). Because of the object-oriented nature of the design, you aren't limited when you want to extend the simulation.

There is nothing particularly sacred or inspired about the way this program was designed. It is an approach that seems to work, but it may have some limitations for the particular type of system you want to model. For example, your idea of a **LifeUnit** may be much broader: you might want to model other animals as well as man, and limit their activities according to what type of animal they are ("a dog cannot buy a newspaper"). For this kind of problem you will want to use inheritance and *virtual* functions (see Chapters 7 and 8), so both people and dogs will be inherited from **LifeUnit**, and they will have some things in common but different other abilities. While you may need to change the design to fit your problem, you will benefit by studying it.

To maximize portability between systems, the program uses the ANSI terminal escape sequences to move the cursor. While this works, it slows the display. You might want to customize the display code (isolated in the **LifeUnit** functions **draw()** and **erase()**) to use whatever high-speed library functions your local platform provides.

While reading the code, you will notice that the variable names are different than you've seen so far in this book. For this example, the Smalltalk naming convention is used, so you can see the difference. Smalltalk variable names do not include underscores, so Smalltalk programmers often simply run the words together, capitalizing the first letter in each word.

A Class to Represent a Single Living Entity

There are two classes in the Life program. The **LifeUnit** class represents an individual entity, and the **LifeField** is a two-dimensional array where all the **LifeUnit**s live. Each **LifeUnit** knows the **LifeField** where it lives and its location in the field, so if you ask a **LifeUnit** whether it will live into the next generation, it can look around to see how many neighbors it will have. A **LifeUnit** can **draw()** and **erase()** itself, and you can ask it if it will be **Alive()** in the next generation.

The header file for the **LifeUnit** class, shown here, also declares a nonmember function **Fertile()** that is used with the address of an empty cell to see if a new **LifeUnit** will appear in the next generation.

```
//: LIFEUNIT.H—An object for the "Life" simulation
#ifndef LIFEUNIT_H_
#define LIFEUNIT_H_
#include <iostream.h>

// Character to indicate a LifeUnit is alive:
const char LifeChar = 'X';

// A happy face on the PC:
// const char LifeChar = '\x01';

class LifeField;  // forward declaration

class LifeUnit {
  // A LifeUnit knows what grid it lives on, and its location:
  LifeField * LF;
  int LRow, LCol;  // location of unit on screen
public:
  void draw() {
    // ANSI Terminal control Commands to put special character
    // at the coordinates. a '\x1b' in a string produces an
    // "escape."  The \x precedes a hexadecimal number.
    cout << "\x1b[" << LRow << ";" << LCol << "H" << LifeChar;
  }
  void erase() {
    // Put a space where the X was:
    cout << "\x1b[" << LRow << ";" << LCol << "H ";
  }
  LifeUnit(int Row_loc, int Col_loc, LifeField * L) {
    LRow = Row_loc;  LCol = Col_loc;
    LF = L;  // Remember what grid you live on!
    draw();
  }
  // Clean things up before the object goes away:
  ~LifeUnit() { erase(); }
  // See if all the conditions are fullfilled so you can live
  // through the next lifecycle.
```

```
    int Alive();  // returns 1 if alive, 0 if dead
};

// returns 1 if pregnant:
int Fertile(int Row, int Col, LifeField & LF);
// Helper function for Alive() and Fertile():
int NeighborAlive(int nr, int nc, LifeField & LF);

#endif // LIFEUNIT_H_
```

The methods for **LifeUnit** include the rules for life. In this case, **Alive()** and **Fertile()** simply check to see how many neighbors the **LifeUnit** has, but you can easily add a more complicated algorithm. Also, if you want, for example, to make the **LifeUnit** infertile during certain periods of life, you can easily add another state variable in the private data and change the **draw()** function so it prints different characters, depending on the state of the variable. Here are the rules of life (as we know it at this point):

```
//: LIFEUNIT.CPP—The Rules for life. Each LifeUnit figures
//. out whether it survives into the next generation.
#include "lifefld.h"

const MinimumNeighbors = 2;
const MaximumNeighbors = 3;
const MinimumParents = 3;
const MaximumParents = 3;

// Checks to see if the specified cell is currently occupied
int NeighborAlive(int nr, int nc, LifeField & LF) {
  if( LF.InRange(nr, nc) )
    // if nonNULL pointer:
    return ( LF(nr, nc) ? 1 : 0 ); // ternary if-else
  return 0;
}

// Counts the number of units surrounding R, C:
int SurroundingUnits(int R, int C, LifeField &LF) {
  return
    NeighborAlive(R -1, C, LF) +
    NeighborAlive(R +1, C, LF) +
    NeighborAlive(R, C + 1, LF) +
    NeighborAlive(R, C - 1, LF) +
    NeighborAlive(R -1, C - 1, LF) +
    NeighborAlive(R +1, C - 1, LF) +
    NeighborAlive(R -1, C + 1, LF) +
```

```
      NeighborAlive(R +1, C + 1, LF);
}

// Modify the follwing two functions to create more complicated
// rules for the simulation.

// Alive() determines whether the LifeUnit stays alive into the
// next generation by checking all around to see how many other
// units are alive.
int LifeUnit::Alive() {
  int Neighbors = SurroundingUnits(LRow, LCol, *LF);
  if( Neighbors >= MinimumNeighbors &&
      Neighbors <= MaximumNeighbors)
    return 1;  // alive
  return 0;  // died of loneliness or overpopulation
}

// Fertile() determines if the conditions are right (presumably
// in an empty cell) for new life. It happens to use the same
// rules as Alive(), but that can easily be changed.
int Fertile(int Row, int Col, LifeField & LF) {
  int Neighbors = SurroundingUnits(Row, Col, LF);
  if( Neighbors >= MinimumParents &&
      Neighbors <= MaximumParents)
    return 1;  // Pregnant
  return 0;  // too few parents, or overcrowding
}
```

A Field Where LifeUnits Live

The **LifeField** is a two-dimensional array the size of an ANSI terminal that holds pointers to **LifeUnit**s. If an array element is zero, it contains no element. If it is nonzero, there is a living **LifeUnit** associated with that space.

Generally, the next state of a simulation depends on the current state and some number of previous states. In this example, the next state only depends on the current state, but you can change that simply by increasing the constant **history**. This value establishes the number of states by creating an array for each count of **history**. In this example, **history** is 2—one array for the current state, and one for the next state. Every time the system is stepped forward, the current state is examined and the next state is created. If **history** were 3, you would create the next state based on the current state and the previous state.

Since the matrices are constantly being recycled, you must make sure you are indexing the proper state. This can be done by thinking of the matrices as being wrapped around into a loop, and using the modulus operator (%) to generate the index. To calculate the index of the next state, you say

```
int NextField = (CurrentField + 1) % history;
```

which makes **NextField** count 0, 1, 2, ..., **history** – 1.

To calculate the index of the **n** previous states, you say

```
(CurrentField + history - n) % history;
```

Here is the header file for **LifeField**:

```
//: LIFEFLD.H—A class to hold a field of LifeUnits
#ifndef LIFEFLD_H_
#define LIFEFLD_H_
#include "lifeunit.h"
#include <stdlib.h>

// This simple simulation assumes a standard ANSI terminal.
// Must have a buffer around field:
const rowmin = 1;
const rows = 25;
const rowmax = rows - 2;
const colmin = 1;
const cols = 80;
const colmax = cols - 2;
// You can have any amount of history in your simulation.
// This example just looks back one state:
const history = 2;

class LifeField {
  LifeUnit * Field[history][rows][cols];
  // The system cycles through arrays. The current time
  // step is given by the following variable:
  int CurrentField; // to select Field[0], Field[1], etc.
  void error(char * msg1 = "", char * msg2 = "") {
    cerr << "LifeField error: " <<  msg1 << " " << msg2 << endl;
    exit(1);
  }
  void RangeTest(int r, int c, char * msg = "") {
    if ( r <= rowmin || r >= rowmax )
      error(msg, "rows out of range");
```

```
      if ( c <= colmin || c >= colmax )
        error(msg, "cols out of range");
    }
public:
  LifeField(); // initialize all pointers to zero
  // select a pointer (zero pointer means there is no
  // LifeUnit in that location). For more sophisticated
  // simulations, you can use the pointer to interrogate
  // the LifeUnit at that location.
  const LifeUnit * operator() (int r, int c) {
    RangeTest(r, c, "operator()");
    return Field[CurrentField][r][c];
  }
  // Add a new LifeUnit to the field:
  void birth(int r, int c, LifeUnit *lu) {
    RangeTest(r, c, "birth()");
    Field[CurrentField][r][c] = lu;
  }
  // Remove a LifeUnit from the field:
  void death(int r, int c) {
    RangeTest(r, c, "death()");
    Field[CurrentField][r][c] = 0;
  }
  // returns 0 if out of range, 1 otherwise:
  int InRange(int r, int c);
  void Randomize(int factor);  // randomly put down LifeUnits
  // The higher the factor, the sparser the randomization
  int NextGeneration();  // returns nonzero if LifeUnits remain
};
#endif // LIFEFLD_H_
```

In the methods for **LifeField**, the function **Randomize()** uses the ANSI C library functions for random-number generation to initialize the **LifeField** with a random pattern of **LifeUnit**s. The random-number functions are **srand()** to "seed" the random-number generator and **rand()** to generate a random number.

This is a "pseudo" random-number generator. It takes the seed, and performs a calculation with it to generate a series of numbers that approximate randomness. However, if you give it the same seed every time, you will get the same series of numbers (try it!). True random number generators use some sort of random physical process to generate numbers. The only "physical process" you have access to in the ANSI C library is time. Although time itself isn't a particularly random process (as far as anyone knows), the time you start the program can be thought of as random. Thus, by seeding the random-number generator with a number created from the current time, you get a different pattern every time. The ANSI C library function **time()** fills its argument with a value representing the current time. This argument is used to seed **srand()**.

The argument to **Randomize()** is an integer that determines how sparsely the **LifeUnit**s will be distributed. The **rand()** function returns a value from 0 to **RAND_MAX** (**RAND_MAX** is defined in the **stdlib.h** header file). **RAND_MAX** is divided by the argument to **Randomize()** to create a value called **cutoff**. The value returned by **rand()** is divided by **cutoff** in an *integer* divide, so if the result of **rand()** is less than **cutoff**, the divide produces a zero (false); if it is greater than **cutoff**, the divide produces a nonzero value (true). The result of the integer division is used in an **if** statement to determine whether to create a new **LifeUnit**.

To dynamically create a new **LifeUnit**, you simply say **new**, call the constructor with the appropriate arguments, and stash the address returned by **new** somewhere so you don't lose it. Here are the methods for **LifeField**:

```
//: LIFEFLD.CPP—Methods for LifeField
#include "lifefld.h"
#include <time.h>  // to seed the random number generator

int LifeField::InRange(int r, int c) {
  if ( r <- rowmin || r >= rowmax )
    return 0;
  if ( c <= colmin || c >= colmax )
    return 0;
  return 1;
}

LifeField::LifeField() {
  // ANSI Clear Screen, Home Cursor:
  cout << "\x1b[2J";  // <ESC>[2J
  // Initialize everything to zero:
  for (int fld = 0; fld < history; fld++) {
    for(int i = 0; i < rows; i++) {
      for(int j = 0; j < cols; j++)
        Field[fld][i][j] = 0;
    }
  }
  CurrentField = 0;
}
```

```cpp
void LifeField::Randomize(int factor) {
  // This is used to turn the random number into a zero or a 1.
  // Increase the divisor for a sparser randomization:
  const cutoff = RAND_MAX / factor;
  // Seed the random number generator using the current time:
  time_t tnow;
  time(&tnow);
  srand(tnow);

  for(int r = rowmin; r < rowmax; r++) {
    for(int c = colmin; c < colmax; c++)
      if ( !(rand() / cutoff) ) { // integer divide
        Field[CurrentField][r][c] = new LifeUnit(r,c, this);
        if (Field[CurrentField][r][c] == 0) {
          cerr << "new failed in randomize()";
          exit(1);
        }
      }
  }
}

int LifeField::NextGeneration() {
  int StillAlive = 0;
  int Change = 0;   // indicates change in the state
  // this calculation makes it count 0, 1, ... history-1
  int NextField = (CurrentField + 1) % history;
  for(int r = rowmin; r < rowmax; r++) {
    for(int c = colmin; c < colmax; c++) {
      // If one is there, and it's alive, copy it:
      if (Field[CurrentField][r][c]) {
        if (Field[CurrentField][r][c]->Alive()) {
          Field[NextField][r][c] = Field[CurrentField][r][c];
          StillAlive++;
        }
        else {
          delete Field[CurrentField][r][c];
          // (The destructor erases the character).
          Field[CurrentField][r][c] = 0;
          Change++;
        }
      } else {   // one isn't currently there.
        // See if the space is ripe for new life:
        if (Fertile(r,c, *this)) {
          Field[NextField][r][c] = new LifeUnit(r,c, this);
          // A Birth!
```

```
                StillAlive++;
            }
          }
        }
    }
    for(r = rowmin; r < rowmax; r++)  // clear CurrentField:
      for(int c = colmin; c < colmax; c++)
        Field[CurrentField][r][c] = 0;
    CurrentField = NextField;  // step forward in time
    if (!Change) return 0;
    return StillAlive;
}
```

The algorithm used here is pretty stupid, since it just marches through all the empty areas calculating the possibility of a birth in each one. A smarter algorithm would do its work in "live" areas and ignore ones that are all empty. You can improve the algorithm, but this usually requires the program to be structured based on some special knowledge about the algorithm. This reduces the general-purpose nature of the design (you could also try redesigning the structure of the program to allow efficiency heuristics to be used).

The function **NextGeneration()** returns 0 when no changes are taking place. You can also use the return value so you can quit when the number of changes drops below a certain value or remains below a certain value for a set number of generations.

Running the Simulation

Here is the program that runs the simulation. It creates a **LifeField** and initializes it by calling **Randomize()** with an integer argument from the command line. As long as the pattern continues to change, **NextGeneration()** is called. Press CTRL-C to end the simulation.

```
//: LIFE.CPP—Test the Life Simulation
#include "lifefld.h"

void main(int argc, char * argv[]) {
  if( argc < 2 ) {
    cerr << "usage: life integer" << endl
         << "The higher the integer, the sparser the field";
```

```
    exit(0);
  }
  int factor = atoi(argv[1]);
  LifeField Simulation;
  Simulation.Randomize(factor);
  while(Simulation.NextGeneration())
    ;
}
```

The ANSI C library function **atoi()** is used on the first command-line argument (all command-line arguments are character strings) to produce an integer.

Life Extension

Here are some ideas for enhancements to the simulation system:

☐ For speed, change the output statements so they use direct commands for your local system. The ANSI terminal sequences are slow (but portable).

☐ Expand the system to use inheritance and virtual functions (Chapters 7 and 8) so you have many different kinds of **LifeUnit**s with different types of interactions. Many video arcade games are simply elaborate simulations.

☐ Give the **LifeUnit** class the ability to move around in a **LifeField**.

☐ Add features to the **LifeField**, such as walls and rooms. A **LifeUnit** would interact with a **LifeField** feature differently than with another **LifeUnit**.

☐ Often, you want to run a simulation to a certain point, then dump the data for analysis, and later restart the simulation from the same point. Create two member functions for **LifeUnit** called **read()** and **write()** that read the private data for a **LifeUnit** from an open file (the filename or **istream** pointer is passed as an argument) and write the contents of a **LifeUnit** to an open file. Create functions for **LifeField** called **read()** and **write()** that open a file and read or write a field full of **LifeUnit** data points.

Arbitrary-Sized Objects

To review what you know so far about why you use dynamic memory allocation:

☐ Objects can be created dynamically when you don't know how many objects you will need until run time.

☐ Objects can be created dynamically when you don't know what the lifetime of the object will be.

There is a third reason you may need to use dynamic memory allocation:

☐ The constructor for an object can use dynamic memory allocation when you don't know how much memory the object will need until run time.

Examples of arbitrary-sized objects abound, once you start looking for them. For example:

☐ In the **matrix** class (in the appendices) you generally don't know how many elements you need to store until the user creates the matrix, or tells the constructor what file the matrix data is in.

☐ The whole idea of a linked list is that it can expand and contract to hold any number of objects.

☐ A class that creates text-based windows might allocate memory to hold the patch of screen the window covers up (so it can be restored when the window is destroyed); the amount of memory allocated depends on the size of the window.

A Dynamically Sized Array

As an example of an arbitrarily sized object, this section presents a dynamically sized array object. A **DynArray** holds an array of pointers to objects; these are **void** pointers so they can point to any type of object (someone outside of the **DynArray** is responsible for keeping track of what kind of objects are stored in the array and casting them appropriately when they are dereferenced).

A **DynArray** can hold any number of pointers, and you don't have to keep track of the current size of the array. Just call the **add()** function with the pointer you want to add as an argument. The **DynArray** will make new space if it needs it, and you don't have to know when or how. In a sense, a **DynArray** is like an infinitely expandable bag. Because it can hold an arbitrary number of elements, it provides the same functionality as a linked list.

This type of object—an object whose purpose is to hold other objects—is often called a *container class*, and is an important part of object-oriented programming. Container classes are the subject of Chapter 10.

A **DynArray** gives you a few improvements over a linked list. While you can move to the top of a **DynArray** and hunt through it by moving to the **next()** element as you would with a linked list, you can also select elements directly using the bracket operator and an index. The **add()** function returns the index of the element you just added. You can also find out the index by calling **index()**, which returns the index value of the current element.

DynArray keeps track of where it is in the array with a private integer **cursor**, and it keeps track of the current size with **size**. The array where the data is stored is represented by a single pointer to a pointer: **void ** array**. Since a pointer can be used as if it were an array name, once memory is allocated for **array** you can think of it like this: **void * array[size]**. When memory is allocated, the **new** operator must be told what kind of objects it is creating (**void ***) and (in the case of an array) how big they are, like this:

```
array = new void*[size];
```

Here is the header file for **DynArray**:

```
//: DYNARRAY.H—Dynamically sized array of object pointers
#ifndef DYNARRAY_H_
#define DYNARRAY_H_

class DynArray {
  // how much to increase the array when it runs out of space:
  enum { chunk = 10 };
  void ** array;  // starting address of array of void pointers
```

```
  int size;  // current size of the array
  int cursor; // to index through the array
  void error(char * msg = "");
public:
  DynArray();
  ~DynArray();
  int add(void *);  // stash an element in the array,
  // increasing the size if necessary. Returns the index.
  // Both remove() functions return 1 if successful:
  int remove(void *);  // remove an element by pointer
  int remove(int);  // remove an element using its index
  // reset the cursor to the first nonzero element at the
  // top of the array:
  void reset();
  void * next(); // return the pointer to the next element
                 // (empty elements are skipped). Returns NULL
                 // at end of array.
  void * previous(); // like next(), but backing up
  int index() { return cursor; } // index of current element
  // return the pointer to the current element:
  void * current() { return array[cursor]; }
  void * top() { reset(); return current(); } // top of list
  void * operator[](int); // element selection
  int count(); // number of "live" items in the array
};

#endif // DYNARRAY_H_
```

When an array element is initialized or cleared, you will see the value 0 cast to a **void** pointer: **(void *)0**. This makes it explicit to the reader that you are dealing with a pointer, and not an integer.

The **add()** function starts at the top of the list and looks for the first empty **array()** space (this automatically recycles spaces when elements are removed). If it finds one, it places the user's **void** pointer in the space and returns the index number of that space. If, however, it reaches the end of **array** before it finds a space, it must extend the array.

The array is extended in increments of **chunk**, a constant that can be changed to optimize efficiency. To extend **array**, a temporary vector **temp** is allocated which is the current **size** plus an additional **chunk**. The old elements are copied into **temp**, the additional **chunk** is initialized to **(void *)**, and the argument to **add()** is inserted at the beginning of the additional **chunk**.

In this scheme, space is never removed from a **DynArray**. Generally, a **DynArray** will expand to whatever size you need and stay there (since it recycles its array elements). This is appropriate for most situations, but if you have an application where a **DynArray** needs to shrink, you can create a function that condenses all the empty spaces out of the array, copies it to a smaller piece of memory, and deletes the larger piece of memory. This function, unfortunately, will mix up all the index values.

The algorithm of searching down the array for the first empty space works fine for small arrays, but if you have a large array with very few empty spaces it becomes inefficient. In this situation you may want to add a second **private** array that contains the index numbers of empty spaces in the first.

The **next()** function moves the cursor to the next nonempty element of **array** and returns the pointer there. If the end of the **DynArray** is reached, it returns **(void *)0**. You can get the address at the current cursor location with the **current()** function, or the index of the location with the **index()** function. Elements may be removed using the overloaded **remove()** function and either the index or the pointer to be removed.

The **reset()** function moves the cursor not just to the top of the array, but to the first nonzero element of the array. This way, you will always have a valid pointer available via **current()** after **reset()**.

Here are the methods for **DynArray**:

```
//: DYNARRAY.CPP—The advantages of an array, with the
//. dynamic flexibility of a linked list.
#include "..\chap_6\dynarray.h"  // to compile remotely
#include <iostream.h>
#include <stdlib.h>  // exit()
#include <string.h> // memset()

void DynArray::error(char * msg) {
  cerr << "DynArray error: " << msg << endl;
  exit(1);
}

DynArray::DynArray() {
  size = chunk;
  cursor = 0;
  array = new void*[size];  // allocate a block of void *'s
  memset(array, 0, sizeof(void*) * size); // zero the memory
}
```

```cpp
// The destructor frees the dynamically allocated memory:
DynArray::~DynArray() {
  delete []array;
  // Note: individual elements are not deleted!
  // We don't know what type they are (only void*).
  // Need templates or virtual functions (future chapters)
}

int DynArray::add(void * new_element) {
  // Put it in the first empty space avaialable:
  for(int i = 0; i < size; i++)
    if(array[i] == 0) {
      array[i] = new_element;
      return i;
    }
  // at this point, no space was found. Add new space:
  int tempsize = size + chunk;  // increase space by chunk
  void ** temp = new void*[tempsize];
  memset(temp, 0, sizeof(void*) * tempsize); // zero the memory
  // copy the old array over:
  for(i = 0; i < size; i++)
    temp[i] = array[i];
  temp[i = size] = new_element;  // put at start of empty space
  delete array;  // free old memory
  array = temp;
  size = tempsize;
  return i;
}

int DynArray::remove(void * rp) {
  for(int i = 0; i < size; i++)
    if( array[i] == rp ) {
      array[i] = 0;
      return 1;
    }
  return 0; // not found
}

int DynArray::remove(int ri) {
  if( ri < 0 || ri >= size)
    error("remove index out of range");
  // check to see if there's an element at that slot:
  if( array[ri] ) {
    array[ri] = 0;
    return 1;
  }
```

```
    return 0; // not found
}

void DynArray::reset() {
  cursor = 0;
  while( (array[cursor] == 0) && (cursor < size - 1) )
    cursor++;  // find the first nonzero element
}

void * DynArray::next() {
  if( cursor == size -1 ) // last element, no next.
    return 0;
  // Not at the end. Increment until you find a nonempty slot
  // or the end:
  while(array[++cursor] == 0)
    if ( cursor == size -1 )  // no more elements in list
      return 0;
  return array[cursor];
}

void * DynArray::previous() {
  if(cursor == 0) return current();
  while(array[--cursor] == 0)
    if(cursor == 0) // top of list
      return 0;
  return array[cursor];
}

void * DynArray::operator[](int x) {
  if(x < 0 || x >= size)
    error("operator[]—index out of range");
  return array[x];  // even if it's empty...
}

int DynArray::count() {
  int cnt = 0;
  for(int x=0; x < size; x++)
    if(array[x])
      cnt++;
  return cnt;
}
```

Notice that the **include** statement for DNYARRAY.H contains path information. This allows you to specify ..\CHAP_6\DYNARRAY.OBJ inside the makefile of another chapter to use **DynArray** in another project. Then **make** can rebuild DYNARRAY.OBJ if necessary, and when it compiles

DYNARRAY.CPP the compiler will know where to look for the header file (otherwise it will get confused while doing a compile from another directory).

To test **DynArray**, a simple class called **string** is created to hold a character string. It relies on getting a pointer to a statically initialized character string, for simplicity. The **string** class overloads the stream output **operator<<()** for simple output.

The test program creates a lot of strings (more than a single **chunk**, so the dynamic sizing can be tested) and puts them into the **DynArray da**. The entire array is printed; then a **string** containing the word "OOPS" is removed from **cp**, and the array is printed again.

To remove the **string** containing "OOPS," the ANSI C library function **strstr()** is used to search for the pattern. The **strstr()** function takes two arguments: a **char** pointer to the string to be searched, and a **char** pointer to the pattern to search for. As mentioned in Chapter 4, the quoted string "OOPS" produces the starting address of the NULL-terminated ASCII character string that has been created statically and stashed in memory somewhere. To generate the address of the string to be searched, the **string** class has a member function **cp** that returns the address of the internal string.

Notice that whenever a pointer from **da** is produced, it must always be cast to a **string** * before it is used; otherwise you will get an error message for attempting to dereference a **void** pointer.

Here is the test program for **DynArray**:

```
//: DYNATEST.CPP—Test program for dynarray.
#include "dynarray.h"
#include <iostream.h>
#include <string.h>
#include <stdlib.h>

// Very simple class to save a string and print
// it with iostreams:
class string {
  char * str;
public:
  string(char * msg = "") { str = msg; }
  char * cp() { return str; }
  friend ostream& operator<<(ostream& s, string * sp) {
    return s << sp->str;
```

```
    }
};

void main() {
  DynArray da;
  da.add(new string("This is a "));
  da.add(new string("test of the "));
  da.add(new string("dynamic array "));
  da.add(new string("class "));
  da.add(new string("to \n"));
  da.add(new string("(OOPS! A Mistake) "));
  da.add(new string("see "));
  da.add(new string("if "));
  da.add(new string("it "));
  da.add(new string("will "));
  da.add(new string("automatically make "));
  da.add(new string("itself bigger "));
  da.add(new string("when it \n"));
  da.add(new string("runs out of "));
  da.add(new string("room."));

  // First, print the whole list:
  da.reset();
  do
    cout << (string *)da.current();
  while( da.next() );
  cout << endl << endl;
  // Now, find the element with the "OOPS":
  da.reset();
  while( strstr(((string *)da.current())->cp(), "OOPS") == 0 )
    if(da.next() == 0) {
      cerr << "OOPS not found" << endl;
      exit(1);
    }
  int rm = da.index(); // number of element to remove
  cout << "removing " << (string *)da[rm] << endl;
  delete (string*)da[rm];  // delete the string object
  if (da.remove(rm))
    cout << "removed successfully!" << endl;
  // Print the whole list again, while deleting the strings:
  da.reset();
  do {
    cout << (string *)da.current();
    delete (string *)da.current();
    da.remove(da.current());
  } while( da.next() );
}
```

Improving **DynArray**

The ANSI C library function **realloc()** takes a block of memory allocated by **malloc()**, **calloc()**, or **realloc()** and expands it or contracts it. If you expand the block and **realloc()** can't find enough space where the block is, it will copy the existing block into a new, larger memory space.

If you look back at the **add()** method for **DynArray**, you can see the same activities taking place, only less efficiently—the block is *always* moved and copied, and the C++ code to perform the copy probably isn't as efficient as **realloc()** (which is often written in assembly language).

Duplicating Space for Strings

The **string** class in the DYNATEST program you just read relies on being initialized with the address of a character string constant. Other programs in this book so far have also made that assumption. What if you want to handle the more general case of *any* type of **char** *? In particular, what if you want to make a **string** object from a local array? You don't want to point to an array that someone else can also change, or which can go out of scope and become invalid.

The solution to this problem is to allocate memory on the free store and copy the string into this private data area. Then you will have two separate copies of the data, and it is unimportant what happens to the data outside the class.

This is another situation where you don't know until run time how big an object will be. When you allocate memory on the free store, you must create enough for the whole string. Fortunately, the ANSI C library provides a package of string-handling functions to make this easy, including **strlen()**, which returns the size of the string (not including the terminating zero; you must add 1 to provide space for it), and **strcpy()**, which copies the contents of its second argument into the contents of the first argument (both arguments are character pointers) *including* the zero terminator.

The modified, general-purpose **string** class looks like this:

```
//: STRING.CPP-String class that handles any type of
//. character pointer argument (static or automatic data)
```

```
#include <iostream.h>
#include <string.h>

// Very simple class to save a string and print
// it with streams:
class string {
  char * str;
public:
  string(char * msg = "") {
    // duplicate the message as private data:
    str = new char[strlen(msg) + 1];
    strcpy(str, msg);
  }
  char * cp() { return str; }
  friend ostream& operator<<(ostream& s, string & sp) {
    s << sp.str;
    return s;
  }
};


void main() {
  char * msg1 = "This is msg1";
  string S(msg1);
  cout << "original msg1: " << msg1 << endl;
  cout << "original S: " << S << endl;
  msg1[0] = 'X';  // NOTE: modifying a string constant
  msg1[1] = 'X';  // is NOT portable.
  msg1[2] = 'X';
  cout << "msg1 after modification: " << msg1 << endl;
  cout << "S after msg1 was modified: " << S << endl;
}
```

The statement

```
str = new char[strlen(msg) + 1];
```

creates a character array on the free store. The size of the array is the
length of the string **msg**, plus one for the terminating zero. The pointer
str holds the address of the character array. The contents of **msg** and
the terminating zero are copied into the newly allocated memory with the
statement

```
strcpy(str, msg);
```

You can also allocate a single instance of a built-in type (as well as an array of built-in types, as shown above). For example, to create a dynamically allocated **double**, you can say

```
double * dp = new double;
```

The ANSI C library provides a function called **strdup()**, which allocates storage for a string *and* copies the string in one step. It returns the address of the allocated storage. However, **strdup()** uses **malloc()**, not **new**, so you must remember to release the storage with **free()**, not **delete**.

Encryption Example with Dynamic String Allocation

Here is the encryption example from Chapter 4, modified to use (more appropriately) dynamic string allocation:

```
//: ENCODE2.CPP—Reimplementation of class encode
//. to use dynamic string allocation.
#define TEST
#include <iostream.h>
#include <string.h>
// The following path is for this book's source-code disk.
// Your directory may be different:
#include "..\chap_4\encode.h"

unsigned char encode::make_key(char * keystring) {
  unsigned char ckey = 0;
  for(char * cp = keystring; *cp != 0; cp++)
    ckey += *cp;  // generate a number from the key
  return ckey;
}

encode::encode(char * msg, char * key) {
  unsigned char ckey = make_key(key);
  encrypted_string = new char[strlen(msg) + 1];
  strcpy(encrypted_string,msg);  // save the message
  for(char * cp = encrypted_string; *cp != 0; cp++)
    *cp += ckey;  // use the key to encrypt the msg
}

char * encode::decode(char * key) {
 unsigned char ckey = make_key(key);
```

```
 for(char * cp = encrypted_string; *cp != 0; cp++)
   *cp -= ckey;  // use the key to decrypt the string
 return encrypted_string;
}

#ifdef TEST

void main() {
  encode hidden_message("This is a test string", "key string");
  cout << hidden_message.decode("key string") << endl;
}

#endif // TEST
```

Notice that the header is the same, so you can use the same programs as you used before with this class. The implementation changed, not the interface, so any program that used this class is unaffected. This is one of the advantages to programming in C++ — changes are localized and don't tend to cause other changes throughout the program.

The Mechanics of Dynamic Object Creation

When you encounter some of the more subtle problems involved with free store, it is helpful to know how C++ manages memory. Two subjects will be examined: the functions that are called when you use **new** and **delete**, and what goes on inside the system.

The Order of Constructor and Destructor Calls

Because C++ has dynamic object creation and not just dynamic memory allocation, constructors must be called so **new** will return the address of a "live" object. Similarly, the destructor for an object must be called before the memory for that object is deallocated, in case cleanup is necessary.

When you use **new** to create an object, enough memory for the data items in the object structure (these items normally live on the stack or in the **static** memory area) is allocated on the free store, and then the constructor for the object is called. In case the object is a conglomeration of other objects, either through class inheritance or because the object contains member objects, the constructors are called in a particular order: first the constructor for the base class is called, then the constructor(s) for the member object(s), and finally the constructor for the derived class.

When you use **delete** to destroy an object that was previously created on the free store, the compiler performs any cleanup specified for the class by calling its destructor. If the object is a conglomeration of other objects, the destructors are called in a particular order, which is the reverse of the order of constructor calls: first the derived class destructor is called, then the member object destructor(s), and finally the destructor for the base class.

Even though inheritance has not yet been explained in detail (see Chapter 7), for the sake of this discussion a small example will be used to show the order of constructor and destructor calls when the object contains a member object and is inherited from another class, which also contains a member object. By running the program you can see what happens:

```cpp
//: ORDER.CPP—The order of constructor and destructor calls
//. for inherited objects and objects with member objects.
#include <iostream.h>

class member {  // to be used as a member object
  int x;  // to remember what object this is
public:
  member(int i) {
    cout << "member constructor called with arg " << i << endl;
    x = i;
  }
  ~member() {
    cout << "member destructor called, x = " << x << endl;
  }
};

class base { // to be used as a base class
  int xx;  // to remember what object this is
  member M;  // a member object
public:
  // Here's how you initialize a member object:
```

```
    base(int a, int b) : M(b) {
      cout << "base constructor called with arguments "
           << a << ", " << b << endl;
      xx = a;
    }
    ~base() {
      cout << "base destructor called, xx = " << xx << endl;
    }
};

// Here's where inheritance happens, as well as another member
// object. Watch carefully!
class derived : public base {  // <--- inheritance!
    int xxx;  // to remember what object this is
    member MM;
public:
    // Here's how constructors for the base class AND the
    // member function are called, before the class body, to
    // remind you they are called before the constructor for
    // this class. This is the "constructor initializer list":
    derived(int a, int b, int c) : base(a,b), MM(c) {
      cout << "derived constructor called with arguments "
           << a << ", " << b << ", " << c << endl;
      xxx = a;
    }
    ~derived() {
      cout << "derived destructor called. xxx = " << xxx << endl;
    }
};

void main() {
  {
    cout << "creating derived X(1,2,3);" << endl;
    derived X(1,2,3);
    cout << "derived X(1,2,3) going out of scope" << endl;
  } // <- destructor called here
  cout << "creating derived * dp = new derived(4,5,6);" << endl;
  derived * dp = new derived(4,5,6);
  cout << "calling delete dp;" << endl;
  delete dp;
}
```

Each constructor and destructor in the above example contains a **cout**
call so you can see the order in which they are called. The **class member**
is used as a member object in both **class base** and **class derived**, to show
the order in which member objects are constructed. The **class base** is

the "base class" for **class derived**, that is, **class derived** inherits **class base**. This hierarchy demonstrates the order of constructor and destructor calls for member objects, base classes, and the member objects contained in a base class.

A member object is used inside an enclosing class just by defining an instance of the member object's class. The member object, however, must be initialized specially. When the body of the enclosing class's constructor is entered, the member object must have already been initialized. To show this initialization, the member object's constructor is called *after* the argument list for the enclosing class's constructor argument list but *before* the body. This is called the *constructor initializer list*, and it looks like this:

```
base(int a, int b) : M(b) {
  //... body of constructor
```

When a class inherits from another class, the base class must be initialized before the body of the derived class's constructor is entered. The constructor for the base class is also called before entering the derived class's constructor body, as shown here:

```
derived(int a, int b, int c) : base(a,b), MM(c) {
  // ... body of constructor
```

The way you specify base-class and member-object constructor calls in a derived class serves as a reminder of the order in which they are called: before the body of the enclosing class and/or derived class constructor is called.

Here is the output from ORDER:

```
creating derived X(1,2,3);
member constructor called with arg 2
base constructor called with arguments 1, 2
member constructor called with arg 3
derived constructor called with arguments 1, 2, 3
derived X(1,2,3) going out of scope
derived destructor called. xxx = 1
member destructor called, x = 3
base destructor called, xx = 1
member destructor called, x = 2
creating derived * dp = new derived(4,5,6);
```

```
member constructor called with arg 5
base constructor called with arguments 4, 5
member constructor called with arg 6
derived constructor called with arguments 4, 5, 6
calling delete dp;
derived destructor called. xxx = 4
member destructor called, x = 6
base destructor called, xx = 4
member destructor called, x = 5
```

At first glance, the order of constructor calls doesn't seem quite right—a member constructor is called *before* the base-class constructor. If you look closely, you'll see that the order is, in fact, correct. The **base** constructor is called, but before it has a chance to print its message it must call the constructor for the member object that is *part of* **base**. Then **base** prints its message, and finally the message from the derived-class constructor is printed. The destructors are called in the same way, in reverse.

Arrays of Objects

If you allocate an array of objects without aggregate initializers, the class that the objects belong to must contain a constructor with no arguments. This constructor is called a *default constructor*. The syntax for allocating an array of objects is, for a class called **object**:

```
object * op = new object[10];  // array of 10 objects
```

When you **delete** an array of objects belonging to a class with a destructor, you must precede the object's address with a set of empty brackets, like this:

```
delete []op;
```

This tells the compiler it needs to set up calls to the destructor for every object in that array, and not just the first object (if you don't give the brackets, the compiler assumes it's just one object). You may see older code that has a number inside the brackets. Earlier versions of C++ required the number so the run-time system would know exactly how many times to call the destructor. However, this introduced a bug potential—you might give one number when the array was created and another when it was destroyed. Thus, the language was changed so the run-time system keeps track of how many objects are in the array, and all you have to do is tell it that an array is being destroyed. It looks up the number and calls the destructor the correct number of times.

You can also use this notation for arrays of built-in types, but built-in types do not have destructors so, like any object without destructors, the argument is ignored. However, it's *always* a good idea to use this notation when destroying arrays, in case you decide to turn the class into a *template* that may use objects of user-defined types that have destructors.

Constructors and destructors are called automatically for every element in an **auto** array, as well as if the array is created with **new** and destroyed with **delete**. The following example illustrates.

```cpp
//: NEWARRAY.CPP—Constructors and destructors are called
//. for every object in an array.
#include <iostream.h>

class BobTheDog {
public: // no data elements!
  //  A constructor with no arguments is necessary
  // to create arrays of objects. A constructor where
  // all the arguments have default values works too.
  BobTheDog() { cout << "constructor called" << endl; }
  ~BobTheDog() { cout << "destructor called" << endl; }
};

void auto_objects() {
  BobTheDog spaniel[5];
}

void dynamic_objects() {
  BobTheDog * mutt = new BobTheDog[8];
  // note the compiler must be told to call
  // the destructor for each element:
  delete []mutt;
}

void main() {
  cout << "calling auto_objects" << endl;
  auto_objects();
  cout << "calling dynamic_objects" << endl;
  dynamic_objects();
}
```

The function **auto_objects()** creates an array on the stack, and you will see a constructor call for each element when the scope is entered and a destructor call for each element at the end of the scope. The function **dynamic_objects()** shows an array of the same object being created on the free store, and then deleted.

If you take the **sizeof(BobTheDog)**, you'll discover that it is *not* zero, as you might expect. This is because an object with no elements may be used inside an array, and if it had zero size, all the objects in the array would have the same starting address.

Internal Operations

When you use **new**, you must give the operator an argument of the data type you want to create so it knows how much memory to allocate. When you call **delete**, however, you only need to give it a starting address (for an array of objects, you must precede the address by [] so the destructor is called for all the objects). You may have surmised that **new** keeps tabs on how much memory is allocated, so the correct amount can be freed by **delete**.

The algorithm for **new** stores the amount of space allocated somewhere in memory. It might be stored next to the allocated block or in a table somewhere—the way **new** works varies between implementations. In addition, the location and amount of space allocated is stored somewhere so subsequent calls to **new** do not allocate the same chunk of memory. If **new** is allocating an array, the number of objects in that array is also stored.

When you free a chunk of memory using **delete**, the system marks that block of memory as available, so the next time **new** is used that memory may be reallocated. Some implementations of C++ immediately write over portions of the deallocated memory. You should realize that it is never safe to use memory after it has been deallocated. After reading this explanation, it may sound like a silly thing to do, but some folks do it anyway. This goes into the same classification of "taboos" as "don't return addresses of local variables."

Heap Fragmentation

If your program does a lot of memory allocation and deallocation, a phenomenon called *heap fragmentation* may result. Eventually, your heap may be so riddled with occupied space that, while enough free space exists to allocate a new chunk, there is no contiguous piece of memory large enough to allocate the size you request.

If you create a program that fragments the heap, you might need to add a routine to perform *heap compaction*. A compactor goes through the heap and moves all the chunks of allocated memory "down" (if you think of the heap as growing "up" from the bottom of memory, and the stack growing "down"), so that large chunks of free memory once again become available. Because a compactor changes all the addresses of the chunks of allocated memory, your program must have intimate knowledge of the compactor and interact with it to keep all the addresses current. Because of this, you can't write a general-purpose compactor and make it part of the language or a library function.

Some operating systems, such as the one for the Apple Macintosh, perform heap compaction for you. To accomplish this they use *double indirection*: whenever you request a chunk of memory from the operating system, you get back *a pointer to a pointer* to that chunk of memory. You must always take the address you get back and dereference it twice. You cannot use the actual address of the chunk of memory, because the operating system may change that address when it performs heap compaction.

Although many operating systems have methods to allocate chunks of memory, C++ and C do not generally go to the operating system when you use **new** and **delete**, although they may certainly be implemented that way. When a program starts, it takes a big chunk of data space. When you allocate free store, the memory is taken from that space, so C++ manages the free store, not the operating system.

NULL Pointers

Generally, the value of NULL for a pointer has special meaning (note the use of 0 instead of NULL in C++ for increased portability, as noted in the previous chapter). It usually means the pointer isn't pointing anywhere. 0 is a convenient value because it is also a logical false, so you can use it in statements like: **while(ptr)** or **if(ptr)**.

Although it's possible to dereference a pointer with a NULL value, you almost never want to. More sophisticated operating systems will trap an attempt to dereference a NULL pointer, but with simpler machines, you may end up in some memory-mapped hardware, or in the operating system itself.

In C++, it is quite natural to use the value 0 to indicate the pointer is empty. This is supported by the special feature that if you call **delete** with a 0 pointer, it has no effect. You don't have to test to see if a pointer is 0 before you call **delete** for that pointer.

ANSI C doesn't actually specify that the value of NULL must be 0. The implementation can use any value for NULL that it needs to. It must convert between that representation and 0 under appropriate circumstances. Normally, you have no portable way of detecting how an implementation represents NULL (again, this is why you should use 0 in C++, since the C++ compiler is guaranteed to treat it properly, while whatever cast is used for NULL might cause problems).

Multiple Deletions

Memory allocated on the free store should only be deleted once. If you call **new** once for a single allocation and **delete** more than once for the same allocation, it can be disastrous.

Changing the Behavior of new and delete

C++ allows you to change the behavior of many aspects of the system. Dynamic memory allocation is no exception. Both **new** and **delete** are considered operators in C++, but you can not only overload them on a class-by-class basis like normal operators—you can also overload the global **new** and **delete**. This gives you complete control over dynamic memory allocation.

Examples of when you might need to do this:

☐ Suppose you are developing code in C++ for an *embedded system* (a program that is burned into ROM or EPROM and used for a specific application like a control system). Embedded systems generally have constraints on the placement and use of memory, so C++'s **new** and **delete** may be inappropriate. You can define a free store in your embedded system by redefining **new** and **delete**.

☐ You may need to implement **new** and **delete** so they work more efficiently for your particular application.

☐ A program that performs dynamic memory allocation can be difficult to debug. You might have access to a C package that provides debugging facilities through rewritten versions of **malloc()** and **free()**. These can be utilized in C++ by redefining **new** and **delete** globally.

Here's an example of global redefinition of **new** and **delete** (you must include NEW.H before doing this):

```
void* operator new(size_t sz) {
  return malloc(sz);   // convenient for bounds-checking malloc
}
void operator delete(void * dp) { free(dp); }
```

The signatures of these functions must be matched exactly—**new** takes a **size_t** argument (the number of bytes it must allocate) and returns a **void*** (which is handed to the constructor by the system); **delete** takes a **void*** (the address of the memory, after the destructor has been called).

Class-by-class overloading of operator **new** will be shown shortly.

Free Store Exhaustion

In some applications, exhausting the free store means you've made an error, and your program has been wildly allocating free store. However, there are many situations when exhausting the free store is a normal and recoverable condition. For example:

- [ ] Your system might be designed to generate garbage, which can be collected to create more room.

- [ ] You might be fragmenting the heap. If you design your system to allow it, the heap can be compacted.

- [ ] You might have taken over free store allocation by redefining **new** and **delete** (demonstrated later in this section) and you might have some method of getting more memory when your local store is exhausted.

- [ ] You might want to use as much memory as possible, to buffer disk I/O, for example. The only portable way to see if a certain amount of memory is available is to call **new** and see if it fails.

When free store is exhausted, the system calls the **_new_handler()** function, which ... does nothing. However, you can change the action of the **_new_handler()** by creating your own function and attaching it with the predefined function **set_new_handler()**, as shown in the following example. When free store is exhausted, your new-handler will be called. For example, if you suspect you are running out of free store, you can make the program print a message and exit, as in this example:

```
//: FSHANDLR.CPP—Adding your own handler, called when
//. free store runs out.
#include <iostream.h>
#include <stdlib.h>
#include <new.h>  // declares set_new_handler()

void no_more_free_store() {
  cout << "You've exhausted the free store!" << endl;
  exit(1);
}

void main() {
  set_new_handler(no_more_free_store);
  while(1)
    new int;  // this loop will exhaust free store!
}
```

Here, **set_new_handler()** takes the address of **no_more_free_store()** and installs it as the function to be called when free store is exhausted. The statement

```
while(1)
  new int;
```

eventually allocates all the free store, so you can see the handler called.

Class-By-Class Overloading of new and delete

When you redefine **new** and **delete** as class members, the compiler will call those functions *only* when you create an object of that class on the free store. This way you can selectively change the meaning of **new** and **delete**—if the global version (which you may also have changed) works fine, then you leave that class as it is. However, if, for example, you're doing a lot of creation and destruction of objects of a particular class and you want to speed up the process, you can take over storage allocation for that particular class.

Notice that you're *only* taking over storage allocation. The compiler calls your **new** to get the storage and then calls the constructor for that storage (so you'd better ensure that the proper amount is allocated!). With **delete**, the compiler first calls the destructor and then calls your **delete** to deallocate the storage.

The syntax for class-by-class **new** and **delete** is the same as the global versions. In the following example, **new** and **delete** are overloaded to report when they are called and then call the global versions:

```
//: OPNEW.CPP—Overloading operator new and delete
#include <iostream.h>
#include <stdlib.h>
#include <new.h>  // new-handler declaration

class X {
  static int visible;
  int i[100];
```

```
public:
  void* operator new(size_t sz) {
    if(visible) cout << "X::operator new" << endl;
    return ::new unsigned char[sz];
  }
  void operator delete(void* dp) {
    cout << "X::operator delete" << endl;
    ::delete(dp);
  }
  static void quiet() { visible = 0; }
};

int X::visible = 1;

unsigned long count = 0;

void memout() {
  cerr << "out of free store after "
       << count << " objects" << endl;
  exit(1);
}

void main() {
  set_new_handler(memout);
  X* xp = new X;
  delete xp;
  X::quiet();
  while(1) {
    new X;
    ++count;
  }
}
```

The class **X** is intentionally made large so it takes up space. The **static** data member **visible** tells the constructor and destructor whether they should print a message. It is initialized to true when the storage for the static member is allocated, and is turned "off" by the **static** member function **quiet()**. The new-handler in this case tells how many objects were created before free store was exhausted.

In **main()**, after the new-handler is set, an object of type **X** is created and destroyed, so you can see that the different versions of **new** and **delete** are indeed called. Then objects are created on the heap (ignoring the return values) until free store is exhausted. You can see from this experiment how much heap space is available in your program.

Notice in **X**'s versions of **new** and **delete** that the global **new** and **delete** are called. If you simply said **new** and **delete** in these situations, the nearest version would be used, and you'd end up with a recursive function call. To specify the global versions, you must use the scope resolution operator with nothing preceding the function name: **::new** and **::delete**.

Trivial Garbage Collection

As a trivial example of a system with garbage collection, the following program defines a class called **garbage**. The **garbage** objects are used for some mysterious purpose and then thrown away. When the system runs out of free store, the **garbage** objects that are no longer in use are freed by the garbage collector. To find out if an object is still in use, the object itself is questioned. The **in_use** variable can be set according to criteria specific to your application.

To store the pointers without muss and fuss, the **DynArray** class defined earlier in this chapter is used. Notice how convenient it is to use the class once it's defined—you just make a **DynArray**, throw pointers in and fish them out later. Whenever an object is created, the **garbage** constructor passes its address to **DynArray::add()** so it is stored in the table.

```
//: GARBAGE.CPP—A simple example of how a garbage
//. collector might work.
#include <iostream.h>
#include <stdlib.h>
#include <new.h>
#include "dynarray.h"

DynArray memtable;  // place for free store pointers

class garbage {
  enum { garbage_chunk = 512 };  // size of an object
  int memory[garbage_chunk];
  int in_use;
public:
  garbage() { in_use = 0; } // we're done, it's dead
  void* operator new(size_t sz) {
    void * g = ::new unsigned char[sz];
    memtable.add(g);
```

```
      return g;
  }
  void operator delete(void* dp) {
    memtable.remove(dp);
    ::delete(dp);
  }
  int alive() { return in_use;}
  int dead() { return !in_use;}
};

void garbage_collector() {
  // print messages at the bottom of the screen using
  // ANSI terminal escape commands:
  cout << "\x1b[25;1H\x1b[KGarbage Collecting...";
  cout << "\x1b[24;40H\x1b[Kitems: " << memtable.count();
  memtable.reset();
  do
    if(((garbage *)memtable.current())->dead()) {
      cout << "\x1b[25;40H\x1b[Kremoving "
           << (long)memtable.current();
      delete (garbage *)memtable.current();
      memtable.remove(memtable.index());
    }
  while( memtable.next() );
  cout << "\x1b[25;22H\x1b[Kdone.";
}

void main() {
  set_new_handler(garbage_collector);
  while(1)
    new garbage;  // this loop will exhaust free store
}
```

Operators **new** and **delete** are overloaded so when a **garbage** object is created on the free store, its address is automatically recorded in the **memtable**. Then, when the system runs out of free store, the new-handler can go through the **memtable** and free any dead **garbage** objects, thereby releasing memory on the heap. When the new-handler returns, the system tries again (successfully, this time) to allocate storage.

The program displays its garbage-collecting activities as they occur. If you are using a PC, you can try different memory models to get an idea of how much free store is allocated for each. Also, the program gives you an idea of how much stack space and heap space is allocated for a program, since you can see the number of chunks allocated before garbage collection occurs; the stack space is roughly the amount left over.

Pitfalls in Dynamic Memory Allocation

When you decide to use dynamic memory allocation (for built-in types) or dynamic object creation (for user-defined types), there are certain potential traps you can encounter. As mentioned before, when you create a variable on the free store, it has an arbitrary lifetime. You are responsible for deleting the variable when you no longer need it. If you don't take care in cleaning up, you may run out of free store.

You must also be sure that a class with a constructor that allocates free store has a complementary destructor that deallocates that free store or (again) you may run out of free store. For an example, look at the destructor for **class DynArray**.

You will encounter more subtle problems when you begin passing object arguments by value into functions and returning object arguments by value from functions. If the object contains pointers to memory on the free store, you will copy the structure that lives on the stack and contains the pointers. This is called a *shallow copy*, since the memory on the free store isn't copied. Assuming your destructor properly deallocates the free store, you will end up returning a structure that has pointers to deallocated free store. This problem is examined in detail in Chapter 9.

Calculating Object Size

You must somehow know or calculate the size of the class when you call **new** or any other function that allocates dynamic memory. As with built-in types, you can usually just give the class name to **new**, and an object of the proper size will be created. The following example is a class that has a pointer to another class, which is created on the free store:

```
//: SIZES.CPP—Object sizes are automatically calculated for
//. you when using "new."

class X {
```

```
  int i, j, k;
// ...
};

class Y {
  long u, v, w;
// ...
};

class Z {
  double a, b, c;
// ...
};

class conglomerate {
  X * xp;
  Y * yp;
  Z * zp;
public:
  conglomerate() {
    xp = new X; // just tell it the class, not the size
    yp = new Y;
    zp = new Z;
  }
};
```

Some classes contain hidden elements (classes with **virtual** functions, described in Chapter 8). Since **new** calculates the size of the class for you, you don't need to concern yourself with what's inside.

Occasionally, you will need to calculate the size of your object while performing dynamic memory allocation. This can be accomplished using the **sizeof** operator. In the following example, a class contains a pointer to a **struct** that contains the size of a vector and the starting address of the vector itself:

```
//: VVEC.CPP—Calculating sizes for dynamic memory allocation
//. using sizeof.
#include <iostream.h>
#include <assert.h>
#include <stdlib.h>

class vvec {
  struct vec {
    int size;  // length of vector
    float v[1]; // trick—this is only the start of the vector
```

```
  } * vv;
public:
  vvec(int sz) {
    vv = (vec *)new char[sizeof(vec) + (sz-1) * sizeof(float)];
    vv->size = sz;
  }
  ~vvec() { delete vv; }
  float& operator[](int i);
};

float& vvec::operator[](int i) {
  if(i > 0 && i < vv->size) return vv->v[i];
  static float d = 0;
  return d;
}

typedef long type;  // try different types for different effects
const BitsInType = sizeof(type) * 8;

void main(int argc, char * argv[]) {
  assert(argc > 1);
  const sz = atoi(argv[1]);
  vvec A(sz);
  for(int i = 0; i < sz; i++)
    A[i] = (type)1 << (i % BitsInType);
  for(i = 0; i < sz; i++)
    cout << "A[" << i << "] = " << A[i] << endl;
}
```

This employs a useful but dangerous trick, which is acceptable only because it is encapsulated inside **class vvec**. Notice that the nested structure **vec** (which is visible only within **vvec**) contains a size indicator and an array of size 1. However, there is only a pointer, and not an object of **vec**, inside **vvec**. In the constructor, memory is allocated to hold a vector of the desired length. Notice the calculation performed,

```
new char[sizeof(vec) + (sz-1) * sizeof(float)];
```

The first part, **sizeof(vec)**, is simply the size of the structure itself, as you would expect. However, the second part, **(sz–1)*sizeof(float)**, takes the constructor argument, **sz**, and uses it to calculate the size of an array of **float** numbers. But why minus 1? This is because **vec** already contains the first element of that array. Now the dynamically allocated **vec** is not an array of size 1, but of whatever size you allocated (good thing C and

C++ don't do any bounds checking, or this wouldn't work!). This trick is used in places where the compiler's code generation may be more efficient (and where that's important).

Notice you could have placed the **size** member inside of the enclosing class. However, what happens if you want to point **vv** to another **vec** object, which may have a different size? It's best to keep all the information about an object tied together with the object itself, so you won't inadvertently forget about it.

The overloaded **operator[ ]** simply returns a reference to the selected element if it is within bounds and to a static **float** if it is out of bounds (other error reporting could be performed here).

In **main()**, an integer argument is picked off the command line (and converted from a string with the ANSI C library function **atoi()**) and used to determine the size of the **vvec A**. Then **A** is filled with interesting numbers, generated by doing a bitwise left-shift of 1 (cast to the appropriate type). Notice the shift value is the index modulo of the number of bits in the type, so when the 1 would normally be shifted off the end this causes it to effectively start over at the bottom. Also notice that **type** is determined by a **typedef**, so you can play with the program by changing **type** to **char**, **short**, **int**, and so on. Also check out the different behavior of **signed** and **unsigned**.

Using References with Dynamic Memory Allocation

It is possible to bind the value returned by **new** to a reference instead of a pointer. For example:

```
//: FREEREF.CPP—Using references for dynamic memory

class marilyn {
  double artist;
public:
  void paint() {}
  void draw() {}
  void tie_dye() {}
};
```

```
void main() {
  // notice you must dereference the address, so the reference
  // sees an object (references must always bind to objects):
  marilyn & mc = *new marilyn;
  // now you can use it just like a scoped object:
  mc.paint();
  mc.draw();
  mc.tie_dye();
  // but you are still responsible for cleaning up:
  delete &mc;
}
```

References can be attractive because they make a dynamically allocated object look like a local object, with the same syntax for calling member functions. They are deceiving because a destructor is called for a local object, while no destructor is called for a reference. Since a reference is less flexible than a pointer (you can't reassign a reference once it has been initialized) it generally isn't very useful in this facility. Again, references seem best left to their intended purpose: as function arguments and for returning addresses.

Placing Objects at Specific Locations

On rare occasions, you need to place objects at specific memory locations, perhaps because there is some hardware there or as part of a specialized memory-management function. C++ provides a way to do this using the *placement syntax* for operator **new** and explicit destructor calls for cleanup. Here's an example for a purely hypothetical piece of hardware (notice that the hardware location was simulated using a piece of memory called PORT) on a machine with memory-mapped I/O:

```
//: PLACE.CPP—Explicit object placement syntax
#include <new.h>

// First, overload operator new so it takes an argument:
void * operator new(size_t, void * p) { return p; }

class IOport {
  unsigned char control; // registers
  volatile unsigned char status;
```

```
    volatile unsigned char data;
public:
  IOport(unsigned char initvalue) {
    control = initvalue; // initialize hardware
  }
  ~IOport() {
    while(status && 0x01) // clear bit
      control = 0x0e;
  }
  unsigned char read() {
    while(status && 0x04) // not ready to read
      ;
    return data;
  }
  void write(unsigned char byte) {
    byte = data;
    control = 0x02; // write byte
    while(status && 0x08) // wait for acknowledge
      ;
  }
};

// Some dummy memory to represent the IO port:
char PORT[sizeof(IOport)];

void main() {
  IOport * port = new(PORT) IOport(0x0f);  // placement syntax
  port->write('h');
  char i = port->read();
  port->IOport::~IOport(); // explicit destructor call

  // same thing with references:
  IOport & port2 = *new(PORT) IOport(0x0f);  // placement syntax
  port2.write('h');
  i = port2.read();
  port2.IOport::~IOport(); // explicit destructor call
}
```

The placement syntax has an expression in parentheses right after the **new** operator. This expression represents the physical location where the memory is located. Notice that you must overload **operator new** so that it accepts this second argument (second, because the first is the size of memory to be allocated and is automatically generated by the compiler). The **operator new** shown here simply returns the value of the second argument (*without* allocating any further memory, notice). The constructor is then called for this memory, instead of the memory that would have been allocated on the heap.

When you want to clean up an object created this way, *don't* call **delete**, which would try to deallocate the memory. Instead you must explicitly call the destructor using a special syntax (which is only provided for complementary use with the placement specifier). Notice that it's just like an ordinary function call except that the class name and the scope resolution operator are used.

In the second part of **main()** you can see the same effect, but using references instead of pointers.

In the class **IOport**, two of the data members are **volatile**. This is a good example of the appropriate use of the keyword **volatile**, because both the **status** and **data** registers are hardware outside the scope of the compiling environment, so the compiler is told it should make no assumptions about those values during optimization. This way, every time the **while** loops are passed through, the registers are actually read.

Makefile for Chapter 6 Examples

Here is the makefile for all the examples in this chapter:

```
# makefile for examples in Chapter 6
# Borland C++ compiler, with the following
# warnings turned off:
# aus: identifier assigned a value which is never used
# eff: code has no effect
# par: parameter "parameter" is never used
CPP = bcc -w-aus -w-eff -w-par
# nmake CPP=cl        # Microsoft C++ command line

.cpp.exe:
        $(CPP) $<

.cpp.obj:
        $(CPP) -c $*.cpp

all:    dave.exe freestor.exe delete.exe life.exe \
        dynatest.exe encode2.exe order.exe \
        newarray.exe fshandlr.exe garbage.exe \
```

```
            sizes.obj vvec.obj freeref.exe string.exe \
            opnew.exe place.exe

life.exe : life.obj lifefld.obj lifeunit.obj
        $(CPP) life.obj lifefld.obj lifeunit.obj

dynatest.exe : dynatest.obj dynarray.obj
          $(CPP) dynatest.obj dynarray.obj $(STRMLIB)

# On a PC, this is much more entertaining when compiled
# with the large memory model:
garbage.exe : garbage.obj dynarray.obj
          $(CPP) garbage.obj dynarray.obj $(STRMLIB)

freestor.exe : freestor.cpp tracker.h
delete.exe : delete.cpp tracker.h
life.obj : lifefld.h lifeunit.h life.cpp
lifefld.obj : lifefld.h lifeunit.h lifefld.cpp
lifeunit.obj : lifefld.h lifeunit.h lifeunit.cpp
dynarray.obj : dynarray.cpp dynarray.h
dynatest.obj : dynatest.cpp dynarray.h
garbage.obj : garbage.cpp dynarray.h
encode2.obj : ..\chap_4\encode.h encode2.cpp
```

CHAPTER

Reusing Code
in C++

Programmers are very familiar with the concept of "reinventing the wheel." Often, it seems like every time you start a new project you end up rewriting a lot of code that you or someone else has written before. The existing code may not be quite right for your application, but it might be too complicated to be worth the effort to figure out how to change it. If you've done this sort of thing before, you know that you can burn up a lot of time trying to figure out how to modify old code—one project can mysteriously turn into several.

The inability to easily reuse code is expensive. Not adding a feature to your program (because learning to use someone's code is too much of a hassle) is unfortunate and probably results in reducing the productivity of the end user. If you must rewrite something from scratch, then you might just find a way to avoid writing it at all.

This chapter focuses on the support in C++ for the reuse of existing code. Classes can be reused in two ways. The first way is by creating *member objects* of other classes inside your new class. This approach, called *composition*, takes the view that an object can be *composed of* other objects. One object can also be a *kind of* another object. This is called *inheritance*. Just as a child inherits traits from its parents, a *derived class* (also called a *subclass* or *child class*) inherits traits from a base class (also called a *superclass* or *parent class*). With composition, you are saying "this class is some of these, and some of those, and one of these." For example, a **building** has **doors** and **windows** and **rooms**. When a class is a *kind*, you are saying "this new class is that old one with some changes." For example, a **skyscraper** is a type of **building**.

This chapter looks at building new classes from old ones using composition or inheritance. Inheritance, however, also creates another kind of relationship. When you inherit a new class from an old one, the new class doesn't just take on the characteristics of the old one. Instances of the new class are also instances of the old class. That is, any functions or operations that worked on objects of the old class work on objects of the new class as well. All classes inherited from the same base class have the same set of functions, or interface, as the base class. This concept of class hierarchy is very powerful, and will be explored in Chapter 8.

This chapter begins by demonstrating the syntax for inheritance and composition, followed by a number of code examples using these techniques. The chapter ends with a discussion of multiple inheritance, which allows you to inherit from more than one base class.

Syntax for Composition and Inheritance

To use a class in C++, you must have the header file containing the class definition and, minimally, the object code file or a library containing the object code file. Coincidentally, this is exactly what you need to derive a new class from an old one or to compose a new class using an object of an existing class—you don't need the source code for the methods (although it can be useful). In the past, vendors of C libraries had the option of providing sources, often at a fee. With C++, any library that can be used can also be easily adapted to solve a new problem, whether or not you have the sources.

There are no new keywords in C++ to create new classes from existing ones using composition and inheritance. However, the syntax is different in two places: the way you describe the makeup of your new class, and the way you specify the constructor calls for the subobjects of your new class. One of the important safety features of C++ is that it can guarantee that all objects in a system are properly initialized (via constructor calls) and properly cleaned up (via destructor calls). The use of improperly initialized variables in a program constitutes an important class of errors, so this is a significant guarantee. The syntax of the constructor initializer list allows you to exactly specify the way constructors for the subobjects of your new class are called.

Composition: Reusing Code with Member Objects

To reuse code with composition, you need only declare an object of a class to be a member of a new class. Creating an object as a member of another class is very different than creating an ordinary (nonmember) object, however. Remember that one of the important features of C++ is that it guarantees that all objects are properly initialized. With composition (and inheritance) this extends to all the subobjects: each part *must* be properly initialized—the compiler guarantees this by ensuring that a constructor is called for each subobject.

With an ordinary object, the constructor is called at the point where you define the object, and you may give an argument list after the identifier. If you do not give an argument list for an ordinary object, the constructor with no arguments or all default arguments is called.

With a member object, you *never* give an argument list at the point the member object is declared in the class structure. The declaration of the member object tells the compiler to add space for the member object in any instances of the new class. However, the constructor cannot be called until the space is actually allocated, which does not occur until you create an instance of the new class and the new class's constructor is called. To control construction of all the subobjects, you use a special syntax in your new constructor, called the *constructor initializer list*.

When the body of the new class's constructor is entered, you must be able to assume that all member objects have been initialized; thus the constructors for all member objects must be called *before* the constructor for the new class. To remind you that constructors for member objects are called before the new class's constructor, the constructor initializer list shows the calls being made *outside* the body of the new class's constructor, after the argument list (and a colon, to indicate the start of constructor calls), and before the opening brace. When calling the member object constructor, you must use the same form as if you were calling the constructor for an ordinary object—the identifier followed by an argument list. The syntax for using member objects is thus

```
class classname {
  // ...
  memberclass member_object_name;
  // ...
public:
  classname(arglist); // constructor
  // ...
};
classname::classname(arglist) : member_object_name(arglist2) {
  // constructor body
}
```

Arglist2 is the argument list for the constructor of the member object; it may or may not contain arguments from *arglist*.

You can use as many member objects as you want in a class. For each member object you add, just add a constructor call to the constructor initializer list, separating it from the other elements with commas. The constructors are called in the order the objects appear in the class declaration. You can also create arrays of member objects inside a class. (As with any array of objects, the constructor with no arguments is used for initialization, so no initializer needs to be specified in the derived-class constructor.)

Inheritance Syntax

You can use inheritance for two reasons. The first, explored in this chapter, is because you have a class that you or someone else wrote and it isn't *quite* right. However, you don't want to throw away the code and rewrite it from scratch. That would require too much time and effort. Inheritance allows you to tweak the existing code by adding functionality here and there. You only change the features you need to and ignore the rest. You don't need to know how the whole thing works. By reusing code with inheritance, you can program faster.

The second reason to use inheritance is to express a problem as a hierarchy of classes. The base class interface is common to all the derived classes. Subclasses can be manipulated using this common interface in some other part of the program. A well-designed program can be extended by simply deriving a new class from the base class—since the program already knows how to talk to any object in a class derived from the base class, the changes are minimal. Creating extensible programs by carefully designing the class hierarchy is investigated in the next chapter.

When you inherit a new class from an old class, you indicate the name of the class you are inheriting from right after the name of the new class, separated by a semicolon. The syntax is

```
class derived_class_name : base_class_name {
  // body of class declaration
};
```

The members of a class default to **private** unless you explicitly declare them **public**. This is also true with inheritance: a base class is **private** unless you explicitly declare it **public**. In the preceding declaration, all the **public** members of **base_class_name** can only be used by member functions of **derived_class_name** and are inaccessible to users of **derived_class_name**. If you want the **public** members of **base_class_name** to be available to users of **derived_class_name**, you must declare

base_class_name public as it is being inherited. Thus, the more common syntax you will see for inheritance is

```
class derived_class_name : public base_class_name {
  // body of class declaration
};
```

When you inherit you get the base-class data elements and base-class member functions in the derived class. Essentially, the base-class structure is copied into the derived-class structure. You can add your own data elements and member functions. Inside the derived-class member functions, you can call **public** base-class member functions and manipulate **public** base-class data elements.

There are some member functions that are *not* automatically inherited into the derived class. Constructors, destructors, and the overloaded **operator=()** all apply to the specific derived-class structure. It would be a mistake to assume that what worked properly for constructing and destructing the base class should also work properly for the derived class. Therefore, the compiler forces you to treat constructors, destructors, and the **operator=()** specially (**operator=()** is usually a combination of destruction and construction. It is covered in Chapter 9).

A new destructor must be created (if one is necessary) for each new derived class, and the destructors for the base classes and member objects are called automatically when an object goes out of scope. Since there is only one constructor for each class, there is no ambiguity (and no arguments), so the compiler can automatically call all the base-class destructors. Note that *all* destructors for all base classes are automatically called by the compiler to guarantee proper cleanup of all parts of an object. The order of destructor calls is from the most derived destructor first to the base destructor last (since each destructor must be able to assume that "baser" objects are still valid). Member-object destructors are called in the *reverse* order that the member objects are declared in the new class.

Constructors, however, are different because they are overloaded and they take arguments. Just as with composition, you use the constructor initializer list to perform the constructor call. This echoes the syntax for inheritance: it starts with a colon and ends with the left brace that opens the body. Here's how it looks for a derived-class constructor:

```
derived_class_name::derived_class_name(arglist1)
        : base_class_name(arglist2) {
  // derived class constructor body
};
```

where *arglist1* is the argument list for the derived-class constructor, and *arglist2* is the argument list for the base-class constructor.

If the constructor for the base class is overloaded, the particular constructor that is called depends on the argument list, just as in any constructor call. If no explicit call is made to the base-class constructor in the derived-class constructor, the base-class constructor with no arguments is called.

If your derived class contains member objects, you must also call their constructors in the constructor initializer list. The list of calls is separated by commas and can be in any order—remember that the order in which you call them in the constructor initializer list is unimportant—making an assumption here can lead to bugs. The member-object constructor calls always occur after the base-class constructor call in the order in which the member objects are declared (*not* the order in which the calls are made!).

The following example demonstrates how constructors and destructors are called in derived classes. All the classes in the example print a message when their constructors and destructors are called, so you can see which ones are called, and in what order. The file begins with a preprocessor macro that, given a name, creates a class with these "message constructors" and "message destructors." There are two constructors so you can see the difference between an explicit constructor call (the constructor with an argument) and an automatic constructor call when no explicit call is made (the constructor with no arguments).

Three classes are created: **base**, **member1**, and **member2**. Three derived classes are then constructed, with **base** used as a base class, and **member1** and **member2** used as member objects. In the first, **derived1**, the constructor explicitly calls the constructors for the base class and member objects using arguments. In the second, **derived2**, no calls are made to the base class or member object constructors. In the third, **derived3**, the constructor calls are intentionally made out of their "proper" order to see what will happen. The output of the program is appended as comments at the end.

```cpp
//: INHTEST.CPP—Demonstration of the order of constructor
//. and destructor calls.
#include <iostream.h>

// A macro to create a class:
#define cldecl(CNAME) class CNAME { \
  int i; \
public: \
  CNAME() { cout << #CNAME "() constructor called" << endl; } \
  CNAME(int) { \
    cout << #CNAME "(int) constructor called" << endl; \
  } \
  ~CNAME() { cout << #CNAME " destructor called" << endl; } \
}

cldecl(base);
cldecl(member1);
cldecl(member2);

// The "regular way":
class derived : public base {
  member1 m1;
  member2 m2;
public:
  derived() : base(1), m1(1), m2(1) {
    cout << "derived constructor called" << endl;
  }
  ~derived() { cout << "derived destructor called" << endl; }
};

// No explicit constructor calls
class derived2 : public base {
  member1 m1;
  member2 m2;
public:
  derived2() {
    cout << "derived2 constructor called" << endl;
  }
  ~derived2() { cout << "derived2 destructor called" << endl; }
};

// Disordered constructor calls:
class derived3 : public base {
  member1 m1;
  member2 m2;
public:
  derived3() : m2(1), m1(1), base(1) {
```

```cpp
      cout << "derived3 constructor called" << endl;
  }
  ~derived3() { cout << "derived3 destructor called" << endl; }
};

void main() {
  {
    cout << "\n\t derived X:" << endl;
    derived X;
  }
  {
    cout << "\n\t derived2 X:" << endl;
    derived2 X;
  }
  {
    cout << "\n\t derived3 X:" << endl;
    derived3 X;
  }
}

/* output from this program:

  derived X:
base(int) constructor called
member1(int) constructor called
member2(int) constructor called
derived constructor called
derived destructor called
member2 destructor called
member1 destructor called
base destructor called

  derived2 X:
base() constructor called
member1() constructor called
member2() constructor called
derived2 constructor called
derived2 destructor called
member2 destructor called
member1 destructor called
base destructor called

  derived3 X:
base(int) constructor called
member1(int) constructor called
member2(int) constructor called
derived3 constructor called
```

```
derived3 destructor called
member2 destructor called
member1 destructor called
base destructor called
*/
```

To test the classes, an instance of each class is put inside its own scope, so you can see all the constructor calls and then all the destructor calls for each object, one at a time. As you can see from the output, the order you write the constructor calls for the inherited class and member objects is unimportant—the compiler always performs the calls the same way. The constructor with no arguments (or all default arguments) is called if no constructor call is explicitly written. The destructor calls are out of your hands, since the compiler always calls the destructors in reverse order to the way the constructors were called.

Composition with Pointers to Objects

By creating an instance of an object as a member of another object, you decide at compile time how your new class will be composed. You can also delay the decision until run time by using, instead of an object, a pointer to an object. This has been called *pluggable pointer composition* because you compose the object at run time by "plugging in" a pointer to an object. It is a very powerful way to add run-time flexibility to your system.

As an example, suppose you have a base class,

```
class base { /* ... */ };
```

two or more classes derived from that base class,

```
class derived1 : public base { /* ... */ };
class derived2 : public base { /* ... */ };
```

and finally, a class with a pluggable pointer for **class base**,

```
class composed {
  base * pluggable;
  // ...
public:
```

```
composed(base * plg) {
  pluggable = plg;
  // ...
}
// ...
};
```

Now you can decide at run time, using the constructor call, what type of object will be used in **class composed**:

```
derived1 X;
derived2 Y;
composed c1(&X), c2(&Y);
```

Here, **c1** is created with a **derived1** object, and **c2** is created with a **derived2** object. This works because a derived-class object is also a member of the base class, so a derived-class pointer can be substituted any place a base class pointer is required. You can even change the object being pointed to after the object is created, so you can modify object behavior after it has been created!

Examples of Composition and Inheritance

The rest of the chapter will consist of various examples demonstrating the use of composition and inheritance.

A Class to Handle Errors

The need to handle errors when building classes is very common. When something goes wrong in an object, you often want to call a function that prints a sensible error message and either recovers to an earlier state or exits the program.

The following class, called **error_handler**, is meant to be used as a member object in other classes. The single argument to the constructor is a string that will be printed for all error messages the new class will issue; it is usually just the class name followed by the word "error" and a colon. The two methods, called **message()** and **terminate()**, take a format string and arguments exactly like **printf()**, so you can print virtually any kind of message with debugging information when an error occurs.

The header file **error.h**, shown here, is the header file for error messaging using the **printf()** approach:

```
//: ERROR.H—A class to perform error management inside other
//. classes. This class demonstrates reuse via member objects.
//. class_msg describes the class error_handler is being used
//. in. terminate() takes arguments just like printf() does.
#ifndef ERROR_H_
#define ERROR_H_

class error_handler {
  char * msg;
public:
  error_handler(char * class_msg) : msg(class_msg) {}
  void message(char * format_string, ...);
  void terminate(char * format_string, ...);
};

#endif // ERROR_H_
```

The constructor simply assigns the pointer from the string argument to the internal **msg** pointer. You'll notice that this assignment takes place in the constructor initializer list, where the constructors for all the base classes and all the member objects are normally called. However, **char *** is a built-in type, so you don't normally think of it as having a constructor. This is true; however, for consistency you can pretend that it *does* have a constructor. The effect of this "pseudo" constructor call is simply assignment.

It is a good practice to initialize all member objects, whether they are user-defined or built-in types, in the constructor initializer list. That way, in the constructor body you'll know that all the member objects are initialized.

Assigning a **char *** to an external string rather than making a local copy in the object assumes that the external string will not be changed over the course of the program. The argument is intended to be the name of the class or program for which the **error_handler** is created, so it is fairly safe to assume that a quoted string constant will be used. If you know this may not be the case, then you should change the code to allocate storage and make a local copy of the argument.

The **message()** and **terminate()** functions print a message to **stderr** (C standard I/O error output) and then continue processing or terminate using **exit()**, respectively. Notice that both use ellipses as trailing arguments. This is ANSI C syntax for a *variadic argument list*, which means "any number or type of arguments," most commonly seen in **printf()**. Indeed, that's why it is used here—so you don't have to learn anything new to use the **error_handler** class.

Notice in **error.h** the "insulation" provided by the preprocessor statements involving the name ERROR_H . This is especially important in such a general-purpose class, since the likelihood is very good that the header file will be included more than once.

To use a variadic argument list, you must call macros in the ANSI C library header file **varargs.h**. This is shown here in the implementation file for **error_handler**:

```
//: ERROR.CPP—The variable argument list for terminate() is
//. implemented using the ANSI C library functions for variable
//. arguments (in stdarg.h) and the associated printf()-like
//. vfprintf() function.
#include <stdio.h>
#include <stdarg.h>
#include <stdlib.h>  // exit()
#include "..\chap_7\error.h"

void error_handler::message(char * format_string, ...) {
  va_list arg_pointer;
  va_start(arg_pointer, format_string);
  fprintf(stderr, "%s error: ", msg);  // class message first
  vfprintf(stderr, format_string, arg_pointer);
  va_end(arg_pointer);
}

void error_handler::terminate(char * format_string, ...) {
  va_list arg_pointer;
  va_start(arg_pointer, format_string);
  fprintf(stderr, "%s error: ", msg);  // class message first
  vfprintf(stderr, format_string, arg_pointer);
  va_end(arg_pointer);
  exit(1);
}
```

The **arg_pointer** is a special type of pointer that indexes through the argument list. Calling the macro **va_start()** sets this pointer up. Then **arg_pointer** is handed to **vfprintf()**, which knows how to select all the arguments in the list. When the function is finished, a call to **va_end()** resets **arg_pointer**. This is important, because it restores the stack to the way it was before the function call.

The file ERRTEST.CPP, shown here, is a simple test that shows how **error_handler** is used inside another class:

```
//: ERRTEST.CPP—Test of printf()-like error messaging
#include "error.h"

class etest {
  static error_handler error;  // only make one for each class
public:
  void demonstration() {
    error.terminate("in function %s, value %d\n",
                    "demonstration", 1);
  }
};

// initialization of static member object:
error_handler etest::error("etest");

void main() {
  etest E;
  E.demonstration();
}
```

Notice that the **error_handler** inside **class etest** is **static**, so only one object will be created, regardless of how many objects of **class etest** are created. Objects like this are sometimes referred to as *class variables*, since they exist for the benefit of the entire class. You won't use storage for that object every time you create an **etest**, which is very important.

The definition for the **static** member **error_handler** reserves storage for the object (in only one place) and calls the constructor for that object before **main()** begins. In addition, the destructor is called after **main()** exits.

Note that in **etest::demonstration()**, calling **terminate()** is just like using **printf()**, which is the desired effect.

The iostream Approach

The **printf()** approach to error messaging works fine and is especially useful when the users are more familiar with **printf()** than with C++. However, the **printf()** approach has several problems, all relating to the variable argument list. First, if "**...**" means "any number or type of arguments," then the compiler suspends all type checking for those arguments. In addition, if you don't have the format string written correctly and you have too few arguments in the list to match the format string, you'll usually get garbage when the function prints. In both of these cases the compiler can't help you because you've effectively told it to buzz off and mind its own business, that you're taking care of this particular argument list. It's bad enough when **printf()** gives problems, but an unintelligible error message is particularly useless.

This lack of type checking in I/O is one of the main reasons iostreams were developed as a standard library for C++. With iostreams, you can say

```
cout << "hello, world, I'm " << 5
    << " on " << ctime(&now) << endl;
```

The object **cout** is the analog of **stdout** in C standard I/O, and the **<<** operator has been overloaded to mean "put to" when used with iostream objects. Every expression in between **<<** operators is evaluated separately.

Notice there are a number of different things going on in this statement. There are two strings, one function, **ctime()**, (from the ANSI C library) that returns a string, an integer (5), and something called a *manipulator*, named **endl**. The manipulator does something to the iostream itself, rather than just put something into the iostream. In this case, it places a newline in the iostream and then flushes the iostream.

There are different functions called for the iostream, depending on whether the argument is a string, an **int**, a **float**, etc. You can even create your own iostream functions when you make a new class, so objects of your class can be sent to an iostream. One of the best things about iostreams is that the compiler determines whether the iostream arguments are properly used, and which function to call. This means that you not only get compile-time error checking, but potentially much greater efficiency than the **printf()** family of functions (which is the other important reason that iostreams were developed). Every time you call **printf()**, the format string and the arguments must be parsed by the function at run time! This is slow, and it means **printf()** must be large. Since all iostream arguments are parsed at compile time, the compiler does the work instead of the printing function, so the functions are much smaller and execution is faster.

In addition, the syntax of an iostream expression is easier to read because you simply see the items to print in the order they are printed.

Adapting iostreams with Inheritance

In the spirit of the **error_handler** class, the following file adapts error reporting to the iostream style:

```
//: IOSERROR.H—Simple error handler using iostreams.
//. Installing static objects of this class in other classes
//. and in programs puts a framework in place, which can be
//. modified later and recompiled for more sophisticated
//. error handling.
#ifndef IOSERROR_H_
#define IOSERROR_H_
#include <iostream.h>
#include <strstream.h>

// Manipulator inserts a newline in the output stream:
inline ostream& nl(ostream& os) { return os << "\n"; }

class ioserror : public ostrstream {
  enum { bsize = 300 };   // a "local const" for the class
  char msg[bsize];   // buffer for holding error messages
  char* classname;   // name associated with this handler
public:
  ioserror(char * class_name);   // name of class/program
  void dump() {
    if(*msg) {   // only dump if there are messages
      clog << nl << classname << " error: " << msg << endl;
    }
  }
};

// Manipulator prints all error messages and exits:
ostream& terminate(ostream& os);

#endif // IOSERROR_H_
```

The **class ioserror** is derived from **ostrstream**, which is a special type of iostream that performs *in-core formatting*. This is just like the ANSI C library function **sprintf()**, which performs a **printf()** to an area of memory instead of standard output. The **class ioserror** keeps all the messages in the buffer **msg**, but because it is derived from **ostrstream** it automatically has all the properties of streams, including all the formatting functions for integers, characters, strings, floats, etc.

In **class ioserror**, you can see the use of **enum** to simulate a local **const**. Inside a class, a **const** creates a local instance that must be initialized in the constructor initializer list and cannot be changed for the life of the object. However, each object of that class can have a different value for the **const**, and the **const** always requires storage, which means the compiler can't use it in a constant expression like an array definition. To create a constant value that is local to a class doesn't require any storage, and can be used in array definitions, this "untagged enumeration" technique is perfect. Its only limitation is that it can only be used with integral values.

Creating Manipulators

One of the odd things about manipulators is that to use them, you don't make a usual function call, with parentheses. You simply give the manipulator's name. This works because the compiler sees a pointer to a function in the iostream list, and it remembers that there's an overloaded **operator<<()** which takes a function pointer. This overloaded **operator<<()** is called an *applicator*, and the only kind of function pointer it accepts is for a function that takes an **ostream&** argument and returns an **ostream&** (**istream** manipulators have **istream** arguments and return values). All the applicator does is call the function and return the **ostream**, but because it's there you can make manipulators.

The simplest manipulator, seen in **ioserror.h**, just puts a newline on the output stream, as shown here:

```
inline ostream& nl(ostream& os) { return os << "\n"; }
```

Note that manipulators cannot be member functions, and thus they can be applied to *any* iostream.

The second manipulator, the critical one for **ioserror**, is **terminate**. When terminate is called, all the stored error messages are printed and the program is terminated.

Now it turns out that you'll want to use the **ioserror** class in several ways, and this will affect the design of **terminate**. First, it will be used inside of other classes, as a localized error-messaging system. If an object of a particular class has a problem, it sends a message to its local error handler. That way, you know which class had trouble. However, classes may report problems without terminating, so you can get more information about the trouble before the program exits. This means that not only will each **ioserror** object have its own local buffer where it stores error messages (the buffer **msg**), but there must be a list of pointers to **ioserror** objects someplace so all the objects will be dumped upon termination.

Secondly, you'll want to use global **ioserror** objects, especially in your **main()** file. That way you can report program errors the same way you report class errors.

There's no guarantee that the **terminate** manipulator will be called anywhere. The **ioserror** objects may simply report errors and expect someone else to call **terminate**. The ANSI C library function **atexit()** takes care of the problem by creating a list of functions to be called when the library function **exit()** is called. The **exit()** function is also called during a normal return from **main()**. The only time **exit()** is not called is when you leave the program using the library function **abort()** (a ruthless and inadvisable practice, especially in C++ since it skips static object destructor calls).

Implementing ioserror

You can see how this all comes together in the file IOSERROR.CPP, shown here:

```
//: IOSERROR.CPP—Implementation of iostream error handler.
//. Also includes a default replacement new_handler
#include "..\chap_7\ioserror.h"  // for remote compilation
#include <stdlib.h>
#include <new.h>

// This is a trivial implementation; for general solutions you
// will probably want to use one with a variable size.
```

```
class eh_list {  // ioserror container class
  static ioserror* list[];
  static int cursor;
public:
  enum { size = 100 };  // number of error handlers
  eh_list() {
    atexit(eh_list::dump);  // execute dump() on exit()
  }
  // Add error handlers as they are constructed:
  static void Register(ioserror* eh) {
    if(cursor < size)
      list[cursor++] = eh;
    else
      clog << "increase eh_list size" << nl;
  }
  // Dump contents of all error handlers:
  static void dump() {
    while(cursor-- > 0)
      list[cursor]->dump();
  }
};

// static data member definitions (initialize everything to 0)
ioserror* eh_list::list[eh_list::size] = { 0 };
int eh_list::cursor = 0;

static eh_list ehandler_list;  // visible only in this file

// Initialize the ostrstream to write to the msg buffer,
// and register this object in the eh_list:
ioserror::ioserror(char * class_name)
  : ostrstream(msg, bsize), classname(class_name) {
    eh_list::Register(this);  // static member function call
}

// The first error handler to terminate dumps the data
// from all the error handlers. No error information is lost.
ostream& terminate(ostream& os) { // manipulator
  exit(1);
  return os;  // dummy return value to satisfy compiler
}

// On a separate issue: a default replacement _new_handler
// so you'll always get a message if you run out of free store.
struct _INIT_NEW_HANDLER {
  void (*old_handler)();
  static void new_handler() {
```

```
    cerr << "Heap Error: out of free store" << endl;
    exit(1);
  }
  _INIT_NEW_HANDLER() {
    old_handler = set_new_handler(new_handler);
  }
  ~_INIT_NEW_HANDLER() {
    set_new_handler(old_handler);
  }
};
// Visible only in this file:
static _INIT_NEW_HANDLER _init_new_handler;
```

The first thing you see in that file is a container class for **ioserror** pointers called **eh_list**. There's a single **static** (visible only in this file) instance of this class called **ehandler_list**. This is where all the objects of class **ioserror** register themselves upon creation; you can see this registration in the **ioserror** constructor. The **eh_list::Register()** function just sticks the pointer in the internal array (after checking to make sure the boundary wasn't exceeded). This is a simple implementation; in a more general one you might want to use a linked list (however, the interface wouldn't change).

The constructor for **eh_list** calls **atexit()** with the address of the **eh_list::dump()** function, so all **ioserror** objects are dumped at program exit. However, treating a member function like **eh_list::dump()** as an ordinary function argument for **atexit()** is normally not possible in C++, where the member function call and the object it is being called for are tightly bound together. How can it happen here? You'll notice that both **eh_list::Register()** and **eh_list::dump()** are declared as **static** member functions. Like **static** member objects, **static** member functions work for the class as a whole, and don't manipulate any nonstatic member data. This means they don't need the address of the object (**this**) secretly passed to them, as happens with ordinary member functions. Instead, a **static** member function looks just like an ordinary global function, with the exception that its name is hidden inside the class.

You can call a **static** member function in the ordinary way, and you can also call it by simply specifying the class name with the scope resolution operator, as seen in **eh_list::eh_list()**. Since it has the characteristics of an ordinary member function, its address can be passed to **atexit()**.

Now you can see that all the **terminate** manipulator needs to do is dump the contents of every **ioserror** object in the list. It does this by calling **exit()**, which executes the functions logged by **atexit()**, including **eh_list::dump()**. Also, even though it will never get there, **terminate** must return its **ostream** argument to satisfy the compiler. The **eh_list::dump()** function simply goes through the list, calling **dump()** for each of the **ioserror** objects (note that this is *not* a recursive call; **eh_list** and **ioserror** each have their own distinct version of **dump()**. The compiler knows which one to call because it knows the type of object). The **ioserror::dump()** function (in **ioserror.h**) will only put information on **clog** if there are messages in the error **msg** buffer. If so, the class name and the string "error:" are sent to **clog** followed by the **msg** buffer.

But it's not finished yet: how do messages get into the **msg** buffer? To understand this, you need to look at the constructor for **ioserror** in IOSERROR.CPP. Notice that the first thing in the constructor initializer list is a call to the base-class constructor **ostrstream(msg, bsize)**. An **ostrstream** is a way to treat a region of memory like an iostream. When this constructor form is used, the programmer is saying what region of memory to use (if the constructor has no arguments, the object creates and manages its own memory). The code used here tells the **ostrstream** to send everything into the buffer **msg** (and to make sure that it doesn't overflow the size of the buffer, **bsize**). Thus, with an **ioserror** object called **error**, if you say **error << "hello";** the string "hello" will end up in the **msg** buffer of that object.

Testing ioserror

The file IOSTEST.CPP, shown here, tests **ioserror** and demonstrates how you should use it in new classes:

```
//: IOSTEST.CPP—Test of ioserror.
//. Demonstrates that errors from all classes are always
//. reported, whether terminate is used or exit() is called.
#include "ioserror.h"
#include <stdlib.h>
#include <conio.h>  // getch()
#include <new.h>

class gonk {
  static ioserror error;
```

```
public:
  void test() {
    error << "oops! number: " << 47 << nl;
  }
};

class boink {
  static ioserror error;
public:
  void test() {
    error << "ack! value: " << 3.14159 << nl;
  }
};

class urp {
public:
  friend ostream& operator<<(ostream& os, urp&) {
    return os << "Urp!" << nl;
  }  // not a member function!!
};

// static data member definitions:
ioserror gonk::error("gonk");
ioserror boink::error("boink");

// global error function:
ioserror error("errstest");

void quit_test(int index) {
  cout << "early exit: press ESC" << endl;
  if(getch() == 27)
    error << "quitting on index " << index
          << nl << terminate;
}

void main() {
  gonk g;
  boink b;
  urp u;
  quit_test(1);
  g.test();
  quit_test(2);
  b.test();
  quit_test(3);
  error << u;  // urp's overloaded operator <<
```

```
  cout << "preparing to exit()" << endl;
  // Exhaust the heap:
  while(1) new int[100];   // bad statement
}
```

Notice that the classes **gonk** and **boink** both contain **static ioserror** objects. **ioserror** objects in your classes should always be **static** so you don't use space in every object; just once for the whole class.

Inside the **test()** member functions, you can see that these objects work exactly the same as iostreams. Each time information is sent to the member **error** objects, it is stored. Only when the **terminate** function is called (or the program quits with **exit()**, which also happens in normal termination) are all the messages printed out.

The class **urp** shows how you can make an overloaded iostream **operator<<()** for your own classes. In **main()**, you can see the call to the output operator, **error << u;**. Note that any action you do with ordinary iostreams, you can do with an **ioserror** object. This is because **class ioserror** is derived from a type of iostream, so it *is* actually a type of iostream. Thus, if you create an overloaded output iostream **operator<<** for a class you make, that operator will work with **ioserror** objects as well. Although it took some thinking, it didn't take much coding and all the power of iostreams is still available.

By putting **ioserror** objects in all your classes, you create a consistent, portable framework for error reporting. Since the member objects are **static**, there is no impact on the size or performance of any objects containing **ioserror**s. All error reporting can use the well-established iostreams format, and new classes with overloaded **operator<<()** functions for iostreams just drop right in. In addition, if you want to modify the way errors are handled, the framework can be modified in one place to make it more powerful, and all the changes will be propagated just by recompiling.

As you can see, adding sophisticated error messages to your classes is very easy. You will find that error messages are exceptionally useful when you start building large projects with many classes. The objects themselves will tell you where the problems are; this will reduce your debugging time greatly. You can also create a stand-alone instance of **error_handler** for use in **main()**.

A Class to Handle Timing

Here's another class you might use to make a member object inside a class. The **class timer** allows you to **start()** timing a process, **mark()** the end of the process, and read the **elapsed_time()** in seconds. It also has a function to **pause()** for a number of seconds. The header file contains all the methods as **inline** functions:

```
//: TIMER.H—A small class to handle delays and timing
#ifndef TIMER_H_
#define TIMER_H_
#include <time.h>

class timer {
  time_t start_time, mark_time;
public:
  void start() { // start the stopwatch
    time(&start_time);
  }
  void mark() {  // mark the time
    time(&mark_time);
  }
  double elapsed_time() { // how many seconds elapsed?
    return difftime(mark_time, start_time);
  }
  void pause(int seconds) {  // wait
    start();
    do
      mark();
    while ( elapsed_time() < seconds );
  }
};

#endif // TIMER_H_
```

The **class timer** uses the ANSI C library functions for keeping time, prototyped in **time.h**. The ANSI committee could not force very stringent requirements on the time functions because some systems might not be able to meet them. As a result, the granularity of the time functions is 1 second. This means that if you ask for a pause of 10 seconds, you will get a pause of no less than 9 seconds and no more than 10 seconds. For many applications, this is fine. If you need higher resolution, you can measure the number of clock ticks using the **clock()** function. The number of clock ticks per second (**CLOCKS_PER_SEC** in **time.h**) is implementation dependent and will often give you a better granularity than the methods used here.

Here is **class timer** modified for (potentially) higher resolution:

```
//: TIMER2.H—Class timer modified to use the (implementation
//. dependent) clock ticks instead of difftime. This should
//. provide higher resolution than timer.h.
#ifndef TIMER2_H_
#define TIMER2_H_
#include <time.h>

class timer {
  clock_t start_time, mark_time;
public:
  void start() { // start the stopwatch
    start_time = clock();
  }
  void mark() {  // mark the time
    mark_time = clock();
  }
  clock_t elapsed_time() { // how many seconds elapsed?
    return (mark_time - start_time)/ CLOCKS_PER_SEC;
  }
  void pause(int seconds) {  // wait
    start();
    do
      mark();
    while ( elapsed_time() < seconds );
  }
};

#endif // TIMER2_H_
```

The implementation of **pause()** is appropriate for a single-tasking environment. In a multitasking environment you may need to be careful that you don't hang up the machine during a **pause()**.

The following program tests **class timer**. It takes an integer from the command line and counts that many seconds. It also checks the elapsed time, and prints it at the end. To see the difference in the two implementations of **timer**, try alternately including **timer.h** and **timer2.h**.

```
//: TIMETEST.CPP—A test for class timer. Takes the pause()
//. argument from the command line.
#include <iostream.h>
#include <stdlib.h>
#include "timer2.h"
#include "ioserror.h"

static ioserror error("timetest");

void main(int argc, char ** argv) {
  if(argc < 2)
    error << "usage : timetest delay_in_seconds" << terminate;
  timer T1, T2;
  T1.start();
  T2.pause(atoi(argv[1]));
  T1.mark();
  cout << "elapsed time: " << (int)T1.elapsed_time()
       << " seconds" << endl;
}
```

Notice that an instance of **class error_handler** is used as an ordinary (nonmember) object to print an error message if the user doesn't supply the right number of arguments.

Here's a more interesting use of **class timer**. It takes a command that you would ordinarily type at the operating system command prompt, executes it using the ANSI C library **system()** function, and then tells you how long it took to execute:

```
//: TIMECOM.CPP—Times the execution of a command.
//. Also demonstrates in-core formatting using iostreams.
#include <stdlib.h>  // system() declaration
#include <iostream.h>
#include <strstream.h>
#include "timer2.h"
#include "ioserror.h"

static ioserror error("timecom");

void main(int argc, char ** argv) {
  if(argc < 2)
    error << nl << "\t usage : timecom command-line"
          << terminate;
  ostrstream command;
  // copy the rest of the line into a single buffer:
  for(int i = 1; i < argc; i++)
```

```
    command << argv[i] << " ";
  command << ends;
  timer T1;
  T1.start();
  cout << command.str() << endl;
  system(command.str());
  T1.mark();
  cout << "elapsed time: " << (int)T1.elapsed time()
       << " seconds" << endl;
  delete command.str();   // clean up ostrstream
}
```

The system command can contain any number of arguments. It is copied into the string stream **command** using ordinary iostream functions. The **str( )** function returns the address of the buffer used by **command.** Once you call **str( )** for a **strstream** object, you are responsible for freeing the storage with **delete.**

Reusing Code with Inheritance

This section examines the way you might start with an existing class that you or someone else has created and build upon it using inheritance. As you look at the code, you might think that it would make more sense to go back and change the base class rather than using inheritance. In fact, once you get the whole system fleshed out it may indeed make sense to go back and collapse the hierarchy into a single class. However:

❑ You might not own the source code to the base class.

❑ Someone else might be using the base class and relying on it, so you cannot change it.

❑ Each class in the hierarchy might represent a distinct concept that is useful by itself, and not as part of a bigger class.

❑ As you are developing the code, inheritance allows you to keep the debugged, working code (in the base class) separate from the buggy new code (in the derived class). Since the new code is smaller and not folded into the mass of code in the base class, you can more easily spot errors.

A Class to Manage the Screen

So far in this book, control of the screen has been implemented via ANSI terminal-control sequences. ANSI terminals are quite common; VT100 terminals or terminal emulators (available on many UNIX machines) use ANSI sequences, and the PC emulates an ANSI terminal when the device driver ANSI.SYS is loaded. However, using ANSI terminal-control sequences isn't particularly general or portable. The example in this section creates a general-purpose screen-control class and isolates the ANSI sequences in the methods. This way, you can change the methods to use more efficient function calls if you desire, without altering the interface. Later, this class will be refined and expanded using inheritance.

The functionality of the base class will be limited. The cursor can be moved, you can erase to the end of the line, clear the whole screen and move the cursor to the "home" position. You can also save and restore the cursor location. Notice that, in the following header file, there is no mention of ANSI terminals, or *any* kind of terminal. This means you can implement the functionality any way you want (or implement it multiple ways for portability between different platforms).

```
//: SCREEN1.H—Simple screen-handling class
#ifndef SCREEN1_H_
#define SCREEN1_H_

class cursor_controller {
public:
  // Simple cursor motion:
  void up(int rows = 1);
  void down(int rows = 1);
  void right(int cols = 1);
  void left(int cols = 1);
  void move(int row, int col); // absolute positioning
  void home() { move(1,1); }
  // Erasing portions of the screen:
  void clear_screen();  // also send cursor "home"
  void clear_eol();  // clear to end of line
  // Saving and restoring the cursor position:
  void save();
  void restore();
};
```

```
#endif // SCREEN1_H_
```

The implementation of **cursor_controller** uses the ANSI control sequences, which always start with an escape character (ASCII 27 or hexadecimal 1B) followed by a left bracket.

This "attention sequence" is combined in the following example into a preprocessor constant called **ATN** (for ATteNtion sequence). **ATN** is included in the print strings using the string concatenation feature of the ANSI preprocessor.

```
//: SCREEN1.CPP—Methods for simple screen control

#include <iostream.h>
#include "..\chap_7\screen1.h"  // for remote compilation
#define ATN "\x1b["

void cursor_controller::up(int rows) {
  cout << ATN << rows << "A";
}

void cursor_controller::down(int rows) {
  cout << ATN << rows << "B";
}

void cursor_controller::right(int cols) {
  cout << ATN << cols << "C";
}

void cursor_controller::left(int cols) {
  cout << ATN << cols << "D";
}

void cursor_controller::move(int row, int col) {
  cout << ATN << row << ";" << col << "H";
}

void cursor_controller::clear_screen() { cout << ATN "2J"; }

void cursor_controller::clear_eol() { cout << ATN "K"; }

void cursor_controller::save() { cout << ATN "s"; }

void cursor_controller::restore() { cout << ATN "u"; }
```

Here is a program to test **cursor_controller**:

```cpp
//: SCR1TEST.CPP—Test for class cursor_controller
#include "screen1.h"
#include <iostream.h>
#include "timer2.h"

timer TT;
cursor_controller cursor;

void message(char * function_name) {
  cursor.save(); cursor.home(); cursor.clear_eol();
  cout << "testing " << function_name;
  cursor.restore();
  TT.pause(2);
}

void main() {
  message("clear_screen");
  cursor.clear_screen();
  message("move");
  cursor.move(12,40);   // center of screen
  message("right");
  cursor.right(20);
  message("left");
  cursor.left(40);
  message("up");
  cursor.up(4);
  message("down");
  cursor.down(8);
  message("clear_eol");
  for(int i = 0; i < 60; i++)
    cout << "X";
  TT.pause(1);
  cursor.left(40);
  TT.pause(1);
  cursor.clear_eol();
}
```

The test program contains a macro to print a message on the screen and delay for a few seconds (using an instance of **class timer**), so the effects of the screen-control commands can be seen. Notice that there is no terminating semicolon in the macro definition. This forces all macro calls to be terminated with a semicolon.

Adding Functionality Through Inheritance

Now suppose you want to control the screen, but the **cursor_controller** class doesn't do quite what you need. In particular, suppose you want to implement character attributes (blink, reverse video, and the like). With C++, you don't have to rewrite the class to add functionality; you simply inherit it into a new class, as shown here:

```
//: SCREEN2.H—Adding new features to cursor_controller
// through inheritance.
#ifndef SCREEN2_H_
#define SCREEN2_H_
#include "..\chap_7\screen1.h"  // base class declaration

class cursor_controller2 : public cursor_controller {
public:
  void normal();  // no attributes
  void high_intensity();
  void blink();
  void reverse();
  void invisible();
};

#endif // SCREEN2_H_
```

Here are the methods for **cursor_controller2**:

```
//: SCREEN2.CPP—Methods for screen control with attributes
#include <iostream.h>
#include "..\chap_7\screen2.h" // for remote compilation
// ANSI terminal attributes:
#define ATTRIBUTE(A) cout << "\x1b[" #A "m"

void cursor_controller2::normal() { ATTRIBUTE(0); }

void cursor_controller2::high_intensity() { ATTRIBUTE(1); }

void cursor_controller2::blink() { ATTRIBUTE(5); }

void cursor_controller2::reverse() { ATTRIBUTE(7); }

void cursor_controller2::invisible() { ATTRIBUTE(8); }
```

When you inherit, you don't need access to the source code for the methods of the base class. You *do* need the header file and the object code for the methods. The derived class uses the declaration of the base class. Thus, the header file for the base class must be included in the header for the derived class because the base class must be declared before the derived class. The object code for the base class must be searched by the linker to resolve all the calls to the methods of the base class. When SCREEN2.OBJ is linked, the object file SCREEN1.OBJ must be searched by the linker (**class timer2** doesn't have an object code file, since it consists solely of **inline** functions).

Here is a program to test **cursor_controller2**:

```
//: SCR2TEST.CPP—Test for class cursor_controller2
#include "screen2.h"
#include "timer2.h"
#include <iostream.h>

timer TT;

#define TEST(feature) \
  cursor.move(12,20); \
  cursor.clear_eol(); \
  cursor.feature(); \
  cout << #feature << " text" ; \
  TT.pause(1); \
  cursor.normal()

void main() {
  cursor_controller2 cursor;
  cursor.clear_screen();
  TEST(normal);
  TEST(high_intensity);
  TEST(blink);
  TEST(reverse);
  TEST(invisible);
  // The finale:
  cursor.move(12,20);
  cursor.clear_eol();
  cursor.reverse(); cursor.blink();
  cout << "That's All, Folks!";
  TT.pause(2);
  cursor.normal();
  // If you don't do a cursor.normal() as the very last
```

```
    // function, the program exits and leaves the attribute !
}
```

The **test()** macro allows you to test all the new features of the class without writing a lot of code. Notice that both the "stringize" and string-concatenation features of the preprocessor are used in the statement:

```
cout << #feature << " text"; \
```

More Improvements to cursor_controller2

The **cursor_controller2** class still lacks polish. The program exits without resetting the screen attributes to "normal." If you forget to do this yourself, the terminal may be left with undesirable attributes. Also, what is to keep the user from declaring more than one instance of **cursor_controller2**? This isn't a windowing system, which allows multiple windows. There is only one screen.

It would be helpful to print an error message if the user tries to move the cursor off the screen. Finally, it would be nice to add some support for display formatting: centering text, drawing vertical and horizontal lines of user-selected characters, and delays to allow end users time to read the screens.

To add these features, **cursor_controller2** will be inherited into a class called **screen_controller**. This new class will contain a member object of **class error_handler** to generate error messages and a member object of **class timer** to allow pausing during output messages. The **screen_controller** will also contain maximum row and column coordinates for the screen to use for bounds checking and display formatting. To prevent more than one instance of **screen_controller** in a program, **screen_controller** will contain a **static** data member that the constructor can examine to ensure no other objects of the class already exist.

Here is the header file for **screen_controller**:

```
//: SCREEN3.H—Inheriting cursor_controller2 and adding
//. more improvements
#ifndef SCREEN3_H_
#define SCREEN3_H_
```

```cpp
#include "..\chap_7\screen2.h"
#include "..\chap_7\ioserror.h"
#include "..\chap_7\timer2.h"

class screen_controller : public cursor_controller2 {
  int rowmax, colmax; // screen boundaries
  static ioserror error;
  timer interval;
  static object_count;  // counts number of instances
public:
  // The defaults are for a "standard" terminal:
  screen_controller(int rows = 25, int cols = 80);
  // but you can change them:
  void setrows(int rows);
  void setcols(int cols);
  int maxrow() { return rowmax; }
  int maxcol() { return colmax; }
  // the destructor cleans up the screen:
  ~screen_controller();
  // moving the cursor to the corners of the screen:
  void upper_left();
  void lower_left();
  void upper_right();
  void lower_right();
  // draw vertical line of lc;
  void draw_vertical(int row, int col, int length, char lc);
  // draw horizontal line of lc:
  void draw_horizontal(int row, int col, int length, char lc);
  // center text on a particular row
  void center(int row, char * text);
  // Replace inherited function with error-checking version:
  void move(int row, int col);
  // built-in time delay function:
  void pause(int seconds = 1);
  // draw a box around the edges of the screen. The characters
  // used for the box are
  //    hor = horizontal line character
  //    ver = vertical line character
  //    ul = upper-left corner character
  //    ur = upper-right corner character
  //    ll = lower-left corner character
  //    lr = lower-right corner character
  void drawbox(int hor, int ver, int ul,
            int ur, int ll, int lr);
};
```

```
// Single global instance of this class:
extern screen_controller screen;

#endif // SCREEN3_H_
```

Notice that one of the member functions in the base class, **move()**, has been redeclared. Whenever you take a function that has been defined in a base class and redefine it in a derived class, you must redeclare it in the derived class. This makes it explicit to both the compiler and the user that the old definition of the function is being replaced. You can still *use* the old definition of the function, however—in the code for **screen_controller::move()** that follows, you will see a call to **cursor_controller::move()**. The scope resolution operator is necessary here because otherwise the compiler would take the nearest function and you would get an infinitely recursive call (well, not actually infinite—only until the stack blows up). The implementation of **screen_controller::move()** is not very efficient because of the error checking and function-call overhead. It is a demonstration of how to make particular function calls rather than how to write efficient code.

The **screen3.h** header file just shown declares a single global instance of **screen_controller** called **screen**, which is defined in the following implementation file:

```
//: SCREEN3.CPP—"Polished" screen controller class methods
#include <iostream.h>
#include <string.h>
#include "..\chap_7\screen3.h"

// definition of static data members:
int screen_controller::object_count = 0;
ioserror screen_controller::error("screen_controller");

// Create a single global instance of screen_controller.
// If the user tries to create another, it generates a
// run-time error message.
screen_controller screen;  // use default parameters

screen_controller::screen_controller(int rows, int cols)
  : rowmax(rows), colmax(cols) {
  if(object_count++) // test, then increment
    error << "Only 1 screen_controller object is allowed."
```

```
          << nl
          << "An object called screen is defined for you."
          << terminate;
    cout << "\x1b[=7l";   // turn off line wrap
  }


  void screen_controller::setrows(int rows) { rowmax = rows; }


  void screen_controller::setcols(int cols) { colmax = cols; }


  screen_controller::~screen_controller() {
    normal();   // return to normal text upon exit.
    cout << "\x1b[=7h";   // turn on line wrap
  }


  void screen_controller::upper_left() { move(1,1); }


  void screen_controller::lower_left() { move(rowmax,1); }


  void screen_controller::upper_right() { move(1,colmax); }


  void screen_controller::lower_right() { move(rowmax,colmax); }


  void screen_controller::draw_vertical(
      int row, int col, int length, char l_char) {
    if(row > rowmax || (row + length) > rowmax)
      error << "draw_vertical: row index out of bounds"
            << terminate;
    if(col > colmax)
      error << "draw_vertical: col index out of bounds"
            << terminate;
    for(int rrow = row; rrow <= row + length; rrow++) {
      // call the more efficient version of move:
      cursor_controller::move(rrow,col);
      cout << l_char;
    }
  }


  void screen_controller::draw_horizontal(
      int row, int col, int length, char l_char) {
    if(col > colmax || (col + length) > colmax)
      error << "draw_horizontal: row index out of bounds"
            << terminate;
    if(row > rowmax)
      error << "draw_horizontal: col index out of bounds"
            << terminate;
    for(int ccol = col; ccol <= col + length; ccol++) {
```

```
    // call the more efficient version of move:
    cursor_controller::move(row,ccol);
    cout << l_char;
  }
}

void screen_controller::center(int row, char * text) {
  move(row, (colmax - strlen(text))/2 );
  cout << text;
}

void screen_controller::move(int row, int col) {
  if(row > rowmax)
    error << "move: row index out of bounds" << terminate;
  if(col > colmax)
    error << "move: col index out of bounds" << terminate;
  // call a base class function:
  cursor_controller::move(row,col);
}

void screen_controller::pause(int seconds) {
  interval.pause(seconds);
}

void screen_controller::drawbox(int hor, int ver,
                    int ul, int ur, int ll, int lr) {
  draw_vertical(0, 0, maxrow() - 1, ver);
  draw_vertical(0,maxcol(), maxrow() - 1, ver);
  draw_horizontal(0, 0, maxcol() - 1, hor);
  draw_horizontal(maxrow(), 0, maxcol() - 1, hor);
  upper_left(); cout << (char)ul;
  lower_left(); cout << (char)ll;
  upper_right(); cout << (char)ur;
  lower_right(); cout << (char)lr;
}
```

Notice the calls to the member object constructors in the constructor for **screen_controller**. Even though the class is inherited, no call to the base-class constructor is made because there is none. There is also no explicit call to the constructor for **interval** because that object has a default constructor that will be called automatically. The constructor first looks at the **static** variable **object_count**. A **static** variable, which is shared by all objects in a class, is initialized at the time it is defined (here, **object_count** is initialized to zero). If **object_count** is nonzero, it means that an instance of this class has already been created, so the user is trying to create a second **screen_controller**. This is an error, so the program is terminated with a message to the user. If **object_count** is zero, this is the first object so **object_count** is set to 1, and a command is given to turn off the line wrap (which causes the screen to shift up at inopportune times).

The destructor returns the cursor type to normal and turns the line wrap back on.

The **draw_vertical()** and **draw_horizontal()** functions can be used to draw lines of arbitrary length starting at arbitrary positions on the screen. They first check the starting and ending positions of the line to make sure it doesn't exceed the boundaries. The **drawbox()** function uses several of the other member functions to draw a border around the edge of the screen. You specify the characters used in the border in the argument list.

The following program uses some of the features of **screen_controller**. Uncomment the two statements at the beginning of **main()** to see the effect of trying to define a second instance of **screen_controller** (other than the one defined in SCREEN3.CPP) and trying to move the cursor out of bounds.

```
//: SCR3TEST.CPP—Test for class screen_controller
#include "screen3.h"

// Characters for making a box with double-line characters
// on the PC. Modify these for your own system.
const ulcorner = 201;
const urcorner = 187;
const llcorner = 200;
const lrcorner = 188;
const hbar = 205;
const vbar = 186;

void main() {
  // generates error message:
//   screen_controller screen2;
  // generates error message when using default screen size:
//   screen.move(26,81);
  screen.clear_screen();
  screen.drawbox(hbar, vbar, ulcorner, urcorner,
                 llcorner, lrcorner);
  screen.center(4, "Demonstration of class screen_controller");
  screen.reverse(); screen.blink();
```

```
screen.center(8, "That's All, Folks!");
screen.move(screen.maxrow() -1, 0);
screen.pause(3);
}
```

The vertical bars, horizontal bars, and corners are specific to the PC. If you are using UNIX, you will want to change them to something appropriate to your terminal.

Initializing static Member Variables

SCREEN3.CPP shows the definition and initialization of a **static** member variable, **object_count**, as part of the startup process (it only happens once, during program initialization). To do this, you use the scope resolution operator in an initialization statement specifying the type, full name (including class name), and initial value. The syntax is:

```
type classname::staticmembername = initialvalue;
```

There can only be one statement of this type for each static data member in a system, thus there is no danger that the user can manipulate private data this way. If there is not precisely one statement of this type, the linker will issue an error.

Initializing static Objects

In plain C, if you want some initialization performed before **main()** is called, the code you must write is very implementation dependent. In C++, you need only create an object with global lifetime; the object can be explicitly global or it can be **static** (all such objects are generally referred to as *static objects*). Before **main()** is called, the constructors for all static objects will be called, so you can put any code you need run before **main()** inside a constructor for a static object. When the program exits, the destructor code for the objects will be called. The **screen** object in SCREEN3.CPP is an example—the destructor always calls the **normal()** member function so the cursor is never left in an unknown state.

If the definition for one object with global lifetime appears before the definition of another in a single file, the first one's constructor is guaranteed to be called first. Other than that, the *order* of constructor calls for objects with global lifetime is not guaranteed in C++. If you have two objects with global lifetime defined in two separate files, you don't know which one will be called first. The only guarantee you get is that they *will* be called before **main()**, and the destructors *will* be called after **main()** (unless you exit the program using the ANSI C library function **abort()**; **exit()** calls the constructors).

If one object depends on another, this can cause problems. The simple solution, if you have enough control of the source code, is to put all objects with global lifetime that depend on each other into a single file and control the order of constructor calls by the order of definition in the file. This doesn't solve the problem of a constructor for an object with global lifetime depending on the existence of an initialized object that is defined in another object file. For instance, if you want to use the **screen** object in a constructor for an object with global lifetime and you don't have control of the sources where **screen** is defined, you've got problems.

A partial solution to this problem, presented by Jerry Schwarz ("Initializing Static Variables in C++ Libraries," *The C++ Report*, Volume 1, Number 2, February 1989), is to add a very simple class (referred to in this discussion as *the initializer class*) to the end of a header file for the object you want to create with global lifetime (which will be referred to here as *the global object*, even though it may also be a **static** member object). You can always do this because you always have access to the header file even if you don't have access to the code for the methods. The initializer class has the sole task of initializing the global object. The global object is represented by a pointer, so the compiler doesn't call the constructor for the global object. The initializer class makes a single instance of the object using **new**.

You must also add a **static** instance of the initializer class, referred to here as *the initializer object*, to the header, so the initializer object is created in every file where you include the header, but the initializer object is invisible outside the file (it has internal linkage). When the program starts up, *one* of the initializer object constructors will be called before any constructor that uses the global object (since the header must appear before the global object's use).

The initializer class contains a **static int** to count the number of times the global object is created. When the program starts, this **int** is initialized to 0. The first time the initializer class constructor is called, the global object is created and the **static int** is incremented. All the other times the initializer class constructor is called, the global object is not created.

As an example, here's what you might add to the header file for **class screen_controller**:

```
class screen_controller { /* ... */ };
// New stuff here:
extern screen_controller * screen;
class screen_initializer {
  static int initialization_count;
public:
 screen_initializer() {
   if(initialization_count) return;
   initialization_count++;
   screen = new screen_controller;
 }
 ~screen_controller() {
   delete screen;
   screen = 0;
 }
};
static screen_initializer screen_init;
```

The destructor relies on the fact that a call to **delete** with an argument of 0 has no effect, so the first call to the destructor will destroy the object while the other calls won't do anything.

Notice that **screen** is now a pointer to an object, and not an object, so the member function calls must be made with the arrow (**->**), not the dot (**.**).

Suggestions for Further Improvements

The error checking is currently quite limited—the user is prevented from moving the cursor off the screen with the **move()** command or the line-drawing commands. You can still move the cursor to the right edge of the screen and then output to **cout**. You can also move the cursor off the screen with the **up()**, **down()**, **left()**, and **right()** commands. Even if **class screen_controller** kept track of cursor coordinates whenever the cursor was explicitly moved with a member function, the implicit cursor motion from a **cout** statement would always make the system lose track of the cursor.

To solve these problems, you need to force all screen output to go through a member function in the class. You could call this member function **print()**. To determine the new cursor position after a **print()** statement, use an **ostrstream** object to print the output into a buffer. Use **strlen()** to measure the length of the buffer and reposition the cursor (assuming it doesn't exceed the boundaries). Finally, send the buffer to the screen.

The approach of keeping track of the cursor has two further advantages: you could **center()** a line without specifying the row number, and the class becomes much more portable. Since all screen I/O goes through the class, you could move code written using class **screen_controller** to a windowing system without too much effort.

Another improvement you might want to make is to replace the existing error function with one that can recover from problems, instead of exiting the program.

Speed is often a problem with screen output. You may want to use a local library of screen output functions to improve the performance. Since C++ classes separate the interface from the implementation, you can reimplement the methods for **class screen_controller** without modifying any programs that use the class. Simply modify and recompile SCREEN3.CPP and relink all the object files to create a new executable file.

In the makefile at the end of this chapter, you will see that any program that uses **screen_controller** must link in **screen1.obj**, **screen2.obj**, and **screen3.obj**. If you have a librarian, it makes sense to combine these three object files into a single library called **screen.lib**.

Storing Objects on Disk

Reusing code with composition means defining a class as an agglomeration of objects. Reusing code with inheritance means

☐ You are adding successive refinements to the meaning of a class, as has been demonstrated up to now in this chapter or

❑ You want to make the subclass a "kind of" the superclass and use the fact that a group of subclasses all belong to the same superclass, as will be shown in the next chapter or

❑ You want to easily add a feature to other classes that has nothing to do with the hierarchy or successive refinement of a class (one of the better arguments for multiple inheritance). This last use will be illustrated in this section.

It is very convenient to be able to store objects on disk and to retrieve them later or with another program. The class developed in this section can be inherited into any class and will give the new class the ability to store itself to disk in a file with other instances of the same class. An instance of this class can also read itself from a file containing other instances of the class. This implementation should only be used for classes whose structures do not contain any pointers. If there are any pointers, the pointer is stored but not the data it points to.

Objects that keep themselves on disk are often referred to as *persistent objects*. The ideal implementation of persistence would be a sort of "superglobal" object, which lived outside the invocation of a *program* just as an ordinary global object lives outside the invocation of any function.

Unfortunately, this turns out to be a lot harder to implement than you might imagine. A particular problem, as mentioned above, occurs when the object contains pointers. Once a pointer is written out to disk and the program terminates, the value of the pointer becomes meaningless. A proper implementation of persistence must have a mechanism to restore meaningful pointers to a persistent object. Many commercial class libraries implement some form of support for persistence, and it's usually ungainly because of the pointer problem.

Using the storable Classes

To implement storability in your new class, you must do two things: create a **static** object of type **storage_file** as a member of your new class, and inherit your class from **class storable**. The **static storage_file** member allows you to successively store objects of your class in the same file after opening the file only once. Because a different **static storage_file** member is defined for each different **storable** subclass, you can have a different file open for each class. You can only have one file open at a time for a class (this makes intermixed reading and writing tedious), but you can open and close several files sequentially in a session.

To store such an object, the user opens a file with a call to the member function **open_file()**, with the filename and the appropriate argument requesting input, output, or append. This function can be called with any object in the class, and the output file remains open and all objects are stored there until the user makes a call to **open_file()** or **close_file()** (or the destructor is called). All files are automatically closed when the program exits. To store an object, the user calls the member function **write_object()**. To retrieve an object (after **open_file()** is called for input) the user creates an object and calls the member function **read_object()**.

Design Considerations

Your new class must be inherited from class **storable** instead of defining a **storable** member object because the member functions of **storable** must have access to **this**. The starting address of the object's structure, **this**, must be given to the functions that read a block of memory from disk and write a block of memory to disk. Of course, the base **class storable** has no way of knowing how big the derived class will be—you must specifically set the size of the object via a member function of **class storable**.

The size of the object is set in the definition of the static data member, and only needs to be done once for each class, with a global statement like

```
storage_file mjm::disk(sizeof(mjm));
```

In addition, the destructor call for the static member **disk** at the termination of the program ensures that all files are cleaned up properly. This cannot be done in the destructor for **storable**, because every time an object belonging to a subclass of **storable** went out of scope, the file would be closed.

The End Record

It is usually necessary to keep information in each file to describe the file's contents. With a **storable** subclass, you never know how many records the file will contain until you've written them all and are closing the file. The information about the file is kept at the *end* of the file. The information is stored in what will be called an *end record*, which is a nested **struct** inside class **storage_file**. You could also reserve space at the beginning before you begin writing records, but the approach used here demonstrates the ability to read a record off the end of the file, as well as the beginning.

In this example, the end record only contains the size of each object in the file and the number of objects in the file. This allows some rudimentary error checking, since you can compare the size of the objects in the file with the size of the object you are trying to read from the file. You can also keep track of how many objects are left in the file. You may want to add information to the end record to indicate the date the file was written, its full path name, machine location, notes about the data, and so on. If you decide to do this, it is important that the size of the end record doesn't change just because you inherit it into a new class, and that any **storable** class can successfully read the end record in any file (so you can generate useful error messages). To do this, you will need to treat the end record as a header block with information leading to more sophisticated data in the file (for instance, the size and location of arbitrary-length text entries).

There are two functions in **class storable** dealing with end records: **close_file()**, which writes the end record out to the file before it closes it, and **get_end_record**, which moves to the end of the file minus the size of an end record, reads the end record, moves back to the beginning of the file and returns the record it read. It also validates the file to make sure you are reading the type of records that match the objects.

In the header file for **class storable**, notice that the constructor must always be handed a pointer to a **storage_file**. This pointer is stored in each object of the derived class; it is the only space overhead in deriving from class **storable**. Here is the header file:

```
//: DISKSTOR.H—A class designed to be inherited by
//. a subclass that needs to store itself to disk and
```

```
//. retrieve itself from disk.
#ifndef DISKSTOR_H_
#define DISKSTOR_H_
#include <iostream.h>
#include <fstream.h>
#include <strstream.h>
#include "ioserror.h"

// Each storable class must contain a static object of struct
// storage_file so all storage for objects of that class goes
// to the same file.

// unopened file pointer:
const ios::open_mode nil = (ios::open_mode)0;

class storage_file {
  static ioserror error;
  enum { bsize = 100 };  // a "local const" for the class
  char file_name[bsize]; // name of file for storage/retrieval
  ostrstream fbuf;  // use streams for the file_name buffer
  fstream file;  // the storage file
  ios::open_mode filemode; // input, output or append?
  struct end_rec {
    int object_size;  // size of objects stored/read
    int object_count; // number of objects stored in file
    end_rec(int sz) : object_size(sz), object_count(0) {}
  } end_record;
  end_rec get_end_record();
public:
  storage_file(int objsize) : filemode(nil),
    fbuf(file_name, bsize), end_record(objsize) {}
  ~storage_file() { close_file(); }  // writes the end_record
  void open_file(char * filename, ios::open_mode om = ios::in);
  void close_file();
  void write_object(unsigned char * adr); // to the file
  // read an object from the file, and return "this":
  storage_file* read_object(unsigned char * dest);
  int& object_count() { return end_record.object_count; }
  const int object_size() { return end_record.object_size; }
};

// A class to be stored on disk must be inherited from
// the following base class:

class storable {
  // costs a pointer, but allows multiple databases:
  storage_file* sfile;
```

```
public:
  storable(storage_file * sf) : sfile(sf) {}
  void open_file(char * filename, ios::open_mode om = ios::in) {
    sfile->open_file(filename, om);
  }
  void close_file() { sfile->close_file(); }
  int& object_count() { return sfile->object_count(); }
  void write_object() { // write the current object to the file
    sfile->write_object((unsigned char*)this);
  }
  void read_object() { // read a record into the current object
    sfile = sfile->read_object((unsigned char*)this);
    // assignment restores value of sfile, which gets
    // overwritten during the read operation.
  }
};

#endif // DISKSTOR_H_
```

Notice that all the work is happening inside class **storage_file**. The **storable** class is really just a wrapper for a pointer to a **storage_file** object and a set of functions that access the object. However, those functions utilize **this**, so they can pass the starting address of the current object for writing to disk and for reading from disk.

Despite the caveat about pointers, you can see that a pointer is actually introduced into the structure. What happens when an object is read back from disk? In **storable::read_object()**, **sfile->read_object()** is called with the address of **this**. The object on disk is read directly into the current object, which certainly destroys the pointer **sfile** by writing a meaningless value over it. Notice, however, that **sfile->read_object()** returns the uncorrupted value of the current **storage_file** pointer, which is assigned back to **sfile**! This technique retains the proper value of **sfile** when an object is restored from disk.

iostream Functions for File I/O

Before you can understand details of the **storage_file** implementation, you need to know about the iostream functions that manipulate files.

The iostream functions used in this class for reading and writing files in binary format mimic those in the ANSI C library that do the same thing, and they have similar names. To understand binary format, consider a floating-point number represented in four bytes in memory. If you want to store this on disk in binary format, those same four bytes will be transferred as four bytes on disk; the floating-point number will not be converted to a sequence of ASCII digits. This method is generally more conservative with time and space, and you don't have to know anything about the data you are storing other than its size. A call to **write_object()** will store an exact image of an object's structure on disk.

The primary iostream functions that are used for **storable** are **open()**, which opens a file; **read()** which reads a block of data from file into memory; and **write()**, which writes a block of data from memory into the file. These functions are analogous to **fopen()**, **fread()**, and **fwrite()** in the ANSI C library. The function **seekg()** is also used to move around in the file—it's analogous to **fseek()** in the ANSI C library.

In the ANSI C file functions, the most important argument is the *file pointer*. The file pointer contains all the information about the file and its current state; in particular, at what point in the file the next read or write will occur. When you call **fread()**, **fwrite()**, or **fseek()**, you move the file pointer. **fread()** and **fwrite()** move the pointer forward according to the size of the block you read or write; **fseek()** moves the file pointer to any point in the file relative to the beginning of the file, the current position of the file pointer, or the end of the file. In the iostream versions, you don't need to pass the file pointer because all that information is implicit in the fstream object you send the messages to.

The **open()** function must know the filename (a character string) and the *access mode*, which tells it to open the file for reading, writing, or appending and specifies whether the file is text or binary. Both **read()** and **write()** need to know where to put the data in memory or where in memory the data is coming from, how big a record is, and how many records to read or write. Here is the syntax for **read()** and **write()**:

```
istream& read(char * destination_buffer, int bytes_to_read);
ostream& write(const char * source_buffer, int bytes_to_write);
```

The **seekg()** function needs to know whether the new position is relative to the beginning of the file (SEEK_SET), the end of the file (SEEK_END), or the current position of the file pointer (SEEK_CUR). Also, **seekg()** must know how far away the file pointer should be from the relative point; this number can be positive or negative. Here is the syntax for **seekg()**:

```
istream& seekg(streamoff relative_movement, ios::seek_dir);
```

Notice that when an enumeration type is shown with a scope resolution operator, as in the iostream enumeration to determine the direction of the seek: **ios::seek_dir** (you can find this in **iostream.h**), it simply means that the enumeration is placed within a **class** or **struct** (a good practice, since it prevents global name clashes).

Here are the methods for **storage_file**:

```
//: DISKSTOR.CPP—Methods for storable base class
#include "diskstor.h"
#include "ioserror.h"
ioserror storage_file::error("storage_file");

// Function to conditionally close file and
// write the end record.
void storage_file::close_file() {
  if(filemode != nil) {
    if(filemode == ios::out || filemode == ios::app) {
      // write the "end record", which holds a value
      // indicating the size of the objects in the
      // file and the number of objects.
      file.write((unsigned char*)&(end_record),
                 sizeof(end_rec));
    }
    file.close();
    filemode = nil;
  }
}

storage_file::end_rec storage_file::get_end_record() {
  end_rec er(0);
  // read the end record to find out size and number of records:
  file.seekg(-(long)sizeof(end_rec), ios::end);
  file.read((unsigned char*)&er, sizeof(end_rec));
  // move back to beginning of file:
  file.seekg(0, ios::beg);
    if(er.object_size != object_size()) {
    error << file_name << " objects wrong size" << nl
      << "object size = 0x" << hex << object_size()
```

```
          << nl << "file object size = 0x"
          << hex << er.object_size << terminate;
    }
    if(er.object_count <= 0)
      error << file_name << " contains 0 objects" << terminate;
    return er;
}

void storage_file::open_file(char *fname, ios::open_mode mode) {
  close_file();
  fbuf << fname;
  filemode = mode;
  file.open(fname, mode | ios::binary);
  if(!file) {
    error << "can't open "<< fname << " for ";
    switch(mode) {
      case ios::in : error << "reading" << terminate;
      case ios::out : error << "writing" << terminate;
      case ios::app : error << "appending" << terminate;
    }
  }
  if(mode == ios::in)
    end_record = get_end_record();
  if (mode == ios::app) {
    get_end_record();  // validate the existing file
    // set file pointer so next write overwrites the end record:
    file.seekg(-(long)sizeof(end_rec), ios::end);
  }
}

void storage_file::write_object(unsigned char * address) {
  if(!file)
    error << "tried to write a file that wasn't open"
          << terminate;
  if(filemode == ios::in)
    error << "tried to write to an input file" << terminate;
  file.write(address, object_size());
  if(file.fail())
    error << " writing to " << file_name << terminate;
  object_count()++;  // another record added
}

storage_file* storage_file::read_object(unsigned char * dest) {
  if(!file)
    error << "tried to read a file that wasn't open"
          << terminate;
  if(filemode == ios::out || filemode == ios::app)
```

```
    error << "tried to read from an output file" << terminate;
if(object_count()) {
  object_count()--;
  file.read(dest, object_size());
  if(file.fail())
    error << "tried to read past end of "
          << file_name << terminate;
} else
  error << "can't read past last record in "
        << file_name << nl;
return this;  // to assign to pointer just overrwritten
}
```

The value **nil** (defined in **diskstor.h**) is used to indicate that there is no file open. In **open_file()**, a call to **close_file()** is made at the beginning of the function. Then **close_file()** checks to see if a file is open. If so, it writes the end record and closes the file.

The **get_end_record()** method returns the end record of the currently open file. It creates an empty end record **er**, seeks to the end of the file *minus* the size of the end record, and reads the record into **er**. Then it compares the object size in **er** to its own object size and checks to see that there is at least one object in the file.

The **open_file** method stores the name of the file in the **ostrstream fbuf** (which is attached to the **char** buffer **file_name** in the constructor) so that it can be used later, in error messages. Then **open()** is called— notice that the desired mode is combined with **ios::binary** with a bitwise OR. If the file is opened for reading, **end_record** is assigned to the value in the file (and validated) with **get_end_record()**. If the file is opened for appending, **get_end_record()** is just used for validation; then the file pointer is moved so it will append the next record directly over the old end record.

Carefully examine the member functions **storage_file::read_object()** and **storage_file::write_object()**. After the error checking, the functions make calls to, respectively, **read()** and **write()**. Notice that the first argument to **read()** and **write()** is the address of the object to be read or written, passed in as **this** by **storable::read_object()** and **store-able::write_object()**. The representation of the object on disk is being read directly into the current object in **storage_file::read_object()**, and the representation is being copied from the current object to disk in **storage_file::write_object()**. This is the reason it is so important to inherit **storable** into a new class rather than making it a member object—a member object would use the member's **this**, which wouldn't be right.

As objects are read from a file, the **object_count** is decremented so the program knows when there are no more objects. As objects are written to a file, the **object_count** is incremented so that when the end record is written, it contains an accurate count of the objects in the file.

Creating a Storable Class

To show you how to make a class with objects that can store themselves to disk and retrieve themselves from disk, here's an example class that contains some integer and floating-point data:

```
//: STORTEST.H—Test for disk-storage classes
#ifndef STORTEST_H_
#define STORTEST_H_
#include "diskstor.h"

class mjm : public storable {
  int i, j, k;
  double monica, matt, mike, maura, mark;
  static storage_file disk;
public:
  mjm() : storable(&disk) { }
  mjm(int ii, int jj, int kk, double d1, double d2,
      double d3, double d4, double d5);
  void print(char * msg = "");
};

#endif // STORTEST_H_
```

The only thing that distinguishes this class from any other is that it contains a **static** instance of **storage_file** and it is inherited from **class storable**. Here is the implementation of **class mjm**:

```
//: STORTEST.CPP—Test for disk-storage classes
#include "stortest.h"
#include <iostream.h>

// static data member initialization:
storage_file mjm::disk(sizeof(mjm));
```

```
mjm::mjm(int ii, int jj, int kk, double d1, double d2,
        double d3, double d4, double d5) : storable(&disk) {
  i = ii;
  j = jj;
  k = kk;
  monica = d1;
  matt = d2;
  mike = d3;
  maura = d4;
  mark = d5;
}

#define PRI(arg) cout << #arg " = " << arg << endl

void mjm::print(char * msg) {
  cout << msg << endl;
  PRI(i); PRI(j); PRI(k);
  PRI(monica); PRI(matt); PRI(mike); PRI(maura); PRI(mark);
}
```

The size of the object is set in the definition of the static data member **storage_file mjm::disk(sizeof(mjm))** (the constructor call sets the size).

The **PRI()** macro to print an integer and the **PRD()** macro to print a floating-point number are simply used to reduce typing and mistakes.

To test **class mjm,** here are two programs. The first, shown here, creates four instances of **mjm** and writes them to disk:

```
//: MJMTEST1.CPP—Driver for disk-storage test class. This
//. program writes a file of objects.
#include "stortest.h"

void main() {
  mjm A(1,2,3, 1.1, 2.2, 3.3, 4.4, 47.0),
      B(4,5,6, 5.5, 6.6, 7.7, 8.8, 47.0),
      C(7,8,9, 9.9, 10.10, 11.11, 12.12, 47.0),
      D(10,11,12, 13.13, 14.14, 15.15, 16.16, 47.0);
  A.print("A");
  B.print("B");
  C.print("C");
  D.print("D");
  A.open_file("mjm.dat", ios::out);  // could use B, C or D also
  A.write_object();
  B.write_object();
  C.write_object();
```

```
      D.write_object();
      D.close_file();   // could use A, B or C also
   }
```

The second test program, shown next, creates four instances of **mjm** and reads them from the same disk file:

```
//: MJMTEST2.CPP—Driver for disk-storage test class.
//. This program reads a file of objects.
#include "stortest.h"

void main() {
   mjm A, B, C, D;
   A.open_file("mjm.dat");   // defaults to "input file"
   A.read_object();
   B.read_object();
   C.read_object();
   D.read_object();
   A.print("A");
   B.print("B");
   C.print("C");
   D.print("D");
}
```

Both programs print out the contents so that you can see that the second program does indeed reconstruct the objects that the first program wrote to the disk.

Suggestions for Improvements

Not all file systems keep track of file systems in units of bytes. This means that when you open a file, the "end" may be further out than where the last record was written. Thus, the implementation shown here may not be portable to all platforms. You can avoid this problem by storing the location of the last record in the beginning of the file.

You might want to modify the end record to include more information. Notice you only need to change the declaration of **end_rec**, since all the reading and writing uses **sizeof()** to determine the size of the record.

Consider what is necessary to allow the system to store and retrieve objects that occupy a piece of memory the size of which is unknown at compile time. Objects like this would consist of a structure containing pointers to data on the free store; this data would have to be stored on disk after the object's structure. The structure, which is always a fixed size, would be read from disk first. From the structure, the size of the arbitrary-sized portion would be determined, so the proper **read()** could be performed to reconstruct the rest of the object.

A List That Can Save and Retrieve Itself

The solutions to certain types of problems can be expressed very cleanly using lists of objects. It can be useful to store entire lists to disk and retrieve those lists from disk. The example presented in this section combines **class storable** with **class DynArray** to create a list that can save and retrieve itself. The objects in the list will be small database records for holding names and addresses; they will belong to **class db_record**, which is inherited from **class storable**. The **class db_list** will be inherited from **class DynArray** to further specify the type of items **DynArray** can hold from **void *** to **db_record *** and to add methods to store and retrieve the entire list. You may find this example useful not only because you can make a general-purpose list that can store and retrieve itself, but also because you can see various methods of building up a complex class out of simpler classes.

The example created from these classes will be a simple flat-file database manager that you can add names to (using DBADD) and look up names in (using DBFIND). In addition, you can take the data from your current database manager, write it out in comma-separated ASCII form (most DBMSs support this), and convert it using DBCONV to the form used in this project so you can use DBFIND to look up names.

Defining the Database

Whenever you create a program, it's important to isolate the things that change from the things that stay the same. That way, all the changes can be kept in one place, under control. In this project, the most important change you will want to make is in the layout of the database. To make this as simple as possible, the database is defined in a single header file as a series of calls to a macro named FIELD:

```
//: FIELDS.H—Field names and sizes for DB example.
//. Only place you need to modify to change the database.
FIELD(last, 20);
FIELD(first, 20);
FIELD(business, 40);
FIELD(address2, 40);
FIELD(street, 40);
FIELD(city, 15);
FIELD(state, 10);
FIELD(zip, 15);
FIELD(phones, 40);
```

The clever thing about this technique is that there is no one definition for FIELD—if you want to use the field names as an identifier, for example, you simply undefine the FIELD macro, and then define it to only use the identifier names. For example, if you wanted to create an enumeration of the above field names you could do it like this:

```
#undef FIELD
#define FIELD(name, size) name,
and then create the enumeration:
enum fieldnames {
 #include "fields.h"
};
```

Notice that the sizes are simply ignored in this case, but you can do some other activity that ignores the names and uses the sizes. Any time you need to use the information in a different way, you just redefine the macro and include the header file again. This powerful technique demonstrates that no matter how problematic the preprocessor can be, it certainly has its moments.

A Class to Hold a Database Record

A database record is a group of string buffers that are encapsulated into an object. Each string buffer is a *field* in the record. You can read or write the strings in the fields. To hold each database record, a class called **db_record** is created. The structure in the class is a fixed size, and you must recompile the program when you add or remove fields—this harks back to the early days of inflexible database managers.

The first definition of the **FIELD** macro allocates private storage for the field (notice the extra character to hold the terminating NULL in the string) and creates three member functions for that field—two to get information into the field (one from an **istream** and one from a **char** pointer) and one to read the information back out. When **fields.h** is included inside the next class, **db_record**, the macro causes this code to be generated inside **db_record** for each field, as shown here:

```
//: DBRECORD.H—Database records using storable class
#ifndef DBRECORD_H_
#define DBRECORD_H_
#include <string.h>
#include "diskstor.h"

// Declare a field and create methods for putting information
// into a field and accessing information in a field:
#undef FIELD
#define FIELD(fieldname, fieldsize) \
private: \
  char fieldname[fieldsize + 1]; \
public: \
  void get_##fieldname(istream& s) { \
    get_field(s, fieldname, fieldsize + 1); \
    fieldname[fieldsize] = '\0'; \
  } \
  void get_##fieldname(char * s) { \
    strncpy(fieldname, s, fieldsize); \
    fieldname[fieldsize] = '\0'; \
  } \
  char * read_##fieldname() { \
    return fieldname; \
  }

class db_record : public storable {
  static storage_file disk;  // for disk storage
  // Input from a stream:
  void get_field(istream& s, char * field, int maxsize);
public:
  char bstart;  // marks the start of the data block
  #include "fields.h"  // the field definitions
  char bend;    // marks the end of the data block
public:
  db_record() : storable(&disk) { erase(); }
  void erase() {
```

```
  // zero the database record block:
    memset(&bstart,'\0', &bend - &bstart);
  }
  void view();  // view record to cout
};

#endif // DBRECORD_H_
```

The constructor calls the base-class constructor for **storable** with the address of its **static storage_file** object. Then it calls **erase()**, which sets the contents of all the data fields to '\0' using the ANSI C library function **memset()**. The **memset()** function must be given a starting address, the value to set the block to, and the size of the block. To calculate the size of the block without knowing the names of the data fields in the block (which could easily change), two dummy pieces of data are placed in the structure: **bstart**, to give the address of the beginning of the block, and **bend**, to get the address of the end of the block. The size of the block is then calculated as **&bend – &bstart**.

The **private** member function **get_field()** gets an input string from the user and truncates it to the proper size before copying it into the appropriate field in the **db_record** object's structure. You can modify **get_field()** to do fancier input handling.

The **view()** function redefines the **FIELD** macro to display all the different fields. This is used when displaying a record.

Here are the remaining methods for **db_record**:

```
//: DBRECORD.CPP—Implementation of class db_record
#include "dbrecord.h"

// static data member definition:
storage_file db_record::disk(sizeof(db_record));

void db_record::get_field(istream& s, char * field, int max) {
  const big = 150;
  static char buf[big];
  s.getline(buf, big);  // get the entire line
  ostrstream in(field, max - 1);
  in << buf << ends;  // truncates the line
}

void db_record::view() {
  // Change FIELD macro to display the different fields:
```

```
#undef FIELD
#define FIELD(fieldname, size) \
  cout << #fieldname ": " \
       << read_##fieldname() \
       << endl;
#include "fields.h"  // DB field definitions
}
```

Note the definition for the static data member **db_record::disk**, where the size of the object is installed in the **storage_file** object.

In the TAWK example in Chapter 11, a different kind of database file is manipulated. In that example, the fields are also objects. You could use that approach here, as well, but the design used here is simpler to understand.

A Class to Make a List of db_records

A **db_record** knows how to store and retrieve itself because it is inherited from class **storable**. To make this system flexible, you must be able to create an arbitrary number of **db_records**—as many as are contained in the database file. The class **DynArray** is used because it can handle any number of objects and the mechanism is hidden. **DynArray** handles **void** pointers. The new list should not accept anything but **db_records**. In the following header file, you can see that **class db_list** is inherited from **DynArray**, and that the methods in **DynArray** that take **void** pointers as arguments or return **void** pointers are redefined to pass or return **db_list** pointers.

```
//: DBLIST.H—A storable list of database records.
#ifndef DBLIST_H_
#define DBLIST_H_
// This file organization corresponds to the source-code
// disk for this book. Yours may be different:
#include "..\chap_6\dynarray.h"
#include "dbrecord.h"

class db_list : public DynArray {
  static ioserror error;
public:
  // Force all member functions of DynArray which handle void *
  // to only use db_record *
```

```
int add(db_record * dbr) { return DynArray::add(dbr); }
int remove(db_record * dbr) { return DynArray::remove(dbr); }
db_record * next()  { return (db_record *)DynArray::next(); }
db_record * current() {
  return (db_record *)DynArray::current();
}
db_record * operator[](int index) {
  return (db_record *)DynArray::operator[](index);
}
// New methods for this class:
void save_list(char * filename);  // save list to a file
void retrieve_list(char * filename); // get from a file
};

#endif // DBLIST_H_
```

The two new member functions, **save_list()** and **retrieve_list()** use local instances of **db_record** called **temp** to open and close the database file and to see if there are any records left. Since all instances of **db_record** have access to the **static** member **struct disk**, it doesn't matter what object you use to manipulate the file—the modifications to the file affect all of the objects in **db_record**. Thus, **temp** is only used to manipulate the file and never contains any valid data.

Here are the new methods for **db_list**:

```
//: DBLIST.CPP—Non-inline methods for db_list
#include "dblist.h"
#include <conio.h>
#include "screen3.h"
// #define DEBUG

ioserror db_list::error("db_list");

void db_list::save_list(char * filename) {  // to a file
  db_record temp;
  temp.open_file(filename, ios::out);
  reset();
  do {
    current()->write_object();
  } while(next());
  temp.close_file();
}

void db_list::retrieve_list(char * filename) { // from a file
  db_record temp;
```

```
  temp.open_file(filename);
  // while there are records left, read them from the file:
  while(temp.object_count()) {
    db_record * dbrp = new db_record;
    dbrp->read_object();
#ifdef DEBUG
    dbrp->view();
    cout << "CR to continue";
    cin.get();
#endif
    add(dbrp);
  }
  temp.close_file();
}
```

The calls to **reset()**, **current()**, and **add()** are calling base-class member functions in **DynArray**.

Adding Records to the Database File

Using **db_record** and **db_list**, you can create a set of utilities to work with your database files. The utilities shown here will add new data to a file; look up data according to a last name, first name, or company name; and convert records from comma-separated ASCII. You may also want to write utilities to sort a file, remove records from a file, edit records, print an envelope, and so on.

The first utility program adds a single record to a file. The file has a fixed name. Both of these decisions were made with the consideration that you will probably have a single database file with all your important names and addresses, and you will probably only add one record at a time. These decisions speed startup and use.

If the program is started and it cannot find the database file (called **namelist.dbf**), it creates one with a single, empty record (so it doesn't contain zero records, which would cause an error), and exits.

Most of the space taken up by the following program is for reading and displaying the information. Because most of the work is hidden in the classes, the key statements are very simple. For example,

```
db_list database;
database.retrieve_list(dbfile);
```

opens the database file and reads it in, and

```
database.add(&new_record);
database.save_list(dbfile);
```

adds the new record and updates the file with the new list.

The **FIELD** macro is redefined so it prompts the user for each field name and captures the response into that field. Then it's redefined to display the record. Here's the program:

```
//: DBADD.CPP—Add a single new record to a database file.
//. Tests db_record & db_list. The name of the database file is
//. hard-wired into this end-user application to reduce typing
//. when adding an entry, but you may want to pick it off the
//. command line.
#include "dblist.h"
#include "screen3.h"

char * dbfile = "namelist.dbf";

void main() {
  // Check to see if file exists. If not, create it.
  // Might want to make this into a member function.
  ifstream tmpfile(dbfile);
  if (!tmpfile) {  // if it doesn't exist, make the file:
    db_record temp;
    cout << "initializing " << dbfile << endl;
    temp.open_file(dbfile, ios::out);
    temp.write_object(); // write an empty record
    temp.close_file();
    return;  // return from main();
  } else
    tmpfile.close();  // if it exists, close it
  // Read file into array:
  db_list database;
  database.retrieve_list(dbfile);
  // add new records:
  db_record new_record;

  screen.clear_screen();

  // Change the FIELD macro to get the different fields:
  #undef FIELD
  #define FIELD(fieldname, size) \
    cout << "enter " #fieldname ": "; \
```

```
      new_record.get_##fieldname(cin)
#include "fields.h"  // the database layout

  screen.clear_screen();

  // Change the FIELD macro to display the different fields:
  #undef FIELD
  #define FIELD(fieldname, size) \
    cout << #fieldname ": " << new record.read_##fieldname() \
        << endl
  #include "fields.h"

  database.add(&new_record);
  database.save_list(dbfile);
}
```

Looking Up Records in the Database File

The next program uses **db_list** to read a database file (the same one created in the above example). It searches for a match among any fields you choose—in this case, the last name, first name, or business name. To find any word in those data fields, the fields are parsed into an object of class **word_array**, defined here by inheriting it from **DynArray**. A **word_array** is simply a collection of discrete words. You use the member function **parse()** to take a string, break it up into words, and add each one to the array. Then the member function **contains()** tells you if the argument you pass it is inside the **word_array**. In the program, the **last**, **first**, and **business** fields are handed to the **word_array wa** for each record and then **wa** is queried to see if it contains the match word.

Notice that **word** has a class of its own. The constructor duplicates its argument with the ANSI C library function **strdup()**, and the destructor frees the memory with **free()** (the use of **delete** here could be disastrous, since **strdup()** uses **malloc()**). The **operator char*()** returns an ordinary string pointer whenever you need it (such as when it's used in an ANSI C library function that needs a **char***). Thus, it's like an ordinary C string, only a bit safer and smarter.

Here's the program:

```
//: DBFIND.CPP—Find a record in the database file created by
//. DBADD.CPP. Uses a linear search, which isn't as slow as it
```

```
//. might seem, since all records are in memory.
#include "dblist.h"
#include "screen3.h"
#include "ioserror.h"
#include <conio.h>
#include <string.h>
#include <stdlib.h>

ioserror error("dbfind");
char * dbfile = "namelist.dbf";

class word {
  char * w;
public:
  word(char * W) : w(strdup(W)) { }
  ~word() { free(w); }
  operator char*() { return w; }
};

class word_array : public DynArray {
public:
  word_array() {}
  ~word_array() {
    for(word* s = top(); s; s = next())
      delete s;
  }
  int add(word* s) { return DynArray::add(s); }
  word* top() { return (word*)DynArray::top(); }
  word* next() { return (word*)DynArray::next(); }
  void parse(const char * argstring) {  // into words
    // duplicate string, since strtok modifies it:
    char * string = strdup(argstring);
    // words are separated by spaces or punctuation:
    char* wrd = strtok(string, " ,.\n");
    while(wrd) {
      add(new word(wrd));
      wrd = strtok(0, " ,.\n");  // continues with same string
    }
    free(string); // release memory
  }
  int contains(char * W) {
    word* wrd = top();
    while(wrd) {
      // == 0 means string match:
      if(!strcmpi(*wrd, W)) return 1;
```

```
      wrd = next();
    }
    return 0;   // no match
  }
  void dump() { // for debugging
    reset();
    word* w = top();
    while(w) {
      cout << (char*)*w << nl;
      w = next();
    }
    cout << "Any key to continue, ESC to quit";
    if(getch() == 27) exit(1);
  }
};

void main(int argc, char ** argv) {
  if(argc < 2)
    error << "usage: dbfind [last|first|business]" << terminate;
  // Read file into array:
  db_list database;
  database.retrieve_list(dbfile);
  // hunt through the database:
  database.reset();
  int found = 0;
  do {
    word_array wa;
    // Look at last, first and business names:
    wa.parse(database.current()->read_last());
    wa.parse(database.current()->read_first());
    wa.parse(database.current()->read_business());
    if(wa.contains(argv[1])) {
      screen.clear_screen();
      database.current()->view();
      cout << "Any key to continue, ESC to quit";
      if(getch() == 27) return;
      found++;
    }
  } while(database.next());
  if(!found) error << "name not found" << terminate;
}
```

For large, sorted files you can improve the speed of the search by utilizing the ANSI C library function **bsearch()** instead of a simple sequential search, as was used here.

Converting from an ASCII file

Virtually all database-management systems have the ability to read and write their data in a comma-separated ASCII format, probably because that is the form that the BASIC programming language has always used as its native mode for data files. The next program allows you to convert the data in your existing database into something that can be utilized by DBADD and DBFIND.

Comma-separated ASCII puts each field inside quotes, separates fields with commas, and puts each record on a single line so all you need to do is read records in a line at a time and then parse the line into fields. Generally when you want to break a line into pieces, the first place to look is the ANSI C library function **strtok()**. However, that wasn't appropriate here, so a function **asctok()** was created, which has a similar syntax—the first time you call it, you give it the buffer you want to parse; when you want to get subsequent words from the same buffer you hand it 0. It returns the starting address of the parsed field (without the surrounding quotes) until it can't find any more fields in the line, when it returns 0. To remember which buffer it is working on, it uses a **static** variable **buf**. This is the C version of **static** variables—the value remains valid between function calls.

Here is the conversion program:

```
//: DBCONV.CPP—Convert comma-separated ASCII database.
//. Converts from your old database.
//. Note: for big databases, you may need to compile
//. everything in a bigger memory model.
#include "dblist.h"
#include "screen3.h"
#include "ioserror.h"
#include <conio.h>
// #define DEBUG

ioserror error("dbconv");
char * dbfile = "namelist.dbf";

// Like strtok, but for comma-separated ASCII files.
// Simple version assumes no embedded quotes in fields.
char * asctok(char* buffer) {
  static char * buf = 0;
  if(buffer) buf = buffer;  // starts a new line
```

```
    if(!buf) return 0;
    char * result = strchr(buf, '\"'); // find opening quote
    if(!result) return 0;
    result++; // move past opening quote
    buf = strchr(result, '\"'); // find closing quote
    *buf = '\0'; // null-terminate the field
    buf++; // move up to the next place
    return result;
}

void main(int argc, char* argv[]) {
    if(argc < 2)
        error << nl << "\t usage: dbconv old_db" << nl <<
        "Where old_db is a database in comma-separated ASCII "
        "format, with the fields in the correct order (see"
        " FIELDS.H).\nThe created file is called "
        << dbfile << nl << "and is accessed with dbfind.exe. "
        "New records can be added with dbadd.exe."
        << terminate;
    ifstream infile(argv[1]);
    if(!infile)
        error << "could not open " << argv[1] << terminate;
    db_record record;

    db_list database;
    const sz = 300;
    char buf[sz];
    while(infile.getline(buf, sz)) {
        // parse the line into a record:
        char * cp = asctok(buf); // gets the first field
        #undef FIELD
        #define FIELD(fieldname, size) \
        if(cp) record.get_##fieldname(cp); \
        cp = asctok(0);
        #include "fields.h"

        #ifdef DEBUG
        screen.clear_screen();
        record.view();
        cout << "\n press a key to continue";
        if(getch() == 27) return;  // from main()
        #endif

        database.add(new db_record(record));
        record.erase();

    }
```

```
database.save_list(dbfile);
}
```

Notice that the **FIELD** macro is once again redefined to perform the task of capturing fields with **asctok()**. Also, the **asctok()** function makes the assumption that there are no embedded double quote marks in the fields (my database manager, for example, substitutes single quotes for double quotes when writing out ASCII files).

It can be very convenient to be able to browse through a file you've just converted to make sure everything works correctly. Here's a program that allows you to move forward and backward through the database, one record at a time:

```
//: DBTEST.CPP—Displays entire database file as a test
#include "dblist.h"
#include "screen3.h"
#include "ioserror.h"
#include <conio.h>

ioserror error("dbtest");
char * dbfile = "namelist.dbf";

void main(int argc, char ** argv) {
  // Read file into array:
  db_list database;
  database.retrieve_list(dbfile);
  // hunt through the database:
  database.reset();
  while(database.current()) {
      screen.clear_screen();
      database.current()->view();
      cout << "Any key: forward record, "
              "b: backward record, ESC to quit";
      switch(getch()) {
        case 27 : return;
        case 'b' : database.previous(); continue;
        default : database.next();
      }
  }
}
```

Although it may seem like reading the entire list in is a slow way to work, in the database defined here, containing nearly 600 records, looking up a name took substantially less time than utilizing the original database manager. Of course, this depends on the hardware and configuration.

Accessing Elements of the Base Class

If you are designing a class that you intend to be inherited, you may want to give the programmer access to **private** elements in your class and at the same time prevent the user of your class from manipulating those elements directly. This is a problem, because **private** elements in the base class cannot be accessed by any functions except members or friends of the base class. This means you can't get access to **private** elements of a class by simply inheriting it.

If you think about it, this makes sense; you don't want the **private** mechanism broken just because a class is inherited. If that were true, then you would no longer have control over what functions could change the **private** data or even know what those functions were.

The use of the keyword **public** while inheriting a class doesn't affect the **private** elements of the base class, either. It only says whether the **public** members of the base class will be **public** in the derived class. If you leave off the **public** keyword when inheriting a class, the **public** elements of that class will only be accessible to members of the derived class, not to users of the derived class.

How, then, do you make elements of the base class **private** to users of the base class but available to members of the derived class? The **protected** keyword has the desired effect. Here is an example of the use of the **protected** keyword:

```
//: PROTECT.CPP—Use of the "protected" keyword
#include <iostream.h>

class base1 {
  int i;  // i is private
public:
  base1(int ii = 0) { i = ii; }
  void print() { cout << "base1 i = " << i << endl; }
};

class base2 {
```

```
protected:
  int i;  // i is private to users, public to inheritors
public:
  base2(int ii = 0) { i = ii; }
  void print() { cout << "base2 i = " << i << endl; }
};

class derived1 : public base1 {
public:
  // this won't work:
// print() { cout << "derived1 i = " << i << endl; }
};

class derived2 : public base2 {
public:
// This will work:
  void print() { cout << "derived2 i = " << i << endl; }
};
```

In **derived1**, the **print()** member function won't work because it cannot access the **private** element **i** in **base1**. In **derived2**, however, **print()** function has access to the **protected** element **i** in **base2**.

It is also possible to use **protected** inheritance to make all members of a base class **protected**.

Disabling Member Functions in an Inherited Class

Sometimes you want to inherit a class, but you don't want the user to be able to use certain functions in the base class. There are two methods for solving this problem. The first is simply to redefine the function in the derived class and make it something innocuous or generate an error message. For example:

```
//: HIDE1.CPP—Redefining a base class function in order
//. to hide it.
#include "ioserror.h"

class base {
  int i, j, k;
public:
```

```
  base(int ii = 0, int jj = 0, int kk = 0) {
    i = ii; j = jj; k = kk;
  }
  void setall(int val) {
    i = j = k = val;
  }
  void nullify() {
    i = j = k = 0;
  }
};

class derived : public base {
  static ioserror error;
public:
  derived(int x, int y, int z) : base(x,y,z) { }
  // setall() is automatically available in derived.
  // To prevent the user from calling nullify(), you can
  // redefine it to generate an error message:
  void nullify() {
    error << "nullify() not available" << nl;
  }
};

// define the static data member:
ioserror derived::error("derived");

void main() {
  base A;
  A.setall(1);
  A.nullify();
  derived B(1,2,3);
  B.setall(2);
  B.nullify();   // this generates a run-time error
}
```

This method works, but you don't know you've done something wrong
until run time.

  If you want the error messages to be generated at compile time, you
can make all the **public** members of the base class **private** in the derived
class. Then you can selectively "export" base class functions by stating
their names in the **public** section of the derived class. In the following
example, the **private** keyword is used explicitly during inheritance. You
don't have to do this, but it reminds the user of the class that those
members are not available.

```
//: HIDE2.CPP—Hiding members by letting the base class be
//. private, and explicitly "exporting" the acceptable
//. functions. This causes compile-time errors if you try
//. to use the unacceptable functions.

class base {
  int i, j, k;
public:
  base(int ii = 0, int jj = 0, int kk = 0) {
    i = ii; j = jj; k = kk;
  }
  void setall(int val) {
    i = j = k = val;
  }
  void nullify() {
    i = j = k = 0;
  }
};

class derived : private base {
public:
  derived(int x, int y, int z) : base(x,y,z) { }
  // all the members of base are private, unless you
  // explicitly "export" them:
  base::setall;
};

void main() {
  base A;
  A.setall(1);
  A.nullify();
  derived B(1,2,3);
  B.setall(2);
//  B.nullify();  // this generates a compile-time error
}
```

Notice that when you are "exporting" a function name, you simply state the name—no argument list is given for functions. This method has the advantage of generating errors sooner in the development cycle (during compilation rather than during execution).

Multiple Inheritance

Multiple inheritance (MI) is a feature added to the C++ language after its initial release (MI was the main feature in AT&T release 2.0) amidst much arguing to and fro. There are people who still claim strongly that you can do everything you need without MI and those who say they run into situations where they absolutely must have it. Both parties have valid points.

MI is something that you should know about, but generally avoid. When you get into a situation where you have no choice but to use it, you'll know. Some situations that formerly required a messy application of MI can now be trivially fixed with templates.

The basic need for MI occurs because in C++, it's possible to grow inheritance hierarchies from scratch. This means you may purchase a class library from vendor A and one from vendor B, each with its own inheritance tree. Because you may want to mix the characteristics of two or more independent class hierarchies, you need to be able to inherit from more than one class at a time.

People with backgrounds in other object-oriented languages, notably Smalltalk, don't understand the need for multiple inheritance at first because some OOP languages require that all class creation be done through inheritance from a leaf on a single, giant tree. Since you're always getting characteristics and behaviors from the roots of the same tree, there is virtually no need to combine types from more than one base class. All classes in Smalltalk have the same class at the very root; it's called "Object."

A C++ class library that mimics the structure of the Smalltalk class hierarchy is often referred to as an "object-based" hierarchy. This has nothing to do with any fundamental concept in object-oriented programming; it is simply a class hierarchy with the class "Object" at its root.

There are two reasons you need multiple inheritance. The first is pragmatic. Sometimes you need to "mix" the characteristics of two types together. For example, you want to put mail objects into a list that only accepts message objects. So you mix the two together to get what you want.

The second, and probably better, use of MI is conceptual, and appears during design. Suppose you're building a system to modify, view, and edit files. Sometimes you might want to edit a file without viewing it (a batch editor), and sometimes you might want to view a file without editing it. It makes sense to create a file viewer and a file editor and combine the two with MI to make a screen editor. Or suppose you're creating an animation system, which is a sequence of displayable, storable shapes. These are examples of how MI can mesh well with your design.

The problem with MI is that it can introduce ambiguities. When you have more than one base class, how do you know which base-class function to call? In addition, you can get multiple instances of the same base class in your final object, which may or may not be a problem. C++ solves these problems with *virtual base classes*, which have a set of rules all their own. When using MI and virtual base classes, you must be extra aware of what is going on; it's not a nice thing to force an application developer, who is using your classes, to understand. Thus, when you use MI you should attempt as much as possible to keep this use hidden within your design.

Multiple Inheritance Syntax

The syntax for MI is just what you'd expect. You list more than one base class and call more than one base-class constructor in the constructor initializer list. For example:

```
//: MI.CPP—Simple multiple inheritance

class base1 { public: base1(int); };
class base2 { public: base2(float); };

class mi : public base1, public base2 {
public:
  mi(int I, float F) : base1(I), base2(F) {}
};
```

Everything else is taken care of for you—since there is only one destructor possible for each base class and destructors never take arguments, the base-class destructor calls happen quietly. Also, you can call member functions in base classes, just like with single inheritance.

Multiple Inheritance Problems

Multiple inheritance can introduce ambiguities. To understand this, some terminology is important.

☐   A *direct base class* is one that is in the base-class list of the current class. You can see it just by looking at the declaration for the current class.

☐   An *indirect base class* is one that is hidden inside a base class that you're inheriting.

The ambiguity problem occurs when you multiply inherit two base classes that both contain the same indirect base class. This brings up another term: your new class contains two *subobjects* of the same indirect base class, because each direct base class contains one subobject. Here's an example:

```
//: IBASE1.CPP—ambiguity in MI

class ibase { public: void print(); };
class A : public ibase {};
class B : public ibase {};
class Q : public A, public B {
public:
//  void f() { print(); } // AMBIGUOUS!
  void f() { A::print(); } // eliminates ambiguity
};
```

The **class ibase** is a direct base class of **A** and **B**, but an indirect base class of **Q**. Now what happens when you call a function that is in the indirect base class (**print()**, in the example)? Which subobject is the compiler supposed to call that function for? The compiler is unable to resolve this and reports an ambiguity error.

One way to solve this problem is simply to specify the subobject for which the function is to be called. This is done as just shown, with the scope resolution operator. This might work, but you must cope with it, and you're left with the annoying duplicate subobject. From one standpoint, the duplicate subobject just takes up space, but what if it represents something that really needs to be shared, like a buffer? In that case, it's very important that everyone use the same space, and the duplicate subobject breaks your program.

The duplicate subobject may also introduce logical ambiguities. As you'll see in Chapter 8, it is very important in object-oriented programming to be able to *upcast* a pointer to a derived-class object into a base-class pointer (it's called "upcasting" because a hierarchy tree is traditionally shown with the base class at the top of the diagram, with the derived classes growing downward). This makes logical sense because, for example, a **triangle** object is also a **shape** object—and **triangle** is inherited from **shape**. In the preceding code, a **Q** object is an **A** and a **B** and also an **ibase**, because it is derived, either directly or indirectly, from those classes. While you can upcast from a **Q** pointer to an **A** or **B** pointer with no problem, the compiler reports an ambiguity error if you try to upcast to **ibase**, as seen here:

```
//: AMBIG.CPP—Ambiguity during upcasting in MI

class ibase { public: void print(); };
class A : public ibase {};
class B : public ibase {};
class Q : public A, public B {
public:
  void f() { A::print(); }
};

void main() {
  Q q;
  Q * qp = &q;
  A * ap = qp; // OK
  B * bp = qp; // OK
  ibase * ip = qp; // error
}
```

The compiler must return a pointer to an **ibase**, but it can't figure out whether you want to upcast to **A**'s **ibase** subobject, or to **B**'s **ibase** subobject. This is a difficult problem, especially when you're using **virtual** functions (described in Chapter 8).

virtual Base Classes

The solution is an extension of the **virtual** keyword, which is primarily used to implement polymorphism. (This is the important meaning of the keyword **virtual**. Its use in multiple inheritance is just to prevent the introduction of a new keyword, because the idea has some vague commonality.) You can create a virtual base class. If you do this, any class that multiply inherits two classes containing the same virtual base class will only get one copy of that subobject, and there will be no ambiguity in either function calls or storage for that subobject. Here's what it looks like:

```
//: IBASE2.CPP—Eliminating MI abiguity
//. using virtual base classes

class ibase { public: void print(); };
class A : virtual public ibase {};
class B : virtual public ibase {};
class Q : public A, public B {
public:
  void f() { print(); } // not ambiguous
};

void main() {
  Q q;
  Q * qp = &q;
  ibase * ip = qp; // no problem!
}
```

The **virtual** base class is implemented as a pointer in the derived class, rather than the non**virtual** approach of embedding the subobject directly in the derived class. This way, if in a multiply inherited derived class more than one base class is inherited from the same root class, they only contain pointers to a single subobject of that root class.

Of course, this doesn't come without a price, which is the way you must initialize **virtual** base classes. To understand this, another new term is necessary: *most derived class*. The most derived class is simply the one that you're currently in. The rule for **virtual** base classes is this: the most derived class is responsible for initializing the **virtual** base class. Here's an example:

```
//: VBASE.CPP—The most derived class must
//. initialize the virtual base class

struct vbase { vbase(int); };

struct d1 : virtual vbase {
  d1(int i) : vbase(i) {}
};

struct d2 : virtual vbase {
  d2(int i) : vbase(i) {}
};

struct most : d1, d2 {
  most(int i) : d1(i), d2(i), vbase(i) {}
};

struct most2 : most {
  most2(int i) : most(i) {}  // error—no vbase() call
};
```

Structs are used here instead of classes, to eliminate the extra **public** keywords that wouldn't add to the example.

Inside the constructor for **d1**, **d1** is the most derived class, so it is responsible for calling the constructor for **vbase**. The same is true for **d2**. This is what you would expect anyway, since **vbase** is the direct base class of **d1** and **d2**. However, in the constructor for **most** you must *still* call the constructor for **vbase**, because **most** is the most derived class while inside its constructor. This makes sense, because there is only one instance of **vbase** since it is a **virtual** base class. How would the compiler know which way to initialize **vbase**, through **d1** or through **d2**? However, the process continues, even though it might seem logically "tied off" at **most**. In **most2**, an error is generated because the constructor has no call to **vbase**. This means that if you install a **virtual** base class in a hierarchy, its effects will be felt forever, by anyone inheriting from that hierarchy (unless the virtual base class has a default constructor). You should give serious thought before saddling the users of your class library with this kind of constraint.

As you can see, multiple inheritance adds significant complexity to inheritance. Fortunately, you aren't forced to use it very often—indeed, before release 2.0 from AT&T, C++ programmers had to find a way around it. An additional feature in the language, the **template** (shown in Chapter 10) removes one more need for multiple inheritance. The best advice, certainly for the new C++ programmer, is to avoid multiple inheritance whenever possible.

Makefile for Chapter 7 Examples

Here is the makefile for all the examples in Chapter 7. You can see that the dependency list for the .OBJ files has gotten quite large, because the projects are being created from many files. The maintenance of the dependency lists in your files can become problematic. There are programs which usually have the name **makedep** (for "make depend" or "make dependency list") which automatically create dependency lists for your files. Borland's version of **make** has a directive (seen here commented out) called .AUTODEPEND, which automatically determines the dependencies of the files, so the long list of .OBJ dependencies shown here is unnecessary when using .AUTODEPEND.

```
# makefile for examples in Chapter 7
# run make -i errors to ignore errors in ambig.cpp & vbase.cpp
# Borland C++ compiler, with the following
# warnings turned off:
# aus: identifier assigned a value which is never used
# eff: code has no effect
# par: parameter "parameter" is never used
# inl: "not expanded inline" warnings
# use huge model (for database examples)
CPP = bcc -mh -w-aus -w-eff -w-par -w-inl
LINK = bcc -mh
# nmake CPP=cl LINK=cl      # Microsoft C++ command line

# turn on Borland autodependency checking:
# .AUTODEPEND

.cpp.exe:
        $(CPP) $*.cpp

.cpp.obj:
```

```
#          $(CPP) -c {$< }      # Borland make speedup
           $(CPP) -c $<

all :    iostest.exe errtest.exe timetest.exe timecom.exe \
         inhtest.exe scr1test.exe scr2test.exe scr3test.exe \
         mjmtest1.exe mjmtest2.exe dbadd.exe dbfind.exe \
         dbconv.exe dbtest.exe protect.obj hide1.exe \
         hide2.exe mi.obj ibase1.obj \
         ibase2.obj

errors: ambig.exe vbase.obj  # compile with: make -i errors

iostest.exe : iostest.obj ioserror.obj
         $(LINK) $**

errtest.exe : errtest.obj error.obj
         $(LINK)  $**

timetest.exe : timetest.obj ioserror.obj
         $(LINK) $**

timecom.exe : timecom.obj ioserror.obj
         $(LINK) $**

scr1test.exe : scr1test.obj screen1.obj
         $(LINK) $**

scr2test.exe : scr2test.obj screen2.obj screen1.obj
         $(LINK) $**

scr3test.exe : scr3test.obj screen3.obj screen2.obj \
               screen1.obj ioserror.obj
         $(LINK) $**

mjmtest1.exe : mjmtest1.obj stortest.obj diskstor.obj \
               ioserror.obj
         $(LINK) $**

mjmtest2.exe : mjmtest2.obj stortest.obj diskstor.obj \
               ioserror.obj
         $(LINK) $**

dbadd.exe : dbadd.obj dynarray.obj diskstor.obj \
               ioserror.obj screen3.obj screen2.obj \
               screen1.obj dbrecord.obj dblist.obj
         $(LINK) $**
```

```
dbfind.exe : dbfind.obj dynarray.obj diskstor.obj \
               ioserror.obj screen3.obj screen2.obj \
               screen1.obj dbrecord.obj dblist.obj
        $(LINK) $**

dbtest.exe : dbtest.obj dynarray.obj diskstor.obj \
               ioserror.obj screen3.obj screen2.obj \
               screen1.obj dbrecord.obj dblist.obj
        $(LINK) $**

dbconv.exe : dbconv.obj dynarray.obj diskstor.obj \
               dbrecord.obj ioserror.obj screen3.obj \
               screen2.obj screen1.obj dblist.obj
        $(LINK) $**

hide1.exe : hide1.obj ioserror.obj
        $(LINK) $**

# obj dependencies:

dynarray.obj : ..\chap_6\dynarray.cpp ..\chap_6\dynarray.h
        $(CPP) -c ..\chap_6\dynarray.cpp

diskstor.obj : diskstor.h ioserror.h diskstor.cpp
mjmtest1.obj : stortest.h diskstor.h ioserror.h mjmtest1.cpp
screen2.obj : screen2.h screen1.h screen2.cpp
protect.obj : protect.cpp
screen1.obj : screen1.h screen1.cpp
timetest.obj : timer2.h ioserror.h timetest.cpp
stortest.obj : stortest.h diskstor.h ioserror.h stortest.cpp
dbfind.obj : dblist.h ..\chap_6\dynarray.h dbrecord.h \
               diskstor.h ioserror.h fields.h screen3.h \
               screen2.h screen1.h ioserror.h timer2.h dbfind.cpp
scr1test.obj : screen1.h timer2.h scr1test.cpp
scr2test.obj : screen2.h screen1.h timer2.h scr2test.cpp
timecom.obj : timer2.h ioserror.h timecom.cpp
screen3.obj : screen3.h screen2.h screen1.h ioserror.h \
               timer2.h screen3.cpp
scr3test.obj : screen3.h screen2.h screen1.h ioserror.h \
               timer2.h scr3test.cpp
mjmtest2.obj : stortest.h diskstor.h ioserror.h mjmtest2.cpp
hide1.obj : ioserror.h hide1.cpp
dbadd.obj : dblist.h ..\chap_6\dynarray.h dbrecord.h \
               diskstor.h ioserror.h fields.h screen3.h \
               screen2.h screen1.h ioserror.h timer2.h dbadd.cpp
dbrecord.obj : dbrecord.h diskstor.h ioserror.h \
```

```
                        fields.h dbrecord.cpp
dbconv.obj : dblist.h ..\chap_6\dynarray.h dbrecord.h \
               diskstor.h ioserror.h fields.h screen3.h \
               screen2.h screen1.h ioserror.h timer2.h dbconv.cpp
errtest.obj : error.h errtest.cpp
iostest.obj : ioserror.h iostest.cpp
ioserror.obj : ioserror.h ioserror.cpp
error.obj : error.h error.cpp
dbtest.obj : dblist.h ..\chap_6\dynarray.h dbrecord.h \
               diskstor.h ioserror.h fields.h screen3.h \
               screen2.h screen1.h ioserror.h timer2.h dbtest.cpp
dblist.obj : dblist.h ..\chap_6\dynarray.h dbrecord.h \
               diskstor.h ioserror.h fields.h screen3.h \
               screen2.h screen1.h ioserror.h timer2.h dblist.cpp
```

CHAPTER

Writing Extensible Programs in C++

*I*n the previous chapter, inheritance was used to modify a class when it didn't fit the needs of the problem at hand. **public**, **private**, and **protected** data and functions can be added through inheritance to increase the functionality of a class, and **public** functions of a base class can be redefined or hidden in a derived class. Using inheritance to modify existing classes is a very powerful way to develop code incrementally, especially since you can inherit a class even if you don't have the source code for the methods of that class. Incremental code development with inheritance also isolates bugs; if you have a working base class you inherit into a derived class that has bugs, you have a reasonable certainty that the bugs were introduced in the methods of the derived class.

Using inheritance to change the functionality of an existing class is an excellent programming aid. One of the great benefits of object-oriented programming, however, is not just in writing code but in *designing* programs. Inheritance is a way of classifying concepts. Many problems can be cast into a hierarchy or tree of these concepts; the tree shows which concepts share common features.

As an example, the following figure shows a hierarchy that illustrates various different kinds of transportation. At the base of the tree, all transportation has certain things in common: a certain number of passengers can be carried, a certain speed may be attained, there is a certain fuel efficiency, and so on. In Figure 8-1, transportation is subdivided into types depending on the medium: water, land, air, space, and other dimensions. All of these types of transportation inherit the characteristics of the base class. The types of transportation are further subdivided according to their specific idiosyncrasies.

Regardless of the specific subclass of transportation you are dealing with, you know it will have the methods available in the base class (unless those methods have been hidden by privately inheriting the base class). This means all modes of transportation have a certain common interface, which is the same as saying that all forms of transportation have certain things in common. By creating this tree of subclasses, you can, for example, always find out how many passengers can be carried by a mode of transportation (assuming there is a method in the base class to tell you this information). A program that manipulates objects of **class transportation** is extensible: all you need to do is derive a new subclass of **transportation**. The program already knows how to handle it.

FIGURE 8-1

A transportation tree

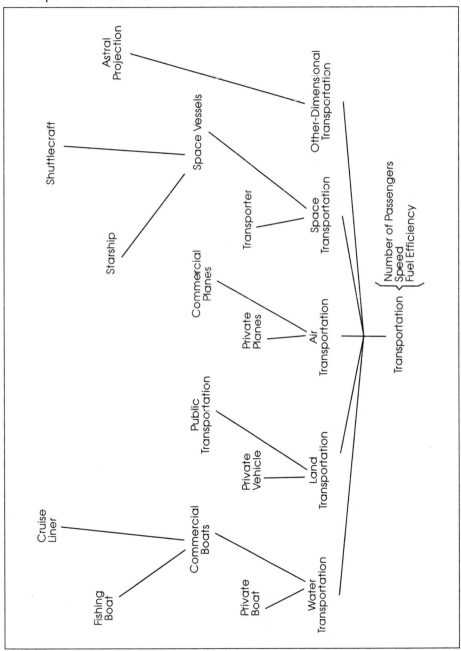

Coding the Transportation Hierarchy in C++

To illustrate this point, a portion of the hierarchy will be turned into C++ code, and a small program will be written to manipulate objects of **class transportation**. The program will be extended by adding a new subclass. Here is the code that implements a portion of the tree:

```
//: TRANSPRT.H—Implementing the transportation tree

class transportation {
  char * name;
  int passengers;
  int speed;
  int fuel_use;   // scale of 0 to 100
  int safety;    // scale of 0 to 100
  int range;
  char * difficulty;
  int expense;    // scale of 0 to 100
  char * comfort;
  char * notes;
public:
  transportation(char * nm, int pass, int spd, int fuel,
    int safe, int rng, char * difficult, int exp, char * comf,
    char * nte) :
      name(nm),
      passengers(pass),
      speed(spd),
      fuel_use(fuel),
      safety(safe),
      range(rng),
      difficulty(difficult),
      expense(exp),
      comfort(comf),
      notes(nte)
      {}
  const char * trans_name() { return name; }
  int num_of_pass() { return passengers; }
  int max_speed() { return speed; }
  int fuel_usage() { return fuel_use; }
  int degree_of_safety() { return safety; }
  int distance_possible() { return range; }
  const char * degree_of_difficulty() { return difficulty; }
  int cost() { return expense; }
```

```cpp
    const char * level_of_comfort() { return comfort; }
    const char * other_observations() { return notes; }
};

class water_transport : public transportation {
  int crew;
  int hulls;
  char * navigation;
public:
    water_transport(char * nm, int pass, int spd, int fuel,
      int safe, int rng, char * difficult, int exp, char * comf,
      char * nte, int crw, int hls, char * nav) :
        transportation(nm, pass, spd, fuel, safe, rng, difficult,
          exp, comf, nte), crew(crw), hulls(hls), navigation(nav) {}
    int crew_complement() { return crew; }
    int number_of_hulls() { return hulls; }
    const char * navigational_system() { return navigation; }
};

class private_boat : public water_transport {
  int owners;
public:
    private_boat(char * nm, int pass, int spd, int fuel, int safe,
      int rng, char * difficult, int exp, char * comf,
      char * nte, int crw, int hls, char * nav, int ownrs) :
        water_transport(nm, pass, spd, fuel, safe, rng,difficult,
          exp, comf, nte, crw, hls, nav), owners(ownrs) {}
    int number_of_owners() { return owners; }
};

class commercial_boat : public water_transport {
  int fare;
public:
    commercial_boat(char * nm, int pass, int spd, int fuel,
      int safe, int rng, char * difficult, int exp, char * comf,
      char * nte, int crw, int hls, char * nav, int fre) :
        water_transport(nm, pass, spd, fuel, safe, rng,difficult,
          exp, comf, nte, crw, hls, nav), fare(fre) {}
    int fare_per_passenger() { return fare; }
};

class cruise_liner : public commercial_boat {
  int feed_rate;
public:
    cruise_liner(char * nm, int pass, int spd, int fuel,
      int safe, int rng, char * difficult, int exp, char * comf,
      char * nte, int crw, int hls, char * nav, int fre,
```

```
      int feeding) :
        commercial_boat(nm, pass, spd, fuel, safe, rng,difficult,
          exp, comf, nte, crw, hls, nav, fre),feed_rate(feeding) {}
    int meals_per_day() { return feed_rate; }
};

class fishing_boat : public commercial_boat {
  int refrigerator_capacity;
public:
  fishing_boat(char * nm, int pass, int spd, int fuel,
    int safe, int rng, char * difficult, int exp, char * comf,
    char * nte, int crw, int hls, char * nav, int fre,
    int refer_cap) :
      commercial_boat(nm, pass, spd, fuel, safe, rng,difficult,
        exp, comf, nte, crw, hls, nav, fre),
        refrigerator_capacity(refer_cap) {}
  int fish_storage_capacity() { return refrigerator_capacity; }
};

// End of that branch of the tree. Now develop a new branch.

class land_transportation : public transportation {
  int wheels;
public:
  land_transportation(char * nm, int pass, int spd, int fuel,
    int safe, int rng, char * difficult, int exp, char * comf,
    char * nte, int whls) :
      transportation(nm, pass, spd, fuel, safe, rng, difficult,
        exp, comf, nte), wheels(whls) {}
  int number_of_wheels() { return wheels; }
};

class private_vehicle : public land_transportation {
  int stereo;
  int sunroof;
public:
  private_vehicle(char * nm, int pass, int spd, int fuel,
    int safe, int rng, char * difficult, int exp, char * comf,
    char * nte, int whls, int ster, int sunrf) :
      land_transportation(nm, pass, spd, fuel, safe, rng,
        difficult, exp, comf, nte, whls),
        stereo(ster), sunroof(sunrf) {}
  int has_stereo() { return stereo; }
  int has_sunroof() { return sunroof; }
};

class public_transportation : public land_transportation {
```

```
    int schedule;  // how often it comes by
public:
  public_transportation(char * nm, int pass, int spd,
    int fuel, int safe, int rng, char * difficult, int exp,
    char * comf, char * nte, int whls, int sched) :
      land_transportation(nm, pass, spd, fuel, safe, rng,
        difficult, exp, comf, nte, whls), schedule(sched) {}
  int regularity() { return schedule; }
};

// And so on, for the other branches of the tree ...
```

The following file contains a function called **print_info()**, which asks a **transportation** object some questions. Every object belonging to a class that has been derived from **transportation** also belongs to **class transportation**. You can pass any object derived from **transportation** to **print_info()**, and the function will work properly.

```
//: TRANSPRT.CPP—Investigates modes of transportation
#include <iostream.h>
#include "transprt.h"

void print_info(transportation & transport) {
  cout << "name = " << transport.trans_name() << endl;
  cout << "number of passengers = "
       << transport.num_of_pass() << endl;
  cout << "maximum speed = "
       << transport.max_speed() << endl;
  cout << "fuel consumption = "
       << transport.fuel_usage() << endl;
}
```

Object Slicing

Notice that in TRANSPRT.CPP, **print_info()** takes an address (as a reference; a pointer may also be used). It's very important to use addresses—pointers or references—when a function is to manipulate an object of a base class *or* any of its derived classes. It's possible to pass an object of a derived class by value to a function which is expecting an object of a base class. However, the compiler will only pass the base-class portion—it will *slice* the object and remove its additional derived-class members as it is passed into the function. Here's a simple example:

```
//: SLICE.CPP—object slicing during argument passing

struct base { int a[10]; };
struct derived : base { int b[10]; };

void f(base) {};

void main() {
  base b;
  derived d;
  f(b);
  f(d);
}
```

Inside **f()** in both function calls, the size of the argument is the same, of course—the size of **base**. The compiler makes no complaints about it. However, in this chapter, base-class function calls can manipulate derived parts of the object; you'll soon see how this happens. If an object is sliced, the derived part may not be there, which would be disastrous. Thus, you should always avoid *object slicing* in these situations by passing an address.

Here's a small program that tests **print_info()** and some of the transportation classes:

```
//: TRANTST1.CPP—Test for print_info() and some of the
//. transportation classes
#include "transprt.h"
void print_info(transportation & transport);

void main() {
  cruise_liner princess("Love Boat", 800, 14, 1, 99,
    5000, "easy", 100, "very comfortable", "", 80, 1,
    "electronic", 4000, 8);
  private_vehicle volkswagen("bug", 4, 55, 25, 5, 400,
    "moderate", 10, "somewhat uncomfortable", "", 4, 1, 1);
  public_transportation bus("greydog", 56, 60, 12, 80, 600,
    "fairly easy", 4, "more uncomfortable", "", 6, 4);
  print_info(princess);
  print_info(volkswagen);
  print_info(bus);
}
```

Now suppose you want to derive a new class from **transportation** and use **print_info()** on that class. The **print_info()** function doesn't need to be changed a bit, as shown here:

```
//: TRANTST2.CPP—Deriving a new class and using print_info()
//. on it. Demonstrates extensibility.
#include "transprt.h"
void print_info(transportation & transport);

class other_dimensional : public transportation {
  int dimension;
public:
  other_dimensional(char * nm, int pass, int spd, int fuel,
    int safe, int rng, char * difficult, int exp, char * comf,
    char * nte, int dim) :
      transportation(nm, pass, spd, fuel, safe, rng,
        difficult, exp, comf, nte), dimension(dim) {}
  int dimension_number() { return dimension; }
};

void main() {
  other_dimensional time_travel("Tardis", 47, 0, 0, 10, 0, "?",
    100, "quite comfortable", "", 7);
  other_dimensional Buckaroo("Overthruster", 1, 0, 0, 1, 0, "?",
    100, "very jarring", "Can cause insanity", 8);
  print_info(time_travel);
  print_info(Buckaroo);
}
```

Any function or program you write that manipulates objects of a base class (via addresses) is extensible. You can add to its capabilities by deriving a new class from the base.

Virtual Functions

Suppose you want to create functions and programs that manipulate base-class objects so those functions and programs are extensible through inheritance. Sooner or later you will run into a problem, which can be illustrated by an example. The **description** class is a simple class that carries a description of itself and a has a method to print the description:

```
//: DESCRIP1.H—A class that contains a self-description.
#ifndef DESCRIP1_H_
#define DESCRIP1_H_
#include <iostream.h>

class description {
protected: // so derived classes have access
  char * information;
public:
  description(char * info) : information(info) {}
  void print() { cout << information << endl; }
};

#endif // DESCRIP1_H_
```

Now suppose you want to extend the abilities of the class, and any function or program using **class description**, by inheriting the class into a more specific form of **description** containing more information. To print the additional information, the **print()** function must be redefined for each new class. Here are some examples:

```
//: DESCRIP2.H—Subclasses of class description
#ifndef DESCRIP2_H_
#define DESCRIP2_H_
#include "descrip1.h"

class sphere : public description {
  float radius;
public:
  sphere(char * info, float rad)
      : description(info), radius(rad) {}
  // redefine the base-class member function:
  void print() {
    cout << information << endl;
    cout << "radius = " <<  radius << endl;
  }
};

class cube : public description {
  float edge_length;
public:
  cube(char * info, float edge) :
    description(info), edge_length(edge) {}
  // redefine the base-class member function:
  void print() {
    cout << information << endl;
```

```
        cout << "edge length = " <<  edge_length << endl;
    }
};


#endif // DESCRIP2_H_
```

So far, things look fine. However, there is a discrepancy between treating an object as a member of the base class and treating it as a member of a derived class. The following test program illustrates the problem:

```
//: DESCRIP.CPP—Test of derived description classes
#include "descrip2.h"

sphere small_ball("mini", 1.0),
       beach_ball("plastic", 24.0),
       planetoid("moon", 1e24);
cube crystal("carbon", 1e-24),
     ice("party", 1.0),
     box("cardboard", 16.0);

description * shapes[] = {
  &small_ball,
  &beach_ball,
  &planetoid,
  &crystal,
  &ice,
  &box
};

void main() {
  // print the descriptions individually:
  small_ball.print();
  beach_ball.print();
  planetoid.print();
  crystal.print();
  ice.print();
  box.print();

  // print all the descriptions in the list:
  for(int i = 0; i < sizeof(shapes)/sizeof(shapes[0]); i++)
    shapes[i]->print();
}
```

When the member function **print()** is called for the specific object, the desired method is used, and all the information about the object is printed. However, when the object is treated as an instance of the base class by calling **print()** for all the pointers in the array **shapes**, the base class method for **print()** is used! This is clearly not the desired effect. What you want in a case like this is the best of both worlds: the common interface provided by the base class, but the different implementations of the methods created in the derived classes.

The problem occurs because the function call to **print()** must be resolved before the program executes. When the compiler generates the call to **print()** for each element of an array of **description** pointers, it generates a call to **description::print()** because that's the only function it knows about in that context. Resolving the function call at compile time is called *early binding* or *static binding*.

To implement a common interface with different implementations for the member functions, the resolution of function calls must be delayed until run time. The goal is to be able to say, "You, you're an object of **class description**; **print()** yourself!" This should not call **description::print()**, but instead **sphere::print()** or **cube::print()**, depending on whether the object is a **sphere** or a **cube**. Resolving a function call at run time is called *late binding* or *dynamic binding*.

To perform dynamic binding of a function in a C++ class, you declare the function with the **virtual** keyword. You can declare any or all of your class member functions virtual. When you declare any functions in a class to be virtual, the compiler secretly adds a data member to the class. This data member is referred to here as the **VPTR**, and is a pointer to a table of function pointers, referred to here as the **VTABLE**. The **VTABLE** contains pointers to all the functions that have been declared virtual in the class, or in any derived classes. Here is a brief example showing evidence of the secret existence of the **VPTR**:

```
//: VPTRSIZE.CPP—sizeof() detects the existence of VPTR
#include <iostream.h>

class novirtual {
  int x;
public:
  void foo() {}
};

class withvirtual {
  int x;
```

```
public:
  virtual void foo() {}
};

void main() {
  cout << "sizeof(novirtual) = " << sizeof(novirtual) << endl;
  cout << "sizeof(withvirtual) = "
       << sizeof(withvirtual) << endl;
}

/* Output of this program on a PC with Borland C++,
   compact model:

sizeof(novirtual) = 2
sizeof(withvirtual) = 4
*/
```

Whenever a call to a virtual function is made in a C++ program, the compiler generates code to treat the **VPTR** as the starting address of an array of pointers to functions. The function-call code simply indexes into this array and calls the function located at the indexed address. This means if you call a virtual member function while treating the object in question as a member of its base class, the correct derived-class function will always be called.

To illustrate this, look at the effect of virtual functions on **class description**. Here is all the code repeated in a single file for the files **descrip1.h**, **descrip2.h**, and DESCRIP.CPP shown previously. Notice the only change to the code is the addition of the keyword **virtual** to the **print()** function in the base class. Everything else is untouched.

```
//: DESCRFIX.CPP—Fixing "description" w/ virtual functions
#include <iostream.h>

class description {
protected: // so derived classes have access
  char * information;
public:
  description(char * info) : information(info) {}
  // ONLY CHANGE IS RIGHT HERE: ADDITION OF "virtual" :
  virtual void print() { cout << information << endl; }
};

class sphere : public description {
  float radius;
```

```cpp
public:
  sphere(char * info, float rad)
     : description(info), radius(rad) {}
  // redefine the base-class member function:
  void print() {
    description::print();
    cout << "radius = " << radius << endl;
  }
};

class cube : public description {
  float edge_length;
public:
  cube(char * info, float edge)
     : description(info), edge_length(edge) {}
  // redefine the base-class member function:
  void print() {
    description::print();
    cout << "edge length = " << edge_length << endl;
  }
};

sphere small_ball("mini", 1.0),
       beach_ball("plastic", 24.0),
       planetoid("moon", 1e24);
cube crystal("carbon", 1e-24),
     ice("party", 1.0),
     box("cardboard", 16.0);

description * shapes[] = {
  &small_ball,
  &beach_ball,
  &planetoid,
  &crystal,
  &ice,
  &box
};

void main() {
  // print the descriptions individually:
  small_ball.print();
  beach_ball.print();
  planetoid.print();
  crystal.print();
  ice.print();
  box.print();
```

```
  // print all the descriptions in the list:
  for(int i = 0; i < sizeof(shapes)/sizeof(shapes[0]); i++)
    shapes[i]->print();
}

/* Output of this program:

mini
radius = 1
plastic
radius = 24
moon
radius = 1e+024
carbon
edge length = 1e-024
party
edge length = 1
cardboard
edge length = 16
mini
radius = 1
plastic
radius = 24
moon
radius = 1e+024
carbon
edge length = 1e-024
party
edge length = 1
cardboard
edge length = 16

*/

/* Output of this program WITHOUT the "virtual" keyword in
   the base class:

mini
radius = 1
plastic
radius = 24
moon
radius = 1e+024
carbon
edge length = 1e-024
party
```

```
edge length = 1
cardboard
edge length = 16
mini
plastic
moon
carbon
party
cardboard
*/
```

You can see from the output that the virtual function is essential for creating objects with the same interface but different implementations.

Inside Virtual Functions

To ensure that you understand this critical concept—virtual functions are the very heart of OOP—consider a second, much simpler example: an abstraction of the often-used "shapes" example. All shapes can be drawn, but circles, squares, and triangles are all drawn differently. To create an extensible program, you want to be able to manipulate generic **shape** pointers and ignore the details of what specific kind of **shape** you're dealing with. Thus, the code that manipulates **shape** pointers will be immune to changes. If you want to extend the system, you only have to derive a new type of **shape**. Here's what it looks like:

```
//: SHAPES.CPP—Very simple polymorphism
#include <iostream.h>

struct shape {
  virtual void draw() {}
};

struct circle : shape {
  void draw() { cout << "circle::draw" << endl; }
};

struct square : shape {
  void draw() { cout << "square::draw" << endl; }
};

struct triangle : shape {
```

```
  void draw() { cout << "triangle::draw" << endl; }
};

void main() {
  shape * list[3] = { new circle, new square, new triangle };
  for(int i = 0; i < 3; i++)
    list[i]->draw();
}
```

The base class **shape** defines the common interface for all specific types of shapes by defining a function **draw()**. Each derived class redefines **draw()** in its own unique way, but it is the same draw function, because the signature is identical.

The **main()** function is where the trouble starts. The definition of **list** is as an array of pointers to **shape** objects. It is initialized with three pointers, one from each specific type. But now all the information about the specific types is lost, since **list** just holds pointers to shapes. The compiler cannot know what the specific types are anymore.

In addition, the C++ compiler is usually very picky about assigning one type of pointer to another. Ordinarily this could be disastrous—you could assign the address of a **rock** to a **bird** pointer, and then you could effectively tell a **rock** to fly. Since **rock** probably doesn't have a **fly()** member function, who knows what actually gets called. Probably you'd crash something.

However, the above assignments go by without a peep from the compiler. This is because an *upcast* is completely safe. You can always cast from a more-derived type like **circle** *up* to a less-derived type like **shape**, and there's no danger (the "up" and "down" comes from the historical practice of drawing hierarchy trees down from the root, the inversion of Figure 8-1). This is because there is no way to remove functions during inheritance, so any functions you can call in the base class must also exist in the derived class. Thus, base-class function calls are always OK. A *downcast*, on the other hand, is not necessarily safe because a **shape** pointer could actually be a **circle** or a **square** or who knows what? (Only you can know that, by installing other information in the object that you query at run time; this is called *run-time type checking*.)

So once the **list** is filled, the compiler has lost all the specific information about the objects; it only knows they are pointers to **shape**s. Now what happens when you call a member function, as in

```
list[i]->draw();
```

The compiler only knows that **list** holds **shape** pointers, so it must call the version of **draw()** defined in the base class (which isn't at all what you want). It turns out that with *this* program, that's not what happens. The best way to see this is to type in the program and then single-step through it with the debugger. You'll see that the right behavior occurs, and this is the key to OOP—you "send a message to an object, and the object figures out what to do with it."

The case where the compiler can only know to call the base-class version of **draw()** is early binding—the compiler figures it out. However, in this case you want the function call to be resolved at run time, so the **virtual** keyword is used in the base class to make this happen. The **virtual** keyword causes late binding.

Mechanics of Virtual Functions

It helps to understand exactly what's going on when virtual functions are set up and called. Consider the most trivial example:

```
struct X {
 int i;
 virtual void f();
 virtual void g();
};
X x, *xp = &x;
xp->g();
```

This generates a virtual call (notice that if you said **x.g()**, the compiler would make a nonvirtual call because it knows the exact type of **x**). Here's a picture of what it looks like:

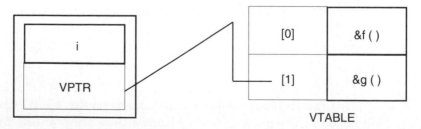

VTABLE

The **i** member is in the structure just like you'd expect. The compiler has secretly inserted the **VPTR** into the structure—this is the equivalent of its "type field." However, the **VPTR** is assigned to an array of pointers to functions called the **VTABLE**, which contains all the virtual function addresses from the structure. The **VPTR** is initialized to the starting address of the **VTABLE**—where else—in the constructor, so there's no chance of making a virtual function call before the **VPTR** has been initialized. (This is accomplished by secret code inserted into the constructor by the compiler. It's also one reason **inline** constructors are not as efficient as you think.)

Neither the **shape** example nor this one has a constructor. Here's a situation where it's critical for proper initialization to occur—if the **VPTR** isn't initialized, you'll have a disaster the first time you make a function call. This is one essential reason why the compiler automatically creates a default constructor if you don't explicitly create any constructors—one job of the generated default constructor is to initialize the **VPTR** (the compiler inserts this initialization in all constructors).

To see what happens in **xp->g()**, it's very helpful to generate assembly language and examine it. Here are the two important statements on the 80*x*86 architecture:

```
mov  bx,word ptr [si+2]
call    word ptr [bx+2]
```

The object address (**this**) is in the source index register **si**. The first statement fetches into the **bx** register the contents of **this** + 2, which is past the data element **i**. In fact, it's the **VPTR**. With the **VPTR** in **bx**, the next statement calls what **bx** + 2 points at. This reaches into the **VTABLE**, gets the second function address (each are of length 2 in this memory model) and calls that function. That's how late binding is implemented. The code effectively says "fetch the **VPTR**. Index into the **VTABLE** by *X* addresses (*X* representing the number of the virtual function, usually in declaration order) and call the function whose address is at that location."

The code generated by the compiler simply goes to the table, fetches the function address, and calls it. It makes no assumption about the **VTABLE** except that the addresses will be in the same order for every **VTABLE**. The actual function called will be determined by the **VTABLE** the **VPTR** indicates, which is different from one type to another. Each time you inherit a new type, the compiler creates a new **VTABLE** for that type. If you don't redefine a function, the compiler uses the function address from the previous class's **VTABLE**. There's a virtual function address in every slot of the **VTABLE**.

Extending the System

Now consider what happens if you want to add a new type of shape to the system.

```
//: SHAPES2.CPP—Extending the system
#include <iostream.h>

struct shape {
  virtual void draw() = 0;  // pure virtual
}; // makes this class pure abstract

struct circle : shape {
  void draw() { cout << "circle::draw" << endl; }
};

struct square : shape {
  void draw() { cout << "square::draw" << endl; }
};

struct triangle : shape {
  void draw() { cout << "triangle::draw" << endl; }
};

// new type of shape:
struct line : shape {
  void draw() { cout << "line::draw" << endl; }
};

void main() {
//  shape s; // error because of pure virtual
  shape * list[4] = {
    new circle, new square, new triangle, new line
  };
  // code where it's used stays the same
  for(int i = 0; i < 4; i++)
    list[i]->draw();
}
```

Ignoring for the moment the modification to the base class, you can see that a new class has been added. Also you can see that the code **list[i]->draw()**, because it's ignorant of specific types, doesn't need to change. Although it's only one line in this program it represents the bulk of the program you ordinarily create and the place where changes are most likely to cause trouble.

The only place in **main()** that had to be modified is where the objects are created. Creation is a special act, and the compiler must know the exact type of the object when it creates it so it can set up the **VPTR** (so other functions can *ignore* the specific type). You'll generally find the two steps to extending a C++ OOP design are to

1. Derive a new type from the common base type and

2. Change the code so that new type can be created

Everything else, if the program is designed properly, will remain the same. If the **shape** base class is used in a computer-aided-design program that only manipulates generic **shape**s, you can derive as many new types of **shape**s as you want without changing the core of the program.

Pure Virtual Functions

The other modification in SHAPES2.CPP is in the base class. Instead of giving **draw()** an empty function body like before, it is defined as

```
virtual void draw() = 0;
```

which seems to imply the function body is assigned to 0; that is, there's *no* function body for this function. That is precisely the meaning, and when the compiler tries to create a **VTABLE** for that class, it cannot find a function address for that particular function, so it has nothing to put into that **VTABLE** position. This means it cannot create the **VTABLE**, which means it cannot create an object whose specific type is **shape**.

A function with its body assigned to 0 like this is called a *pure virtual function* (it only works with virtual functions inside classes). Any class that contains one or more pure virtual functions is called a *pure abstract base class*. An abstract base class is one that is only meant to be used as an interface to other classes derived from it. Formerly, you could only say a class was abstract and put error functions in one or more base-class members that would produce messages at run time. With pure virtual functions you can enforce the abstractness of a base class with error messages at compile time.

Of course, the pure virtual functions must be redefined in a derived class before you can make an instance of that derived class. If you don't define one or more pure virtual functions in a derived class, then *that* class is also pure abstract.

Rules for Virtual Functions

If you are redefining a virtual function in a derived class, you must redeclare the function in the derived-class definition. The prototypes for the base-class version of a virtual function and all the derived-class versions must be identical for the virtual function to work properly. This makes sense; otherwise it wouldn't be a "common interface." Your

Virtual Functions and Efficiency

You may wonder why the programmer is given the option of making a function virtual—why not just let the compiler create *all* functions as virtual? This was another language design decision made in favor of run-time efficiency. As you can see in the assembly code above, a virtual function requires an extra dereference to make a function call. The language defaults in favor of maximized efficiency, which is accomplished through early binding. If the default were to late binding, then even C **struct**s would acquire a **VPTR** when used in a C++ program, and even the simplest functions in a class would have the overhead of virtual functions (not only would this make **inline** functions meaningless, it would make them impossible). The C++ approach means the programmer is forced to be aware of the difference between early and late binding, and to know when to apply late binding. Several other object-oriented languages, Smalltalk in particular, always use late binding, so the programmer never has to think about it.

compiler may or may not issue a warning message if you use a new function signature when redefining a virtual function (something to the effect that you are "hiding" the virtual function in the base class). Note you *can* change the prototype for a nonvirtual derived-class member function that has been defined in the base class. This is essentially the same as declaring a new function. If you change the prototype of a nonvirtual function, the original function in the base class is not hidden.

You cannot have virtual constructors, but you *can* have virtual destructors. In fact, virtual destructors are essential to the solution of some problems. It is also possible to have virtual operator overloading.

An Extensible Menu System

As a useful example of extensible programming, consider the problem of building menus. Adding functionality to menus is a typical task, and you want it to be as painless as possible. In addition, while the process of selecting one menu item is identical to the process of selecting any other menu item (that is, the interface is the same), what happens when a menu item is selected can vary widely. This sounds like virtual functions could be used to advantage.

The menu system will be broken into two parts. The fundamental unit will be the **class menu_item**, which represents a single item on the menu and its associated functionality. These fundamental units will be contained by a second class called **menu_driver**, which manages a group of **menu_items**. A class that has the sole task of holding objects of another class is often called a *container class* (see Chapter 10).

Different types of **menu_item** will be derived from the base class. The **menu_item** will contain functions to display the item and to test to see if a keystroke matches the item's **activation_letter**. If a match is made, the **virtual execute()** function is called.

Isolating Nonportable Code

Before launching into the menu system, a separate problem must be solved. ANSI C doesn't provide any library support for *raw I/O* because it's usually system dependent. The lack of raw I/O means you cannot, for example, just grab a keyboard character—you must wait until an entire line is entered followed by a carriage return. Many compiler vendors and/or operating systems *do* provide functions that grab keyboard keys, but they are of course nonportable. A good way to handle a problem like this is to isolate the nonportable code. The following header file isolates the nonportable function to get a character from the keyboard.

```
//: GETKEY.H—Isolation of nonportable console I/O.
//. Many packages for the PC use getch() to do "raw" I/O
//. from the keyboard. You may need to investigate your
//. system to find out how to grab a keyboard character
//. without waiting for a carriage return.
#ifndef GETKEY_H_
#define GETKEY_H_

#ifdef __BORLANDC__  || _MSC_VER
#include <conio.h>
inline int get_console_key() { return getch(); }
#else
// if all else fails, force the user to enter a CR after
// the character:
inline int get_console_key() { return getchar(); }
#endif

#endif //  GETKEY_H_
```

The macro **get_console_key()** is simply redefined for the local environment. You will see this header file used several places in the menu system.

A Class to Represent a Single Menu Entry

Here is the header file for **menu_item**:

```
//: MENUITEM.H—Class to represent a single item on the menu
#ifndef MENUITEM_H_
#define MENUITEM_H_

class menu_item {
  char activation_letter;
  char * item_name;
  char * item_description;
```

```
public:
  menu_item(char activ_let, char * name, char * descrip) :
    activation_letter(activ_let), item_name(name),
    item_description(descrip) {}
    // menu action is empty for the base class:
  virtual const char * execute() = 0;
  void display(int line_number);
  int execute_if_match(char test_char);
};

#endif // MENUITEM_H_
```

Notice that the function **execute()** is declared as **virtual**. The function **execute_if_match()** compares its argument to **activation_letter**. If there is a match, it calls **execute()**, which must be redefined in a derived class (examples will be shown in a test program). The **execute()** can be anything.

Here are the methods for **menu_item**:

```
//: MENUITEM.CPP—Methods for single menu item.
//. This header file organization is for the book's
//. source-code disk. Yours may be different.
//. Use the screen controller from Chapter 7:
#include "getkey.h"
#include "menuitem.h"
#include "..\chap_7\screen3.h"
#include <iostream.h>
// Use the error handler from Chapter 7:
#include "..\chap_7\ioserror.h"
static ioserror error("menu_item: ");

const key_col = 1;  // column for activation letter
const name_col = 4; // column for item name
const descr_col = 20;  // column for item description

void menu_item::display(int line_number) {
  screen.move(line_number, key_col);
  screen.clear_eol();
  screen.reverse();
  cout << activation_letter;
  screen.normal();
  screen.move(line_number, name_col);
  screen.high_intensity();
  cout << item_name;
  screen.normal();
```

```
    screen.move(line_number, descr_col);
    cout << item_description;
}

int menu_item::execute_if_match(char test_char) {
  const char * return_message;
  if(test_char == activation_letter) {
    if(*(return_message = execute()) != '\0') {
      error << "\n" << return_message << "\n"
            << "any key to continue ";
      get_console_key();
    }
    return test_char;
  }
  return 0;  // not a match
}
```

Two of the classes from Chapter 7 are being reused here: **class screen_controller** (which automatically defines a single object called **screen** and prevents you from creating any other instances) and **class ioserror** (to report errors). The instance of **ioserror**, **error**, is declared **static** so it has file scope (internal linkage) and will not interfere with any other file using the same name for its **ioserror**.

The **display()** function simply prints the line of information on the screen via the **screen** object. The **execute_if_match()** function calls **execute()** if the key pressed matches **activation_letter**. The **execute()** function returns a pointer to a **const** character string. If this string is empty, it means the function has executed successfully. If the string is not empty, there was a problem and the string contains an error message, which is printed. The **execute_if_match()** function returns the key pressed if the key matches with **activation_letter**, and 0 if there is no match (and no call to **execute()**).

A Class to Manage a Collection of Menu Entries

Now that the base class for a menu entry has been defined, a container class can be created to manipulate an array of pointers to **menu_item**. Since you usually do not create a menu at run time (although this can be desirable), the array of **menu_item** pointers will be created globally, and the starting address of the array will be handed to the constructor along with the size of the array and a headline to print at the top of the menu. Here is the header file for **class menu_driver**:

```
//: MENUDRIV.H—Container class for menu_item. Displays
//. a menu on the screen and gets a response.
#ifndef MENUDRIV_H_
#define MENUDRIV_H_
#include "menuitem.h"

const char quit_character = 'q';
const char forward_screen = '+';
const char backward_screen = '-';

// spacing for menu items:
const linespacing = 2;

class menu_driver {
  menu_item ** menu; // array of pointers to menu items
  char * headline;  // to print at the top of the screen
  int total_items; // total number in menu
  int items_per_page; // how many you can fit in a screen
  int current_page; // current screen of commands
  int max_pages;    // maximum number of screens
public:
  menu_driver(char * head, menu_item ** menu_array, int size);
  void display_current_page();
  int get_and_execute(); // get a command and do it, return key
  void run() {
    do
      display_current_page();
    while(get_and_execute() != quit_character);
  }
  void dump(); // for testing
};

#endif // MENUDRIV_H_
```

The value of **linespacing** is used by the constructor to calculate the number of menu items per page. The argument **size**, the size of the menu array, is used to calculate the total number of menu items, which is used to calculate the number of pages. These calculations and the value of **current_page** are used to move back and forth through the menu pages. The **display_current_page()** function clears the screen, writes the headline, all the menu items that will fit on the page, and a line at the bottom telling the user how to quit or move forward or backward through the menu pages (if there is more than one page). The user moves through the menu pages or quits by selecting one of the character constants **forward_screen**, **backward_screen**, or **quit_character**.

The **get_and_execute()** function waits for a keystroke and, after checking that it doesn't match with **forward_screen**, **backward_screen**, or **quit_character**, tests each **menu_item** on the current screen of the array until it finds a match. It returns the value of the keystroke if it is **forward_screen**, **backward_screen**, **quit_character**, or a successfully completed function; otherwise it returns 0.

Here are the methods for **class menu_driver**:

```cpp
//: MENUDRIV.CPP—Methods for menu_driver class
//. This header file organization is for the book's
//. source-code disk. Yours may be different.
#include <iostream.h>
#include "..\chap_7\screen3.h"
#include "menudriv.h"
#include "getkey.h"
const lines_per_page = 25;

menu_driver::menu_driver(char * head, menu_item ** menu_array,
                         int msize)
  : menu(menu_array), headline(head), current_page(0) {
//    items_per_page = (screen.maxrow() - 4) / linespacing;
// the above line doesn't always work with static objects
// because the screen object may not get initialized before
// this object.
    items_per_page = (lines_per_page - 4) / linespacing;
    // 2 lines for the top and two for the bottom. Notice the
    // integer divide truncates any remainder.
    // The total number of items is the size of the list
    // divided by the size of a single item (the first one):
    total_items = msize / sizeof(*menu);
    max_pages = total_items / items_per_page;
    if(total_items % items_per_page) // if there's a remainder
      max_pages++;
}

void menu_driver::display_current_page() {
  screen.clear_screen();
  screen.home();
  screen.reverse();
  screen.center(1, headline);
```

```cpp
   int line = 3;   // current line to write on
   screen.normal();
   for(int i = current_page * items_per_page;
       (i < (current_page + 1) * items_per_page)
       && (i < total_items) ;
       i++ ) {
     menu[i]->display(line);
     line += linespacing;
   }
   screen.move(screen.maxrow(), 1);
   screen.reverse();
   cout << quit_character;
   screen.normal();
   cout << " to quit     ";
   if(current_page < max_pages - 1) {
     screen.reverse();
     cout <<  forward_screen;
     screen.normal();
     cout << " for next screen    ";
   }
   if(current_page > 0 ) {
     screen.reverse();
     cout << backward_screen;
     screen.normal();
     cout << " for previous screen    ";
   }
}

int menu_driver::get_and_execute() {
   int key = get_console_key();
   switch(key) {
     case quit_character: return quit_character;
     case forward_screen:
         if(current_page < max_pages - 1)
           current_page++;
         return forward_screen;
     case backward_screen:
         if(current_page > 0)
           current_page--;
         return backward_screen;
   }
   // only look at the items on this page:
   for(int i = current_page * items_per_page;
     (i < (current_page + 1) * items_per_page)
     && (i < total_items) ;
     i++ )
       if(menu[i]->execute_if_match(key))
```

```
        return key;
    return 0;   // nothing found to execute
}

void menu_driver::dump() {
    cout << "menu = " <<  menu << endl;
    cout << "headline = " <<  headline << endl;
#define PR(x) cout << #x " = " << x << endl;
    PR(total_items);
    PR(items_per_page);
    PR(current_page);
    PR(max_pages);
    get_console_key();
}
```

In the constructor, you might wonder why the size of the **menu_item** pointer array must be passed into the function. The reason is that an array identifier is different than a pointer to an array. If you take the **sizeof()** an array identifier, you get the size of the entire array. If you take the **sizeof()** a pointer to an array, you get the size of the pointer. When you pass an array identifier to the constructor as the argument **menu_array**, the starting address of the array is produced and assigned to the **menu_array**. At that point, inside the function, you have no way of figuring out how big the array is, since all you have is a pointer. Thus the size of the array must be taken and passed to the constructor. The constructor uses this information to determine the number of menu items per page and the number of pages.

The constructor contains a "wart" in the commented-out line:

```
// items_per_page = (screen.maxrow() - 4) / linespacing;
```

which has been replaced with the calculation:

```
items_per_page = (lines_per_page - 4) / linespacing;
```

The first calculation depends on a global object; the second doesn't. The reason the change was made will be discussed later.

The **display_current_page()** function is primarily a series of calls to the **screen_controller** object **screen**. After the screen is cleared and the headline is written, the **display()** function is called for each **menu_item** on the page. At the bottom of the page, the **quit_character** is printed with a message. If there are more pages, the user is told how to move forward, and if this isn't the first page, the user is told how to move backward.

In **get_and_execute()**, the **quit_character**, **forward_screen**, and **backward_screen** selections are handled in a **switch** statement; each of the cases returns from the function, so no **break** statement is needed. If the function makes it through the **switch** statement, the selected key is tested against all the menu items *on the current page* with the **menu_item::execute_if_match()** function. Because only the items on the current page are checked, you can reuse activation letters from page to page.

The **dump()** function has been included for debugging.

Testing the Menu System

To test the menu system, subclasses with different definitions of **execute()** must be derived from the base **class menu_item**. A global array of pointers to instances of these subclasses must be created, and the starting address of the array must be handed to the constructor for **menu_driver**, along with the array size and a headline.

The subclasses derived from **menu_item** in the following example show only a small sample of the possible ways you can redefine **menu_item**. Essentially, any time you want a new type of menu functionality, you should derive a new subclass. Notice in particular the derived **class submenu**, which allows you to create a menu that is activated by selecting an item from another menu.

```
//: MENUTEST.CPP—Test for the menu_driver class
//. note screen size can be changed by commands to the
//. screen object before initializing the menu.
#include "getkey.h"
#include "menudriv.h"
#include "..\chap_7\screen3.h"
#include <time.h>
#include <iostream.h>
#include <strstream.h>
#include <stdlib.h>

// First, derive some subclasses of menu_item to perform
// different kinds of actions:
```

```
class display_time : public menu_item {
public:
  display_time() :
    menu_item('t', "display time", "shows the time and date") {}
  const char * execute() {
    time_t now;
    time(&now);
    screen.clear_screen();
    screen.move(10, 10);
    cout << "current time is " << ctime(&now);
    screen.move(12, 10);
    cout << "any key to continue";
    get_console_key();
    return "";  // execution finished OK
  }
} disp_time;  // instance of display_time

// a class to view environment variables:
class environment : public menu_item {
  char * envname;
public:
  environment(char kn, char * en) :
    menu_item(kn, en, "displays this environment variable"),
    envname(en)
    {};
  const char * execute();
};

const char * environment::execute() {
  screen.clear_screen();
  screen.move(10, 10);
  char * envstr = getenv(envname);
  if(envstr == 0)
    return "Environment variable not found";
  cout << "environment variable "
       << envname << " is " << envstr;
  screen.move(12, 10);
  cout << "any key to continue";
  get_console_key();
  return "";  // execution finished OK
}

environment path('p', "PATH"), // instances of this class
            library('L', "LIB"),
            includes('i', "INCLUDE"),
            foo('f', "FOO"); // for testing the error system
```

```cpp
class system_command : public menu_item {
protected:
  char * command_name;
public:
  system_command(char ck, char * cname) :
    menu_item(ck, cname, "the system executes this command"),
    command_name(cname) {}
  const char * execute();
};
const char * system_command::execute() {
  screen.clear_screen();
  if(system(command_name)) // non-0 means error
    return "error executing system command";
  screen.move(screen.maxrow(), 1);
  screen.reverse();
  cout << "any key to continue";
  screen.normal();
  get_console_key();
  return "";   // execution finished OK
}
system_command directory('l', "ls"),
               fulldirect('a', "ls -l"),
               subtree('s', "ls -R"),
               sysdate('d', "DATE");

// Here's a second tier of inheritance.
// A system command with a single command-line argument:
class syscom_1arg : public system_command {
  char * argprompt;
public:
  syscom_1arg(char ck, char * cname, char * argp) :
    system_command(ck, cname), argprompt(argp) {}
  const char * execute();
};

const char * syscom_1arg::execute() {
  const bsize = 50, cbsize = 100;
  char buf[bsize], cbuf[cbsize];
  screen.clear_screen();
  screen.move(10,10);
  cout << argprompt << " : ";
  cin.getline(buf, bsize);
  ostrstream strbuf(cbuf, cbsize); // in-memory stream buffer
  strbuf << command_name << " " << buf;
  if(system(cbuf)) // nonNULL means error
    return "error executing system command";
```

```
    screen.move(screen.maxrow(), 1);
    screen.reverse();
    cout << "any key to continue";
    screen.normal();
    get_console_key();
    return "";  // execution finished OK
}

syscom_1arg emacs('e', "emacs", "name of file to edit"),
            changedir('c', "cd", "directory to change to"),
            more('m', "more", "name of file to view");

// Here's a class that is a gateway to another menu:
class submenu : public menu_item {
  menu_driver newmenu;
public:
  submenu(char smk, char * smd, char * head,
          menu_item ** sma, int size) :
    menu_item(smk, "sub-menu", smd), newmenu(head, sma, size)
    {}
  const char * execute();
};

const char * submenu::execute() {
  newmenu.run();
  return "";  // execution finished OK
}

// Here are three classes to display data in
// different number formats. They will be placed
// in the submenu. First, a base class to build the others
// with:

class display_number : public menu_item {
  enum { bsize = 100 };
  char buf[bsize];
  char * description;
protected:
  int decimal;
public:
  display_number(char nc, char * nn, char * nd,
    char * descrip) :
    menu_item(nc, nn, nd), description(descrip) {}
  void get_decimal() {
    screen.clear_screen();
    screen.move(10, 10);
    cout << "decimal value: ";
```

```cpp
    cin.getline(buf, bsize);
    decimal = atoi(buf);
    screen.move(11, 10);
    cout << description << " : ";
  }
  void finish() {
    screen.move(12, 10);
    cout << "any key to continue";
    get_console_key();
  }
};

class display_binary : public display_number {
public:
  display_binary() :
    display_number('b', "display binary",
                   "converts decimal to binary",
                   "binary value") {}
  const char * execute();
};

const char * display_binary::execute() {
  get_decimal();
  // Assume 8-bit bytes here:
  for(int i = 8 * sizeof(int) - 1; i >= 0; i--)
    cout << ((decimal & (1 << i)) ? '1' : '0');
  finish();
  return "";  // execution finished OK
}
display_binary disp_binary;

class display_hex : public display_number {
public:
  display_hex() :
    display_number('h', "display hex",
                   "converts decimal to hex",
                   "hex value") {}
  const char * execute() {
    get_decimal();
    // change format with manipulators:
    cout << "0x" << hex << decimal << dec;
    finish();
    return "";  // execution finished OK
  }
};
display_hex disp_hex;
```

```
class display_octal : public display_number {
public:
  display_octal() :
    display_number('o', "display octal",
                   "converts decimal to octal",
                   "octal value") {}
  const char * execute() {
    get_decimal();
    // change format with manipulators:
    cout << "0" << oct << decimal << dec;
    finish();
    return "";  // execution finished OK
  }
};
display_octal disp_octal;

// the array holding the submenu menu_item pointers:
menu_item * submenu_array[] = {
  &disp_binary,
  &disp_octal,
  &disp_hex
};

// create an object to perform the submenu function:
submenu number_conversion('n',
  "convert from decimal to other number formats",
  ">>> Number Conversion <<<",
  submenu_array, sizeof(submenu_array));

// The array holding all the menu_item pointers:
menu_item * tstmenu1[] = {
  &disp_time,
  &number_conversion,
  &path,
  &library,
  &includes,
  &foo,
  &directory,
  &fulldirect,
  &subtree,
  &changedir,
  &sysdate,
  &emacs,
  &more
};

void main() {
```

```
menu_driver menu(">>>>  A test menu  <<<<",
                tstmenu1, sizeof(tstmenu1));
menu.run();
}
```

The first class, **display_time**, has such a limited and focused functionality that you wouldn't ever make more than one instance of it. Since it's so focused, it doesn't need any arguments, either. Of course, not using any arguments puts some limitations on the flexibility of choosing activation keys for the other menu items. The **display_time** class uses the ANSI C library functions for time, located in **time.h**.

The **class environment** will display a selected environment string using the ANSI C library function **getenv()**. The name of the environment variable is displayed as part of the menu display line. This class also demonstrates the use of the error function—if the environment variable is not found (as will probably be the case with **foo**), an error message is returned. You can test it by selecting **FOO** from the menu.

The **class system_command** uses the ANSI C library function **system()** to send a command to the operating system. The name of the command is stored in a **protected** data area (so it can be accessed by derived classes) and used on the menu display line. When you select the **system_command** object from the menu, the screen is cleared and the command is run. If **system()** returns a nonzero value, there was a problem executing the command so an error message is returned; otherwise the output is held on the screen until the user presses a key. Four instances of **system_command** are defined: three with the **ls** listing program available on all UNIX machines and on MS-DOS as an add-on or from the public domain, and one with the DATE command. You may have to change the commands used here to suit those available on your local system.

The **class syscom_1arg** is derived from **system_command**. A **syscom_1arg** object executes a system command that takes a single command-line argument. The constructor takes an extra argument, which is a string to prompt the user for the extra command-line argument. The **execute()** function prompts the user for the argument and builds the command from the program name and the user-supplied argument by using a string stream to print the formatted string into a buffer called **cbuf**. Then **cbuf** is handed to **system()** to execute the command. Three instances of this class are created, one each to run **emacs** (an editor), **cd** (change directory), and **more** (view a document a page at a time). All three of these programs are available in one form or another on both UNIX and MS-DOS.

The next class, **submenu**, is particularly interesting because it is a **menu_item** that has as a member object an instance of **menu_driver**, which means it is a menu item that selects another menu! As you can see, **execute()** simply runs the menu. To demonstrate the **submenu** function, three subclasses of **menu_item** are created to perform data conversion from decimal to binary, hexadecimal, and octal. (As an exercise, create subclasses to convert numbers in the other direction and add them to the submenu.)

First, **class display_number** is derived from **menu_item** so the common activities of the classes won't have to be repeated. All the number conversion classes are derived from **display_number** and use the **get_decimal()** and **finish()** functions from **display_number**. The number conversion classes are **display_binary**, **display_hex**, and **display_octal**, and the instances of those classes are **disp_binary**, **disp_hex**, and **disp_octal**. An array of **menu_item** pointers called **submenu_array[]** is created from the addresses of those instances, and an instance of **submenu** called **number_conversion** is initialized with this array. The **number_conversion** is now a **menu_entry**, which is a gateway to another menu.

Finally, the array of **menu_item** pointers called **tstmenu1[]** is created from the addresses of all the instances of **menu_item** that have been previously defined (including, you will notice, **number_conversion**). In **main()**, an instance of **menu_driver** called **menu** is initialized with this array, and the **run()** function is called for the menu. As you can see, all the work is in setting up the menu—running it is a snap!

You will notice, as you derive your own subclasses of **menu_item** and add instances of them to the menu system, that it is very difficult to break the system by adding new subclasses. Any problems you have will be isolated to the new code you write, not the way your code interacts with the rest of the system—the interaction is fixed by the inheritance hierarchy.

Initialization of Static Variables

The "wart" that was mentioned in MENUDRIV.CPP occurs because the line that was commented out,

```
// items_per_page = (screen.maxrow() - 4) / linespacing;
```

depends on the object **screen** being initialized before the calculation is performed. The **screen** is a global object, and its lifetime lasts throughout the whole program. The ANSI C specification describes variables like these as having *static storage duration* (note that **static** variables that are local to a function or class also have static storage duration). C++ programmers often refer to these variables as "static variables" (yet another confusion to the use of the word **static**). What they mean is "static storage duration."

The only guarantees about initialization of static variables is that variables occurring earlier in a file will be initialized first, and all static variables will be initialized before **main()** is entered. There are no rules about the order of initialization across different files. In MENUTEST.CPP, as long as all the **menu_driver** objects were created inside **main()**, the **screen** object was certain to be initialized, so any calculation in the constructor that depended on **screen** works fine. However, to add a **submenu** object to the main menu, the **submenu** object must be created as a global object so its address can be taken and added to **tstmenu1**. This means the constructor for **menu_driver**, which is used to create a member object in **submenu**, must be called for a static object. When this was attempted, the above commented-out calculation did not work because the **screen_controller** constructor had not yet been called for the **screen** object, so **screen** was not initialized and the calculation produced the wrong answer.

The solution used in MENUDRIV.CPP robs the system of its flexibility. You can no longer call **screen.setrows()** and **screen.setcols()** at the beginning of **main()** and change the size of the screen. There is no solution in sight in terms of changes to the language. The only way to recapture the flexibility of this system is to rewrite **menu_driver** to dynamically build its own array of **menu_items** at run time (using **DynArray** from Chapter 6, or something like it). This would allow all **menu_driver** objects to be created inside **main()** or the scopes of other functions, so it would be guaranteed that **screen** was properly initialized whenever the **menu_driver** constructor was called. A **menu_driver** that can be created at run time also has a greater flexibility than the one shown in this system, since you could also construct new menus "on the fly," based on user input or other dynamic considerations.

The inability to control the order of initialization of static objects is *not* currently addressed in draft-ANSI C++, so you'd better learn to live with it.

Improvements You Might Want to Add to the Menu System

Simple improvements include adding page numbers or other messages that change depending on what page you are on at the top of the menu. You might want to allow a string representation of a key with no printable representation (such as ESC or the function keys on the PC). You might also want to add a way to force a page break in menu pages, so you can group menu items logically on separate pages.

Abstract Classes

In the previous example, **class menu_item** is an abstract class (because **execute()** is pure virtual, it is a pure abstract class). An abstract class is one with no instances, and is not designed to be used to create objects. An abstract class is only designed to be inherited. It specifies an interface at a certain level of inheritance, and provides a form upon which other classes can be created. In the previous example, all the derived menu items are treated by **class menu_driver** as members of the abstract base **class menu_item**. The abstract class is the most important class in the example, because it is the pathway to extending the system. To create a new type of menu item that can be used by the existing system, you must derive it from the abstract **class menu_item**.

Abstract classes have other benefits. Because an abstract class provides a framework upon which you can build other classes, you don't have to use the C programmer's trick of creating skeleton code and then copying and modifying the skeleton to create new functionality. One problem with the skeleton code is if you want to change the skeleton, the changes must be propagated by hand throughout the system—an error-prone process at best. In addition, you don't know if you have bugs in the original skeleton or in the modified versions. By using an abstract class, you can change the interface and immediately propagate the changes throughout the system with no errors. All changes made by the programmer who derived the new class are shown explicitly in the code for the derived class, and any bugs that show up are almost always isolated in the new code.

An Abstract Class to Aid Debugging

Suppose you want to build a project consisting of a large number of classes, possibly using a large number of programmers. If you want to make sure every class in your project has a common debugging interface, a good approach is to create an abstract class from which all the other classes in your project will be inherited. Since anyone who creates a new class for your project must inherit from your base class, they are not free to create a different interface, so you are guaranteed that all objects in the project will respond to the same debugging commands. Here's an example of an abstract base class for debugging:

```
//: DEBUG1.H—Pure abstract class for debugging
#ifndef DEBUG1_H_
#define DEBUG1_H_

class debuggable {
public:
  virtual void dump() = 0;  // dump contents of an object
};

#endif // DEBUG1_H_
```

If someone derives a new class from **debuggable** and doesn't redefine **dump()**, the compiler will issue an error message when they try to create an object of that new class (which still contains a pure virtual function).

Here are some examples of classes derived from **debuggable**:

```
//: DBGTEST.CPP—Testing class debuggable
#include "debug1.h"
#include <iostream.h>

class X : public debuggable {
  int i, j, k;
public:
  X(int ii = 0, int jj = 0, int kk = 0) {
```

```
    i = ii; j = jj; k = kk;
  }
  // Other member functions ...
  void dump() {
    cout << "i = " << i
         << ", j = " << j
         << ", k = " << k << endl;
  }
};

class Y : public debuggable {
  float f, g, h;
public:
  Y(float ff = 0.0, float gg = 0.0, float hh = 0.0) {
    f = ff; g = gg; h = hh;
  }
  // Other member functions ...
  void dump() {
    cout << "f = " << f
         << ", g = " << g
         << ", h = " << h << endl;
  }
};

void main() {
  X x(1,2,3);
  Y y(4.1, 5.2, 6.3);
  x.dump();
  y.dump();

  // you can also treat x & y as members of debuggable:
  debuggable * dba[2];
  dba[0] = &x;
  dba[1] = &y;
  dba[0]->dump();
  dba[1]->dump();
}
```

Any objects in your system can be dumped, and you can add the object addresses to a list of **debuggable** pointers and call **dump()** for members of the list.

The abstract class becomes very powerful when you have it integrated into your system and you want to change the interface. Imagine how difficult this would be with a conventional language—first, you would have to make sure the debugging interface was properly implemented in all parts of your system. If you ever wanted to change the interface, you would have to check each separate part to make sure the new interface was properly added. A headache like this would probably keep you from doing it in the first place. With abstract classes in C++, you simply change the abstract class and recompile the system. The new interface automatically propagates through the system; when the virtual function(s) added in the new interface are redefined in the derived classes, the compiler ensures strict conformance to the interface.

For example, suppose you wanted to add a function called **trace()** to **class debuggable**:

```
//: DEBUG2.H—Changing the interface of an abstract class
#ifndef DEBUG2_H_
#define DEBUG2_H_

class debuggable {
public:
  virtual void dump() = 0;  // dump contents of an object
  virtual void trace() = 0;
};

#endif // DEBUG2_H_
```

When this is used in DBGTEST.CPP, the virtual function **trace()** must be redefined in **class X** and **class Y**. The compiler will tell you if you forget to make a definition somewhere. (If you want **trace()** to be optional, you can give it an empty function body in the base class.) This means you can design the debugging framework into your classes, and even change the framework midway through your project without any problems.

An Abstract Class for Garbage Collection

Suppose you want to create a more general version of the garbage-collection system suggested in Chapter 6. That example showed only one type of garbage object. In practice, you might want to collect the garbage generated by many different classes. This is another situation where an abstract class is appropriate.

The following header file contains the redesigned abstract class for classes that create objects to be collected by a garbage collector. There are only three member functions in the abstract class: the constructor, which adds the pointer to the object to a list used by the garbage collector, a virtual function to determine whether the object is "dead" (ready to be collected), and a virtual destructor:

```
//: GARBAGE2.H—Abstract class for objects designed to be
//. destroyed by a garbage collector
#ifndef GARBAGE2_H_
#define GARBAGE2_H_

class garbage {
public:
  // This will always be called when the class
  // is inherited, even if the programmer forgets to make
  // the explicit call to the base-class constructor:
  garbage();
  // It is very important that the destructor be virtual,
  // so the derived class is destroyed properly by the
  // garbage collector:
  virtual ~garbage() {}
  // You must redefine this in your derived class so it
  // determines (by some algorithm) whether your object is
  // alive or dead:
  virtual int dead() { return 1; }
};

#endif // GARBAGE2_H_
```

Because the destructor is virtual, the actual destructor for the derived class will be called by the garbage collector. This is very important because the abstract class knows nothing about the intricacies of destroying the derived-class object. Virtual destructors make things work properly.

The trickiest function in any garbage-collection scheme is the one that tells the garbage collector whether this object can be safely destroyed. It is the subject of much debate and many papers and algorithms, and will not be discussed here. If you can figure out whether your object is not being used, then the function **dead()** should return a nonzero value. If the object is still in use, **dead()** should return 0 (false).

Here are the methods for the abstract **garbage** class, and an example you can use by defining the preprocessor macro **EXAMPLE**:

```cpp
//: GARBAGE2.CPP—Methods for improved garbage collection
#include "garbage2.h"
#include <iostream.h>
#include <stdlib.h>
#include <new.h>  // set_new_handler() prototype
#include "..\chap_6\dynarray.h"
// The follwing #define creates an example:
#define EXAMPLE

// The following #define should be set to 0 after testing:
#if 1
#include "..\chap_7\screen3.h"
#define DISPLAY(arg) arg;
#else
#define DISPLAY(arg)
#endif

static DynArray memtable;  // place for free store pointers

// the constructor simply adds the object address to the array:
garbage::garbage() {
  memtable.add(this);  // save the pointer
}

void garbage_collector() {
  DISPLAY(screen.move(screen.maxrow(), 1));
  DISPLAY(screen.clear_eol());
  DISPLAY(screen.reverse());
  DISPLAY(cout << "Garbage collecting...");
  DISPLAY(screen.normal());
  memtable.reset();
  do
    if(((garbage *)memtable.current())->dead()) {
      DISPLAY(screen.move(screen.maxrow() -1, 1));
      DISPLAY(cout << "removing " << memtable.current());
      delete (garbage *)memtable.current();
      memtable.remove(memtable.index());
    }
  while( memtable.next() );
  DISPLAY(screen.move(screen.maxrow(), 22));
  DISPLAY(screen.reverse());
  DISPLAY(cout << "...done");
  DISPLAY(screen.normal());
}
```

```
// set_new_handler() is the function that sets the
// "new-handler" to the function of your choice.
// Here's a class whose only job is to initialize the
// "new-handler" to the garbage_collector()
class init_garbage_collector {
public:
  init_garbage_collector() {
    set_new_handler(garbage_collector);
  }
};

#ifdef EXAMPLE

#define chunk 512

class garbage_obj : public garbage {
  int memory[chunk];
public:
  // redefinition of the dead() virtual function:
  int dead() { return 1; }
};

void main() {
  // couldn't make this global, because of
  // order-of-initialization (conflicts with ioserror):
  init_garbage_collector handler_initializer;
  // This continues until you interrupt the program.
  // Control-C often does the trick.
  screen.clear_screen();
  while(1)
    new garbage_obj;  // this loop will exhaust free store!
}

#endif // EXAMPLE
```

If you don't want to see the activities of the garbage collector, you should comment out the line

```
#define DISPLAY
```

The **memtable** is an instance of **class DynArray** (from Chapter 6) used by **class garbage** to store pointers to **garbage** objects when they are created. The garbage collector hunts through **memtable** to find objects that can safely be destroyed. The garbage collector asks each object in the table if it is **dead()**; if it is, the object is destroyed by calling its (virtual) destructor via **delete**. Notice you can only create **garbage** objects on the free store.

The C++ function **set_new_handler()** must be called before the program starts to install the garbage collector. This way, the garbage collector will be called when the free store is exhausted. So the user doesn't have to worry about this task, a special class is created called **init_garbage_collector**. This class has a single instance called **handler_initializer**. The sole task of **handler_initializer** is to call **set_new_handler()** and install the garbage collector. This technique of creating a special class and a single instance is very useful for pre- and post-**main()** initialization and cleanup. Whenever you do something like this with global objects, however, you run the risk of getting snagged by the order of initialization of static objects.

To test the garbage collector and to show you how to use it, a simple class called **garbage_obj** is created. Its sole purpose is to take up space and exhaust the free store so the garbage collector will be called. The **main()** function consists of an infinite loop that calls **new** to create new **garbage_obj**s.

Simulation Using Abstract Classes

As a final example for this chapter, consider the simulation problem introduced in Chapter 6 as the Life program. The Life simulation was somewhat limited in flexibility because inheritance and virtual functions had not been introduced at that point in the book. Now that you know about these very important features of C++, you can see a more flexible implementation of a simulation problem.

The abstract class that will be the fundamental unit in this example is called **simulation_unit**. A **simulation_unit** knows where it is on a grid and how to **display()** and **erase()** itself from the screen. A **simulation_unit** can also move itself about on the grid (unlike **LifeUnit**s, which were stationary), and it has a member function called **cycle()**, which causes it to move through a step of its existence. Here is the header file for **class simulation_unit**. Notice that most of the functions are virtual:

```
//: SIMULATE.H—A pure abstract base class for simulation
#ifndef SIMULATE_H_
#define SIMULATE_H_
const xsize = 25;
const ysize = 80;

class simulation_unit {
protected:
  int x,y; // location on grid
public:
  virtual void display() = 0;
  virtual void erase() = 0;
  simulation_unit(int x_loc, int y_loc) : x(x_loc), y(y_loc) {
    // display();
    // OOPS!  The above would be a classic mistake. In
    // constructors and destructors, the virtual mechanism
    // doesn't work. This call would resolve to the local
    // version of display(), which is a pure virtual (and
    // thus would halt the machine). display() must be called
    // in all the derived-class constructors!
  }
  virtual ~simulation_unit() { erase(); }
  virtual void cycle() = 0; // execute one cycle of activity
  void move(int x_steps, int y_steps); // to a new location
};

extern simulation_unit * s_grid[xsize][ysize];

#endif // SIMULATE_H_
```

If **simulation_unit** were derived into a class to simulate the Life game, for example, **cycle()** would be redefined to look at the nearest neighbors and decide whether it will live to the next generation. The simulation presented here, however, is quite different than Life because it exists on a passive grid (called **s_grid**, for simulation grid), and the **simulation_unit**s initiate all activities, while Life was created with an active grid—the grid controlled the creation and destruction of **LifeUnit**s. This was not necessarily the best solution, but it solved the problem of figuring out who was to decide when to create and destroy **LifeUnit**s.

If you were to create Life using the simulation in this section, the classes derived from **simulation_unit** would have to work it out among themselves how objects are to be created and destroyed. This might seem more realistic for many types of problems, but it is a more difficult problem to solve, since it requires that each object be, essentially, an independent task. In this example, the problem of objects negotiating with each other to determine the outcome of a particular transaction will be completely skirted. With classes derived from **simulation_unit**, objects can perform imperious actions (they can even destroy one another!) but there is no facility for negotiated behavior. As in real life, it seems much easier to act first and ask questions later (albeit far less civilized).

In **simulate.h**, you can see definitions for the size of the display. Because **s_grid** is an array, it must be declared with constant indices. This can be eliminated with more programming if it becomes a problem, but it would not have added to the understanding of the current example.

An additional class is included in the file to initialize the **s_grid**. The **class init_grid** has a single global instance called **grid_initializer**. The entire effect of **grid_initializer** takes place in the constructor, where all the elements of **s_grid** are set to 0. The **s_grid** could have been encapsulated in a class of its own, but since all the grid elements are **public** anyway and it would have required an extra level of indirection, nothing would be gained by doing so.

Here is the file containing the definition of **s_grid**, **init_grid**, and the **move()** method for **simulation_unit**:

```cpp
//: SIMULATE.CPP—Simulation_unit methods
#include "simulate.h"
#include <iostream.h>

// For simplicity, a global array is used:
simulation_unit * s_grid[xsize][ysize];

// A class whose sole task is to initialize grid[][]
// before main is entered:
class init_grid {
public:
 init_grid();
};
init_grid grid_initializer;  // single global instance

// constructor does the initialization:
init_grid::init_grid() {
    for(int i = 0; i < xsize; i++) {
      for(int j = 0; j < ysize; j++)
        s_grid[i][j] = 0;
    }
}
```

```
void simulation_unit::move(int x_steps, int y_steps) {
  int x_new = x + x_steps;
  int y_new = y + y_steps;
  if (x_new < 0 || x_new >= xsize)
    cerr << "move: x coordinate out of bounds";
  if (y_new < 0 || y_new >= ysize)
    cerr << "move: y coordinate out of bounds";
  if(s_grid[x_new][y_new] == 0) { // place is currently empty
    s_grid[x][y] = 0; // leave old place
    erase();  // erase old place on screen
    s_grid[x = x_new][y = y_new] = this; // land in new place
    display(); // display new place on screen
  }
}
```

The responsibility for making sure that the arguments to **move()** do not attempt to go out of bounds is left to the caller—**move()** will say you're trying to go out of bounds, but it won't do anything about it. The **move()** function, however, will only place the object at the destination if there isn't an object currently at the destination. If the current object is a chess piece, for example, and it is taking another piece from the board, it is responsible for destroying that piece and clearing the position before moving. When a **move()** is successful, it is quite simple: the old position is cleared (set to 0), the old place on the screen is erased, the new grid position is set to **this**, the internal object coordinates are set to the new position, and the object's symbol is displayed at the new position on the screen.

To test the simulation system, two classes are derived from **simulation_unit** in the following file. The first class, **pop_around**, simply jumps around the screen in random leaps. The **virtual cycle()** function calculates a landing point within the bounds of the screen and tries to jump there using **move()**. Of course, **move()** only moves the object to the destination if no one is already there.

The second class, **crawl_around**, can only move one step at a time diagonally to its present position. It's interesting to see the patterns in the random-number generator when you only have **crawl_around** objects.

Both **pop_around** and **crawl_around** use the ANSI C library function **rand()** pseudorandom number generator to calculate their next position. The pseudorandom number generator is seeded by calling **srand()** with some integral argument. As with the Life example in Chapter 6, this seed is obtained from a number generated by the ANSI C library **time()** function (it is based on the current time). The seeding is accomplished before **main()** is entered by creating a class called **init_random** with a single global instance called **random_number_initializer**. The seeding takes place in the constructor for **init_random**.

Here is the file to test the system containing the class definitions for **pop_around**, **crawl_around**, **init_random**, and the **main()** file:

```
//: SIMTEST.CPP—Simple test of simulation class. First,
//. classes must be derived from the abstract simulation_unit
#include "simulate.h"
#include "..\chap_7\screen3.h"
#include "..\chap_7\ioserror.h"
#include <iostream.h>
#include <stdlib.h>  // srand() and rand()
#include <time.h>  // to seed the random-number generator
#define DOPOPS    // Comment out to remove pops
#define DOCRAWLS  // Comment out to remove crawls

// This class generates objects that jump around on the
// screen:
class pop_around : public simulation_unit {
public:
  void display() {
    screen.move(x,y);
    cout << "@";
  }
  void erase() {
    screen.move(x,y);
    cout << " ";
  }
  pop_around(int xi, int yi) : simulation_unit(xi, yi) {
    display();
  }
  enum direction { pos = 0, neg = 1 };
  void cycle() {
    // Generate two random numbers, one to control x-motion
    // and one to control y-motion. The possible motion in
    // any direction is factored in.
    // First, choose a direction to move—0 means positive,
    // 1 means negative. Note that a zero value for x or y
    // must move in a positive direction and a size-1 value
    // for x or y must move in a negative direction (otherwise
    // divide-by-zero happens in a later calculation).
```

```
      direction x_direction, y_direction;
      if ( x <= 0 )
        x_direction = pos;   // must move positively
      else if ( x >= xsize - 1 )
        x_direction = neg;   // must move negatively
      else
        x_direction = (direction)(rand() % 2);
      if ( y <= 0 )
        y_direction = pos;   // must move positively
      else if ( y >= ysize - 1 )
        y_direction = neg;   // must move negatively
      else
        y_direction = (direction)(rand() % 2);
      // Now generate a random amount to move in that direction.
      // The amount of space left in that direction is used
      // in the calculation. Note the use of the ternary
      // if-else operator.
      int x_jump = x_direction ?
        ( -rand() % x) /* neg calculation */
        : (rand() % (xsize - x -1)); /* pos calculation */
      int y_jump = y_direction ?
        ( -rand() % y) /* neg calculation */
        : (rand() % (ysize - y - 1)); /* pos calculation */
      move(x_jump, y_jump); // won't move anyplace if
      // there's already something at the destination.
    }
};

// Objects of this class move one step at a time:
class crawl_around : public simulation_unit {
public:
  void display() {
    screen.move(x,y);
    cout <<"*";
  }
  void erase() {
    screen.move(x,y);
    cout <<" ";
  }
  crawl_around(int xi, int yi) : simulation_unit(xi, yi) {
    display();
  }
  void cycle() {
    // random number decides which direction the step is in
    int x_step = (rand() % 2) ? -1 : 1;
    if ( x + x_step < 0 ) x_step = -x_step;
    if ( x + x_step >= xsize ) x_step = -x_step;
```

```
      int y_step = (rand() % 2) ? -1 : 1;
      if ( y + y_step < 0 ) y_step = -y_step;
      if ( y + y_step >= ysize ) y_step = -y_step;
      move(x_step, y_step);
   }
};

// This class is just to initialize the random-number generator
// before main() is entered:
class init_random {
public:
   init_random() {
      // Seed the random-number generator using the current time:
      time_t tnow;
      time(&tnow);
      srand(tnow);
   }
} random_number_initializer; // single global instance

static ioserror error("simtest");

// initialize grid with pop_around and crawl_around objects,
// and make it run.
void main(int argc, char * argv[]) {
   if(argc < 3)
      error << "usage:\n\t"
         "simtest pop_factor crawl_factor\n"
         "Where pop_factor determines the density of pop_around\n"
         "objects, and crawl_factor determines the density of\n"
         "crawl_around objects on the display." << terminate;
   screen.clear_screen();
   // Convert the command-line arguments into factors that will
   // turn the random number into a zero or 1, to decide whether
   // to place an object at that point in the grid:
   int pop_factor = RAND_MAX / atoi(argv[1]);
   int crawl_factor = RAND_MAX / atoi(argv[2]);
   // randomly lay down objects in the grid:
   for(int x = 0; x < xsize; x++) {
      for(int y = 0; y < ysize; y++) {
#ifdef DOPOPS
         if( !(rand() / pop_factor) ) // integer divide
            if(!s_grid[x][y])  // make sure place is empty
               s_grid[x][y] = new pop_around(x,y);
#endif
#ifdef DOCRAWLS
         if( !(rand() / crawl_factor) )
            if(!s_grid[x][y])  // make sure place is empty
```

```
            s_grid[x][y] = new crawl_around(x,y);
#endif
    }
  }
  // to run the simulation, random x,y locations are chosen and
  // if there's a simulation_unit there, its virtual cycle()
  // is called. The values xrand and yrand take the value
  // returned by rand() and turn it into a number
  // between 0 and xsize for x, or 0 and ysize for y.
  int xrand = RAND_MAX / (xsize - 1);
  int yrand = RAND_MAX / (ysize - 1);
  while(1) {
    int x_location = rand() / xrand;
    int y_location = rand() / yrand;
    if(s_grid[x_location][y_location])
      s_grid[x_location][y_location]->cycle();
  }
}
```

In **main()**, **pop_factor** and **crawl_factor** are created from the value of **RAND_MAX** (the largest number the random-number generator will create; contained in **stdlib.h**) and the command-line arguments. The **pop_factor** and **crawl_factor** control the number of **pop_around** and **crawl_around** objects that are placed on the grid; the command-line arguments give the user control over the numbers.

In this implementation of the simulation, the location to be "cycled" is chosen randomly; you can perform your cycling in many other different fashions if you want.

Suggestions for Further Developments

You might want to add a piece of **private** data to the derived classes **pop_around** and **crawl_around** so they can hold unique symbols that will be printed on the screen by **display()**. This way you can visually track the motion of the objects. Keep in mind there's nothing here that says an object must only be one character position. You can use up any number of positions, but you might want to make sure objects can't overlap each other on the screen. There's also nothing that says you are limited to text for your **display()** function. If you have access to a graphics package, you can easily use that.

You might also want to try creating an arcade-type simulation where the objects run around eating each other, shooting each other, or some other hostile activity. Without the ability to negotiate, that's about the level at which you find yourself.

Construction and Destruction

Constructors and destructors, since they perform the special acts of birth and death for an object, are very different from ordinary member functions, as you've seen before. This is also true where virtual functions are concerned. Inside a constructor or destructor, the virtual mechanism doesn't work—there is no late binding inside constructors or destructors. This has a number of implications that can cause you problems if you don't understand them.

Suppose you create a constructor and destructor for the **shape** example. Inside the constructor you think, "Well, one thing I'd like to do when I'm creating this object is to draw it." So naturally you call the **draw()** member function inside the constructor. Inside the destructor, you decide erasing is a proper activity. So you very sensibly write the following program:

```
//: SHAPES3.CPP—Virtual functions in constructors/destructors
#include <iostream.h>

struct shape {
  virtual void draw() {}
  virtual void erase() {}
  shape() { draw(); }
  virtual ~shape() { erase(); }
};

struct circle : shape {
  void draw() { cout << "circle::draw" << endl; }
  void erase() { cout << "circle::erase" << endl; }
};

struct square : shape {
  void draw() { cout << "square::draw" << endl; }
  void erase() { cout << "square::erase" << endl; }
};
```

```
struct triangle : shape {
  void draw() { cout << "triangle::draw" << endl; }
  void erase() { cout << "triangle::erase" << endl; }
};

void main() {
  circle C;
  square S;
  triangle T;
}
```

But when you compile and run it, nothing happens. That's because inside the constructor and destructor, only the "local" versions of the functions are called. Late binding doesn't take place.

To understand why, remember how constructors and destructors work. When an object is being created, the base-class constructor is called first, then the next-derived constructor, and so on until you get to the most-derived constructor. Briefly, the object is constructed from the "bottom up." Inside the base constructor, if a virtual call *were* made, it would bind to a function defined in a more-derived class. This function would assume it could manipulate all the elements in that more-derived class. But you're still in the base-class constructor, and those elements haven't been initialized by the more-derived constructor yet! This would be a very unsafe thing to do. Therefore the only versions of virtual functions that can be called in a constructor are the "local" versions, because those only manipulate elements in the current class, which are safe.

You can look at it another way. When you're in a constructor, the **VPTR** is assigned to the local **VTABLE**, because while you're in the constructor that's what type the object *is*. The constructor cannot know this object will eventually become a **circle** rather than a **triangle**. That only occurs when this constructor finishes, and the next-derived constructor is called as part of the sequence. Then that constructor wakes up with and sets *its* **VPTR** to *its* local **VTABLE** and proceeds. (It is more likely the compiler will simply make a direct call in the constructor rather than going through the **VPTR**).

The same logic works for the destructor. Since the object is destroyed from the "top down" (from the most-derived destructor to the base-class destructor), by the time you get to the base class most of the object has been destroyed. If you were able to make a virtual call from the base-class destructor, the call would bind to a more-derived function, which would assume it could manipulate elements that had already been destroyed.

Most compilers don't give you any warnings about this, since it's certainly not illegal or illogical to want to call local versions of a function inside a constructor or destructor. It's just that you need to be aware of it and not expect virtual behavior where it won't happen, or else you'll end up with a confusing bug.

A Halting Problem

Because the virtual mechanism doesn't happen inside constructors and destructors, you can get an interesting problem, shown here:

```
//: HALTING.CPP—a halting problem with pure virtuals

class halt {
public:
  virtual void go() = 0;
  halt() { go(); }
};

class halt_and_catch_fire : public halt {
public:
  void go() {} // pure virtual defined
};

void main() {
  halt_and_catch_fire hcf;
}
```

The identifier is a reference to a mysterious, undocumented assembly-language command on an early mainframe called **hcf** (halt and catch fire). Programming legend has it the command caused the machine to stop processing and conflagrate. This program will compile and link but causes a run-time error. When the base-class constructor is called as part of the normal sequence of construction, it calls the local version of **go()**, which is pure virtual and doesn't have a function body. Although it's fairly clear here, the problem can develop more subtle forms, if you call an ordinary member function in the constructor, and *that* calls a pure virtual function. It's one to watch for.

Pure Virtual Destructors

Although you can have virtual destructors, you cannot have pure virtual destructors. Most compilers accept them, however, so you can write the following:

```
//: PVDEST.CPP—You can't have pure virtual destructors
#include <iostream.h>

struct base {
  virtual ~base() = 0;  // compiler accepts, but not linker
};

struct derived : base {
  ~derived() { cout << "~derived" << endl; }
};

void main() {
  delete new derived;
}
```

The compiler will accept the code and make its normal sequence of destructor calls, including a call to the base-class constructor. The linker, however, will be unable to resolve that call.

Makefile for Examples in Chapter 8

Here is the makefile for all the examples in this chapter.

```
# makefile for examples in Chapter 8
# Borland C++ compiler, with the following
# warnings turned off:
# aus: identifier assigned a value which is never used
# eff: code has no effect
# par: parameter "parameter" is never used
# inl: "not expanded inline" warnings
CPP = bcc -w-aus -w-eff -w-par -w-inl
# nmake CPP=cl  # Microsoft C++ command line

.cpp.exe:
        $(CPP) $<
```

```
.cpp.obj:
        $(CPP) -c $<

all :   slice.exe trantst1.exe trantst2.exe descrip.exe \
        vptrsize.exe descrfix.exe shapes.exe shapes2.exe \
        menutest.exe dbgtest.exe garbage2.exe simtest.exe \
        shapes3.exe halting.exe pvdest.exe

trantst1.exe : trantst1.obj transprt.obj
        $(CPP) $**

trantst2.exe : trantst2.obj transprt.obj
        $(CPP) $**

menutest.exe : menutest.obj menudriv.obj menuitem.obj \
                screen3.obj screen2.obj screen1.obj \
                ioserror.obj
        echo $** > menutest.rsp
        $(CPP) @menutest.rsp

garbage2.exe : garbage2.obj dynarray.obj \
                screen3.obj screen2.obj screen1.obj \
                ioserror.obj
        $(CPP) $**

simtest.exe : simtest.obj simulate.obj screen3.obj \
                screen2.obj screen1.obj ioserror.obj
        $(CPP) $**

transprt.obj : transprt.h transprt.cpp
trantst1.obj : transprt.h trantst1.cpp
trantst2.obj : transprt.h trantst2.cpp
descrip.obj : descrip2.h descrip1.h descrip.cpp
menuitem.obj : getkey.h menuitem.h ..\chap_7\screen3.h \
                ..\chap_7\screen2.h ..\chap_7\screen1.h \
                ..\chap_7\ioserror.h ..\chap_7\timer2.h \
                ..\chap_7\error.h menuitem.cpp
menudriv.obj : ..\chap_7\screen3.h ..\chap_7\screen2.h \
                ..\chap_7\screen1.h ..\chap_7\ioserror.h \
                ..\chap_7\timer2.h menudriv.h menuitem.h \
                getkey.h menudriv.cpp
menutest.obj : getkey.h menudriv.h menuitem.h \
                ..\chap_7\screen3.h ..\chap_7\screen2.h \
                ..\chap_7\screen1.h ..\chap_7\ioserror.h \
                ..\chap_7\timer2.h menutest.cpp
dbgtest.obj : debug1.h dbgtest.cpp
garbage2.obj : garbage2.h ..\chap_6\dynarray.h \
```

```
                       ..\chap_7\error.h ..\chap_7\screen3.h \
                       ..\chap_7\screen2.h ..\chap_7\screen1.h \
                       ..\chap_7\ioserror.h ..\chap_7\timer2.h \
                       garbage2.cpp
simulate.obj : simulate.h simulate.cpp
simtest.obj : simulate.h ..\chap_7\screen3.h \
               ..\chap_7\screen2.h ..\chap_7\screen1.h \
               ..\chap_7\ioserror.h ..\chap_7\timer2.h \
               ..\chap_7\error.h simtest.cpp
screen1.obj: ..\chap_7\screen1.cpp ..\chap_7\screen1.h
             $(CPP) -c ..\chap_7\screen1.cpp
screen2.obj: ..\chap_7\screen2.cpp ..\chap_7\screen2.h \
             ..\chap_7\screen1.h
             $(CPP) -c ..\chap_7\screen2.cpp
screen3.obj: ..\chap_7\screen3.cpp ..\chap_7\screen3.h \
             ..\chap_7\screen2.h ..\chap_7\screen1.h
             $(CPP) -c ..\chap_7\screen3.cpp
ioserror.obj:   ..\chap_7\ioserror.cpp ..\chap_7\ioserror.h
             $(CPP) -c ..\chap_7\ioserror.cpp
error.obj:    ..\chap_7\error.cpp ..\chap_7\error.h
             $(CPP) -c ..\chap_7\error.cpp
dynarray.obj: ..\chap_6\dynarray.cpp ..\chap_6\dynarray.h
             $(CPP) -c ..\chap_6\dynarray.cpp
```

If you are using a dependency-list generator tool, and you want the dependency list to be generated properly when you are using header files from other directories, you must examine those other header files. If they include any *other* header files, those *other* header files must be described in such a way that the dependency generator can find the *other* files. This usually requires using the double dots in the path to mean "the directory above this one" enough times that you can get to a common directory between where you are and where the other files exist, and then specifying the path from there. In the source-code listing disk for this book, all the code for each chapter is placed in a subdirectory by itself, and all these subdirectories are off of a single main directory. Thus, the header files in Chapter 7 include entries such as:

```
#include "..\chap_7\screen1.H"
```

so they can be included in files in other directories, and everything will work fine.

CHAPTER

Arguments and Return Values

The primary activity in object-oriented programming is creating new classes of objects. Program complexity is generally hidden in these objects; writing the **main()** function consists of managing objects.

Creating a new class of objects is effectively an extension to the language. This is different from "extensible languages" in that the new class of objects must be truly integrated into the compiling environment rather than casually added to the language. In C++, new types of objects are made as *first class* as possible. First class means objects of a user-defined type are treated identically to objects of a built-in type. Although classes in C++ are not completely first class, it usually appears that they are: static type checking is performed, objects are initialized and cleaned up, operators may be used with the objects (if operators have been defined for the class), and so on.

This chapter focuses on a more complex issue of creating a first-class user-defined type: passing objects to functions and returning objects from functions. For simple classes, the passing and returning of objects is transparent, but when a class becomes more complex, a number of issues arise that can be quite confusing to the new C++ programmer. This chapter will teach you to build complex classes that can be passed and returned correctly.

Passing by Name, by Value, or by Reference

A *function frame* is the scope where all the function variables are manipulated; it is bounded by the opening and closing braces of the function. The function communicates with the "outside world" in one of two ways: by changing values that are global to the function or through passing and returning. Passing and returning moves values across the boundaries of the function frame.

Information can be moved across the frame boundary in two ways:

1. A copy of the entire variable is made. This is called *pass by value*. Since a copy of the variable is made, the variable may be changed inside the function frame without affecting the variable it was copied from.

2. Only the address of the variable is transferred across the boundary. This is called *pass by name* when a pointer is passed and *pass by reference* when a reference is used; in both cases an address is manipulated. (However, **inline** functions may be treated differently. Some implementations treat references to built-in types as aliases.)

Addresses are passed for two reasons: the first is simply for efficiency. If you know the variable will only be read (and this can be enforced by using the **const** keyword in the argument list), then it is generally faster to pass the address when using objects larger than a pointer. There is an additional benefit to passing an address. The address you pass is for an *initialized* object, and the size of the address is always the same, so there are none of the problems (described in this chapter) involved with copying and initialization. If the programmer can avoid passing or returning objects by value, the problems described here can be ignored.

The second reason for passing an address is to physically manipulate the object that the address points to (that is, change an object that is global to the function). Normally, the results of a function call should be expressed through the function's return value, but there are situations where this is unsatisfactory (for example, the function may need to have an effect on more than one object). If object addresses are passed, the function may directly affect any number of objects on the other side of the function frame boundary.

Pass by Reference

It is said that all argument passing in C is pass by value (since you explicitly declare pointers and pass addresses). C++ adds a new type of argument passing: pass by reference.

Passing by reference is the same as declaring an argument to be a pointer and then passing an address. With references, however, the compiler does all the work for you—it forces the address to be passed into the function (even though the user doesn't explicitly take the address). Inside the function you can manipulate the item as if it were an object. This is a big improvement, since a lot of errors when using C libraries can be attributed to confusion over whether to pass an address.

Since the C++ compiler handles the details for you when you pass by reference, fewer mistakes are made. Thus, pass by reference is the preferred scheme whenever you won't be modifying the argument.

When to Pass by Value

There are cases when you genuinely need a copy of an object to be created inside the frame of a function. You may need to modify the object, and you don't want the original touched. In these cases, you must pass the object by value.

If the compiler passes an **int**, **float**, or other built-in type by value, it knows what to do: a copy of the data is pushed on the stack before the function is called. When passing a type that you've created, however, the compiler has no idea how to handle it—you may require all kinds of complicated initialization.

Since the copy constructor is critical, it is one of the few functions that the compiler will generate for you automatically in certain cases when you don't define it yourself (the others are the default constructor—if no other constructors have been defined—and the **operator=()**). If you have a "simple" class that only contains variables of built-in types and none of the member data are pointers, the automatically generated copy constructor will simply be a *bit copy* (so it duplicates the behavior in C). A bit copy copies all the bytes of the old structure into the new structure. If the class contains member objects with copy constructors, those copy constructors will be called in the generated copy constructor. Both the bit copy of built-in types and the generated calls to all the copy constructors for member objects are called *memberwise initialization*.

When pointers are involved, memberwise initialization performs a *shallow copy*, since they ignore anything but what is in the class structure. With pointer members, a *deep copy* is usually required to allocate free memory and copy the items that are pointed to. To accomplish this, you must define your own copy constructor to take over those activities and prevent the default version from being generated.

Hidden Activities in C

Arguments and return values are transparently controlled by the compiler in C. Since the user can define new types in C++, it is important to understand the way arguments are passed and values are returned.

How C Arguments Are Passed

When a function is called, the caller pushes arguments on the stack and an assembly language CALL is executed. In plain C the last argument in the list is pushed first, and most C++ implementations follow this scheme.

Inside the function call, the stack pointer is moved down to make space for local variables, and the arguments are used right on the stack. After the call is completed, the caller cleans the arguments off the stack. This reduces the risk (in old C) of crashing the system by calling a function with the wrong number of arguments, because the caller always pushes and cleans the same number of arguments. In ANSI C (and C++), function prototyping allows the compiler to generate error messages if the function call is made with an incorrect number or type of arguments.

The C compiler knows the sizes of all built-in types and how to pass them by pushing them on the stack. There are a finite number of built-in types, and they are all known when the compiler is written so dealing with pass by value is a straightforward problem. Structures are simply pushed on the stack piece by piece. Passing by name means a pointer is pushed on the stack.

How Values Are Returned in C

In plain C, values are normally returned in registers. The compiler writer decides which registers will be used to return an **int**, a **short**, a **double**, and so on. It is important that values be returned in registers because C is designed to be *reentrant*: it can be interrupted at any point without destroying data. Well-behaved interrupts always save the register contents, so returning values in registers is safe. If, however, a compiler were created that returned values on the stack, the process would occur as follows: the return value would be pushed on the stack, then the stack pointer would be restored to the point *above* the return value where the return address is located so an assembly language **return** could be performed (the return address woud be popped off the stack into the instruction pointer).

Since the stack space where the return value lived would be *below* the stack pointer in this hypothetical compiler, that stack space might be overwritten by an interrupt routine *after* the return from the function but *before* the caller had a chance to retrieve the result. This would not allow programming with interrupts. Since C and C++ are both intended to be used as systems programming languages, interrupts must be supported, thus values are returned in registers.

The Problem with Structures

You might wonder what happens when the return value is too large to fit into the register set—particularly when the return value is a **struct**, as is the case when we return an instance of a class (physically, a class looks like a structure). The original solution (and the one most old C compilers followed) in plain C was to copy the return value to a global static data area, return from the function, and then copy the global static data area into the destination **struct**. This, of course, is a non-reentrant solution. If an interrupt happens during a return, it is possible the global static data area contents might be overwritten. Since most system-level programmers don't return **struct**s from functions this un-feature of C has gone largely unheralded.

Because of the way **struct**s are returned, the statement

```
A = B = C;
```

is not allowed if **A**, **B**, and **C** are structures (that is, **struct**s are not completely first class). It is allowed for other types in C. Fortunately, many C compilers have fixed this problem.

Some C compilers and all implementations of C++ use a different scheme to return **struct**s (and objects, which are just glorified **struct**s). The address of the destination **struct** is secretly passed into the function (possibly in registers). The function copies the return value directly into the destination before exiting. Not only is this more efficient (it eliminates a copy) it is reentrant.

You should be aware that the "new, improved" solution to structure copying doesn't necessarily happen automatically in all C++ implementations. The only time you are guaranteed to avoid the global **static** data area when returning an object is when a copy constructor and an **operator=()** is defined for the object's class (both are described in this chapter).

Hidden Activities in C++

C++ also performs "hidden" activities when handling arguments and return values. Built-in objects (such as **int**, **float**, **long**, and **char**) are treated just as they are in C. The compiler writer knows about these types and can build passing and returning rules into the compiler. The compiler writer doesn't, however, know anything about the new types *you* define.

Since an object looks like a **struct** when it is just sitting in memory, the easy way out is to handle arguments and return values as if an object *is* a **struct**. When the user doesn't intervene, this is exactly what the C++ compiler does, and if there are member objects, those constructors are called as well. But if the class contains pointers to other items, a simple structure copy will not usually be what you want.

When copying is inappropriate and/or initialization and cleanup must occur when variables are being passed into or out of a function frame, C++ allows the user to implicitly take over the hidden activities that occur by defining a function that is automatically called by the compiler to perform argument passing and value returns. This function is called the *copy constructor*.

Dangers of Returning Addresses

The novice programmer might wish to avoid all this trouble by only passing and returning addresses of objects. Passing the address of objects *into* a function frame is a very good idea and should be practiced whenever possible (preferably using references), but passing the address of a variable that is local to the function frame *out* of the function frame is usually a bad idea (see the function **oname()** in MMTRACE.CPP later in this chapter for an example of when it is acceptable). Once a variable goes out of scope, it is never reliable to use that variable, even if the variable is immediately copied.

This means that any object requiring initialization or cleanup that is passed or returned by value from a function must have a copy constructor.

The Copy Constructor X(X&)

The copy constructor handles three cases: two for copying, and one for initialization. It is a constructor that takes as its argument a reference to an object of the same class as itself.

Let's look at the simplest case first: initialization. The copy constructor is called when you want to declare and initialize an object from another object of the same type. Here's an example:

```
//: CI.CPP—An example of the copy constructor
//. being used for initialization.
#include <iostream.h>

class ci {
  int i;
public:
  ci(int j) { i = j; }
  // copy initializer:
  ci(ci & rv) {
    cout << "copy initializer called" << endl;
    i = rv.i; // copy in the rvalue
  }
};
```

```
void main() {
  ci original(1);
  ci copy1(original); // copy initializer called.
  ci copy2 = original; // here, too
}
```

Notice that we can use the more common type of constructor call (**copy1**) or the more confusing equal sign. The reason it's confusing is that most people get familiar with the **operator=()** being called whenever the compiler encounters an **=** sign used with that class. Here is the single case when **operator=()** is *not* called:

```
classname object = object;
```

The reason it's an exception is that the object on the left is being created; it doesn't have an existing value as it does with

```
object - object;
```

You cannot call the member function **operator=()** for an object that hasn't been constructed yet! Thus a constructor is necessary.

If no objects of the class will be passed or returned or created from other objects in the class, it is not necessary to define a copy constructor. In the preceding example, if the declaration and initialization proceeds as follows,

```
classname object1;
classname object2;
object1 = object2;
```

the copy constructor is not called (**operator=()** is called instead, if it has been defined; more about that later).

Copying into and out of Functions

The second and more complicated use of the copy constructor is passing by value and returning a value from a function. If a copy constructor is available, it is automatically called by the compiler whenever an object is passed or returned by value.

The copy constructor must perform all the initialization necessary when creating one object from another. When passing objects into a function frame, the object on the inside (the local, or *automatic*, variable) must be initialized from the object on the outside. When returning objects out from a function frame, the object on the outside must be initialized from the object on the inside. Initialization often means simply copying, but it can mean much more, as the example later in this chapter will show.

As an example of a class that requires a copy constructor, consider an integer vector, shown here:

```
//: VEC.CPP—Integer vector illustrates the copy constructor
#include <iostream.h>
#include <stdlib.h>

class vec {  // an integer vector
  int size;
  int * vp;
public:
  vec(int i = 0, int j = 0);
  vec(vec & rv);
  ~vec() { delete vp; }
  vec operator=(vec & rv);
  void print(char * msg = "");
  int & operator[](int x);
  int length() { return size; }
};

vec::vec(int i, int j) {
  vp = new int[size = i];
  for (int x = 0; x < size; x++)
    vp[x] = j;
}

vec::vec(vec & rv) {
  vp = new int[size = rv.size];
  for (int x = 0; x < size; x++)
    vp[x] = rv.vp[x];
}

vec vec::operator=(vec & rv) {
  delete vp; // release old memory
  vp = new int[size = rv.size];
```

```
    for (int x = 0; x < size; x++)
        vp[x] = rv.vp[x];
    return *this;  // return a copy of this object
}

void vec::print(char * msg) {
    cout << msg;
    for(int x = 0; x < size; x++)
        cout << vp[x] << " ";
    cout << endl;
}

int & vec::operator[](int x) {
    if ( x >= size) {
        cout << "vec index out of range";
        exit(1);
    }
    return vp[x];
}

// pass in by value, return by value:
vec func1(vec value) {
    if (value.length() >= 1)
        value[0] = 0;
    return value;
}

void main() {
    vec A(4,3);
    vec B;
    A.print("A: ");
    B.print("B: ");
    B = func1(A);
    A.print("A after func1: ");
    B.print("B after func1: ");
}
```

The copy constructor is used to pass a **vec** by value to **func1()** and to return a **vec** from **func1()**. It is essential here, since the compiler would default to simply copying the source object structure into the destination object structure, and the dynamically allocated memory (which is destroyed when **value** goes out of scope in **func1()**) isn't reproduced for the returned value. The pointer to the memory would be copied, but when the free store was released it would either be written over immediately (depending on the implementation of **new** and **delete**) or written over when **new** is called at some unknown later time.

When you define a copy constructor, you take all responsibility for the process—the default memberwise initialization isn't performed. As you can see in the copy constructor for **class vec**, the value of **size** is copied just as it would be in the default case, but new memory is allocated, initialized, and assigned to **vp**.

Object Assignment

The **operator=()** function is another situation where the compiler creates a default function if assignment is used and no **operator=()** has been defined. Like memberwise initialization, this default does a bit copy for built-in types and calls the **operator=()** for member objects—the process is referred to as *memberwise assignment*. This is often an equally satisfactory solution for simple objects, but when pointers and more elaborate initializations occur, an **operator=()** must be defined.

Unique Characteristics of operator=()

Assignment falls into an odd category by itself, and the programmer must be aware that **operator=()** is unlike any other operator or member function.

operator=() *Cannot Be Inherited*

Although **operator=()** is not a constructor in the usual sense, *it does not inherit* (just as constructors do not inherit). Assignment must perform the same duties as both the destructor and the copy constructor. To perform these duties, **operator=()** must have specific knowledge of the derived class (the derived class often contains new elements), thus an inherited **operator=()** is incorrect.

operator=() *Is Destruction + Copy Initialization*

As you can see in **class vec**, assignment is nearly identical to copy construction. The difference is this: the copy constructor is a *constructor*, so you must assume the object has never been initialized. Assignment, however, is simply another function called for an initialized object, so the object is "live," and the initialized parts must be coped with properly. In **class vec**, memory has been allocated when **operator=()** is called, and that memory must be freed before assigning **vp** to a new vector.

Here's a general guideline to follow: when defining an **operator=()**, you must perform the duties of the destructor on the current object before performing the duties of the copy constructor with the argument to the right of the equal sign. Thus the **operator=()** for a complicated object often looks like the code for the destructor followed by the code for the copy constructor.

operator=() *Has a Return Value*

The **operator=()** has another difference from the copy constructor. It has a return value (constructors have *no* return value). The return value can be anything, but the most common practice is to return a copy of the newly assigned-to object by saying **return *this**. This allows sequential assignment to be performed (as in **A = B = C;**); as noted before, this kind of structure assignment is not always allowed in C. The result of the assignment may also have a member function called (as in **if ((A=B).is_ok())** ...)

Temporary Variables

The statement

```
B = func1(A);
```

from the previous listing is actually rather elaborate and can cause confusion, especially if you print a message whenever destructors get called. This statement causes "hidden" objects to be created!

In C, a function can be called for its return value or for its side effects (modifications to its arguments or to global data). Thus the user must always have the option of ignoring the return value. The compiler knows how to ignore return values in C, but C++ objects are generally more complicated, so a "temporary variable" is created by the compiler to catch the return value as the function passes it out. A reference to this return value is then passed to **vec::operator=()**. As you just read, **operator=()** usually has a return value; this value is assigned to a *second* temporary variable. In fact, for any function that returns an object by value, the compiler generates a temporary variable when the function is called (if the object's class has a copy constructor).

If **func1()** is being called for its side effects,

```
func1(A);
```

the temporary variable is simply ignored after the return value is copied into it. Note that, as it is written, **func1()** has no side effects.

The address of the temporary variable is secretly passed into **func1()** so the result can be copied into it at the end. Thus the code generated for a call to **func1()** will show an extra argument being passed.

Walking Through an Assignment

Here's a review of the statement

```
B = func1(A);
```

At the beginning of the function, stack space is allocated for the **struct** of the local object **value**. The copy constructor is called for **value** with **A** as an argument so **A** can be reproduced in the local frame. The address of the temporary variable (which has storage allocated *outside* the function, before the call is made) is also passed into the function. At the end of the function, the copy constructor is called for the temporary variable with **value** as an argument. The copy constructor copies the return value out of the function frame. Since the return value of **func1()** is being used here, its address (the address of the temporary variable) is passed to the next function in line, **vec::operator=()**.

The **operator=()** is called as a member function for **B**. Since **B** will be re-bound to new data, the old representation of **B** must be cleaned up first. In this case, "cleanup" simply means deleting the free memory allocated for the vector. New memory is then allocated to hold the new vector and the data is copied in, just as it happens with the copy constructor. Finally, **operator=()** returns a copy of itself by calling the copy constructor for a second temporary variable with its own address (***this**) as an argument. This last temporary variable is unused, so it is ignored (except by the destructor, which cleans it up at the end of the scope).

If the subject is not yet transparent (it took the author over a month to figure it out!), examples later in this chapter generate output to show the creation and use of temporary variables.

An Example of Deep Copy: Class **matrix**

A **matrix** class is a good example of the proper use of the copy constructor. Since it is never known until run time how large or what dimensions a matrix will be, the data space for the matrix must always be dynamically allocated. In addition, matrices are often too unwieldy to copy around when passing and returning, so this example will simply move a pointer around.

Reference Counting

Since a pointer is moved, the bulk of the matrix data lives in the free store, so the program must be very careful not to delete "live" data from the free store. The destructor must ensure that no objects are pointing to the data before it is released. To accomplish this, a technique called *reference counting* is used. The reference counter tells how many objects are currently using the data. Since the reference count must be associated with data rather than any particular object, it is allocated on the free store as part of the structure that also contains information about the size of the matrix and a pointer to the actual matrix data. This structure is called a **matrep** in the program, for "matrix representation."

The **matrix** objects only contain a pointer to a **matrep**; the rest of the information is in the **matrep** itself, on the free store.

When a new object is tied to a particular **matrep**, the reference count is increased. When an object is untied, the reference count is decreased. Whenever the reference count is decremented it is tested—if it goes to zero, the **matrep** and the matrix data are deleted. Notice that the destructor simply decrements the reference count, and only deletes the data if the subsequent reference count is zero. The copy constructor simply increments the reference count of the argument and copies the pointer.

operator=( ) and Element Selection

The **operator=()** follows the general guidelines: first, cleanup is performed (just as in the destructor); then the object's pointer is copied from the argument, and the new reference count is increased to indicate another object is using the data (as is done in the copy constructor). Finally, a copy of the object is returned.

The function **val()** allows element selection. It returns a reference to an element in the matrix. Since the reference is not declared as a **const**, the element may be read or written. Notice that **val()** also performs bounds checking to make sure the user isn't trying to index outside the matrix. This error checking is quite valuable, but it slows down the process a fraction. The member functions all directly access the elements, ensuring that the indexes don't go out of bounds. The speed of element selection can be increased by making the function **val()** an **inline**.

Matrix Multiplication and Addition

The **operator*()** and **operator+()** functions define multiplication and addition for the matrices. The next implementation file to be shown, MMATRIX.CPP, shows how the proper definition of the copy constructor is critical for complicated classes. Both functions create their results in a local **matrix** and then return that local variable.

When either **operator*()** or **operator+()** is called, the compiler creates a temporary variable and secretly passes its address as an argument. When the local **matrix** variable is created, there is only one object using the dynamically allocated portion, so the reference count is 1 (see the constructor definition). At the **return** statement, the compiler calls the copy constructor for the temporary variable, with the local variable as an argument. The copy constructor copies the pointer from the local variable to the temporary variable and increments the reference count. At that point, the reference count is 2. After the **return** statement, the destructor is called by the compiler. The destructor decrements the reference count to 1 but doesn't destroy the dynamically allocated portion of the matrix, since the temporary variable is still using it. This way, the matrix is returned very quickly without destroying and reallocating memory, and copying the entire matrix.

Messages to Temporary Variables

In **main()**, the matrix functions are exercised. The last statement shows how you can call a member function for a temporary variable: the function **print()** is called for the result of **B*identity**. Understanding the concept of the temporary variable makes it much easier to determine what is happening here. In particular, if you call a member function that changes the result, it will have no effect, since the action will be on the temporary variable. For example:

```
(B*identity).val(1,1) = 0;
```

will set element 1,1 of the temporary variable to 0 and promptly forget about that matrix (until cleanup time). It is a perfectly valid statement, but it makes no logical sense.

A Complete matrix Class

This code only shows a framework for a matrix class, but it shows the portion that is most relevant to C++ programming. The remainder of the class is primarily mathematical and not appropriate to the subject of this chapter. The complete **matrix** class is given in Appendix B.

Think About It

While studying this code, remember that what is going on here isn't trivial. It may take awhile before you understand it all.

Here is the header file:

```
//: MMATRIX.H—Simple matrix class to show "deep copy"
//. complexities. See text for description of reference counting

class matrix {
  // A structure to hold matrix information. This structure
  // is always created on the free store.
  struct matrep {
    double **m; // pointer to the matrix
    int r,c;    // number of rows and columns
    int n;      // reference count
  } *p;
  void error(char * msg1, char * msg2 = ""); // private function
public:
  matrix(int rows = 1, int columns = 1, double initval = 0);
  matrix(matrix& x); // copy constructor
  ~matrix();
  matrix operator=(const matrix& rval); // matrix assignment
  matrix operator+(const matrix& rval); // matrix addition
  matrix operator*(const matrix& rval); // matrix multiplication
  double & val(int row, int col); // element selection;
  // can be used to read or write an element.
  void print(const char * msg = "");
};
```

Here is the implementation file:

```
//: MMATRIX.CPP—Implementation of simple matrix
#include <stdio.h>
#include <iostream.h>
#include <iomanip.h>
#include <stdlib.h>
#include "mmatrix.h"

void matrix::error(char * msg1, char * msg2) {
  cerr << "matrix error: " << msg1
       << "   " << msg2 << endl;
  exit(1);
}

matrix::matrix(int rows, int columns, double initval) {
```

```
    // create the structure:
    p = new matrep;
    // allocate memory for the actual matrix:
    p->m = new double *[rows];
    for (int x = 0; x < rows; x++)
      p->m[x] = new double[columns];
    p->n = 1;  // so far, there's one reference to this data
    p->r = rows;
    p >c = columns;
    for (int i=0; i< rows; i++) {
      for (int j = 0; j < columns; j++)
        p->m[i][j] = initval;
    }
}

matrix::matrix(matrix& x) {
  x.p->n++; // we're adding another reference.
  p = x.p;  // point to the new matrep.
}

matrix matrix::operator=(const matrix& rval) {
  // clean up current value:
  if(--p->n == 0) {  // If nobody else is referencing us...
    for (int x = 0; x < p->r; x++)
      delete p->m[x];
    delete p->m; // ...nobody else can clean us up...
    delete p;
  ]
  // connect to new value:
  rval.p->n++;  // tell the rval it has another reference
  p = rval.p;  // point at the rval matrep
  return *this;
}

matrix::~matrix() {
  if (--p->n == 0) { // if reference count goes to 0
    for (int x = 0; x < p->r; x++)
      delete p->m[x];
    delete p->m; // delete data
    delete p;
  }
}

double & matrix::val(int row, int col) {
  if (row < p->r && col < p->c)
    return (p->m[row][col]);
  else
```

```
      error("index out of range");
    static double dummy(0);
    return dummy;
}

matrix matrix::operator*(const matrix& rval) {
  if( p->c != rval.p->r)
    error("# rows of second mat must equal "
          "# cols of first for multiply!");
  matrix result(p->r, rval.p->c);
  for(int row = 0; row < p->r; row++) {
    for(int col = 0; col < rval.p->c; col++){
      double sum = 0;
      for(int i = 0; i < p->c; i++)
        sum += p->m[row][i] * rval.p->m[i][col];
      result.p->m[row][col] = sum;
    }
  }
  return result; // Returning a local variable?
  // copy constructor happens before the destructor,
  // so reference count is 2 when destructor is called,
  // thus destructor doesn't free the memory.
}

matrix matrix::operator+(const matrix& rval) {
  if(( p->r != rval.p->r) || ( p->c != rval.p->c))
     error("must have equal dimensions for addition!");
  matrix sum(p->r,p->c);
  for (int i=0; i< p->r; i++) {
    for (int j = 0; j < p->c; j++)
      sum.p->m[i][j] = p->m[i][j] + rval.p->m[i][j];
  }
  return sum; // see note for operator*()
}

void matrix::print(const char *msg) {
  if (*msg) cout << msg << endl;
  for (int row=0; row< p->r; row++){
    for (int col = 0; col < p->c; col++)
      cout << setw(12) << setprecision(6)
           << p->m[row][col];
    cout << endl;
  }
}
```

```
void main() {
  matrix A(4,4,3);
  matrix B(4,4);
  int w = 0;
  for (int u = 0; u < 4; u++) {
    for (int v = 0; v < 4; v++)
      B.val(u,v) = w++;
  }
  matrix identity(4,4);
  for(int i = 0; i < 4; i++)
    identity.val(i,i) = 1;
  matrix C = B + A;
  A.print("A:");
  B.print("B:");
  C.print("C = A+B:");
  (B*identity).print("B*identity:");
}
```

Caveat

It is not a good idea to have two objects pointing to the same data (unless one of those objects is a temporary variable, in which case it is the compiler's responsibility). This is often called *aliasing*. With aliasing, any change one object makes in the data is reflected in the other object, with unpredictable results.

There are two ways to prevent this. One is to disallow **matrix** assignments like

```
A = B;
```

To do this you will have to build in a scheme to distinguish temporaries from "real" variables.

The second way is to create a scheme that allocates new memory and duplicates the object whenever the user attempts to write to a memory space that has two objects using it. Both techniques involve overhead and careful bookkeeping. It has been suggested that reference counting is not always the best solution to the kind of problem **class matrix** has (that is, passing and returning large amounts of data).

Tracing the Creation and Destruction of Objects

It can be confusing to try to imagine how a complex program works. Since each object has a unique identifier (its address, available via the keyword **this**), it is possible to display all the calls of the constructors and destructor. The following modified **matrix** class shows both user-created variables and compiler-created temporary variables. The logic of **class mmtrace** is the same as **class matrix** except for the addition of the tracing information.

User-created variables are identified by their variable names; a string with the name is an argument to the constructor. When the normal constructor is called, the string is always present. When the copy constructor is called, however, the name string for the current object may be empty, indicating a temporary variable. If this is the case, the **hidden** flag is set.

The private member function **oname()** returns a pointer to a string that describes the object. Notice this function is one of the unusual cases when it's acceptable to return an address. The address is either **name**, which is valid outside the scope of **oname()**, or the address of **static char buf[20]**. Since **buf** is static, it is also valid outside the scope of **oname()**. The return value is declared **const** so the string may not be modified.

The **oname()** function checks to see if the object is associated with a variable name; if so, the address of **name** is returned. If the **hidden** flag is set, the variable is described as "hidden," and the object address (**(int)this**) is given to give it a unique identifier. This information is placed in the static buffer by building an **ostrstream** object using the buffer. Anything sent to the **ostrstream** will end up, formatted, in its associated buffer.

The function **object_data()** is called to display information about an object. To help clarify the trace, a tiny class called **tformat** with a single instance called **TAB** is used to perform indentation.

The program output is the trace of a single expression,

```
E = A + B + C + D;
```

where all the elements are matrices.

Here's the header file:

```
//: MMTRACE.H—Matrix class with tracing to show
//. initialization & destruction
class mmtrace {
  char * name; // to keep track of which object this is
  int hidden; // indicates a hidden variable
  struct matrep {
    double **m; // pointer to the matrix
    int r,c;    // number of rows and columns
    int n;      // reference count
  } *p;
  void error(char * msg1, char * msg2 = ""); // private function
  const char * oname(); // an identifier string for the object
public:
  mmtrace(char * object_name,
    int rows = 1, int columns = 1, double initval = 0);
  mmtrace(mmtrace& x); // copy constructor
  ~mmtrace();
  mmtrace operator=(mmtrace& rval); // matrix assignment
  mmtrace operator+(mmtrace& rval); // matrix addition
  void object_data(char * msg); // trace information
};
```

Since the definition of **struct matrep** is inside the class, it is scoped inside the class and has better hiding and encapsulation.

Automatically Creating a Trace File

In two of the examples in this chapter, a file is opened with the same name as the source file containing **main()**, and all the output which would normally go to **cout** is sent to this trace file instead. It is helpful to mechanize this process by creating a class in a header file.

The ANSI C preprocessor provides a macro **__FILE__** that produces the name of the file. Unfortunately, it always produces the name of the file it's in. If it's in an **include** file, it has no idea who is including the file. Thus, to get the name of the file containing **main()** while inside an include file, you must force the programmer to first set the name of the file, *before* including the file. So the use of this class will always look like this:

```
char* basename = __FILE__;
#include "trace.h"
```

This way, **basename** has the name of the enclosing file.

Here's the header file:

```
//: TRACE.H—Automatically create a trace file
//. you must precede the inclusion of this file with
//. char* basename = __FILE__;
//. to capture the name of the enclosing file
#ifndef TRACE_H_
#define TRACE_H_
#include <fstream.h>
#include <string.h>
#include <ctype.h> // toupper()
#include <assert.h>

// Portable function to force a string to uppercase:
inline void upcase(char * p) {
  while(*p) { *p = toupper(*p); p++; }
}

struct _tracefile {
  ofstream file;
  _tracefile() {
    char tracename[20]; strcpy(tracename, basename);
    char name[20]; strcpy(name, basename);
    char * p = strrchr(tracename, '.');  // Find the last period
    strcpy(p + 1, "OUT"); // output file name extension
    upcase(tracename);
    upcase(name);
    file.open(tracename);
    assert(file);
    file << "//: " << tracename << " — Output of " << name
         << endl;
  }
  ~_tracefile() { file.close(); }
} _TRACE;
// Send all output to the trace file:
#define cout _TRACE.file
#endif // TRACE_H_
```

The first **inline** function forces a string to uppercase. There are implementations of similar functions in various compiler libraries, but none agree on name. For portability, it is best to simply code the function.

The **struct _tracefile** contains an instance of an **ofstream**. This is not initialized in the constructor initializer list; or rather, the default constructor is used there, which doesn't open a file. Fortunately, there's also the **open()** function that lets you open the file later if you don't have all the information at first, as is the case here. The filename is created by taking the **basename**, finding the last period in it, and replacing the existing extension (presumably .cpp) with a new one, .out. This is the file name used for the output file (successful opening is checked with **assert()**). Both filenames are forced to uppercase, and the first line in the file is created.

The statement **#define cout _TRACE.file** takes everything that was normally sent to **cout** and sends it to the trace file.

Matrix Trace Implementation

Here's the implementation file, which also uses **trace.h**:

```
//: MMTRACE.CPP—Trace generation for matrix class
//. to show initialization and destruction
#include <iostream.h>
#include <strstream.h>
#include <fstream.h>
#include <string.h>
#include <stdlib.h>
#include "mmtrace.h"
// Open a trace file and send all output to it:
char* basename - __FILE__;
#include "trace.h"

// a tiny class to perform indentation
class tformat {
  int depth;
public:
  tformat() : depth(0) {}
  void operator++() { depth += 2; }
  void operator--() { depth -= 2; }
```

```cpp
    // define postfix versions:
    void operator++(int) { operator++(); }
    void operator--(int) { operator--(); }
    void indent() {
      for (int i = 0; i < depth; i++ )
        cout << " ";
    }
} TAB;

void mmtrace::error(char * msg1, char * msg2) {
  cerr << "matrix error: " << msg1
       << "   " <<   msg2 << endl;
  exit(1);
}

// returns a character pointer to a printable
// description of the object
const char * mmtrace::oname() {
  if (!hidden) return name; // visible; has a name
  const bufsz = 20;
  static char buf[bufsz]; // static data in a function
  ostrstream obuf(buf, bufsz);
  obuf << "temporary:this = " << (unsigned int)this << ends;
  return buf;
}

void mmtrace::object_data(char * msg) {
  TAB.indent();
  cout << msg << ": [" << oname()
       << "], p = " << (int)p << endl;
}

mmtrace::mmtrace(char * object_name,
    int rows, int columns, double initval)
      : hidden(0), name(strdup(object_name)) {
  p = new matrep;
  p->m = new double*[rows];
  for (int x = 0; x < rows; x++)
    p->m[x] = new double[columns];
  p->n = 1;  // so far, there's one reference to this data
  p->r = rows;
  p->c = columns;
  for (int i=0; i< rows; i++) {
    for (int j = 0; j < columns; j++)
      p->m[i][j] = initval;
  }
  object_data("constructor called");
```

```cpp
  TAB++;
}

mmtrace::mmtrace(mmtrace& x) : hidden(1) {
  // in this example, copy constructor is only used
  // to initialize temporary variables.
  name = strdup("temporary");
  object_data("before copy-init");
  x.object_data("copying from");
  x.p->n++;      // we're adding another reference,
  p = x.p;       // so increase the count.
  object_data("after copy-init");
}

mmtrace mmtrace::operator=(mmtrace& rval) {
  object_data("op= before assignment");
  rval.object_data("op= argument");
  rval.p->n++;
  TAB.indent();
  cout << "before decrement, reference count = "
       << p->n << endl;
  if(--p->n == 0) {
    TAB.indent();
    cout << "op= releasing old contents of ["
         << oname() << "]" << endl;
    for (int x = 0; x < p->r; x++)
      delete p->m[x];
    delete p->m;
    delete p;
  } else {
    TAB.indent();
    cout << "[" << oname()
         << "] contents not released" << endl;
  }
  p = rval.p;
  object_data("op= returning *this");
  return *this;
}

mmtrace::~mmtrace() {
  object_data("destructor called");
  TAB.indent();
  cout << "before decr, reference count = " << p->n << endl;
  if(--p->n == 0) {
    TAB.indent();
    cout << "destructor releasing contents of ["
         << oname() << "]" << endl;
```

```
      for (int x = 0; x < p->r; x++)
        delete p->m[x];
      delete p->m;
      delete p;
    } else {
      TAB.indent();
      cout << "contents of [" << oname()
           << "] not released" << endl;
    }
    free(name);
    TAB--;
}

mmtrace mmtrace::operator+(mmtrace& rval) {
  if(( p->r != rval.p->r) || ( p->c != rval.p->c))
     error("must have equal dimensions for addition!");
  object_data("in op+ called for");
  rval.object_data("op+ argument");
  mmtrace sum("op+ local: sum",p->r,p->c);
  for (int i=0; i< p->r; i++) {
    for (int j = 0; j < p->c; j++)
      sum.p->m[i][j] = p->m[i][j] + rval.p->m[i][j];
  }
  TAB.indent();
  cout << "in op+; returning sum" << endl;
  return sum;
}

// Macro prints a statement; then executes it.
// '#' before arg turns it into a string:
#define TRACE(arg) TAB.indent(); cout << #arg << endl; arg

void main() {
  TRACE(mmtrace A("A",4,4,3));
  TRACE(mmtrace B("B",4,4));
  TRACE(mmtrace C("C",4,4,5));
  TRACE(mmtrace D("D",4,4,6));
  TRACE(mmtrace E("E"));
  TRACE(E = A + B + C + D);
  TAB.indent();
  cout << "After E = A + B + C + D" << endl;
  E.object_data("E");
  TAB.indent();
  cout << "Program finished, time for cleanup" << endl;
}
```

Here is the output from this program, so you can see how the expression is evaluated by the compiler and how variables are created and destroyed:

```
//: MMTRACE.OUT—Output of MMTRACE.CPP
mmtrace A("A",4,4,3)
constructor called: [A], p = 5880
  mmtrace B("B",4,4)
  constructor called: [B], p = 6056
    mmtrace C("C",4,4,5)
    constructor called: [C], p = 6232
      mmtrace D("D",4,4,6)
      constructor called: [D], p = 6408
        mmtrace E("E")
        constructor called: [E], p = 6584
          E = A + B + C + D
          in op+ called for: [A], p = 5880
          op+ argument: [B], p = 6056
          constructor called: [op+ local: sum], p = 6636
            in op+; returning sum
            before copy-init: [temporary:this = 654], p = 3030
            copying from: [op+ local: sum], p = 6636
            after copy-init: [temporary:this = 654], p = 6636
            destructor called: [op+ local: sum], p = 6636
            before decr, reference count = 2
            contents of [op+ local: sum] not released
          in op+ called for: [temporary:this = 654], p = 6636
          op+ argument: [C], p = 6232
          constructor called: [op+ local: sum], p = 6818
            in op+; returning sum
            before copy-init: [temporary:this = 654], p = 20547
            copying from: [op+ local: sum], p = 6818
            after copy-init: [temporary:this = 654], p = 6818
            destructor called: [op+ local: sum], p = 6818
            before decr, reference count = 2
            contents of [op+ local: sum] not released
          in op+ called for: [temporary:this = 654], p = 6818
          op+ argument: [D], p = 6408
          constructor called: [op+ local: sum], p = 7000
            in op+; returning sum
            before copy-init: [temporary:this = 654], p = 21076
            copying from: [op+ local: sum], p = 7000
            after copy-init: [temporary:this = 654], p = 7000
            destructor called: [op+ local: sum], p = 7000
```

```
          before decr, reference count = 2
          contents of [op+ local: sum] not released
        op= before assignment: [E], p = 6584
        op= argument: [temporary:this = 654], p = 7000
        before decrement, reference count = 1
        op= releasing old contents of [E]
        op= returning *this: [E], p = 7000
        before copy-init: [temporary:this = 654], p = 11698
        copying from: [E], p = 7000
        after copy-init: [temporary:this = 654], p = 7000
        destructor called: [temporary:this = 654], p = 7000
        before decr, reference count = 3
        contents of [temporary:this = 654] not released
      destructor called: [temporary:this = 654], p = 7000
      before decr, reference count = 2
      contents of [temporary:this = 654] not released
    destructor called: [temporary:this = 654], p = 6818
    before decr, reference count = 1
    destructor releasing contents of [temporary:this = 654]
  destructor called: [temporary:this = 654], p = 6636
  before decr, reference count = 1
  destructor releasing contents of [temporary:this = 654]
  After E = A + B + C + D
  E: [E], p = 7000
  Program finished, time for cleanup
  destructor called: [E], p = 7000
  before decr, reference count = 1
  destructor releasing contents of [E]
destructor called: [D], p = 6408
before decr, reference count = 1
destructor releasing contents of [D]
destructor called: [C], p = 6232
before decr, reference count = 1
destructor releasing contents of [C]
destructor called: [B], p = 6056
before decr, reference count = 1
destructor releasing contents of [B]
destructor called: [A], p = 5880
before decr, reference count = 1
destructor releasing contents of [A]
```

After all the constructors are called, the evaluation of **A + B + C + D** proceeds from left to right. First, **operator+()** is called for **A** with an argument of **B**. Inside the function **operator+()**, the constructor is called for the local variable **sum**. The **sum** is returned by calling the copy constructor for a temporary variable with **sum** as the argument. The destructor is called for **sum** when it goes out of scope, but the reference count is 2, since the temporary variable is also using it. Next, **operator+()** is called for the temporary variable with **C** as the argument.

Each local **sum** is bound by the copy constructor to a new temporary variable until the expression has been evaluated. The temporary variable representing the sum is passed to **operator=()** called for **E**.

Notice the result of **operator=()** is also bound to a temporary variable; this is the effect of the statement **return *this;** in the definition for **operator=()**. This final temporary variable is not used in this code.

You can see that destructors are called for the temporary variables, as well as the visible ones, and that the reference count works out correctly.

*Returning Objects with *new*

The **new** keyword creates and initializes (by calling the appropriate constructor) an object on the free store. This section shows why you should never return an object created on the free store *by value* (that is, **return *new ...**).

More About References

In addition to their use in argument passing, references can be created as independent variables. A variable created this way looks and acts exactly like a regular object, but it is actually an address (or an alias, for inline functions in some implementations of C++). The compiler quietly performs all the proper dereferencing.

It isn't usually very useful to declare reference variables other than as function arguments or return values. Reference variables initialized with ***new** are an exception.

All references *must* be initialized. The address contained in a reference must always point to an initialized object. The following is an error (except in a class declaration; see Chapter 4):

```
int & intref;  // ERROR: must be initialized to something
```

There are two correct ways to initialize references. The first is to bind the reference to a named object, as shown here:

```
//: REF1.CPP—Binding a reference to an initialized object
#include <iostream.h>

class RC {
  int i;
  char * name;
public:
  // The compiler allocates space for the name string, so
  // assigning "name" (instead of allocating space and
  // copying) is a safe thing to do:
  RC(char * nm,int j = 0) { name = nm; i = j; }
  void set(int k) { i = k; }
  void print(char * msg = "") {
    cout << msg << ": " << name << " : i = " << i << endl;
  }
};

void main() {
  RC A("A",5);   // create an object
  RC & B = A;    // create a reference
  A.print("A after initialization");
  B.print("B, a reference to A");
  B.set(20);     // changing B ...
  A.print("A after B.set(20)");   // ... also changes A!
}
```

The output generated by this program is

```
A after initialization: A : i = 5
B, a reference to A: A : i = 5
A after B.set(20): A : i = 20
```

The object **A** is created, then a reference **B** is made from **A**. Notice that a reference is treated by the compiler as an *object*, not an address, thus the *value* of **A**, and not the address of **A**, must be used in the expression.

The above situation is subject to the same caveats as given for the **matrix** class, when reference counting was used. Since **A** and **B** point to the same object, changing **A** or **B** will modify that object. This is generally more confusing than it is useful.

Proper Use of *new

The second and more practical way to use an independent reference is to initialize it with a variable created on the free store. Since destructors are never called for references unless the user explicitly calls **delete()**, the reference created this way is not subject to the normal scoping rules, so it "lives" until the user explicitly destroys it. Scoping may also be disabled by using pointers in a similar fashion, but the syntax is easier to read with references.

When initializing a reference from an object created on the free store, keep in mind that the keyword **new** returns an *address*, and a reference must be initialized with an *object*. Thus the address returned by **new** must be dereferenced with a *, as shown here:

```
//: REF2.CPP—Reference bound to a free-store object
#include <iostream.h>

class RCF {
  int i;
public:
  RCF(int j = 0) { i = j; }
  ~RCF() { cout <<"destructor called!"; }
};

void main() {
  RCF & C = *new RCF(47);
  // destructor is never called for a reference
}
```

In this above program, the destructor will never be called.

When initializing a reference, the compiler quietly takes the address of the source object, so the address of the object that is actually on the free store is bound to **C**.

Improper Use of *new

It might be tempting for the new C++ programmer to return an object created on the free store instead of worrying about reference counting or creating a copy constructor that performs proper deep copying. It seems to be a very neat solution: since the destructor is never called (destructors are not automatically called for objects created on the free store), there is no need to worry about the copy constructor. The statement

```
return *new classname(arguments);
```

seems to work just fine.

The problem with the statement can be seen by executing the following program:

```
//: STARNEW.CPP—Why return *new is usually bad
#include <iostream.h>

class starnew {
  int * intarray;
  char * chararray;
public:
  void data(char * msg = "") {
    cout << msg << ":\n\tthis = " << (unsigned int)this
         << " intarray = "<< (int)intarray
         << " chararray = "<< (int)chararray << endl;
  }
  starnew(int intsize, int charsize) {
    intarray = new int[intsize];
    chararray = new char[charsize];
    data("constructor called");
  }
  starnew(starnew &rval) {
    rval.data("argument of copy-constructor");
    intarray = rval.intarray;
    chararray = rval.chararray;
    data("after copy-constructor");
  }
  ~starnew() {
    delete intarray;
    delete chararray;
    data("destructor called");
  }
};

starnew return_starnew() {
  cout << "return_starnew, before return *new starnew(5,5);"
       << endl;
  return *new starnew(5,5);
```

```
}

void main() {
  starnew A = return_starnew();
  A.data("A");
  starnew & B = *new starnew(6,6);
  B.data("B");
  delete &B; // explicit destructor call for reference
}
```

The problem can be seen in the trace generated by program execution:

```
return_starnew, before return *new starnew(5,5);
constructor called:
    this = 4302 intarray = 4310 chararray = 4324
argument of copy-constructor:
    this = 4302 intarray = 4310 chararray = 4324
after copy-constructor:
    this = 65522 intarray = 4310 chararray = 4324
A:
    this = 65522 intarray = 4310 chararray = 4324
constructor called:
    this = 4334 intarray = 4342 chararray = 4358
B:
    this = 4334 intarray = 4342 chararray = 4358
destructor called:
    this = 4334 intarray = 4342 chararray = 4358
destructor called:
    this = 65522 intarray = 4310 chararray = 4324
```

Inside the function **return_starnew()**, an object is created on the free store, and a pointer to that object is produced by **new**. When the pointer is dereferenced and returned via **return *new**, a copy of the structure (a shallow copy *only*) is returned and copied into **A**'s structure. The copy includes pointers to the two arrays, so when a destructor is called for **A**, the two arrays are destroyed. *However*, the original structure created on the free store is *never destroyed!* In fact, you couldn't destroy it if you tried, since the address of that structure is immediately lost when the **return *new** statement is executed. Thus, no destructor is ever called to free the memory allocated for the structure inside the function **return_starnew()**.

A program written using **return *new** will work fine until some number of free-store allocations and deallocations have occurred; then it will run out of memory. This occurs because all the structures left lying around in the free store eventually fill it up or fragment it so much that no block of memory can be found of the desired size.

The example also shows the creation and destruction of a reference **B**. This is the proper way to call a destructor for a reference.

An OOP Interpreter Foundation in C++

The last example in this chapter answers the question: how do you create an object-oriented framework for an interpreter so it can easily be extended to handle new classes? The solution may enlighten you about some aspects of C++ and OOP design.

Smalltalk Solution

The solution came from the design of Smalltalk. It turns out that Smalltalk must live with this problem all the time: it's an interpreted language, and you are constantly adding new classes to it, so the interpreter is extensible. How does the interpreter know whether it's passing around a big object like a matrix, or a small object like an integer? How does it know what messages those objects can receive?

Smalltalk makes all objects the same size. Each of these objects has a common interface, and can receive any kind of message—only when the program runs do the messages get resolved, so you don't know until run time whether a message you send to an object has an associated method (the famous "method not found" error). All objects are inherited from the same base class, which is usually named **Object** (thus, C++ class hierarchies that follow this model are often referred to as "Object-based" hierarchies—it's just because of the name, not any abstract concept). The Smalltalk interpreter simply passes **Object**s around and sends messages to **Object**s, and polymorphism takes care of the rest.

The C++ solution shown here follows the same path. The analog of **Object** is **class number**, which contains a single pointer and has no **virtual** functions, so each object of this class is the size of a single pointer, and passing it around is very efficient. The pointer points to an object that contains all the information about the specific number, including its type, its data, an identifier, and so on. It's actually a pointer to a base class, called **num**, that is a common interface to all representations of numbers, each of which is derived from **num**. The common interface contains **virtual** functions for all the operations you want to perform, including addition, subtraction, and the like. For simplicity, this example only shows addition, but you can add other operators by following the same form.

The **class number** has all the operations in **class num** because the interpreter will only deal with **number** objects when it creates expressions. All a **number** object does is call the **num** version of the functions polymorphically through its pointer. However, **class number** also handles assignment, destruction, and copy construction—tricky business.

Since **class number** contains a pointer, any time you assign one **number** to another, create a new **number** from an existing one (copy construction), or destroy a **number**, you run into the problem of aliasing. What happens if more than one **number** object points to the same **num** object? This happens regularly in this scheme, as you will see later from the program's output.

To ensure that you don't destroy a **num** object that is still being used by one or more **number** objects, reference counting is again employed. A variable called **refcount** is placed inside **class num**. Each time a **number** object attaches its pointer to a **num** object, it increments that **num**'s **refcount**. The **number** destructor decrements the **refcount** and, if it goes to 0, destroys the **num**. If it's not 0, it means some other **number** is still using that **num**.

The maintenance of the **refcount** and the passing of the various messages through to the **num** are all that **class number** does, so it's very simple. There are two other issues before you can understand the code: type checking and object creation.

Type Checking

Normally, the C++ compiler is ferocious about type checking. It won't let you get away with *anything*, especially some of the very questionable things C allows. Here, however, you don't want to worry about specific types until run time, because the interpreter must be able to send messages to any type of object and let the object figure out what to do with it. Thus, it must tell two **number** objects to add themselves and let the objects worry about whether they are compatible types or not. Although you normally want the safety of the compiler's type checking, it must be effectively disabled here so the interpreter can be easily extended.

This "disabling" has already taken place, since the interpreter will only use **number** objects. Now the type checking must happen at run time. When a function (including an operator) is called, it must check to see that its argument is compatible with the object it was called for—in this example, compatibility will mean that it's an equivalent type, but you could also do conversions. The **virtual** function **typecheck()** in **class num** will perform the testing by checking a **type** variable inside **num**. The function is **virtual** in case you want to redefine it in a derived class to mean "compatible" instead of "equivalent."

When any function is called by the interpreter, it is simply passing **number**s. It doesn't pay attention to their specific type. So inside the **integer** addition function, for example, you must figure out whether you're adding to an **integer**, and then perform the cast every time you use that pointer. To make things simpler, each class has a **cast()** function that checks the type and performs a cast to a type of that class if it is safe. This is the function where you would perform type conversions if you desire. To use this function inside the **integer::operator+(num * arg)** function, for example, you start off by saying

```
integer * Arg = cast(arg);
if(Arg) // ...
```

If the **cast()** is unsuccessful, it returns 0 (and issues an error message; exceptions will be preferable when they are available). From then on, you have a pointer to an **integer**, and you don't have to perform any casting, since it was all done at the beginning.

Object Creation

In any extensible C++ program, there is one spot where things can't happen automatically: the constructor. After the object is created, all the code that uses objects can be identical regardless of type because of polymorphism, but when the object is created, you (and the compiler)

must know the exact type, since otherwise it can't set up the **virtual** mechanism properly. It would be nice to have "virtual constructors" in the language, but it's a conundrum: how can you "send a message to an object and let the object figure out what to do with it" when the object isn't there yet?

There are a number of variants of the virtual constructor solution. The simplest technique is used in this example: the **number** constructor just takes a pointer to the **num** object that the **number** will hold. This produces some funny-looking constructor calls, for example:

```
number X(new integer(0, "X"));
```

Remember, however, that the interpreter will be generating this constructor call (albeit using pointers, since it can't use identifiers) so it doesn't matter if it looks strange. Also, the simplicity of the design is appealing.

The second argument is the identifier, so the **num** always knows what it is.

The Example

NUMTERP.CPP contains the complete program to demonstrate this design. It should work with any C++ compiler.

One of the first things you will notice in this example is all the support for tracing the output. This is critical because the type checking and object handling that the compiler would ordinarily do has been taken over, so you must be able to see exactly what's going on to ensure that the proper behavior is taking place. Several preprocessor macros facilitate this. **TRACE** uses the ANSI C preprocessor "stringizing" feature to turn its argument into a string, which it sends to **cout**. Then it duplicates its argument. This allows you to print out the statement before it is executed. **MSG** sends its argument to **cout** (**MSGC** omits the **endl** so you can continue the next message on the same line), and **DBUG** just duplicates its argument. The macros are redefined when debugging is turned off; **TRACE** just duplicates its argument (without printing anything), and the others do nothing. Notice that this is a much more readable way of inserting debugging code than putting a bunch of ugly **#ifdef/#else/#endif** sets throughout your program.

There's also a conditionally defined function called **buildID()**, which takes three arguments and builds an identifier string from them. This is used to give an identifier to a return value. For example, when you say **A + B**, the identifier for the resulting temporary object is **(result of A + B)**. That way, the trace is much more readable.

The **buildID()** function creates its string in a static data area that is big enough so the largest conceivable string can be created. Then this storage is associated with an **ostrstream** object like this:

```
ostrstream omsg(buf, msglen);
```

Now **omsg** can be treated just like any other **ostream** object (**cout**, for example). The only difference is that you terminate it with **ends** (to put the '\0' in) rather than the traditional **endl** (which puts out a newline and flushes the buffer). The **ostrstream** object knows how big the buffer is and will not write past the end. You must duplicate the memory pointed to by the return value of **buildID()**; otherwise it will change in the next call to the function. The duplication is performed in the **num** constructor initializer list by a call to the common library function **strdup()**, which allocates storage with **malloc()** and copies the string. Since **malloc()** is used instead of **new**, the **num** destructor must use **free()** instead of **delete** to release the memory. The cast to **void*** is necessary because **id** is a **const char***, which doesn't implicitly convert to a non**const** pointer like **void***.

When debugging is turned on, a trace file is created (as in MMTRACE.CPP), and all the output that would normally go to **cout** goes to the trace file instead, so you automatically get a complete trace in NUMTERP.OUT.

NUMTERP.CPP is shown here:

```
//: NUMTERP.CPP—Framework for numerical interpreter
#include <iostream.h>
#include <fstream.h>
#include <strstream.h>
#include <string.h>
#include <stdlib.h>
#include <float.h> // declaration of FLT_MAX
#include <limits.h> // declaration of INT_MAX
#define DEBUG
```

```
#ifdef DEBUG
// Create a trace file, and send all data to it:
char* basename = __FILE__;
#include "trace.h"
// A macro to see what's going on, and three to control
// the insertion or removal of debugging code (easier
// to read than all the #ifdef/#endif statements; also
// allows you to change the ostream destination)
#define TRACE(arg) cout << #arg << endl; arg;
#define MSG(arg) cout << arg << endl
#define MSGC(arg) cout << arg
#define DBUG(arg) arg
// Builds a string identifier for the return value.
// op is the operator being applied: " + ", " * " ...
char * buildID(const char* arg1, const char * op,
               const char * arg2) {
  const sz = 200; // overly large so you never run out
  static char buf[sz];
  ostrstream omsg(buf, sz);
  // to prevent overlong lines:
  char * nl = strchr(arg1, '\n'); // find old newline
  if(nl) while(*++nl == ' ') ; // move past leading spaces
  else nl = (char *)arg1;
  omsg << "\n  (return val of " << nl << op << arg2
       << ")" << ends;
  return buf; // must be duplicated outside
}
#else
#define TRACE(arg) arg;
#define MSG(arg)
#define MSGC(arg)
#define DBUG(arg)
char * buildID(const char*, const char*, const char*) {
  return "";
}
#endif

// Abstract base class for numerical representation:
class num {
  int refcount; // reference count
  int type;
  static int objcount; // total number of objects
protected:
  const char* id; // identifier
public:
```

```cpp
    virtual int typecheck(num * arg) {
      if(type != arg->type) {
        cerr << "incompatible types" << endl;
        return 0;
      }
      return 1;
    }
    virtual num* operator+(num*) = 0;
    // other operators here
    // ...
    num(int t, const char* ID)
        : refcount(0), type(t), id(strdup(ID)) {
      MSG("creating " << id << ", count = " << ++objcount);
    }
    virtual ~num() {
      MSG("destroying " << id << ", count = " << --objcount);
      free((void*)id); // release malloced identifier memory
    }
    virtual ostream& printstream(ostream&) = 0;
    void incr_ref() {
      refcount++;
      DBUG(dump());
    }
    num * decr_ref() {
      if(!--refcount) {
        delete this;
        return 0;
      }
      DBUG(dump());
      return this;
    }
    const char* ident() { return id; }
    void dump() {
      cout << id << " rc=" << refcount << endl;
    }
};

int num::objcount = 0; // initialize static data member

// Constant-sized object to hold pointer to num:
class number {
  num * n;
public:
  number(num* N) : n(N) {
    DBUG(dump("in number constructor for "));
    n->incr_ref();
  }
```

```
  ~number() {
    MSGC("in ~number: ");
    if(n) n = n->decr_ref();
    else cerr << "error: null n pointer" << endl;
  }
  number operator+(number arg) {
    MSG("in number::operator+ ");
    return number(n->operator+(arg.n));
  }
  number operator=(number arg) {
    DBUG(arg.dump("in number::operator= with arg "));
    if(!(n->typecheck(arg.n))) return number(n); // error
    TRACE(n->decr_ref()); // & conditionally delete old num
    TRACE(n=arg.n); // attach to new representation
    TRACE(n->incr_ref()); // rvalue num has another reference
    TRACE(return number(n));
  }
  number(number& N) {
    MSG("in number copy-constructor ");
    n = N.n;
    n->incr_ref();
  }
  friend ostream& operator<<(ostream& os, number& N) {
    return N.n->printstream(os);
  }
  void dump(char * msg = "") { cout << msg; n->dump(); }
};

// Different types of numerical representations:
class integer : public num {
  int i;
  integer* cast(num* arg) {
    if(typecheck(arg))
      return (integer*)arg;  // perform a "downcast"
    return 0;
  }
public:
  enum { Integer = 1 };
  integer(int X, const char * ID) : i(X), num(Integer, ID) {
    MSG("integer constructor for " << ID);
  }
  num* operator+(num* arg) {
    integer* Arg = cast(arg);
    MSGC("in integer::operator+ for " << id);
    MSG(" with arg " << Arg->id);
    if(Arg) return
      new integer(i + Arg->i, buildID(id, " + ", Arg->id));
```

```
      return new integer(INT_MAX, "error");
  }
  ostream& printstream(ostream& os) {
    return os << i;
  }
};

class floating : public num {
  float i;
  floating* cast(num* arg) {
    if(typecheck(arg))
      return (floating*)arg; // perform a "downcast"
    return 0;
  }
public:
  enum { Floating = 2 };
  floating(float X, const char* ID)
      : i(X), num(Floating, ID) {}
  num* operator+(num* arg) {
    floating * Arg = cast(arg);
    if(Arg) return
      new floating(i + Arg->i, buildID(id, " + ", Arg->id));
    return new floating(FLT_MAX, "error");
  }
  ostream& printstream(ostream& os) {
    return os << i;
  }
};

class vector : public num {
  int * v;
  int size;
  int sizecheck(vector* arg) {
    if(size != arg->size) {
      cerr << "different vector sizes" << endl;
      return 0;
    }
    return 1; // means OK
  }
  vector* cast(num * arg) {
    if(typecheck(arg))
      return (vector*)arg; // perform a "downcast"
    return 0;
  }
public:
  enum { Vector = 3 };
  vector(int sz, int val, const char* ID)
```

```
        : size(sz), v(new int[sz]), num(Vector, ID) {
          MSG("in vector constructor for " << ID);
          for(int i = 0; i < size; i++)
            v[i] = val;
      }
    ~vector() { delete []v; }
    vector(vector* arg, char* ID)
        : size(arg->size), num(Vector, ID) {
        MSGC("in vector constructor from a vector pointer");
        MSC(" with arg " << arg->id);
        v = new int[size];
        for(int i = 0; i < size; i++)
          v[i] = arg->v[i];
      }
    num* operator+(num* arg) {
        vector * Arg = cast(arg);
        MSGC("in vector::operator+ for " << id);
        MSG(" with arg " << Arg->id);
        if(!Arg || !sizecheck(Arg))
          return new vector(0, "error");
        vector * va = new vector(Arg, buildID(id, " + ", Arg->id));
        for(int i = 0; i < size; i++)
          va->v[i] += v[i];
        return va;
      }
    ostream& printstream(ostream& os) {
        for(int i = 0; i < size; i++) {
          os << v[i];
          if(i < size -1) os << ", ";
        }
        return os;
      }
};

void main() {
  TRACE(number A(new integer(1, "A")))
  TRACE(number B(new integer(2, "B")))
  TRACE(number X(new integer(3, "X")))
  TRACE(X = A + B + X)
  DBUG(X.dump("X is now "));
  cout << X << endl;

#if 0 // Other examples not shown in trace:
  TRACE(number C(new floating(1.129f, "C")))
  TRACE(number D(new floating(3.14159f, "D")))
  TRACE(number Y(new floating(0, "Y")))
  TRACE(number V1(new vector(10, 10, "V1")))
```

```
      TRACE(number V2(new vector(10, 7, "V2")))
      TRACE(Y = C + D)
      DBUG(Y.dump("Y is now "));
      cout << Y << endl;
      cout << "V1 = " << V1 << endl;
      cout << "V2 = " << V2 << endl;
      TRACE(number V3(new vector(10, 9, "V3")))
      cout << "V3 = " << V3 << endl;
      TRACE(V3 = V1 + V2 + V3);
      DBUG(X.dump("V3 is now "));
      cout << "V3 = " << V3 << endl;
#endif
}
```

The Core of the Design

The best place to start understanding the design is in the second class, **number**. This is the second class because it holds a pointer to the first class, **num**. Of course, they could have been declared in a different order if all the functions hadn't been defined as **inline**, but that wouldn't have added to the clarity.

The **class number** is surprisingly simple. Its only member is **n**, the **num** pointer. This is initialized to the pointer you hand it when you create the object, as in **number X(new integer(0, "X"))**. The constructor also calls a function **num::incr_ref()** for **n**, which increments the reference counter to indicate that one object is using this **num** (notice that the **num** constructor initializes **refcount** to 0).

The **number** destructor checks to see if **n** is nonzero (which is an error, and shouldn't happen); then it calls **num::decr_ref()** for **n**. This decrements the reference count and returns the pointer to the same **num** object if the reference count is still nonzero. If the reference count goes to zero, the **num** is deleted by its own member function, by calling **delete this** (the **num** destructor is **virtual**, so the correct behavior will take place); then 0 is returned. The return value is assigned back to **n**, so **n** automatically becomes 0 when the object is destroyed, but keeps its value otherwise.

The **operator=()** and copy constructor are always handled by **number**; they are never defined in the specific types of **num** objects. This is because **number** objects are responsible for maintaining the proper reference counts, which are ignored in the **num** class; the reason the reference count is in **num** is because the count must be attached to the object being referenced. In the copy constructor **number(number&)**, you can see how simple the process is: **n** (from the object being created) is attached to the argument's **n**, and then the reference count is incremented to indicate that an additional **number** object is using that **num** object now. The **operator=()** is identical, *except* that the lvalue is a constructed object, so its **n** is pointing to a **num** object before it is attached to the rvalue's **num**. So before it is detached, the reference count must be decremented and that **num** destroyed if no one else is using it.

The **number::operator+()** is the one example of the kind of operation you'll want your interpreter to do. You can see that all it does is defer the operation to its **n** pointer by calling the **virtual** function **operator+**. All operators return **num** pointers to their results—sometimes these are the same as the object, as in **X += B;** often they are new **num** objects created on the heap.

Keeping Track of Objects

The last function in **number**, called **dump()**, prints an optional status message and then calls the **dump()** function for **n**. This is used inside the **DBUG** macro in various places to illuminate the trace. **num::dump()** prints out the **num** object identifier and the current reference count for that object.

The object identifier string differentiates one object from another inside the trace. In the example shown here, the identifier has the same name as the **number** object when it is created, but because pointers can be reassigned, this can change (as will be shown in the trace). Also, temporary objects don't have ordinary identifiers, so **buildID** is used to manufacture them.

The class **num** also contains a **type** field; this is simply an integer. Each time you create a new class, you define a unique integer to identify that class; in these examples an untagged **enum** is used inside each new class to attach a more meaningful name to the number. You could also create a global **enum** with all the identifiers, but the technique shown encapsulates all the changes needed to create a new numerical data type within the new class.

The **type** field is used to compare one type to another to see if they agree; **typecheck()** performs this function. You could also redefine **typecheck()** so it knows about possible conversions—for example, that it's legal to convert an **integer** to a **floating**. Then the **cast()** function in the particular class could perform the conversion (this can be mechanized somewhat by using a table of pointers to conversion functions).

To easily show that all the **num** objects that are created are also destroyed, a **static** data member called **objcount** is created inside **num**. The debug code inside the **num** constructor increments and displays this value, and the debug code in the destructor decrements and displays the value.

Creating Specific Data Types

The **number** class only acts as a constant-size container that holds a pointer to a **num** object. However, the **num** class itself is a pure abstract base class and only acts as an interface. Thus, you can't create objects of type **num**—you must create objects of classes *derived* from **num**. This is where the real work is done, and the way you extend the interpreter is by deriving new types. That's the goal of any object-oriented design: extensibility is achieved by deriving new types from existing types and leaving the code untouched that controls the interface types.

For simplicity, this example only contains three numerical types: **integer**, **floating**, and **vector**. In addition, the only operation defined on those types is **operator+()**, just to show how it's done—all other operations follow the same framework, except for **operator=()**, which is defined in **class number**. Note that all three types are inherited from **num** so they get all its functionality and members. All three classes follow the same form: they add their particular data representations, constructors, destructors, **operator+()**, and **printstream()** functions.

The **integer** and **floating** types are virtually identical except for their data representations and that **integer** contains tracing statements. Both also include **cast()** functions, which call **typecheck()** to ensure that the arguments have identical type. If so, a "downcast" is performed, which means that a cast is forced from a more general base type to a more specific derived type (the directions "up" and "down" come from the traditional display of a class hierarchy growing down from its base class).

Normally, this is not a safe thing to do because how can you know that a **num** pointer is actually pointing to an **integer** and not a **vector**? In this case, the type is known, because it was checked by the call to **typecheck()**. The compiler will happily allow you to perform an "upcast" without an explicit cast, because it *knows* that for example a **floating** is also a **num**, but it knows nothing about the other direction, so the only way to safely downcast is if you acquire some information at run time that lets you know it is OK. If you get this information, the compiler forces you to use an explicit cast.

The **cast()** function is used inside any operation on the type that takes an argument. Instead of checking the argument and performing the downcast inside the code, the check and cast are performed once upon entry to the function by creating a pointer to the specific type and attempting to generate the address by using **cast()**. If the function fails, it returns 0, so the new pointer can be checked. If it is successful, you know it's the proper type from then on, so no cast is necessary for the rest of the function.

The vector *Class*

In many situations, if you have a new data type you want to add to the interpreter you can just embed it as a member object of a subclass of **num**, as was done with **integer** and **floating**. The **class vector** is an example of a new type built from scratch in a subclass of **num**. It's a fairly typical implementation of a vector that sizes itself when it is created (you could make it into a template for a vector that holds an arbitrary type). The constructor allocates storage for the vector in the constructor initializer list (the "pseudoconstructor call" **v(new int[sz])** assigns the result of **new** to **v**), and the destructor (which is called *first* in the chain of destructor calls for a **num**) frees the storage with **delete []v**. Note that the empty-brackets syntax is used here to force the destruction of all elements of the array, even though there is no destructor for **int**—this is a good practice to follow in case you turn the class into a template, which may be used for objects that have destructors.

The second constructor is used inside the various functions of **vector** when they want to clone a new **vector** given a pointer to an existing one; you can see it used inside **operator+()**. Notice that the **for** loop inside the two constructors and **operator+()** can be replaced with the ANSI C library function **memcpy()**, which is usually a much more efficient way to copy chunks of memory (and easier to make **inline**—some compilers have trouble doing this).

Testing the Framework

In **main()**, all the statements are traced so you can see what's going on when objects are created, destroyed, added, and assigned. When building a framework like this, it is critical you verify that it's working properly at each step, and a debugger isn't as useful as the system shown here because it doesn't produce the specific output helpful when you are trying to understand the mechanism. This trace was used to ensure that the design was correct.

The most complicated expressions are for the **integer** and **vector** types. For the **integer**s, it looks like this:

```
X = A + B + X;
```

The compiler resolves this into something like this:

```
number temp(X.operator=((A.operator+(B)).operator+(X)));
```

These are all calls to **number** functions, not **integer** functions, because the interpreter must not have to know the specific types it's manipulating. The system relies on the polymorphic calls through the **num** pointer inside the **number** object to handle the details.

The **A + B + X** is evaluated left to right. Because the **operator=()** returns a copy of itself (so you can use expressions like **A = B = X**), the compiler sets up a temporary value to receive the result.

In an expression like this, it's critical to ensure that the **num** objects are passed around, created, and destroyed properly so no **number** ends up pointing to a destroyed **num** object. You can see this is the case in an edited excerpt of the output trace:

```
X = A + B + X
(1) in number copy-constructor, X refcount = 2
(2) in number copy-constructor, B refcount = 2
```

```
(3)  in integer::operator+ for A with arg B
(4)  creating (return value of A + B)
(5)  integer constructor for (return value of A + B)
(6)  in number constructor for (return value of A + B)
     refcount = 0
(7)  (return value of A + B) refcount = 1
(8)  in ~number: B refcount = 1
(9)  in integer::operator+ for
     (return value of A + B) with arg X
(10) creating (return value of (return value of A + B) + X)
(11) integer constructor for
     (return value of (return value of A + B) + X)
(12) constructor for number
     (return value of (return value of A + B) + X)
(13) (return value of (return value of A + B) + X) refcount = 1
(14) in ~number: X refcount = 1
(15) in number::operator= with arg
     (return value of (return value of A + B) + X)
         refcount = 1
(16) n->decr_ref()
(17) destroying X
(18) n=arg.n
(19) n->incr_ref()
(20) (return value of (return value of A + B) + X) refcount = 2
(21) return number(n)
(22) constructor for number
     (return value of (return value of A + B) + X)
(23) (return value of (return value of A + B) + X) refcount = 3
(24) in ~number:
     (return value of (return value of A + B) + X) refcount = 2
(25) in ~number: (return value of (return value of A + B) + X)
     refcount = 1
(26) in ~number: destroying (return value of A + B)
(27) X is now (return value of (return value of A + B) + X)
     refcount = 1
```

To understand why **X** is passed in by value first in (1), consider what the compiler does to evaluate the expression

```
(A.operator+(B)).operator+(X)
```

When making a member function call, the compiler secretly passes the address of the object (**this**) as the first argument, so inside the compiler this function call ends up looking something like this (implying the name mangling):

```
number_operatorplus(&(A.operator+(B)), X)
```

Since arguments are pushed right to left, **X** is passed first (using the copy constructor to pass by value), and *then* the compiler discovers it must evaluate **A.operator+(B)** in order to produce the address of the current object. So it starts that process in (2) by passing **B** (again using the copy constructor). In both cases, the same physical **num** representation is used when passing the **number** by value, so you have two **number** objects—the one outside the function and the one passed into the function—pointing to the same **num**, so that **num** has a reference count of two in each case (the increment occurs in the **number** copy constructor).

In (3) through (7), a new **num** is created to hold the return value of the addition (so the arguments remain untouched), and a temporary **number** is created to be the return **number**; the constructor for this temporary is what increments the reference count to 1. You can see that the function is finished in (8) because the destructor for the local copy of **B** is called, which reduces the reference count to 1 but doesn't destroy the **num** because the original **B number** is still using it.

There's something particularly interesting happening here. You might think that the **return** statement inside **number::operator+()**

```
return number(n->operator+(arg.n));
```

would create a local temporary, construct it, copy it out to the outside temporary with the copy constructor, and then destroy the local temporary. However, you can see from the trace that none of this activity occurs by (8). The compiler is smarter than that—because it sees the constructor call in a **return** statement, it constructs the return value directly into the outside variable (in this case, the temporary **number** created by the compiler to hold the return value). This eliminates a lot of redundant creation and destruction

In (9) you can see that the return value of **A + B** has now become the current object. In (10) through (13) a new result is created that represents **A + B + X**. Again, this is constructed directly into the outside temporary that was created to hold the result, because in (14) only the local copy of **X** is destroyed. That terminates the addition expression.

In (15) you can again see something interesting occurring: the **number::operator=()** function takes its argument by value, but no copy constructor is called. You can see the same thing happen with addition if you expand the expression to something like **A + B + (X + Z)**. The temporary that is created by **(X + Z)** is *not passed in using the copy constructor*. Because the compiler builds the temporaries to evaluate the expression, it knows exactly how they are used and can take shortcuts when passing them.

In (16) through (20), you can see the assignment taking place—the old **num** reference count is decremented (it goes to 0 so it is destroyed), **n** is attached to the rvalue's **num**, and its reference count is incremented. Then the return value of **operator=()** is created, again directly into the outside temporary, in (21) through (23). This return value is never used, so the compiler immediately destroys it in (24). In (25), the temporary representing **(A + B + X)** (the result of the addition that was passed to **operator=()**) is destroyed—in both these cases, the only thing that happens is the reference count of the **num** is decremented, because **X** is still using that object. In (26) the temporary from **(A + B)** is destroyed, and in (27) you can see that **X** is now assigned to the result of the calculation, with a reference count of 1.

Here's the entire trace output of the program:

```
//: NUMTERP.OUT—Output of NUMTERP.CPP
number A(new integer(1, "A"))
creating A, count = 1
integer constructor for A
in number constructor for A rc=0
A rc=1
number B(new integer(2, "B"))
creating B, count = 2
integer constructor for B
in number constructor for B rc=0
B rc=1
number X(new integer(3, "X"))
creating X, count = 3
integer constructor for X
in number constructor for X rc=0
X rc=1
X = A + B + X
in number copy-constructor
B rc=2
in number::operator+
in integer::operator+ for A with arg B
creating
```

```
  (return val of A + B), count = 4
integer constructor for
  (return val of A + B)
in number constructor for
  (return val of A + B) rc=0
  (return val of A + B) rc=1
in number copy-constructor
X rc=2
in number::operator+
in integer::operator+ for
  (return val of A + B) with arg X
creating
  (return val of (return val of A + B) + X), count = 5
integer constructor for
  (return val of (return val of A + B) + X)
in number constructor for
  (return val of (return val of A + B) + X) rc=0
  (return val of (return val of A + B) + X) rc=1
in number::operator= with arg
  (return val of (return val of A + B) + X) rc=1
n->decr_ref()
X rc=1
n=arg.n
n->incr_ref()
  (return val of (return val of A + B) + X) rc=2
return number(n)
in number constructor for
  (return val of (return val of A + B) + X) rc=2
  (return val of (return val of A + B) + X) rc=3
in ~number:
  (return val of (return val of A + B) + X) rc=2
in ~number: destroying
  (return val of A + B), count = 4
X is now
  (return val of (return val of A + B) + X) rc=2
6
in ~number:
  (return val of (return val of A + B) + X) rc=1
in ~number: B rc=1
in ~number: destroying A, count = 3
```

By studying this and playing with the program, you'll learn more about the activities of the compiler than you ever wanted!

Building the Interpreter

This is just the framework for the interpreter, but it turns out to be the hard part. To put the rest of the interpreter together and make it easily extensible, you should use a compiler-compiler like YACC. Numerous examples exist of how to use this language to create interpreters, and you can get a free version of YACC called Bison (from the Free Software Foundation) from a number of sources including the C Users Group (2601 Iowa, Lawrence, KS 66046 (913) 841-1631). However, if you want a truly object-oriented solution, you should consider Yacc++ from Compiler Resources (3 Proctor Street, Hopkinton MA 01748 (508) 435-5016).

Makefile for Chapter 9 Examples

Here is the makefile for all the examples in this chapter:

```
# makefile for examples in Chapter 9
# Borland C++ compiler, with the following
# warnings turned off:
# aus: identifier assigned a value which is never used
# eff: code has no effect
# par: parameter "parameter" is never used
# inl: "not expanded inline" warnings
CPP = bcc -w-aus -w-eff -w-par -w-inl
# nmake CPP=cl      # Microsoft C++ command line

.cpp.exe:
        $(CPP) $<

.cpp.obj:
        $(CPP) -c $<

all: mmtrace.exe mmatrix.exe ci.exe vec.exe ref1.exe \
     ref2.exe starnew.exe numterp.exe

numterp.exe : trace.h numterp.cpp
mmatrix.exe : mmatrix.h mmatrix.cpp
mmtrace.exe : mmtrace.h trace.h mmtrace.cpp
```

CHAPTER

Containers and Templates in C++

*C*ertain types of classes just beg to be used in many situations, not just in a single case. The most common of these are *container classes*, which are used to contain other objects. You especially need container classes when creating objects on the heap using **new**—there's got to be a place to put the objects while you're using them, since you've taken over the management of object creation and destruction from the compiler and you're responsible for everything. You've seen a useful example of containers in Chapter 6: the **DynArray**, which was reused in Chapter 7. This chapter will emphasize containers, an associated concept called *iterators*, and teach you how to use the support built into C++ for creating general-purpose containers and iterators.

It becomes quite tedious to create a new container class for every type you want to store. This is especially annoying because you should only need to design the container once and then use it in various situations. This an important part of the object-oriented philosophy, so it seems like it ought to work here, too. This uncovers a definite need.

The designers of C++ were aware of this need, too. In his first edition, Stroustrup (Bjarne Stroustrup, *The C++ Programming Language*, 1st edition, Addison-Wesley 1986, sections 1.16 and 7.3.5) included the solution developed at Bell Labs. This was the creation of "generic classes" with parameters indicating what types they deal with. The *parameterization* was implemented using the preprocessor. In this chapter this method is used to create a class, called **gstackq** (which is a generic class that looks like both a stack and a queue), that can hold any other type. This *parameterized type* can then easily make a **gstackq** of (for example) **shape**s and a **gstackq** of **string**s. Once the original parameterized **gstackq** is created, you don't need to think about it anymore, you can just use it. Thus parameterized types allow you to create not a single class, but a specification for a family of classes.

Although the preprocessor approach is clever and will work with virtually any version of C++, it is painful to write and read. It is only included here so you will understand it if you encounter it in old code, not so you will write code using this technique (unless you only have an old version of C++ available!). This chapter focuses on a more modern way to create parameterized types. A feature called *templates* has been added to later versions of C++, and is part of the ANSI C++ draft. Using templates is a much easier way to create parameterized types, and it has other interesting effects that will be explored, including template functions.

First, here's an overview of the concepts of container classes.

Containers and Iterators

Container classes are made to serve; they don't have any role other than to hold objects. The only analogy in C is an array, but a container is usually much more sophisticated than an array. Generally, a container will always have some way to put things into it and take things out of it (which makes sense, since it only holds things). All other functionality is adjunct to putting in and taking out.

The way items are inserted, inspected, and removed from a container is a design issue. The first impulse when creating a container class is to make all the operations pertaining to it part of the class. Often this makes sense. For example, here's a simple container class that holds integers and contains an index to the current element:

```cpp
//: INTCONT.CPP—Simple integer container with internal index
#include <iostream.h>
#include <string.h>  // memset()

class intcontainer {
  int* array;
  int index, next_empty;
  const size;
public:
  intcontainer(int sz) : size(sz), index(0), next_empty(0) {
    array = new int[sz];
    memset(array, 0, size * sizeof(int));
  }
  ~intcontainer() { delete []array; }
  void add(int I) {
    if(next_empty < size) array[next_empty++] = I;
    else
      // error handling goes here ...
      ;
  }
  void reset() { index = 0; }
  int next() {
    if(index < next_empty) return array[index++];
    else
      // error handling goes here ...
```

```
      return array[index];
  }
  int end() const { return index >= next_empty; }
};

void main() {
  intcontainer X(20);
  for(int i = 0; i < 20; i++)
    X.add(1 << i);
  X.reset();
  while(!X.end())
    cout << X.next() << endl;
}
```

The **1 << i** provides interesting values. Can you explain why the output looks the way it does?

In the constructor, **memset()** is an ANSI C library function that sets a number of bytes (the third argument) to a value (the second argument) starting at a particular memory location (the first argument). You can use a **for** loop here, but **memset()** is usually faster, and it is a simple function call so the compiler doesn't have any trouble inlining it (most compilers can't **inline for** loops).

In the constructor, you see the following:

```
intcontainer(int sz) : size(sz), index(0), next_empty(0)
```

This *constructor initializer list* is the place to initialize all member objects (and base-class objects, if you're using inheritance). The initialization for these **int**s looks like constructor calls, even though **int** is a built-in type and not a class. This is allowed in the constructor initializer list so you can initialize all member objects, even if they're built-in types, before you enter the constructor body. That way, you know everything has been set up properly. Initialization of built-in types this way simply means assignment (with constants and references, of course, it literally means initialization).

This class works fine, and containers are often designed this way. However, what happens if you want to look at more than one spot in the container at once? Perhaps you'd like to compare elements in one part of the container with those in another part. The container fails because you cannot look at more than one place at once, and this is because the concept of manipulating or controlling the container is bound in too tightly with the container itself. There's only one index, and the user is powerless to change the situation. What's needed is a way to separate the concept of containment from the concept of control. This is sometimes called *control abstraction*, and it's accomplished with an *iterator*.

You can think of an iterator the same way you think of an array index in C. If you create an array:

```
int A[20];
```

the array simply holds elements; it has nothing to do with selecting them. You can use multiple indices like this,

```
A[I] = 100;
cout << A[X];
```

and the array has no problem with it (unlike the container class).

To solve the problem with the container, you need a separate data type that can "iterate" through the container. In effect, it must act somewhat like the simple array index in C. It would be nice to increment this iterator, have it return the current object, and have it indicate if it's at the end. Here's one way to do it for the **intcontainer**:

```
//: INTITER.CPP—Integer container with iterator
#include <iostream.h>
#include <string.h>  // memset()

class intcontain {
  int* array;
  const size;
public:
  intcontain(int sz) : size(sz) {
    array = new int[sz];
    memset(array, 0, size * sizeof(int));
  }
  ~intcontain() { delete []array; }
  friend class intiterator;
};

class intiterator {
  intcontain& container;
  int* data;
public:
  intiterator(intcontain& ic) : container(ic), data(ic.array) {}
  int end() const {  // is it at the end?
```

```
    return (data - container.array) >= container.size;
  }
  void reset() { data = container.array; } // top of list
  int operator++() {  // prefix operator
    if(!end()) {
      data++;
      return 1;
    }
    return 0;  // Means: past end of list
  }
  int operator++(int) { return operator++(); } // postfix
  operator int() const { return *data; }  // type conversion
  void insert(int X) { *data = X; }
};

void main() {
  intcontain X(20);
  intiterator I(X);
  for(int i = 0; !I.end(); I++, i++)
    I.insert(1 << i);
  I.reset();
  while(!I.end()) {
    cout << I << endl;
    I++;
  }
}
```

The container is trivial; it only initializes itself. All the control activities are now inside the iterator, which behaves somewhat like a simple integer index in a C array.

The iterator must be given permission to access the private elements inside the container. This is done with the **friend** declaration at the end of **class intcontain**. The iterator must know who it refers to, so it contains a reference to an **intcontain** called **container**. The C++ compiler ensures that a reference inside a class is initialized before it can ever be used by forcing the initialization to take place in the constructor initializer list like this:

```
intiterator(intcontain& ic) : container(ic), data(ic.array) {}
```

Again, the initialization of **data** is the same as a simple assignment—it could have been done in the constructor body. However, it is good practice to initialize all members before entering the constructor body whenever this is possible. This makes it easier to prevent "used before initialized" errors.

Prefix and Postfix

Notice the two definitions of **operator++()**. The first one is the typical, old-style version of the function. Prior to AT&T 2.1, this worked for both the prefix (**++X**) and postfix (**X++**) calls. However, to be compatible with C, sometimes you want prefix and postfix to work differently, so a second form was introduced. When the compiler sees the postfix form used, it makes a call to **operator++(int)** by passing it a single integer argument. The value of this argument is fixed by the compiler, and you always ignore it; its only use is to distinguish between prefix and postfix operators (the same is also true for **operator--()**). Here, the postfix version is simply aliased to the prefix version with an **inline** function (which means there is no overhead, since the compiler does all the substitution).

In **main()**, you can see how the two classes work. As before, the container **intcontain X** is created with a specified size. The iterator **I** is created by giving its constructor the **intcontain** object as an argument, so **I** can bind itself to **X**. From then on, all the work is done using the iterator, and the container becomes a passive vessel. Creating more than one iterator to simultaneously view other parts of the container is easy (imagine looking up several words at a time in a dictionary object so you can display them all at once on a screen).

The automatic type-conversion **operator int()** will extract an **int** from the iterator whenever it is used where an **int** is expected. This means that you can send data to **cout** by just giving the name of the iterator. Notice that **operator int()** doesn't have any return type specified; that's because its name is also its return type. This is a special case that only applies to automatic type-conversion operators.

Introducing Templates

Let's look at a very simple example of a container class that simply holds pointers to **int**s:

```
//: QUE.CPP—Very simple queue
#include <iostream.h>

class queue {
  enum { size = 10 };
  int *q[size];
  int in, out; // indexes
public:
  queue() : in(0), out(0) {}
  void add(int * i) {
    q[in++] = i;
    if(in >= size) in = 0;  // wrap
  }
  int* get() {
    if(out == in) return 0;
    int *result = q[out++];
    if(out >= size) out = 0;
    return result;
  }
};

void main() {
  int I[] = { 1, 3, 5, 7, 11, 13 };
  queue iq;
  for(int i = 0; i < sizeof(I)/sizeof(I[0]); i++)
    iq.add(&I[i]);
  for(int* p = iq.get(); p; p = iq.get())
    cout << "iq.get() = " << *p << endl;
}
```

This class creates a queue, so you can retrieve things in the same sequence you put them in.

The size of the queue is established by the enumeration **size**, which is hidden inside the class—a good thing to do so you don't "pollute" the global name space. An enumeration must be used inside a class instead of a **const**, since a **const** may have a different value for different objects. Thus it requires space, and its value cannot be used by the compiler to establish array sizes, as is done here.

The implementation of the **queue** is hidden, and it isn't really important. You could use a linked list if you wanted, and the user wouldn't see any difference in the interface. In addition, you would certainly want more error-checking code (which is left out here for the sake of brevity).

In **main()**, the test for the **queue** stores pointers, not the objects themselves. In the definition for **I**, the compiler automatically counts the number of elements in the initialization list and allocates the proper amount of memory. When printing, the **for** loop calls **get()** until a zero pointer is returned to indicate the **queue** is empty.

Now this is all very nice, but chances are you don't want to store **int**s. You probably have your own class you want to store in a container. Traditionally, you have two choices. You can take this **queue**, adapt it for your new class, and adapt it again for other new classes (and of course, make up new names for the types of queues as you go) or you can automate the process using the preprocessor to make substitutions in a big macro. This second approach was described by Stroustrup. It's a clever use of the preprocessor, but difficult to create and use and abominable to look at. Plus you can't use comments, so it's hard to understand.

Fortunately, people realized how important container classes are and that the language needs to support them directly, rather than forcing programmers to flounder around with the preprocessor. Thus the *template* was born, and is now implemented in compilers conforming to draft-ANSI C++.

Templates in C++

Templates allow you to define how a family of classes can be created. Creating a template is quite easy; you make a class using an unspecified type (call it **T**, here) wherever appropriate and then precede the class declaration with

```
template<class T>
```

When defining a member function outside the class declaration, you must give the compiler the same notification and you must follow the class name with the type. The beginning of a definition looks like this:

```
template<class T> returntype classname<T>::membername(arglist) {
```

Whenever you define an object of a class, you must specify the type using the same angle-bracket syntax, like this:

```
classname<type> object_identifier(arglist);
```

That's all there is to it. The compiler takes care of all the details for you: it creates all the necessary definitions whenever it sees you use a new type, and it makes sure there are no multiple definitions if you use the same type in two different files. This process of creating a class from a template is called *instantiation*. You can create class templates just like any other class (you can use comments, for example). The only significant difference is that the compiler doesn't perform error analysis on the template until you actually instantiate one. For this reason, some people suggest creating an ordinary class before turning it into a template. However, this isn't as critical as when using macros, because when you do instantiate a template, the compiler can go right back to the template declaration and show you exactly where the error is.

Here's a simple example showing the syntax of a template:

```
//: SIMTEMPL.CPP—Very simple use of templates
#include <iostream.h>

template<class T>
class Array {
  T* a;
  int size;
public:
  Array(int);
  T& operator[](int index);
};

template<class T>
Array<T>::Array(int sz) : a(new T[size = sz]) {
  for(int i = 0; i < size; i++)
    a[i] = 0;
}

template<class T>
T& Array<T>::operator[](int index) {
  if(index >= 0 && index < size)
    return a[index];
```

```
    clog << "Array::operator[] index out of bounds\n";
    return *new T;   // throw-away object on heap
    // (assumes a default constructor)
}

void main() {
  Array<int> I(10);   // Template "instantiation"
  for(int i = 1; i < 11; i++) {
    I[i] = (2 << i);
    cout << I[i] << endl;
  }
}
```

The template for **class Array** can hold any type (including, as you can
see in **main()**, a built-in type like **int**). The constructor allocates a
specified number of **T** pointers and initializes them to 0. The overloaded
operator[] returns a reference to an arbitrary type, so you can both read
and write into the array. Notice the definition of **operator[]**, however. It
performs error checking so you cannot travel out of bounds. If you do, it
logs the error into the **iostream clog** (which prints the error out at a later
time).

This brings up an interesting aside. When, in a container class, you
are supposed to return a reference to an object, what happens when you
cannot locate a valid object? The compiler demands that you return a
reference to an object, since that's what you told it you were going to do
when you gave it the function's return value. One alternative is to make
a special, static "dud" object as a private member of the class. This dud
can be given error information when it is created, so anyone receiving it
can discover that it's the dud value and something has gone wrong.
However, that presumes you know enough about the type you're using
to set up the dud properly. In a parameterized type, it's best to make as
few assumptions as possible about the type you're manipulating. It's
often safe, however, to assume there is a default constructor for the type
(a constructor with no arguments or with all default arguments). Making
that assumption, when an error is encountered, it's logged and the
following return value is used in this statement:

```
return *new T;
```

Notice that since this is a return by reference, an address and not a copy
is used (so the problem described in Chapter 9 doesn't occur here).

This returns a reference to a valid object, but the object isn't part of the array, as the user might expect. If the user goes on to read or assign to that value, it won't be in the array. In addition, the user doesn't know that this object was created on the free store with **new**, and will thus not know to delete it. This is definitely not the correct behavior. However, the error message was logged and will show up. Since there's already a problem, you shouldn't necessarily expect perfect behavior on the part of the program from then on. Your goal should be to get the message out, and if the program only limps along after that, so what? It's broken. This way, you may get more information than if the program simply printed one message and then terminated. Of course, when exception handling is implemented, you'll have an alternate way to return from a function, and you won't have to worry about returning a dud value.

A Very Simple String Class

To make the examples more interesting, let's use a very simple string class:

```cpp
//: OSTRING.H—Very simple string class
#ifndef OSTRING_H_
#define OSTRING_H_
#include <string.h>
#include <stdlib.h>
#include <iostream.h>

class String {
  char *s;
public:
  String(char * S = "") : s(strdup(S)) {}
  // copy constructor:
  String(const String& rv) : s(strdup(rv.s)) {}
  void operator=(const String& rv) {
    free(s);
    s = strdup(rv.s);
  }
  ~String() { free(s); }
  operator const char*() const { return s; }
  friend ostream& operator<<(ostream& os, const String& S) {
    return os << S.s;
  }
  void print(char* msg = "") {
    cout << msg << s << endl;
```

```
    }
};

#endif // OSTRING_H_
```

The constructor duplicates the **char*** (in the constructor initializer list), and the destructor releases the memory with **free()**, not delete, since **strdup()** uses **malloc()**. Note that you can use **malloc()** and **free()** alongside **new** and **delete**, but never on the same piece of memory!

The copy constructor **String(String&)** is used if a **String** is ever passed or returned by value. This constructor tells the compiler how to make a copy of the **String**, since otherwise it would just copy the structure directly (sometimes called a *bitwise copy*) and you'd end up with two pointers looking at the same physical memory on the heap. This gets very confusing when one of them destroys the memory, so the **String** just takes the safe approach and makes a new copy on the heap for every **String** in existence.

The **operator=()** is just like the copy constructor, except its **lvalue** is an object that already has a value and a piece of memory on the heap. This memory must be destroyed before getting new memory to make a copy of the object on the right side of the = sign. You can find out more about the copy constructor and **operator=()** in Chapter 9.

The **operator char*()** performs automatic type conversion. Whenever you use an object of type **String** in a function that wants a **char***, the compiler automatically converts the object by calling **operator char*()**. Notice there is no return value specified, because the name of the operator is the return value.

The **operator<<()** function isn't a member function at all! Even though it's declared and defined inside the class body, the keyword **friend** makes it an ordinary global function, not a member function. The **friend** also says that this function has special permission to access private elements of **String**. This function is an example of how you make your own **operator<<()** for iostreams. The first argument is what appears on the left side of the << (this is a global function, remember, so there are two arguments). The second argument is what appears on the right side. This function will be matched by the compiler if it sees an **ostream** on the left, followed by <<, followed by a **String** on the right. All the function does is send the contents of the **String** to the **ostream** and return the **ostream** (so it can be used in chained expressions).

A Queue Template

Here's the queue implemented with templates:

```cpp
//: QUE2.CPP—Simple queue using templates
#include <iostream.h>
#include "ostring.h"

template<class T> class queue {
  enum { size = 10 };
  T *q[size];
  int in, out; // indexes
public:
  queue() : in(0), out(0) {}
  void add(T * i) {
    q[in++] = i;
    if(in >= size) in = 0;  // wrap
  }
  T* get() {
    if(out == in) return 0;
    T *result = q[out++];
    if(out >= size) out = 0;
    return result;
  }
};

void main() {
  int I[] = { 1, 3, 5, 7, 11, 13 };
  queue<int> iq;  // an int queue
  for(int i = 0; i < sizeof(I)/sizeof(I[0]); i++)
    iq.add(&I[i]);
  for(int* p = iq.get(); p; p = iq.get())
    cout << "iq.get() = " << *p << endl;

  String S[] = { "this", "is", "a", "queue", "too" };
  queue<String> sq; // a string queue
  for(i = 0; i < sizeof(S)/sizeof(S[0]); i++)
    sq.add(&S[i]);
  for(String* sp = sq.get(); sp; sp = sq.get())
    cout << "sq.get() = " << *sp << endl;
}
```

That's all there is to it. Now if you want to create a new type of queue, it's trivial. Here's how to create the **int** queue from before:

```cpp
queue<int> iq;
```

You can also make a queue for **String**s:

```
queue<String> sq;
```

These are both tested inside **main()**.

Parameterized Types with the Preprocessor

The original parameterized types used preprocessor macros, which is why they didn't catch on so well. It's tedious to create and debug these kinds of parameterized types, and it requires a bit of extra understanding on the part of the user. It was definitely better than nothing, and you will no doubt see the macro forms of parameterized types in some older pieces of code. Thus, it's helpful to look at and understand how they work (but you shouldn't use the preprocessor approach to write new parameterized types unless you can't get your hands on a compiler that supports templates).

The goal here is to create, for example, a macro that makes a specific type of **gstackq**, given a parameter. The user will have to do this:

```
declare(gstackq, String)
```

to make available a type of **gstackq** that holds string objects. Of course, this will only declare the new type, but it won't make any objects of that type. You have to do this in the place you'd normally make an object. But you must also specify the specific type of the stack (that is, you must tell the compiler this is the type of **gstackq** that holds **String**s) like this:

```
gstackq(String) strstack;
```

This creates a new object called **strstack**. Notice how the syntax for the definition of a parameterized type using macros is very similar to the template form—templates have angle braces where macros use parentheses. This was intentional, so there would be very little syntax change when going from macros to templates.

The preprocessor must do a lot of name pasting to keep everything distinct. It has to create something the compiler will accept, which is just an ordinary name.

The easiest way to create a parameterized type is to start with an ordinary class, get it to work the way you want, and then convert it to a macro. Two things must be observed when doing this. First, comments cannot be placed inside macros (which of course makes the code harder to understand). Second, debugging is much harder after you've turned it into a macro, since the macro is preprocessed onto a single line and the compiler just gives you an error for that line. One approach to debugging is to run the preprocessor, go into the intermediate file, and put line breaks in appropriate places in the expanded macro. When you run the compiler on the intermediate file, you'll get a more meaningful error message.

For the **gstackq**, let's look at an ordinary implementation first. This is a stack designed to hold strings:

```
//: STACKQ.CPP—Works like a stack and a queue.
//. Implemented as a singly linked list. Note: incrementing
//. the iterator moves down from top of stack!
#include <iostream.h>
#include <string.h>
#include <stdlib.h>
#include "ostring.h"
#pragma warn -inl  // ignore "not expanded inline" warnings

// a stack/queue container for strings:
class String_stackq {
  // A nested type:
  struct String_node { // a link in the list
    String * obj;  // the data
    String_node * next; // next link in the list
    String_node(String* o, String_node * n) : obj(o), next(n) {}
  };
  String_node *head;
public:
  String_stackq() : head(0) {}  // create an empty list
  void push(String* t) {  head = new String_node(t, head); }
  String* pop() {  // pop from the top of the list
    if(head) {
      String_node* old = head;
      String* retval = old->obj;
      head = head->next;
```

```
        delete old;
        return retval;
      }
      else
        return 0;
    }
  String* pull() {  // pull from the end of the queue
    if(!head) return 0;
    String_node* cursor = head;
    String* retval;
    if(head->next == 0) {
      head = 0;
      retval = cursor->obj;
      delete cursor;
      return retval;
    }
    while(cursor->next != 0)
      cursor = cursor->next;
    retval = cursor->obj;
    String_node* previous = head;
    while(previous->next != cursor)
      previous = previous->next;
    previous->next = 0;
    delete cursor;
    return retval;
  }
  friend class String_stackq_iterator;
};

// an iterator to look inside the list:
class String_stackq_iterator {
  String_stackq::String_node *current;  // full nesting
  String_stackq &stack;
public:
  String_stackq_iterator(String_stackq& sl)
    : stack(sl), current(sl.head) {} // init to the head
  String* operator++() {
    if(current) current = current->next;
    return current ? current->obj : 0;
  }
  // Post-increment form:
  String* operator++(int) { return operator++(); }
  void reset() { current = stack.head; }
  // Automatic type conversion:
  operator String*() {
    return current ? current->obj : 0;
  }
```

```cpp
  // "Smart pointer":
  String* operator->() {
    return current ? current->obj : 0;
  }
  int remove() {
    if(!current) return 0;
    if(current == stack.head) return (int)stack.pop();
    String_stackq::String_node* cursor = stack.head;
    while(cursor->next != current) cursor = cursor->next;
    cursor->next = current->next;
    delete current;
    return 1;
  }
};

char* test[] = {
"Hello", "this", "is", "a", "test",
"to", "see", "if", "it", "works"
};

const size = sizeof(test)/sizeof(test[0]);

main() {
  String_stackq X;
  for(int i = 0; i < size; i++)
    X.push(new String(test[i]));
  String* tp = X.pop();
  while(tp) {
    tp->print();
    delete tp;
    tp = X.pop();
  }
  for(i = 0; i < size; i++)
    X.push(new String(test[i]));
  tp = X.pull();
  while(tp) {
    tp->print();
    delete tp;
    tp = X.pull();
  }
  for(i = 0; i < size; i++)
    X.push(new String(test[i]));
  String_stackq_iterator I(X);
  ++I; ++I;   // preincrement
  cout << "removing: ";
  I->print();   // uses "smart pointer"
  cout << endl;
```

```
I.remove();
I.reset();
while(I) {
  I->print();
  I++;  // post-increment
}
return 0;
}
```

Key Points

Pragmas

Notice the expression **#pragma warn -inl** in STACKQ.CPP. A *pragma* expresses some nonstandard feature about a compiler. In this case, it tells the Borland C++ compiler not to generate warning messages about not expanding **inline** functions. A **pragma** is ignored by the compiler if it doesn't understand the directive, which means it is easier to port code from one compiler to another while using the specific bells and whistles of a particular compiler.

The container class is called **String_stackq**. It is not a parameterized type—you're not there yet. This is only a container for **Strings**. Internally, it has the form of a linked list because a linked list can expand and contract easily. Of course, you could also implement it some other way and do your expansion and contraction in big chunks (this might be more efficient).The **String_node** is a single link in the linked list, and it is created as a nested class.

Nested classes have several implementations, depending on the version of C++ you are using. Pre-AT&T 2.0-conforming compilers don't allow nested classes; AT&T 2.0-conforming compilers allow nesting, but the nested class is treated as if it were declared globally. In AT&T 2.1-conforming compilers and on, the nested class is treated as you would expect from the syntax; that is, the class declaration is an element of the enclosing class and is subject to the scoping and privacy rules of any other element of the class.

This means if you have a nested class,

```
struct X {
    struct Y {};
};
```

and you want to create a Y object, you must use scoping, as follows:

```
X::Y yy;
```

String_stackq *Member Functions*

There are only four member functions for the **String_stackq**: a constructor that creates an empty stack, **push()** to put a new element on the top of the stack, **pop()** to remove an element from the top of the stack, and **pull()** to remove an element from the other end of the stack so it looks like a first-in, first-out (FIFO) queue. All these functions perform the "usual" activities involved in maintaining a linked list. You might have to stare at them for a while or put some print statements in if you haven't experienced a linked list before.

The most succinct of these functions is **push()**, which reads as follows:

```
head = new String_node(t, head);
```

This creates a new node using the information you give it in **t**, and links it into the top of the list all in one motion. The trick is that it's using the constructor for **String_node** to perform all the initialization and handing the constructor the old **head** to use for its **next** pointer. The newly created object is then assigned to **head**, which links it in to the top of the list, and this effects the "push."

The **pop()** function has it easy, since it is removing the element at the head of the list. The hard job in a singly linked list is removing an element somewhere else than the head, which is what **pull()** must do. The problem is that you must unthread the element from the list: you've got to find the element whose **next** points to the removed element. In a doubly linked list, this would be easy—you'd just look backward using the "previous" link (which you don't have). However, in a singly linked list you can only look forward, so the only way to find the element whose **next** points to you is to start back at the beginning of the list and move down it, examining each **next** pointer. How efficient this is compared to maintaining a doubly linked list depends both on the size of the list and how often you remove elements from the middle. It's convenient to have both the singly and doubly linked versions in your class library so you can determine the most efficient one.

stackq *Iterator*

The **String_stackq** is not so "pure" as the **intcontain** and **intiterator** pair shown earlier. In particular, **String_stackq** has a way to **push()**, **pop()**, and **pull()**. This doesn't violate good design simply because there can be only one "top" for a stack, and one "bottom" for a queue, so you don't need more than one way to look at it. Indeed, if you're only using this class as a stack or a queue, you won't need an iterator at all. The iterator adds the ability to look at and manipulate elements in the middle of the list.

Most of the elements in **String_stackq_iterator** are similar to those in **intiterator**—the constructor, the two forms of **operator++()**, the **reset()** function, and automatic type conversion via the **operator string*()**. In addition, there are two other functions: **operator->()** (the so-called *smart pointer*) and **remove()**, which unlinks an element from anywhere in the list.

The smart pointer is useful as a syntactic device—it allows you to treat an object as a pointer. It also gives you access to the operation so you can insert your own error-checking code or any other manipulation you desire. Here, if a **String_stackq_iterator** is treated as a pointer by dereferencing it with the **->**, the compiler will call the **operator->()** function. **operator->()** must return either a pointer to another class (which is what happens here, by returning a pointer to the contained class) or an object or reference that has an **operator->()**. The compiler will automatically do a whole sequence of dereferences. In this case, the returned **String*** will be produced and that will in turn be dereferenced, all in a single statement.

You can see this used in **main()**, in the following statement:

```
I->print();
```

This gets the **string*** that **I** is currently pointing to and it calls **print()**. You can see how much more pleasant the syntax becomes in some situations when using smart pointers.

The other function of interest is **remove()**. This deals with the same problem encountered in **String_stackq::pull()**: how do you remove an element that is not at the top of a singly linked list? The answer for both functions is that you must start at the top of the stack and hunt through it until you find the element *behind* the one you want to remove. First, of course, you must check to see that:

1. You're pointing at a valid element. If not, do nothing.

2. You're not at the head of the stack. If so, just use the **pop()** function.

At this point, do the following:

1. Create a **String_node*** (notice the scope resolution to handle full nesting) and set it to the top of the stack.

2. Start moving through the stack, looking to see if the **next** pointer is identical to the element you want to remove.

3. Once a match occurs, you can thread the previous element's **next** past you to point to the current element's **next**, thus removing the current element from the list. The same logic described here for **remove()** also applies to **pull()** (although the latter function must also return the contents of the element it pulled).

Here's what a removal looks like in a singly linked list:

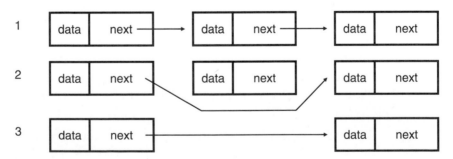

The tests performed in STACKQ.CPP's **main()** ensure that the **String_stackq** and associated iterator work properly. An array of character strings is used to fill the **String_stackq X**, and these are popped and printed. The process is then repeated but using the **pull()** function instead. (Notice that in both cases you are responsible for calling **delete()** for the objects when you're finished with them—the container doesn't take any responsibility for the lifetime of the objects it contains.) Finally, a **String_stackq_iterator** is created and exercised by removing an element from the middle of the list. It is also used to travel through the list and print the elements (using its smart pointer).

Parameterizing the stackq

Now you have a nicely working, debugged stack/queue with an iterator. But alas, it only works for the silly **String** class, so it isn't very useful for general programming. Here's where parameterization is critical for reusing containers and iterators. If you can create something that contains not a **String**, but an arbitrary type to be determined later, you will have a container and iterator that can easily be reused in many situations. That's the goal.

Preprocessor Parameterized Types

First, the problem will be solved the "old" way, using the macros in **generic.h** (a standard **include** file that comes with your compiler). To do this, you must turn the entire class into a macro and replace all the instances of **String** with the place holder for the type parameter (just called **type**, here). In the process of turning it into a macro, you must remove all comments (an unfortunate side effect). Here's what it looks like:

```
//: GSTACKQ.H—Generic singly linked list
//. works like a stack and a queue. Use like this:
//. class yourtype { /* your type body */ };
//. declare(gstackq, yourtype)   // creates the class
//. gstackq(yourtype) X;          // makes an object
//. gstackq_iterator(yourtype) I(X);  // makes an iterator
//. X.push(new yourtype(args));  // adds one
//. yourtype * yt = X.pop();      // gets one off the top
//. yt = X.pull();                // gets one off the bottom
//. Note: incrementing iterator moves down from top of stack!
//. Also: your compiler may not fully support nested classes.
#pragma warn -inl  // ignore "not expanded inline" warnings
#ifndef GSTACKQ_H_
```

```
#define GSTACKQ_H_
#ifndef TEMPLATES  // if templates aren't available...
#include <generic.h>  // use generic macros

#define gstackq(type) name2(type, gstackq)
#define node(type) name2(type, node)
#define gstackq_iterator(type) name2(type, gstackq_iterator)

// Can't have comments inside a macro!
#define gstackqdeclare(type)                                      \
class gstackq(type) {                                             \
  struct node(type) {                                            \
    type * obj;                                                  \
    node(type) * next;                                          \
    node(type)(type* o, node(type) * n) : obj(o), next(n) {}   \
  };                                                             \
  node(type) *head;                                             \
public:                                                          \
  gstackq(type)() : head(0) {}                                  \
  void push(type* t) {  head = new node(type)(t, head); }       \
  type* pop() {                                                  \
    if(head) {                                                   \
      node(type)* old = head;                                   \
      type* retval = old->obj;                                  \
      head = head->next;                                        \
      delete old;                                               \
      return retval;                                            \
    }                                                            \
    else                                                         \
      return 0;                                                  \
  }                                                              \
  type* pull() {                                                 \
    if(!head) return 0;                                          \
    node(type)* cursor = head;                                  \
    type* retval;                                               \
    if(head->next == 0) {                                       \
      head = 0;                                                  \
      retval = cursor->obj;                                     \
      delete cursor;                                            \
      return retval;                                            \
    }                                                            \
    while(cursor->next != 0)                                    \
      cursor = cursor->next;                                    \
    retval = cursor->obj;                                       \
    node(type)* previous = head;                               \
    while(previous->next != cursor)                             \
      previous = previous->next;                                \
```

```
      previous->next = 0;                                          \
      delete cursor;                                               \
      return retval;                                               \
    }                                                              \
friend class gstackq_iterator(type);                               \
};                                                                 \
                                                                   \
class gstackq_iterator(type) {                                     \
  gstackq(type)::node(type) *current;                              \
  gstackq(type) &stack;                                            \
public:                                                            \
  gstackq_iterator(type)(gstackq(type)& sl)                        \
    : stack(sl), current(sl.head) {}                               \
  type* operator++() {                                             \
    if(current) current = current->next;                           \
    return current ? current->obj : 0;                             \
  }                                                                \
  type* operator++(int) { return operator++(); }                  \
  void reset() { current = stack.head; }                           \
  operator type*() {                                               \
    return current ? current->obj : 0;                             \
  }                                                                \
  type* operator->() {                                             \
    return current ? current->obj : 0;                             \
  }                                                                \
  int remove() {                                                   \
    if(!current) return 0;                                         \
    if(current == stack.head) return (int)stack.pop();             \
    gstackq(type)::node(type)* cursor = stack.head;                \
    while(cursor->next != current) cursor = cursor->next;          \
    cursor->next = current->next;                                  \
    delete current;                                                \
    return 1;                                                      \
  }                                                                \
};

// To be continued ...
```

The backslash is required at the end of every line in a macro to continue the macro (it puts the entire macro on a single line!). Notice there is a preprocessor statement (after the usual "header file insulation") that tests to see if **TEMPLATES** is defined. If your compiler supports C++ templates, you should **#define TEMPLATES** before including this header file (you can also do it on the compiler command line), so you use the template version of this class instead. You'll see this later, in the second half of this file.

Generic Macros for Parameterized Types

Old-style parameterized types are built using the "generic" macros in the C++ header file **generic.h**. Here's what they look like:

```
// token-pasting macros
#define name2(z, y)      name2_x(z, y)
#define name2_x(z, y)    z##y
// macros for declaring and implementing classes
#define declare(z, y) name2(z, declare)(y)
#define implement(z, y) name2(z, implement)(y)
```

The macros require an extra level of indirection because of the way the ANSI C preprocessor works.

In addition to the macros in **generic.h**, you must also define several others to create the parameterized type. The simplest one, shown here, creates the full type name:

```
#define gstackq(type) name2(type,gstackq)
```

This turns **gstackq(string)** into **stringgstackq**, a unique name for the new type.

The creator of the parameterized type must supply this macro and at least one other: the macro that makes the specific class. Here's the beginning of the macro:

```
#define gstackqdeclare(type) \
class gstackq(type) {  \
```

The rest of the macro is just like a regular class declaration, except you use the argument **type** every place you want the parameter to be used (as an argument or return value, for example). Notice that the preprocessor will also expand the **gstackq(type)** macro to generate the proper identifier for the class.

Now if you call the macro **declare(gstackq, String)**, the following happens: first, the preprocessor expands the **declare** macro to

```
name2(gstackq, declare)(String)
```

Then it expands the **name2** macro to produce

```
gstackqdeclare(String)
```

which is finally expanded to the full class declaration, with **String** replacing **type** everywhere. The advantage of using this system is you have a consistent syntax when declaring all of your parameterized types.

If you can create the class with all **inline** functions, then the **gstackqdeclare()** macro (or its equivalent for your particular class) is all that is necessary. However, if you need to create non-inline functions, you must do similar work for the **implement()** macro so that all the member functions are defined. This can cause problems if the class is used the same way in different files of the same project; the linker will give multiple-definition errors (another problem that templates solve).

The **name2** macro is used to create the three macros **gstackq(type)**, **node(type)**, and **gstackq_iterator(type)**. The end user uses these macros to refer to stacks and iterators specified to handle a specific type. For example, a **gstackq** designed to hold a **String** is referred to as **gstackq(String)**. The **name2** macro turns this into the internal name **Stringgstackq** (which you never have to use, since you should always use the macro form).

Throughout the **gstackqdeclare()** macro, the specific **String** has been replaced with the generic type. However, any type within the macro that is itself parameterized must use a macro to generate its full name; for example, **node(type)**.

That's all there is to creating a macro. It seems simple enough, but it is usually much more annoying because the preprocessor is involved, so its actions are out of the control of the compiler. If an error occurs, it's hard to find, and if you want to add a new feature to your parameterized type you must modify the macro and then debug it inside the macro (which is a particular problem, since the entire macro ends up on one line, so the compiler will give you a single line number for something that contains many "real" lines of code). The creation and use of parameterized types is much easier and more robust using templates.

gstackq *as a Template*

Now consider how **gstackq** should look when using templates. This is the continuation of **gstackq.h**, which is a single header file that creates

gstackq as both a generic type (for those compilers that don't have templates) and as a template (for those that do).

```
//: GSTACKQ.H—File continued; alternative using templates

#else // templates available

template<class type> class gstackq {
  struct node {
    type * obj;
    node * next;
    node(type* o, node * n) : obj(o), next(n) {}
  };
public:
  node *head;
public:
  gstackq() : head(0) {}
  void push(type* t) {  head = new node(t, head); }
  type* pop() {
    if(head) {
      node* old = head;
      type* retval = old->obj;
      head = head->next;
      delete old;
      return retval;
    }
    else
      return 0;
  }
  type* pull() {
    if(!head) return 0;
    node* cursor = head;
    type* retval;
    if(head->next == 0) {
      head = 0;
      retval = cursor->obj;
      delete cursor;
      return retval;
    }
    while(cursor->next != 0)
      cursor = cursor->next;
    retval = cursor->obj;
    node* previous = head;
    while(previous->next != cursor)
      previous = previous->next;
    previous->next = 0;
```

```
      delete cursor;
      return retval;
   }
friend class gstackq_iterator<type>;
};

template<class type> class gstackq_iterator {
   gstackq<type>::node *current;   // For full nesting
   // node * current;   // pre AT&T 2.1 nesting
   gstackq<type> &stack;
public:
   gstackq_iterator(gstackq<type>& sl)
      : stack(sl), current(sl.head) {}
   type* operator++() {
      if(current) current = current->next;
      return current ? current->obj : 0;
   }
   type* operator++(int) { return operator++(); }
   void reset() { current = stack.head; }
   operator type*() {
      return current ? current->obj : 0;
   }
   type* operator->() {
      return current ? current->obj : 0;
   }
   int remove() {
      if(!current) return 0;
      if(current == stack.head) return (int)stack.pop();
      gstackq<type>::node* cursor = stack.head;
      while(cursor->next != current) cursor = cursor->next;
      cursor->next = current->next;
      delete current;
      return 1;
   }
};

#endif // TEMPLATES
#endif // GSTACKQ_H_
```

Notice that it's almost identical to the version using generic macros, but it's a lot easier to read and understand. It takes the parameterization that you've just seen using preprocessor macros and brings it into the realm of the C++ compiler, where it is vastly easier to write, use, and debug parameterized types. There's another benefit: it's much easier for people who make browsers to include a template in their class database. Macros are very difficult to detect when building a browser!

While it has been suggested that you use the process shown earlier to create templates (create an ordinary class; then convert it) it is easily conceivable that you can create a template from scratch, whereas it would be a nightmare to create a macro-based parameterized type from scratch. In addition, templates have other interesting abilities: you can use nonclass arguments to templates (such as an **int**) and you can create function templates that instantiate ordinary functions. You'll see some of the uses of these later.

Testing gstackq

Here's a test program that reproduces the actions of STACKQ.CPP. The program exercises the generic macro or the template, depending on whether you leave in or comment out the **#define TEMPLATES** line:

```
//: STACKTST.CPP—Test for gstackq generic type
//#define TEMPLATES
#include "gstackq.h"
#include <new.h>
#include <iostream.h>
#include <string.h>
#include <stdlib.h>
#include "ostring.h"

char* test[] = {
"Hello", "this", "is", "a", "test",
"to", "see", "if", "it", "works"
};

const size = sizeof(test)/sizeof(test[0]);

#ifndef TEMPLATES
declare(gstackq, String);
#endif

void main() {
#ifdef TEMPLATES
  gstackq<String> X;
#else
  gstackq(String) X;
#endif
  for(int i = 0; i < size; i++)
    X.push(new String(test[i]));
  String* tp = X.pop();
```

```
  while(tp) {
    tp->print();
    delete tp;
    tp = X.pop();
  }
  for(i = 0; i < size; i++)
    X.push(new String(test[i]));
  tp = X.pull();
  while(tp) {
    tp->print();
    delete tp;
    tp = X.pull();
  }
  for(i = 0; i < size; i++)
    X.push(new String(test[i]));
#ifdef TEMPLATES
  gstackq_iterator<String> I(X);
#else
  gstackq_iterator(String) I(X);
#endif
  ++I; ++I;
  cout << "removing: ";
  I->print();  // uses "smart pointer"
  cout << endl;
  I.remove();
  I.reset();
  while(I) {
    I->print();
    I++;
  }
}
```

The file is very similar to STACKQ.CPP, except for the **#ifdef**s to do the appropriate thing, depending on whether macros or templates are used. Notice that when templates are used, no declaration corresponding to the **declare()** macro is necessary. The compiler automatically handles the declaration and implementation (that is, the instantiation) of the specific type whenever it sees you using it. In addition, using templates of the same type in different files will not cause multiple definition errors; these are resolved for you.

The **gstackq** class was created after many attempts at building reusable container classes. Since it has the effect of being a stack, a queue, and a linked list all at once, you should find it a useful, general-purpose tool.

Template Arguments

A template can have multiple arguments, and the arguments to a template don't have to be classes. You can also use built-in types. This is helpful in the following program, which uses an **int** template argument to determine the size of a buffer, making it more efficient:

```
//: ARGS.CPP—Template arguments can be built-in types
//. Here, sz is treated as a genuine const inside the class
#include <iostream.h>
#include <stdlib.h>

template<class T, int sz> class buffer {
  T v[sz];  // automatic array initialization
  void error(char * msg = "") {
    clog << endl<< "buffer error: " << msg << endl;
    exit(1);
  }
public:
  T& operator[](int index) {
    if(index < 0 || index >= sz) error("out of bounds");
    return v[index];
  }
  void dump(char * msg = "");
};

// defining a template function outside the class:
template<class T, int sz> void buffer<T,sz>::dump(char * msg) {
  if(*msg) cout << msg;
  for(int i = 0; i < sz; i++)
    v[i].print();  // it doesn't know whether "print()" exists!
}

struct Char {
  char c;
  Char(char C = 0) : c(C) {}
  void print() { cout << c; }
};

void main() {
  buffer<Char, 20> buf1;
  buffer<Char, 20> buf3;
  buffer<Char, 100> buf4;
```

```
//  buf1 = buf4;  // error

  buf1[0] = 'h';  // overloaded operator[]
  buf1[1] = 'e';
  buf1[2] = 'l';
  buf1[3] = 'l';
  buf1[4] = 'o';
  buf3 = buf1;  // operator= automatically generated
  buf3.dump();
  buf1[21] = 'x';  // out of bounds
}
```

The **operator[]** calls **error()** if the index is out of bounds, and **error()** aborts the program. This is an alternative to the previous method of returning an anonymous value created on the heap. It has the advantage of terminating the program right away, but the disadvantage that you don't get to see how many times the program goes out of bounds before finishing.

In the definition for **buffer<T,sz>::dump()**, notice that all the arguments must be given inside the angle brackets when creating a non-inline definition, even if those arguments aren't used inside the function. The arguments are required so the compiler can generate the proper name (similar to what the macros were doing).

Since **T v[sz]** inside buffer is an array of objects, not an array of pointers, the default constructor (the constructor with no arguments, or with all default arguments) is called for every object in the array. This means that all objects of **struct Char** will be initialized to 0 by their constructor when **Char** is used as the first argument to a buffer template.

Now you can see something a little more subtle. If the arguments between two instantiations of a template don't match exactly, you have two completely different types! This makes sense, as you can see in **main()**. If **buffer<Char, 20>** were the same as **buffer<Char, 100>,** then, when you went to copy one to the other, it would be a disaster because the two objects are of different sizes! Thus the statement **buf1 = buf4** generates a compiler error message.

However, it is possible to assign **buf3 = buf1**, and the proper behavior occurs (bitwise copy) even though there is no explicit **operator=()**! This is because the C++ compiler will automatically generate default versions of two functions: **operator=()** and the copy constructor (which would be **buffer(buffer&)** in this case). It turned out that the lack of these functions

const *in Classes*

In an ordinary array, you can use a **const** in C++ (not in C) to determine the size of the array. The compiler will perform the substitution of the **const** for you. However, inside a class the concept of **const** changes its meaning: it becomes a value that cannot be changed and occupies storage (just like the meaning in C). Thus, the compiler cannot know the value of the **const** at compile time (because you may want different **const** values in different objects), which means you cannot use it in an array definition inside a class. Before templates, you had two ways to solve this problem. You could either use a **const** outside the class (not so great, because you then pollute the global name space) or use an untagged **enum** inside the class, like this:

```
class X {
  enum { sz = 10; }
  int Z[sz];
// ...
```

Now **sz** is a name that is local to the class and is treated by the compiler as a true constant.

With templates, you have a third way to create a constant inside a class. The template argument **sz** will be substituted, using its actual value, inside the template by the compiler. This is quite nice because it means you can determine the size of the object at compile time with an argument to the template, and put the entire object on the stack, instead of determining the size at run time and putting part of it on the heap (plus the overhead involved in calling **new**). Of course, it's also a limit—you no longer have the choice of making different-sized objects at run time.

caused so much difficulty and confusion (because they are needed in situations where you either assume they're there, or don't expect them to be needed) that it was necessary for the compiler to generate them automatically. If you need a more sophisticated copy constructor or **operator=()**, you can write it yourself, and the compiler won't generate it for you.

The queue *Template with a Size Argument*

You can also modify the simple queue class that you saw earlier so it takes a size argument, as follows:

```
//: QUE3.CPP—Simple queue with integer template argument
//. Shows non-inline function definitions

template<class T, int size> class queue {
  T *q[size];
  int in, out; // indexes
public:
  queue() : in(0), out(0) {}
  void add(T * i);
  T* get();
};

template<class T, int size>
void queue<T, size>::add(T * i) {
  q[in++] = i;
  if(in >= size) in = 0; // wrap
}

template<class T, int size>
T* queue<T, size>::get() {
  if(out == in) return 0;
  T *result = q[out++];
  if(out >= size) out = 0;
  return result;
}

void main() {
  queue<float, 10> fq1, fq2;
  queue<float, 11> fq3;
  fq1 = fq2;  // OK—same type
//  fq3 = fq1;  // error—different type
}
```

The previous comments concerning type equivalence also apply here.

Templates and Hardware

The ability to use a nonclass type in a template suggests another use, and the solution to a problem that has plagued hardware-oriented folks ever since C++ came out. It seems that you ought to be able to make an object that represents a piece of hardware—in effect, an object that "sits" on a particular piece of hardware—by knowing that hardware's I/O address or memory-mapped I/O address. Then if you had a bunch of similar hardware, sitting in different locations, you could just make an object for each location. Although it's possible to do this in a crude fashion by storing the hardware address in the object, this isn't very efficient (especially when the compiler uses a macro to write directly to I/O ports), and it never seemed quite "right." However, with templates you can do this:

```
//: HARDWARE.CPP—Templates and fixed hardware locations

template<int address> class UART {
public:
  UART() { /* initialize hardware */ }
  void send(unsigned char byte) {
      *(unsigned char*)address = byte;
  }
};

void main() {
  UART<0x2450> UART1;
  UART<0x2650> UART2;
  UART1.send('h');
  UART2.send('i');
}
```

This template doesn't take a user-defined type, just an **int**. The expression in **send()** should reduce to an assembly language statement (and the inline prevents argument-passing overhead!)—very efficient. The same should be true for compilers that substitute macros for I/O port reads and writes. Please note that this is only demonstration code; it is not meant to work with an actual UART (that program would be much longer and more complex).

As an alternative, see the use of the placement syntax for **operator new** in Chapter 6.

Static Members in Templates

When you place a **static** data member in a class, only one piece of storage is allocated for that member, and the storage is shared by all objects of that class. Thus, **static** data members can be thought of as a way to communicate between objects of a class. This is true even with inheritance; all objects of a class and all objects of any subclasses share the same storage for a **static** data member.

Templates work differently. Whenever you instantiate a template, you get a different space for all **static** storage. Here's a demonstration:

```
//: STATICT.CPP—Templates & static members
#include <iostream.h>

template<class T, int init> class foo {
  static int i;
public:
  void set(int x) { i = x; }
  void print() { cout << "i - " << i << endl; }
};

template<class T, int init> int foo<T,init>::i = init;

void main() {
  foo<int, 1> I;
  foo<int, 1> J;
  foo<char, 2> U,V;
  J.print();   // prints "1"
  V.print();   // prints "2"
  I.set(100);
  U.set(47);
  J.print();   // prints "100"
  V.print();   // prints "47"
}
```

Notice that the **static** data member, which must be defined (that is, storage must be allocated and any initialization performed) outside the class, must also use the full template syntax.

Although **I** and **J** are defined using separate template specifications, those specifications are identical, so the compiler knows to use the same actual class for both. This means that the same **static** data storage is used for both. You can see this because, even though **I.set(100)** sets the static member to 100, **J.print()** prints out the value. This same printing test shows that the actual class for **U** and **V** is a different one than for **I** and **J**, because the template specification is different.

How Template Member Functions Are Generated

In QUE3.CPP the definitions for **queue<T, size>** are not **inline**, but they still appear before they are used in **queue<float, 10>** and **queue<float, 11>**. The compiler must know how to generate all the member functions for all the variations of the **queue** class. As long as the member functions all appear before **queue** objects are created, there's no problem.

But what if, for some reason, you must separate the interface and the implementation? With an ordinary class, you place all the member function definitions in a separate .CPP file and put the class declaration in a header file. You can do the same thing with templates, but this puts the compiler in a quandary.

To understand this, suppose you have a template class named **bob**, and you put the declaration only into a header file called **bob.h** and the implementation of the member functions into BOB.CPP. Now you want to use the template in another file, called MAIN.CPP. Here's what it looks like:

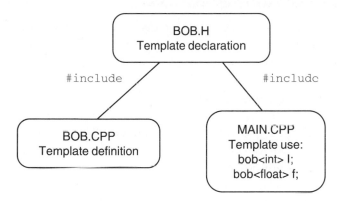

When BOB.CPP is compiled, the compiler has all the template definitions available, so it can generate any of the necessary member function definitions. However, it doesn't know *what definitions are needed* while it's compiling BOB.CPP—it won't know until it compiles MAIN.CPP, at which time it doesn't have the template definitions available!

The Clairvoyant Compiler

The ultimate solution to this problem is intended to be with the compiler. Ideally, the compiler will just "know" how to generate the function definitions, regardless of where the template definitions are. Unfortunately, this is a tricky problem to solve and so, for a while anyway, some compilers will force *you* to keep track of and be responsible for the generation of function definitions. Although this can be annoying, it is still far better than not having templates available at all.

There are several approaches to the management of templates, each of which solves a different problem. As mentioned earlier, the nicest solution is simply to place all definitions in the header file containing the template. Then everything works transparently. You'll see how to solve the "bob" problem next, and finally, in the following section on function templates you'll see how to solve the problem of specialized definitions used with general templates.

The Borland Solution

Borland C++ doesn't magically generate template definitions in the "bob" problem. Instead, you will get a link error, complaining that one or more functions haven't been defined. To solve the problem, you use *compiler switches* controlled by **pragma**s. Templates are controlled by the **–Jg** family of switches:

-Jg   The default value. Whenever you use a template, definitions will be generated at that point. If the identical function is created from the template in separate files, the linker will merge them so there will be no multiple definition errors. This works just fine as long as all the definitions are **inline** in the header file.

-Jgd   Just like **–Jg**, except the linker will not merge multiple definitions. This is used when you want to generate a single definition for a particular use of a template.

-Jgx   The compiler will not generate definitions when a template is used. Instead, it will generate external references to the functions generated by the template. In the file where the template function definitions are available, you must cause the correct definitions to be generated.

By using the **–Jgd** and **–Jgx** switches along with one extra trick, you can properly create the template definitions. The extra trick is you have to tell the compiler to generate the definitions *in the definition file*. To do this without creating any instances, you use a **typedef**, like this:

```
typedef bob<int> dummy_bobi;
```

This appears inside of BOB.CPP, so it isn't visible anyplace else. You aren't actually going to use the name **dummy_bobi**, but it tells the compiler that it will be used someplace, so it had better generate the **bob<int>** definitions. Here's what the files will look like when the proper **pragma**s and **typedef**s are in place:

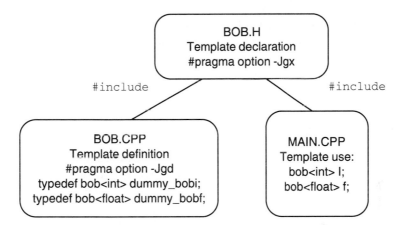

Now whenever the header file is included, any template use will generate external references because of the **#pragma option –Jgx**, *except* in BOB.CPP, the definition file. Here, the **typedef**s are preceded by **#pragma option –Jgd**, so those definitions will actually be created and they will be public (so the linker will be able to find them when it sees the references in MAIN.CPP).

The drawback to this approach is that every time you introduce a new template usage, you must go to BOB.CPP and edit the file. If your template use involves a user-defined type (**String**, for example), the header must be included in BOB.CPP, and a new **typedef** (**typedef bob<String> dummy_bobString;** for example) must be added. This adds a fair bit of management overhead. Worse, it requires an extra level of understanding on the part of the user of the template. It certainly doesn't contribute to ease of library use (one of the major C++ goals). This is why automatic creation of definitions for templates is an important goal.

To be fair, automatic definition creation is a difficult task, and the ARM states (Ellis & Stroustrup, *The Annotated C++ Reference Manual*, Addison-Wesley 1990. Section 14.5c) that the simplest mechanism is to "leave the problem to the programmer," so the approach used by Borland is fully within the boundaries of a proper implementation of templates. The AT&T compiler solves the problem at the linker end—if the linker can't resolve a function call that it knows (by special tagging information mangled into the function name) comes from a template, it restarts the compiler and hands it this new template information so the compiler will instantiate that template. Then the linker tries again—it can go through several iterations before it succeeds. One hopes more elegant solutions are forthcoming. (Again, none of this is an issue in the common case of putting all the template definitions in the header file.)

A Specific Example

To see exactly how to use the **pragma**s, let's look at an example that is modified from the **DynArray** class in Chapter 6. Now that you know what a container class is, it becomes very clear that **DynArray** is such a class (even though it just looked like a dynamically sized array to begin with). Therefore, it seems a prime candidate to be a template. Here is the header file, including the necessary pragma:

```
//: TDYNA.H—Dynamically sized array of object pointers
//. Modified to use templates.
#ifndef TDYNA_H_
#define TDYNA_H_

template<class T, int chunk = 10>
class DynArray {
  T ** array;  // starting address of array of T pointers
  int size;  // current size of the array
  int cursor; // to index through the array
  void error(char * msg = "");
public:
  DynArray();
  ~DynArray();
  int add(T *);  // stash an element in the array,
  // increasing the size if necessary. Returns the index.
  // Both remove() functions return 1 if successful:
  int remove(T *);  // remove an element by pointer
  int remove(int);  // remove an element using its index
  // reset the cursor to the first nonzero element at the
  // top of the array:
  void reset();
  T* next(); // return the pointer to the next element
             // (empty elements are skipped). Returns NULL
             // at end of array.
  int index() { return cursor; } // index of current element
  // return the pointer to the current element:
  T * current() { return array[cursor]; }
  T * operator[](int); // element selection
  int count(); // number of "live" items in the array
```

```
};

#pragma option -Jgx  // to generate external references
// must use
// #pragma option -Jgd
// inside class definition file after inclusion of this file,
// before "dummy" typedefs so public definitions for class
// members are generated.

#endif // TDYNA_H_
```

Notice how the trailing argument in the template declaration has a default value. Default values are as convenient in templates as they are in ordinary functions.

The **#pragma option –Jgx** at the end of the header file will cause any file in which it is included to generate external references to all template usage. Thus, in the implementation file, **#pragma option –Jgd** must be used to cause the member functions to be generated. Here's the implementation file; notice that **ostring.h** must be included so the compiler knows what to do with the **String** in the "dummy **typedef**":

```
//: TDYNA.CPP—The advantages of an array, with the
//. dynamic flexibility of a linked list.
//. Modified to use templates.
#include "tdyna.h"
#include <iostream.h>
#include <stdlib.h>  // exit()

#pragma option -Jgd  // to generate public definitions
#include "ostring.h"
// generate definition:
typedef DynArray<String> dummy_type_string_vector;

template<class T, int chunk>
void DynArray<T, chunk>::error(char * msg) {
  cerr << "DynArray error: " << msg << endl;
  exit(1);
}

template<class T, int chunk>
DynArray<T, chunk>::DynArray() {
  size = chunk;
  cursor = 0;
  array = new T*[size];  // allocate a chunk of pointers
  memset(array, 0, sizeof(T*) * size); // zero the memory
```

```
}

template<class T, int chunk>
DynArray<T, chunk>::~DynArray() {
  for(int i = 0; i < size; i++)
    delete array[i];
  delete array;
}

template<class T, int chunk>
int DynArray<T, chunk>::add(T * new_element) {
  // Put it in the first empty space avaialable:
  for(int i = 0; i < size; i++)
    if(array[i] == 0) {
      array[i] = new_element;
      return i;
    }
  // at this point, no space was found. Add new space:
  int tempsize = size + chunk;  // increase space by chunk
  T ** temp = new T*[tempsize];
  memset(temp, 0, sizeof(T*) * tempsize); // zero the memory
  // copy the old array over:
  for(i = 0; i < size; i++)
    temp[i] = array[i];
  temp[i = size] = new_element;  // put at start of empty space
  delete array;  // free old memory
  array = temp;
  size = tempsize;
  return i;
}

template<class T, int chunk>
int DynArray<T, chunk>::remove(T * rp) {
  for(int i = 0; i < size; i++)
    if( array[i] == rp ) {
      delete array[i];  // must have been made on the heap!
      array[i] = 0;
      return 1;
    }
  return 0; // not found
}

template<class T, int chunk>
int DynArray<T, chunk>::remove(int ri) {
  if( ri < 0 || ri >= size)
    error("remove index out of range");
  // check to see if there's an element at that slot:
```

```
  if( array[ri] ) {
    delete array[ri];  // must have been made on the heap!
    array[ri] = 0;
    return 1;
  }
  return 0; // not found
}

template<class T, int chunk>
void DynArray<T, chunk>::reset() {
  cursor = 0;
  while( (array[cursor] == 0) && (cursor < size - 1) )
    cursor++;  // find the first nonzero element
}

template<class T, int chunk>
T * DynArray<T, chunk>::next() {
  if( cursor == size -1 ) // last element, no next.
    return 0;
  // Not at the end. Increment until you find a
  // nonempty slot, or the end:
  while(array[++cursor] == 0)
    if ( cursor == size -1 )  // no more elements in list
      return 0;
  return array[cursor];
}

template<class T, int chunk>
T * DynArray<T, chunk>::operator[](int x) {
  if(x < 0 || x >= size)
    error("operator[] — index out of range");
  return array[x];  // even if it's empty...
}

template<class T, int chunk>
int DynArray<T, chunk>::count() {
  int cnt = 0;
  for(int x=0; x < size; x++)
    if(array[x])
      cnt++;
  return cnt;
}
```

To create new **DynArray** types, you must modify TDYNA.CPP, include the header file for your new type, and create a "dummy **typedef**." This is unfortunate, since the type is generally used in some other file and there's no intuitive connection between using the type in one file and modifying a separate file to allow its use. You can see the usage in the test file for the **DynArray** template shown here:

```
//: TDYNATST.CPP—Test program for template DynArray.
#include "tdyna.h"
#include "ostring.h"

void main() {
  DynArray<String> da;
  da.add(new String("This is a "));
  da.add(new String("test of the "));
  da.add(new String("dynamic array "));
  da.add(new String("class "));
  da.add(new String("to \n"));
  da.add(new String("(OOPS! A Mistake) "));
  da.add(new String("see "));
  da.add(new String("if "));
  da.add(new String("it "));
  da.add(new String("will "));
  da.add(new String("automatically make "));
  da.add(new String("itself bigger "));
  da.add(new String("when it \n"));
  da.add(new String("runs out of "));
  da.add(new String("room."));
  // First, print the whole list:
  da.reset();
  do
    cout << *da.current();
  while( da.next() );
  cout << endl << endl;
  // Now, find the element with the "OOPS":
  da.reset();
  while( strstr(*da.current(), "OOPS") == 0 )
    if(da.next() == 0) {
      cerr << "OOPS not found" << endl;
      exit(1);
    }
  int rm = da.index(); // number of element to remove
  cout << "removing " << *da[rm] << endl;
  if (da.remove(rm))
    cout << "removed successfully!" << endl;
  // Print the whole list again:
  da.reset();
  do
    cout << *da.current();
```

```
    while( da.next() );
}
```

This file is nearly identical to DYNATEST.CPP in Chapter 6, with the exception of the way the **DynArray** is created. The dummy type declaration in TDYNA.CPP is:

```
typedef DynArray<String> dummy_type_string_vector;
```

This **typedef** name is never intended to be used, so it should be as unlikely as possible. The sole reason it's there is to tell the compiler to generate the function definitions for the array.

Again, this is not the suggested design approach for templates in general. Normally, *all* the declarations and definitions should go in the header file. Even if the file is included in more than one place and identical classes are instantiated in more than one file, the linker will merge the duplicate definitions.

A Better Design

Although the template version of **DynArray** shown above is workable, it has a major design flaw. This is seen when you instantiate a number of different **DynArray** types. For each one, you generate all the code for a complete new **DynArray**. Now, you might think this is precisely what templates are meant to do—generate modified classes so you don't have to—and so you don't cause errors while making the modifications by hand. This is certainly true, but you don't want to abandon everything else just because templates are available. In particular, you don't want to miss the fact that, in the above example, there's a lot of code in common, regardless of the type of template being instantiated. This is especially obvious because void pointers are being used, so the implementation doesn't care what type of pointers it's handling.

Code commonality is expressed through inheritance. Using inheritance, you can create a simple template that inherits from the **DynArray** in Chapter 6, as shown here, rather than reimplementing the entire class (as shown in the preceding example):

```
//: TDYNAINH.H—DynArray using inheritance and templates.
//. More sensible, since it prevents code duplication.
#ifndef TDYNAINH_H_
```

```
#define TDYNAINH_H_
#include "..\chap_6\dynarray.h"

template<class T>
class DynArrayT : public DynArray {
public:
  DynArrayT() : DynArray() {};
  int add(T * t) { return DynArray::add(t); }
  int remove(T * t) { return DynArray::remove(t); }
  int remove(int i) { return DynArray::remove(i); }
  T* next() { return (T*)DynArray::next(); }
  T * current() { return (T*)DynArray::current(); }
  T * operator[](int i) { return (T*)DynArray::operator[](i); }
};

#endif // TDYNINH_H_
```

Not only is this much smaller, but creating a new instantiation involves almost no code. The only function that creates code is the constructor (even though it looks empty, hidden code is created to perform special constructor operations). The rest of the functions generate no code overhead at all, but simply cause the compiler to perform type checking while calling the base-class functions.

In addition, you can see that the need for the **pragma** switches has been obviated, since all the template function code is inlined in the header file. This approach is obviously far superior to the prior example. You should always be on the lookout for ways to simplify your code, especially with inheritance. As you can see here, templates are no substitute for inheritance, but the two can be used together quite profitably.

You can use TDYNATST.CPP to test this approach by including the new header file and linking DYNARRAY.OBJ from Chapter 6.

Function Templates

A *class template* defines a family of classes. It's also possible to make a *function template* that defines a family of functions. The following example creates a single Quicksort that will sort any type of array. You can see here that the template syntax is virtually identical—the only difference is that you're defining functions instead of classes:

```
//: TQSORT.H—Quicksort using function templates
#ifndef TQSORT_H_
#define TQSORT_H_

template<class T>
inline  void swap(T& a, T& b) {
  T tmp = a;   // copy constructor
  a = b;       // operator=
  b = tmp;
}

// A quicksort:
template<class T>
void quicksort_(T L[], const int r, const int l) {
  if(r > l) {
    T v = L[r];   // copy constructor
    int i = l -1, j = r;
    for(;;) {
      while(L[++i] < v)  ;  // operator <
      while(v < L[- j])  ;  // (operator > not required)
      if(i >= j) break;
      swap(L[i], L[j]);
    }
    swap(L[i], L[r]);
    quicksort_(L, i-1, l);
    quicksort_(L, r, i+1);
  }
}

#pragma option -Jgx
// The following has an external definition, and
// shouldn't be automatically generated from the template.
// Special version for arrays of char* :
void quicksort_(char* L[], const int r, const int l);
#pragma option -Jg
// Go back to automatic definition generation.

// Wrapper for the first call:
template<class T> void quicksort(T L[], int size) {
  quicksort_(L, size - 1, 0);
}

#endif // TQSORT_H_
```

The first function, **swap()**, is very simple—all it does is exchange the values of two variables. It performs an exchange of the actual variables, rather than copies, because references are used for the arguments. The **swap()** function is used inside the **quicksort_()** routine. The reason there are two functions, **quicksort_()** and **quicksort()**, is that this is a recursive sort and the first call must be made using the less-than-transparent form of the recursive call. Other sort routines simply work with the size of the array, and with an additional template, the problem was easily fixed; **quicksort()** creates the first call to **quicksort_()**, which then proceeds to call itself recursively with the appropriate arguments.

Note that the **quicksort_()** function only relies upon the existence of **operator<()** for the type it is sorting. It is slightly easier to read if you use both **operator<()** and **operator>()**, but this way is easier to use in some cases. You won't know if the necessary operator is defined for the type you want to sort until the template is actually instantiated for that type.

You can see that, following the template implementation of **quicksort_()**, there is a nontemplate function declaration bearing the same name, but with **char*** as its type. This was added because if the template implementation is used to sort an array of **char***, it ends up sorting based on the pointer addresses and not on the values of the strings. This isn't what you want. Fortunately, C++ allows us to add any number of nontemplate functions with the same name and specific argument lists (the normal overloading mechanism is used here). If the compiler sees your definitions, it won't automatically instantiate a template for that particular signature. However, this is another case where you must take over control of template instantiation.

Here's the reason. As you saw earlier, if you even mention a function or class, the compiler will instantiate the template for that function or class. This is why the "dummy **typedef**" is used—a **typedef** only creates an alias, but the mere fact that the compiler sees the template used, even in a **typedef**, forces it to create the necessary functions.

In the header file you see the following declaration:

```
void quicksort_(char* L[], const int r, const int l);
```

Now in any ordinary situation, this really *would* be a declaration. However, the compiler is seeing this after it sees a template with the same name and number of arguments. Naturally it thinks you want it to make the function for you. So it does, and if you've defined it somewhere else, you get a multiple-definition error at link time.

To solve this problem with Borland C++, this declaration needs to be preceded with **#pragma option –Jgx** so it will simply make external calls to that function and not try to generate it from the template. After the declaration, you go back to automatic template instantiation with **#pragma option –Jg**.

Here's the special version of **quicksort_()** to handle character strings:

```
//: TQSORT.CPP—Implementation of Quicksort for char*
#include "tqsort.h"
#include <string.h>

// Special version for arrays of char* :
void quicksort_(char* L[], const int r, const int l) {
  if(r > l) {
    char* v = L[r];
    int i = l -1, j = r;
    while(1) {
      while(strcmp(L[++i], v) < 0)  ;
      while(strcmp(v, L[--j]) < 0)  ;
      if(i >= j) break;
      swap(L[i], L[j]);
    }
    swap(L[i], L[r]);
    quicksort_(L, i-1, l);
    quicksort_(L, r, i+1);
  }
}
```

The difference here is that the ANSI C library function **strcmp()** is used instead of the less-than operator.

The compiler will try to select a previously defined function before it will generate its own from a template, so in this case the special **char*** version of the Quicksort will be used. You can see how it works in the following file, which tests the sort in several ways:

```
//: SORT.CPP—Test of function template Quicksort
#include <time.h>
#include <stdlib.h>
#include <iostream.h>
#include <string.h>
#include <conio.h> // kbhit()
#include <dos.h>  // delay()
#pragma warn -inl
#include "tqsort.h"
```

```
void test_quicksort(int display = 0) {
  const sz = 500;
  int X[sz], Y[sz];
  for(int i = 0; i < sz; i++)
    X[i] = Y[i] = rand() % 100;
  quicksort(X, sz);
  for(i = 0; i < sz -1; i++)
    for(int j = i + 1; j < sz; j++)
      if(X[i] > X[j]) cerr << "quicksort error";
  if(display) {
    for(i = 0; i < sz; i++)
      cout << X[i] << " ";
    cout << endl << endl;
    delay(1000 * display);  // display = delay in seconds
  }
}

char * strarray[] = {
  "this", "is", "an", "array", "of", "char", "pointers"
};
const sasz = sizeof(strarray)/sizeof(strarray[0]);

void main() {
  srand((unsigned)time(new time_t)); // seed random generator
  while(!kbhit()) test_quicksort(3); // no arg for no output

  char alpha[] = "zqrabctuvswxydefmnoghipqrjkl";
  quicksort(alpha, strlen(alpha));
  cout << alpha << endl;

  quicksort(strarray, sasz);  // special version called
  for(int i = 0; i < sasz; i++)
    cout << strarray[i] << endl;
}
```

The first function, **test_quicksort()**, creates an array of random integers and sorts them. Then it checks to make sure they are in ascending order. This automatically tests the routine. If you give it a nonzero argument, it will print the results of the sort and then pause for the same number of seconds as the argument.

In **main()**, **test_quicksort()** is called over and over until you press a key, so the routine can be continuously tested. Then an array of characters is sorted and printed, and finally the special version of the sort routine is automatically called when sorting an array of character strings.

Templates and Pointers to Members: The "Apply" Function

You normally think of a pointer as something that holds the address of an object (in the purest sense of the word "object": "a region of storage"). This means a pointer can hold the address of a variable or of a function (which also occupies storage). These "traditional" pointers can only point to physical locations in memory. A structure in ANSI C simply gives a specification for layout and data types, but you don't have any specific addresses until you make objects of those structures. At that point, the address of a structure member can have as many values as there are objects. In ANSI C, this concept is partially coped with using the **offsetof()** macro, which produces the physical offset in bytes of the structure member from the beginning of the structure. This way, you can take the address of an object and calculate where a particular structure member sits.

In C++, a structure (**struct** or **class**) appears to have function members as well as data members. However, the function members don't actually occupy storage in the structure (this would be wasteful and redundant); they are instead conceptually contained in the structure by the way they are scoped. Physically, however, they exist just like an ordinary global function (albeit with a funny name produced by mangling). This makes the generalized concept of a pointer to a class member a bit more difficult, since the compiler must determine whether it needs to offset into a physical object or go find a function somewhere. In both cases, dereferencing this *pointer to member* is tied to the **this** pointer of the object (**this** is secretly passed to all member functions, and is the starting address of the current object).

A class is just a way to create new objects and has no physical embodiment until objects of that class are created. Similarly, a pointer to a class member represents not an address of a physical element but instead the place where that element will be for any particular object. Because of this, you cannot dereference a pointer to a member by itself—it must always be associated with an object.

When you define a pointer to a member, it must be given the exact type of the member it will point to, as well as the class name. Here is an example showing the syntax of pointers to members:

```
//: PTRMEMB.CPP—Pointers to members

class I {
  int i;
public:
  int v;
  I(int ii = 0) : i(ii), v(ii) {}
  int mul(int x) { return i * x; }
};

void main() {
  int I::* ptr_mem_int = &I::v;              // (1)
  int (I::* ptr_mem_func)(int) = &I::mul;    // (2)

  I a(4);
  a.*ptr_mem_int = 12;                       // (3)
  int b = (a.*ptr_mem_func)(47);             // (4)

  I * c = &a;
  c->*ptr_mem_int = 44;                      // (5)
  (c->*ptr_mem_func)(b);                     // (6)
}
```

To use a pointer to a member, you must first create an object of the class associated with that pointer, and then dereference the pointer using the object. Lines (1) and (2) show the definition and initialization of a pointer to member of type **int**, and a pointer to member of type **function** (which takes an **int** argument and returns an **int**). The initialization could have been done separately from the definition, but it's always best to initialize at the point of definition, so you don't have an uninitialized pointer available.

The pointer-to-member syntax is quite straightforward—everywhere you would normally use a * to define a pointer, you must precede this with the class name and the scope resolution operator.

Dereferencing a pointer to member also follows a consistent syntax. Where you would ordinarily just use member selection with the ., you must add the pointer dereference *, as seen in (3) and (4). If you have a pointer to an object, member selection with **->** must be followed by the pointer dereference *****, as shown in (5) and (6).

Pointers to members are useful if you want, for example, to create a function that will apply an operation to all the elements in a list. Suppose you have a class that has three member functions with identical arguments and return values, as in the following:

```
class dweeb {
  // ...
public:
  // ...
  void spin();
  void dodge();
  void feint();
};
```

Now suppose you have some sort of container class called **dweeblist** that is filled with **dweeb** objects. A pointer to the current **dweeb** object is produced with a member function **current()**. You can define a function that applies a member function (which is passed as an argument) to all the **dweeb** objects in **dweeblist** and then call this function for a **dweeblist dl** like this:

```
//: DWEEB.CPP—Pointers to members & the "apply" function
#include <iostream.h>

class dweeb {
public:
  void spin()  { cout << "spinning!" << endl; }
  void dodge() { cout << "dodging!" << endl;  }
  void feint() { cout << "feinting!" << endl; }
};

template<int sz> class dweeblist {
  dweeb list[sz];
  int cursor;
public:
  dweeblist() : cursor(0) {}
  void reset() { cursor = 0; }
  dweeb * current() { return &list[cursor]; }
  void next() { cursor++; }
  int end() { return cursor >= sz; }
  void apply(void (dweeb::* df)()) {
    reset();
```

```
    while(!end()) {
      (current()->*df)();
      next();
    }
  }
};

void main() {
  dweeblist<7> dl;
  dl.apply(&dweeb::spin);
  dl.apply(&dweeb::dodge);
  dl.apply(&dweeb::feint);
}
```

Typically, the kind of function you'd want to **apply()** to every object in a list would be something like **draw()**, for a computer-aided design program.

Pointers to members have fairly limited use, but they can be quite helpful when you want to delay the selection of a specific function until the program is running. Obviously, there are other more direct ways to accomplish the same thing, but this is more elegant and, as in the above case, may be simpler for the user. The concept of "applying" a function to every object in a list is easier to understand than worrying about the mechanics of creating an iterator and stepping through the list, calling the function for each object in the list. It is also briefer to write and easier to read, and thus less error prone (be aware, however, that the iterator approach may run faster!).

A pointer to a member of a base class can be converted to a pointer to a member of a class derived from that base if the base class is public in the derived class and the conversion is not ambiguous. A pointer to a member can be cast into an integral type (this can be used in place of the ANSI C library function **offsetof()**), to a pointer to another member, or to a pointer to a function. If you try to assign a virtual member function to a pointer to a member function, the result will be 0.

One drawback to the above example is that you must know the precise signature of the member function you wish to call via the pointer to member. This makes it quite difficult to come up with a generic container class with an **apply()** function, because you'd have to create an exhaustive set of overloaded **apply()** functions. With templates, however, this problem can be solved fairly easily, as shown here:

```
//: PMEM.CPP—Pointers to members & templates
//. The "apply" function.
#include "ostring.h"

template<class T, int sz>
class bag {
  T* t[sz];
public:
  bag() { memset(t, 0, sizeof(T*) * sz); }
  void set(int i, T* ip) {
    if(i < 0 || i >= sz)
      cerr << "bag boundary exceeded" << endl;
    else
      t[i] = ip;
  }
  T* operator[](int i) {
    if(i < 0 || i >= sz) {
      cerr << "bag boundary exceeded" << endl;
      return 0;
    }
    else
      return t[i];
  }
  int size() { return sz; }
};

template<class B, class T, class X>
void apply(B& b, void (T::*pmf)(X), X x) {
  for(int i = 0; i < b.size(); i++)
    if(b[i]) (b[i]->*pmf)(x);
}

template<class B, class T, class X, class Y>
void apply(B& b, void (T::*pmf)(X, Y), X x, Y y) {
  for(int i = 0; i < b.size(); i++)
    if(b[i]) (b[i]->*pmf)(x, y);
}

class String2 : public String {
public:
  String2(char* s) : String(s) {}
  void print2(int i, char * s) {
    cout << i;
    print(s);  // base-class function
  }
  void test(int) {}
  void test2(float, float) {}
```

```
};

void main() {
  bag<String2, 10> B;
  for(int i = 0; i < B.size(); i++)
    B.set(i, new String2("world!"));
  apply(B, &String2::print, "Hello, ");
  apply(B, &String2::print2, 47, " What a ");
  apply(B, &String2::test, 1);
  apply(B, &String2::test2, 1.1F, 2.2F);
}
```

Now the **apply()** function will automatically be instantiated for member functions that take one argument (the first **apply()** template) or two arguments (the second). Since the types of the arguments are in the template, they can be anything. The only limitation here is in the return value. An independent template argument cannot specify the return value for a template function, for the same reason that two overloaded functions cannot differ only by their return values. The return value isn't mangled into the function name, and thus functions that differ only by their return value are not distinct, and don't overload. Thus you must still exhaustively create template definitions to cover differing return values.

This is not as big a problem as it seems because when you **apply()** a function to every element in a list, the return values are discarded anyway. The difficulty occurs when you're using someone else's class that has a member function that wasn't designed to be applied this way. In that case, you may not be using it properly.

Notice you can't make **apply()** a member function of **class bag**. That's because you cannot nest template declarations. For the same reason, you can't make it a **friend** function of **bag**. (These restrictions exist in the draft-ANSI C++ specification at the time of this writing. However, they might be relaxed by the ANSI committee in the future. The problems associated with relaxing them have not been fully determined, and it is much easier to allow behaviors later than to disallow behaviors once they've been determined to be problematic.)

The **apply()** function can be a very convenient and useful notation. However, make sure you profile your program to make sure that **apply()** isn't too much of a hog; in many cases it is significantly faster to use iterators.

Functor Generation with Templates

A *functor* is a class whose sole purpose is to contain a function. That is, the only reason you create an object of that class is to call its function. A functor serves the same role as a function, but you can create it, pass it as a parameter, and treat it in all other ways as an object. If you use inheritance with a functor, you can reduce code duplication by putting common code into a base class. Using virtual functions, you can gain the same run-time flexibility with functors that is possible with pointers to functions.

Consider a problem that occurs with functors: where you would normally simply write a function, you must now create a whole class. This is tedious, and it might just be tedious enough that you'll design the program some other way rather than taking advantage of functors. This is especially true when you're creating an application framework, and the end user is required to create the functor classes.

Fortunately, templates can be used to solve this problem. As seen in the Quicksort example, if the compiler knows that you've created a function for a specific argument list, it won't generate one for you (it doesn't create one when sorting character strings). Thus, if you create a template for the functor and define all the necessary functions *except* the "special function" that the functor class is created for, that function is the only one that needs to be defined and the notation cleans up quite nicely, as seen here:

```
//: TFUNCTOR.CPP—Functor generation with templates
#include <iostream.h>

template<int> class functor {
public:
  void print(char * msg = "") {
    cout << "functor " << msg << endl;
  }
  void description();  // defined elsewhere
};

void functor<1>::description() {
  cout << "this is functor 1" << endl;
}

void functor<2>::description() {
  cout << "this is functor 2" << endl;
```

```
}

void functor<3>::description() {
  cout << "this is functor 3" << endl;
}

void main() {
  functor<1> A;
  functor<2> B;
  functor<3> C;
  A.print("A"); A.description();
  B.print("B"); B.description();
  C.print("C"); C.description();
}
```

The **int** in the **functor** class is merely used to differentiate one functor from another (you could also use an enumeration, if you wanted more textual information). Notice that the **print()** function is defined by the template, but the **description()** function is not, so it must be defined elsewhere. If you don't define it, the linker will complain when you try to call it.

Templates and Inheritance

Inheritance used in a template can provide some very powerful mechanisms for creating code. For example, suppose you want to create a stack class, but you want to allow the user to select the way the stack is implemented—with a simple fixed-size array, an array allocated on the heap, or with a linked list:

☐ The fixed-size array is the fastest, both in initialization time and in access time, so it is best for objects that are created rapidly, in large numbers, especially if they are passed around by value.

☐ The heap-allocated array has fast access time, but slower startup time, since **new** must be called (although the speed can be increased by providing a custom **operator new**). However, you can determine the size at run time, although it is fixed after creation.

☐ The linked list is the most flexible, since it creates space on the heap for each element you place in it, so it "never" runs out of space (assuming, of course, you don't run out of heap space). It is also the slowest, and passing it by value (copying it) is a nightmare.

Thus, it's important to know how you're going to use the stack before you decide on the underlying implementation, and only the programmer knows that. Here's a way to allow the programmer to select the implementation:

```
//: IMPCTRL.CPP—Implementation control with templates
#include <iostream.h>
#include "..\chap_7\ioserror.h"  // for heap checking

class base_container {
public:
  virtual void add(void*) = 0;
  virtual void* get() = 0;
};

class fixed_array : public base_container {
  enum { sz = 100 };
  void *a[sz];
  int cur;
public:
  fixed_array(int) : cur(0) {}  // dummy argument
  void add(void* d) {
    if(cur < sz) a[cur++] = d;
    // else: do error processing
  }
  void* get() {
    if(cur <= 0) return 0; // more error processing
    return a[--cur];
  }
};

class heap_array : public base_container {
  void **a;
  const sz;
  int cur;
public:
  heap_array(int size) : sz(size), cur(0), a(new void*[sz]) {}
  void add(void* d) {
    if(cur < sz) a[cur++] = d;
    // else: do error processing
  }
  void* get() {
```

```
        if(cur <= 0) return 0; // more error processing
        return a[--cur];
    }
};

class list : public base_container {
    struct node {
        void * data;
        node * next;
        node(void* d, node* nxt) : data(d), next(nxt) {}
    } *head;
public:
    list(int) : head(0) {}   // dummy argument
    void add(void* d) { head = new node(d, head); }
    void* get() {
        if(head == 0) return 0;
        void* d = head->data;   // get data
        node* p = head;   // save old head
        head = head->next;   // move head to next node
        delete p;   // delete old head
        return d;
    }
};

template<class Type, class Form, int sz = 0>
class stack : private Form {   // private inheritance
public:
    stack() : Form(sz) {}
    void push(Type* d) { Form::add(d); }
    Type* pop() { return (Type*)Form::get(); }
};

void main() {
    stack<int, fixed_array> F;
    stack<int, heap_array, 100> H;
    stack<int, list> L;
    for(int i = 0; i < 100; i++) {
        F.push(new int(i));
        H.push(new int(i));
        L.push(new int(i));
    }
    for(i = 0; i < 100; i++)
        cout << *F.pop() << "\t"
             << *H.pop() << "\t"
             << *L.pop() << endl;
}
```

The template uses **private** inheritance to inherit an implementation rather than an interface. If you've been wondering why **private** inheritance exists, this is an ideal example. It allows you to use inheritance to build underlying portions of a class rather than to create types from other types. This is sometimes referred to as the distinction between *subclassing* and *subtyping*.

Templates in Libraries

One of the places you'll commonly see templates used is in libraries from compiler vendors and third-party library vendors. With these kinds of tools available, you can almost always avoid writing (and debugging!) your own container classes. Instead, you can go to the reference manual and find the type of container to suit your need. With templates, instantiating a container to manage your particular class becomes effortless.

The following example creates a nicely formatted directory listing under MS-DOS. It uses a template from the Borland class library, called **BI_ISListImp**. This name follows a convention used at Borland. The **BI** stands for Borland International. The **I** stands for "indirect," meaning that this takes pointers rather than the objects themselves. **S** indicates the list is sorted. **List** differentiates this from an array or some other representation, and **Imp** stands for "implementation" (the reason for this is not clear). You will often see this sort of naming convention from vendors to prevent their class names from clashing with other vendors (since classes exist in a single name space). However, they usually provide a header file with simplifying **typedef**s, so you don't actually have to type the names if you don't want to.

Since you are using a sorted list, the list must have a way of determining how to sort the elements. For this, the template requires that the objects it manipulates have an **operator<()** and an **operator==()** defined. The basic DOS directory structure, defined in the Borland header file (not ANSI C) **dos.h**, is **struct ffblk**. This is used in the functions **findfirst()** and **findnext()** that take a pointer to an **ffblk** and fill it with the next directory entry that matches the wildcard specified in the first argument. However, **ffblk** is a simple **struct** that comes from a C library, so it doesn't have member functions, particularly not the ones you need to put the object in a **BI_ISListImp**. This is remedied with inheritance into class **dfile** (just because a **struct** comes from a C library doesn't mean you can't inherit it!). Now a **dfile** can be passed to any function that expects an **ffblk**, and that function won't know the difference.

In addition, you can add member functions, as you can see here:

```
//: TDIR.CPP—Sorted directory listing program
//. using Borland container class templates.
#include <listimp.h>  // Borland list template header
#include <shddel.h>    // deletion control
#include <dir.h>
#include <dos.h>
#include <string.h>
#include <iostream.h>
#include <conio.h>
#pragma warn -inl

class dfile : public ffblk {
public:
  dfile(dfile& df) : ffblk(df) {
    strlwr(ff_name);  // force to lower case
  }
  dfile() {}  // Must explicitly create default constructor
  int operator==(dfile& df) {
    return !strcmp(ff_name, df.ff_name);
  }
  int operator<(dfile & df) {
    return strcmp(ff_name, df.ff_name) < 0;
  }
  friend ostream& operator<<(ostream& os, dfile& df) {
    int whitespace = sizeof(df.ff_name)
                      - strlen(df.ff_name) + 1;
    if(df.ff_attrib == FA_DIREC) {  // directory
      os << "[" << df.ff_name << "]";
      whitespace -= 2;
    } else
      os << df.ff_name;
    for(int i = 0; i < whitespace; i++)
      os << ' ';  // fill out the rest of the space
    return os;
  }
};

class dir : public BI_ISListImp<dfile> {
  int size;  // number of dfile items
```

```
public:
  dir(char * afn = "*.*") : size(0) { // file descriptor
    dfile f;
    int done = findfirst(afn, &f, FA_DIREC);
    while(!done) {
      if (f.ff_name[0] != '.') {  // don't add '.' or '..'
        add(new dfile(f));                        // (1)
        size++;
      }
      done = findnext(&f);
    }
  }
  ~dir() { flush(TShouldDelete::Delete); }
  int count() { return size; }
};

void main(int argc, char * argv[]) {
  const scrlen = 24;
  dir D(argc > 1 ? argv[1] : "*.*");              // (2)
  // number of initializers = number of columns:
  BI_IListIteratorImp<dfile> it[] = { D, D, D, D, D };
  const cols = sizeof(it)/sizeof(it[0]);          // (3)
  int startpoint = D.count() / cols;              // (4)
  if(D.count() % cols) startpoint++;              // (5)
  for(int i = 0; i < cols; i++)
    for(int j = 0; j < startpoint * i; j ++)      // (6)
      it[i]++;
  for(int k = 0; k < startpoint; k++) {           // (7)
    for(int i = 0; i < cols; i++) {
      if(it[i]) cout << *it[i].current();
      it[i]++;
    }
    cout << endl;  // end of each line
    static int lnum = 0; // output paging
    if(++lnum >= scrlen) { getch(); lnum = 0; }
  }
}
```

In addition to the two operators, **dfile** also contains a copy constructor and a **friend** function. The copy constructor **dfile(dfile&)** is called whenever a **dfile** object is passed by value, which happens later in (1). This copy constructor first calls the base-class version and then forces the filename string to lowercase with a call to the Borland (non-ANSI C) library function **strlwr()**.

You might notice there's no copy constructor for **ffblk**. This is true, but the compiler will automatically generate one for you if it doesn't exist. The default action is a memberwise copy, which means that the copy constructors for each member are called. Since there are no copy constructors defined for the members of **ffblk**, the copy defaults to a bitwise copy, which is a simple copy of every element in the structure. Thus, this copy constructor performs a bitwise copy via the base-class copy constructor and then modifies the filename field with **strlwr()**.

The **friend** function is an overloaded **operator<<()** to work with **ostream**s. This means that a **dfile** object can be placed directly on an output stream. It is useful here not only because it allows subdirectories to be displayed differently than ordinary files, but also because it fills the space on the right side of the filename when it prints. Notice that this is not a member function, even if it appears as an **inline** inside the class declaration. The **friend** keyword distinguishes it as a global function. Because it is a global operator, it must have two arguments, one that goes on the left side of the **<<** and one that goes on the right.

Although you can simply make a list directly from the template as **BI_ISListImp<dfile>**, it would need to be initialized separately. It's much more robust to inherit from the template, as seen in **class dir**, and then perform all the initialization in the constructor. In addition, the template class doesn't keep track of how many elements it has, so data member **size** is added, and the elements are counted as they are added. **count()** returns the number of elements.

When **findfirst()** and **findnext()** (the Borland library functions to find the files) are called in the constructor for **dir**, they fill the **ffblk** with an uppercase filename. However, in (1) the copy constructor is called, so the name is automatically converted to lowercase.

In the destructor for **dir**, you can see the **BI_ISListImp<dfile>::flush()** function is called with an argument that tells it to call **delete** for all the pointers contained in the list. This is yet another solution to the "who owns the objects in a list?" question: let the user decide. As a default, the **flush()** function won't call **delete**, so you are responsible for getting the objects deleted some other way. However, in this case the list is specifically told to **delete** all the objects.

The **main()** function takes two arguments in this case. This is how the command line is passed into the program. The first argument, tradition-ally called **int argc**, is the number of items on the command line: 1 if there are no arguments (just the command itself), 2 if there is one argument, and so on. The second argument, traditionally called **char ** argv** or **char* argv[]** (which are equivalent as arguments), is an array of pointers to character strings. Each character string pointed to in the array represents a single item on the command line. Thus, the expression

```
for(int i = 0; i < argc; i++) cout << argv[i] << " ";
```

will print out all the items on the command line, starting with the command itself.

When **dir D** is defined in (2), its constructor gets an argument that is produced by a ternary **if-then-else** expression, the **?:** form. If there is an argument on the command line, that argument is used for the constructor argument. If not, ***.*** is used, indicating all files should be found. This one definition creates the sorted list and fills it with directory items. All you have to do now is use it.

Although the list is sorted, printing it out from left to right isn't very helpful. To be readable, it needs to be broken into a number of lists, with the lists printed side by side. This turns out to be easily done with iterators, which allow us to look at more than one place in a list at any one time. The list doesn't even have to be broken up. All you need to do is create an iterator for each column you want to display and position that iterator at the beginning of the appropriate part of the **dir** list.

The definition for **it[]** uses automatic counting and aggregate initialization; each of the **D**s is given to the corresponding **it** as its constructor argument. In (3), the number of columns is calculated from the size of the **it** array. You may think this looks funny at first, but it allows the array size to be determined in only one place—by the number of arguments in the aggregate initialization list. Everything else is based on that value. This means that you can change the number of columns without having to hunt through your code looking for dependencies. This is a good practice to do whenever possible, because it allows the code to be rapidly changed without introducing bugs.

Lines (4) and (5) show the calculation of **startpoint**, which is the offset into the **D** list used to position the iterators. This is simply the number of elements in the list divided by the number of columns, as seen in (4). However, that's an integer division, and there may be some elements left over, which would get left out of the display. To correct this, line (5) checks to see if there's a remainder and adds 1 to **startpoint** if there is.

Next you must move the respective iterators to the appropriate starting points. This is accomplished by looping through all the iterators, and for each one incrementing the iterator by **startpoint** times the number of that column, as seen in (6). You'll notice that the zero iterator isn't moved at all.

The columns are printed out in (7) by looping from 0 to **startpoint**, printing out all of the corresponding column elements for each one. Finally, output that is longer than **scrlen** is paged using the **static int lnum**. This *could* have been defined at the top of **main()**, but it's more convenient and maintainable to define it as close as possible to the point of use. Since the variable is **static**, it isn't initialized to 0 on each pass through it, but only once at the initialization of the whole program.

Rethinking Existing Code

After discovering templates, situations might present themselves in a new and more elegant light. For example, consider the database table example BRACKETS.CPP from Chapter 5. Since both **record** and **table** have the identical form, it makes sense to turn them into a template. That program can be turned into a more useful tool, which reads one file into a table and a second file into a list. Then it checks to see if each word in the list exists in the table and reports on those that don't (a version of this program was used in the preparation of this book, to ensure that each .CPP file in a directory was represented in the **makefile**). Here is the header file containing the **flexvector** template and the **field** class:

```
//: FLEXVECT.H—flexvector template and field class
#ifndef FLEXVECT_H_
#define FLEXVECT_H_
#include <string.h>
#include <stdlib.h>
#include <iostream.h>
#pragma warn -inl

template<class T, int bumpsize = 10>
class flexvector {
```

```
  T ** Array;
  int size;
  void copygrow(int newsize) {
    T** temp = new T*[newsize];
    for(int i = 0; i < size; i++)
      temp[i] = Array[i];
    while(i < newsize)
      temp[i++] = new T;
    size = newsize;
    delete []Array;
    Array = temp;
  }
public:
  flexvector() : size(0), Array(0) {}
  ~flexvector() {
    for(int i = 0; i < size; i++)
      delete Array[i];
    delete Array;
  }
  T& operator[](int i) {
    if(i < 0) { cerr << "flexvector: negative index"; exit(0); }
    if(i >= size) copygrow(i + bumpsize);
    return *Array[i];
  }
  int Size() { return size; }
};

class field {
  char * data;
public:
  field(char * d = "") : data(strdup(d)) {}
  ~field() { free(data); }
  void operator=(char * d) {
    free(data);
    data = strdup(d);
  }
  int contains(field& f) {
    // find f.data inside data:
    return (int)strstr(data, f.data);
  }
  operator int() { return strlen(data); }
  friend ostream& operator<<(ostream& os, field& f) {
    return os << f.data;
  }
};

#endif // FLEXVECT_H_
```

Here's the program to check the list of words against the file:

```cpp
//: INFILE.CPP—Revision of BRACKETS.CPP from Chapter 5
//. Reads a file into a table; checks to see if each word
//. in a list in a second file is contained in the first.
#include <string.h>
#include <stdlib.h>
#include <fstream.h>
#include "..\chap_7\ioserror.h"
ioserror error("infile");

template<class T, int bumpsize = 10>
class flexvector {
  T ** Array;
  int size;
  void copygrow(int newsize) {
    T** temp = new T*[newsize];
    for(int i = 0; i < size; i++)
      temp[i] = Array[i];
    while(i < newsize)
      temp[i++] = new T;
    size = newsize;
    delete []Array;
    Array = temp;
  }
public:
  flexvector() : size(0), Array(0) {}
  ~flexvector() {
    for(int i = 0; i < size; i++)
      delete Array[i];
    delete Array;
  }
  T& operator[](int i) {
    if(i < 0) { cerr << "flexvector: negative index"; exit(0); }
    if(i >= size) copygrow(i + bumpsize);
    return *Array[i];
  }
  int Size() { return size; }
};

class field {
  char * data;
public:
  field(char * d = "") : data(strdup(d)) {}
  ~field() { free(data); }
  void operator=(char * d) {
    free(data);
```

```cpp
        data = strdup(d);
    }
    int contains(field& f) {
      // find f.data inside data:
      return (int)strstr(data, f.data);
    }
    operator int() { return strlen(data); }
    friend ostream& operator<<(ostream& os, field& f) {
      return os << f.data;
    }
};

class table : public flexvector< flexvector<field> > {
public:
  int contains(field& f) {
    for(int i = 0; i < Size(); i++) // all rows in table
      for(int j = 0; j < operator[](i).Size(); j++) // columns
        if(operator[](i).operator[](j).contains(f))
          return 1;
    return 0;
  }
};

void main(int argc, char* argv[]) {
  if(argc < 3)
    error << "usage: infile mainfile comparefile" << terminate;
  ifstream mainfile(argv[1]);
  if(!mainfile)
    error << "can't open " << argv[1] << terminate;
  const bsz = 120; char buf[bsz];
  table Table;
  int lines = 0;
  while(mainfile.getline(buf, bsz)) {
    int j = 0;
    char * p = strtok(buf, " \t\n");
    while(p) {
      Table[lines][j++] = strlwr(p); // lower case comparison
      p = strtok(0, " \t\n");
    }
    lines++;
  }

  ifstream comparefile(argv[2]);
  if(!comparefile)
    error << "can't open " << argv[2] << terminate;
  flexvector<field> List;
  int lsize = 0;
```

```
while(comparefile.getline(buf, bsz)) {
  char * p = strtok(buf, ".,;:\'\" \t\n"); // no punctuation
  if(p) List[lsize++] = strlwr(p);  // lower case comparison
  // One word on each line of the list
}

for(int k = 0; k < List.Size(); k++) {
  if(!Table.contains(List[k]))
    cout << List[k] << " not in " << argv[1] << endl;
}
}
```

The two classes **record** and **table** from the Chapter 5 example have been turned into the template **flexvector**, which you can see has the identical form. The **class field** is the same as before, and it has an additional member **contains()**, which checks to see if the argument field is contained inside the current object.

Look carefully at the new definition of the **table** class—it inherits from a class that turns out to be just like the old **table** class, created by instantiating one **flexvector** inside another,

```
flexvector< flexvector<field> >
```

but note how space was left between the right-side delimiters. If you didn't do this, the compiler would see a right-shift operator (this drawback to using angle-braces as delimiters was not considered too annoying).

The creation of **class table** instantiates the base class *and* inherits from it, all in one line. Then it adds an additional member function **contains()**, which determines whether a **field** object is contained anywhere within the table.

In **main()**, the file denoted by the first argument is read into the table using **strtok()** to tokenize the words in the file, as in BRACKETS.CPP, except that the words are forced to lowercase using the ANSI C library function **strlwr()** so that all the comparisons will be case insensitive (you could also leave it as a user option with a command-line flag). The file denoted by the second argument is read into the one-dimensional **flexvector** called **List**. Notice in the **strtok()** statement that only the first word on the line is used (because there are no succeeding **strtok()** calls) and that punctuation is also used in the set of delimiters, so for example "FOO.CPP" would be read into **List** as "foo" (**strlwr()** is used here, too).

Once the **Table** and **List** are filled, the comparison is quite straight-forward—you simply ask **Table** if it contains each word in **List**.

A Batch Editor

The **flexvector** template can also be used in an even more useful program: a batch editor. While **AWK** (mentioned earlier in this book) is very useful for activities where you need to modify entire groups of files, it has a sequential nature that can be limiting—it only reads forward, a line at a time. If you need to do something to a portion earlier in a file based on what happens later in a file it becomes difficult or impossible in **AWK**. To solve this more general editing problem, here's a program that reads the entire file in all at once so you can edit it and then write it out:

```
//: BATEDIT.CPP—Using a flexvector to make a file editor.
//. Designed for batch editing tasks of files
#include "flexvect.h"
#include <fstream.h>
#include <ctype.h>
#include "..\chap_7\ioserror.h"
ioserror error("batedit");
const bufsz = 120;

// Similar to strtok() but also gets chunks of white space.
// First call, argument is buffer, subsequent calls with
// no argument use same buffer.
char * nextToken(char * buf = 0) {
  static char* p = 0;
  static char returnbuf[bufsz];
  if(buf) p = buf; // starting a new buffer
  if(*p == 0) return 0; // end of buffer
  char * rp = p;
  if(isspace(*p))
    while(isspace(*++p) && *p != '\0')
      ; // move past space
  else // OR
    while(!isspace(*++p) && *p != '\0')
      ; // move past word
  for(int i = 0; rp < p; i++, rp++)
    returnbuf[i] = *rp; // copy result
  returnbuf[i] = '\0';
  return returnbuf; // must copy this; changed next call
```

```
}

void main(int argc, char* argv[]) {
  if(argc < 2)
    error << "usage: batedit editfile" << terminate;
  ifstream editfile(argv[1]);
  if(!editfile)
    error << "can't open " << argv[1] << terminate;
  char buf[bufsz];
  flexvector< flexvector<field> >  Table;
  int lines = 0;
  while(editfile.getline(buf, bufsz)) {
    int j = 0;
    char * p = nextToken(buf);
    while(p) {
      Table[lines][j++] = p;
      p = nextToken();
    }
    lines++;
  }

  // Entire file is in memory now as a collection of words and
  // space blocks, so you can perform editing functions here...

  // Print entire file:
  for(int k = 0; k < lines; k++) {
    for(int i = 0; Table[k][i]; i++)
      cout << Table[k][i];
    cout << endl;
  }
}
```

The primary difference here is the function **nextToken()**, which is vaguely similar to the ANSI C library function **strtok()**. **nextToken()** takes an argument of the buffer you want to "tokenize," which in this case simply means break up into words and chunks of space. The important thing that **nextToken()** does that **strtok()** doesn't easily do is return those chunks of white space as tokens. Since this is a text editor, all characters are important.

To keep track of the buffer, **nextToken()** uses a **static** pointer **p** to the buffer, just like **strtok()** does. However, **nextToken()** doesn't touch the external buffer; it just reads it. Each resulting token is placed in a **static** buffer called **returnbuf**, and that buffer's starting address is returned from the function (thus you must copy it, lest it be overwritten at the next function call). Since **p** is **static**, it only needs to be reassigned when you pass a nonzero pointer to **nextToken()**. Each subsequent time the function is called, **p** is moved forward to the beginning of the next chunk of interest.

To delimit words from chunks of spaces, the ANSI C library character classification function **isspace()** is used. If you start with a space, **p** is moved forward until it isn't a space, but if you start with a nonspace, **p** is moved forward until it *is* a space. Before any of this happens, the pointer **rp** is assigned to **p**, so the result is that **rp** and **p** bound the chunk of interest, which is then copied into the **static** return buffer. Notice that at this point **p** is ready for the next function call.

In **main()**, **nextToken()** is used instead of **strtok()** to break the input into words and chunks of space. Once the entire file is read in, you can do anything you want to it on a word-by-word basis. The only thing done here, as a proof, is to write the file back out again. To test it, run the program on itself and use a file-comparison program to prove to yourself the results are identical.

Now you can perform tricky maneuvers like removing the extra newlines at the ends of files. However, what's shown here is only the most basic beginning of what you can do with this program. You might think there needs to be more functionality in the classes, since for example there is no direct facility in **flexvector** for inserting words. Look carefully before adding a lot of member functions, though—in this case insertion can also be thought of as replacing an existing word with that word and some other text.

Template Power

Templates are an orthogonal new idea in C++. They aren't ordinary classes, and you certainly can't think about them in the same way you think about inheritance. Inheritance and templates both allow you to create new classes from an existing framework, but inheritance relates the new class to the existing class, where a template is simply a way of manufacturing new classes. In fact, you can almost think of **template** as the keyword that supports container classes.

Templates are an extremely useful feature, and they fill in a hole in C++ (albeit a subtle hole) that required programmers to generate work-arounds, usually involving the preprocessor. Once again, a feature in C++ has managed to wrest control away from the notorious preprocessor.

Makefile for Chapter 10

Here is the makefile for the examples in this chapter. It uses the Borland **.AUTODEPEND** directive to turn on automatic dependency checking, so you don't have to explicitly write out all the dependencies:

```
# makefile for examples in Chapter 10
CLASSLIB = \borlandc\classlib\lib\tclasss.lib
CINCLUDE = -I\borlandc\classlib\include
CPP = bcc -w-inl

# turn on borland autodependency checking:
.AUTODEPEND

.cpp.exe:
        $(CPP) $*.cpp

.cpp.obj:
        $(CPP) -c {$< }

all:    intcont.exe intiter.exe que.exe \
        simtempl.exe que2.exe stackq.exe \
        stacktst.exe args.exe que3.exe \
        hardware.exe statict.exe tdynatst.exe \
        sort.exe ptrmemb.exe dweeb.exe \
        pmem.exe tfunctor.exe impctrl.exe \
        tdir.exe tdyntst2.exe infile.exe batedit.exe

tdynatst.exe : tdynatst.obj tdyna.obj
  $(CPP) $**

sort.exe : sort.obj tqsort.obj
  $(CPP) $**

tdyntst2.exe : tdyntst2.obj dynarray.obj
  $(CPP) $**
```

```
dynarray.obj : ..\chap_6\dynarray.cpp

tdir.exe : tdir.cpp
  $(CPP) $(CINCLUDE) $** $(CLASSLIB)

ioserror.obj : ..\chap_7\ioserror.cpp

infile.exe : infile.obj ioserror.obj
  $(CPP) $**

batedit.exe : batedit.obj ioserror.obj
  $(CPP) $**
```

CHAPTER

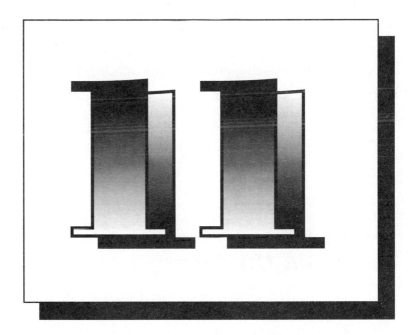

Complete Examples

*T*his chapter contains examples to help you learn to create polished programs and to demonstrate object-oriented design. The first section contains some iostream utilities, including a technique to handle command-line arguments in a generic fashion.

The second section reads and manipulates a comma-separated ASCII database file according to a script file. This section demonstrates techniques of parsing and recursive analysis.

The third section is a clock-based control system. It parses a user script and creates a linked list of generic event objects. These objects are continuously tested; when an object is ready, it is run and removed from the list. This example demonstrates virtual functions, parsing, and linked lists.

The fourth section is a fun example that draws snakes that crawl around on the screen. Each snake is a recursive collection of segments.

The chapter concludes with an implementation of the classic "shape" example in a polymorphic class hierarchy. Three examples of this are shown: a shape editor, a random shape-generating program, and a graphic simulation (based on the example in Chapter 8) that moves shapes randomly around the screen.

Iostream Utilities

Iostreams have been used throughout the book as parts of other programs. This section explores the power of iostreams by showing some small, useful utilities that can be quickly created using that library.

Manipulating Files with Iostreams

Opening an **iostream** file is just a matter of creating an **fstream** object. The file is automatically closed when the object goes out of scope. You can check to see if the file is properly opened using the overloaded **!** operator. All the other standard iostream functions are available when using **fstream**s. Here's a simple example that copies a file:

```
//: SCOPY.CPP—Copies a file from arg1 to arg2
//. and makes an extra copy in TMP.$$$
#include <fstream.h>
#include "..\chap_7\ioserror.h"
const char* tfile = "TMP.$$$"; // name of temp file

ioserror error("scopy");

void main(int argc, char * argv[]) {
  if(argc < 2) error << "usage: scopy from to" << terminate;
  ifstream in(argv[1]);
  if(!in) error << "couldn't open " << argv[1] << terminate;
  ofstream out(argv[2]);
  if(!out) error << "couldn't open " << argv[2] << terminate;
  ofstream tmp(tfile);
  if(!tmp)  error << "couldn't open " << tfile << terminate;

  char c;
  while(in.get(c)) {
    out.put(c);
    tmp.put(c);
  }
}
```

As a second example, consider how easy it is to create a program that stores the current working path in a file and later retrieves it. This way, you can quickly return to your current project directory if you leave it:

```
//: RECALL.CPP—Saves your directory location
// An example of iostream simplicity
#include <fstream.h>
#include <stdlib.h>
#include <dir.h>
#include "..\chap_7\ioserror.h"
const char * path = "\\tmp\\last.$$$";
ioserror error("recall");

void main(int argc, char* argv[]) {
  const sz = 100;
  char buf[sz];
  if(argc > 1)  // store the current path
    if(*argv[1] != 's')
      error << "usage: \n\trecall \nto return to last stored "
      "path OR: \n\trecall s \nto store the current path.\n"
      "You must have a TMP directory off your root directory."
      << terminate;
```

```
  else {
    getcwd(buf, sz);
    ofstream dirloc(path);
    if(!dirloc) error << "couldn't open " << path
                      << terminate;
    dirloc << buf << endl;
    return;
  }
  ifstream dirloc(path);
  if(!dirloc) error << "couldn't open " << path << terminate;
  dirloc.getline(buf, sz);
  chdir(buf);
}
```

Since **iostream** handles all the file opening, reading and writing, and closing for you *and* it uses the same convenient syntax, it becomes effortless to write a program that uses files for data storage.

An "Alias" for MS-DOS

Here are a pair of programs that demonstrate, among other things, the use of string streams. These allow you to write to a buffer in memory as easily as writing to any other type of stream. The ALIAS program takes a command you type on the command line and turns it into a batch file, which it stores in your batch directory. If you precede the alias name with a +, it will also prompt you for a line of help information, which it puts into a file for later use by the BHELP program. If you put a ; in the line, it separates commands in the batch file. A ~ generates commands to change to the current drive and directory. If the batch file already exists, the program asks you before overwriting it.

Both ALIAS and BHELP have some information in common; particularly directory paths, as shown here:

```
//: ALIAS.H—Common information for ALIAS.CPP and BHELP.CPP

const char* bat_dir = "C:\\ABAT\\"; // alias batch directory
const char* hname = "BHELP.TXT"; // help filename
const char* tmpname = "TMP.$$$"; // temporary filename
const bufsz = 120;   // buffer size
const screenlength = 24;
```

Of course, this wouldn't work in ANSI C because **const**s are global, so multiple definition errors would occur. In C++, **const**s are **static**, so this is not a problem. The ALIAS program is shown here:

```
//: ALIAS.CPP—Create a batch file from a command line
//. Also creates supporting help file.
#include <fstream.h>
#include <iostream.h>
#include <strstream.h>
#include <stdio.h>
#include <string.h>
#include <direct.h>
#include "alias.h"

void main(int argc, char* argv[]) {
  if(argc < 3) {
    cerr << "usage: alias name command-line\n"
         << "alias +name command-line\n"
         << "creates a batch file in " << bat_dir
         << "  from command-line.\n';' separates commands. "
         << ". means change to current drive & directory\n"
         << "+name also adds a help entry for the alias.\n"
         << "BHELP.EXE provides help for current batch files."
         << endl;
    return;
  }
  // point past + if it exists:
  char * alias = (*argv[1] == '+' ? argv[1] + 1 : argv[1]);
  char fname[bufsz]; // buffer to hold batch file path & name
  ostrstream fn(fname, bufsz); // create batch filename:
  fn << bat_dir << alias << ".bat" << ends;
  char buf[bufsz]; // general-use buffer
  { // Check for existence of file:
    ifstream test(fname);
    if(test) {
      cout << "overwrite " << fname << "? (y/n) ";
      cin >> buf;
      cin.ignore(); // discard remaining input characters
      if(*buf != 'y') {
        cerr << "terminating without creating file" ;
        return;
      }
    }
  } // "test" closed here
  if(*argv[1] == '+') {
    // Create filename:
```

```
        char helpname[bufsz];
        ostrstream hn(helpname, bufsz);
        hn << bat_dir << hname << ends;
        // open file for reading, copy all lines except
        // help entries which match current alias name:
        {
          ifstream helpfile(helpname);
          ofstream tmp(tmpname);
          while(helpfile.getline(buf, bufsz)) {
            if(strstr(buf, alias) == buf) continue; // discard
            tmp << buf << endl; // no match, keep line
          }
          cout << "help line: ";
          cin.getline(buf, bufsz); // get help text
          tmp << alias << ": " << buf << endl;
        } // both files closed. Move tmp to helpfile:
        remove(helpname);
        rename(tmpname, helpname);
      }
      ofstream ofile(fname);
      if(!ofile) { cerr << "couldn't open " << fname; return; }
      for(int i = 2; i < argc; i++) {
        switch(*argv[i]) {
          case ';' : ofile << endl; break;
          case '~' : ofile << (char)(_getdrive() + 'A' - 1)
                           << ":" << endl;
                     ofile << "cd " << getcwd(buf, bufsz) << endl;
                     break;
          default  : ofile << argv[i] << " ";
        }
      }
      ofile << endl;
    }
```

In the preceding program, the lines:

```
char fname[bufsz];
ostrstream fn(fname, bufsz);
fn << bat_dir << alias << ".bat" << ends;
```

create and use a string stream **fn** from an ordinary character buffer
fname. The string stream object is created for output (thus the o).
Everything you send to **fn** will end up in **fname**. The **bufsz** is used so **fn**
doesn't write past the end of **fname**. When you send information to **fn**
and you want to put in a \0 string terminator, you use **ends** instead of
endl.

At this point, **fname** contains the filename and path. Then the file is opened as an input file, to see if it already exists. If it does, you are queried to see if you want to overwrite it. Notice the file is automatically closed by the **test** destructor because of the enclosing braces; they are there just to force **test** out of scope.

The **istream** member function **ignore()** is very useful when you're capturing user input because of the way **iostream** works. If you ask for a character, you'll get a character, even though the user must enter a character and press carriage return before the information is sent to **cin**. The newline is still in the buffer, and the next time you get input from **cin**, you'll get anything else in the buffer after your original character, and the newline. This is often not what you want, so **ignore()** allows you to throw away all the current input.

The help file is opened and each line is copied into a temporary file, *unless* the first word on that line is the same as the current alias name, in which case the line is not copied. Then the user is prompted for a new help line which is added to the file. The ANSI C library function **remove()** deletes the old help file, and **rename()** changes the temporary file to the help file.

Finally, the batch file itself is opened, and the command line arguments are sent to the file, except if the argument is a ; (which produces a new line in the batch file) or a ~ (which generates commands to change to the drive and directory that ALIAS was invoked from). If you think of other output you'd like ALIAS to automatically add, you can easily add the code to generate it here.

The BHELP program simply opens the help file and prints it out (if there are no arguments) or prints any lines that contain a matching word to the command-line argument:

```
//: BHELP.CPP—Access "alias" help system
#include <fstream.h>
#include <iostream.h>
#include <strstream.h>
#include <string.h>
#include "alias.h"

void main(int argc, char* argv[]) {
  // create help filename and open file:
  char helpname[bufsz];
  ostrstream hn(helpname, bufsz);
```

```
hn << bat_dir << "BHELP.TXT" << ends;
ifstream helpfile(helpname);
if(!helpfile) {
  cout << "could not open " << helpname;
  return;
}
char buf[bufsz];
if(argc < 2) {
  cerr << "alias commands available: "
       << "(type 'bhelp word' for lookup on 'word')" << endl;
  int linecount = 1;
  while(helpfile.getline(buf, bufsz)) {
    cout << buf << endl;
    if ( ++linecount % screenlength == 0 ) {
      cout << "press CR to continue:";
      cin.ignore(); // ignore input line
      linecount = 0;
    }
  }
  return;
}
strlwr(argv[1]);
int found = 0;
while(helpfile.getline(buf, bufsz)) {
  if(strstr(strlwr(buf), argv[1]) == 0) continue; // no match
  found++;
  cout << buf << endl; // match
}
if(!found) cout << "no help found for " << argv[1] << endl;
}
```

Both the command-line argument and the input string are forced to lowercase with the commonly available function **strlwr()**, to eliminate case sensitivity.

Marking Words in a File

Here's a program that further demonstrates the use of string streams. It places any markers you choose on specific words in a file.

```
//: WORDTAG.CPP—Tags selected words in a text file
//. Example of iostream file and buffer handling
#include <strstream.h>
#include <fstream.h>
#include <string.h>
```

```
const char* startmark = "<(";
const char* endmark = ")>";
const marklength = strlen(startmark) + strlen(endmark);

void main(int argc, char *argv[]) {
  if(argc < 4) { cerr <<
    "Usage: wordtag word infile outfile\n"
    "word is bracketed by '" << startmark << "' and '"
    << endmark << "' wherever it is\n"
    "encountered as infile is written to outfile."
    << endl;
    return;
  }
  const char* word = argv[1];
  const wordsize = strlen(word);

  ifstream in(argv[2]);
  if(!in) {
    cerr << "could not open input file " << argv[2] << endl;
    return;
  }

  ofstream out(argv[3]);
  if(!out) {
    cerr << "could not open output file " << argv[3] << endl;
    return;
  }

  const bufsize = 200;
  char buf[bufsize], outbuf[bufsize];

  while(in.getline(buf, bufsize)) {
    char * found = buf;
    while(found = strstr(found, word)) {
      *found = '\0'; // terminate string
      ostrstream output(outbuf, bufsize);
      output << buf << startmark << word
             << endmark << found + wordsize << '\0';
      memcpy(buf, outbuf, bufsize);
      found += wordsize + marklength;
    }
    out << buf << endl;
  }
}
```

After opening the input and output files, each string is read in until the
end of the file is encountered with the **while(in.getline(buf, bufsize))**

(note this will not overwrite the buffer). For each line, a pointer called **found** is set to the beginning of the buffer, then moved forward with a call to the ANSI C library function **strstr(found, word)**, which finds the first occurrence of **word**, searching from **found**. Since the result is assigned back to **found**, the pointer is moved forward to the beginning of the first word. At that point the line is terminated by inserting a \0 (yes, right into the buffer). The **ostrstream output** is created, and the first part of the line is inserted, followed by the marked word, followed by the rest of the line *after* the word. Then the whole line is copied back into **buf** with the ANSI C library function **memcpy()**, and **found** is moved forward past the word and its marks. At this point the search is repeated for more words in the buffer until the end is reached, at which point it is sent to the output file.

A Tool to Check Line Widths

The following program checks the widths of your listings and creates a batch file to edit the files that contain lines that are too long:

```
//: WIDTH.CPP—Verifies that no line is wider than maxwidth
#include <fstream.h>
#include <string.h>
#include <direct.h>
const int maxwidth = 64;   // maximum line width

ofstream names("names.bat");
ofstream tmp("tmp.tmp");

class fileinfo : ffblk {
  int done;
public:
  fileinfo(char * afn) {
    done = findfirst(afn, this, 0);
  }
  operator char*() { return (done ? 0 : ff_name); }
  int operator++() { return (done = findnext(this)); }
  int operator++(int) { return operator++(); }
  friend ostream& operator<<(ostream& os, fileinfo& fi) {
    return os << fi.ff_name;
  }
};
```

```
void checkfiles(char * afn) {
  const sz = 100;
  char buf[sz];
  fileinfo files(afn);
  while (files) {
    ifstream in(files);  // open an input file
    int found _ 0;
    int linecount = 0;
    while ( in.getline(buf,sz) ) {
      linecount++;
      if ( strlen(buf) > maxwidth ) {
        cout << "in " << files << ", line "
          << linecount << " is too long by "
          << strlen(buf) - maxwidth << " characters" << endl;
        cout << buf << endl;
        tmp << "in " << files << ", line "
          << linecount << " is too long by "
          << strlen(buf) - maxwidth << " characters" << endl;
        if(!found) {
          found++;
          names << "emacs " << files << " tmp.tmp" << endl; }
      }
    }
    files++; // get the next filename
  }
}

void main() {
  checkfiles("*.cpp");
  checkfiles("*.h");
  checkfiles("makefile");
}
```

After opening the batch file and the text file in which to store the line width messages, the **ffblk** struct (from **dir.h**, used with **findfirst()** and **findnext()**) is inherited into a new class called **fileinfo**, so the entire **ffblk** struct is copied into **fileinfo**. The constructor calls **findfirst()** to get the first filename (notice it passes **this** as the address of the **ffblk**, since the current class is inherited from **ffblk**, so it *is* an **ffblk**!). Then, every time you call **operator++()** (note both the pre- and postfix versions are defined) the next filename is fetched by calling **findnext()**. When you want the name of the file, simply use the object and the **operator char*()** will produce the name. Finally, the overloaded **ostream** output operator puts the filename on an output stream.

The **fileinfo** class is used inside **checkfiles()** to step through all the possible filenames, given an ambiguous filename. Each file is opened, and all its lines are read in one at a time and checked with the ANSI C library function **strlen()**. If one is too long, its position in the file is noted, printed to standard output and to the TMP.TMP file, and the filename is placed in the batch file (the "emacs" editor is invoked by the batch file, but you can use your own favorite).

A Program to List Files

This program sends any number of files to standard output after adding headlines and line numbers. It is intended that the output be redirected to your printer, as in:

```
list file1 file2 file3 > PRN:
```

(or piped to a print spooler in UNIX).

There are several lines in the program that are specific to a particular printer (in this case, the Hewlett-Packard LaserJet). The line

```
const pagelength = 95;
```

gives the number of lines in a page; since compressed print is used here there are more lines than on a typical page.

The lines:

```
cout << escape << "&15C";
cout << escape << "(s16.66H";
```

send escape codes to initialize the LaserJet, and the line:

```
cout << escape << "E";
```

ejects the last page and resets the printer.

To manage paging, a class called **pager** is created, and a single instance **line** is made. When **line** is incremented (using **operator++()**), it checks to see if the number of lines, **linecount**, is greater than **pagelength**. If so, it ejects the page, increments the number of pages,

pagecount, and generates a new headline. Every time the file is changed, the member function **name()** changes the name so the headline can reflect the new filename.

Class **pager** also maintains a time when the listing started, to print in the headline. ANSI C time function declarations are contained in the header file **time.h**. Consult your local manual for a full description of the time functions.

```cpp
//: LIST.CPP—Produce program listings on a HP LaserJet
// Change the escape sequences for your favorite printer
#include <stdlib.h>
#include <iostream.h>
#include <fstream.h>
#include <string.h>
#include <time.h>
const pagelength = 94;  // number of lines per page
const tabsize = 8; // number of spaces in a tab
const char escape = char(27); // Escape character

// In the date and time function, the structure element
// tm_wday is a number representing the day of the week.
// This array converts a number in tm_wday to a weekday name.
char * weekday[] = {
  "Sunday",
  "Monday",
  "Tuesday",
  "Wednesday",
  "Thursday",
  "Friday",
  "Saturday",
};

// Class to hide the details of paging the output
class pager {
  int linecount;  // count lines per page
  int pagecount; // pages for whole job
  char * filename;
  time_t ltime;  // holds encoded time
  tm t; // the time and day
  int namecount; // counts the number of times the name()
                 // function has been called.
public:
  pager() {
    linecount = pagecount = 1;
    filename = (char *)0;
```

```
    namecount =0;
    time(&ltime); // get time
    // convert time & make a local copy:
    t = *localtime(&ltime);
  }
  void header();  // print the header at the top of a page
  void tab(int i = 1) {
    for(int j = 0; j < i * tabsize; j++)
      cout.put(' ');
  }
  void eject() {
    cout << '\f'; // Form Feed
    pagecount++;
    linecount = 2;
    header();
  }
  // add one to the linecount and conditionally eject:
  void bumpline() {
    if ( ++linecount % pagelength == 0)
      eject();  // and print new header
  }
  void operator++() { bumpline(); }
  void operator++(int) { bumpline(); }  // postfix version
  void name(char * fn) {  // change name
    // the first 2 times, don't print the name. This would
    // generate duplicates for the first file in the list:
    if (namecount++ >= 2) {
      cout << "\nFILE: " << fn;
      bumpline();
      cout << endl; bumpline();
      cout << endl; bumpline();
    }
    delete filename; // free old name (delete 0 has no effect)
    filename = new char[strlen(fn) + 1];
    strcpy(filename,fn); // attach new name
  }
} line;  // declare a global

void pager::header() {
  cout << "FILE: " << filename;
  tab(2);
  int hr = t.tm_hour, pm = 0;
  int hour = hr > 12 ? (pm++, hr -12) : hr;
  cout << weekday[t.tm_wday] << ", " <<
```

```
      t.tm_mon << "/" << t.tm_mday << "/" << t.tm_year <<
      "   " << hour << ":" <<
      (t.tm_min < 10 ? "0" : "") << t.tm_min << " " <<
      (pm ? "pm" : "am");
   tab(2);
   cout << "page " << pagecount << "\n\n";
}

void main(int argc, char * argv[]) {
   const int bsize = 100;
   if (argc < 2) {
      cerr << "usage: list filelist\n";
      exit(1);
   }
   // these two lines are HP LaserJet-specific:
   cout << escape << "&l5C";  // 5/48" (approx 10 lines/inch)
   cout << escape << "(s16.66H"; // small typeface
   line.name(argv[1]); line.header(); // first page header
   // do for all files:
   for (int filenum - 1; filenum < argc; filenum++) {
      ifstream infile(argv[filenum]);
      line.name(argv[filenum]); // change & print the name
      int count = 1;  // count of lines in file
      char buf[bsize], c;
      while(infile.getline(buf,bsize)) { // reads each line
         // until '\n' or line size == bsize
         cout << count++ << ": " << buf << endl;
         line++;  // count lines & automatically page
      }
   }
   // this line is HP LaserJet-specific:
   cout << escape << "E";  // eject page and reset printer
}
```

Notice that the member function **name()** changes the name in the **pager** object and prints the new filename. The first time you call **name()**, it sets the name for use by the headline. The second call to **name()** is also for the first file, but after the **while** loop. You don't want the name printed in either case because the name is printed at the top of the first page. A counter, **namecount**, keeps track of the number of times the function has been called. After two times, the filename is printed.

Command-Line Processing

C and C++ contain convenient facilities for processing arguments on the command line. Arguments are usually filenames, but often some form of flags (or switches) are also needed to allow the user options in the way the program operates.

The code presented here includes a class to make the handling of flags easy. This class can be modified to manage flags for any other program by simply creating your own header file to define the flags. The class makes the main program much clearer, and the template reduces errors.

When a C or C++ program starts, the command line is passed to the **main()** routine in the form of two arguments. As with any argument list in a function, you may call the arguments anything you want as long as they are of the correct type. Traditionally, however, the arguments are called **argc** (for "argument count") and **argv** (for "argument values"). The **argc** is an integer that tells the number of arguments in the command line including the program name (**cat filename** has an **argc** of 2). The **argv** is an array of character pointers that point to strings of the names on the command line, including the program name. You may see **main()** declared in two equivalent forms: **main(int argc, char ** argv)** or more typically **main(int argc, char * argv[])**. In either case, **argv[0]** produces a character pointer to the program name string, **argv[1]** points to the first argument, and so on. Command-line processing consists of determining the number of arguments (via **argc**) and processing each one (via their character strings in **argv**).

As an example, here's a program that simply lists its arguments:

```
//: ARGLIST.CPP—List command-line arguments
#include <iostream.h>

void main(int argc, char * argv[] ) {
  for(int i = 0; i < argc; i++)
    cout << "arg[" << i << "] is : " << argv[i] << "\n";
}
```

Command-Line Flags

A program often has a number of options. These options may be set by a configuration file, interaction with the user, or via arguments on the command line. Command-line flags are usually differentiated by a leading character; for this example, + will turn the flag on (enable the desired option) and - will turn the flag off (disable the option).

The programs in this section demonstrate a system to easily add flag options to the command line. To change the flag options, edit a special file containing calls to a macro called **FLAG**. For the first program, the file looks like this:

```
//: TSTFLAG.H—Flag definitions for CLTEST.CPP
// This file defines the command-line flags
// needed for a program; this is the only place
// flags need to be set up.

FLAG(var1)
FLAG(var2)
FLAG(var3)
FLAG(var4)
FLAG(var5)
```

The **FLAG** macro is redefined and the header file included any time you need to do something with the flags. This "flag-definition header file" is used in the program's header file as follows:

```
//: CLFLAGS.H—Class to manage command-line flags
// NOTE: the file FLAGFILE (a #define on the compiler
// command line) is different for each program. This
// is controlled in the makefile

#ifndef FLAGFILE
// The "error" preprocessor directive emits error
// messages during compilation
#error FLAGFILE must be defined on the
#error command line with -DFLAGFILE=filename
#endif

#define xstringize(a)    #a
#define stringize(a)     xstringize(a)

#undef FLAG
#define FLAG(name) name,

enum FLAG_NUMBER {
  #include stringize(FLAGFILE)
  FLAG_COUNT_
```

```
};

class CL_flags {
  int flag_value[FLAG_COUNT_];
 public:
  CL_flags();
  int is_flag(char * cl_arg); // true if a flag
  void set(FLAG_NUMBER n) { flag_value[n]++; }
  void clear(FLAG_NUMBER n) { flag_value[n] = 0; }
  int is_on(FLAG_NUMBER n) { return flag_value[n]; }
  int is_off(FLAG_NUMBER n) { return !flag_value[n]; }
  // returns a character representation of the flag:
  const char* str(int n);
};

extern CL_flags flag;
```

The **stringize()** function takes the command-line definition and turns it into a character string (using **xstringize()**) so it can be used in the **#include** statement.

In this file, the **FLAG** macro is redefined to reproduce its argument followed by a comma. When the FLAGFILE is included, an enumeration is created. Note that FLAGFILE is defined on the compiler command line so **cflags.h** can be the same, no matter what program you're setting up the flags for. If the header file defining the flags hasn't been included, an error message is emitted using the **#error** directive. You can use this directive any time you want to send a message to the person compiling the program.

The class **CL_flags** keeps track of the number and value of all the flags. The **flags** object is declared as **extern** in the header file and defined in the definition file; you simply reference it in your program. Once the object is initialized, you can set or clear flags, and you can test to see if a flag is on or off. Because of the **enum**, you can refer to flags by their name; this makes the program much easier to read and write.

The **is_flag()** function checks to see if the argument is a flag using the ANSI C library function **strcmp()** to compare strings, and it sets or clears the corresponding flag number according to whether the character leading the flag is + (to set the flag) or - (to clear it). The rest of the program can simply query the **CL_flags** object to see whether a particular flag is set or cleared.

Here is the implementation for **CL_flags**:

```
//: CLFLAGS.CPP—Manages command-line flags
#include <string.h>
#include <iostream.h>
#include <stdlib.h>
#include "clflags.h"

CL_flags flag; // Single flag object used in program

#undef FLAG
#define FLAG(name) #name,

static const char * FL_STRING[] = {
  #include stringize(FLAGFILE)
};

CL_flags::CL_flags() {
  for (int i = 0; i < FLAG_COUNT_; i++)
    flag_value[i] = 0; // clear all flags
}

int CL_flags::is_flag(char * cl_arg) { // true if a flag
  if ( cl_arg[0] != '-' && cl_arg[0] != '+')
    return 0; // not a flag
  for (int i = 0; i < FLAG_COUNT_; i++) {
    // note we must start the comparison at the character
    // after the '+' or '-' by adding 1 to the pointer:
    if ( strcmp( FL_STRING[i], cl_arg + 1 ) == 0) {
      switch (cl_arg[0]) {
        case '+' : set((FLAG_NUMBER)i); break;
        case '-' : clear((FLAG_NUMBER)i);
      }
      break; // quit "for" loop
    }
  }
  if ( i == FLAG_COUNT_ ) {
    cerr << "command-line error: flag not found: "
      << cl_arg << "\n"
      << "available flags are:\n";
    for (int j = 0; j < FLAG_COUNT_; j++)
      cerr << "\t" << FL_STRING[j] << "\n";
    cerr << "+ to turn on, - to turn off\n";
    exit(1);
  }
  return 1; // return true since it was a flag
}

const char* CL_flags::str(int n) {
```

```
  if(n < 0 || n >= FLAG_COUNT_) return "flag # out of range";
  return FL_STRING[n];
}
```

Here, the **FLAG** macro is redefined so the flags get string representations, and those strings are placed in an array of character pointers (using aggregate initialization). In the redefinition of the **FLAG** macro, the preprocessor "stringizing" directive **#** is used to turn the identifier into a string.

An alternative design might hand **argc** and **argv** to the constructor and let it hunt through the command line for flags. When it finds a flag, it can remove it from the command line and adjust **argc** and **argv** accordingly. Although this is more automatic, it doesn't have the same level of flexibility. With the design shown here, the *order* of the flags on the command line can be important. You can turn a feature on for one file and turn it off for the next one. This can be very useful.

The constructor turns all the flags off. **Is_flag()** checks to see if an argument is a flag; if so the flag value is noted and a Boolean true (nonzero value) is returned so the user can ignore the argument. If an unknown flag is encountered an error message is printed along with a list of the acceptable flags.

Here's an example using **CL_flags**:

```
//: CLTEST.CPP—Test clflags
#include "clflags.h"
#include <iostream.h>

void main(int argc, char * argv[]) {
  for (int i = 1; i < argc; i++)
    if ( ! flag.is_flag(argv[i]))
      cout << "argument " << i << " isn't a flag\n";
  for (i = 0; i < FLAG_COUNT_; i++)
    cout << "flag " << flag.str(i) << " is "
    << (flag.is_on((FLAG_NUMBER)i) ? "ON" : "OFF") << "\n";
}
```

It prints out the state of the arguments that are flags and the arguments that aren't flags. With this program, you can turn a flag on and off, and (since it processes the flags all at once) it will only notice the final value.

To compile any program using **CL_flags**, you must specify on the compiler command line the name of the file containing the flag names. This is done by setting a preprocessor definition on the command line, like this:

```
-DFLAGFILE=tstflag.h
```

You must also generate and link an .OBJ file with a different name for each project. The makefile at the end of the chapter shows how this is done for the example programs.

A Simple Utility

The next example also uses the **CL_flags** system. It takes standard input, processes it according to the flag settings, and sends the result to standard output. The flags default to "option disabled." The effect of each flag is as follows:

+zero:	Zero the high bit of each character (high bits are set by some word processors)
+number:	Put line numbers on the output
+upcase:	Make all characters uppercase
+downcase:	Make all characters lowercase
+xtab:	Expand tabs to spaces

If you want to number the lines of a file called INFILE and send the result to a file called OUTFILE, type

```
format +number < infile > outfile
```

The program uses a set of plain C functions declared in the file **ctype.h** to convert the letter cases.

The flag-name header file is shown here:

```
//: FORMFLAG.H—Flag definitions for the format program
```

```
FLAG(zero)
FLAG(number)
FLAG(upcase)
FLAG(downcase)
FLAG(xtab)
```

The format program, shown here, just interrogates the flags to see what is to be done with each input character:

```
//: TFORMAT.CPP—Format input according to command-line flags
//. Send result to standard output
#include "clflags.h"
#include <iostream.h>
#include <ctype.h> // toupper() & tolower()

void main(int argc, char * argv[]) {
  for (int i = 1; i < argc; i++)
    flag.is_flag(argv[i]); // process flags
  char c;
  int linecount = 1;
  if (flag.is_on(number))
    cout << linecount << ": ";
  while( cin.get(c) ) {
    if (flag.is_on(zero))
      c &= 0x7f; // zero the high bit
    if (flag.is_on(upcase))
      c = toupper(c); // all but a-z are unchanged
    if (flag.is_on(downcase))
      c = tolower(c); // all but A-Z are unchanged
    if (c != '\t' || flag.is_off(xtab))
      cout.put(c); // ordinary output
    else {
      for (int x = 0; x < 8; x++)
        cout.put(' '); // expand tabs to spaces
    }
    if ( c == '\n' ) {
      linecount++;
      if (flag.is_on(number))
        cout << linecount << ": ";
    }
  }
}
```

Improvements

There are two modifications you can make to the **CL_flags** system. First, you can add a default message, which is printed whenever an incorrect flag is used. The message should be constructed at compile time from a text file, and the user should be able to call it via a member function.

The second modification is to allow arguments to flags. For example:

```
programname size=20
```

This means you must differentiate between on/off flags and variable flags and look for an = in the flag.

Not all programs use all the features of an object-oriented programming language. Many, such as this one, benefit from encapsulation but don't use inheritance or virtual functions.

TAWK: A Simple Database Interpreter

Most microcomputer database management systems will read and write records in a "comma-separated ASCII" format. This is probably an artifact from the days when BASIC (which uses that format) was the only common tongue on microcomputers. Comma-separated ASCII files are useful not only because they allow the records from one database to be moved to another, but because they can be manipulated using programming languages.

Here's an example of a comma-separated ASCII file:

```
"Robert Jones", "Bob's Bagels","423 Main","Clover", "CA"
"Julia Zompstien", "Julie's Tabouleh","147 Elm","Clover", "CA"
"Otis Careen", "Zoom Espresso","301 Mt. View","Clover", "CA"
"Jim Cliff","Jimmy's Jamaican Food","901 Garden","Clover","CA"
"Juan Ortez","Thai Palace","700 Rushing Creek","Clover","CA"
"Tran Phin","Vietnam Garden","90 Center Street","Clover","CA"
```

Each field in a record is delimited by double quotes. The fields are separated from each other by commas, and each record is terminated by a newline. Commas are allowed inside fields, but double quotes are not.

While BASIC automatically reads and writes these records, other languages must be programmed to do so. In C++, this tedious task can be encapsulated into several classes; the user of the class doesn't need to worry about the details. In the first part of this project, two classes are created: the constructor for class **field** reads a single quoted and comma-separated field and makes an object from it. The constructor for class **csascii** opens a comma-separated ASCII file and reads records (as arrays of field objects) one at a time until the file ends. A simple application is shown that uses the classes to search through a database file for a last name.

Database files must often be manipulated or output in an organized way as a "report." It becomes tedious to write and compile code for each different report, and nonprogrammers must often design reports. A common solution to a problem like this is the creation of a "scripting language" specifically tailored to the task at hand. The second part of this project is the creation of a very simple language that outputs the comma-separated ASCII records to standard output according to a script in a separate file.

The program is called "TAWK" for "tiny AWK," since the problem it solves is vaguely reminiscent of the "AWK" pattern-matching language found on UNIX (versions of AWK have also been created for DOS). It demonstrates one of the thornier problems in computer science: parsing and executing a programming language. The data-encapsulation features of C++ prove very useful here, and a recursive technique is used to read arbitrarily long fields and records (note the other solution, presented in Chapter 7 as the function **asctok()** in DBCONV.CPP).

Recursive Descent

A *recursive-descent* algorithm is very useful if you don't know how long or complicated a statement will be when you start looking at it. In programming languages, for example, recursive-descent parsers are often used in expression evaluation, since expressions can contain other expressions. In this project, the expressions aren't particularly complicated, but you don't know how long a string of text is going to be.

When scanning an expression using recursive descent, a central function is used. This function munches along absorbing input until it runs into a delimiter indicating a change in the type of input (white space, for example, or a number). At this point it might call another function to eat the white space or to get the string of digits and turn it into a number. Then if the expression is finished it will just return. If the expression *isn't* finished (and here's the tricky part) it *calls itself.* That is, it *recurses.* Every time it encounters a new expression within the one it's evaluating, it just calls itself to evaluate the expression.

When solving more complex problems (such as a programming language), a set of functions is used. Each function may call any of the others during expression evaluation.

At some point the evaluation must bottom out. When this happens, the function performs some termination activities and then returns. As the stack unwinds from all the recursive calls, the tail end of each function call performs some operation to store the information it was able to glean, and then it returns. When the function finally completes, the expression has been evaluated.

Recursive scanning is used in three places in this project. The **field** class, which creates an object containing a single quote-delimited field, has a recursive function **field::getfield()** (shown in file FIELD.CPP) to read one character at a time, keeping track of the number of characters encountered, until the end of the field. When the closing quote is encountered, memory is allocated for exactly the right number of characters and the function returns. As it unwinds, characters are placed in the object's data buffer. Using recursive descent means there are no restrictions on the field size, assuming you have an infinite stack. For very large records, **field::getfield()** may need to be changed so it doesn't blow up the stack.

The **token** class (in file **parse.h**) uses recursive descent in a more sophisticated way. When a **token** object is created by handing it an input stream (via the constructor function **token::token(istream & input)**), it reads the input stream until it has scanned a complete token. When the constructor completes, a new token has been created.

A *token* is a group of symbols representing a single concept. A C++ compiler uses a large number of tokens: { means "begin a scope," **'for'** means "start a for loop," **'foo'** means "a variable."

TAWK has a much smaller number of tokens. All tokens in TAWK are delimited by the @ sign, which starts a new command. When @ is encountered, it is pushed back onto the input stream (for use in the next **token** object), and the current token is completed. The central recursive function for **token** is **token::get_token()**, shown later in file PARSE.CPP.

The class **parse_array** builds an array of tokens by recursively calling **parse_array::build_array()**. This function makes a new token and then looks at the token to decide what to do next.

The two programs (LOOKUP and TAWK) are built from several classes. Each of these classes will be examined.

Class field

Here is the declaration for class **field**:

```
//: FIELD.H—Used by csascii class to build a single field.
//. Fields are collected by csascii to create a record.
#include <iostream.h>
#include <fstream.h>

class field { // one field in a comma-separated ASCII record
  ifstream * input; // where to get the data
  char * data;
  int length, fsize;
  int end_of_file;  // flag to indicate the end of file happened
  void getfield();  // recursive function to read in a field;
          // treats data, length & input as globals
  int infield; // flag used by getfield() to determine whether
        // it's inside a quoted field
public:
  field(ifstream & instream);
  ~field();
  friend ostream& operator<<(ostream &s, field & f) {
    s << f.data;
    return s;
  }
  int eof() { return end_of_file; }  // to check for end
  int size() { return fsize;}
```

```
  int last_length() { return length; }
  char * string() { return data; }
};
```

Here are the definitions for class **field**:

```
//: FIELD.CPP—Definitions for class field
//. A recursive scanning scheme is used because field
//. length is always unknown.
#include "field.h"

field::field(ifstream & instream) {
  input = &instream;
  length = 0;
  end_of_file = 0; // set flag to say "we're not at the end"
  infield = 0; // set flag to say "we're not inside a field"
  data = 0; // to show no memory has been allocated
  getfield();  // recursively get characters until end of field
}

field::~field() {
  delete data;  // if no memory has been allocated,
                // this will have no effect.
}

// A Comma-separated ASCII field is contained in quotes to allow
// commas within the field; these quotes must be stripped out
void field::getfield() {
  char c = input->get();
  // This happens when Descending:
  if(c == EOF) {
    end_of_file++;  // just say we reached the end...
    return;
  }
  else  // watch out for the UNIX vs. DOS LF/CR problem here:
    if (((c != ',') || infield) && (c != '\n')) {
      if ( (c != '"') && (c != '\r')) // watch for quotes or CR
        length++;  // no quotes—count this character
      else {
        if ( c == '\"')
          infield = !infield;  // if we weren't inside a field
          // and a quote was encountered, we are now inside
          // a field. If we were inside a field and a quote
          // was found, we're out of the field.
        c = 0; // a quote or CR; mark it so it isn't included
      }
      getfield();  // recursively get characters in field
```

```
    // after returning from function call, we jump past
    // the following "else" part to finish the recursion
  }
  else { // This happens once, when the terminator is found:
    fsize = length;  // remember how long the string is
    data = new char[length + 1]; // space for null terminator
    data[length] = '\0';  // highest index is "length"
      // when you allocate an array of length + 1
    length--;  // notice we don't insert the delimiter
    // Now the first "if" statement evaluates to TRUE and
    // the function rises back up.
    return;
  }
// This happens when Ascending:
if ( c ) // if it wasn't a quote or CR,
  data[length--] = c;  // put chars in as we rise back up...
}
```

The field object doesn't control opening or closing files; it is simply handed an **istream** from which it takes its input. If it finds the end of input, it just makes an internal note (by setting its **end_of_file** flag) and returns. It's up to the caller to check for end of file with the function **field::eof()**.

The **operator<<()** is overloaded so a field object may be put to a stream output object. When this occurs, the **data** field is copied to the output.

The field constructor **field::field(istream & instream)** initializes all the variables to 0 and sets the member **istream * input** equal to **instream**. This allows **field::getfield()** to treat **input** as a global variable and get the next character. The last thing the constructor does is call the recursive function **field::getfield()**, which recurses until it reaches the end of the field. When the constructor finishes, the field is complete.

The function **field::getfield()** reads a character from the input stream. If it isn't an end-of-file, it checks for terminators, which include a comma if not enclosed by quotes (determined by a special flag **infield**) or a carriage return, which delimits the entire record. If no terminator is found, the function counts the current character and calls itself to get the next character. If a terminator is found, memory is allocated to hold the string (using the C++ dynamic-memory allocation keyword **new**) and the string terminator \0 is inserted. As the function returns from calling itself, each character is inserted, from right to left, into the buffer.

Memory is not always allocated for a field. The constructor for a field object sets the **data** pointer to 0. If memory is never allocated, the destructor will **delete** a NULL pointer, which is defined to have no effect.

Class csascii

Here is the **csascii** (for comma-separated-ASCII) class declaration:

```
//: CSASCII.H—Manipulates comma-separated ASCII databases
#include <iostream.h>
#include <fstream.h>
#include "field.h"

class csascii {  // manipulates comma-separated ascii files,
// generated by most database management systems (generated and
// used by the BASIC programming language). Each field
// is separated by a comma; records are separated by newlines.
  int fieldcount;
  field ** data; // an array to hold the entire record
  ifstream * datafile; // file with comma separated ASCII input
  int readrecord(); // private function to read a record
 public:
  csascii(const char * filename); // Open file, get first record
  ~csascii(); // destructor
  int next(); // get next record, return 0 when EOF
  field & operator[](int index); // select a field
  int number_of_fields() { return fieldcount; }
};
```

Here's the definition file for **csascii**:

```
//: CSASCII.CPP—Comma-separated ascii database definitions
//. manipulation class
#include <stdlib.h>
#include "csascii.h"
#include <fstream.h>

int csascii::readrecord() {
  for (int fieldnum = 0; fieldnum < fieldcount; fieldnum++ ) {
    data[fieldnum] = new field(*datafile);
    if (data[fieldnum]->eof()) return 0;
  }
```

```cpp
    return 1;
}

csascii::csascii(const char * filename) {
  int quote = 0;
  fieldcount = 0;
  // first, determine the number of fields in a record:
  {
    ifstream infile(filename);
    if(!infile) {cerr << "could not open "<< filename; exit(1);}
    char c;
    while(infile.get(c), c != '\n') {
      // keep track of being inside a quoted string:
      if (c == '\"') quote = !quote;  // invert the flag
      // fields are delimited by unquoted commas:
      if ( c == ',' && !quote)
        fieldcount++;
    }
  }  // infile goes out of scope; file closed
  fieldcount++; // last field terminated by newline, not comma
  // an array of field pointers:
  data = new field*[fieldcount];
  // reopen at start; dynamically allocate so it isn't scoped:
  datafile = new ifstream(filename);
  readrecord();
}

csascii::~csascii() {
  for (int i = 0; i < fieldcount; i++ )
    delete data[i];  // free all the data storage
  delete []data;  // general form for array deletion
  delete datafile; // calls ifstream destructor to close file
}

int csascii::next() {
  if(data)
    for (int i = 0; i < fieldcount; i++ ) {
      delete data[i];  // free all the data storage
      data[i] = 0;
    }
  return readrecord(); // 0 when end of file
}

field & csascii::operator[](int index) {
  if (index >= fieldcount) {
    cerr << "index too large for number of fields in record";
    exit(1);
```

```
  }
  return *(data[index]);
}
```

The constructor opens the input file, counts the number of fields in a record, and closes the file. It then creates an array of pointers to field objects, reopens the file and reads the first record in. Every time **csascii::next()** is called, a new record is read until the end of the file.

The **operator[]()** is overloaded so the individual fields may be selected from each record. This function checks to ensure that the index is within bounds.

Notice that in **csascii::csascii()**, the file is closed implicitly by putting braces around the first clause in the constructor where the fields are counted. When the **istream** object goes out of scope, the file is closed. This is the only purpose for putting the braces there. Anytime you want to control the destruction of a local variable, simply put it in braces.

Testing field *and* csascii

Here is a short program to show the use of class **csascii**:

```
//: LOOKUP.CPP-Use of csascii to find name in a database
//. Combines fields so you can search on all fields in a record
#include "csascii.h"
#include <string.h>
#include <stdlib.h>
#include <conio.h>
#include <strstream.h>
const char ESC = char(27);  // Escape character
const char* dbfile = "PPQUICK.ASC";

void main(int argc, char ** argv) {
  if (argc < 2) {
    cerr << "usage: lookup lastname\n";
    exit(1);
  }
  char * target = strlwr(argv[1]);
  // create object & open file:
  csascii file(dbfile);
  do {
    const bsize = 150; char buf[bsize];
```

```
   ostrstream combined(buf, bsize); // for combining the fields
   for(int i = 0; i < file.number_of_fields(); i++)
     combined << file[i];
   combined << '\0';
   if (strstr(strlwr(buf),target)) {
     cout << ESC << "[2J"; // ANSI clear screen
     for (int i = 0; i < file.number_of_fields(); i++)
       cout << file[i] << endl;
     cout << ESC << "[7m" << "press any key"
          << ESC << "[0m"; // ANSI display reverse video
     if( getch() == 27) break;
   }
 } while (file.next());
}
```

The **csascii** object **file** is created by giving it the name of the comma-separated ASCII file PPQUICK.ASC. Then the records are read one at a time, and field 0 is compared to the first argument on the command line (presumably the last name of the person in the database). When a record is found, it is displayed on the screen (notice the use of the ANSI screen-control codes). A flag called **found** is set to indicate at least one record is found, so when no more matches occur the program knows to exit (it is assumed the file has been sorted by the database manager).

The ANSI C library function **strcmp()** has been used here for compatibility. To ignore upper- or lowercase in the comparisons, some compilers provide a special function.

TAWK: Tiny AWK

The TAWK language is a tiny database processor, vaguely like AWK—a "Tiny AWK."

The TAWK language

TAWK has a syntax as follows:

tawk *tawkfile csafile*

csafile contains comma-separated ASCII records. Each field in a record is contained in quotes, and each record is delimited by a newline. These are standard records that can be generated by the BASIC language and most database management systems.

tawkfile is a file that contains formatting commands. Each record in the *csafile* is read, and fields in the record are printed out according to the formatting commands in the *tawkfile*.

Everything in the *tawkfile* (characters, spaces, and newlines) is printed literally except for the following:

@(n)   Print field number *n*; @(3) prints field 3 of the current record. The first field in a record is field 0.

@<n>   Print an ASCII character number *n*; @<27> prints the escape character.

@!   This line is a comment until the end of the line.

@?nn@: (then *statements*) @~ (else *statements*) @   An   **if-then-else** conditional. If field *nn* is not empty, the **then** statements are executed; otherwise the **else** statements are executed. A conditional must have all three parts, but the statements may be empty. Conditionals can be nested.

@Preamble, @preamble, @P, or @p   When a TAWK file is begun, all statements until @main are considered to be part of the preamble. The preamble is only executed once, at the beginning of the program. The preamble must be strictly text, it cannot contain field numbers or conditionals. The @preamble statement is optional; @preamble is assumed until @main.

@Main, @main, @M, or @m   The main section is executed once for each record in the file. All statements between @Main and @Conclusion are part of the main section. @Main may contain field numbers and conditionals. The @main statement is required.

@Conclusion, @conclusion, @C, or @c   The conclusion is executed after the last record in the database file is read and the file is closed. The conclusion, like the preamble, may only contain text. All other characters on the same line as @preamble, @main, or @conclusion are ignored. The @conclusion statement is required.

@end   This must be at the end of the TAWK file.

@@   Print an @.

Here is an example TAWK file:

```
@! A comment, which isn't printed
@! The @preamble is optional, but promotes understanding
@main
    This is field 1: @(1)
    This is field 10: @(10)
    @?4@: @(4) @~Field 4 is empty @.
    print an escape: @<27>
    Regenerate comma-separated ASCII record:
"@(0)","@(1)","@(2)","@(3)"
@conclusion  This is a comment
That's all, folks!!
@end
```

You can see that each TAWK command consists of an @ sign and a single character (in the case of @() and @<>, the commands are @(and @<, and the) and > are used by the function that reads the number to find the end).

Using TAWK

The execution of a TAWK script parallels the compilation or interpretation of other programming languages. The TAWK script is parsed into arrays of tokens when the program starts up. An execution routine steps through the arrays and performs actions based on the tokens to "run" the TAWK script.

Here are the declarations for class **token** and class **parse_array**:

```
//: PARSE.H—Class to parse a tawk script file
//. Creates a structure which can be used at
//. run time to "execute" the tawk script.
#include <iostream.h>
#include <fstream.h>

// types of tokens the scanner can find:
enum tokentype {
  fieldnumber, string, if_, else_, endif_, phase_change
};
```

```
// preamble and conclusion of the tawk script are only executed
// once, while main is executed once for every data record
enum phase { preamble, tmain, conclusion};

class token {
  tokentype ttype;
  union {  // an "anonymous union"
    int fieldnum;  // if type is a fieldnumber
    unsigned char * literal; // if type is a string
  };
  int if_level;  // if this is an if_, then_, or else_
  // private functions:
  void get_token();  // recursive descent scanner
  // Functions to help in scanning:
  void getnext(char & c); // used by get_token();
  unsigned char get_value(char delimiter, char * msg);
  void dumpline(); // for @! comments
  void error(char * msg = "", char * msg2 = "");
 public:
  token(ifstream & input);
  ~token();
  friend ostream & operator<<(ostream &s, token &t);
  int field_number() { return fieldnum; }
  int token_type() { return ttype; }
  int nesting_level() { return if_level;}
};

// The following is called a "container class," since its sole
// purpose is to hold a list of objects (tokens, in this case):
class parse_array {
  token ** tokenarray; // an array of token pointers
  ifstream * parse_stream;
  int token_count;
  int end; // the size of the array
  phase p_section; // of the program (preamble, etc.)
  void build_array(); // another recursive function
 public:
  parse_array(ifstream & input);
  ~parse_array();
  int size() { return end; } // how big is it?
  token & operator[](int index); // select a token
  phase section() { return p_section; }
};
```

Here are the definitions for **token** and **parse_array**:

```
//: PARSE.CPP—Class parse function definitions
#include "csascii.h"
#include "parse.h"
#include <ctype.h>
#include <stdlib.h>

// The following have file scope which means no one outside
// this file can know about them. This is the meaning when a
// variable outside all functions is declared "static."
static ifstream * tokenstream;
static int length; // to remember size of string
static int line_number = 1;  // line counting for errors
static int if_counter = 0; // monitors "if" statement nesting
static phase program_section = preamble;  // ... until @main
static int end_of_file = 0; // zero means not end of file

token::token(ifstream & input) {
  // initialize values and start the descent
  tokenstream = &input;
  length = 0;
  get_token();  // recursively get characters to end of token
}

token::~token() { // delete heap if any has been allocated:
  if (ttype == string)
    delete literal;
}

void token::error(char * msg, char * msg2) {
  cerr << "token error on line " << line_number << ": "
       << msg << " " << msg2 << "\n";
  exit(1);
}

ostream & operator<<(ostream &s, token &t) {
  switch (t.ttype) {
    case string:
      s << (char *)t.literal;
      break;
    case fieldnumber: // only for testing
      s << " fieldnumber: " << t.fieldnum << endl;
  }
  return s;
}

// Get a character from the tokenstream, checking for
// end-of-file and newlines
```

```
void token::getnext(char & c) {
  if(end_of_file)
    error("attempt to read after @end statement\n",
        "missing @conclusion ?");
  if((tokenstream->get(c)).eof() )
    error("@end statement missing");
  if (c == '\n')
    line_number++; // keep track of the line count
}

// See text for description of tokens
void token::get_token() {
  char c;
  // This happens when Descending:
  getnext(c);
  if ( c == '@') {
    if (length == 0) { // length 0 means start of token
      getnext(c);
      switch(c) {
        case '!': // comment
          dumpline(); // dump the comment
          get_token(); // get a real token
          break;
        case 'p' : case 'P' : // preamble statement
          if ( program_section != preamble )
            error("only one preamble allowed");
          dumpline(); // just for looks, ignore it
          get_token(); // get a real token
          break;
        case 'm' : case 'M' : // start of main loop
          dumpline(); // toss rest of line
          program_section = tmain;
          ttype = phase_change;
          return; // very simple token
        case 'c' : case 'C' : // start conclusion
          dumpline();
          program_section = conclusion;
          ttype = phase_change;
          return; // very simple token
        case 'e' : case 'E': // end statement
          end_of_file++;  // set flag
          ttype = fieldnumber; // so destructor doesn't
                     // delete free store for this token.
          if (if_counter)
            error("unclosed 'if' statement(s)");
          return;
        case '(' :
```

```
        if ( program_section == preamble ||
          program_section == conclusion )
         error("@() not allowed in preamble or conclusion");
        fieldnum = get_value(')',"@()");
        ttype = fieldnumber;
        // This is a complete token, so quit
        return;
      case '<' :
        c = get_value('>',"@<>");
        length++;
        get_token(); // get more...
        break;
      case '?' : // beginning of an "if" statement
        if ( program_section == preamble ||
          program_section == conclusion )
         error("@? not allowed in preamble or conclusion");
        fieldnum = get_value('@',"@?@");
        ttype = if_;
        getnext(c);   // just eat the colon
        if(c != ':')
           error("@? must be followed by @: (then)");
        if_level = ++if_counter;  // for nesting
        return;
      case '~' : // the "else" part of an "if" statement
        ttype = else_;
        if_level = if_counter;
        return;
      case '.' : // "endif" terminator of an "if" statement
        ttype = endif_;
        if_level = if_counter--;
        if(if_counter < 0)
           error("incorrect nesting of if-then-else clauses");
        return;
      case '@' : // two '@' in a row mean print an @
        length++;  // just leave '@' as the value of c
        get_token();
        break;
      default:
        error("'@' must be followed by:",
        "'(', '<', '?',':','~','.','p','m','c' or '@'");
    }
  } else { // an @ in the middle of a string; terminate
    // the string. Putback() is part of the stream class.
    // It is only safe to put one character back on the input
    tokenstream->putback(c); // to be used by the next token
    // allocate space, put the null in and return up the stack
    literal = new unsigned char[length + 1]; // space for \0
```

```
      literal[length--] = '\0'; // string delimiter
      ttype = string; // what kind of token this is
      return; // back up the stack
    }
  } else { // not an @, must be plain text
    length++;
    get_token();
  }
  // This occurs on the "tail" of the recursion:
  if(length >= 0) literal[length--] = c;
  // (put chars in as we rise back up)
}


// This function is used by get_token when it encounters a @(
// or a @< to get a number until it finds "delimiter."
// If an error occurs, msg is used to notify the user what
// kind of statement it is.
unsigned char token::get_value(char delimiter, char * msg) {
  char c;
  char buf[5];
  int i = 0;
  while(getnext(c), c != delimiter) {
    if (!isdigit(c))
      error("must use only digits inside", msg);
    buf[i++] = c;
  }
  buf[i] = 0;
  return atoi(buf);
}


void token::dumpline() { // called when @! encountered
  char c;
  while(getnext(c), c != '\n')
    ; // just eat characters until newline
}


// Since there's no way to know how big a parse_array is
// going to be until the entire tawkfile has been tokenized,
// the recursive approach is again used:

parse_array::parse_array(ifstream & input) {
  parse_stream = &input;
  token_count = 0;
  p_section = program_section; // so we know at run time
  build_array();
}
```

```
void parse_array::build_array() {
  token * tk = new token(*parse_stream);
  if( ! end_of_file && tk->token_type() != phase_change) {
    // normal token, not end of file or phase change:
    token_count++;
    // recursively get tokens until eof or phase change:
    build_array();
  } else { // end of file or phase change
    // only done once per object:
    // allocate memory and return up the stack
    tokenarray = new token * [end = token_count];
    memset(tokenarray, 0, end * sizeof(token*));
    if(token_count) token_count--; // only if nonzero
    return;
  }
  tokenarray[token_count--] = tk;  // performed on the "tail"
}

parse_array::~parse_array() {
  for (int i = 0; i < end; i++)
    delete tokenarray[i];
  delete tokenarray;
}

token & parse_array::operator[](int index) {
  if ( index >= end || tokenarray[index] == 0) {
    cerr << "parse_array error: index " << index
         << " out of bounds\n";
    exit(1);
  }
  return *tokenarray[index];
}
```

Here is the **main()** function for **TAWK**:

```
//: TAWK.CPP—Parses a tawk script and reads an ascii file
//. Generates results according to the tawk script.
#include "csascii.h"
#include "parse.h"
#include <fstream.h>
#include <stdlib.h>
#include <conio.h>  // DOS only—for getch(). Must use a
                    // local key-capture function for UNIX.
const char ESC = char(27);

void main (int argc, char * argv[]) {
  int screen = 0;  // flag set true if screen output desired
```

```
if (argc < 3) {
  cerr << "usage: tawk tawkfile datafile\n" <<
      "trailing -s pages output to screen";
  exit(1);
}
if (argc == 4) {
  if (argv[3][0] != '-') {
    cerr << "must use '-' before trailing flag\n";
    exit(1);
  } else
  if (argv[3][1] != 's') {
    cerr << "'s' is only trailing flag allowed";
    exit(1);
  } else
    screen++; // set screen output flag true
}
ifstream tawkfile(argv[1]);
if(!tawkfile) { cerr << "couldn't open " << argv[1]; exit(1);}
parse_array Apreamble(tawkfile);  // the @preamble
parse_array Amain(tawkfile);  // the @main section
parse_array Aconclusion(tawkfile); // the @conclusion
csascii datafile(argv[2]); // make a comma-separated ASCII
                           // object from the second arg
// ------  @preamble ------
for (int i = 0; i < Apreamble.size(); i++)
  cout << Apreamble[i]; // preamble can only contain strings
if(screen) {
  // ANSI reverse video sequence:
  cout << ESC << "[7m" << "press any key" <<
    ESC << "[0m";
  getch();
}
// ------ The Central Loop (@main) -------
do {  // for each record in the data file
  if(screen) cout << ESC << "[2J"; // ANSI clear screen
  for(int i = 0; i < Amain.size(); i++) {
    switch(Amain[i].token_type()) {
      case fieldnumber:
        cout << datafile[Amain[i].field_number()];
        break;
      case string:
        cout << Amain[i];
        break;
      case if_: {
        int fn = Amain[i].field_number();
        if (datafile[fn].size() == 0) { // conditional false
          int level = Amain[i].nesting_level();
```

```
                // find the "else" statement on the same level:
                while ( !(Amain[i].token_type() == else_
                    && Amain[i].nesting_level() == level))
                        i++;
              } // conditional true—just continue
              break;
            }
            case else_: { // an "if" conditional was true so skip
              // all the statements in the "else" clause
              int level = Amain[i].nesting_level();
              // find the "endif" statement on the same level:
              while ( !(Amain[i].token_type() == endif_
                  && Amain[i].nesting_level() == level))
                      i++;
              break;
            }
            case endif_: // after performing the "else" clause
              break; // ignore it; only used to find the end
              // of the conditional when "if" is true.
            default: // should never happen (caught in parsing)
              cerr << "unknown statement encountered at run time\n";
              exit(1);
          }
        }
        if(screen) {
          cout << ESC << "[7m" <<
            "press a key (ESC quits)" << ESC << "[0m";
          if( getch() == 27) break;
        }
      } while (datafile.next()); // matches do { ...
      // ------ @conclusion ------
      for ( i = 0; i < Aconclusion.size(); i++)
        cout << Aconclusion[i]; // contains only strings
    }
```

The TAWK script is parsed into three different **parse_array**s, one each
for the **@preamble**, **@main**, and **@conclusion**. These arrays are executed
using the database file as input.

Class **token**

Each token must be a particular type. The kind of information a token
contains depends on what type it is. In TAWK, the possible token types

are as follows: a field number (for printing out a field or testing if a field is empty in an **if** statement), a string (simple text including nonprintable characters), parts of a conditional statement (**if, else**, and **endif**), or a phase change, which indicates a transition from **@preamble** to **@main** or **@main** to **@conclusion**. Since a phase change is never executed but is simply used to terminate the creation of a **parse_array**, it isn't a token in the same sense as the others, but some form of communication was necessary, and this seemed the cleanest.

The different types of tokens and phases are enumerated in the **tokentype** and **phase** declarations. The phase information is kept by the main program, but each token contains a **tokentype** identifier. Since a token can never be a field number and a string at the same time, the data container in a token is combined into an *anonymous union*, which is like a regular union only it has no name. The union is used to save space.

A token also contains information about the level of **if** statement. Because **if** statements can be nested, each token that is an **if, else**, or **endif** must have information about the nesting level. If the conditional evaluates to false (that is, the field is empty), the interpreter must hunt through tokens in the **parse_array** until it finds the **else** statement *at the same level*, and continue executing statements from there.

While **token::get_token()** is performing its recursive scanning, it calls several other functions, which are made private, since they aren't needed by the user. **Token::get_next()** gets a character and tests for end-of-file (which is an error condition, since an **@end** statement should always terminate the **tawk** script). **Token::get_value()** is used for the @() and @<> statements. **Token::dumpline()** is called for comments.

The PARSE.CPP file starts with a number of **static** variables defined at file scope. This means they are not visible outside the file. When the constructor is called, it establishes the source of input characters (**tokenstream**), sets the **length** of the string which has been read so far to 0, and begins the recursive by calling **token::get_token()**.

There are three possibilities in **token::get_token()**:

1. The next character in the input stream is an @ and the current **length** is 0. This indicates the beginning of a command; the next character will determine what the command is. In this case, a large **switch** statement is executed.

2. The next character is an @ and the **length** is not 0. This means the scanner is in the middle of a string, and a command is starting. In this case, the @ is pushed back onto the input stream (for use by the next token), space is allocated for the string and the "unwinding" of the stack is started with a **return**.

3. The next character is not an @. This means it must be plain text. In this case, **token::get_token()** calls itself to get more characters.

Class parse_array

The class **parse_array** is a *container class*, since it is only used to contain objects of another class (**token**). There is no way to know how many tokens a **parse_array** will contain, so the recursive approach is used again. The constructor initializes some variables and calls the recursive function **parse_array::build_array()**, which keeps getting tokens and calling itself until a phase change or the end of the input (an **@end** statement). At this point, it allocates space to hold all the tokens (which it has been counting during the descent) and ascends, storing a token on each function return.

The individual tokens in a **parse_array** can be selected using brackets ([ ]) because the bracket operator has been overloaded in **parse_array::operator[ ]( )**. Since **token** has a stream function defined, tokens can be put directly to **cout**.

Executing a TAWK Script

TAWK.CPP contains the **main()** function. After the command-line arguments are checked, the **tawk** script is opened and three **parse_arrays** are created, one each for the **@preamble**, **@main**, and the **@conclusion**. The second command-line argument is used to create a **csascii** object.

At the beginning and end of the script execution, the preamble and conclusion **parse_arrays** are simply sent to standard output (**cout**). Since they can only contain text, no other action is necessary.

The central loop executes the statements in the **@main** phase for each record the **csascii** object reads from the database file. After a record is read, the type of each token in **parse_array Amain** is used in a **switch** statement to choose the proper action. Strings are sent to **cout**, and field numbers send the selected field to **cout**.

In an **if** statement, if the selected field is empty in the current record, the **parse_array** index is incremented until the **else** token at the same level is found. If the field is not empty, no action is taken (the following statements are executed). When an **else** is encountered, it means the **if** evaluated to true, so the **else** clause is skipped over until the **endif** of the same level is found.

Example TAWK Scripts

Here are some example TAWK scripts. The first reformats a file with six fields into one with five fields, combining the last two fields. If both of the last two fields are not empty, a space is inserted between them:

```
@! REFORM.TWK
@! A TAWK script to reformat a comma-separated ASCII file
@! with 6 fields. This creates a new CS-ASCII file with
@! fields 4 and 5 combined.
@main
"@(0)","@(1)","@(2)","@(3)","@(4)@?4@: @~@.@(5)"
@conclusion
@end
```

The next script prints out the contents of the comma-separated ASCII file used as an example earlier:

```
@! A comment, which isn't printed
@! The @preamble is optional, but promotes understanding
@main
        This is field 0: @(0)
        This is field 1: @(1)
        This is field 2: @(2)
        This is field 3: @(3)
        This is field 4: @(4)
        @?2@: @(2) @~Field 2 is empty @.
```

```
print an escape: @<27>
        Regenerate comma-separated ASCII record:
"@(0)","@(1)","@(2)","@(3)"
@conclusion  This is a comment
That's all, folks!!
@! The @conclusion isn't necessary if you don't have one
@end
```

The following script shows the usefulness of the preamble and conclusion. It creates a tiny phone list on an HP LaserJet printer. The preamble and conclusion are used to send special control codes to the printer. The use of nested **if-then-else** statements is shown here: if field 3 exists, it is printed followed by a carriage return and a test to see if field 4 exists, which is printed with a linefeed if it does (nothing happens if it isn't). If field 3 doesn't exist, field 4 is tested and printed with a linefeed; else only a linefeed is printed. When everything is completed a "reset" is sent to the LaserJet.

```
@! WALLET.TWK
@! TAWK file to create a tiny phone listing for a wallet
@! on a Hewlett-Packard Laserjet-compatible printer
@! From a comma-separated ASCII file generated by a DBMS
@preamble
@<27>&l5C@! approximately 10 lines per inch
@<27>(s16.66H@! small typeface, built into Laserjet
@main
@! last, first, (area code) phone1
@(0),@(1) (@(2))@?3@:@(3)
@! phone2, if it exists
@?4@:@(4)
@~@.@~@?4@:@(4)
@~
@.@.@conclusion
@<27>E @! Reset the Laserjet
@end
```

If you want a further challenge, try adding a "goto" system to TAWK. You will need to create a label command and a **goto** command. Gotos can be executed from **if-then-else** statements.

Hiding Complexity in TAWK

The **main()** program for TAWK is actually quite small for what it does. Because the details are hidden in the **csascii** and **parse_array** objects, one can imagine creating a much more sophisticated program without losing control of the complexity. This is typical of C++; indeed, the language was designed to allow one programmer to handle the same amount of code that previously required several. The compiler supports the creation of large projects by hiding initialization and cleanup and enforcing the correct use of user-defined types.

A Clock-Based Control System

This project parses an ASCII "script file" to create a list of events it constantly checks. When an event is ready, the program runs it and removes it from the list.

The program is designed to be easy to modify, even for the novice C++ programmer. The modification process is straightforward, and several examples are given. In addition, there are a number of interesting techniques demonstrated, both in C++ and plain C.

This project is quite complete: with a very small amount of customization, you can turn it into a deliverable package that allows customers to configure their own control systems to run selected events at certain times. An inexpensive computer, along with whatever control hardware you need becomes a stand–alone, time–based controller!

The program design can be changed to add hardware events (in addition to clock events). Some degree of interrupt support is even conceivable.

This isn't the ultimate real-time control system. The adequacy of the system depends on the speed of the computer and the speed/accuracy requirements of your problem. Many problems simply don't require a complicated, preemptive control system.

CONTROLR Manual Page

The **CONTROLR** program has its own scripting language. Here's the "manual page". The syntax for running the program is

controlr *scriptfile* [r | n]

scriptfile is an ASCII file containing commands and comments. Each line in the file can be empty, or contain a single command (including a comment) or contain a comment alone. A comment is started with a single quote (') and continues to the end of the line.

The second argument is optional, as follows:

r reprints the script file in a form readable by **controlr** and quits.

n turns off the event display to speed things up.

 Warning   Reboot is required to get out of program when the n flag is used!

There are two types of commands: system commands (which control the execution of the program) and controller commands (which control the target devices).

CONTROLR System Commands

Available system commands are

```
cycle(CC:CC:CC)
force(FF:FF:FF)
align(AA:AA:AA)
```

which mean the following:

CC:CC:CC is the cycle time. The cycle command restarts the system after each cycle period.

FF:FF:FF is the force time. The force command restarts the system at the force time.

AA:AA:AA is the align time. If the align hours are nonzero, the system restarts on the hour (even if the align hours are greater than zero). If the align hours are zero, but the align minutes are nonzero, the system restarts every even multiple of the align minutes. If align hours and minutes are zero, the system restarts every even multiple of the align seconds.

If there are no system commands, the events in a script will only run once.

It doesn't make any sense to have more than one "cycle" command (only the shortest cycle will ever get used), but you can use as many "force" commands as you want. If any of the force commands are in the future, they are added to the list.

CONTROLR Controller Commands

Controller commands consist of the command word (specified by the programmer), optional modifiers, and optional comments. The command word and modifiers may appear in any order on the line.

If a command word appears alone, as in

```
LIGHT_ON
```

that command is executed immediately, upon startup. Thus it is an initializer.

A controller command may have three types of modifiers. All consist of a single character and a time argument. The characters and their meanings are shown here:

+   The event occurs at the startup time plus the modifier time.

@   The event occurs at the modifier time.

R   The event time (relative or absolute) is randomized by adding a time between zero and the modifier time.

Here is an example script:

```
'This is a comment
@align(00:00:15) 'repeat each 15 seconds, on the 15-second mark
```

```
LIGHT_ON     'start with light on
LIGHT_OFF  +00:00:02  'light off 2 seconds after start
LIGHT_ON   +00:00:02 R00:00:08  'on between 2 and 10 seconds
+00:00:12 LIGHT_OFF  ' order doesn't matter
LIGHT_OFF @12:00:00 'light off at noon
LIGHT_ON @12:45:00 R00:30:00 'on at 12:45 + up to 30 minutes
```

Using the CONTROLR Program

Here's a sample script file:

```
'TSTSCRPT : A sample script for CONTROLR.EXE
cycle(00:03:00)  ' restart every 3 minutes
force(  16:15:00  ) 'restart at an absolute time
force(  21:20:00  ) 'notice spaces are ignored
force(  21:25:00  )
align(00:05:00)   ' restart on the five-minute mark
'''''''     start up conditions   ''''''''''
LIGHT_ON
THERMOSTAT_NIGHT
BELL
''''''''''''''''''''''''''''''''''''''''''''
LIGHT_OFF  +00:00:10  ' light off ten seconds after startup
THERMOSTAT_DAY +00:00:15 ' heater high 15 seconds after startup
THERMOSTAT_DAY @13:50:00 ' heater high at 1:00 pm
LIGHT_ON      +00:00:30 R00:00:10 'light on 30 secs after start
LIGHT_OFF @14:00:00 R01:00:00 '2 pm plus up to 1 hour
R00:00:10 +00:01:00 GREENHOUSE_WATER_ON ' order is unimportant
R00:00:10 +00:01:30 GREENHOUSE_WATER_OFF
```

To modify the program for your own use, edit the file CONTROLR.CPP (shown later in this chapter). Two preprocessor macros are used in the file: **EVENT_TYPE** and **MAKE_EVENT**. You can see how a new kind of event is added to the system by looking at the example definitions at the beginning of CONTROLR.CPP (**LIGHT_ON**, **LIGHT_OFF**, **BELL**, and so on).

Each definition consists of a call to the **EVENT_TYPE** macro followed by member definitions for *name::action()* and *name::description()*, where *name* is what you've called the new kind of event. The **action()** function is run when the event is "ready" (in this case, when the clock time is greater than or equal to the event time), and the **description()** is used to describe the event on the display.

Remove all the event definitions except for **system_restart**. Now create your own definitions.

For each **EVENT_TYPE** macro call and associated definitions, you also need to add a **MAKE_EVENT** call further down in the program. If you search for the label **CREATE:** you will see a **while(1)** loop containing a number of **MAKE_EVENT** definitions that correspond to the **EVENT_TYPE** definitions at the beginning of the file. The arguments to the macro are the class name and a string that is the command name used in the script file. Remove these macro calls and replace them with your own.

Recompile the program with C++ by typing **make**. That's all there is to it.

Object-Oriented Event Control

This program is a true OOP design, since it manipulates generic objects. Each object belongs to the pure abstract base class, **event** (see the file **event.h**), and to a specific derived class that has special properties in two virtual functions, **description()** and **action()**. A virtual function is declared in the base class and defined in the derived class, so two objects can have the same interface but different implementations.

Objects of the base class are kept in a list and constantly checked to see if they are ready to run ("ready" in this case is only tied to the clock. To modify the system to respond to hardware events, make **ready()** a virtual function and redefine it in a derived class to test hardware). When an event is ready, its **action()** is performed and it is removed from the list.

A Class to Manage Time

Here is the header file **event.h**, which contains two class definitions: class **time_point**, to represent a single point in time, and class **event**, to represent a single event:

```
//: EVENT.H—Event classes
//. Each event object has a scheduled time, and a virtual
```

```cpp
//. function to be executed at that time. The event class
//. should be derived into a class with the desired
//. "action" function; a list of events is managed in main().
#include <iostream.h>
#include <iomanip.h> // setw()

// A point in time:
class time_point {
  int hours;
  int minutes;
  int seconds;
public:
  time_point(); // get current time
  void normalize ();
  // set a specific time:
  time_point ( int hr, int min = 0, int sec = 0 ) {
    hours = hr; minutes = min; seconds = sec;
    normalize();
  }
  // the copy-constructor: (create one point from another)
  time_point (time_point & rv);
  time_point (char *);  // from string, i.e.: "09:45:23"
  void randomize(time_point & random_f);
  // compare one time point to another:
  void operator=(time_point & rv); // assignment
  int operator>=(time_point & rv);
  time_point operator+(time_point & rv);
  void display(){
    cout << setw(2) << setfill('0') << hours << ":"
         << setw(2) << setfill('0') << minutes << ":"
         << setw(2) << setfill('0') << seconds;
  }
  int & hr() { return hours; }
  int & min() { return minutes; }
  int & sec() { return seconds; }
};

// an event object is scheduled to occur at some point in time:
class event {
  time_point event_time; // when the event should happen
public:
  // note the initialization of the member object:
  event() : event_time() {}; // no arguments—do it now
  event(time_point & tp)  : event_time(tp) {} ; // absolute
  event(time_point & tp, time_point & rst_time) // from restart
    : event_time(tp + rst_time) {}
```

```
    event(time_point & tp, time_point & rst_time,
          time_point & random_f)
      : event_time(tp + rst_time) {
        event_time.randomize(random_f);
      }
    // "ready" is true if event is ready to run:
    int ready(time_point & now) {
      return now >= event_time;
    }
    void display() { event_time.display(); }
    // The following function is redefined for each specific
    // subclass:
    virtual void action()  = 0;
    // This is optionally redefined so you can see what
    // events are waiting to be run:
    virtual void description() {
      cout << "no description" << endl;
    }
};

// This macro derives a new class from class event. It saves
// typing and errors when you want to make a new type of event.
// To use it: EVENT_TYPE(event_class_name);  you must also
// define a function for the new action which is to happen
// when the event is ready to run:
// void event_class_name::action() { /* defintion here */ }
// See the examples in CONTROLR.CPP

#define EVENT_TYPE(ENAME) class ENAME : public event { \
  public: \
  ENAME() : event() {} \
  ENAME(time_point & p) : event(p) {} \
  ENAME(time_point & p, time_point & s) : event(p,s) {} \
  ENAME(time_point & p, time_point & s, time_point & r) \
        : event(p,s,r) {} \
  void action(); \
  void description(); \
};
```

Class **event** contains a member object, called **event_time**, that belongs to class **time_point**. Various **time_point**s can be assigned, added, and compared to see if one is greater than or equal to another, and "randomized" (increased by a random amount of time, bounded by a random factor). Once class **time_point** is defined, details of time calculations can be ignored.

The **setw()** and **setfill()** iostream manipulators set the output width and fill characters, respectively.

Each object in class **event** is associated with a single **time_point**. When the clock time is greater than or equal to the **event_time**, the member function **ready()** returns true. This way you can ask an event if it's ready to run.

To create a new type of event, a new class must be inherited from **class event** so the virtual functions **description()** and **action()** may be redefined. This inheritance is always the same except for the name, so the code to inherit a new subtype is packaged into the macro **EVENT_TYPE**, defined in **event.h** and used in CONTROLR.CPP (this could also be a class template). Notice that a macro can be continued as long as you keep putting backslashes at the end of each line.

Here are the definitions:

```cpp
//: EVENT.CPP—Definitions for event.h
//. (class event functions are all inline).
#include "event.h"
#include <time.h>
#include <stdlib.h> // for rand(), srand(), atoi()

// Correct the time so hours < 24, minutes & seconds < 60
void time_point::normalize () {
  if ( seconds >= 60 ) {
    minutes += seconds / 60; // integer division
    seconds = seconds % 60; // integer remainder
  }
  if ( minutes >= 60 ) {
    hours += minutes / 60;
    minutes %= 60; // short form of " = minutes % 60 "
  }
  if ( hours >= 24 ) {
    hours %= 24;
  }
}

time_point::time_point() { // get current time
  time_t ltime;  // holds encoded time
  struct tm *t; // the time and day
  time(&ltime); // get time
  t = localtime(&ltime); // convert time
  hours = t->tm_hour;
  minutes = t->tm_min;
```

```
    seconds = t->tm_sec;
}

time_point::time_point (time_point & rv) {
  hours = rv.hours;
  minutes = rv.minutes;
  seconds = rv.seconds;
}

void time_point::operator=(time_point & rv) {
  hours = rv.hours;
  minutes = rv.minutes;
  seconds = rv.seconds;
}

time_point::time_point (char * ts) {
  hours = atoi(ts);
  ts += 3; // move pointer past first ':'
  minutes = atoi(ts);
  ts += 3; // move pointer past second ':'
  seconds = atoi(ts);
  normalize();
}

void time_point::randomize(time_point & random_f) {
  time_point now;
  // seed the random number generator:
  srand(now.hours + now.minutes + now.seconds);
  // create a random number between 0 and 1:
  float r = (float)rand()/(float)32767;
  seconds += (int)(r * random_f.seconds);
  minutes += (int)(r * random_f.minutes);
  hours += (int)(r * random_f.hours);
  normalize();
}

int time_point::operator>=(time_point & rv) {
  if ( hours > rv.hours )
    return 1;
  if (hours < rv.hours)
    return 0;
  // here, hours == rv.hours
  if ( minutes > rv.minutes )
    return 1;
  if ( minutes < rv.minutes )
    return 0;
  // here, minutes == rv.minutes
```

```
    if ( seconds >= rv.seconds  )
      return 1;
    return 0; // seconds < rv.seconds
}

time_point time_point::operator+(time_point & rv) {
  time_point sum(0);
  sum.seconds = seconds + rv.seconds;
  sum.minutes = minutes + rv.minutes;
  sum.hours = hours + rv.hours;
  sum.normalize();
  return sum;
}
```

You might want to improve the **randomize()** function. Notice you can change the implementation without modifying the interface so the rest of the program is unaffected.

A C++-Oriented Linked List

Object-oriented programs often manage an arbitrary number of generic objects (from classes that use polymorphism, also known as virtual functions). A linked list is often the best way to handle these objects.

Here is a linked-list template for this project. This container assumes it "owns" the objects that it holds, so when they are removed they are destroyed.

```
//: LINKLIST.H—A self-contained linked list
//. The first object must be created as a named variable
//. with no arguments. This is the name of the list.
//. All the rest are created with "new" and arguments,
//. but the return value of "new" is never used (normally
//. a no-no).
#include <iostream.h>
#include <stdlib.h>

template <class Type>
class LinkList {
  // the start of all members of this class:
  static LinkList<Type> * head;
  // used to step through the list:
  static LinkList<Type> * cursor;
```

```
      LinkList * next_el; // link to the next element
      Type * ddata; // holds the information in this node
      void error(char * msg = "") {
        cout << "list error: " << msg << endl;
        exit(1);
      }
public:
    LinkList() { // create a named list (don't use "new")
      next_el = 0;
      ddata = 0; // to mark end of list
      // point to yourself as the only element:
      cursor - head = this;
    }
    LinkList(Type * info) {
      ddata = info;
      // insert this element at the head of the list:
      next_el = head;
      head = this;
    }
    ~LinkList() {
      // cout << "list destructor" << endl;
      LinkList<Type> * current = head, * old = head;
      while ( current != this ) {
        // find our place in the list, and the element before
        if (current -- 0) error("can't delete nonexistent link");
        old = current;
        current = current >next_el;
      }
      if ( this == head )
        head = next_el;  // move head to next link
      old->next_el = next_el; // unlink this from list
      delete ddata;   // assume ownership
    }
    Type * data() { return ddata; }
    void reset() { cursor = head; }
    LinkList * next() { // step through the list
      // return the current element and step forward one,
      // if we can.
      LinkList<Type> * llp = cursor;
      if (cursor->next_el != 0)
        cursor = cursor->next_el;
      if (llp->ddata != 0)
        return llp;
      else // tail element has empty ddata pointer (don't use it)
        return 0;
    }
    void print(char * msg = "") {
```

```
    cout << msg << " " << ddata << endl;
  }
  void dumplist() {
    reset();
    LinkList<Type> * llp;
    while( (llp = next()) != 0 )
      llp->print();
  }
};

template<class Type> LinkList<Type> * LinkList<Type>::head;
template<class Type> LinkList<Type> * LinkList<Type>::cursor;
```

This linked list uses the unique features of C++ to advantage, in particular constructors, destructors, and static class variables.

Many linked lists define a link element and then a container to manage the links. The class **LinkList** *contains itself*. It does this by using a **static** data member for the **head** pointer (the pointer to the beginning of the list) like this:

```
static LinkList<Type> * head;
```

The **LinkList** constructor with no arguments points **head** to an empty element (used to indicate the end of the list). The constructor with an argument, **LinkList(Type * info)**, should only be called with the **new** keyword, which creates an object on the heap. The **new** keyword normally returns the address of the object it created and in most cases if you lose this address you can never release that heap space. Here, however, the constructor ties the element into the linked list by inserting it at the head, so the address isn't lost. So the proper way to add an element to the list is to simply call **new** and ignore the return value (a process that normally invites disaster).

Notice the **cursor** pointer is also static. This means there is only one cursor for the entire list (although you could certainly create a similar container/iterator pair).

Removing Elements with delete

Most linked lists have a function to unlink elements. This linked list is unique because it uses the destructor to remove objects neatly from the linked list. If you call **delete** with a pointer to a **LinkList,** the destructor removes that **LinkList** from the list and deletes the data. This produces very tidy code when using the linked list (see the last part of CONTROLR.CPP).

Here's a test for **LinkList** to ensure that it works properly:

```
//: LINKTEST.CPP—Test of linked list
#include "linklist.h"
#include <string.h>

class string {
  char * s;
public:
  string(char * st) : s(strcpy(new char[strlen(st) + 1], st)) {}
  ~string() { delete s; }
  operator char*() { return s; }
  friend ostream& operator<<(ostream& os, string* S) {
    return os << S->s;
  }
};

typedef LinkList<string> strlink;

void main() {
  strlink stringlist;
  new strlink(new string("first"));
  new strlink(new string("second"));
  new strlink(new string("third"));
  new strlink(new string("fourth"));
  new strlink(new string("fifth"));
  new strlink(new string("sixth"));
  stringlist.dumplist();
  stringlist.reset();
  stringlist.next();
  strlink * rmd = stringlist.next();
  delete rmd;
  cout << "----------" << endl;
  stringlist.dumplist();
  stringlist.reset();
  while ( ( rmd = stringlist.next() ) != 0 )
    delete rmd;
  stringlist.dumplist();
}
```

This test uses yet another version of a **string** class. This one is different because instead of using the non-ANSI library function **strdup()** (which uses **malloc()**), it uses **new** to allocate the memory and the ANSI C library function **strcpy()** to copy it. Also, note the **ostream** output function takes a pointer, not a reference, to conform to the way the **LinkList** function **print()** uses its data.

The example simply adds a group of **string** objects to a list, removes one in the middle, and then removes them all.

Parsing the Script

Here is the file, CONTROLR.CPP, that contains the subclass definitions of the **event**s, the parser, and the list manager.

Notice at the beginning of **main()** the program tests for a single trailing flag **-s**. You can improve the program by using the **CL_flags** system shown at the beginning of this chapter.

```
//: CONTROLR.CPP—The main controller.
//. Parses a file of commands and creates a list of events.
//. When it is time to run an event, the event's action is
//. executed and the event is removed from the list.
#include <iostream.h>
#include <fstream.h> // file iostreams
#include <string.h>
#include <setjmp.h> // setjmp() & longjmp()
#include <stdlib.h>
#include "event.h"
#include "linklist.h"

jmp_buf system_restart_buf; // for setjmp & longjmp

typedef LinkList<event> event_el;
event_el event_list;

// To add a new type of event, mimic the following definitions
// (call the macro EVENT_TYPE and create an action for your new
// event) and add a new macro call of MAKE_EVENT in the
// "while(1)" loop with the comment "CREATE."  That's all there
// is to extending the system. (The description() definition is
// optional).

EVENT_TYPE(light_on);
void light_on::action() {
  // put hardware control code here to physically
```

```
  // turn on the light.
}
void light_on::description() {
  cout << "light is on" << endl;
}
// End of a user-defined event definition.
// More user-defined event definitions:
EVENT_TYPE(light_off);
void light_off::action() {
  // put hardware control code here to physically
  // turn off the light.
}
void light_off::description() {
  cout << "light is off" << endl;
}


// an example of an action() which inserts a new
// one of itself into the event list:
EVENT_TYPE(bell);
void bell::action() {
  // ring bell every 10 seconds:
  cout << char(7) << endl;
  time_point now;
  new event_el(new bell(now + time_point(0,0,10)));
}
void bell::description() {
  cout << "ring bell" << endl;
}



EVENT_TYPE(greenhouse_water_on);
void greenhouse_water_on::action() {
  // put hardware control code here
}
void greenhouse_water_on::description() {
  cout << "greenhouse water is on" << endl;
}

EVENT_TYPE(greenhouse_water_off);
void greenhouse_water_off::action() {
  // put hardware control code here
}
void greenhouse_water_off::description() {
  cout << "greenhouse water is off" << endl;
}

EVENT_TYPE(thermostat_night);
```

```cpp
void thermostat_night::action() {
  // put hardware control code here
}
void thermostat_night::description() {
  cout << "thermostat on night setting" << endl;
}

EVENT_TYPE(thermostat_day);
void thermostat_day::action() {
  // put hardware control code here
}
void thermostat_day::description() {
  cout << "thermostat on day setting" << endl;
}

// The above EVENT_TYPEs are just examples, but the following
// is used by the system:
EVENT_TYPE(system_restart);
void system_restart::action() {
  event_list.reset();
  // remove all entries from the list:
  event_el * ep;
  while ( (ep = event_list.next()) != 0)
    delete ep;
  // "nonlocal goto" back to beginning of main():
  longjmp(system_restart_buf,1);
}
void system_restart::description() {
  cout << "system restart" << endl;
}

// This specifies when an event is to happen.
// relative: from system startup time
// absolute: 24-hour clock time
enum whenis { now, relative, absolute, unassigned };

// A "token" structure to hold the information in
// the line from the event description file:
struct tk {
  whenis when;
  int randomize;
  char * descriptor;
  time_point etime;
  time_point randomization;
  tk() : when(unassigned),
         randomize(0), descriptor("") ,
         etime(0), randomization(0)
```

```
        {}
  ~tk() { if ( when != unassigned )
          delete descriptor;
  }
  void display();
};


// output the event description in such a way
// that it can be reparsed by this program:
void tk::display() {
  if ( when != unassigned ) {
    cout << descriptor;
    int dl = 25 - strlen(descriptor);
    for (int i = 0; i++ < dl; cout.put(' ') )
      ;
    if(when == relative) cout << "+";
    if(when == absolute) cout << "@";
    if ( when != now) {
      etime.display(); cout << "\t";
    }
    if(randomize) {
      cout << "R";
      randomization.display();
    }
    cout << endl;
  }
}

void main (int argc, char * argv[]) {
  if ( argc != 2 && argc != 3 ) {
    cerr << "Usage: controlr <scriptfile> [r|n]\n"
      "Second argument is optional. r reprints the\n"
      "script file in a form readable by this program.\n"
      "n turns off the event display to speed things up.\n"
      "Warning: reboot is required to get out of program\n"
      "when the n flag is used!\n"
      " <scriptfile> is an ASCII file containing controller"
      " commands\n";
    exit(1);
  }
  int evdisplay = 1; // flag means "display events"
  int reprint = 0; // flag means reprint script file & quit
  if ( argc == 3 ) {
    if ( *argv[2] == 'n' )
      evdisplay = 0;
    if ( *argv[2] == 'r' )
```

```
        reprint++;
}
// set the restart buffer so longjmp comes back here:
setjmp(system_restart_buf);
time_point startup_time;  // time at startup or restart
{ // forces istream eventscript out of scope at closing
  // brace, which closes file so it is reopened when
  // this scope is entered again.
ifstream eventscript(argv[1]);
if (!eventscript) {
  cerr << "cannot open " << argv[1] << endl;
  exit(1);
}
// for use by strtok(), the token grabber. Tokens are
// whitespace or paren delimited:
const char * delimit = " \t\n\r()";
const int BSIZE = 100;
char buf[BSIZE], c;
while( eventscript.getline(buf,BSIZE) ) {
  { // to force tk token out of scope after each loop
  tk token; // to save information about event
  char * tokptr = strtok(buf, delimit); // get first token
  while ( tokptr != 0 ) { // do for all tokens in line
    if ( * tokptr == '\'' ) { // start of comment
      break; // throw away to end of line
    }
    if ( strcmp(tokptr,"cycle") == 0 ) {
      // make cycle time from next token:
      time_point cycle_time(tokptr = strtok(0, delimit));
      if (reprint) {
        cout << "cycle(";
        cycle_time.display();
        cout << ")" << endl;
      }
      cycle_time = cycle_time + startup_time;
      // enter it into the event list:
      new event_el(new system_restart(cycle_time));
    } else
    if ( strcmp(tokptr,"force") == 0 ) {
      // make force time from next token:
      time_point force_time(tokptr = strtok(0, delimit));
      if (reprint) {
        cout << "force(";
        force_time.display();
        cout << ")" << endl;
      }
      // if we aren't already past the force_time,
```

```
      // enter it into the event list:
      if ( ! (startup_time >= force_time))
        new event_el(new system_restart(force_time));
    } else
    if ( strcmp(tokptr,"align") == 0 ) {
      // make align time from next token:
      time_point align_time(tokptr = strtok(0, delimit));
      if (reprint) {
        cout << "align(";
        align_time.display();
        cout << ")" << endl;
      }
      if ( align_time.hr() != 0 ) { // XX:00:00 align to hours
        align_time.hr() = startup_time.hr() + 1;
        align_time.min() = align_time.sec() = 0;
      } else {
        align_time.hr() = startup_time.hr();
        if ( align_time.min() != 0 ) { //00:XX:00 align minute
          int next_min =
            ( (startup_time.min()/align_time.min()) + 1 )
              * align_time.min();
          if (next_min > 60 )
            align_time.hr()++;
          else
            align_time.min() = next_min;
          align_time.sec() = 0;
        } else { // 00:00:XX align seconds
          align_time.min() = startup_time.min();
          if (align_time.sec() != 0) {
            int next_sec =
              ( (startup_time.sec()/align_time.sec()) + 1 )
                * align_time.sec();
            if (next_sec > 60 )
              align_time.min()++;
            else
              align_time.sec() = next_sec;
          }
        }
      }

      align_time.normalize();
      new event_el(new system_restart(align_time));
    } else
    if ( *tokptr == '+' ) {
      token.when = relative;
      token.etime = time_point(++tokptr);
    } else
```

```
      if ( *tokptr == '@' ) {
        token.when = absolute;
        token.etime = time_point(++tokptr);
      } else
      if ( *tokptr == 'R' || *tokptr == 'r' ) {
        token.randomize++;
        token.randomization = time_point(++tokptr);
      } else {
        // it wasn't anything else—assume a name
        token.descriptor = new char[strlen(tokptr) + 1];
        strcpy(token.descriptor,tokptr);
      }
      tokptr = strtok(0, delimit); // get next token
    }
    // line parsed. Now perform actions based on token.
    if(!*token.descriptor)
      // A line with an empty descriptor means a comment line
      // or a system command (which was executed in the parser).
      // Go back to beginning of while loop and get next line:
      continue;
    // If the token isn't empty but it isn't relative or
    // absolute, it means the event should happen now:
    if(token.when != relative && token.when != absolute)
        token.when = now;
    if(reprint)
      token.display();


    // add an event to the list. First, a macro which creates
    // the right event based on the token information. This
    // saves a great deal of typing and mistakes. The final
    // "break" gets out of the "while(1)" loop which follows.
    // The macro is placed here instead of at the beginning of
    // the file (as is conventional) because it makes the code
    // easier to understand.
    //    STRING is the string the parser finds in the
    // script file. ENAME is the name of the class.
#define MAKE_EVENT(STRING,ENAME) \
if (strcmp(token.descriptor,STRING) == 0) { \
  switch(token.when) { \
    case relative:  \
        if (token.randomize)  \
          new event_el(new ENAME( startup_time, \
                              token.etime, \
                              token.randomization)); \
        else \
          new event_el(new ENAME(startup_time, token.etime)); \
        break; \
```

```
    case absolute: \
        if (token.randomize) \
          new event_el(new ENAME(token.etime, \
                                  time_point(0), \
                                  token.randomization)); \
        else \
          new event_el(new ENAME(token.etime)); \
        break; \
    case now: \
        new event_el(new ENAME); \
  } \
  break;  \
}
// End of macro definition


    // Create the event and add it to the list, using the
    // information parsed from the script file.
    // CREATE:
    while(1) {
      // When a match is found, a "break" statement in the
      // macro jumps out of the "while(1)" loop.
      MAKE_EVENT("LIGHT_ON", light_on);
      MAKE_EVENT("LIGHT_OFF", light_off);
      MAKE_EVENT("BELL", bell);
      MAKE_EVENT("GREENHOUSE_WATER_ON", greenhouse_water_on);
      MAKE_EVENT("GREENHOUSE_WATER_OFF", greenhouse_water_off);
      MAKE_EVENT("THERMOSTAT_DAY", thermostat_day);
      MAKE_EVENT("THERMOSTAT_NIGHT", thermostat_night);
      // if there wasn't a match, it's an error:
      cerr << "unrecognized line in " << argv[1] << "\n";
      token.display();
      exit(1);
    } // end of "while(1)"
    } // end of tk token scope (token destroyed)
  } // all lines in file are parsed
  } // end of scope enclosing istream eventscript
  if (reprint) exit(0);  // just reprint script
  cout << char(27) << "[2J"; // ANSI clear screen
  // The list of events has been completely built.
  // Now loop through the list and look for events to be run.
  while(1) {
    { // this '{' forces "current_time" to go out of scope so it
      // is destroyed and created for each pass through the loop
      time_point current_time;
      if (evdisplay) {
        cout << char(27) << "[s"; // ANSI save cursor position
```

```
      cout << char(27) << "[1;40H"; // move cursor to 1,40
      cout << char(27) << "[7m"; // reverse video
      current_time.display();
      cout << " started: "; startup_time.display();
      cout << char(27) << "[m"; // no attributes
      cout << char(27) << "[u"; // restore cursor position
    }
    event_list.reset();
    event_el * ep;
    while ( (ep = event_list.next()) != 0) {
      if ((ep->data())->ready(current_time)) {
        if(evdisplay) {
          cout << "\nRUNNING an event:" << endl;
          (ep->data())->description();
        }
        (ep->data())->action(); // run the event
        delete ep; // remove event from list
        // print out remaining list times and descriptions:
        if(evdisplay) {
          cout << "\n\n Event list:" << endl;
          event_list.reset();
          while ( (ep = event_list.next()) != 0) {
            (ep->data())->display();
            cout << " ::: ";
            (ep->data())->description();
          }
        }
      }
    }
  } // close of "current_time" scope
} // end of while(1) looping through event list
}
```

After the subclasses are derived, you will see a definition for a **struct** called **tk** (for "token"). A **tk** is a place to store all the information about a particular event while parsing a line. When the parser is finished with the line, a new **event** can be created based on the information in the **tk**.

This approach has several advantages. It generally separates the analysis from the action (except for system commands, which can easily be added to **tk**) to keep the code easy to understand and maintain. By creating an internal representation instead of executing events as soon as you figure out what they are, you allow the possibility of saving the internal representation of the entire file (instead of handling it a line at a time, as is done here) so the design can easily be changed to allow faster system restarts.

The iostreams are used for console and file I/O. In **main()**, the script file is opened as an **ifstream,** and one line is read at a time using the member function **getline()** until the file ends. The ANSI C function **strtok()** breaks each line into pieces; **strtok()** is a very useful function when you want to parse input. The function name means "break a string into tokens" (the word "token" as used here means "a piece of text"). The **strtok()** function looks for a single character terminator from among the characters you give it in the second argument. The possible terminators (given by the constant string **delimit**) are white space (space, tab, linefeed, carriage return) or an open or closing parenthesis.

The first time you call **strtok()** for a line, you give it the starting address of the buffer as the first argument. For subsequent calls using the same line, give it **0** as the first argument. **strtok()** will return a pointer to a NULL-terminated string token until it can't find any more (in which case it returns **0**).

Each token is analyzed in a large **if-else** statement until the entire line has been parsed.

System Commands

You can see that the system commands (**force**, **cycle**, **align**—commands that modify the control system) are handled differently in the parser than the control commands (which modify the system being controlled). System commands are executed by the parser (*execute* in this case means "an event is added to the event list"). Control commands require string matching and argument checking before an event can be added to the event list.

Parser Improvements

You can improve the design of the parser by adding **cycle, force**, and **align** to the enumeration **whenis**. During parsing, simply assign **token.when** to the type of system command and **token.etime** to the time and delay the event creation until after the parsing is completed. This improvement is also the first step necessary to allow you to turn the entire file into a representation in memory.

One system command you may want to add is "commandfile" to change the name of the controller script file used when the system restarts.

Adding an Event to the List

After each line is parsed, an event is added to the list based on the information in the line. The macro **MAKE_EVENT** compares the **token.descriptor** to a string; if there is a match it makes a new **event**. This occurs inside what appears to be an infinite **while** loop. You can think of it as a **case** statement that matches strings (instead of integral values, as an ordinary **case** does); it was implemented this way to simplify the addition of new event types. An **if-else** construct would not have fit neatly into a macro (since **else** would occur at the end of the macro). By using a **break** at the end of the macro to jump out of the **while(1)** loop the code fits together nicely.

Managing the List

After the script file is parsed and the list is constructed, the program loops through the list looking for events to run. At the beginning of each loop, a new **current_time** object is created, and all the **event** objects in the list are tested with their **ready()** functions, using **current_time** as the argument.

Notice the extra set of braces in the final **while(1)** loop. The only purpose of these braces is to force **current_time** out of scope at the end of the loop. When it goes out of scope, the destructor is called, and when the loop is started again, the constructor is called. This updates **current_time.** The trick of forcing an object to go out of scope (and thus calling a constructor or destructor) is used several places in the program.

The list is reset, and each element is tested against the current time until there are no more elements in the list. If one is found, it is run and removed from the list. This abbreviated code is executed when the n command-line option is used.

Design Guidelines

When designing an object-oriented system, it is important that your concept of an object encompasses all the possible uses for that object. In this system, for example, an **action()** can be anything, including restarting the system (see **EVENT_TYPE(system_restart)** in **CONTROLR.CPP**). Notice also the flexibility of the system: the action of one event can add other events to the list, as shown in **EVENT_TYPE(bell)**.

The system restart commands are necessary for two reasons: you might want to create a process that repeats itself, and there may be a power failure and you want the controller to resynchronize itself.

Restarting the System

To make a system command just another type of **event**, **system_-restart::action()** must be able to jump to the beginning of the **main()** function. This isn't as easy as using **goto**, since any labels in **main()** are outside the scope of **system_restart::action()**.

C solves this kind of problem with a concept called *nonlocal goto*, implemented with the library functions **setjmp()** and **longjmp()**. The **setjmp()** function stores the contents of the stack and the program counter in a type of structure called a **jmp_buf**. When **longjmp()** is called with that same structure as an argument, it goes back to the spot **setjmp()** was called and restores the same stack. With the exception of the return value of **setjmp()**, it looks exactly like the first time **setjmp()** was called. Notice that **longjmp()** is called inside the **system_restart::-action()** function, which has no idea where the jump will end up. Because **setjmp()** is called at run time and can be called in several different spots, you can not only jump *anywhere*, you can decide at run time where you will jump.

Increasing Restart Speed

The controller script file is reopened and reparsed every time the system is restarted. If this isn't as quick as you'd like (if you are restarting at very short intervals), you can rewrite the parsing section to store the information in a linked list of **tk** pointers. When the system restarts, you won't have to open and reparse the file. Just build the new list of events from the list of **tk** pointers. If you're a very good programmer, you can create an image of the list and duplicate it using **memcpy()** when the system is restarted. This is more complicated than it sounds, and not for the faint of heart.

A second, much quicker alternative is to create a small disk cache, just large enough to hold the script file.

If you are concerned about the execution speed of the events, use the n command-line flag to eliminate display. Screen display can be notoriously slow. This option, unfortunately, requires you to reboot the system to get out of the program (or kill the process, in UNIX). You can fix this in MS-DOS by adding the non-ANSI C statement **if(kbhit()) exit(0);** inside the last **while(1)** loop.

Advantages of Object-Oriented Design

Pay special attention here to the ease with which you can extend the system. Extending the system consists essentially of deriving a new data type from the base class **event** (you must also add a line at the **CREATE:** label, but there is no thinking involved). Since the system already knows how to handle **event**s, you only need to focus your efforts on what is new; the rest of the program doesn't break because you've added a new data type.

The idea of designing a program for extensibility is often new to users of traditional procedural languages. Those languages make the implicit assumption that a program will be designed once and never changed. Experience has shown that modifying programs is a rule, rather than an exception. When you design a program, look for items that can be thought of as objects, and see what those objects have in common. Create a base class containing all those common features as virtual functions, and create code to manage objects of that base class. You will find yourself building programs that are much easier to read, maintain, and extend.

Remember, however, that the real point of object-oriented programming is not virtual functions, operator overloading, and the like. Those are just features in a language to support object-oriented programming.

The point is to distinguish the parts of the program that are least likely to change from those that are most likely to change.

Snakes on the Screen

This program generates snakes that crawl around on the screen. Each snake is an object made of other objects called segments. To demonstrate the snakes, you indicate on the command line how many snakes you want, how big they are, and a delay factor (if you want to slow things down). Each snake is denoted by a different ASCII character. You can even make 200 snakes of length 1 and watch a bunch of characters run around on the screen (also try 1 snake of length 100).

The program will work on any platform as long as you have ANSI terminal emulation. You can also easily rewrite the very brief **segment::draw()** and **segment::erase()** routines to support graphics.

The header file contains the class definitions for **point** (to hold X-Y information), **segment** and **snake**. The **point** is a **struct** for the convenience of having coordinate information packaged together without the bother of private data. The constructor simply initializes the data elements **x** and **y** using the initializer list. The == operator is overloaded to determine whether one **point** is equivalent to another—this is important when preventing a snake from backtracking over itself. Finally, **random_point()** is a **static** member function that returns a **point** that is created randomly. This function creates a temporary object by calling the **point** constructor; no identifier is necessary since the object is immediately returned (by value).

Here is the header file:

```
//: SNAKE.H—Snake program declarations
#include <stddef.h>  // size_t definition

struct point {  // coordinate representation
  int x, y;
  point(int xi = 0, int yi = 0) : x(xi), y(yi) {}
  int operator==(point rval) {  // test equivalence
    return x == rval.x && y == rval.y;
  }
  static point random_point();  // generate random point
```

```
};

class segment {
public:
  enum direction { UP, DOWN, RIGHT, LEFT };
private:
  segment * previous;
  point sp;    // position on screen
  char pattern; // to display on the screen
  direction heading; // "tendency of motion" of the snake
  void erase();
  void checkheap(); // make sure this is on the heap!
public:
  void draw();
  // redefine operator new for this class ONLY:
  void * operator new(size_t sz);
  segment(point p, char ptrn);
  segment(segment * prv, direction dir);
  ~segment() { erase(); }
  int shed_tail(); // go back to the tail and drop it off
  point seg_point() { return sp; }
  int cross_over(point); // is this point an existing segment?
  direction path() { return heading; }
  void redraw_tail(); // redraw everything from here back
};

class snake {
  segment * head;
  int length, maxlength;
public:
  snake(point p, int size, char ptrn);
  void crawl(segment::direction);
  void slither();
};
```

Segments

The **segment** class contains a pointer to the **previous** segment in the list. This way, any segment can send a message to the segment behind it ("drop the tail off, pass it on!"). There is a **point** object so the segment knows where it is located on the screen; it needs to draw itself and prevent the snake from running over itself (although other snakes may slither over it). There is a variable called **pattern**, which is displayed on the screen. Finally, there is a variable called **heading** of the enumerated type **direction**. This variable is used to determine where the snake is going so it can (usually) continue in that direction.

 Note The original design didn't include **heading**. It was added after the system was running and the snakes were doubling back on themselves, which looked ugly. This is one good reason you should get your system working as soon as possible—you *can't* know some things while you're designing, only after you see it working.

Local Enumerations

Notice that **enum direction** is inside the class definition, and is local to the class. The enumeration tag and the names are local to the class, so they don't pollute the global namespace—you must refer to them as **segment::UP**, and so on. Preventing namespace pollution is a very important feature of C++. One of the reasons big projects get out of hand is simply because they eventually get too many names to manage.

Class Overloading of new

Here, **new** is overloaded because **segment** objects must never be created on the stack, only on the free store. To signal the programmer **segment::operator new()** puts a "signature" in the dynamically allocated memory. The function **segment::checkheap()** looks for this signature; if it doesn't find it, a message is sent to the programmer. It isn't foolproof, but it will usually detect misuse. The reason all segments must be created on the heap is they are only destroyed by **segment::shed_tail()** when it calls **delete**.

segment *Constructors*

There are two constructors for **segment**. The first is for the initial segment of the snake; it establishes the starting point and the pattern to be used. The second constructor makes a segment that is linked to an existing segment and in a specified direction. Note that both constructors call **checkheap()** to ensure that the object was created on the free store. The first constructor is straightforward, but the second must "wrap" the coordinate of the new segment around the display screen if it goes off the edge. In addition, the **draw()** method isn't called in the second constructor. This is because you can create a new segment that may cross over an old segment of the same snake. The calling function must check the new segment before actually drawing it.

Here is the implementation file:

```cpp
//: SNAKE.CPP—Drawing snakes on the screen
// Assumes ANSI terminal or ANSI.SYS on a PC
#include "snake.h"
#include <stdlib.h>
#include <iostream.h>
#include <time.h>
#include <string.h>  // memset()
const height = 23; // screen height
const width = 78; // screen width
const char escape = char(27);  // escape character

point point::random_point() {
  return point(rand() % width, rand() % height);
}

void * segment::operator new(size_t sz) {
  void * tmp = ::new unsigned char[sz];  // use global new()
  memset(tmp, 'x', sizeof(segment)); // fill with x's
  return tmp;
}

void segment::checkheap() {
  if(pattern != 'x') { // check for memset pattern
    cerr << "can only create segments on the heap!";
    exit(1);
  }
}

segment::segment(point p, char ptrn)
  // capriciously choose old heading:
  : sp(p), previous(0), heading(LEFT) {
  checkheap();
  pattern = ptrn;
  draw();
}
```

```
segment::segment(segment * prv, direction dir)
  : previous(prv), sp(prv->sp), heading(dir) {
  checkheap();
  pattern = previous->pattern;
  // create new segment in appropriate direction & wrap:
  switch (dir) {
    case UP :    if(--sp.y < 0) sp.y = height;   break;
    case DOWN :  if(++sp.y > height) sp.y = 0;   brcak;
    case LEFT :  if(--sp.x < 0) sp.x = width;    break;
    case RIGHT : if(++sp.x > width) sp.x = 0;    break;
  }
}

// Recursive function to go back to the beginning of the
// sequence of segments, to find the tail and remove it:
int segment::shcd_tail() {
  if (previous == 0) {
    delete this;  // 0 means we're at the tail
    return 1; // indicates to next call 'up' that tail was found
  }
  // recursive call until tail is found:
  if(previous->shed_tail()) // 1 means the call removed the tail
    previous = 0;
  return 0; // means the call didn't remove the tail
}

// Recursive check to see if p crosscs an existing segment:
int segment::cross_over(point p) {
  if(prcvious == 0) return p == sp;
  if(p == sp) return 1;
  // recursive call to go to the end, or a cross point:
  return(previous->cross_over(p));
}

// Recursively redraw entire snake:
void segment::redraw_tail() {
  draw();
  if(previous == 0) return;
  previous->redraw_tail();
}

void segment::draw() {
  // move cursor:
  cout << escape << "[" << sp.y << ";" << sp.x << "H";
  cout << pattern;
}
```

```
void segment::erase() {
  // move cursor:
  cout << escape << "[" << sp.y << ";" << sp.x << "H";
  cout << ' ';
}

snake::snake(point p, int size, char ptrn)
  : length(0), maxlength(size) {
  head = new segment(p, ptrn);
}

// Just mindlessly goes where you tell it:
void snake::crawl(segment::direction dir) {
  head = new segment(head,dir);
  if(++length >= maxlength) {
    --length;
    head->shed_tail();
  }
}

// Find its own way, tending to the current path:
void snake::slither() {
  const int chance = 10; // 1 in 10 chance to change directions
  segment::direction old = head->path();
  // Choose a new direction by throwing the dice to decide
  // whether to actually change direction. If so, choose
  // a new direction randomly:
  segment::direction dir;
  if (rand() % chance != chance/2)
    dir = old; // change only if magic number is rolled
  else {
    dir = (segment::direction)(rand() % 4);
    head->redraw_tail();  // occasionally redraw everything
  }
  segment * new_seg = new segment(head, dir);
  // ensure new segment doesn't cross over existing snake:
  if(head->cross_over(new_seg->seg_point())) {
    delete new_seg;
    return;  // new direction causes cross-over
  }
  // successfully found new direction
  head = new_seg;
```

```
  head->draw();
  if(++length >= maxlength) {
    --length;
    head->shed_tail();
  }
}

static void pause(int rate) {
  for (int i = 0; i < rate; i++)
    ;
}


void main(int argc, char * argv[]) {
  if( argc < 4 ) {
    cerr << "usage: snake num_of_snakes size_factor pause_rate"
         << endl << "CTRL-BREAK to quit";
    exit(1);
  }
  cout << escape << "[=7l"; // turn off ANSI line wrap
  cout << escape << "[2J"; // clear screen
  // seed the random number generator:
  srand(time(new time_t));
  // Create a whole nest of snakes:
  const num_of_snakes = atoi(argv[1]);
  const size_factor = atoi(argv[2]);
  const pause_rate = atoi(argv[3]);
  snake ** snakes = new snake*[num_of_snakes];
  for(int i = 0; i < num_of_snakes; i++)
    snakes[i] = new snake(point::random_point(),
#if 0  // for randomly chosen sizes:
        rand() % size_factor, i + '0');
#else  // for fixed sizes: (avoid the bell)
        size_factor, ((i + 1) % 254 == 7) ? 1 : (i + 1) % 254);
#endif
  while(1){
    for(i = 0; i < num_of_snakes; i++) {
      snakes[i]->slither();
      pause(pause_rate);
    }
  }
}
```

Recursive Member Functions

The next three functions are quite entertaining. All of them are recursive, but they recurse back down the snake toward the tail. It is as if you are traversing a linked list, but since each link is an object with its own member functions, you can do it recursively.

The function **segment::shed_tail()** must do three things. If the current segment is the tail (in which case the **previous** pointer will be 0), the tail is deleted (thus the reason for forcing segments to be made on the heap). However, if the tail was just deleted, the segment just up from the tail is the new tail. Thus, when the tail is deleted, the recursive function returns a 1 to tell the next segment up that it should set its **previous** pointer to 0 to indicate it is the new tail. Finally, if nothing happens, it returns a 0 to tell the next segment up to do nothing but return 0 in turn.

The **segment::cross_over()** function takes its argument, a **point**, and checks to see if it's equivalent to the segment's point. If so, it returns 1 to indicate yes (which means the point isn't a good choice). If not, it calls **previous->cross_over()** to check back until a crossover point or the tail is found.

The **segment::redraw_tail()** function calls **draw()** and then recursively calls itself until the tail is encountered, thus redrawing the entire snake. **draw()** and **erase()** are the only functions that do any output; if you want to adapt the program to a new system, you only have to change these (and a couple of minor places in **main()**).

The snake Class

The **snake** object is quite simple. A **snake** consists of a pointer to a **segment** called **head**, and numbers indicating the current length and maximum length. There is a single constructor that creates a new **segment** for the **head**, and initializes **length** and **maxlength**. After that, the snake will **crawl()** in any **direction** you say. The **snake::crawl()** simply assigns **head** to a new **segment**, which is made from the previous **head** (thus chaining the snake together). If the snake is too long, the tail is shed.

snake::slither() is a more interesting function. It "throws dice" using the ANSI C library function **rand()**, which generates random numbers, to decide whether or not to change directions. Thus the statement

```
if (rand() % chance) != chance/2)
```

creates a random number between 0 and **chance**, and tests to see if it is equivalent to **chance/2**. Thus, in a perfect distribution you have a 1 in **chance** probability the statement will be true.

If the above **if** statement is true, **snake::slither()** will just make the snake continue in the same direction by using the old direction (thus you can make the snakes do more twists and turns by reducing **chance**). If it is false, a random number between 0 and 4 is generated and cast into a **direction** (to indicate one of the directions in **segment**). Note that C++ forces you to explicitly cast an integer into a **enum**; it won't just allow you to sneak it by—better type checking! When the snake turns, it is also redrawn, just because it only happens occasionally (redrawing the whole snake every time it moves slows things down significantly).

Next, a new **segment** is created, but it isn't assigned to the head—yet. First, you must test to ensure that the new segment won't cross over an existing segment. If it does, the segment is deleted, and the function returns without doing anything. The next call to **slither()** will try again with a new direction. When running the simulation, you will see that sometimes a long snake can coil in upon itself and be unable to move.

A Flexible main()

One of the important features supported by C++ is a "dynamic programming style." This means determining the conditions (the number and type of objects in your system) of a program at run time rather than compile time. By delaying more of the decisions about the system, you allow new discoveries and adjustments to be made *after* the system is finished. Not only does this mean modifications may sometimes be made to the program without reprogramming, it also means the user may discover things about the system the programmer never thought of (these may work themselves back into a future version of the program). Whether designers like it or not, all programs go through iterations of use, learning, and redesign. This is one of the reasons existing design techniques don't always work so well—they provide good structure and documentation, but not good design flexibility.

In **main()**, you can see that the user determines the number of snakes, the size of the snakes, and the speed of the simulation on the command line. After the ANSI C random-number generator is seeded using the current time, the arguments are picked off the command line, and an array of pointers to snakes is created on the heap (astute readers will notice this space is never freed—sloppy, but not too bad, since it's such a small variable. It's not something you want to make a general habit of, though). The **#ifdef** statements determine whether the sizes of the snakes are chosen randomly or are a fixed size (both options use **size_factor**).

The delay is introduced with the function **pause()** (defined just before **main()**), which uses a very primitive loop (not a good idea on multitasking systems). The rate can be adjusted by the user, on the command line, for various processor speeds and quantities of snakes.

Projects Using Graphic Shapes

In the final projects for this chapter, you'll see all the features of object-oriented programming: data abstraction, inheritance, polymorphism, and a dynamic programming style. These features will be used in a graphic **shape** hierarchy containing virtual functions for drawing, erasing, moving, resizing, and so on. Numerous different types of shapes are inherited from the base class, all with different characteristics and behaviors.

The **shape** hierarchy will be used in several program examples. The first is a shape editor—you can create as many shapes as you like and step through the list of shapes and edit each one (moving it, changing its background, making it larger or smaller, and so on). The second example places random shapes in random places on the screen. The final example revisits the simulation problem in Chapter 8 by creating a simulation unit represented by a **shape** on the screen. The shapes move randomly about the screen; you can create your own simulation units with more interesting rules.

You'll also see how the complexity of some components—in particular, the graphics library (the Borland Graphics Interface is used here)—can be encapsulated to make a library much easier to use and port to other platforms that may have a different graphics library available. The use of the graphics concepts are all you see, hidden away from their implementation.

Encapsulating the BGI

The first class takes the tedious initialization required for the Borland Graphics Interface (BGI) and encapsulates it into an object. The only reason for doing all this is to "hide" the BGI initialization; you'll only create one instance of **Graphics** in each program. Using BGI becomes remarkably simple, however, since all you have to say is

```
Graphics BGI(bgi_path);
```

The **bgi_path** is the path where the graphics drivers are stored. If the object cannot find the right driver in that path, it automatically tries the local directory.

Here's the class interface for **Graphics**:

```
//: BGI.H—Class to "wrap" around Borland Graphics Interface
#ifndef BGI_H_
#define BGI_H_
#include <graphics.h>

class Graphics {
  static int gdriver;
  static int gmode;
  static int errorcode;
  static int X_max;  // maximum graphics screen coordinates
  static int Y_max;
public:
  static COLORS maxcolor;
  // Constructor default: request auto detection
  Graphics(char * path = "", graphics_drivers gdriv = DETECT);
```

```
~Graphics() { close(); }   /* clean up */
static void close() { closegraph(); }
static int xmax() { return X_max; }
static int ymax() { return Y_max; }
// Text output (in graphics mode) on the bottom line:
static void bottomprompt(char * prompt);
};
#endif // BGI_H_
```

All the information necessary to start and run the BGI is contained in this class, along with some other information you almost always need to know (**X_max**, **Y_max**, and **maxcolor**). These are automatically initialized and available whenever you use this class.

Notice that all the functions and data are **static** (with the exception of constructors and destructors, which cannot be). This means only one instance of each data element will be created, and the functions can be accessed without respect to any particular object.

The difference between **maxcolor** and **xmax()** and **ymax()** is that **maxcolor** can be accessed directly (and thus changed) while the access functions protect their values from being changed.

Here's the implementation for **Graphics**. At the beginning of the file are the **static** data member definitions:

```
//: BGI.CPP—Methods for Borland Graphics Interface "wrapper"
#include "bgi.h"
#include <iostream.h>
#include <stdlib.h>
#include <conio.h>

// static data member definitions:
COLORS Graphics::maxcolor;
int Graphics::gdriver, Graphics::gmode,
    Graphics::errorcode,
    Graphics::X_max, Graphics::Y_max;

Graphics::Graphics(char * path, graphics_drivers gdriv) {
  // initialize graphics and local variables:
  gdriver = gdriv;
  initgraph(&gdriver, &gmode, path);
  // read result of initialization:
  errorcode = graphresult();
  while (errorcode != grOk) {  /* an error occurred */
    // try again with local directory:
```

```
        initgraph(&gdriver, &gmode, ".");
        errorcode = graphresult();
        if(errorcode == grOk) break;
        cerr << "Graphics error: " << grapherrormsg(errorcode)
             << endl << "Press any key to halt:";
        getch();
        exit(1); /* terminate with an error code */
    }
    X_max = getmaxx();
    Y_max = getmaxy();
    maxcolor = (COLORS)getmaxcolor();
}

void Graphics::bottomprompt(char * prompt) {
    const clipping = 1;   // clipping on
    setviewport(0, Y_max - textheight(prompt),
                X_max, Y_max, clipping);
    clearviewport();
    outtextxy(0,0, prompt);
    setviewport(0,0, X_max, Y_max, clipping);
}
```

Notice all the work is done in the constructor; these are the tedious things you normally have to do every time you use the BGI.

The **bottomprompt()** function is a way to print a message at the bottom of the screen. It uses a viewport at the screen bottom and the default graphics text. If you need to do iostream-style output, create an intermediate buffer and use it for a **ostrstream** object, like this (after including **strstream.h**):

```
const sz = 80;
char buf[sz];
ostrstream output(buf, sz);
output << "an integer " << 47 << " a string " << "47" << endl;
Graphics::bottomprompt(buf);
```

A Generic Shape Class

The goal of this project is to use polymorphism; that is, to avoid any concern with specific types and instead treat everything as generally as possible. To do this, the essence of the project is distilled into a single concept. Here, the program manipulates shapes. A shape can do such things as draw itself, erase itself, move itself, and resize itself. These activities will probably be different for specific types of shapes, so the proper functions need to be called even if you're treating an object as a generic shape (that is, accessing the object via a shape pointer). Virtual functions are used to create a common interface for a group of subtypes (here, **Circle**s, **Square**s, and **Rectangle**s are all shapes you can **draw()**). You can call a virtual function for any object without knowing its exact type, and the proper method will be used.

Here's the header file for class **shape**:

```
//: SHAPE.H—Abstract base class for all shapes
#ifndef SHAPE_H_
#define SHAPE_H_
#include "bgi.h"

class shape {
protected:
  COLORS line_color, fill_color;
  fill_patterns fill_pattern;
  int xcoord, ycoord;  // "center" coordinates
  int x_proportion, y_proportion;  // determines size of shape
public:
  shape(int xc, int yc, int xscale, int yscale,
        COLORS fc = BLACK, fill_patterns fp = SOLID_FILL,
        COLORS lc = Graphics::maxcolor);
  virtual ~shape() {}  // virtual destructor
  virtual void draw();
  virtual void erase();
  virtual void moverelative(int x, int y) {
    erase();
    xcoord += x;
    ycoord += y;
  }
  virtual void moveabsolute(int x, int y) {
    erase();
    xcoord = x;
    ycoord = y;
  }
  void setxsize(int xs) { x_proportion = xs; }
  void setysize(int ys) { y_proportion = ys; }
  virtual void setsize() {}; // change to a new size
  virtual void edit();  // modify a shape according to user
  virtual void fillcolor(COLORS fc = BLACK);
  virtual void fillpattern(fill_patterns fp = SOLID_FILL);
};
```

```
#endif //  SHAPE_H_
```

As you can see from the constructor, you initialize a shape by providing it with coordinates and X and Y proportions (which determine its size). You can optionally tell it what colors and fill patterns to use; if you don't, default values are used.

The destructor for **shape** is also virtual. This ensures that proper cleanup will take place, even if you call the destructor via a pointer to the base class as will be done here.

Shape Implementation

Here's the implementation file for class **shape**:

```
//: SHAPE.CPP—Methods for generic shape class
#include "shape.h"
#include <conio.h>

const size_step = 5;  // for increasing or decreasing size

shape::shape(int xc, int yc, int xscale, int yscale,
             COLORS fc, fill_patterns fp, COLORS lc)
     : xcoord(xc), ycoord(yc),
       x_proportion(xscale), y_proportion(yscale),
       line_color(lc), fill_color(fc), fill_pattern(fp)
   {}

void shape::draw() {
  // call this, then your specific drawing function
  setsize();
  setcolor(line_color);
  setfillstyle(fill_pattern, fill_color);
}

void shape::erase() {
  // call this, then your specific drawing function
  setcolor(BLACK);
  setfillstyle(SOLID_FILL, BLACK);
}

void shape::edit() {  // change characteristics
```

```
while(1) {
  Graphics::bottomprompt(
  "p: pattern, c: color, s: size, q to quit");
  switch(getch()) {
    case 'p' : fill_pattern=(fill_patterns)(fill_pattern + 1);
               fillpattern(fill_pattern);
               draw();
               break;
    case 'c' : fill_color = (COLORS)(fill_color + 1);
               fillcolor(fill_color);
               draw();
               break;
    case 's' : Graphics::bottomprompt(
               "X for larger xval, x for smaller,"
               "Y for larger yval, y for smaller, q to quit");
               for(int rsp=getch(); rsp!='q'; rsp=getch()) {
                 switch(rsp) {
                   case 'X': x_proportion += size_step; break;
                   case 'Y': y_proportion += size_step; break;
                   case 'x': x_proportion -= size_step; break;
                   case 'y': y_proportion -= size_step; break;
                 }
                 if(x_proportion <= 0) x_proportion = 1;
                 if(y_proportion <= 0) y_proportion = 1;
                 erase();
                 setsize();  // virtual function call
                 draw();
               }
               break;
    case 'q' : return;
    default  : break;
    }
  }
}

void shape::fillcolor(COLORS fc) {
  fill_color = fc;
  if(fill_color > Graphics::maxcolor)
    fill_color = BLACK;  // wrap around "corner"
}

void shape::fillpattern(fill_patterns fp) {
  fill_pattern = fp;
  if(fill_pattern >= USER_FILL)
    fill_pattern = EMPTY_FILL;  // wrap around "corner"
}
```

Notice that you only use the keyword **virtual** in the class declaration, not the member function definition.

The **const size_step** defaults to internal linkage in C++—it isn't visible outside this file. Thus you may use the same name somewhere else without a collision.

Even though **draw()** and **erase()** are virtual functions, they can still be called explicitly by their redefined children (using the scope resolution operator), so it's useful for them to have a standard activity. In addition, placing common functionality in the base class reduces code size.

The call to the static function **Graphics::bottomprompt()** doesn't refer to a specific object. It doesn't need to, since the function refers to the entire class (and a **static** function has no **this**).

The **edit()** function changes colors, patterns, and sizes and depends heavily on virtual functions, in particular for sizes. The **edit()** changes the proportions and then calls **setsize()**, which reshapes the specific type of object.

Specific Types of Shapes

Now that the basic framework is laid out, some specific shapes can be created. The BGI has two basic types of shapes that can be drawn and filled in with patterns: ellipses and polygons. These suggest equivalent classes derived from **shape**, and all other types are derived from one of these two.

First, here's an **Ellipse** (note the uppercase E, to differentiate it from the BGI library function **ellipse()**) and a specific type of **Ellipse**, a **Circle**:

```
//: ELLIPSE.H—Ellipses and circles are types of shapes
#ifndef ELLIPSE_H_
#define ELLIPSE_H_
#include "shape.h"

class Ellipse : public shape {
protected:
  int xradius, yradius; // Ellipse radii from center
public:
  Ellipse(int xc, int yc, int xrad = 10, int yrad = 10,
```

```
          COLORS fc = BLACK, fill_patterns fp = SOLID_FILL,
          COLORS lc = Graphics::maxcolor);
  ~Ellipse() { erase(); }
  void draw();
  void erase();
  void setsize();
};

// A Circle is an Ellipse with only one radius
class Circle : public Ellipse {
public:
  Circle(int xc, int yc, int radius = 10) :
    Ellipse(xc, yc, radius, radius) {}
  void setsize();
};

#endif // ELLIPSE_H_
```

The virtual functions **draw()** and **erase()** are only redefined for **Ellipse**, not **Circle**. The redefinition works for both classes (this is another facet of code reuse).

The **draw()** and **erase()** functions must call the specific BGI drawing functions. The **setsize()** function proportions the radii of an **Ellipse** differently from a **Circle**. You can see this in the implementation:

```
//: ELLIPSE.CPP—Methods for ellipses and circles
#include "ellipse.h"

Ellipse::Ellipse(int xc, int yc, int xrad, int yrad,
        COLORS fc, fill_patterns fp, COLORS lc)
  : shape(xc, yc, xrad, yrad, fc, fp, lc),
    xradius(xrad), yradius(yrad) {}

void Ellipse::draw() {
  shape::draw();
  fillellipse(xcoord, ycoord, xradius, yradius);
}

void Ellipse::erase() {
  shape::erase();
  fillellipse(xcoord, ycoord, xradius, yradius);
}

// Set the size based on the proportions:
void Ellipse::setsize() {
```

```
  xradius = x_proportion;
  yradius = y_proportion;
}

// Notice a circle's size only depends on x_proportion:
void Circle::setsize() {
  xradius = yradius = x_proportion;
}
```

The virtual function late-binding mechanism is not used inside constructors and destructors. The "most local" function is called via static binding. This is done because, for example, a constructor could otherwise call a function for an object that hasn't yet been initialized. Thus, you cannot call **draw()** in the base class **shape()** constructor and expect a virtual call.

Polygons

The BGI polygon is more complicated: it requires an array of X-Y pairs as the vertices of the polygon. Since the general-purpose **Polygon** class cannot know how many vertices a polygon will have until the point at run time when you create it, this array must be allocated dynamically using **new**, and copied from an array the user hands to the constructor. You can see the way this works for an unspecified type of **Polygon** in the SHED.CPP program, shown later. However, for particular types of polygons (squares, rectangles, triangles) you *do* know how many points you have so it would be redundant to force the user to make an array and pass the array and the size to a square, for example.

This problem is solved by creating a **static** array of X-Y pairs to pass to a **Square** constructor (for example). The values of the points are unimportant, since they are calculated by other means, but it is important to pass a valid array address to **Polygon**. A **static** array produces a valid address without wasting space with multiple arrays.

Here's the header file for **Polygon** and its derived classes:

```
//: POLYGON.H—Shapes for squares, rectangles, triangles, etc.
#ifndef POLYGON_H_
#define POLYGON_H_
#include "shape.h"
```

```
#include <string.h>

class Polygon : public shape {
protected:
  // array of points determining the corners:
  int * relative_vertices;
  // relative_vertices[0] and [1] are the "anchor coordinates"
  void translate();
private:
  int * actual_vertices; // actual coordinates of the corners
  int vcount;   // number of vertices
public:
  Polygon(int vnumber, int * vertices, int xc, int yc,
          int xsize = 10, int ysize = 10,
          COLORS fc = BLACK, fill_patterns fp = SOLID_FILL,
          COLORS lc = WHITE);
  ~Polygon();
  void draw();
  void erase();
  void moverelative(int x, int y) {
    shape::moverelative(x, y);
    translate();
    setsize();
  }
  void moveabsolute(int x, int y) {
    shape::moveabsolute(x, y);
    translate();
    setsize();
  }
};

class Rectangle : public Polygon {
protected:
  static int corners[8];
public:
  Rectangle(int xc, int yc, int xsize = 10, int ysize = 20);
  void setsize();
};

class Square : public Rectangle {
public:
  Square(int xc, int yc, int size = 10);
  void setsize();
};

class Triangle : public Polygon {
  static int corners[6];
```

```
public:
  Triangle(int xc, int yc, int size = 10);
  void setsize();
};

#endif // POLYGON_H_
```

Again, notice that some virtual functions that must be reimplemented in **Polygon** from **shape** don't need to be changed again for **Rectangle**, **Square**, and **Triangle**. The **setsize()** function seems to be the one that must always be redefined; this makes sense because it takes the internal **x_proportion** and **y_proportion** sizes (defined way back in **shape**, as **protected** data members for access in derived classes such as these) and adjusts the specific shape to conform.

Here are the methods for class **Polygon**:

```
//: POLYGON.CPP—Methods for class polygon
#include "polygon.h"
#include <string.h>

// Static data member initialization:
int Triangle::corners[6], Rectangle::corners[8];

Polygon::Polygon(int vnumber, int * vertices, int xc, int yc,
                 int xsize, int ysize,
                 COLORS fc, fill_patterns fp, COLORS lc)
      : shape(xc, yc, xsize, ysize, fc, fp, lc),vcount(vnumber){
  if(vcount <= 0) vcount = 1;  // must have at least one vertex
  relative_vertices = new int[vcount * 2];
  actual_vertices = new int[vcount * 2];
  memcpy(relative_vertices, vertices, vcount * 2 * sizeof(int));
  translate();  // calculate actual_vertices
}

void Polygon::translate() {
  memcpy(actual_vertices, relative_vertices,
         vcount * 2 * sizeof(int));
  for(int i = 0; i < vcount * 2; i += 2) {
    actual_vertices[i] += xcoord;
    actual_vertices[i+1] += ycoord;
  }
}

Polygon::~Polygon() {
  erase();
```

```
    delete relative_vertices;
    delete actual_vertices;
}

void Polygon::draw() {
  shape::draw();
  fillpoly(vcount, actual_vertices);
}

void Polygon::erase() {
  shape::erase();
  fillpoly(vcount, actual_vertices);
  drawpoly(vcount, actual_vertices); // erase "trailing" line...
}

Rectangle::Rectangle(int xc, int yc, int xsize, int ysize)
  : Polygon(4, corners, xc, yc, xsize, ysize) {
    setsize();  // virtual mechanism not active in constructors
}

void Rectangle::setsize() {
  relative_vertices[0] = 0;
  relative_vertices[1] = 0;
  relative_vertices[2] = x_proportion;
  relative_vertices[3] = 0;
  relative_vertices[4] = x_proportion;
  relative_vertices[5] = y_proportion;
  relative_vertices[6] = 0;
  relative_vertices[7] = y_proportion;
  translate();
}

Square::Square(int xc, int yc, int size) :
  Rectangle(xc, yc, size, size) {
    setsize();  // virtual mechanism not active in constructors
}

void Square::setsize() {
  relative_vertices[0] = 0;
  relative_vertices[1] = 0;
  relative_vertices[2] = x_proportion;
  relative_vertices[3] = 0;
  relative_vertices[4] = x_proportion;
  relative_vertices[5] = x_proportion;
  relative_vertices[6] = 0;
  relative_vertices[7] = x_proportion;
  translate();
```

```
}

Triangle::Triangle(int xc, int yc, int size) :
  Polygon(3, corners, xc, yc, size) {
    setsize();  // virtual mechanism not active in constructors
}

void Triangle::setsize() {
  relative_vertices[0] = 0;
  relative_vertices[1] = 0;
  relative_vertices[2] = x_proportion;
  relative_vertices[3] = 0;
  relative_vertices[4] = x_proportion/2;
  relative_vertices[5] = y_proportion;
  translate();
}
```

The **new** keyword is used to create local space for the array of points, and the ANSI C library function **memcpy()** rapidly copies the values from the argument into the local array. Notice that the array simply shows points relative to a local origin. To create the actual array of points to hand to the BGI **fillpoly()** function, a second array is created. The **translate()** function adds the values of the origin's **xcoord** and **ycoord** to each vertex. This means that to move the object, you simply erase it, change the coordinates, call **translate()**, and draw it—which is precisely what **moverelative()** does. Notice, however, that any shapes derived from **Polygon** do not need to redefine the **translate()** function. This is a good design indicator—as you create more specific types, you need to redefine less virtual functions.

The **setsize()** function does the work in the constructors for the derived classes **Rectangle**, **Square**, and **Triangle**. It sets the values of the relative vertices and then simply calls **translate()** to calculate the values of the actual vertices.

Container Classes

The class **SHlist** is inherited from the Borland container class **BI_ListImp** to create a container class to hold **shape** pointers. In this class, the member function **drawlist()** has been overloaded to create two versions. In the version with no arguments, an iterator (an object with the job of indexing through a container) is created to point to the elements of the list (again by instantiating the appropriate template), and it is initialized by handing it ***this**, the current object. The iterator sets itself up to point to the top of the list, and the postincrement operator produces the address of the current object *before* the increment. Testing the value in the **while** loop produces true or false indicating whether the iterator has reached the end of the list (this uses the automatic type conversion **operator int()** defined for the iterator).

The second version of **drawlist()** takes a single argument, which is a reference to another iterator. This iterator points to the shape you're currently interested in, which should be drawn last (so it is on top). A local iterator is created from the argument, and it is incremented (to move past the current element); then every shape is drawn until the end of the list. The local iterator is restarted so it points to the top of the list, then every element is drawn until the one corresponding to the argument has been displayed. Notice the following code:

```
do
   if(it)  it.current()->draw();
while(it++ != Cur.current());
```

The **if** is required to handle the case of the empty list. In the **while** conditional, the **operator++** produces the pointer to the **shape** object *before* incrementing, so it must be compared with the pointer to **Cur**, produced with **current()**. Because the value produced by the postincrement is the one before the increment, the matching element will be displayed before the test returns false.

The Shape Editor SHED

Now there are enough tools to bring everything together into the shape editor. One of the important features of this editor is that it must be extensible; that is, you must be able to easily add new types of shapes. This is where all the work done setting up a polymorphic system pays off: there's only one point where you need to know the specific type of shape, and that's in the constructor. Once you've created the shape, you can call any of its polymorphic functions and the right thing will automatically happen, as if by magic!

To make adding new types of shapes easy, all the constructor calls are in one place, inside the **makeshape()** function, which is responsible for making all the objects. The **makeshape()** function returns a pointer to a generic shape it creates on the heap via **new**. All you have to do is tell the function what type of shape you want to create and it makes one for you.

Here's the code for the shape editor:

```
//: SHED.CPP—Graphic shape editor
#define EXTEND  // to add a new feature to the system
#include "polygon.h"
#include "ellipse.h"
#if defined(EXTEND)
#include "circbox.h"  // An "extension" to the system
#endif
#include "doskey.h"
#include <listimp.h> // list template
#include <shddel.h>   // deletion control

// BGI initialization:
Graphics BGI("c:\\borlandc\\bgi\\"); // path with BGI files

shape * makeshape() {
  const x = Graphics::xmax()/2, y = Graphics::ymax()/2;
  while(1) {
    Graphics::bottomprompt(
      "c: circle, e: ellipse, r: rectangle, "
      "s: square, t: triangle"
#if defined(EXTEND)
      ", b: circlebox"  // must also extend the menu
#endif
    );
    switch(get_doskey()) {
      case CAP_C: case LC_C: return new Circle(x, y, 10);
      case CAP_E: case LC_E: return new Ellipse(x, y, 10, 30);
      case CAP_R: case LC_R: return new Rectangle(x,y);
      case CAP_S: case LC_S: return new Square(x, y);
      case CAP_T: case LC_T: return new Triangle(x, y);
      // Must also extend the switch statement:
#if defined(EXTEND)
      case CAP_B: case LC_B: return new circlebox(x,y, 10);
#endif
      default: break;
    }
  }
}
```

```
}

// Derive class from template instantiation:
class SHlist : public BI_ListImp<shape*> {
public:
  void drawlist() { // draw the entire list
    BI_ListIteratorImp<shape*> it(*this);
    while(it) (it++)->draw();
  }
  void drawlist(BI_ListIteratorImp<shape*>& Cur) {
    BI_ListIteratorImp<shape*> it(Cur);
    it++; // draw Cur element last
    while(it) (it++)->draw();
    it.restart();
    do
      if(it) it.current()->draw();
    while(it++ != Cur.current());
  }
  ~SHlist() { flush(TShouldDelete::Delete); }
};

void main() {
  SHlist shapelist;

  // Create some default shapes:
  int verts1[] = { 0, 0, 0, 20, 50, 50, 75, 0 };
  shapelist.add(new Polygon(
          sizeof(verts1)/(sizeof(verts1[0]) * 2),
          verts1, 100,300, 20,20, WHITE, HATCH_FILL));
  shapelist.add(new Ellipse(200,200,50, 75, WHITE, HATCH_FILL));
  shapelist.add(new Ellipse(100,200,70, 75, WHITE, HATCH_FILL));
  shapelist.add(new Square(300,300, 100));
  shapelist.add(new Circle(350,350, 47));


  BI_ListIteratorImp<shape*> sh(shapelist); // points to top
  shapelist.drawlist(sh);
  while(1) {
    Graphics::bottomprompt(
      "a: add shape, r: remove, n: next shape, "
      "arrow keys: move, e: edit, esc to quit");
    const move_factor = 20;
    switch(get_doskey()) {
      case CAP_A      : // Add a shape
      case LC_A       : shapelist.add(makeshape()); // to top
```

```
                              sh.restart();   // iterator to top
                              sh.current()->draw();
                              break;
        case CAP_R          : // Remove the current shape
        case LC_R           : if(sh) {
                                  delete sh.current();
                                  shapelist.detach(sh.current());
                              }
                              sh.restart(); // point to valid item
                              shapelist.drawlist(sh);
                              break;
        case CAP_N          : // move to next valid shape in the list
        case LC_N           : sh++;
                              if(!sh) sh.restart();
                              if(!sh) return;  // empty list
                              sh.current()->draw();
                              break;
        case LEFT_ARROW     : if(sh)
                                  sh.current()->moverelative(
                                    -move_factor, 0);
                                  shapelist.drawlist(sh);
                              break;
        case RIGHT_ARROW    : if(sh)
                                  sh.current()->moverelative(
                                    move_factor, 0);
                              shapelist.drawlist(sh);
                              break;
        case UP_ARROW       : if(sh)
                                  sh.current()->moverelative(
                                    0, - move_factor);
                              shapelist.drawlist(sh);
                              break;
        case DOWN_ARROW     : if(sh)
                                  sh.current()->moverelative(
                                    0, move_factor);
                              shapelist.drawlist(sh);
                              break;
        case CAP_E          :
        case LC_E           : if(sh) sh.current()->edit();
                              shapelist.drawlist(sh);
                              break;
        case ESCAPE         : return;
        default             : break;
      }
    }
  }
}
```

You'll notice that **makeshape()** forces the user to select a proper shape, because it must return a valid shape pointer (which is immediately added to the **shapelist**).

The **main()** function is remarkably simple, as you'll often find it is with C++ programs—the work goes into designing the objects, and using them is easy. A container called **shapelist** is created, and some shapes are placed in the list (including an oddly shaped polygon made using a custom array of vertices). Then, a **while** loop executes user commands until the user presses ESC to leave the program. The user commands can request the next shape (with N), movement (with the arrow keys), addition or removal of the current shape (A or R), and editing of the current shape (E). All user commands generate virtual function calls—notice the pointer **sh** points to a generic shape object, and you can't find mention of anything but generic shapes inside the **while** loop.

The creation of the iterator is very location specific. If you create it before any shapes are added to **shapelist**, it will point to the top of the empty list. After adding elements, you must remember to **restart()** the iterator to the top of the list, or else it will remain pointing at a zero element and you'll get undesirable results. However, if you wait until later before creating the iterator, it will point to a nonzero element in the first place. This is another example indicating that it is best to delay the creation of objects until right before you use them (and of course, until you have all the necessary information to create the object).

Keyboard Scan Codes

There are two additional items here. The first is the **doskey.h** include file, which contains a function to retrieve the scan code (not the letter representation of the key pressed) from the keyboard. This is important to allow use of the arrow keys and others on the keyboard. The **bioskey()** function captures the scan codes by making a DOS BIOS call. Here's **doskey.h**, with definitions for the keys in this program:

```
//: DOSKEY.H—Scan codes returned by BIOS
//. Allows reading of cursor pad, ctrl, alt, shift, etc.
//. Not a complete set.
#ifndef DOSKEY_H_
#define  DOSKEY_H_
```

```
#include <bios.h>

enum doskey {
  CAP_A = 0x1e41, // Capital letter A
  LC_A = 0x1e61, // Lowercase letter a
  CAP_B = 0x3042,
  LC_B = 0x3062,
  CAP_C = 0x2e43,
  LC_C = 0x2e63,
  CAP_E = 0x1245,
  LC_E = 0x1265,
  CAP_N = 0x314e,
  LC_N = 0x316e,
  CAP_P = 0x1950,
  LC_P = 0x1970,
  CAP_R = 0x1352,
  LC_R = 0x1372,
  CAP_S = 0x1f53,
  LC_S = 0x1f73,
  CAP_T = 0x1454,
  LC_T = 0x1474,
  LEFT_ARROW = 0x4b00,
  RIGHT_ARROW = 0x4d00,
  UP_ARROW = 0x4800,
  DOWN_ARROW = 0x5000,
  ESCAPE = 0x11b
};

inline doskey get_doskey() {
  while(!bioskey(1));  // wait for a keypress
  return (doskey)bioskey(0);
}

#endif  DOSKEY_H_
```

This is the program used to print out the key values as you press them:

```
//: KEYREAD.CPP—Basic key-capture program
#include <fstream.h>
#include <bios.h>

void main(void) {
    ofstream out("key.tmp");
    char ch;
    while(1) {
      cout << "Input a character:";
```

```
    while(!bioskey(1));
    int key = bioskey(0);
    cout << "key = 0x" << hex << key << endl;
    out << "key = 0x" << hex << key << "," << endl;
    if(key == 0x11b) return; // escape to quit
  }
}
```

Extending the Program

The second new item in SHED.CPP is activated by uncommenting the line:

```
// #define EXTEND  // to add a new feature to the system
```

This displays what may be the most important and exciting feature of object-oriented programming: extensibility. Extensibility means that once you've gone to all the trouble of setting up your program to use virtual functions, as done here, you can almost effortlessly add new features to it. Adding new features to an existing program is a constant process that happens as the needs of customers change. Extensibility doesn't cost much—a little more thought during design (which soon becomes natural), and the benefits are tremendous: in minutes, you can experiment with new features that might have taken hours or days to add with a non-OOP design.

To add a feature, you simply derive a new subtype. Here, it must be derived from **shape**, since that's what the system handles. You could create a different type of **Polygon** (a pentagon, for example) but for something a little different this project will combine two existing shapes, a **Circle** and a **Square**, to create a new shape, **circlebox**:

```
//: CIRCBOX.H—Combined circle and square
#include "polygon.h"
#include "ellipse.h"

class circlebox : public shape {
  Circle C;
  Square S;
public:
  circlebox(int xc, int yc, int size = 10) :
    shape(xc, yc, size, size),
```

```
      C(xc, yc, size), S(xc, yc, size + 20) {
   }
   void setsize() {
     C.setxsize(x_proportion);
     C.setsize();
     S.setxsize(x_proportion + 20);
     S.setsize();
   }
   void draw() {
     S.draw();
     C.draw();
   }
   void erase() {
     S.erase();
     C.erase();
   }
   void moverelative(int x, int y) {
     shape::moverelative(x,y);
     S.moverelative(x,y);
     C.moverelative(x,y);
   }
   void fillcolor(COLORS fc = BLACK) {
     shape::fillcolor(fc);
     S.fillcolor(fc);
     C.fillcolor(fc);
   }
   void fillpattern(fill_patterns fp = SOLID_FILL) {
     shape::fillpattern(fp);
     S.fillpattern(fp);
     C.fillpattern(fp);
   }
};
```

You can see that **circlebox** is composed of a **Circle** and a **Square**. A **circlebox** could conceivably be created using multiple inheritance—this would say: "a **circlebox** is a kind of **Circle** and a kind of **Square**." However, this would introduce a number of problems. Both **Circle** and **Square** have some identical functions, like **setsize()**, which would have to be disambiguated using the class names and the scope resolution operator. That's fairly easy to do, but a more difficult problem is the fact that two subobjects of class **shape** would be introduced, and when the **circlebox** pointer is upcast to assign it to a **shape** pointer (while adding it to the container), the compiler wouldn't know which subobject to use for the representative **shape**. You can, of course, make **shape** a virtual base class, but this adds another burden since it must always be initialized by the most derived class. Here, it's much easier to use composition instead of multiple inheritance (the easiest solution to many problems often involves avoiding multiple inheritance).

Just creating the new type isn't enough to add it to the system. You must also insert at least one place where an object of that new type will be created (and, in SHED.CPP, an entry must be added to the "new shapes" menu). This is the constructor call you see inside **makeshape()**:

```
#if defined(EXTEND)
    case CAP_B: case LC_B: return new circlebox(x,y, 10);
#endif
```

Remember the constructor is the only place where the exact type of the object must be known. The constructor is where the object's future behavior is established.

Design of the Base Type

Notice how important the design of the base type is (in this case, **shape**). If the base type isn't designed properly, you will have problems extending the system. However, don't agonize too long over the base type's design—remember that part of the object design process happens when you extend the system and discover a flaw in your thinking. You can go back and change the design. (For example, **shape** was modified several times while creating this system.)

Random Shape Generation

As an example of code reuse, this example will randomly generate shapes and put them on the screen, removing them some time later. Of course, the **shape** hierarchy can remain in place exactly as it stands; the only change necessary is to the driver program.

A New Container Template

Once again, a container class is necessary to hold the shapes as they are created. But instead of using a predefined container, here's one created from scratch. It is the same type of container/iterator pair, but much simpler (and probably faster, for that reason). It also comes with much less baggage, so it is useful in many places where you just want a quick container but don't want to pay much for it. This class should come in handy for a lot of general uses (dare I suggest you put it in your INCLUDE directory?). The definition looks like this:

```
//: SLISTT.H—Extremely simple linked list template
//. Template argument determines list ownership
#ifndef SLISTT_H_
#define SLISTT_H_
#include<stdlib.h>

template <class T, int owns = 1>  // default to owning objects
class slistt {
  struct link {
    T * data;  // pointer to the actual T
    link * next;  // next link in list
    link(T * sh, link * nx)
      : data(sh), next(nx) {}
    ~link() { if (owns) delete data; }
  };
  link *head;  // head always points to the top of the list
public:
  // initialize an empty list:
  slistt() : head(0) {}
  // insert a new link in at the head:
  T * add(T * sh) {
    head = new link(sh, head);
    return sh;
  }
  ~slistt(); // remove elements until the list is empty
  friend class slistIterator<T, owns>;
};

template <class T, int owns>
slistt<T, owns>::~slistt() {
  while(head) { // while there are elements left at the top
    link* l = head->next; // remember the next position
    delete head; // delete the top
    head = l;
  }
}

template <class T, int owns = 1>
class slistIterator {
```

```
    slistt<T, owns>::link * cursor;
    slistt<T, owns>& list;
public:
  slistIterator(slistt<T, owns>& SL)
      : list(SL), cursor(SL.head) {}
  // top() and ++ return the current T, or 0 for the end:
  T * top() { // go to top of the list
    cursor = list.head;
    return cursor ? cursor->data : 0; // return data if nonzero
  }
  T* tail() {  // go to last valid element
    if(!cursor) cursor = list.head;
    while(cursor->next) cursor = cursor->next;
    return cursor ? cursor->data : 0;
  }
  T * operator++() {  // Only move forward if cursor isn't 0:
    if(cursor) cursor = cursor->next;
    return cursor ? cursor->data : 0;
  }
  T* operator++(int) { // postfix version
    slistt<T, owns>::link * cur = cursor;
    if(cursor) cursor = cursor->next;
    return cur ? cur->data : 0; // return data before increment
  }
  // Type conversion operator returns current pointer:
  operator T*() { return cursor ? cursor->data : 0; }
  // Smart Pointer:
  T* operator->() {
    return cursor ? cursor->data : (exit(1), (T*)0);
  }
  void remove();  // remove the current element
};


template <class T, int owns>
void slistIterator<T, owns>::remove() { //delete current element
  if(!cursor) return;  // nothing to remove (or at end of list)
  slistt<T, owns>::link *cur, *drag;
  cur = drag = list.head;
  while(cur != cursor) {
    drag = cur;
    cur = cur->next;
  }
  // special case—object at the head of the list:
  if (cur == list.head) {
    list.head = list.head->next;
    cursor = list.head;
```

```
      delete cur;
      return;
    }
  drag->next = cur->next;   // thread past deleted node
  delete cur;
  cursor = drag; // back up to previous element
}

#endif // SLISTT_H_
```

The ownership issue is again addressed in this template; you control ownership with a flag during template creation; the default is to the **slistt** owning the objects it contains, and destroying them when either a link or the container is destroyed. Also there is no option here of putting the objects themselves in the container; everything is a pointer (which is simpler and certainly the more common case).

The container is implemented as a linked list, so there is no size consideration. The **link** structure is nested, so it is invisible (and inaccessible) to the outside. The sole member of **slistt is head**, a pointer to the "top" link in the list (the last one entered; it acts like a push-down stack) which is initialized to 0 to indicate an empty list. Inserting a new link with the **add()** function is a trivial and foolproof process, and cleaning up the list with the destructor is simply a matter of "popping" all the links off the list and destroying them.

The iterator **slistIterator** is a **friend** of **slistt**, so it has access to private members. It is initialized to a specific **slistt** object, and is tied to that **slistt** for its lifetime (this is ensured by using a reference member **list**, instead of a pointer). The **cursor** is moved around in the list by the functions **top()**, **tail()**, and **operator++()**. Note the prefix version of **operator++()** returns its pointer *after* moving forward, and the postfix version returns the pointer *before* moving forward. The **operator T*()** performs automatic type conversion whenever an **slistIterator** object is used where a **T*** is expected.

The only function here that's tricky is **remove()**. Since it's a singly linked list, you must start at the top and work your way down, keeping track of the element right behind you, until you find the one you want to remove. Then you remove that element and thread the one behind you to point to the one in front of you.

Here's a program to test the linked list. It reads a text file, creating a **string** object for each line and inserting the result into an **slistt**. Then it copies the strings into a second **slistt** to reverse their order, and (to ensure that **remove()** works properly when the iterator points to the tail of the list) removes all the elements from the end of the first list:

```
//: SLTEST.CPP—Test of list template
#include <assert.h>
#include <fstream.h>
#include <string.h>
#include <stdlib.h>
#include "slistt.h"

class string {
  char * st;
public:
  string(char * s) : st(strdup(s)) {}
  ~string() { free(st); }
  friend ostream& operator<<(ostream& os, string* s) {
    return os << s->st;
  }
};

void main(int argc, char** argv) {
  assert(argc == 2);  // proper number of arguments
  slistt<string> strings;
  slistt<string, 0> strings2; // no ownership
  ifstream in(argv[1]);
  assert(in);  // make sure file is open
  const sz = 100; char buf[sz];
  while(in.getline(buf, sz))
    strings.add(new string(buf));
  slistIterator<string> it(strings); // associated iterator
  while(it)  // type conversion to pointer
    strings2.add(it++);  // to reverse the order
  slistIterator<string, 0> it2(strings2);
  while(it2)
    cout << it2++ << endl;
  cout << "***********************" << endl;
  it.tail();  // remove items from tail to reverse order
  while(it) {
    cout << it << endl;
    it.remove();
  }
}
```

The **slistt** container and its iterator should come in handy in many situations where you need to manipulate an indeterminate number of objects.

Creating the Program

Here is the container and the **shape** hierarchy used to create the random shapes. Notice the inheritance of **slistt** to make a custom **ShapeList**:

```
//: RNDSHAPE.CPP—Creating random shapes
#include <conio.h>
#include <dos.h>
#include <stdlib.h>
#include "polygon.h"
#include "ellipse.h"
#include "circbox.h"
#include "slistt.h"

Graphics BGI("c:\\borlandc\\bgi\\");

enum shapetypes { Scircle, Sellipse, Srectangle,
                  Ssquare, Striangle, Scirclebox,
                  MAXSHAPE };  // tag for counting

shape * MakeRandomShape() {
  const x = rand() % Graphics::xmax();
  const y = rand() % Graphics::ymax();
  switch((shapetypes)(rand() % MAXSHAPE)) {
    default:  // just default to "Circle"
    case Scircle: return new Circle(x, y, 10);
    case Sellipse: return new Ellipse(x, y, 10, 30);
    case Srectangle: return new Rectangle(x,y);
    case Ssquare: return new Square(x, y);
    case Striangle: return new Triangle(x, y);
    case Scirclebox: return new circlebox(x,y, 10);
  }
}

COLORS color = BLACK;
```

```
class ShapeList : public slistt<shape> {
public:
  void add(shape * s) {
    slistt<shape>::add(s);
    s->fillpattern(SOLID_FILL);
    s->fillcolor(color);
    s->draw();
  }
  void drawlist() {
    slistIterator<shape> it(*this);
    while(it) (it++)->draw();
  }
  void fillcolor(COLORS fc = BLACK) {
    slistIterator<shape> it(*this);
    while(it) (it++)->fillcolor(fc);
  }
};

void main() {
  ShapeList shapelist;  // holds all the shapes
  const shapecount = 25;
  for(int i = 0; i < shapecount; i++)
    shapelist.add(MakeRandomShape());
  int count = 0;
  const clearcount = 20; // before changing color
  slistIterator<shape> sh(shapelist);
  sh.tail(); // always points to tail
  while(!kbhit()) {
    shapelist.add(MakeRandomShape()); // add to head
    sh.remove(); // remove shapes from tail
    if(++count % clearcount == 0) {
      count = 0;
      clearviewport();
      // Change color and redraw:
      color =(COLORS)( (color + 1) % Graphics::maxcolor);
      shapelist.fillcolor(color);
      shapelist.drawlist();
    }
  }
}
```

A Simulation with Shapes

As a final project, a graphic simulation will be created based on the simulation class presented in Chapter 8. A modified version of this is combined with the shape hierarchy to create a program that generates a desired number of shapes (specified on the command line) at random locations on the screen. Then it repeatedly tells each shape to **cycle()** itself to produce the simulation. There is only one type of simulation class here, but you can easily derive others and give them other movement rules.

In Chapter 8, the simulation grid was effectively used as a container. Now, however, better containers are available; the **slistt** class will be used to store the pointers as they are placed in the simulation grid. Then an **slistIterator** will pass through the list and **cycle()** each element.

The cycling will move each element one step in a random direction. In Chapter 8, everything was in text mode so each grid element corresponded to a physical location on the screen. In graphics mode, however, the granularity of the screen is much smaller and doesn't correspond to the grid elements. Two functions, **xform_x()** and **xform_y()**, take the grid-based coordinates and translate them into graphics coordinates for use when moving a shape. If you want to cause the shapes to move in smaller increments, increase the **xsize** and **ysize** granularity of the grid.

As in RNDSHAPE.CPP, the shapes are created randomly by the function **MakeRandomShape()**, but this time a random fill color is also chosen to make it easier to track the shapes as they move around the screen.

An especially interesting technique is shown in the initialization of the simulation grid:

```
simulation_unit * s_grid[xsize][ysize] = {0};
```

This uses aggregate initialization in a helpful way. If no initialization were specified, the pointers in **s_grid** would contain garbage values. It is important they be initialized to 0, but tedious to write out every element in the aggregate initialization. You could, of course, loop through and initialize the values (risking the usual off-by-one errors), but fortunately C++ provides a better way. The above expression *appears* to only initialize the first element because only one element is specified. However, when the compiler sees one or more element values provided in the aggregate initialization list, *but not all of them*, it initializes the remainder to 0. Thus this is a very succinct and elegant way to initialize array elements to 0.

Here is the graphics simulation program:

```
//: GSIM.CPP—Graphics version of simulation from Chap 8
#include <iostream.h>
#include <stdlib.h>
#include <time.h>
#include <conio.h>
#include "polygon.h"
#include "ellipse.h"
#include "slistt.h"
const xsize = 25; // Grid granularity
const ysize = 80; // Grid granularity
Graphics BGI("c:\\borlandc\\bgi\\");

enum shapetypes {
  Srectangle, Ssquare, Striangle,
  MAXSHAPE,  // tag for counting (move down for other shapes)
  Scircle,
  Sellipse,
};

shape * MakeRandomShape() {
  const x = rand() % Graphics::xmax();
  const y = rand() % Graphics::ymax();
  shape * s;
  switch((shapetypes)(rand() % MAXSHAPE)) {
    default:  // just default to "Circle"
    case Scircle: s= new Circle(x, y, 10); break;
    case Sellipse: s = new Ellipse(x, y, 10, 30); break;
    case Srectangle: s = new Rectangle(x,y); break;
    case Ssquare: s = new Square(x, y); break;
    case Striangle: s = new Triangle(x, y); break;
  }
  s->fillpattern(SOLID_FILL);
  s->fillcolor((COLORS)(rand() % Graphics::maxcolor));
  return s;
}
```

```
class simulation_unit {
protected:
  int x,y; // location on grid
public:
  virtual void display() = 0;
  virtual void erase() = 0;
  simulation_unit(int x_loc, int y_loc) : x(x_loc), y(y_loc) {}
  virtual ~simulation_unit() {}
  virtual void cycle() = 0; // execute one cycle of activity
  void move(int x_steps, int y_steps); // to a new location
};

// For simplicity, a global array is used:
simulation_unit * s_grid[xsize][ysize] = {0};

void simulation_unit::move(int x_steps, int y_steps) {
  int x_new = x + x_steps;
  int y_new = y + y_steps;
  if (x_new < 0 || x_new >= xsize)
    cerr << "move: x coordinate out of bounds";
  if (y_new < 0 || y_new >= ysize)
    cerr << "move: y coordinate out of bounds";
  if(s_grid[x_new][y_new] == 0) { // place is currently empty
    s_grid[x][y] = 0; // leave old place
    erase();  // erase old place on screen
    s_grid[x = x_new][y = y_new] = this; // land in new place
    display(); // display new place on screen
  }
}


inline int xform_x(int x) {
  return (x * Graphics::xmax())/xsize;
}
inline int xform_y(int y) {
  return (y * Graphics::ymax())/ysize;
}

// Objects of this class move one step at a time:
class crawl_around : public simulation_unit {
  shape* s;
public:
  crawl_around(shape* S, int xi, int yi)
    : s(S), simulation_unit(xi, yi) {
      display();
  }
```

```
      void display() {
        s->moveabsolute(xform_x(x),xform_y(y));
        s->draw();
      }
      void erase() { s->erase(); }
      void cycle() {
        // random number decides which direction the step is in
        int x_step = (rand() % 2) ? -1 : 1;
        if ( x + x_step <= 0 ) x_step = -x_step;
        if ( x + x_step >= xsize ) x_step = -x_step;
        int y_step = (rand() % 2) ? -1 : 1;
        if ( y + y_step <= 0 ) y_step = -y_step;
        if ( y + y_step >= ysize ) y_step = -y_step;
        move(x_step, y_step);
      }
    };

  void main(int argc, char * argv[]) {
    slistt<simulation_unit> simlist;
    slistIterator<simulation_unit> simit(simlist);
    srand(time(new time_t)); // seed random number generator
    if(argc < 2) {
      BGI.close(); // so message shows up in text mode
      cerr << "usage:\n\t"
        "gsim quantity steps\n"
        "'quantity' is the number of shapes on display\n"
        "'steps' is the randomization factor for the number\n"
        "of steps each shape takes when it is selected."
        " (optional, defaults to 1)";
      return;
    }
    const steps = (argc == 3 ? atoi(argv[2]) : 1 );
    const quantity = atoi(argv[1]);
    // randomly lay down objects in the grid:
    for(int i = 0; i < quantity; i++) {
      int placed = 0;
      do { // keep trying until you find an empty spot
        int x = rand() % xsize;
        int y = rand() % ysize;
        if(!s_grid[x][y]) { // make sure place is empty
          s_grid[x][y] = new crawl_around(MakeRandomShape(),x,y);
          simlist.add(s_grid[x][y]);
          placed++;
        }
      } while(!placed);
    }
    while(!kbhit()) {  // main simulation loop
```

```
      simit.top(); // repeatedly pass through list
      while(simit) {
        // calculate number of steps to take:
        int count = (steps == 1 ? 1 : rand() % steps);
        for(int i = 0; i < count; i++)
          simit->cycle(); // cycle the object
        simit++; // go to next one in list
        if(kbhit()) return;
      }
    }
}
```

Inside the main loop, the iterator is repeatedly passed through the list. For each element, a number of steps is calculated either randomly or (if **steps** from the command line is 1) as the value 1. The **simulation_unit** is cycled that number of times.

The program is quite mesmerizing to watch and play with, but it is just the beginning—a framework. You can easily modify this program to create further interesting simulations.

Makefile for Chapter 11

Here is the makefile for the projects in this chapter:

```
# Makefile for programs in Chapter 11
# For the programs using the command-line system, the
# FLAGFILE must be defined on the command line for
# the system to work properly.
CPP = bcc -w-inl          # Borland C++
# nmake CPP=cl MSC=        # Microsoft C++ command line

!IFNDEF MSC # Borland C++
all: cltest.exe tformat.exe alias.exe arglist.exe scopy.exe \
     recall.exe width.exe wordtag.exe list.exe snake.exe \
     controlr.exe eventtst.exe linktest.exe \
     cstest.exe tawk.exe lookup.exe envelope.exe \
     shed.exe keyread.exe rndshape.exe sltest.exe \
     gsim.exe
RO=o  # Rename object file
INCLUDE=\borlandc\classlib\include
!ELSE # Microsoft C++ 7.00
all: cltest.exe tformat.exe alias.exe arglist.exe \
```

```
        wordtag.exe list.exe snake.exe \
      cstest.exe tawk.exe lookup.exe envelope.exe
RO=Fo # Rename object file
!ENDIF


.cpp.exe:
        $(CPP) $<


.cpp.obj:
        $(CPP) -c -I$(INCLUDE) $<


cltest.exe : cltest.obj clftst.obj
        $(CPP) $**
cltest.obj : cltest.cpp clflags.cpp clflags.h tstflag.h
        $(CPP) -c -DFLAGFILE=tstflag.h cltest.cpp
clftst.obj : clflags.cpp clflags.h tstflag.h
        $(CPP) -c -DFLAGFILE=tstflag.h \
              -$(RO)clftst.obj clflags.cpp
tformat.exe : tformat.obj clformat.obj
        $(CPP) $**
tformat.obj : tformat.cpp clflags.cpp clflags.h formflag.h
        $(CPP) -c -DFLAGFILE=formflag.h tformat.cpp
clformat.obj : clflags.cpp clflags.h formflag.h
        $(CPP) -c -DFLAGFILE=formflag.h \
              -$(RO)clformat.obj  clflags.cpp
scopy.exe : scopy.obj ioserror.obj
        $(CPP) $**
recall.exe : recall.obj ioserror.obj
        $(CPP) $**
ioserror.obj : ..\chap_7\ioserror.h ..\chap_7\ioserror.cpp
        $(CPP) -c ..\chap_7\ioserror.cpp
controlr.exe : controlr.obj event.obj
        $(CPP) $**
eventtst.exe : eventtst.obj event.obj
        $(CPP) $**
cstest.exe : cstest.obj csascii.obj field.obj
      $(CPP) $**
tawk.exe : tawk.obj parse.obj csascii.obj field.obj
      $(CPP) $**
lookup.exe : lookup.obj csascii.obj field.obj
        $(CPP) $**
envelope.exe : envelope.obj csascii.obj field.obj
        $(CPP) $**
snake.exe : snake.h snake.cpp
shed.exe: shed.obj ellipse.obj polygon.obj shape.obj bgi.obj
```

```
   $(CPP) $** graphics.lib \borlandc\classlib\lib\tclasss.lib
rndshape.exe: rndshape.obj ellipse.obj polygon.obj \
              shape.obj bgi.obj
   $(CPP) $** graphics.lib
gsim.exe: gsim.obj ellipse.obj polygon.obj shape.obj bgi.obj
   $(CPP) $** graphics.lib


clflags.obj : clflags.h clflags.cpp
event.obj : event.h event.cpp
alias.obj : ..\chap_7\ioserror.h alias.cpp
eventtst.obj : event.h eventtst.cpp
linktest.exe : linklist.h linktest.cpp
cstest.obj : csascii.h field.h cstest.cpp
parse.obj : csascii.h field.h parse.h parse.cpp
field.obj : field.h field.cpp
recall.obj : ..\chap_7\ioserror.h recall.cpp
rndshape.obj : polygon.h shape.h bgi.h ellipse.h \
               circbox.h slistt.h rndshape.cpp
envelope.obj : csascii.h field.h envelope.cpp
ellipse.obj : ellipse.h shape.h bgi.h ellipse.cpp
keyread.obj : keyread.cpp
shape.obj : shape.h bgi.h shape.cpp
sltest.obj : slistt.h sltest.cpp
wordtag.obj : wordtag.cpp
csascii.obj : csascii.h field.h csascii.cpp
scopy.obj : ..\chap_7\ioserror.h scopy.cpp
snake.obj : snake.h snake.cpp
polygon.obj : polygon.h shape.h bgi.h polygon.cpp
controlr.obj : event.h linklist.h controlr.cpp
tawk.obj : csascii.h field.h parse.h tawk.cpp
shed.obj : polygon.h shape.h bgi.h ellipse.h \
           circbox.h doskey.h shed.cpp
bgi.obj : bgi.h bgi.cpp
lookup.obj : csascii.h field.h lookup.cpp
```

APPENDIX

Exception Handling

*E*xception handling is the last "major" feature to be added to ANSI C++ (although there are certainly a number of other issues that must be addressed), and it has been accepted into draft ANSI C++, so anyone may implement it and claim conformance to the draft. However, it's a hard feature to implement, and at this writing, no commonly available compiler contains exception handling, so all the examples in this section are untested.

Exceptions will change the way you program and the way you think about programming. In the same way that the class changes the way you think about data structures and data types, exceptions change the way you think about flow of control. With exceptions, the question, "What happens if something goes wrong" comes to the forefront (from its previously relegated spot of "I'll cross my fingers" or "I'll think about it later").

An *exceptional condition* is a disastrous situation that occurs during the normal flow of events and prevents the program from continuing. When a program encounters an exceptional condition, it is critical that it be dealt with somehow (a common unacceptable reaction of many programs in this situation is to die). There are several problems when writing functions which generate exceptional conditions.

The first is that the programmer may simply ignore an exceptional condition that might be generated by a function. This is one of those places where the design of C (and most languages) tends to be optimistic and assumes errors won't happen, and if they do that they can be easily handled by checking a return value or some global flag. Unfortunately, functions with return values that can be used to carry error information are special cases, and programs that check those values are even more of a special case. Using a global flag that is set when something goes wrong has the same problem—users typically ignore the value of the flag and continue processing as if nothing had happened.

It turns out that the failure of *any* function is difficult to handle. In addition, different exceptional conditions may require different return information. A good example of this is the constructor—the constructor has no return value to flag an error, and returning from a constructor (even if this is done after setting a "bad" flag) can place you right in the middle of code that assumes that the constructor call was successful. In the most general situation, you must be able to assume that the function cannot even return properly, but that instead it must be aborted.

A good exception-handling mechanism must cope with all these problems. Aborting from the middle of a function without going through the normal return mechanism is particularly problematic because simply leaping out of a function will miss destructor calls for objects that had been constructed at the time the exception occurred. This approach of "leaping" out of the middle of a function is commonly used in C, and is one of the important uses for **setjmp()** and **longjmp()**, the "nonlocal goto" functions. These functions assume that by reconstructing the stack frame at the point of the **setjmp()**, the entire system state will be restored. This may be true in a C program, where all the variables are built-in types and can be erased by simply moving a stack pointer. But in C++, you are creating objects that may have destructors. So what happens if you're part of the way through a block, and you encounter an exception that means you cannot continue processing that block? The objects that have been successfully constructed must be destroyed, but the destructors must not be called for the objects that haven't been constructed. If you were to follow the C approach, you would create a few objects, hit an exceptional condition, and **longjmp()** out of there, leaving behind objects that were created but never destroyed. Thus, C's exception-handling approach is too primitive to employ.

There is one other issue in exception handling for C++: the language supports a distinct boundary—the **class**—between the creators of some pieces of code and the users of that code. If you are creating a class that might generate exceptions, you cannot assume the user will be diligent about checking or responding to those exceptions. If an exception is generated, but not caught someplace, the system cannot simply ignore it (as so often happens with the return values or global flags of C functions). There must be some kind of notification and/or termination of the program.

C++ *Exceptions*

The exception-handling scheme accepted by the ANSI C++ committee looks like an alternate return mechanism. Except for constructors and destructors, all functions can return a value. The type of the value must be specified in the function declaration. But if you're inside a floating-point divide function and you have a problem, you don't really want to return a value. Instead, you may want to return a completely different type of object; a string, for example, that says "divide overflow." In fact, you may want to return a different type of object for every different type of problem. That's one of the facts of life: when you hit an exception, all bets are off, and everything has changed.

One of the striking things about C++ exceptions is that they allow you to return *any* type of object from a function, regardless of what the function return type is. In fact, programmers will certainly be tempted to use exception handling in other ways than it was intended (this is discouraged).

The other fascinating feature of exceptions is that if you've constructed some of the objects in a block, but not all, and you hit an exception, the only destructors called are for the objects which have been constructed! Thus, exception handling is an alternate way to leave a scope (other than the typical one of just reaching the closing brace).

Syntax

When a function returns using the exception-handling mechanism, it's referred to as *throwing* an exception, represented by the C++ keyword **throw** (and don't think you're being original by naming your exceptions "up" or "cookies" or "doughnuts"). A collection of statements which may generate exceptions is placed in a *try block*, prefaced with the keyword **try**. Following the try block, the programmer places a series of *handlers*, each of which begins with the keyword **catch**. Each handler takes an argument of a different type, corresponding to the different types that may be thrown in the try block. It is somewhat reminiscent of a **switch** statement.

Here's a very simple example:

```
class overflow {
public:
  overflow(float, float);
};

float mydiv(float a, float b) {
  if(b == 0) throw "division by zero";
  String s("hello");  // has a destructor
```

```
    if(a > TOOBIG && b < TOOSMALL) throw overflow(a,b);
    return a/b;
}

void main() {
  try {
    mydiv(1,2);
  }
  catch(char* p) {
    cerr << p << endl;
  }
  catch(overflow o) {
    // handle overflows
  }
}
```

The class **overflow** is created especially to distinguish this type of exception. Inside **mydiv()**, two types of exceptions can occur: one that throws a **char***, and one that **throws** an **overflow** object. In the **try** block, **mydiv()** is called (although you can have any number of expressions), and both types of exceptions are handled in the **catch** statements. If the **char*** is thrown, you end up in the **char*** handler, and if **overflow** is thrown, you end up in the **overflow** handler. In **mydiv**, the **String** object **s** is always cleaned up properly; if the first **throw** is activated, the object is not destroyed because it hasn't been constructed, but if the second **throw** occurs, the destructor *is* called.

Exceptions can be thrown from any function, including class member functions.

You can specify what types of exceptions may occur in the function declaration (this is optional, but I personally feel you should be forced to do it). For **mydiv()**, the declaration looks like this:

```
float mydiv(float, float) throw(char*, overflow);
```

This way, the user of the function can see by its declaration how it can act. It's possible for the programmer to lie, and throw an exception that isn't in the specification. If this occurs, the special function **unexpected()** is called; the action of the function can be set to anything you desire with **set_unexpected()**. It's generally considered a design error (or at least, bad form) if you throw something that isn't in the exception specification.

Note that the user isn't *forced* to have a handler for every type of exception, or to even worry about exception handling at all. Of course, you don't want to revert to the barbarism of C's error handling, so *something* must still happen when an exception is thrown. This "something" is the special function **terminate()**, which can also be set to anything you want with **set_terminate()**. That way, *something* will always happen when an exception occurs.

APPENDIX

The matrix Class

*T*his appendix contains the full source code for a class to create and manipulate mathematical matrices. The structure of this class was introduced in Chapter 9; this appendix fleshes it out with a full set of operations, including **inverse()** and **determinant()**. The **matrix** class follows strict portability guidelines so you can use it with any C++ compiler.

Note that although this matrix has been tested (notably, by the readers of the first edition of the book), it is presented here for learning purposes only. If you are doing serious scientific calculations, you should acquire a supported commercial library like Rogue Wave's MATH++. This contains matrices and many other mathematical tools for computing (Rogue Wave, P.O. Box 2328, Corvallis OR 97339, (503) 754-3010).

Using matrices, you can easily construct matrix equations like

```
A = B.determinant() * C + D;
```

An equation like this allows you to focus on the mathematical problem instead of the programming problem.

The algorithms for the **inverse()** and **determinant()** (using LU decomposition) are translated from *Numerical Recipes*, by William H. Press and Brian P. Flannery (Cambridge University Press, 1987), which uses FORTRAN. If you want further information on matrix manipulation and numerical methods in general, consult their later book *Numerical Recipes in C* (Cambridge University Press, 1988). Since the algorithms were not developed by this author, they may not work correctly in all situations—you should not trust the results until you verify them with an independent test. The test shown here simply multiplies a matrix by its inverse to check for the *identity matrix* (a matrix with 1s along its diagonal, and 0s everywhere else), which should always be produced.

Standard Matrix Files

For ease of testing, one of the matrix constructors will read from an ASCII text file following a "standard" format (this is shown in the ANALYZE.CPP program). Comments in this file format begin with # and continue to the end of the line. The file must contain a header block and a data block. The two blocks are separated by three colons (:::). At this point, the header block only needs to contain information about the number of rows and columns in the matrix. The constructor only searches for **r**, **c**, and **=**, so you can say

```
r = 3 c = 3
```

or

```
rows=3 columns=3
```

You must list rows before columns. This can be changed by modifying the constructor.

In the data block, data are separated by spaces. All data are treated as floating-point numbers, whether or not they contain decimal points and exponents. Newlines are ignored in the data block.

The member function **write_standard()** writes a matrix to a file in the standard format, adding date and time information and a message, if you desire. (You can also add information about the path the matrix is located in if you use platform-specific function calls.)

Other constructors create different types of matrices. For example:

```
matrix ID("I", 10); // a 10 x 10 identity matrix
// init each element of a 10 x 10 matrix to 3.14:
matrix F(10, 10, 3,14);
```

You can also create a matrix from an array of **double**s:

```
double dd[] = { 1.1, 2.2, 3.3, 4.4, 5.5, 6.6, 7.7, 8.8, 9.9 };
matrix A(3, 3, dd);
```

A *column vector* is a matrix with one column. Because default arguments are used, a vector definition looks quite sensible, as shown,

```
matrix vec(3); // vector with 3 elements
```

You can multiply a matrix by a column vector in

```
matrix result = A * vec;
```

Row vectors are not quite as obvi either):

```
matrix rowvec(1,3); // row vector with 3 elements
matrix rowresult = rowvec * A;
```

Speed Improvements

Since **double** values are twice as large as **float** values, calculations may take significantly longer (depending on the implementation). For most problems, the use of **double** is overkill; you will never need that level of precision. You should see speed improvements by changing all the **double** declarations to **float**. Even better, consider changing the implementation to a **template** so you can easily make matrices of any type!

An obvious way to speed things up is to add a hardware floating-point coprocessor to your system and recompile the code using the proper flag to force inline generation of calls to the floating-point coprocessor.

Code for the matrix Class

This appendix is provided to give you an example of the structure of a larger class. Other than the description of the design in Chapter 9, a thorough explanation of the code will not be given.

Declaration

ᵃder file must be included in all programs that create and use
#ᵈotice that the header file includes no other header files—this
ᵖilation of programs using the **matrix** class much faster.

```
class matrimatrix class from design in Chapter 9
  struct matrep
    double **m; // 
```

the matrix

```
  int r,c;     // number of rows and columns
  int n;       // reference count
} *p;
void error(char * msg1, char * msg2 = ""); // private function
public:
 matrix(int mrows = 1, int columns = 1, double initval = 0);
 matrix(int mrows, int columns, double* initvalues);
 matrix(char * flag, int dimension); // create an ident matrix
 matrix(char * matfile); // read from a "standard" matrix file
 matrix(matrix& x); // copy-constructor
 ~matrix();
 int rows() const {  return p->r; };  // rows in matrix
 int cols() const {  return p->c; };  // cols in matrix
 matrix operator=(const matrix& rval); // matrix assignment
 // Write a "standard" matrix file:
 void write_standard(char * filename, char * msg = "");
 matrix operator+(const matrix& rval); // matrix addition
 matrix operator+(const double rval); // scalar addition
 matrix operator-(const matrix& rval); // matrix subtraction
 matrix operator-(const double rval); // scalar subtraction
 matrix operator-(); // unary minus
 matrix operator*(const matrix& rval); // matrix multiplication
 matrix operator*(const double rval); // scalar multiplication
 double & val(int row, int col); // element selection;
 // can be used to read or write an element.
 matrix transpose(); // transpose a square matrix
 double determinant();
 matrix inverse();
 double mmin();  // find minimum element in the matrix
 double mmax();  // find maximum element in the matrix
 double mean(); // average all the elements of the matrix
 double variance(); // statistical variance of all elements
 void print(char * msg = ""); // print matrix with a message

private: // functions used by inverse() and determinant()
 void switch_columns(int col1, int col2);
 void copy_column(matrix& m, int from_col, int to_col);
 matrix scale(); // Scale a matrix (used in L-U decomposition)
 void deepcopy(matrix& from, matrix& to); // make an image
 matrix lu_decompose(matrix& indx, int& d );
     // Returns the L-U decomposition of a matrix
 void lu_back_subst(matrix& indx, matrix& b);
     // Uses L-U decomposition for matrix inverse
 double & mval(int row, int col) {
   return (p->m[row][col]);
 } // used by matrix functions which KNOW they aren't
 // exceeding the boundaries
```

```
};

#endif // MATRIX_H_
```

matrix *Methods*

Here are the member function definitions for the **matrix** class, which must be compiled and linked to any program using matrices.

```
//: MATRIX.CPP—Full matrix class from design in Chapter 9
#include <stdlib.h>
#include <iostream.h>
#include <fstream.h>
#include <iomanip.h>
#include <string.h>
#include <math.h>
#include <time.h>
#include "matrix.h"
const double tiny = double(1e-20);
const double limit = double(1e-14);
#define WID setw(6)
#define PREC setprecision(3)

void matrix::error(char * msg1, char * msg2) {
  cerr << "matrix error: " << msg1 << " " << msg2 << endl;
  exit(1);
}

matrix::matrix(int mrows, int columns, double initval) {
  // create the structure:
  p = new matrep;
  p->r = mrows;
  p->c = columns;
  // allocate memory for the actual matrix:
  p->m = new double *[mrows];
  for (int x = 0; x < mrows; x++)
    p->m[x] = new double[columns];
  p->n = 1;   // so far, there's one reference to this data
  for (int i=0; i< mrows; i++) {
    for (int j = 0; j < columns; j++)
      mval(i,j) = initval;
  }
}
```

```cpp
matrix::matrix(int mrows, int columns, double* initvalues) {
  // create the structure:
  p = new matrep;
  p->r= mrows;
  p->c = columns;
  // allocate memory for the actual matrix:
  p->m = new double *[mrows];
  for (int x = 0; x < mrows; x++)
    p->m[x] = new double[columns];
  p->n = 1;  // so far, there's one reference to this data
  int c = 0;
  for (int i=0; i< mrows; i++)  {
    for (int j = 0; j < columns; j++)
      mval(i,j) =  initvalues[c++];
  }
}


// create an identity matrix:
matrix::matrix(char * flag, int dimension) {
  if (flag[0] != 'I')
    error("to create an identity matrix: "
          "matrix(\"I\",dimension)");
  p = new matrep;
  p->r = dimension;
  p->c = dimension;
  p->m = new double *[dimension];
  for (int x = 0; x < dimension; x++)
    p->m[x] = new double[dimension];
  p->n = 1;
  for (int i=0; i< dimension; i++) {
    for (int j = 0; j < dimension; j++)
      mval(i,j) = (i == j ? 1 : 0);
  }
}


// error message when trying to read a "standard"
// matrix file:
static char nonstandard[] =
" is a 'non-standard' file. A 'standard' matrix file must\n"
"start with the dimensions of the matrix, i.e.:\n"
"\t rows=12 columns=14\n or abbreviated:\n\t r=12 c=14\n"
"Notice rows appear before columns, and chars are lower case\n"
"comments follow '#' signs to end of line, data follows :::\n";


// read from "standard" matrix file:
matrix::matrix(char * initfile) {
  ifstream from(initfile);
```

```
if(!from)
  error("cannot open matrix initializer file",initfile);
const bsize = 120;
char buf[bsize], *cp, *cp2;
int rfound = 0, cfound = 0, colonsfound = 0;
p = new matrep;
    /* Parse file initialization header  */
while(from.getline(buf, bsize)) { // for each header line
  // Remove comments with ANSI C library function "strpbrk()":
  if( ( cp = strpbrk(buf,"#")) != 0 ) // look for comments
    *cp = '\0';   // terminate string at comment
  if( ( cp = strpbrk(buf,"r") ) != 0 )
    if ( ( cp2 = strpbrk(cp, "=")) != 0 )
      if ( ( cp = strpbrk(cp2, "0123456789")) != 0 ) {
        p->r = atoi(cp);
        rfound++;  // flag to say rows were found
      }
  if( ( cp = strpbrk(buf,"c") ) != 0 )
    if ( ( cp2 = strpbrk(cp, "=")) != 0 )
      if ( ( cp = strpbrk(cp2, "0123456789")) != 0 ) {
        p->c = atoi(cp);
        cfound++;  // flag to say cols were found
      }
  if ( strstr(buf,":::") != 0 ) {
    colonsfound++;
    break; // ... out of "while" loop
  }
}
if ( !rfound || !cfound || !colonsfound ) {
  cerr << initfile << nonstandard;
  exit(1);
}
p->m = new double *[p->r];
for (int x = 0; x < p->r; x++)
  p->m[x] = new double[p->c];
p->n = 1;  // so far, there's one reference to this data
for (int row = 0; row < p->r; row++) {
  for(int col = 0; col < p->c; col++) {
    const nbsz = 20; char nb[nbsz];
    from >> nb; // scan for space-delimited string
    mval(row,col) = atof(nb); // convert it to a double
    if(from.bad())
      error("problem with matrix initializer file",initfile);
  }
}
}
```

```
matrix::matrix(matrix& x) {
  x.p->n++; // we're adding another reference.
  p = x.p;  // point to the new matrep.
}

matrix::~matrix() {
  if (- p->n -- 0) { // if reference count goes to 0
    for (int x = 0; x < rows(); x++)
      delete p->m[x];
    delete p->m; // delete data
    delete p;
  }
}

matrix matrix::operator=(const matrix& rval) {
  // clean up current value:
  if(--p->n == 0) {  // If nobody else is referencing us...
    for (int x = 0; x < rows(); x++)
      delete p->m[x];
    delete p >m; // ...nobody else can clean us up...
    delete p;
  }
  // connect to new value:
  rval.p->n++;  // tell the rval it has another reference
  p = rval.p;  // point at the rval matrep
  return *this;
}

void matrix::write standard(char * filename, char * msg) {
  ofstream to(filename);
  if(!to)
    error("cannot open or create matrix output file",filename);
  to << "# " << filename
     << ": matrix file written in \"standard\" format" << endl;
  time_t clock;
  time(&clock);
  to <<  "# " << asctime(localtime(&clock));
  to <<  "# " << msg << endl;
  to << "rows= " << rows() << " columns= " << cols() << endl;
  to <<  ":::" << endl;
  for (int row = 0; row < rows(); row++){
    for(int col = 0; col < cols(); col++)
      to << WID << PREC << mval(row,col) << "   ";
    to << endl;
  }
}
```

```
matrix matrix::operator+(const matrix& arg) {
  if(( rows() != arg.rows()) || ( cols() != arg.cols()))
    error("must have equal dimensions for addition!");
  matrix sum(rows(),cols());
  for (int i=0; i< rows(); i++) {
    for (int j = 0; j < cols(); j++)
      sum.mval(i,j) = mval(i,j) + arg.p->m[i][j];
  }
  return sum; // see note for operator*()
}

matrix matrix::operator+(const double arg) {
  matrix sum(rows(),cols());
  for (int i=0; i< rows(); i++) {
    for (int j = 0; j < cols(); j++)
      sum.mval(i,j) = mval(i,j) + arg;
  }
  return sum; // see note for operator*()
}

matrix matrix::operator-(const matrix& arg) {
  if(( rows() != arg.rows()) || ( cols() != arg.cols()))
    error("must have equal dimensions for subtaction!");
  matrix sum(rows(),cols());
  for (int i=0; i< rows(); i++) {
    for (int j = 0; j < cols(); j++)
      sum.mval(i,j) = mval(i,j) - arg.p->m[i][j];
  }
  return sum; // see note for operator*()
}

matrix matrix::operator-(const double arg) {
  matrix sum(rows(),cols());
  for (int i=0; i< rows(); i++) {
    for (int j = 0; j < cols(); j++)
      sum.mval(i,j) = mval(i,j) - arg;
  }
  return sum; // see note for operator*()
}

matrix matrix::operator-() {
  matrix unaryminus(rows(),cols());
  for (int i=0; i< rows(); i++) {
    for (int j = 0; j < cols(); j++)
      unaryminus.mval(i,j) = -mval(i,j);
  }
```

```
      return unaryminus;
  }

  matrix matrix::operator*(const matrix& arg) {
    if( cols() != arg.rows())
      error("# rows of second mat must equal "
            "# cols of first for multiply!");
    matrix result(rows(),arg.cols());
    for(int row = 0; row < rows(); row++) {
      for(int col = 0; col < arg.cols(); col++){
        double sum = 0;
        for(int i = 0; i < cols(); i++)
          sum += mval(row,i) * arg.p->m[i][col];
        result.mval(row,col) = sum;
      }
    }
    return result; // Returning a local variable?
    // copy constructor happens before the destructor,
    // so reference count is 2 when destructor is called,
    // thus destructor doesn't free the memory.
  }

  matrix matrix::operator*(const double arg) {
    matrix result(rows(),cols());
    for (int i=0; i< rows(); i++) {
      for (int j = 0; j < cols(); j++)
        result.mval(i,j) = mval(i,j) * arg;
    }
    return result;
  }

  double & matrix::val(int row, int col) {
  //  if (row >= 0 && row < rows() && col >= 0 && col < cols())
    if (row < 0 || row >= rows() || col < 0 || col >= cols())
      error("index out of range");
    return (mval(row,col));
  }

  matrix matrix::transpose() {
    if(rows() != cols())
      error("matrix must be square to transpose!\n");
    matrix trans(rows(),cols());
    for (int row = 0; row < rows(); row++) {
      for(int col = 0; col < cols(); col++)
        trans.mval(col,row) = mval(row,col);
    }
```

```
    return trans;
}

double matrix::mmin() {
  double temp;
  if(rows() <= 0 || cols() <= 0)
    error("bad matrix size for min()");
  double minimum = mval(0,0);
  for (int row = 0; row < rows(); row++) {
    for(int col = 0; col < cols(); col++)
      if ((temp = mval(row,col)) < minimum)
        minimum = temp;
  }
  return minimum;
}

double matrix::mmax() {
  double temp;
  if(rows() <= 0 || cols() <= 0)
    error("bad matrix size for max()");
  double maximum = mval(0,0);
  for (int row = 0; row < rows(); row++) {
    for(int col = 0; col < cols(); col++){
      if ((temp = mval(row,col)) > maximum)
        maximum = temp;
    }
  }
  return maximum;
}

double matrix::mean() {
  int row, col;
  double sum = 0;
  for (row = 0; row < rows(); row++) {
    for(col = 0; col < cols(); col++)
      sum += fabs(mval(row,col));
  }
  return sum/(row * col);
}

double matrix::variance() {
  int row, col;
  double s_squared = 0;
  double mn = mean();
  for (row = 0; row < rows(); row++) {
    for(col = 0; col < cols(); col++){
      double temp = mval(row,col) - mn;
```

```
        temp *= temp;
        s_squared += temp;
      }
    }
  s_squared /= row * col -1; // number of elements minus one
  return s_squared;
}

double matrix::determinant() {
  if(rows() != cols())
    error("matrix must be square for determinant()");
  matrix indx(cols()); // create the "index vector"
  matrix B(cols()); // see pp 38. in Numerical Recipes
  int d;
  // perform the decomposition once:
  matrix decomp = lu_decompose(indx,d);
  double determinant = d;
  for(int i=0; i < cols() ; i++)
    determinant *= decomp.mval(i,i);
  return determinant;
}

matrix matrix::inverse() {
  if(rows() != cols())
    error("matrix must be square for inverse()");
  matrix Y("I",rows()); // create an identity matrix
  matrix indx(cols()); // create the "index vector"
  matrix B(cols()); // see Press & Flannery
  int d;
  // perform the decomposition once:
  matrix decomp = lu_decompose(indx,d);
  for(int col = 0; col < cols(); col++){
    B.copy_column(Y,col,0);
    decomp.lu_back_subst(indx,B);
    Y.copy_column(B,0,col);
  }
  return Y.transpose();
}

void matrix::print(char *msg) {
  if (*msg) cout << msg << ":" << endl;
  for (int row=0; row< rows(); row++){
    for (int col = 0; col < cols(); col++) {
      double result = mval(row, col);
      if(fabs(result) < limit) result = 0;
      cout << WID << PREC << result << "   ";
```

```
    }
    cout << endl;


  }
}

/***********************************************************
The private support functions for determinant & inverse.
************************************************************/

// copy the from_col of mm to the to_col of "this"
void matrix::copy_column(matrix& mm, int from_col, int to_col){
  if(rows() != mm.rows())
    error("number of rows must be equal for copy_column()");
  for(int row=0; row < rows(); row++)
    mval(row,to_col) = mm.mval(row,from_col);
}

void matrix::switch_columns(int col1, int col2) {
  matrix temp(rows());
  for(int row = 0; row < rows(); row++)
    // temporarily store col 1:
    temp.mval(row,0) = mval(row,col1);
  for(row = 0; row < rows(); row++)
    mval(row,col1) = mval(row,col2); // move col2 to col1
  for(row = 0; row < rows(); row++)
    mval(row,col2) = temp.mval(row,0); // move temp to col2
}

// make an image of a matrix (used in L-U decomposition)
void matrix::deepcopy(matrix& from, matrix& to) {
  if(from.rows() != to.rows() || from.cols() != to.cols())
    error("matrices must be equal dimensions for deepcopy()");
  for(int row = 0; row < from.rows(); row++) {
    for(int col = 0; col < from.cols(); col++)
      to.mval(row,col) = from.mval(row,col);
  }
}

// scale a matrix (used in L-U decomposition)
matrix matrix::scale() {
  double temp;
  if(rows() <= 0 || cols() <= 0)
    error("bad matrix size for scale()");
  if(rows() != cols())
    error("matrix must be square for scale()");
```

```cpp
  matrix scale_vector(rows());
  for (int col = 0; col < cols(); col++){
    double maximum = 0;
    for(int row = 0; row < rows(); row++)
      if ((temp = (double)fabs(mval(row,col))) > maximum)
      maximum = temp;   // find max column magnitude in this row
    if(maximum == 0)
      error("singular matrix in scale()");
    scale_vector.mval(col,0) = 1/maximum; // save the scaling
  }
  return scale_vector;
}


matrix matrix::lu_decompose(matrix& indx, int& d ) {
/*
 Returns the L-U decomposition of a matrix. indx is an output
 vector which records the row permutation affected by the
 partial pivoting, d is output as +-1 depending on whether the
 number of row interchanges was even or odd, respectively.
 This routine is used in combination with lu_back_subst to
 solve linear equations or invert a matrix.
*/
  if(rows() != cols())
    error("Matrix must be square to L-U decompose!\n");
  d = 1; // parity check
  int row,col,k,col_max; // counters
  double dum; // from the book — I don't know significance
  double sum;
  double maximum;
  matrix lu_decomp(rows(),cols());
  // make a direct copy of the original matrix:
  deepcopy(*this,lu_decomp);
  matrix scale_vector = lu_decomp.scale(); // scale the matrix
  // The loop over columns of Crout's method:
  for(row = 0; row < rows(); row++){
    if (row > 0) {
      // eqn 2.3.12 except for row=col:
      for (col = 0; col <= row-1; col++) {
      sum = lu_decomp.mval(row,col);
      if(col > 0) {
        for(k = 0; k <= col-1; k++)
          sum -= lu_decomp.mval(row,k)*lu_decomp.mval(k,col);
        lu_decomp.mval(row,col) = sum;
      }
      }
    }
```

```
// Initialize for the search for the largest pivot element:
maximum = 0;
// i=j of eq 2.3.12 & i=j+1..N of 2.3.13:
for(col=row; col <= cols()-1; col++){
  sum = lu_decomp.mval(row,col);
  if(row > 0){
  for(k=0; k <= row-1; k++)
    sum -=  lu_decomp.mval(k,col) * lu_decomp.mval(row,k);
  lu_decomp.mval(row,col) = sum;
  }
  // figure of merit for pivot:
  dum = scale_vector.mval(col,0) * fabs(sum);
  if (dum >= maximum){ // is it better than the best so far?
  col_max = col;
  maximum = dum;
  }
}
// Do we need to interchange rows?
if(row != col_max) {
  lu_decomp.switch_columns(col_max,row); // Yes, do so...
  d *= -1;  // ... and change the parity of d
  // also interchange the scale factor:
  dum = scale_vector.mval(col_max,0);
  scale_vector.mval(col_max,0) = scale_vector.mval(row,0);
  scale_vector.mval(row,0) = dum;
}
indx.mval(row,0) = col_max;
// Now, finally, divide by the pivot element:
if(row != rows() -1){
  if(lu_decomp.mval(row,row) == 0)
    lu_decomp.mval(row,row) = tiny;
  // If the pivot element is zero the matrix is
  // singular (at least to the precision of the
  // algorithm). For some applications on singular
  // matrices, it is desirable to substitute tiny for zero
  dum = 1/lu_decomp.mval(row,row);
  for(col=row+1; col <= cols()-1; col++)
  lu_decomp.mval(row,col) *= dum;
  }
}
if(lu_decomp.mval(rows()-1,cols()-1) == 0)
  lu_decomp.mval(rows()-1,cols()-1) = tiny;
return lu_decomp;
}
```

```
void matrix::lu_back_subst(matrix& indx, matrix& b) {
/*
 Solves the set of N linear equations A*X = B. Here "this"
 is the LU-decomposition of the matrix A, determined by the
 routine lu_decompose(). Indx is input as the permutation
 vector returned  by lu_decompose(). B is input as the
 right-hand side vector B, and returns with the solution
 vector X. This routine takes into  account the possibility
 that B will begin with many zero elements, so it is efficient
 for use in matrix inversion. See pp 36-37 in
 Press & Flannery.
*/
  if(rows() != cols())
    error ("non-square lu_decomp matrix in lu_back_subst()");
  if(rows() != b.rows())
    error("wrong size B vector passed to lu_back_subst()");
  if(rows() != indx.rows())
    error("wrong size indx vector passed to lu_back_subst()");
  int row,col,ll;
  int ii = 0;
  double sum;
  for(col=0;col < cols(); col++){
    ll= (int)indx.mval(col,0);
    sum = b.mval(ll,0);
    b.mval(ll,0) = b.mval(col,0);
    if (ii >= 0)
      for(row = ii; row <= col-1; row++)
      sum -= mval(row,col) * b.mval(row,0);
    else if(sum != 0)
      ii = col;
    b.mval(col,0) = sum;
  }
  for(col = cols() -1; col >= 0; col--){
    sum = b.mval(col,0);
    if (col < cols() -1)
      for (row = col + 1; row <= rows()-1; row++)
      sum -= mval(row,col) * b.mval(row,0);
    // store a component of the soln vector X:
    b.mval(col,0) = sum/mval(col,col);
  }
}
```

Testing the matrix *Class*

The following program exercises some of the features of **class matrix**. You can get much more sophisticated, as in the matrix equation at the beginning of this appendix.

```
//: ANALYZE.CPP—Exercise the features of the matrix class
#include <iostream.h>
#include <iomanip.h>
#include <stdlib.h>
#include "matrix.h"

void main(int argc, char * argv[]) {
  if (argc != 2) {
    cerr << "usage: analyze matrix_file_name";
    exit(1);
  }
  matrix  m(argv[1]);
  m.print("m is");
  matrix minv = m.inverse();
  minv.print("inverse of m is");
  (m * minv).print("m * m.inverse()");
  cout << "determinant = " << setw(12)
       << setprecision(6) << m.determinant() << endl;
  cout << "min = " << setw(12)
       << setprecision(6) << m.mmin() << endl;
  cout << "max = " << setw(12)
       << setprecision(6) << m.mmax() << endl;
  cout << "mean = " << setw(12)
       << setprecision(6) << m.mean() << endl;
  cout << "variance = " << setw(12)
       << setprecision(6) << m.variance() << endl;
  m.write_standard("test.$$$", "this is a test");
}
```

The following file is an example in standard matrix file format that was used for testing. To try it, type **analyze test.std**.

```
# TEST.STD: a file in "standard" matrix format
# A large matrix for testing the inverse function
r = 7 c = 7
# (elements must be separated by at least one white space)
:::
3       -5       6       4       -2       -3       8
1        1      -9      15        1       -9       2
```

2	-1	7	5	-1	6	11
-1	1	3	2	7	-1	-2
4	3	1	-7	2	1	1
2	9	-8	11	-1	-4	-1
7	2	-1	2	7	-1	9

Makefile for the matrix *Class*

Here is the makefile for the examples in this appendix:

```
# makefile for matrix class
CPP = bcc
# nmake CPP=cl # Microsoft C++ command line

all : analyze.exe

analyze.exe : analyze.obj matrix.obj
        $(CPP) $**

matrix.obj: matrix.cpp matrix.h
        $(CPP) -c matrix.cpp

analyze.obj: analyze.cpp matrix.h
        $(CPP) -c analyze.cpp
```

Index